Christ the Original Mystery

Esoterism and the Mystical Way

JEAN BORELLA

Christ the Original Mystery

Esoterism & The Mystical Way

With Special Reference to the Works of René Guénon

Translated by
G. John Champoux

Originally published in French as
Ésotérisme guénonien et mystère chrétien
© Éditions L'Age d'Homme,
Lausanne, Switzerland, 1997
English translation © Sophia Perennis 2004
First English edition published as
Guénonian Esoterism and Christian Mystery 2004
Second English edition published as
Christ the Original Mystery: Esoterism and the Mystical Way
© Angelico Press / Sophia Perennis 2018
All rights reserved

Series editor: James R. Wetmore

No part of this book may be reproduced or transmitted,
in any form or by any means, without permission

For information, address:
Angelico Press
169 Monitor St.
Brooklyn, NY 11222
angelicopress.com

ISBN 978-1-62138-343-7 (pbk)
ISBN 978-1-62138-342-0 (cloth)
ISBN 978-1-62138-341-3 (ebook)

Cover Image:
Scheme of Christian Kabbalism
from Heinrich Khunrath, *Amphiteatrum
sapientiae aeternae*, n.d. (detail)
Cover Design: Michael Schrauzer

Select Bibliography

Le sens du surnaturel, Éd. de La Place Royale, 1986 (re-edition Ad Solem, 1996, L'Harmattan, 2012); *The Sense of the Supernatural*, T & T Clark, 1998.

Histoire et théorie du symbole, L'Âge d'Homme, 2004 (re-edition of *Le mystère du signe*, Maisonneuve et Larose, 1989).

Ésotérisme guénonien et mystère chrétien, L'Âge d'Homme, 1997; *Guénonian Esoterism and Christian Mystery*, Sophia Perennis. 2004; new edition, *Christ the Original Mystery: Esoterism and the Mystical Way*, Angelico, 2018.

Symbolisme et réalité, Ad Solem, 1997; *Symbolism and Reality*, Angelico, 2016 in tandem with *The Crisis of Religious Symbolism*, 2016.

Penser l'analogie, Ad Solem, 2000, L'Harmattan, 2012.

The Secret of the Christian Way: A Contemplative Ascent Through the Writings of Jean Borella, edited and translated by G. John Champoux with a Foreword by Wolfgang Smith, State University of New York Press, 2001.

Lumières de la théologie mystique, L'Âge d'Homme, 2002.

Le Poème de la Création. Translation of Genesis 1–3, Ad Solem, 2002.

Un homme une femme au Paradis: Sept méditations sur le deuxième chapitre de la Genèse, Ad Solem, 2008.

La crise du symbolisme religieux, l'Harmattan, Paris, 2008 (corrected and enlarged re-edition of 1990 L'Âge d'Homme edition); *The Crisis of Religious Symbolism*, Angelico, 2016.

Amour et Vérité: La voie chrétienne de la charité, L'Harmattan, 2011 (revised edition of *La charitié profanée*, Éd. du Cèdre, 1979); *Love and Truth: The Christian Path of Charity*, Angelico, forthcoming.

Aux sources bibliques de la métaphysique, L'Harmattan, 2015.

Marxisme et sens chrétien de l'histoire, L'Harmattan, 2016.

Sur les Chemins de l'Esprit Itineraire d'un Philosophe Chretien, L'Harmattan, 2018.

Abbreviations Used

D.A.C.L. = *Dictionnaire d'Archéologie Chrétienne et de Liturgie* (Cabrol-Leclerc, Paris).

D.H.G.E. = *Dictionnaire d'Histoire et de Géographie Ecclésiastiques* (Baudrillart).

D.T.C. = *Dictionnaire de Théologie Catholique* (Vacant-Mangenot).

P.G. = Migne, *Patrologiae Cursus completus* — Series graeca, Paris.

P.L. = Migne, *Patrologiae Cursus completus* — Series latina, Paris.

CONTENTS

General Introduction: *A Guénonian Interpretation of Christianity—Is It Legitimate?* 1

I. NATURE OF THE ESOTERIC PERSPECTIVE

1 • *Esoterism: History and Idea* 13
   From Adjective to Noun [14]—Definition and Situation of Esoterism [21]—How the Sacred Sciences are Dependent on Hermeneutics [26]—Some Illustrations of This Doctrine [28]—Appendix: The Notion of Hermeneutics [31]

2 • *Esoterism in Its Essence and in Its Existence* 34
   Introduction: Triangular Structure of the Hermeneutic Field [34]—On Essence and Existence [36]—On Intellect and Concept [40]—Ideal Esoterism and the Ego's Illusions [44]—The Intuition of Essences as Semantic Experience [47]—Did Guénon Teach the Doctrine of Absolute Esoterism? [52]

3 • *Esoterism-Exoterism: A Living Dialectic* 55
   A Triple-Termed Dialectic [55]—Divine Revelation Converts the Outer to the Inner [57]—Esoteric Veiling and Metaphysical Unveiling [62]—Real Esoterism and Formal Esoterism [71]—A Feeble Imitation: The Grail Legend [76]—Conclusion: The Church is Only One [83]

II. RENÉ GUÉNON AND CHRISTIANITY: A CRITICAL EXAMINATION

Introduction: Direct Refutation & Indirect Refutation 89

4 • *Christian Esoterism According to Guénon* 92
   Appendix: 'Religion': History and Etymology [96]

5 • *Jewish Esoterism or New Covenant?* 99
   Christianity is a Universal Religion From Its Beginnings [99]—
   An Examination of Proofs Alleged By Guénon: The Innovation of
   Nicea [106]—Nicene 'Dogmatism' [121]—Dogmatic Mystery and
   Baptismal Mystery [133]—The Torn Veil [139]—The Eschatological Economy of Christianity [149]

6 • *Sacraments and Sacramentals* 152

7 • *The Nature of the Sacraments is Immutable* 157
   On the Nature of the Sacraments [157]—On the Sacramental
   Character [159]—In Itself, Sacramental Grace Is Not Susceptible
   To More Or Less [163]—Guénon's Thesis Is Triply Unacceptable
   [166]—Conclusion: The Sacramental Order is Incorruptible [179]

III. CHRISTIANITY IN ITS MYSTERY

Introduction: The Christian Mystery Speaks of Itself 185

8 • *Mystery and Doctrine* 192
   The Mystery of 'Christianity' [192]—The 'Mysteries' of Paganism
   [201]—The Theological 'Mysterion' in the New Testament [220]—
   The Triple 'Mysterion' of Christian Doctrine [228]—The Christian
   Mystery and the Esoteric Traditions of Rabbinism [239]—Secret
   Traditions in Clement of Alexandria [248]—Esoterism and Knowledge in Origen [260]—Doctrinal Esoterism of the First Centuries
   [277]

9 • *Sacramental Initiation & the Discipline of the Arcane* . 296
   Introduction: A Manifest Esoterization [296]—Mysteries, Sacraments, and Initiation [298]—The Discipline of the Arcane [310]—
   Sacramental Doctrine [338]—Dionysian Theology and Christian
   Initiation [350]—Conclusion: A Certain Spirit of Esoterism [375]
   —Appendix I: On the Silently Recited Canon of the Mass [378]—
   Appendix II: The Degrees of Salvation [383]—Appendix III: Operative Habitus and Entitative Habitus [385]—Appendix IV: St Symeon the New Theologian and Baptism in the Spirit [386]—Appendix V: The Three Stages of the Mystical Way and the Three Parts of

Philosophy [387]—Appendix VI: Infant Baptism in the Church Fathers [388]—Appendix VII: The Nature of Monastic Consecration According to Catholic Doctrine [389]

10 • *The Mystical Way* 394

Introduction: Listening to the Christian Word [394]—What the Fathers Understood by 'Mystical' [397]—The Nature of Mystical Contemplation [405]—From Adjective to Noun [411]—Break or Continuity in the Mystical Tradition [426]—Acquired Contemplation and Infused Contemplation [437]—The Way of Christ and 'Guénonian' Mysticism [441]—The Word of the Mystics and the Divine Essence [458]—Appendix I: Concerning the 'Evangelic Pearl' [482]—Appendix II: Is St John of the Cross a Voluntarist? [483]

Scriptural Index 485

General Index 489

General Introduction

A Guénonian Interpretation of Christianity—Is It Legitimate?

RENÉ GUÉNON'S WORK is generally considered the chief expression of traditional esoterism in the twentieth century. This verdict, heard among good historians and many scholars, Antoine Faivre for example,[1] cannot be seriously disputed since they are in fact surveying the currents of thought so designated, currents extolled since the beginning of the nineteenth century by numerous authors who no doubt inspired Guénon, but whom he surpasses by the breadth of his intellectual genius and the unique character of his position. It is not surprising then that a work of such importance has become known to a large and admiring readership, including—necessarily—many Christians. All have found within it a decisive 're-evaluation' of the nobility and the understanding of their own religion. Guénon's message has thus rendered an invaluable service to some of our contemporaries. In a world devoted to the most anti-spiritual rationalism ever seen, he has reminded us with exceptional force that religion is the keeper of a Knowledge before which all modern science and philosophy are only an 'ignorant knowledge'.[2]

From of all this, no less than from his teachings on metaphysics and symbolism, a Christian can draw the most substantial profit. In many respects, then, the reading of Guénon remains advantageous.

---

1. Antoine Faivre, 'L'ésotérisme chrétien du XVIe au XXe siècle', in *Histoire des religions, Encyclopédie de la Pléiade*, vol. II, pp 1,358.
2. This expression (*savoir ignorant*) is taken from Guénon's *The Crisis of the Modern World* (Hillsdale: Sophia Perennis, 2004), p 54, where it is further characterized as 'knowledge of an inferior order confining itself entirely to the lowest level

Christ the Original Mystery

But what must also be considered is that for the majority of his Christian readers, with the obvious exception of those who have rejected him, the importance of his work is not limited to the light he sheds on ideas of tradition, revelation, the sacred, spiritual knowledge, or even the symbolic language of various traditions, for he is often attributed an *authority* having power over their own religion. In their eyes, Guénon's doctrine is the definitive means for interpreting the Catholic faith, in such a way that the particulars of the Catholic faith can be understood in their true light only by the principles and categories of this doctrine, and especially by a clear distinction between esoterism and exoterism. As a result—a result of which Christian readers seem to be unaware—what the Catholic faith says *about* itself is found to be, if not disqualified, at least *neutralized*. The teachings of Christianity are of course not rejected as to their stated contents, but it is denied, either implicitly or explicitly, that the Catholic Church is in possession of the most profound understanding of these teachings. Like a donkey burdened with relics, this Church, reduced to pure exoterism, is ignorant of the metaphysical nature of the treasures deposited within her, as well as the true import of the means of grace she administers, which are said to be revealed only through initiatic rites, rites about which this Church no longer has the least idea. This is why such Christians feel the need to proceed with a general reinterpretation of Christianity, and in particular with putting the nature of her rites into Guénonian terminology and into accord with the criteria of his teaching.

The exactness of the foregoing description should not be seriously objected to. But if the attitude thus characterized adequately expresses the deep-seated conviction of 'Guénonian Christians', then, at least in anticipation of a judgement, the problem of its legitimacy should be raised. This problem can certainly be resolved in

---

of reality, knowledge ignorant of all that lies beyond it, of any aim more lofty than itself, and of any principle that could give it a legitimate place, however humble, among the various orders of knowledge as a whole. Irremediably enclosed in the relative and narrow realm in which it has striven to proclaim itself independent, thereby voluntarily breaking all connection with transcendent truth and supreme wisdom, it is only a vain and illusory knowledge, which indeed comes from nothing and leads to nothing.' 'Skilled ignorance' might convey the sense more aptly. ED.

General Introduction

the affirmative, but only provided one accepts that the problem can be formulated, accepts that a 'Guénonization' of Christianity is not self-evident. This is precisely the object of my study.

From this standpoint the first question is that of the relationship between hermeneutics and revelation, since the Guénonization of Christianity under discussion rightly consists in setting up Guénonian doctrine as the supreme hermeneutic of Christian revelation.[1] In support of this it can be granted that it is quite normal that a revelation require one or more interpretations. So why not think about Christianity with the help of the Muslim Guénon, since St Thomas Aquinas clearly did so with the help of the pagan Aristotle?

Presented thus the issue raised is immense.[2] In a sense, it represents the most fundamental problem to confront a believing philosopher, which is to say every person insofar as he both believes and thinks. In this work I will broach the issue under only one of its truly essential aspects, that is, the relationship between the natural universality of the hermeneutic intelligence and the supernatural singularity of revelation. With Guénon this is to be dealt with first.

Far from denying the role of metaphysical doctrine in the understanding of revelation, it seems that in order to be understood, every religious language, considered in its direct appearance, must become 'spirit and life' in those *thinking* beings who receive it and speak about it—must become a 'speculative hermeneutics', a 'metalanguage' of an intellectual nature, suitable for communicating its meaning and for making possible its assimilation. This is one necessity imposed on all religions. Revelation shows and speaks, but we still need to understand what we see and listen to what is said. Objective revelation on the one hand, speculative hermeneutics on the other: these are the two poles between which religious *life* is coordinated and unfolds. Without hermeneutics, revelation 'says' nothing; without revelation, hermeneutics has nothing to say.

---

1. On the notion of hermeneutics, see the appendix to chap. I, p31.
2. To this I have devoted portions of two earlier books, *Le mystère du signe* (Paris: Maisonneuve & Larousse, 1989), reprinted under the title *Traité du signe symbolique* (forthcoming), and *La crise du symbolisme religieux* (Lausanne, Switzerland: L'Age d'Homme, 1990).

Christ the Original Mystery

Some may object that, as necessary as a speculative hermeneutic might be—that is, an organized metaphysics expressing itself in ordered discourse—it is not always sufficient to make a revealed fact (a *revelatum*) intelligible since it itself might need to be explained. Proceeding further, it might even be asked whether this is the case with *every* hermeneutic and whether it always requires a second explanation; it would serve no purpose, as I have nevertheless just done, to bring religious life back to the 'revelation-hermeneutics' dialectic. This objection is important, and answering it will let us distinguish a major feature of speculative hermeneutics, to which we will return again and again in the course of this work, but which must be brought up briefly here. I do not reject the idea that interpretation might be to a certain degree indefinite, not only 'extensively', as it does not exhaust its object, there always remaining something more to be said, but also 'intensively' because it itself can always be further explained. And yet observe how the secondary interpretations of a primary doctrinal interpretation are generally effected with the help of the words and syntax of the metaphysical language chosen for this speculative hermeneutics, which are formulated in various ways: the explanation varies, but by means of the same explanatory language. And when it happens that we change our metaphysics to gain a better understanding, leaving behind for example the metaphysics of Plato or Aristotle for that of Shankara, we still remain within the bounds of speculative discourse. The reason for this is that (and this is a major trait which I would like to stress) by right and by principle speculative discourse is a metalanguage unto itself, possessing its own explicit meaning within itself and having no need for another language—whichever one it might be—to unveil it, at least to the extent that the hermeneutic adequately speaks the language of the natural intelligence and is nothing but the most direct expression of this intelligence.

We need to agree that an intellection—and even a simple concept—'speaks its own language', that it is semantically transparent to itself and is known at the same time that it knows. Intellective activity is characterized by this: intellection is intelligible. At least this is true for intellection in its essence, if not in all of its applications. Besides, how could it be otherwise since absolute explanations are

General Introduction

not given intentionally? One explanation can have need of another, and so forth, but there comes a moment when the intellect stands alone and naked before its object. Nothing else can understand in its place; it alone grasps what it grasps, understands what it has learned, digests semantically what it has passively received.

Still, it needs to receive something, an object must be given to it. The intellect knows itself only in knowing, that is to say in the act of intellection, which it produces under the effect of the object to be known: it is the object's revelation that reveals the intellect to itself. That the intellect is intelligible to itself thus in no way entails its self-sufficiency. The intellect is always itself in all its acts, but it is itself only in its relationship with the what is given it: it knows its identity only in its active relationship with the alterity of its object—just as the eye's ability to see 'sees' only in the act of perceiving something. This means there is no metaphysics without a supernatural revelation to be understood, that is to say interpreted. Assuredly, metaphysics is in principle the native tongue of pure intelligence, but this tongue would not speak if it did not have the supernatural revelation of religion here below or the natural revelation of creation in the Earthly Paradise to talk about.

The intellect therefore speaks its own language; which means that no one can teach it this language. Truly, the intellect is itself language, or *logos*. However, since we are not dealing with pure intellect but with a composed metaphysical discourse, with terms (words or concepts) ordered according to set relationships (as is always the case in human cultures), a perfect naturalness, and therefore the perfect universality of such a speculative hermeneutic, can no longer be maintained. The undeniable plurality of metaphysical discourses is opposed to their being strictly equivalent (as if content could be completely alien to the form which embodies it). Undoubtedly we should recognize that these discourses aspire to the same and unique Truth, since there should be a (relative) possibility of translating them into each other—otherwise they could not even be classified under the same concept of metaphysics. But this focal point, this 'Orient' of all metaphysics should be attained doctrinally: no super-discourse is capable of saying or expressing it, and hence no metaphysical doctrine is normative for other doctrines.

It might be objected, however, that in saying this I seem to be positioning my own discourse precisely as normative with respect to all the others. But this is a sophism, for this 'position' is actually a 'negation'. In other words, as Plato (in his *Parmenides*), Damascius, Nagarjuna, or Meister Eckhart inform us, speech can speak of the Beyond of every word, thought, or being (except to contradict, in its very utterance, the Unspeakable about which it is speaking) only by erasing and denouncing from within itself its own statement. This speculative humility should not be considered just a kind of psychological precaution against the eventuality of intellectual pride; it is also and first of all a strict consequence *intrinsic* to the very being of the discourse, like a shadow cast on human speech by the transcendence of the 'beyond-everything'. Therefore there is no explicit supreme doctrine, which means that no doctrinal formulation can explicitly assure the correct understanding of a metaphysical teaching, and that, in particular, certain apparently negative, or even in some respects 'nihilistic' discourses run the risk of being taken the wrong way, without it being possible to prevent this error through a more explicit discourse.

But on the other hand, the transcendence of the absolutely Ineffable liberates as it were the plurality of metaphysical traditions. In any case, it opens the field to a *possible* plurality, which after the fall of Adam and still more after the Tower of Babel will become a *de facto* plurality. But neither is this *de facto* plurality an extrinsic feature of metaphysical doctrines, an ultimately negligible feature, as if the multiplicity of these doctrines had no other interest than to provide Guénonians an occasion to show their unanimity. It should be envisioned within and for itself. We see then that the principle of universal translatability suffers some limitations, since translation always incurs a loss or change of meaning (hence the frequent need to use new terms), and since the various intellectual languages do not have the same aptitude for stating the true meaning of such or such a revelation; a diversity of 'hermeneutic capacity' is also the raison d'être for the plurality of doctrinal languages.

And so, with no universal metaphysical doctrine—not even the Vedanta—to provide the speculative key to every possible revelation, we must place ourselves in a state of intellective virginity and strip

General Introduction

ourselves as much as possible of acquired languages, so as to give the divine Word every chance of being heard, of semantically resounding within us according to Its truth and Its intelligible mode. For the Word also has a way to say what It says, and that is already a hermeneutic, an interpretation of the *revelatum*. Just as there is not, in the reality of our human existence, any pure intellection, since intellection is always actualizing itself as intellection *of* something, neither is there any pure revelation, any pure revealed Object. Every revelation includes a certain comprehension of itself, this being the mode under which it presents itself to men and with the help of which it is made understandable to them. We *have* to be attentive to this hermeneutic mode, for, being willed by God, it must put forth its semantic roots into the intellect of the believer. Surely an apprenticeship in more than one metaphysical language can be useful, or even necessary, to till the intellective earth, to rid it of its brambles and weeds, to improve it and break it up further. But this preparatory labor must not lead to substituting the tares of human discourses for the wheat of the divine Word.

The preceding considerations seemed necessary for an understanding of what will follow, for I intend to critically examine the theses upheld by Guénon on the subject of Christian esoterism and the (for him) exoteric nature of the sacraments. Now, such an examination clashes directly with the conviction that Guénon's doctrine provides its readers with the principles and criteria to ultimately settle the debate. So strong is this conviction that without their knowing it for some it has succeeded in completely stifling the *sensus christianus*. Deaf and blind to the *language* of their own religion, which they have so often mouthed without understanding it, they judge the data of Christianity according to Guénon's doctrine, stipulating that this data be retranslated into his language. Such behavior is quite surprising. Granted, the language of Western *philosophy*, the language of such or such a *theology*, or even *theology in general*, may be rejected in order to think about the *revelatum*. But how is it possible to similarly reject the very language of the *revelatum* and that of the Church entrusted by Christ to transmit it (the Councils). It is God Himself who has *so* revealed Himself. This *so* is the only means we have of reaching an understanding. To imagine that the

Church knows not what it says when it speaks this language and explains its terms, that it is reserved to an elite to delve into their authentic significance—this would be to deny at once the *revelatum*, the *revelatio* and the *Revelatus*.

It will perhaps be objected that it is not a question of rejecting the language of revelation, but simply of speaking about it in a different way. *A priori*, why could the language of Guénon not be as apt—and perhaps even more so—as that of Aristotle or Plato for gaining an understanding of the faith? I would in fact agree that such might be the case; at least I do not deny it *a priori*. I even think Guénon's work in general quite useful with respect to a criticism of the modern world, or an understanding of sacred symbolism and metaphysical doctrine. In this last domain it has furnished certain keys without which it would be hard to truly understand Plato, and even Aristotle. However, this adoption of the Guénonian hermeneutic is legitimate only provided that the doctrine of the faith as formulated by Church and Scripture be spared, since this formulation has been guaranteed by divine *authority* and is identical to revelation insofar as it is revealed: it is therefore prior with regard to every hermeneutic that takes it for an object. Now in this respect Guénon's work has not failed to pose some delicate problems, to the point that it seems to see Christian dogma as an exteriorization—under the form of 'mysteries'—of esoteric truths. But concerning two principal mysteries, those of the Trinity and the hypostatic union (Incarnation), Guénon has never indicated the metaphysical notions of which these dogmas are the exoteric presentation. On the other hand, Guénon has developed his thought on the history of Christian esoterism and the nature of the sacraments rather extensively, and so it is this that must be examined if we are to appreciate its hermeneutic relevance with respect to Christianity.

Yet to treat of Christian esoterism supposes that we have already answered the question raised by the notion of esoterism as such, and it is to this that the book's first part is devoted. We must first strive to situate this notion, surveying it historically within its own framework and according to the function that can be attributed to it. Next, the consequences implied by this characterization with respect to the two major trends that can affect esoterism will be shown: its

General Introduction

absolutization on the one hand, as seen in certain religious movements claiming a 'pure spirit' exclusively for themselves, and its institutional hardening on the other, as observed in the appeal of more or less secret organizations and strongly hierarchized parallel churches. This will then provide the opportunity to specify the relationships that the esoteric perspective maintains with metaphysics as well as with exoterism, striving always to present things in their living reality rather than under their formal definition.

After these rather theoretical considerations I will in the second part critically examine Guénon's views on Christianity. These theses will be first summarized as exactly as possible, and then confronted, on certain essential points, with the actual facts imparted to us by the New Testament, church literature of the early centuries, historical science, and Catholic theology.

It is, however, impossible to rest content with a critical examination of Guénon's theses. It is in fact not enough merely to tell what is unacceptable in the vision he offers of the Christian religion; I must also try to respond to the positive needs conveyed by this vision. There is no systematic anti-Guénonism here; in no way do I seek to burn something I in any case never adored, but only to challenge whatever seems incompatible with Christian truth.[1] Now this challenge is not concerned with the search for an esoteric perspective, which is no more nor less than a search for the heart and for spiritual interiority. I must demonstrate, then, that such a 'spirit of esoterism' is actually present in Church tradition, and that this spirit is summarized and completed in what this tradition calls the 'mystery of Christ'. This will be the focus of the last and most important part of the book, which could just as well be entitled: *From Esoteric Perspective to Christian Mystery*.

---

1. Moreover, the present work is only the development of what I said in the afterword to volume two of the Abbé Henri Stéphane's *Introduction à l'ésotérisme chrétien* (Paris: Dervy, 1983).

I

The Nature of the Esoteric Perspective

1

Esoterism: History and Idea

Guénon's way of dealing with questions is seldom historical.[1] He generally presents the ideas he uses as so many universal concepts, existing 'from all eternity', devoid of genealogy, in the way mathematicians usually introduce those factors deemed indispensable to their arguments. His definitions of terms used are generally stated as if they were self-evident and were being imposed in a thoughtful spirit of rigor and precision.

Thus Guénon always opposes the concepts *substance* and *essence* in the way Aristotle opposes *matter* and *form*. This illuminating distinction can be supported on some etymological grounds. However the distinction seems to ignore that the term *essentia* (probably due to Cicero) and the term *substantia* (proposed by Seneca) are attempts to render into Latin the single and unique term *ousia*, the most literal French equivalent of which would be *étance*. About this Guénon says nothing, so that his reader remains convinced that he has only given a more metaphysical meaning to the Western tradition's philosophical vocabulary, whereas he has changed this vocabulary to the point of making it not readily understandable to a reader of St Augustine, St Thomas, Eckhart, or Nicholas of Cusa.

The case is not the same for the word 'esoterism', for which Guénon is careful to indicate the historical origins: this term, he tells us, was first employed in certain philosophical schools of Greek

---

1. Exceptions are: *Theosophy: History of a Pseudo-Religion* and *The Spiritist Fallacy* (Hillsdale, NY: Sophia Perennis, 2004).

antiquity.[1] Since a Greek word is involved here, this is an incontestable and obvious fact. And yet, as we shall see, it is not strictly accurate, since the term 'esoterism' and the general idea that it designates are totally absent from Greek literature!

Now it is precisely here that the difficulty lies. How do we establish historically the legitimacy of esoterism as a general concept and its elevation into a major category of sacred doctrine, when it is authorized by a time-honored use that is actually not so? And if such a concept is in fact something modern—it is even partly Guénon's creation—how are we to apply it to Christianity, for example, which has never made use of it? Has not Guénon himself taught us that there is always a risk of error in the use of improper terminology? Do we not see him object to the term 'Sufism' as non-traditional, preferring *tasawwuf* as the only orthodox one? Do not be mistaken. I am not denying an author the right to use language as it suits him, nor the right to raise into a general category that which only existed as an adjective. This would be absurd and amount to denying all possibility of self-expression. I am only saying that the question should be posed for itself and not be ignored: for this is a real problem, so real that Guénon himself made a case for it—but this had to do with the word 'occultism'.

From Adjective to Noun

If we carefully examine the all too concise indications provided by Guénon[2] and inquire what historians have to say, we learn that the case is not the same for the noun 'esoterism' as for the adjective 'esoteric': only the latter was used in ancient times and attested to by philosophic literature; the former was totally unknown (although *esoterismos* would have been possible).

---

1. *Introduction to the Study of the Hindu Doctrines* (Hillsdale, NY: Sophia Perennis, 2004).

2. For 'esoterism' we follow Jean-Pierre Laurant, *L'ésotérisme chrétien en France au XIXe siècle*, L'Age d'Homme, coll. 'Politica Hermetica', 1992, pp 19 sq. and pp 42 sq. For 'esoteric', numerous items of information will be found in P. Riffard, *L'ésoterisme*, Laffont, coll. 'Bouquins', pp 70 ff.

Esoterism: History and Idea

As for the adjective *esoterikos*, its seems to appear first in the Aristotelian circles of the first century after Christ. An early instance is found in a rather caustic work by Lucian of Samosata entitled *Philosophers for Sale* (c. AD 166). Lucian advises that whoever wants to buy a slave should choose one that is a disciple of Aristotle. In this way, he tells us, one gets two for the price of one:

> one seen from without, another from within... [we] give the first the name 'exoteric' and the second the name 'esoteric'.[1]

The Aristotelian School, perhaps following its founder's directions, distinguished in the writings of the master two kinds of texts: works widely published (and today lost) qualified as *exoteric*, and more demanding treatises hardly disseminated outside the School (the only ones that have come down to us) called *acroamatics*, meaning 'relating to an oral teaching'. The distinction between these two categories of writings has stirred much debate, among ancient Greek and Latin commentators as well as modern ones.[2] Lucian's text can be understood as an ironic allusion to this distinction. It also bears witness to a change in terminology, *esoteric* now being contrasted with *exoteric*, and no longer *acroamatic*. Everything transpires as if this adjective, which Aristotle uses in the quite profane sense of 'exterior' or 'public', in the end gave rise to its inverted double. Is Lucian its inventor? Quite unlikely. In any case, thirty years later the term has gained currency, as is proven by Clement of Alexandria, who provides, under the form of a neuter plural substantivized adjective (*ta esoterika*, 'the esoterics [books]'), the first instance of *esoterikos*, taken in a noble sense as designating the category of writings Aristotle reserved for the intelligent.[3] From that time on, however, the term will only be used in a restricted and quasi-technical way.[4]

---

1. *Philosophes à vendre et autre écrits*, 26, trans. Eugène Talbot, Éditions Rivages, 1992, p32. Some hold the opinion that Lucian invented the term himself.
2. Octave Hamelin provides essential pieces to this dossier in *Le système d'Aristote* (Alcan, 1920), pp45–59.
3. V *Stromata*, 9, 58. According to A. Méhat (*Études sur les 'Stromates' de Clément d'Alexandrie* [Paris: Seuil, 1966] p54), this Stromata dates from around AD 200.
4. A few modern authors, such as the Italian philosopher and theologian Gioberti (*Filosofia della Revelazione* [Turin, 1856], p131), and, under his influence,

Christ the Original Mystery

As for the noun 'esoterism', every effort to find evidence going back to the eighteenth century has remained futile. In the current state of research, it is acknowledged that the term appeared for the first time in 1828, under the pen of the French historian Jacques Matter in his *Histoire critique du gnosticisme et de son influence*. It was the mystical socialist Pierre Leroux who, around 1840, guaranteed its spread in his famous work *De l'Humanité* by so characterizing Pythagorean doctrine.[1]

This origin is important for the subject at hand, for it shows in what milieu the concept of esoterism as a general category of religious thought was elaborated, once we admit—and how can we deny it?—the correlation that joins the term to the notion it indicates. This milieu is a socialistic romanticism that will inspire the Revolution of 1848, a nebulous ideology in which the religion of Humanity and the cult of democracy are combined with confused speculations on the Trinity, women, and progress (both industrial and social). Add a penchant for secret societies and we have an idea of this more or less Saint-Simonian mythology which excited the imagination of Michelet, George Sand, Alexander Dumas, Victor Hugo, and the Abbé Constant (Eliphas Lévi).[2] Such is the fertile soil from which this term has sprung. Doubtless, those making use of it see 'esoterism' as the source of that religiosity of the future which the impending universal revolution demands and which the Catholic Church no longer seems able to provide. One might indeed, they think, find a few elements of it in Church doctrine, provided one knows how to divine these elements beneath the veil of the dogmas in which clerical incomprehension has clothed them. At the time, this esoterism, extracted from the superstitions of formal religion by

---

Rabbi Benamozegh, attempted to reinstate the use of 'acroamatics': cf. Paul Vuillaud, *La Kabbale juive* (Plan de la Tour: Éditions d'Aujourd'hui, 1976), vol. 1, p39.

1. Laurant, op. cit., lists the following: Jacques Matter, 1828; Jacques Etienne Marconis de Nègre, *L'Hiériphante: développements complets des mystères maçonniques*, 1839; Pierre Leroux, *De l'Humanité* (vol. 2, pp397), 1840; J.B. Richard de Randonvilliers, *Dicitionnaire des mots nouveaux*, 1842. 'Esoterism' makes its first appearance in English in 1835.

2. Philippe Murray's book, *Le dix-neuvième siècle à travers les âges*, Denoël, 1984, conveys suggestive information on these matters.

Esoterism: History and Idea

their pains-taking efforts, revealed its identity with the common basis of all human beliefs which it would (presumably) one day replace.

Having thus acquired both identity and consistency, the notion of esoterism attained the rank of a universal category of religious thought, and therefore a necessary category. Henceforth, its presence or absence in a particular religion will define whether that religion is complete or incomplete. By virtue of its hidden nature, the presence of esoterism obviously cannot be noticed through mere external observation, which anyone could validate. An innate aptitude is required here, an aptitude whose possession is never guaranteed regardless how many are inclined to think themselves endowed with it. To form an exact idea of esoterism, to discern its traces in such or a such a religion is, in all likelihood to lay oneself open to many errors. Consequently, this idea should only be handled with prudence, even with reticence. But to the contrary, it is alluded and appealed to on every occasion in order to qualify or disqualify the most diverse manifestations (whether authentic or not) of the sacred.[1] Everything is explained and justified (or condemned) in the name of esoterism (or its absence) as if the mere pronunciation of the word were a valid argument. Faced with this excess, it is undeniable that the coining of the noun 'esoterism' has favored the inflation (and therefore the devaluation) of the concept so designated, and has thus endowed it with a kind of timeless necessity. But at the same time it is surprising that no one (not even Guénon) has asked how humanity has for millennia been able to do without so seemingly necessary a notion.

There is nothing exceptional in the development we have briefly retraced. And as we will see in this book's last chapter, it was the same for the word 'mystic' which, exclusively an adjective until the end of the sixteenth century, became a noun only in the seventeenth. It was then that one begins to hear of the 'mystical', before the notion attained its vaguest generality, in the nineteenth, with the birth of

---

1. Browse through any major French bookstore or book catalogue and you will see what disparities are covered by the label 'Esoterism': it has supplanted all other designations (occultism, magic, alchemy, religious symbolism, astrology, etc.).

'mysticism'. Perhaps some will deem that we overwork this purely terminological development to draw excessive conclusions that should be worthless against the obvious need for the idea of esoterism, since its late appearance is only the explicit naming of something that always implicitly existed. The response to this objection I will leave to Guénon himself. True, this response is not concerned with the appearance of the term esoterism, but the term 'occultism'. However, I do not see what can prevent it being applied here. As we know, 'occultism', like esoterism and mysticism, is an invention of the nineteenth century. Eliphas Lévi seems to have used it first, in 1856 at the beginning of *Dogma et ritual de la haute magie*.[1] On this subject Guénon remarks:

> If the word is new, it is because what it designates is also new. Prior to this there were 'occult sciences'... But there was never an effort to unite all of them into a single body of doctrine, which would essentially imply the dominance of occultism.[2]

We can gauge the thrust and consequences of such a text if we apply it to the term 'esoterism', which also led to the formation of a single idea, a term which until that time had only been in adjectival use.

But some will say that if this is all that is to be concluded on the subject of esoterism, why bother discussing it further? Or more seriously: is it not vain to propose to define it, if there is precisely nothing to define but a quite indistinct haze of elements lacking real unity, which would risk bestowing an illusory existence upon a mere mental creation?

A reply to this objection would demand a study, both scholarly and speculative, of the relationships that connect the history of ideas to the history of these words. Such an undertaking would mean a considerable digression. I will just say that if the need to designate by an abstract term something that was previously simply the object of an adjectival usage incontestably betrays a loss of intuitive knowledge, then the need to confer on this abstract term a more precise

---

1. *Transcendental Magic: Its Doctrine and Ritual*, tr. A.E. Waite (London: Rider and Company, 1896), p 5.
2. *The Spiritist Fallacy*, p 52.

meaning is all the more urgent. During times of spontaneous adjectival usage, everyone knows what they are saying when they decide that 'this is beautiful' or 'that is courageous,' but there comes a day when someone asks 'what is *beauty?*' or 'what is *courage?*', and certainty gives way to doubt. Henceforth, knowledge will if still possible pass through the mediation of a concept, and therefore through the need for philosophical elaboration: when the wine is drawn, drink we must. In other words, we have no choice. From the time the general idea of esoterism makes its appearance, like that of occultism, the mystical, and even mysticism, from the time it enters into intellectual commerce and circulates in every domain, we can assuredly reject it and deny its validity, but we can no longer ignore it; its very adversaries are compelled to use it. At a later stage in its diffusion (as is the case today) the word tends to be incorporated in our daily speech. And in the course of this work so we shall see that it spontaneously flows from the pens of certain Christian historians of the sacraments, theologians, philosophers, and historians of religions as an accepted term understood by everyone, and that its wide diffusion makes it less compromising. In this respect anyone can see that 'esoterism' has had greater success than 'occultism' with the general public, but also with experts and specialists, who find it a useful category for the history of religions. This means that the word has lost most of its original connotation, inasmuch as the nebulosity of the mystical socialism from which it sprang has been somewhat dissipated over time,[1] whereas the term 'occultism' remains fraught with its original sense and continues to refer quite directly to the knowledge and practice of the 'occult sciences'.

I am thus far from rejecting a term of such current usage. Assuredly, its drawbacks are numerous, not the least of which leads us to believe that this esoterism is the appanage of an 'organization' institutionally distinct from the official Church and characterized as exoteric, or that there is a real possibility of actually practicing esoterism 'in itself', but if we guard against these two nearly opposite tendencies (to harden esoterism into an institution or to dissolve it into an

---

1. It has been replaced today by pseudo-scientific wonders and 'New Age' animism.

ideal), the term can prove useful and even irreplaceable. Clearly, it will signify that the visible forms of religion conceal a more profound and more inward dimension that we are called to seek out. Now this idea is valuable, for only what we have personally and actively discovered is truly ours. It is, in fact, in the course of a long and arduous quest that we are transformed and discover ourselves while thus seeking, and so come to true knowledge [in the original French: *'co-naissance'*, i.e., both 'knowledge' and 'being-born-together']. Otherwise we remain strangers to what we have passively received without the participation of our inner being. The secret of the divine message is communicated only to one who devotes himself to it and, in faith, opens the secret of his heart to it. And even if only in a theoretical way, we still need to know that the words of the message are 'spirit and truth', that our attention needs to be vigilant, and that we need to be awakened by our most inward and most profound seeking—the seeking for the Spirit. The term esoterism is apt for the opening of our consciousness to the presence of the Spirit hidden in revealed forms and sometimes under the appearance of the most baffling symbols. Clearly then, the opposition 'exoterism-esoterism' plays the same role as the Pauline opposition of the letter and the spirit, and is in this respect just as legitimate, but with the already alluded to reservation that one neither absolutizes nor institutionalizes it. We illusorily absolutize it when, after the fashion of certain self-styled 'spiritual' groups or certain gnosticizing doctrines such as the philosophy of Hegel, we dream of practising a pure esoterism divested of any form and free of all reference to any revelation whatsoever. There are abundant examples of this. On the other hand, we unduly institutionalize it when we view it as an opposition between a would-be 'exoteric Church' (the 'Church of Peter') and a no less would-be 'esoteric Church' (the 'Church of John'), a distinction both modern and contrary to Scripture (1 Cor 1:12–13) but quite widespread among those with a fondness for esoterism.

The two following chapters will offer an opportunity to refute both these deviations in turn. But first let us try to *situate* the notions of esoterism and exoterism in a sufficiently plausible way so as to satisfy the needs of the philosopher, concerned about the truth of the thing, and the needs of the historian of religions, preoccupied with suitable classifications. True, these two points of view are not entirely conciliable. The historian intends to pass judgement on the nature of the religious or para-religious phenomena he studies. He is content to make inquiries and describe them as exactly as possible. He is however constrained to classify them, to rank them in various categories, so as to identify them, and therefore, whatever he does do, he is obliged to provide a characteristic definition. Now such a definition necessarily has a bearing on the essence of what is to be defined, an essence that cannot simply be acquired at the end of an inquiry (in Greek *historia* means 'inquiry'), however meticulous—and the more meticulous the inquiry, the more unlikely this will be, for then the sheer variety of cases will elude the inevitable simplifications of our conceptual frameworks. Thus the historian, whether he recognizes it or not, cannot avoid having a theoretical bias about the nature of things, and it is better to recognize this and deal with the question head-on if one is anxious to avoid as much as possible contradictions, ambiguities, and confusions. In short, one cannot do without a philosophical definition of esoterism that in some respects still conveys the vision one has of its essence, *a priori*, and is not just the result of abstraction and generalization from observed cases. On this subject we can even criticize the philosophers and ridicule their pretension. In reality, no one is exempt. But it is also true that philosophers should stick to solid religious facts, which most often are known to us in any precise way only from the works of historians of religion. Here we have a kind of 'circle' from which we seem unable to escape entirely. Such is the lot of all human knowledge, which demands a kind of endless 'fine tuning' between the conceptual and the observed order of things, or, if you like, between the order of essences and the order of existences.

Definition and Situation of Esoterism

Having provided these methodological precisions, we now come to the very notion of esoterism such as I propose to define it, which means such as I propose to situate it. This is in fact the only means at our disposal for avoiding two almost antagonistic deviations: the absolutizing of esoterism and its institutionalization. Thus defined in itself, and situated with respect to the genre from which it is derived, I believe the idea of esoterism will have some chance of escaping the risks of inflation and hardening which characterize it.

We start with its etymology—left aside until now—not because it conceals a mysterious and highly symbolic significance, but because it provides an interesting detail which should never have been lost from sight. This etymology is well known and presents no mystery insofar as it is most likely a question, as mentioned, of a scholarly and late formation modelled on the pre-existing adjective: *esoterikos*. *Esoterikos* breaks down into three elements: *eso-*, *-ter*, and *-ikos*. *Eso* or *eiso*, is a preposition or adverb meaning 'within' or 'inside', originally with an idea of movement; *-ter* should be related to *-teros*, a suffix marking the comparative in Greek. Moreover, in the Acts of the Apostles (16:24) we find the adjective *esoteros* used in the sense of an 'inner'[1] place. And finally, the termination *-ikos* indicates the adjective with a nuance of specificity. The complete word signifies, then, 'that which has a comparatively more interior quality of being.'

Two major ideas, it seems, are to be drawn from this etymological analysis (besides that of interiority, which obviously represents the essential theme): first, the idea of an oppositive comparison, and second, the idea of movement, displacement. These two ideas, directly signified by the morphological structure of the term, should never be lost from sight. As for the first, it indicates that the adjective 'esoteric' always qualifies something by opposition to the contrary quality, which could be designated as 'exoteric'. These two terms are therefore relative to each other and form a pair: 'esoteric' should not signify 'that which possesses the quality of absolute interiority' or 'supreme' interiority, but 'that which is more interior than that which was just spoken of.' This consideration is likewise valid for 'exoteric', also a comparative possessing only a relational significance: there is no absolute exoterism any more than there is an

---

1. 'We need to relate comparatives with *-teros* to Latin words like *al-ter*, *u-ter*, etc.... these Latin forms are from true comparatives,' in P. Crouzet, P. Andraud, and A. Font, *Grammaire grecque*, E. Privat and H. Didier, 1926, p 66.

Esoterism: History and Idea

absolute esoterism. These are commonsense and perfectly logical considerations.[1] This oppositive situation of the two notions was not lost on Guénon: 'where there is no exoterism,' he writes,[2] 'there is no longer any occasion to speak of esoterism either.' This is the case, he thinks, with the Hindu tradition.

Some will perhaps object that by making esoterism correlative to exoterism we place both on the same level, whereas to the very extent that esoterism is something more interior and more profound than exoterism, esoterism is superior to it and does not stem from the same order. This objection expresses the incontestable truth that for we humans, fallen and relatively exterior beings that we are, the divine and the sacred are from the first truly more 'interior' and 'within'; and so much the more does one who is converted from without to within and breaks away from the exteriority of appearances know, by the same token, both exterior *and* interior which, at least for him, cease being in opposition. Without dwelling on a point to which we shall soon return, I can say that this objection describes the principle of an ideal esoterism rather than its actual process. To speak of esoterism is necessarily to speak of a surpassing of exterior appearances, which means, for anyone who experiences the need to accomplish this surpassing, that appearances are still not entirely transparent, that they constitute a veil which must be lifted, torn, or (according to one striking image) a shell that must be transpierced—in short that there is still a difference between these two sides of the real, between exterior and interior, and therefore that the esoteric as such is defined only with respect to the exoteric it strives to surpass. If this surpassing were perfectly accomplished and realized there would no reason to speak of esoterism, for the appearances themselves would be the most hidden of depths, the relative itself would be entirely immanent to the Absolute. Meanwhile, and if we wish to retain an acceptable and clear meaning for the term esoterism, it behooves us to situate it dialectically with respect to its opposite. Thus, superior as it may be, the esoteric perspective as such

---

1. Even in English 'interior' and 'exterior' were originally comparatives and only make sense with respect to one another.
2. *Introduction to the Study of the Hindu Doctrines*, p109.

nonetheless remains on the same side as the exoteric perspective with respect to what surpasses both, which is the very knowledge of Self 'realized' by the Absolute when it begets its Word, for only from the point of view of the Absolute—which is not a point of view—do all differing points of view cease.

A second idea suggested by the formation of the adjective *esoterikos* is, as mentioned, concerned with the dynamic character of the opposition it maintains with *exoterikos*. This character proceeds moreover from my previous remarks, and we will return to this second point also in a coming chapter. For now it will be enough to say that this idea of movement, displacement, or progression is included in the idea of a surpassing of appearances that is inherent to the notion of esoterism. What the term indicates is that esoterism resides in the surpassing itself, that it always remains related to what it surpasses, and therefore that the need for this surpassing is permanent. Illusion, as I have said, consists in forgetting this surpassing in order to see nothing but the ideal intention that orients it. So here, by setting up a statically formal distinction between the esoteric and exoteric perspectives, we risk forgetting here-below that we are all exoterists in some respects, in St Paul's words 'carnal', and that we must ceaselessly convert ourselves, turn our hearts toward the Spirit, or rather let the Spirit effect this return within us, for it is he who converts the exterior into the interior, he who has us proceed 'from faith to faith' (Rom. 1:17), *ex fide in fidem* (with the accusative of motion!), who accomplishes within us the 'passage', the Lord's 'Pasch', leading us from a still exterior faith to an already interior faith. And this passage lasts as long as does our state of being a *traveller*.

These remarks suggested by the etymological makeup of the term lead to an observation that is simple and even banal, but for this very reason quite incontestable. The legitimacy of the distinction into exoteric and esoteric perspectives is relative to a diversity of degrees in our human understanding of divine revelation. This diversity of *degrees in the receiving of* the saving Word is affirmed many times in the Christian Scriptures: Christ himself makes a case for it in the famous parable of the Sower, and St Paul's teaching constantly invites us to examine ourselves with regard to it. But as we shall see

Esoterism: History and Idea

explicitly throughout this work, what is excluded for Christianity is to base this diversity of degrees upon an irreducible differentiation of human natures which would in principle consign some to exoterism and others to esoterism. Moreover, as Christ warns us, neither mental skill nor book-learning have anything to do with it, but foremost and essentially purity of heart. This does not mean that stupidity is welcome here; to the contrary, great intelligence is required, but a profound intelligence, an intelligence that is perception of being and discernment of truth. As for knowledge, it is not necessarily an obstacle to the extent that it is subordinated to faith and does not impede intellective vision.

Having understood then that there are 'those who are without' (Mark 4:11), who are taught in parables, who 'see and do not perceive,' who cannot be 'converted' (4:12), and those to whom is communicated 'the mystery of the Kingdom' (provided we recognize that the same person can belong at once, though not under the same relationship, to both categories), we are authorized to admit the legitimacy of a distinction between exoteric and esoteric perspectives. This distinction, expressing a difference in degrees of understanding, quite logically and quite simply leads to the main place where this distinction is valid, and therefore to the realm to which these two categories of exoterism and esoterism apply (this is what we call 'situating' esoterism): this place is *hermeneutics*.

If there is in fact a general science for the understanding of a cultural object, the name that best suits it is hermeneutics.[1] And as a consequence, to the very extent that the esoterism/exoterism distinction draws its legitimacy from the existence of a scale of degrees in the understanding of the revealed message, this distinction then necessarily is itself hermeneutic in nature and should be appreciated at the core of the general realm of hermeneutics.

Moreover, as we have explained in *Le mystère du signe*,[2] hermeneutics must not be reduced solely to the interpretation of sacred scripture. Ritual and liturgical practice, no less than our spiritual

---

1. See appendix to the present chapter, p31.
2. Paris: Maissonneuve et Larose, 1989, pp229–241, [reprinted under the title: *Traité de signe symbolique* TR].

life, constitute the supreme achievement of sacred hermeneutics understood in its most profound sense; to truly comprehend divine revelation is not only to interpret God's Word according to its different levels of meaning, it is also and above all to obey this Word's commandments, accomplish its rites, and realize the will of heaven within our very being. Without doubt, anyone who accepts this way of seeing things will more easily receive our thesis that esoterism and exoterism share the hermeneutic field, and that it is this which characterizes it.

Such is my conclusion: except for some blurring of these ideas due to circumstances, exoterism and esoterism have a precise and legitimate sense only as different 'hermeneutic modes' of one and the same cultural object: the revealed message. This does not mean that every extension of these terms outside the realm in which they are naturally situated is devoid of significance. But this extension always runs the risk to which every designation is exposed when it no longer refers to the reality it is charged with designating: instead of being used with understanding, words then start thinking and functioning on their own and our minds become confused.

How the Sacred Sciences are Dependent on Hermeneutics

In the next two chapters I shall explain some of the consequences implicit to my definition. First, however, let us anticipate one quite valid objection: if esoterism is to be regarded as a hermeneutic mode of a revealed message, what then of sacred sciences such as alchemy, music, architecture, numerology, grammar, etc., which seem unsuited to a hermeneutic framework, since they are not ordered as such to a particular revealed message? And likewise, if we admit, as we should, that metaphysics is the ultimate degree of speculative hermeneutics, what about certain metaphysical traditions, such as Platonism and Aristotelianism, which have not been constructed with a view to interpreting any revelation whatsoever? To truly answer these questions to any possible extent would demand explanations both lengthy and relatively foreign to the subject of this

Esoterism: History and Idea

book.[1] For now let us summarize the solution that seems to impose itself and to which we shall return in following chapters.

Every science, whether metaphysical or cosmological (the sacred sciences), can in principle be considered as a hermeneutic of the real granted to the human intellect, be it the conditioned real (the world), or the unconditioned Real (the divine Principle). This means firstly that the intellect always enters into the cognitive act under the effect of an encountered object (whatever it might be), and secondly that cognition is never a simple registering of what is, but always and at the same time its interpretation, in other words, making sense of it. Clearly, then, neither Plato nor Aristotle intended in philosophizing to interpret a revealed message that was lacking; nevertheless their philosophies are in many respects presented as a 'theology' of man, of the world, and of their common principle, and these are the objects that act as revealed data. Has not Plato said that the world is the most beautiful of visible gods?[2] The same observations might be made with respect to the various sacred sciences. It should also be added that all these sciences (whether metaphysical or cosmological) have given effective service to particular historical religious messages such as Judaism, Christianity, and Islam.

---

1. I intend to deal with them in a forthcoming work: *La Porte du Ciel. Fondements scripturaires de la tradition métaphysique* (to be published by Ad Solem).

2. This theme is expounded by Timaeus of Locres at the beginning of his explanation of cosmology in the dialogue of the same name. It is possible that Plato was aware of the somewhat abnormal character of the situation of metaphysics in Greek culture—it could not be the hermeneutics of a sacred revelation, which it lacked, and could not fulfill the function of classical mythology, which it rejected. Thus Plato puts the following words addressed to Solon in the mouth of an Egyptian priest: 'You Hellenes are never anything but children, and there is not an old man among you... In mind you are all young; there is *no old opinion handed down* [the French translation includes 'de bouche à oreille', i.e., 'from mouth to ear' TR] *by ancient tradition, nor any science which is hoary with age*' (*Timaeus* 22b, *The Collected Dialogues of Plato*, ed. E. Hamilton and H. Cairns, trans. B. Jowett, Bollingen Series LXXI [Princeton: Princeton University Press, 1961], p1157). Festugière even thinks that Plato's deep intention in *Timaeus* and *Laws* was to found a new astral religion upon the ruins of mythology: 'The mythological gods had had their day: Plato founds a new religion based on recent advances in astronomical science' (*La révélation d'Hermès Trismégiste*, vol. II, *Le Dieu cosmique*, Les Belles Lettres, 1986, p100).

One difficult question remains however, that of the origin of these sciences. As a study of the various religions shows, these sciences have in fact quite often preceded the appearance of the great revelations whose hermeneutic servants they have become, or if they have not preceded them, they at least stem from independent sources. Moreover, science is universal whereas a religion always constitutes a single and unique manifestation. But there should be nothing surprising in this situation once we admit, as I have already expressed on other occasions, that a religion can be defined as the meeting between a vertical revelation, come from on high, and a horizontal cultural tradition, come from humanity's origins and therefore from the Adamic age. Surely the modes of this revelation can in each instance be quite varied, just as the primordial cultural tradition has been considerably diversified, changed, altered, and even partially lost or unilaterally enriched through the ages. But a revealed message is always inserted within a pre-existing culture (be it only a pre-existing language) which it transforms by endowing it with a sacred center, reorganizing it by making it serve as its own elucidation.[1]

I do not think, therefore, that anyone can call back into question our hermeneutic characterization of esoterism. There is nothing very unexpected in this characterization. It is basically even quite banal, and we encounter it, either implicitly or explicitly, in many religions and in numerous authors, particularly Guénon. And, to close, this is what I would like to show.

Some Illustrations of This Doctrine

Hindu tradition will be considered first because it is so significant in this respect. In addition, Guénon has been most specific on the subject of the relationships between revelation (the *Veda*) and the various modes of its hermeneutics.[2] As we know, three categories of

---

1. I have broached this point in *Le mystère du signe*, especially pp 245–7, and in *La crise du symbolisme religieux* (Lausanne: L'Age d'Homme, 1990) *passim*.
2. *Introduction to the Study of the Hindu Doctrines*, pp 230–238.

Esoterism: History and Idea

'points of view' on revealed doctrine are to be distinguished: the *vedanga*, the *upaveda*, and the *darshana*. The six *vedanga*, or 'limbs of the *Veda*', are comprised of the sciences needed for the ritual acts of the Vedic scriptures: phonetics, astrology, ritual, grammar, 'etymology', and prosody.[1] The *upaveda*, or 'secondary knowledges', are connected to the four *Veda* and are the most exterior of their applications. There are four principal ones: medicine, connected to the *Rig Veda*; martial arts, connected to the *Yajur Veda*; music, connected to the *Sama Veda*; and architecture and mechanics, connected to the *Atharva Veda*.[2] But there are many other *upaveda* whose principles and rules are expressed in the *shastras* (treatises) and *sutras* (summaries). Finally the six *darshana* (*darshana* derives from the root *drish* = 'to see', and means 'view', 'perspective'), which represent the six basic domains or six major interpretive modes of revealed doctrine, are generally grouped in pairs: *Nyaya* ('method' or logic) and *Vaisheshika* (elementary differentiation or analysis); *Samkhya* (synthetic enumeration) and *Yoga* ('union'); *Mimamsa* (profound reflection) and *Vedanta* ('end of the Veda'). These last two *darshana* (and this is important here) can be designated by the name *Mimamsa* alone, a *Purva-Mimamsa* (*purva* = 'first') being then distinguished from an *Uttara-Mimamsa* (*uttara* = 'second', cf. the French *outre* [= beyond]). *Mimamsa* (in which we recognize *manas* = 'thinking faculty') means literally 'the fact of willing to think intensely,' and can be translated as 'investigation', 'interpretation', 'explanation', and 'exegesis'. It deals with research into 'points of ritual open to doubt' and the establishing of a 'rational hermeneutics of sacred texts.'[3]

---

1. *Shihsha, jyotisha, kalpa, vyakarana, nirukta*, and *chhandas* respectively; on Hindu grammar, cf. *Le mystère du signe*, pp190–9.

2. *Ayurveda, Dhanurveda, Gandharvaveda*, and *Sthapatyaveda* respectively. These *upaveda* also receive the name *upanga* ('secondary members'). Alchemy should be added to the *Ayurveda*, which uses mercury (*rasa*) to concoct an 'elixir of long life', allowing one to follow, in good health, the very long path leading to deliverance. Cf. Louis Renou and Jean Filliozat, *L'Inde classique*, t.II, in cooperation with Paul Demiéville, Olivier Lacombe, Pierre Meile, French Far Eastern School, 1985 (distributor: Adrien Maisonneuve), §1687, p167. The *Ayurveda* is likewise sometimes attached to certain parts of the *Atharva Veda*.

3. Ibid., §1370, p8.

Christ the Original Mystery

Such is the traditional way in which Hindu orthodoxy presents the organically formed picture of the ensemble of the sacred sciences. And so we see how pure metaphysics has itself been designated as 'hermeneutics', *mimamsa*, and as 'ultimate hermeneutics' since it receives the name *Vedanta*, the 'end' (*-anta*) of 'revealed knowledge' (*veda*). This metaphysics almost never assumes the form of a synthesizing and deductive *ex cathedra* explanation in the manner of Aristotle's *Metaphysics*, Proclus' *Elements of Theology*, or Guénon's *Multiple States of the Being*, but, as with Shankara in particular, is most often presented under the form of a *Commentary* (*bhashya*) on revealed texts (*shruti*): *Upanishads, Bhagavad Gîta*, or canonical treatises (*smriti*), chiefly the *Vedanta-sutra* or *Brahma-sutra*, a book containing the five hundred and fifty aphorisms (*sutras*) in which the traditional metaphysical interpretation of the *Veda* is summarized.[1]

If we turn now to the esoteric tradition of Judaism, the Kabbalah, as made known in the *Zohar*, we likewise see that it essentially consists in a commentary on Holy Scripture, chiefly the book of *Genesis*, the beginning of *Ezechiel*, and the *Song of Songs*. As for *Tasawwuf*, Islamic esoterism, it is easy to see that it amounts in essence to a spiritual and metaphysical reading of the Koran. As Titus Burckhardt says: 'Since Sufism represents the inner aspect of Islam, its doctrine is in substance an esoteric commentary on the Koran.'[2] And this is true not only for metaphysical doctrine but also for cosmological doctrine and the sacred sciences. Guénon himself affirms this in connection with one 'traditional science', chirology, which might be thought of, by reason of its secondary nature, as foreign to revelation; but this is not so: 'These few indications,' writes Guénon,

> as brief as they are, will show how a traditional, regularly constituted science is attached to principles of a doctrinal order

---

1. The word *Vedanta* is applied then to three different things: to the *Upanishads*, to the canonical treatises expressing principles and their interpretation (*Vedanta-sutras*), and to the traditional explanation of these canons (the *Vedanta* in the classical sense of the term).

2. *Introduction to Sufi Doctrine*, trans. D.M. Matheson (Wellingborough, Northamptonshire: Thorsons, 1976), p41.

and is entirely subject to them; and at the same time they will serve to illustrate the truth we have so often affirmed, that such a science is strictly bound to a definite traditional form so that it would be quite unusable outside the civilization for which it was intended.[1]

As for Christianity, the remainder of this work will make it sufficiently clear that, insofar as it is legitimate to speak of an esoteric teaching, it chiefly concerns the interpretation of the Scriptures, especially the New Testament parables, as well as the unwritten doctrine of Christ summarized in the various *Creeds*. This interpretation, seen in its full (theological, ecclesial, liturgical, and even mystical) breadth, puts in play all the sacred sciences, from metaphysics to cosmology, from architecture to music, from anthropology to angelology.

My conclusion seems then to have imposed itself with sufficient certainty. Although it may be quite banal, as I have said, attentively considered and some of its implied consequences unraveled, we immediately see how it somewhat modifies widely accepted ideas on these matters, leading us, in particular, not to a dualist conception of the religious sphere, divided into exoterism and esoterism, but to a *triangular* one. This will be the focus of the next chapter.

Appendix: *The Notion of Hermeneutics*

Hermeneutics is a major 'philosophical locus' today, but it has not always been so. Traditionally, Catholic theologians call hermeneutics the art that delineates the rules for interpreting Holy Scripture and exegesis the application of these rules (Abbé Berthier, *Abrégé de théologie dogmatique et morale*, E. Vitte, 1927, no. 214). The word *hermeneutics* is a substantivized adjective transliterating the Greek *hermeneutike* (s.e. *tekhne*): (art) of interpreting (Plato, *Statesman*, 260D). It derives from the verb *hermeneuein*, meaning 'interpret',

---

1. *Insights into Islamic Esoterism and Taoism*, Sophia Perennis, 2001, p36.

'explain', and refers to Hermes, interpreter and messenger of the Gods, master of the secrets of speech and the power of signs, whose name is related to *herma*, which designates any object serving as a point of support or way-marker, especially raised and occasionally ithyphallic stones—which is not unrelated to Shiva's *lingam*, a Sanskrit word which at first meant 'sign'. Hermes is the son of Zeus and the nymph Maia (*Homeric Hymns*, Mercury, I, 1), just as Ganesh ('Lord' = *isha* of 'categories' = *gan*) is the son of Shiva and Parvati; both are 'logothetes', heavenly revealers of the signs for speech and writing, of the arts and sciences. In Christian revelation the function of Hermes has devolved to St Paul, who is so designated by the inhabitants of Lystra 'because he was chief speaker' (Acts 14:11). Alone or nearly so among the Fathers, Origen and St Augustine have elaborated a precise 'general theory' of hermeneutics (*On First Principles*, IV, 8–27; *On Christian Doctrine*, II and III), without however 'naming' this science in itself. The Latins usually speak of *interpretatio, intelligentia, expositio, enarratio, commentarium, lectio*, etc., but never *hermeneutica*. Even when Catholic writers, at the time of the Reformation, felt the need to compose treatises on biblical hermeneutics specifically, they used the term neither in Latin (*interpretatio* being the preferred term), nor in French (where either *explication* or *intelligence* of the Scriptures was chiefly used). Of the three hundred and seven Catholic treatises on exegesis recorded between 1528 and 1900, we have counted only forty-four (or less than a third) including in their titles the word *hermeneutica*, which appeared for the first time only in 1751, in *De Verbo Dei scripto et tradito seu Introductio in hermeneuticam sacram utriusque Testamenti* by Corbinien Thomas (Salzburg). On the other hand, of the eighty-two Protestant treatises between 1567 and 1900, we find forty (about half) with 'hermeneutics' in the title, the first published in 1654: *Hermeneutica sacra*, by J.C. Dannhauer (Strasbourg). Incontestably the use of the term comes from Protestants wishing to distance themselves from an overly Catholic Latin terminology by making use of a Greek word. It has, however, been imposed on the Catholics themselves, who have ended up integrating it into the technical vocabulary of theology, making a place for it next to the hallowed term 'exegesis', which basically designates the hermeneutic act. Thus Leo XIII, in his encyclical on Holy Scripture, *Providentissimus Deus,* speaks of 'hermeneutic rules' ['laws of interpretation' in the English text TR]. In French, the adjective 'hermeneutic' is recorded for the first time in 1777, in the *Supplément* to the *Encyclopédie* of Diderot and d'Alembert. As for the noun, it first appeared in 1852 in Cellérier's *Manuel d'herméneutique biblique,* published in Geneva.

This historical data (cf. E. Mangenot's article 'Herméneutique', in Vigouroux's *Dictionnaire de la Bible,* vol. III, 1903, COL. 612–33) shows that the use of the word 'hermeneutic' correlates with the formation of the concept of a special science for biblical interpretation. Such a concept then attracted the attention of philosophers to the interpretive act as such: what are we doing when we read a text, biblical or not? It was the Protestant philosopher and theologian, Schleiermacher, who first formulated the need for a general hermeneutics (1819): 'There exists as yet no general hermeneutics, which is the art of understanding, only various specialized hermeneutics' (*Hermeneutik,* edited by Kimmerle, Academy of Cultural Sciences at Heidelberg, 1959, p79). This theme will be taken up again by Dilthey, who develops it into a general method for the cultural sciences ('sciences of the spirit' in German, *Geisteswissenschaften*) in his *Origin and Development of Hermeneutics* (1900). Starting with Dilthey, then with Husserl and above all Heidegger, philosophical reflection on the act of interpreting—the act by which we confer such or such a significance not only on some cultural factor but even on all the facts of our existence—attained its greatest generality: man is not simply a recorder of facts, he understands and interprets them as signs with a certain existential meaning. Here hermeneutics is identical to philosophy itself. However, along with Gadamer and Ricoeur, I believe there is no 'hermeneutics of *dasein*', of the basic interpretation of our experience of existing, that is not given form by a certain cultural tradition and that necessarily calls to mind a revelation. The comprehending of self and world, our 'reading' of life and things, always transpires on the basis of and with the help of the keys to a universal symbol-bearing tradition.

2

Esoterism in Its Essence and in Its Existence

Introduction:
Triangular Structure
of the Hermeneutic Field

L ET US NOW SEE what consequences are implied by the conclusions just established. If the true locus for esoterism as well as for exoterism is hermeneutics, then (contrary to what is ordinarily supposed) not two but three terms are involved here: there is the revealed message, and there are the two dimensions of its hermeneutic. Such is the true concept to be held in this respect. Very often, though, matters are portrayed quite differently, even among Guénonians (I do not say Guénon himself). Usually everything transpires as if the traditional form itself were cut in two, as though this form henceforth would only exist as two parts, an exoteric one and an esoteric one. Divided like this, the very being of the traditional form would be 'exhausted'. This view is inexact and leads to numerous difficulties from which we can escape only by accepting that in the *revelatum* (the revealed data) there is a sacred reality that is neither exoteric nor esoteric in itself. The hermeneutic field is entirely ordered to and relative to its divine Object, and this is its raison d'être. In itself, this Object is independent of these various hermeneutic modes, which means that, if such should be the case, it becomes esoteric or exoteric only in terms of the way it is *seen* by

Esoterism in Its Essence and in Its Existence

someone. Only turn back to the Hindu idea of the unique *Veda* or revelation of Total Knowledge, and the multiple *darshana* or 'points of view' on revelation, and you will understand that this is indeed how things are presented in the traditional order. When we distinguish esoterism from exoterism, we have not exhausted the revealed Object; to the contrary, once considerations about either one have been set aside, everything essential still remains: the gift of the divine *revelatum* itself.

Besides, seeing that both esoteric and exoteric perspectives are relative to the divine *revelatum*, they are also relative to and make sense only with respect to each other, as Guénon himself recognized. This means, in particular, that we cannot simply identify exoterism with the *revelatum* as it actually presents itself to be seen and believed. This is an abuse of language and an often encountered confusion to be carefully avoided: the *revelatum* is the manifestation of divine Truth in our human world; it is neither esoteric nor exoteric in itself, and it would be quite ridiculous to pretend to measure it by the standards of our own categories. But this is not all. Since every esoteric perspective remains relative to the *revelatum* upon which it is based, and thus to the exoteric perspective from which it is to be distinguished, one should not imagine beyond this relative esoterism a supposedly absolute or total esoterism independent of every fixed religious form.

This attitude, encountered in certain religious groups in the name of the transcendence of the Spirit, or even among certain thinkers, like Hegel, who speaks of 'absolute spirit',[1] does not seem to correspond to any real possibility: every esoterism actually practiced and practicable is situated within the framework of a revelation and searches out its inner meaning. One might contrast to this the privileged relationship esoterism maintains with the 'essence' to the extent that this hermeneutic mode is rightly characterized by a search for the essential beneath the formal appearances every revelation necessarily assumes, for otherwise it would be indistinguishable from all of the others. In order to go right to the end of this perspective in obedience to a specific inspiration, must one then surpass the *revelatum* itself in its characteristic identity to gain access to its unique and supraformal essence? In other words, if a seeking for what is essential is indeed the essence of esoterism, are we not being led by the essence of esoterism towards an 'esoterism of the essence' that transcends every revealed form? But in that case let us no longer speak of the essence of esoterism, let us admit that there is neither essence nor true definition of this idea, and that the only thing left is in fact a mere label, whereas if such an essence (which consists in surpassing such or such a revealed form for the sake of its essential contents) does indeed exist, should we not conclude that true and absolute esoterism consists in surpassing the form as such towards the essence of all revelation?

To decide on this point demands, then, that we broach the question of the relationship between essence and existence, a philosophical question if ever there was one, but one impossible to avoid.

On Essence and Existence

In certain respects, the idea of an essence for esoterism might seem arguable. Esoterism is not a natural being, like a rose, a cat, or a man,

---

1. Hegel defines essential religion as the 'awareness of *absolute* truth' (*Encyclopédie des sciences philosophiques en abrégé*, Gallimard, §552, p471; or again: 'the concept of true religion, that is to say that which has absolute spirit for contents' (§564, p484). But religion is still situated within a representational element (it utilizes revealed forms and symbols). Only (Hegelian) philosophy actualizes the perfect transparency of spirit to itself and therefore realizes the content of religion, the truth of the spirit become absolute in reality. However, the perfect actualization of the content of religion in philosophy, that is to say the self-knowledge of the spirit that is no longer foreign to itself, that is itself possessed in a perfect transparency, is only accessible to a few and is only actualized within the philosophic sanctuary: 'the reconciliation (which philosophy effects with religion) . . . is without exterior universality. In this respect, philosophy is a *sanctuary apart* and its servants form an isolated clergy who cannot go along with the world, and which has to preserve the realm of truth' (*Philosophie de la Religion*, ed. Ilting, p708). Clearly, this is absolute esoterism, a thesis that has been maintained in our own day by Frithjof Schuon in *Esoterism as Principle and as Way* (Hillsdale, NY: Sophia Perennis, 1981). He distinguishes the 'historical esoterisms' (Pythagorism, Vedanta, Zen), which do not much interest him, from 'esoterism as such, which we would willingly call *sophia perennis* and which in itself is independent of particular forms, since it is their essence', (p7), 'absolute esoterism' (p26). Just as absolute spirit is only formulated in Hegelian philosophy, so absolute esoterism is identified in fact with the Schuonian *sophia*.

Esoterism in Its Essence and in Its Existence

nor an artificial, technological being like a table or a house. These beings have a separate, immediately observable existence. Each can be the object of a definition and so to each can be assigned an objective essence that determines its nature and makes it what it is. It is not the same for esoterism which is not in any respect an individual and separate reality. It is however a cultural reality, one which exists to the extent that a human being makes it exist by focusing on it. And this is what philosophy calls an 'accidental being', namely, something which in order to exist here-below needs to be maintained in being by another being, a real subject existing within itself (what philosophy calls a 'substantial being', a being subsisting within itself and by itself). Thus here-below the color red does not exist within itself, but only *in* the poppy or *in* the blood.[1] Nevertheless, to belong to the class of accidental beings does not imply an absence of essence. There are indeed red or white, circular or rectilinear essences that do not, however, subsist by themselves here-below. It is the same for cultural realities which only exist as human 'artifacts'. But this does not for all that prevent their being defined and distinguished according to their respective essences.

Esoterism is a human artifact (at least in its actual, culturally set practice) consisting of a certain spiritual attitude that can be defined and distinguished from other attitudes and to which an essence can therefore be assigned. As for this essence, we might say that in the final analysis it consists in that operational mode by which the Holy Spirit summons the heart-intellect to enter into the interior of the *revelatum*. And so esoterism is at once a human procedure and a divine operation that gives form to and transforms our intellect by pneumatizing it.

In a certain way accidental beings are closer to essence than substantial beings, which are themselves closer to existence. To the extent that to be real, to exist, is to be a subsistent individual (*a* tree,

---

1. 'Accidental' because in Latin *accidere* means 'to come to' (something else): in order to be, accidental being needs to 'come' into another being which is itself a substantial being. And as for the hierarchy of beings: an accidental being can be more noble and perfect than the substantial being into which it 'comes'. Thus a circular figure can give form to some worthless material, just as divine grace (which has an accidental being within the person who receives it) is more noble than its receptacle.

a cat, *a* man), an accident (redness, circularity, mathematical activity) possesses, as the Scholastics say, a 'deficient' being. But being independent *as to its essence* of its various existential actualizations, here-below it displays characteristics analogous to those displayed by an essence: one particular poppy is not another one, and yet the same redness exists and is to be seen in both. Colors are, moreover, one of the symbols best suited for giving us some idea of just what an essence is.

This property of accidental being is somehow redoubled in the case of esoterism, since esoterism is itself defined as a seeking for the essence in the religious order, in the order of the *revelatum*. This is precisely why it is good to pay close attention and not lose sight—in the name of the sublimity or transcendence of the essential contents—of the limits imposed by existential conditions on its actualization here-below. In other words and to summarize in a brief formula: an essential esoterism *exists* not simply because esoterism has an essence; or again: an essential religion exists not simply because religion has an essence.

Such a state of affairs is obvious when a natural subsistent being or an artificial object is involved. No one imagines that he will one day encounter in some garden the essential rose and breathe its scent, or own the essential table and write or take a meal upon it. All roses participate in the rose in itself, and all tables in the table in itself, but neither are a part of empirical and earthly realities. Of course it can also be said that we breathe the scent of the rose in itself and write on the table-essence, since both the one and the other establish the specific reality of every rose and every table. But here-below we cannot enter into relationship with the essence *as such*, only with the essence insofar as it is present in a given rose or table to which it gives form.

Such a state of affairs seems less obvious when we deal with that particular category of accidents called human operations and activities, which do not exist in the manner of a thing nor in the *static* manner of a physical accident (like redness and circularity).[1] These

---

1. At least in appearance and according to a rather elementary but, for now, sufficient approach. In reality, the color red is also an energetic vibration.

Esoterism in Its Essence and in Its Existence

operations exist only insofar as a human being performs them. Now, to perform them—and this is the case with all of our acts—an act of will is not enough. We also have to represent to ourselves what we want to do, have an idea of it. We have to conceptualize the goal and those means that lead to it. There is no operation without a concept to guide and give it form all the way through to its actualization. And what is this concept if not the mental form which the essence of the operation assumes when we think about it? This is already true for manufacturing activities: to build a table is to have in mind the model of a table and, in the final analysis, the table's essence. This is even truer for moral or spiritual activities, where what is being actualized, in whatever way, is man himself, and even deified man. The leading idea, the conceptual representation presiding over and directing our acts then acquires a vital importance. With it we are entering into an eminently subjective and personal relationship insofar as, without it, without our love, it loses all reality and life. Thus an inspiring idea somehow becomes our most precious and most intimate possession, the very heart of our endeavor.

And yet, however intense this subjective appropriation may be, we should not forget that we are initially dealing with a concept. Surely, our gaze is toward the essence: in loving, love's essence; in combat, the essence of courage; in writing a poem, the essence of poetry; in understanding the depths of the *revelatum*, the *revelatum*'s essence; etc. But this essence is necessarily present to our minds under the form of the idea we have of it, under the form of a concept. Clearly, we are seeing the essence itself and not the concept, although by means of this concept and through it. Moreover, this is why conceptions formed of an ideal essence to be actualized vary according to cultures and persons, which proves that the concept is only a certain 'view' of the essence and is not identical to it. True, it has a certain number of characteristics in common with the essence: like it, the concept is intelligible; like it, the concept is universal. The concept of a table (in principle) reminds us of every table and, before every object of this nature, lets us judge that *this* is a table, just as a table's essence is present, in various degrees, in all tables given form by it. Likewise, the concept of esoterism (in principle) reminds us of every cultural object of this nature and lets us say: this has to do with esoterism, just as esoterism's essence is present in various degrees in all historically actualized forms of interiorizing hermeneutics. But the concept's universality should not mislead us: it is not the positive universality of the essence considered within itself in its full reality; it is a negative universality, or even a universality by abstraction, that is to say (somehow) by 'ontological delocalization'.[1] Some remarks of a more technical nature are needed here.

On Intellect and Concept

How do we form the concept of esoterism? As with every concept, we do so by reflecting on our experience of certain hermeneutic and spiritual practices within which we discern common characteristics forming a sufficiently unified and identifiable whole. We can be guided in thinking about this by an inspiration coming from above, or more simply by a spontaneous opening of our intellect (only spirit recognizes spirit); but we nevertheless begin with real experiences and received information. From this concrete data we then extract the few universally present elements and, *being guided by a certain supra-conceptual intuition in this matter*, we form a concept of it. There is nothing mysterious, or at least nothing exceptional, about this abstractive process which is that of the thinking (and not the angelic) intellect. It is characteristic of human knowledge in general. As Ruyer says, man is a 'universal reader'. Human, that is to say speculative knowledge is precisely that capacity possessed by a being

---

1. Guénon would say 'general' and not 'universal' here, because he places the universal and the individual in opposition and because the general does not cause us to leave the individual behind. Without rejecting Guénon's distinctions, I am following the Scholastic practice, which designates by the term *universalia* (the 'universals') that which will be called 'general ideas' later. Considered in itself, the concept seems to refer to a realm intermediate between the order of essences (really universal) and the order of individual beings (a molecule, a tree, a cat, a man). This intermediate realm is that of thought. It is universal then insofar as it looks to the essence, and is only general insofar as a class of individuals is concerned. — On the problem of universals, cf. François Chenique, *Éléments de logique classique*, Dunod, 1975, chap. VI, which makes allowance for Guénon's point of view.

Esoterism in Its Essence and in Its Existence

of nature—man—for possibly entering into relationship with all reality, whatever it might be, and becoming aware of its existence. In other words, man is that being for whom everything that is not exists for him.

Here-below this capacity is unique. Non-human beings (atoms, molecules, cells, plants, animals) 'know' of other beings only what is directly concerned with their own being, only what enables them to be formed and become. Their 'world' is their very being and whatever, of the greater world, is indispensable to them: they know or rather recognize of the real only what constitutes their own reality. For a tree, only that aggregate of factors needed for it to exist is 'real': the rest is as if it were not. Doubtless, it would be appropriate to envision in this connection a gradation from atom to animal,[1] a gradation according to which the world is 'enlarged' as we ascend the ladder of being. But in general we can conclude that its own nature is a non-human earthly creature's vision of the real. Here there is identity or near-identity of being and knowing precisely because this knowing is strictly limited to being.

Man on the contrary can know all because his knowledge actualizes a *non-ontological mode* of relationship with everything.[2] Surely, one can say 'the [intellective] soul is all that it knows,' since, as we have said, the act of knowing operates by a certain participation of a knowing intellect in the intelligible form of a known being. But we can say this only provided that along with Aristotle we add 'somehow', which Guénon always fails to mention when citing this proposition (to my knowledge, inexactly). After having concluded: 'in a sense (*pos*) the soul is all existing things,' Aristotle specifies: 'the stone does not exist in the soul, but only the form of the stone.'[3] The identity through knowledge spoken of by Guénon in this connection should be clearly grasped. It is not 'purely theoretical', as he thinks (by seeing the proof of the incompleteness of Western

---

1. To be complete, this description should also consider the rapport of a being with its environment; cf. Guénon, *The Great Triad*, chap. 13.
2. This non-ontological mode of relationship to every possible being and to all beings is directly bound up with the experience of the sign (*Le mystère du signe*, pp120–132).
3. *On the Soul*, III, 8, 431B and 432A.

metaphysics);[1] on the contrary, it is altogether real: when it receives within itself the intelligible form extracted from a known being, the intellect quite really becomes this form. But this intellect, or this intellective soul, is not itself the human being, it is only *that by which* humans know: 'the soul is the instrument whereby man ... thinks.'[2] The identification spoken of by Aristotle does not then directly refer to spiritual or metaphysical realization; to the contrary, it is almost natural and constitutes the very process of human knowledge. It transpires in a speculative mode—the Scholastics say 'intentional' mode—and is only possible because in a world saturated with individual beings the reality of human thought produces a deontologized 'place', a kind of existential no man's land where beings, insofar as they are known, are as it were torn out of their cosmic determinacy, their 'being-there' (*Da-sein*), their ontological site, and accede to a certain universality. When something of the relatively universal occurs to the thinking intellect in a world where whoever says *being*, says *such or such a being*, surely this is something almost miraculous, almost supernatural.

Just because we are capable of imagining the essence does not mean that we can gain access to this essence as such in the fullness of its reality. Some will no doubt object that to deny the possibility of this access is to deny the intellect, reducing knowledge solely to its rational, reflexive, and discursive mode. We shall see in a moment how far I am from denying the reality of an intellectual intuition of essences. But it seems that this intuition, as certain as it might be, nonetheless remains most obscure and very imperfect. The essence

---

1. *Introduction to the Study of the Hindu Doctrines*, pp 92–92. As for the incompleteness (real or assumed) of Western metaphysics, it concerns Aristotle's rather than Plato's doctrine, about which Guénon quite inexplicably says nothing here.

2. *On the Soul*, I, 4, 408B, 15. In other words, a human being is not identical with his intellect. If the human being was wholly intellect, the act of knowing would make it ontologically identical with the intelligible. But the intellect is a power of the soul, and not its very being. Certainly, as Meister Eckhart says: 'There is a power in the soul, of which I have spoken before. If the whole were like it, she would be uncreated and uncreatable, but now [*Translator's note:* in Libera's French translation] this is not so.' Sermon Twenty-Four, *Meister Eckhart, Sermons and Treatises*, trans. and ed. M.O'C. Walshe (Longmead: Element Books, 1979); 'now', that is to say insofar as we are here-below.

Esoterism in Its Essence and in Its Existence

is glimpsed rather than seen and remains beyond our reach even though entirely given. Moreover, if such an intuitive knowledge were integral and perfect, as it is for angelic knowledge (hence its mastery over cosmic beings and processes), our understanding and mastery of the world would be equally perfect, and those traditional cultures where we are assured such a mode of knowledge still exists would provide us with an example, but so far...

Does the doctrine we uphold break with Tradition? Or does it fall back to an exclusively exoteric position? Such objections will not fail to be made. And they will be contradicting not only what Aristotle and St Thomas Aquinas teach, but even Dante himself, whose authority in the matter of esoteric doctrine is recognized by everyone. In fact we read in *The Banquet*, on the subject of purely intelligible realities, called 'separated substances' (i.e., separated from matter) by Aristotle and identified with the angels by theology:

> I declare that our intellect cannot reach up to certain things, such as substances devoid of matter, owing to a lack in the power from which it draws forth whatever it sees: that power, the imagination, is physical, and therefore as regards the kind of knowledge just spoken of, it cannot be of help because it lacks the wherewithal. And although we can to some extent *speculate about such things*, we cannot know them directly, nor fully understand them.[1]

Clearly then there is a certain intuition of essences (I have emphasized the passage affirming this), but an intuition that is imperfect and as it were impotent to seize its object. The only means which we have for knowing these essences is through their effects: 'It should be

---

1. *The Banquet*, III, IV, 9; trans. C. Ryan (Saratoga, CA: Anma Libri, 1989), p87. Dante is following Aristotle's teaching which asserts that the soul cannot think without images (*On the Soul*, III, 7, 431A, 15). The imagination is to be understood here as the faculty for forming images, for having internal representations of objects in their absence. Linked to memory, it is that sense memory intermediate between the sensory and the intelligible. It provides the intellect with a 'substitute matter' upon which to base its thought; it provides our thought with that presentation of objective reality needed to accomplish its activity. Here we see the importance of the symbolic function in metaphysics.

explained here that the most appropriate way to describe all those things which defeat our intellect in that it cannot grasp what they are, is to consider the effects they produce; adopting this approach, we can come to some knowledge of God, of the separate substances, and of prime matter.'[1] Of course it is not to be excluded that, quite exceptionally,

> the 'intellect plunges to such a depth' in its desire, which is God, 'that after it the memory cannot go'.... When the human intellect is exalted in this life, on account of the natural relation and affinity that it has to the separated intellectual substance, it is exalted to such a degree that after return the memory waxes feeble, because it has transcended human bounds.

This is why St Paul, having come back from his rapture (2 Cor. 12:3–4) could not recount what he had heard.[2] Such are the truths taught to Dante by his 'lady' who 'is the lady of the intellect, who is called Philosophy,'[3] and the secret of which is love for the divine *Sophia*:

> For ... Philosophy is a loving exercise of wisdom, which is found supremely in God—since in Him are found wisdom and love and activity at their most sublime... Divine Philosophy, then, pertains to the divine essence.[4]

Ideal Esoterism and the Ego's Illusions

Returning to the task at hand, we conclude that it would be an illusion to believe that our intellective capacity to conceive of esoterism can put us in the actual presence of essential or absolute esoterism

---

1. Ibid., III, VIII, 15; RYAN, p99.
2. *Epist.* x, 28 (to Can Grande), trans. Chas. S. Latham, reproduced in *Aids to the Study of Dante*, by Charles Allen Dinsmore (Boston: Houghton Mifflin Company, 1903), p282.
3. *The Banquet*, III, XI, 1; Ryan, p104.
4. Ibid., III, XII, 12–13; Ryan, pp109–10; a few lines later Dante speaks of the 'marriage' of Wisdom to the Divine Essence.

Esoterism in Its Essence and in Its Existence

('esoterism as such') and warrant our living and practicing it if we feel daring enough to do so. In reality this illusion, to be met with among those who lay claim to the 'freedom of the Spirit', is fed by the psychic powers of the individual being. As I mentioned, it is human will and energy that gives life and reality here-below to this hermeneutic operation named esoterism and the concept of which is formed in our own minds. Only insofar as we conceive of it does esoterism appear to have characteristics belonging to the essence, or even to the Idea in the Platonic sense of the term. And this operation is clearly driven and oriented towards its actualization by an *ideal* esoterism. This is, after all, the situation of all human undertakings in the moral and spiritual order, of all operations not accomplished by the producing of a physically distinct object—in the order of art (*techne*) as much as in the course of more ordinary work. In technical operations, the end sought for is the production of such or such an object and not the object in itself. The object produced, by dint of its own reality, somehow spares the artisan from being charmed by the glimpsed mirage of some ideal object. In the moral, political, or religious order this is not so: no extra-human object results from operations of this order, no object which would rightfully condone or condemn such operations. They are always found to be handed over to themselves and always faced with the ideal to which they strive to be conformed. Hence the temptation of absolutism, totalitarianism, puritanism, and fanaticism, a temptation that stems from wanting to confer the perfection and necessity of the essence on human forms. Nothing is more common than to succumb to it, and political and religious history provide us with dreadful examples. Likewise, some are led in the name of the pure truth of esoterism to reject the multiplicity of existing forms, or in any case to reduce them to the unity and simplicity of a diagram, to the essentiality of an abstraction, which the power of our ambition or spiritual desire clothes with a sacred appearance, a kind of mysterious aura in which we think we see the holy presence of God. Bereft as it is of any sensory appearance, an abstraction provokes of itself its own *esthetization*. Actually existing religious forms impose on our sense of the sacred their concrete manifestations, which sometimes enrapture and sometimes baffle but which fix and direct our spiritual gaze, preventing its straying. To the contrary, the more we elevate ourselves in thought toward the essences, the more we find occasion to exalt in our sense of the sublime, to give free rein to our 'spiritual imagination' and to compensate for the lack of the numinous presence of concepts by means of pictorial and (above all) the most impressive verbal figures.

Thus our attraction for the Spirit, with which our own spirit exhibits a kind of connaturality, can make us forget our present condition, and the intoxication of the perfume it communicates to our soul can make us unconscious of our limitations. Now, however spiritual our intellect might be, it remains the intellect of a human being. It does not exist 'all alone' as such, but only insofar as we give it being through our own existence. Our intellectual vision can be of a supreme beauty, and yet it takes place in a created and contingent being. It is this created and contingent being that must be saved, and can be so only if it commits itself, as such, to the path of its salvation. And here 'as such' means: 'with one's naked being,' 'with one's being divested of all its powers,' even the intellective power. This is why there is no other way, for a single and contingent being, than that which passes through the singleness and contingency of a *revelatum*.

Certainly we can speak of integral metaphysics, of a supreme and universal *Sophia*. But, as Dante says, this perfect philosophy is only found realized in God, in the Divine *Logos*, the Wisdom and Knowledge of the Father, whose sole Hermeneut is the Holy Spirit. Catholic doctrine is not unaware of this: it calls this supreme gnosis of God 'archetypal theology'. But it distinguishes this from 'ectypal theology or the theology of creatures', which includes two modes, according to which God, in heaven, communicates his knowledge to the spirits of the blessed (ectypal theology is then 'conformed as to its manner of knowing' to archetypal theology), or according to which, on earth, this knowledge is bestowed in 'revelation by word and by faith'; in this last mode, we still must distinguish the case of a miraculously (grace-) infused theological science from an ordinarily acquired one.[1]

---

1. M.J. Scheeben, *La Dogmatique*, French trans. from German by the Abbé Belet, Victor Palme, vol. 1, 1877, p3.

Esoterism in Its Essence and in Its Existence

Lacking these distinctions and precautions, the idea of essential esoterism as norm and guide for a spiritual practice presents the gravest of dangers. Being nothing but an idea, a mental anticipation of archetypal theology, it lacks that real presence needed for arousing a personal response and the commitment of our selves. Venerated as an interior revelation kept by the Spirit for the rare few of the elite, it plunges our soul into a pseudo-sacred dream which justifies all pride and, sometimes, shamelessness. But where then does the 'weight of reality'—a living and fascinating reality—which this idea seems to conceal in the eyes of its adepts, come from, even though by itself it is only a simple abstraction? Actually, this weight of being comes from the very being of those who have embraced it. By the power of their imagination, they project upon it their own individual reality's living strength and density of being. Thus projected, the individuality is enlarged, becomes inflated, and identifies itself esthetically with the universal dimensions of the essence instead of noughting itself before it. This means that we can escape this illusion only by accepting to live the way of the Spirit within a recognized distinction and tension between our human existence and the transcendence of the essence, which is to say in poverty. Undoubtedly, moments of fullness and grace do occur in which existence seems to miraculously *coincide* with the essence. But this coincidence cannot be posed as a normative principle for the spiritual life without there being a human individuality to illusorily realize it for his own benefit. I say 'illusorily' because, with this self-inflation to the dimensions of universal esoterism, the individual imagines that he has actually abolished his own limits when he has in fact only lost sight of them.

The Intuition of Essences As Semantic Experience

Should what has just been explained lead to a denial of every intuition of essence beyond the realm of human knowledge? Not at all. Besides, if intellectual intuition 'is not ours,' as Kant maintains, the illusion of a direct and living access to the essence would not even occur. Precisely because we have a certain perception of the essence, we imagine ourselves capable of living this essence in an essential mode. This illusion is not in the perception itself, but in the conviction that our being is on the same high level as our vision.[1] It is important, then, that we try to at least briefly specify what this intuition is because, for tenuous as it might be, it constitutes something quite basic to our cognitive acts, something that quite closely affects our life and our very being.

Everyone has surely had a certain vital experience of the essence which we will call the 'semantic experience' (*semantic* signifying 'what is of a meaningful nature'). In other words, we think every intellect, in the act by which it conceives what the essence of something is, meets with a certain experience of meaning, an experience of the intelligible, without which a concept could never be formed. As I have stressed, and as it seems Dante himself maintains, to abstract a few schematic features, selected more or less arbitrarily from the thing perceived, to form a concept is not enough. There must also emerge from the elements reunited in this way *a* meaning, an *intelligible* unity, something the intellect can acquiesce in, say yes to, because it recognizes itself there, because it makes sense *to it*. For in the final analysis there is no other 'criterium for truth', no other means of knowledge than this acquiescence of the intellect, this experience that it has of being in agreement with itself, with its own intellectual nature. And this cannot be acquired, taught, or demonstrated; it is intuitive, direct, impossible to generate: the very life of the intellect passing from potency to act.

Let us focus on this semantic experience or experience of the intelligible a little more attentively. What is intelligible, that is to say graspable by the intellect, or again, what endows the intellect with the possibility of producing an intellective act, is first of all something in which no contradiction resides. We can know only the noncontradictory, and the features selected as constituting the concept should be compatible with each other: both a circle and a square are

---

1. Schopenhauer notes that anyone who contemplates (by intellectual intuition) momentarily forgets, as in esthetic contemplation, everything which forms his individuality (*Die Welt als Wille und Vorstellung*, III, §34). Kant's citation is drawn from *The Critique of Pure Reason*, Ak. III, 209.

Esoterism in Its Essence and in Its Existence

intelligible, a square circle is not. However, non-contradiction defines only a relatively extrinsic intelligibility, since it is only the condition required for intelligibility, and to be recognized needs only an analysis of those elements making up the essence and their coherence. But once this condition is fulfilled, there is still left to be considered a grasping of the essence in its 'thusness', in its own nature, in its contents as such (*ut sic*). This grasping, this apprehension is performed by our understanding in an intuitive and synthetic act of *contemplation*. The intellect receives within itself the revelation of the essence as meaning, thusness as meaning, since our understanding can receive nothing within itself save by the mode of intelligibility, by what 'makes sense', by what awakens a 'semantic echo' within it. In other words, it can only receive what 'says something to it', what 'speaks to it'. And this is intrinsic intelligibility.

What brings this word to our hearing, the 'milieu' that makes the semantic echo awakened in us resound, is what is called the agent intellect, which is nothing but a certain permanence of the intellective nature 'in act' subsisting in our soul. This simply means that just as our eyes know how to exercise by nature the act of seeing, so our intellect knows spontaneously how to 'react intelligibly' when it receives (passive intellect) any form whatsoever. It has not learned this, and cannot learn it from anyone, since every apprenticeship presupposes such an innate sense of know-how. The agent intellect is therefore the activity of the intellective nature as such: when the passive intellect receives nothing, when it sleeps in a deep sleep ignorant of everything, the agent intellect is awake, solitary, in the pure light of the *Logos*. When the passive intellect is awakened by its encounter with things and receives them within itself, it is this agent intellect that illumines them intelligibly and reveals them to us in their intrinsic intelligibility, an intrinsic intelligibility we are so to say unaware of because it is the very depths of our entire cognitive life: we are immersed in meaning as is a fish in water; everything makes sense to us and is known (exists for us) only insofar as it makes sense.

This is why we forget to be surprised by it. But there is a kind of continuing miracle here. Since nothing is known by us except what makes sense *to us*, except what is known, how are we in a position to semantically welcome all possible forms of being, forms of which we have had no *a priori* idea, forms we are incapable of imagining and the existence of which we had to *learn*, revealed to us through the experience of our senses? Left to its own resources, how could an intellect have invented the rose, the horse, the mountain, or the least blade of grass? And yet from the moment we are informed of their existence, we accept, welcome, and grasp them in their own natures, just as they are, in their thusness, their intrinsic intelligibility, even if it happens that their extrinsic intelligibility causes problems (which is what science is concerned with).

The semantic experience of thusness is something so radical and so original, then, that it escapes our attention. It escapes our attention insofar as an intrinsic meaning is involved—not the extrinsic (or transitive) meaning which makes something intelligible by connecting it to something else. Thusness is rightly untranslatable and therefore, somehow, unable to be formulated. The rose 'speaks rose', like the French speak French; it does not speak 'oak' or 'star'. And this is precisely why, although we can speak of the rose otherwise than as 'rose', our experience of it is completely distinct and recognizable in its unspoken and obscure identity. How then can we doubt we are perceiving in its essence, the rose *as such*, the rose *in itself* revealed in this fontal experience? Does not the word 'essence' designate precisely what a thing is *in itself*? And yet what has been bestowed on the intellect is not the very being of the essence; it is the essence as meaning, the essence as 'semantic presence' in the intellect, not the essence in its own reality, which exists only in God. In the semantic experience we indeed perceive however obscurely the essence of the rose as the raison d'être of all perceived roses. But we still do not see the essence as the transparent identity of both being and raison d'être, for as St Paul teaches, 'We see now through a glass in a dark manner' (1 Cor. 13:12). To intellectively perceive the transparent identity of the being of the rose and its raison d'être would be to perceive *uno intuitu* both the rose's reality and the hidden root by which it eternally flowers out of the divine *Sophia*; it would be to understand, in seeing the rose, why the rose is a rose, that is to say why the rose is without a why. Such a knowledge surpasses our creaturely condition. Or at the very least the semantic experience represents

Esoterism in Its Essence and in Its Existence

only a reduced though faithful image, for the rose tells me a 'something' I cannot repeat in any language, or—which amounts to the same thing—a 'something' I will never finish saying. This experience is necessarily the common act of the one who receives this meaning (understanding) and intrinsic intelligibility (*the* rose). Without this common act there would be no meaning, for only what makes sense *for* me makes sense to me. Thus, in the experience of meaning, subject is joined to object: a semantic and non-ontological union, the only one we are capable of.

What I have so painstakingly described is, however, commonplace and quite ordinary. It is akin to becoming conscious (a consciousness super-conceptual in its depths) of a certain 'poetic' presence in things. And what is in fact intuited in this way is not the concept, a mental form, but a meaning inherent in its contents, its 'fundamental message', which transcends the conceptual form with which it is clothed in the act of thinking about it. Not being an abstractly objective form, this is precisely why this semantic experience can imbue with its intuitive, unformulable light, or if you prefer with its semantic savor, those important events *lived* by a human subject in the course of his earthly existence: no one can love, be a father or contemplate a mountain without 'living' the essence of love, paternity, or mountain—but each time and only through its existential presentation.

In the same way, no one endowed with any metaphysical awareness whatsoever can live such a particular esoterism without receiving from it the revelation of esoterism as such, the revelation of pure and transcendent spiritual interiority. There remains however that this experience is only bestowed (and still only under a certain mode) in an encounter with such or such an esoterism, and not contrary to it or outside of it, and that it only has operative power with a view to our sanctification through the grace of the *revelatum*.

To Philip, who asks him 'Show us the Father,' Christ replies: 'Who has seen me has seen the Father' (John 14:8). It is certainly necessary to have a sense of the Father in order to see him 'in the *Son*', but it is only '*in* the Son' that he is visible and we can go to him. Setting aside the revealed form to gain access to the essence, or to maintain it only as a concession to our weakness, is to deprive ourselves of the only *medium* through which it radiates and touches us; it is to break a mirror in the hope of attaining the image reflected within it, to break a jar the better to drink of its water. The need for a *medium* does not spring from some accidental limitation of the human receptacle but from its status as creature. In this creaturely state the intrinsic universality of intellection is, *of itself,* foreign to the singleness of created being. That which can establish a relationship, then, between a single being and its intellect is the Holy Spirit, and the spiritual way *is* this very relationship. The work by which the Holy Spirit effects this relationship, a work thanks to which intellect is united with personal being and descends into the heart, is the revealed 'form'. In this case it was Christ who was 'formed' by the 'operation of the Holy Spirit' in the womb of the Blessed Virgin Mary.[1] Thus is brought about what might be called the pneumatization of the intellect. Metaphysically, we might say: it is not the essence that is outside of existence, it is existence that is outside of the essence and is this very 'outside of' (*ex-sistere* = 'to be held outside of'). This is why, although existence is immediately present in the essence, when man is involved, the essence is present to the existence (first noetically, and then really) only through a mediation and a revealed mediation, that is to say a form in which the essence has become existence so that existence might rediscover its essence: 'No one cometh to the Father but by me' (John 14:6).

Did Guénon Teach the Doctrine of Absolute Esoterism?

Before closing this chapter, I should reply to an objection sometimes brought against me: the thesis of an esoterism both absolute and independent of all religious forms would only be an outgrowth of what Guénon himself has said. In fact we read in *Perspectives on Initiation* the following remark:

---

1. As I wrote in *La Charité profanée,* pp352–3, it is the Holy Spirit who, in creation, actualizes the cosmological union of form and matter, and, more generally, essence and existence.

Esoterism in Its Essence and in Its Existence

esoterism is not the 'interior' aspect of a religion as such, but is essentially something other than religion, even when its base and support are found therein.[1]

But this remark does not have the significance claimed for it by some. Clearly, here as elsewhere, Guénon uses the word 'religion' in the particular and restrictive sense by which he always characterizes it, emphasized here by the 'as such' following the word. According to this meaning, the term 'religion' is to be applied exclusively to the *Abrahamic exoterisms*: every exoterism is not religious (Confucianism for instance), but, according to Guénon, every religion is exoteric. To assert that esoterism is not the interior part of religion as such is, to use Guénon's language, evident 'by definition'—a call to arms directed against the partisans of 'mysticism'. But in no way does this mean that, for him, esoterism is not the 'interior side' of a *traditional form* (exoterism, whether religious or not, being the exterior side, its 'mystical' aspect included). According to Guénon, then, esoterism should not be independent of the traditional form, and it is not difficult to find explicit confirmations of this doctrine in his work, one of the clearest of which is provided by his famous article 'The Necessity for Traditional Exoterism', in which we read:

> where exoterism and esoterism are directly linked to the constitution of a traditional form in such a way as to be as it were the two faces, exterior and interior, of one and the same thing, it is immediately comprehensible to everyone that one must first adhere to the exterior in order subsequently to be able to penetrate to the interior, *and that there can be no other way than this*.[2]

The concept of an absolute and independent esoterism is therefore baseless in light of Guénon's precaution.

Is this to say in turn that the concept of an esoterism hermeneutic in nature, such as I have expressed it, has any better claim? Without

---

1. Page 20 (Hillsdale, NY: Sophia Perennis, 2004).
2. *Initiation and Spiritual Realization* (Hillsdale, NY: Sophia Perennis, 2004), p 42; my emphasis in the last part of the sentence.

a doubt: Guénon everywhere repeats that esoterism consists in penetrating 'the profound meaning of a tradition,'[1] and this agrees fully with my concept. On the other hand, he frequently mentions the 'complementary aspects' of one and the same doctrine, and logically maintains, as stated, that wherever this single doctrine is lacking (this is the case of Taoism with respect to Confucianism) it is improper to speak *stricto senso* of either esoterism or exoterism.[2] But our concept differs from his on an important point the consequences of which will be explained in the next chapter: it is 'triangular', whereas Guénon's concept seems to be rather 'bipolar' or two-sided. For myself the *revelatum* is ontologically *one*, esoterism and exoterism being only *hermeneutic perspectives*, not objects or things. According to Guénon, to the contrary, it seems that esoterism and exoterism of themselves *constitute* the entire reality of the *revelatum*, like the recto and verso of a single sheet of paper. This two-sided opposition tends to reify the two terms, insofar as they are quite often applied to institutions. However their concepts are handled, what transpires is that we no longer have a very good idea of just what is involved, and so lose sight of the revelation itself: the gift of God, his saving creation, the center that everyone looks to, the sacred form assumed by the manifestation of the Word in whom abides all the treasures of grace.

Not only must we conclude that esoterism is such only with respect to exoterism, and vice versa, but even that they are both relative to that of which they form a dual hermeneutic, upon which they depend, and which is their norm. It is this *revelatum* that endows them with meaning because it orients and illumines them. Undoubtedly, it so happens that metaphysical hermeneutics suffers from having to subject itself to the contingency of a single revealed form. But this suffering, even this passion, is saving: it alone enables the intellect to serve its apprenticeship to being by crucifying its concepts upon the cross of sacred realities.

---

1. Ibid., p 42.
2. *Introduction to the Study of the Hindu Doctrines*, pp 56–57, 65.

3

Esoterism-Exoterism: A Living Dialectic

A Triple-Termed Dialectic

AT THE END of the previous chapter I suggested that Guénon's two-sided concept might reinforce the opposition between exoterism and esoterism. We risk losing sight of their nature as hermeneutic perspectives: each of these modes is entitatively posited in its pure and exclusive reality, and we see conferred on them the nature of an objective, nearly autonomous form, a form completely definable institutionally, and surveyable. That Guénon's readers readily avail themselves of these categories and peremptorily pass judgment on the esoteric or exoteric character of those doctrines and rites known to them is quite noticeable: they imagine themselves endowed with more than sufficient discernment.

If we think through the consequences of the previously mentioned triadic concept, we see how it enables us to avoid such a 'reification' of perspectives, preserve the living and active nature of these hermeneutic *operations*, and forestall their being transformed into abstract forms, or even into a simple labeling process. For if esoterism and exoterism are truly relative to the *revelatum* toward which they direct their gaze, then they are also truly relative to each other, and by the mediation of their *sole* object enter into a living relationship. Otherwise, were the two to *constitute* the totality of the revealed form, like the two sides of a medal, they would never encounter each other, they would always oppose each other as antagonistic forms.

Christ the Original Mystery

Guénon has of course repeatedly stressed that esoterism should not be contradictory to exoterism, such a distinction moreover 'implying comparison and correlation.'[1] Without doubt this distinction is itself characterized as a 'contingent distinction' that is effaced and dissolved 'in the unity of the Principle' once access is gained to the reality for which exoterism and esoterism are only two differing modes of approach. However, contingent as they may be, the distinction is so expressly drawn that esoterism does risk appearing to be the 'contradictor' of exoterism. This is certainly not Guénon's view, but it is a possibility inherent to the way things are presented, since, if 'esoterism is *essentially* something other than religion,' as Guénon states,[2] this is because they have nothing essential in common. But this is untrue: they have at least the *revelatum* in common, unless of course we conclude that the *revelatum* is inessential.

We get an even clearer idea of both if we consider the image of the circle taken by Guénon as a symbol for the relationships of esoterism to exoterism in his article 'The Shell and the Kernel'. The circumference represents the *sharī'ah* or 'exterior law'; the radius represents the *ṭarīqah* or interior 'way';[3] the center represents the *ḥaqīqah*. This latter term rightly designates the essence of something, its quiddity, or even the contents subjacent to any expression whatsoever, or to a symbol seen in its true reality.[4] Now the question at hand involves an intrinsic reality for which esoterism and exoterism are only modes of approach. This is indeed a triple-termed concept, and I think that it needs to be so. But this is perhaps not enough, for we should inquire into the nature of this *ḥaqīqah*. If the term refers

---

1. 'The Shell and the Kernel' in *Insights into Islamic Esoterism and Taoism* (Hillsdale, NY: Sophia Perennis, 2004), p9.

2. Cf. n2 of chap. 2, p51.

3. Guénon specifies in a note (op. cit., p10, n5) that the names *sharī'ah* and *ṭarīqah* both contain (in Arabic) the idea of 'wayfaring' and therefore of 'movement'. This linguistic remark is in complete agreement with the dynamic concept we are trying to express.

4. In her monumental thesis *La distinction de l'essence et de l'existence d'après Ibn Sînâ* (Desclée de Brouwer, 1937), Anne-Marie Goichon makes an illuminating study of this philosophical term (pp 29–38), summarized in a table (p 48). The Sufi lexicon confers a transcendent and mystical significance on *ḥaqīqah*.

Esoterism-Exoterism: A Living Dialectic

to 'principial unity' itself, which is none other than the Reality-Truth of the Divine Essence, we should not situate it on the same plane as that of the circumference and the radius corresponding to the plane of *traditional economy*. Surely we must 'situate' the *ḥaqīqah* at the apex of a true perpendicular to the circle's plane and passing through its center. The circle's center can be regarded then as the trace of the vertical on this plane, its image, or even as the projection and descent of this apex onto the very plane of traditional economy: ultimately, it symbolizes what we are calling the *revelatum*. And so I am explicitly stressing that, on the plane where esoterism and exoterism are distinguished from each other, they are relative *in the very order of traditional economy* to a third term in which they find their unity *hic et nunc* because it constitutes their sole object. Otherwise, were it only from the point of view of the supreme *ḥaqīqah* that their distinctions are abolished, then on the very plane of the traditional form their separateness will be deemed irreducible and transformed into an opposition. This why, despite Guénon's just-mentioned ternary, it is right to speak of a 'two-sided' concept.

Nevertheless, the representation of esoterism and exoterism, depicted by the radius and the circumference respectively, should be somewhat modified, and their dynamic synthesis realized under the form of a concentric spiral, an involuted combination of circumference and radius. This would show that exoterism and esoterism are hermeneutic *operations*, 'wayfarings' and *living* pathways, not fixed geometric determinations. Although useful for defining directions, these determinations are inadequate for getting a clear idea of the spiritual life, which is both circular and radial.

Divine Revelation
Converts the Outer to the Inner

One of the major conclusions that spring from the foregoing considerations is the impossibility of setting static boundaries for two mutually exclusive realms, of dividing the field of a traditional form so that one could say esoterism is here and exoterism there. In other words, there is no pure and absolute exoterism any more than there is a pure and absolute esoterism. Nowhere in religion (in the non-Guénonian sense of the term) is it correct to assert: this is exclusively exoteric and that exclusively esoteric. None of a revealed form's constituent elements, either by itself or by virtue of its own nature, should be ranked in either realm. What is exoteric or esoteric is not such or such a constituent element, but the hermeneutic intention according to which an element is viewed.

But it will be asked, then, what determines the nature of this intention? Lacking a fixed determining principle, how do we discriminate between intentions, how do we 'discern the spirits', and does this distinction still make any sense? As for the 'direction' of the hermeneutic gaze, of course it does. After all, this distinction is none other than that of the letter and the spirit spoken of by St Paul on many occasions: the letter 'exteriorizes' whereas the spirit 'interiorizes', and the exterior is not the interior. But, as a function of a soul's spiritual becoming and the transformations of its hermeneutic gaze, there is a shifting frontier between the two realms when, advancing in this science of the spirit symbolized by Jacob's ladder, we gain access to a new rung of this science and at the same time hearken back to the previous rung: as 'interior' as it may have seemed, the knowledge just surpassed now reveals itself as relatively 'exterior' to that knowledge into which God is leading us. Let me try to be more precise.

There is at once a difference of nature between esoterism and exoterism as to their determining principles, and a difference of degree as to the becoming of a human being who follows the sacred way traced out by revelation. We do not meet with absolute discontinuities in the supernatural order any more than we do in the natural; or rather it is only from the lower point of view that the higher can seem completely other and even inaccessible or non-existent, or in any case unknown as to its true nature. But from the point of view of the higher degree, the lower degree appears as what it is: a rung on the ladder uniting heaven and earth, for every true surpassing integrates what is surpassed without destroying it. At the same time, and paradoxical as it might seem, it is only then, and from the point of view of esoterism, that the exoteric nature of the just-surpassed degree is revealed. There is exoterism, then, only with respect to

Esoterism-Exoterism: A Living Dialectic

esoterism. For the exoterist, there is only the obvious revelation; or rather, to be an exoterist is precisely to believe that there is no esoterism. That is to say, since the exoterist *as such* is unaware of it, save for exceptions, he believes that in religion there is only that which one sees and conceives. Forcing the point somewhat, it could be argued that the exoterist believes only what he sees, while the esoterist sees only what he believes. In a certain way, the esoterist is a conscious exoterist.

From this it follows that esoterism and exoterism are *formally* distinct realities, at least in principle, for as we shall see[1] it can happen that these two realms present themselves both with clearly identifiable exterior marks and in an institutional setting. This by no means signifies that we can speak of either the reality of esoterism or the reality of exoterism, but only that we should not necessarily think of them as instituted and 'officially' recognized forms. Hence the esoterism-exoterism division is not a preliminary required for every reflection on religious traditions, just as, inversely, the *apparent* absence of 'esoteric' forms or institutions in a religion should not mean that it is *really* devoid of any esoteric understanding. There is no true religion without interiority.

In reality, the first distinction to be made on this subject is that which establishes the divine act of revelation between the sacred and the profane. Yes, 'divine act', for it is this which, through its merciful irruption here-below, 'actualizes' in some manner the dispersive exteriority of our worldly scope and casts it out of the 'inner place', outside of its own earthly manifestation, outside of the consecrated enclosure (that can be the size of a subcontinent, for example India) that defines this very manifestation, an enclosure that man only penetrates to gather together his being and unite it to the One. This place is at the foot of Jacob's ladder, which was 'standing upon the earth, and the top thereof touching heaven,' with 'the angels of God ascending and descending by it . . . How terrible is this place! This is no other but the house of God, and the gate of heaven' (Gen. 28:12–7). Such is the chief biblical symbol, after Noah's rainbow, for what Christians will later name a *religion* and a Church. Now, with respect

---

1. Cf. infra, pp71–76.

to the profane world, religion is of itself already something esoteric, of itself already a conversion from the exterior to the interior, even in its lowliest and most elementary aspects; *of itself* already, simply by its visible presence *hic et nunc*, an 'immanent' hermeneutic that completely turns the flesh of the cosmos inside-out and turns it back towards its intelligible origin.[1] The distinction within the very bosom of religion itself between esoterism and exoterism is secondary with respect to the distinction between sacred and profane, and is only a consequence and as it were an 'echo' of it within the bosom of the religious sphere, precisely to the extent that exoterism is built up through a 'worldly' or 'profane' hermeneutic of revelation. The existence of such a hermeneutic is almost inevitable, given the spiritual limitations of every human collectivity: it can hardly not but occur. This is why there must be in the revelation itself formal elements for the nurturing of exoterism, elements that do not far exceed the limits of a common understanding of the sacred. Nevertheless, it is important to stress, as we have done, that never in any authentic revelation have there been purely exoteric elements, that is to say elements exactly fitted to and justifying the limits of 'worldly' understanding. What in fact would such an understanding be? By definition, it would simply regard its object as a being of this world that is nothing more than it seems to be, its essence wholly identical to its physical presence, to its sensory 'being-there' or its conceptual formulation. This is precisely the profane man's vision when he casts a glance on things and beings: for him their physical or mental presence points to nothing but their existence in the *hic et nunc*. Such should not be the vision of a religious man. For him, beings, things, and the words of revelation are manifestations of the transcendent Invisible One. But the gaze of a profane man can nevertheless carry over into the enclosure of religion and confine the Transcendent to its manifestation, not to identify himself with it—this would be idolatry, which is a perversion and a sin and no longer stems from legitimate exoterism—but to reduce the Transcendent to what is indicated by the revelatory form. Thus one grasps the literal meaning of

---

1. An explanation of this hermeneutic reversal is given in *La crise du symbolisme religieux* (Lausanne: L'Age d'Homme, 1990), pp337–67.

Esoterism-Exoterism: A Living Dialectic

a text without suspecting that this meaning is itself the sign of a loftier meaning. The literalist does not confuse meaning with its language-based formulation, he does not identify ideas and the words expressing them, but he confines this meaning to what the words seem to say. Likewise the exoterist—and to some extent we are all exoterists—is someone who limits the divine to what the sacred forms manifest of it, and therefore also to what it is possible for a human being to manifest of it formally, which means that in his spiritual *life* and morality this being will realize from revelation only what can be translated into visible acts and natural human feelings.

Clearly, pure exoterism is in reality an extreme point of view almost impossible to maintain. This point of view, at least in Christianity, is in fact constantly belied by the sacred forms themselves which, far from fitting within the limits of worldly understanding, always and *visibly* surpass it in such a way as to warn us, mercifully, that there is a 'surplus of meaning', a something we have not grasped and for which we should still be seeking. If this were not so, if sacred forms were exactly fitted to the exoteric understanding to be had of them when we abide by their visibility, then God would be a deceiver, and the exoterist would be justified in not seeking further and more profoundly—which is completely contradictory. A divine revelation should not consist only in uprooting us from the world's profanity in order to *install* us statically within a sacred world, in the bosom of which we could continue to lead almost the same life we led in the profane world. To enter into revelation is not merely to change objects as we do furniture. It is to be converted. Not to be converted once, but to be converted always. Sacred forms, rites, symbols, and the Scriptures are basically *conversion-makers*, which means that we are never done with converting, never done with understanding, because they perplex and surpass all understanding.

Paradoxically, a purely exoteric exoterism would be an absolute esoterism, an esoterism so esoteric, so hidden, that it would be strictly invisible, indiscernible, and unsuspected. While we are in the visible, manifested order, the only means for totally hiding something would be to make it completely visible, in such a way that no one would suspect that there was something hidden: complete visibility would be equivalent to complete occultation. But this is cosmologically impossible: manifestation, by the very fact that it is a manifestation, should not be entirely *here*, entirely displayed, entirely visible, entirely free of its invisible roots, detached from 'that'—forever unmanifestable—which it manifests. This is why the fundamental law of all esoterism is that it should make visible something of the not-visible, unveil something of the veiled.

Esoteric Veiling and Metaphysical Unveiling

However, as I have stressed already and will show at somewhat greater length, there is one realm in which such a veiling is no longer truly possible, that is, the realm of pure metaphysical doctrine. With the concepts and principles rightfully making up its language, we are in the 'element of transparency' to the extent that this language is the language of the intellect, for the intellect is one with its act of intellection and is to be found at the heart of what it knows. Here esoterism as such somehow becomes invisible, the (conceptual) forms charged with expressing it (and therefore with pointing it out) being themselves the most transparent there are. And so is realized the highest degree of intelligibility that a mode of expression can attain. Doubtless, a concept is still a sign, a mental symbol, since it is not the actual thing that it makes known. But it is a diaphanous sign, a 'formal' sign as the Scholastics say,[1] a sign that is only one with its own meaning. Of the three terms that make up the sign (signifier, meaning, and referent), in the case of a conceptual sign the first two are indistinguishable.[2] How then will the marks of its esoteric nature

---

1. Joannis a Sancto Thoma, O.P., *Cursus Philosophicus Thomisticus* (Madrid, 1637), new edition, P.B. Reiser, vol. I, Ars Logica, (Rome: E. Marietti, 1930; L.I., chap. II, pp 9–10, and Log. II, Q. XXI and XXII, pp 646–722.

2. On the definition and structure of a symbolic sign, cf. *Le Mystère du signe*, especially chapters IV, V and VI. I did not, in that work, bring up the Scholastic distinction of formal sign (concept) and instrumental sign. Let us remember, then, that the formal sign is so qualified because by its very 'form' (the concept 'table' is the form of the act by which I think 'table') it expresses what it means. The instrumental sign is so named because this sign is an instrument, a means, through which

Esoterism-Exoterism: A Living Dialectic

become apparent in metaphysical discourse? This is impossible. Who has not been struck by the following peculiarity. When we read a work on alchemy or some Masonic ritual we are undoubtedly dealing with a very esoteric text. But when we read Guénon's *The Multiple States of the Being*, we hardly encounter anything but the clearest and most abstract, the most 'open', language which in principle anyone can understand without initiation by his unaided intellect, and yet this book deals with subjects incomparably more elevated than the first two kinds of works.

Certainly one can *label* a metaphysical discourse: 'Warning, esoterism,' or even 'What I am going to say conceals a deeper meaning.' But it is precisely a label that is involved here, something pointing out esoterism and external to the discourse itself, something no more metaphysical than the word *Plums* on a jar of preserves! Whereas the expressive strategy of a symbolic language—the language of Revelation—is entirely different: here, the symbols to be deciphered, and therefore the indicators of esoterism, are part of the language itself. *Of themselves* they make obvious the impossibility (or insufficiency) of the literal sense.

Metaphysical discourse, and more generally philosophical discourse,[1] brings us to the uttermost bounds of hermeneutics. Moreover, its raison d'être is precisely to be the 'last hand' played by human thought in its effort to explain. To see in it the ultimate hermeneutic, as the etymological meaning of its Hindu designation

---

it has to pass to gain access to the knowledge of a thing: smoke as the sign of a fire, or his effigy as the sign of the emperor. A mental sign makes known what it signifies *first* and is revealed to be a sign—so transparent is it—only on reflection. The instrumental sign is known to be a sign *first* and only reveals what it signifies afterward. Cf. J. Maritain, *Quatre essais sur l'esprit dans sa condition charnelle*, Alsatia, 1956, pp71–2.

1. Along with the best European (Greek and Medieval) tradition, I consider metaphysics the loftiest part of theoretical (or speculative) philosophy, the loftiest knowledge which strives, in every domain, to see beings, things, and their existential conditions from the most universal point of view, that of their principles and causes as well as of their nature and ontological level. Therefore, we can concede that, as such, (perennial) philosophy presents itself as the supreme instance of hermeneutic: it receives the name metaphysics when its object is itself of a nature both metaphysical and transcending the order of created existence.

invites us to do (*vedānta* = 'end' (*-anta*) of 'knowledge' (*veda*), 'final doctrine') is to assign it the place and function of an ultimate *interpreting*, which cannot be *interpreted* by something endowed with a greater hermeneutic capacity, since what constitutes the specificity of the philosophical and especially the metaphysical form of knowledge is that they intend to make their statements as transparent and intelligible as possible, thanks to the abstract level of their concepts and the logic of their interconnectedness.[1] Considering the content of metaphysics we can speak of 'absolute esoterism', but if we consider its form, we could just as well speak of 'absolute exoterism', it being given that by definition and at least in principle, there is no longer anything of the hidden within it. Such a language is doomed to transparency and unveiling insofar as it is true that the first philosophy—which is what Aristotle called metaphysics—is also the final speculative philosophy. As a result, the same (metaphysical) text will appear ineffably deep to some while others will see it only as a purely formal stating of a logical axiom: the formula 'being is being' for instance.[2] Moreover, such cases are not rare in the history of Western thought. Plato's dialogue *Parmenides* offers a classic example. We can read this text, as do many of our contemporaries and a few of the ancients,[3] as a dizzying and tedious exercise in dialectic, a kind of sterile game. We can even see in it a self-destruction of the Platonic system by its aging author, who has become skeptical. But we can also, along with Plotinus, Syrianus, Proclus, or Damascius, consider this vexing dialogue to be the zenith of and key to the whole of Platonic 'theology'. Without doubt in our opinion it is the Neoplatonists—or rather the Platonists, for the term 'Neoplatonist' is late—who are right. But such divergent readings of one and the same 'purely' metaphysical or (if you like) philosophical text, obviously shows that it cannot of itself indicate the sense in which it

---

1. On the 'interpreting/interpreted' distinction, present under another form in St Augustine (*De doctrina christiana*, II, 3, 4; see *Le mystère du signe*, pp139–143.

2. Cf. René Guénon, *The Symbolism of the Cross*, chap. 17, fourth, revised edition, trans. Angus Macnab (Hillsdale, NY: Sophia Perennis, 2004), pp91–94; and François Chenique, *Éléments de logique classique*, Dunod, tome 1, p107.

3. Pico della Mirandola, for example, in his *De Ente et Uno*; cf. H. de Lubac, *Pie de la Mirandole*, Aubier, 1974, p267.

Esoterism-Exoterism: A Living Dialectic

should be understood. And so each of us must rely solely on our unadorned intellective capacity. And doubtless this is ultimately the true nature of the dialectic or 'skepticism' at work here. In other words, neither dialectic nor skepticism are *a priori* interpretive keys *obviously by themselves*. By definition, *interpreting* should be more intelligible and explicit than the *interpreted*. Is this the case with dialectic and the skeptical attitude? I doubt it. However, this is what those who use these categories without inquiring into their nature tacitly presuppose. Now, if they had posed this question and brought it to its conclusion, perhaps they would have glimpsed how this essence was basically none other than that of 'negative theology', the radical apophatism employed by true Platonists. They would have understood that no language-based formulation (= no mental form) can speak *the* Truth, nor infallibly indicate the true reading of what is said, be it even the formulation of the metaphysical theory of Ideas, whose exoteric idolatry Plato meant to decry. As long as we are within the order of symbolic language, we think that every mode of expression includes signs, and even signatures, which we need only follow to be led with some certainty toward their real significance. But this is not so for metaphysical language. It alone, because it is the ultimate language, the language-limit, lays bare the limitation of all language. This language abandons us on the shores of silence, alone with the Alone, to our risk and peril, there where no path has been traced in advance across the face of the abyss, there where only the Spirit will bear us up if only we dare step forward.

In short, metaphysical language can indicate that it is surpassed esoterically only by suggesting its own obliteration. It does this not only by providing positively for the indication of this need, for this would be at once too easy and too *ineffective* to the very extent that such an 'indicator of esoterism' would remain *external* to the operation it designates (and in this respect many texts do this fluently, cheaply bestowing on themselves a certificate of apophatism by speaking without cease of the 'ineffable' or the 'inexpressible'.) Much more difficult and drastic is the strategy of a metaphysical text that organizes and sets to work dialectically on its 'self-abolition'.[1] By default, we readily admit that a resolutely 'cataphatic' or 'affirmative' style is worth more than such a fluency with the ineffable. And yet it also risks being an illusion-monger because it maintains that human logic can 'account for' transcendence, thus substituting for the sacred forms of revelation the mythology and even the idolatry of concepts.

We have shown from the point of view of esoterism the consequences implied for metaphysical discourse by its situation as ultimate interpreter. Now we must study this decisive characteristic in itself and inquire into its origins. But there is nothing mysterious here; it simply springs from the essential relationship that such a discourse maintains with the intellect. It is the intellect that necessarily constitutes the ultimate interpretive instance at our disposal. Metaphysical discourse with its vocabulary and syntax is in this respect nothing but the *formal expression of the intellect's self-understanding when it works at understanding its object* (Being, beings, and worlds). As such, metaphysics, as the intellect's self-knowledge in act, is therefore the agent for the interpretation of the intellect by itself. In a word, it is the science of the intellect in the dual sense of this formula: a science belonging to the intellect and a science dealing with the intellect. This self-interpretation of the intellect, out of which metaphysical science is formed, implies no idealist solipsism, since the intellect gains access to its identity only under the effect of its object and in a relationship of otherness to this object.

Doubtless it is not uncommon that metaphysical discourse makes use of symbolism. We are even told that this is the mode of expression best adapted to a knowledge of metaphysical realities. Now, every symbolism can (or should) be interpreted, and so also the discourse making use of it. But this objection is easily refuted once we distinguish a materially metaphysical discourse from a formally metaphysical one. Every discourse whose subject (matter) is composed of a reality of the metaphysical order is materially metaphysical. What is formally metaphysical is solely the mode of expression

---

1. This formula is borrowed from Guy Bugault, who applies it to the dialectics of Nagarjuna (2nd–3rd century), one of the greatest scholars of Madhyamika Buddhism: 'Nagarjuna', in the review *Les Études philosophiques*, Oct.–Dec. 1983, p400. Likewise see, by the same author: *L'Inde pense-t-elle?* (Paris: P.U.F., 1994), devoted in part to Nagarjuna.

Esoterism-Exoterism: A Living Dialectic

which, so to say, makes use of intellectual forms by which we apprehend the real and which the intellect extracts by reflecting upon itself. They are called concepts (categories, notions, ideas, principles, relationships...).[1] As we know, these intellectual forms represent the highest degree of abstraction, which means that they are formed at the end of a cognitive process which retains of the real only what there is within it of the purely intelligible. Is there need to stress that 'abstract' is in no way synonymous with unreal, but designates something of the real seen 'apart from'? Thus, to think about the idea of being as such, we have to abstract it (= extract it) from every known being; and in order to know this idea, to recognize it and grasp its significance, this idea has to be united, by awakening to it, with the innate sense of being that the intellect bears within itself.

Having made these distinctions, it is not hard to understand that a materially metaphysical discourse cannot but be so formally in a way both continuous and including properly symbolic components, which could therefore form the object of an interpretation. We should go even further and affirm that there exists no formally pure metaphysical discourse. And the majority of our concepts, even the most abstract, in fact reveal to our examination the weft of the symbolic diagram out of which its fabric is composed: 'the soul never thinks without a mental image' Aristotle tells us.[2] However, neither is this an objection, for what matters here is the nature of the intention that determines the nature of the intellectual act and distinguishes it from all the others. Now in this respect no doubt the intellect in its metaphysical act takes aim at pure intelligibility, even if it hits it with precision only intentionally. Basically, this means that metaphysical science is always a task to be accomplished rather than a body of knowledge acquired once for all and transmitted with the aid of formulas.

---

1. This is why the Scholastics say that metaphysics, like science, is situated at the level of 'secondary intentions'. They call *intention* every act of the spirit *tending towards* (*in-tendere*) an object: the primary intention is the one by which I think about a thing. But then, because I am a spirit, a being endowed with consciousness and freedom, I can turn back *upon* this first act and, in its turn, take it as the object of my thought: this is secondary intention.

2. *De Anima*, 431A, 16.

Christ the Original Mystery

One last objection to be made is that, even taken formally, a metaphysical discourse can occasionally be the object of an interpretation, if for example it is obscure or too elliptical. This is a much more admissible objection, since no discourse says it all: by definition, speech never exhausts being. The most explicit discourse still conceals something of the unsaid. But this indefinite explanation either only develops what the text states in the course of the text, or expresses it differently, with an alternate conceptual device. In both cases the explanatory discourse belongs to the same interpretive instance as the discourse to be explained; it belongs to metaphysics, and by no means consists in clarifying it starting with a hermeneutic instance endowed with a superior interpretive ability. To explain a metaphysical text is still a metaphysical act, at least, obviously, when we make an appeal to straightforward symbolic and synthetic teaching modes, modes that are sometimes more effective than a long discourse, for sometimes we cannot 'see the forest for the trees.' Actually, the two modes (symbolic and intellectual) are indispensable: the symbolic makes us see, the intellective makes us understand. Anyone who sees is reassured in what he has seen by an interior word.

I am, then, quite far from wanting to reduce by however much the value of metaphysical doctrine, which is rightly unsurpassable. But its place in the first rank of hermeneutic instances, and which in many respects earns it the title of absolute esoterism, demands a ransom: it is also the most ontologically dependent on its object. Without a being given to interpret, no interpretation. And, if metaphysics is the preeminent interpreter, then it is also the most destitute of the interpreted, the hermeneutic most beggarly of its object, the one having more need than any other that its object be given to it. The symbolic mode of expression is of itself already a certain interpretation of the reality it expresses, therefore also an interpreting. Thus, to symbolize the mystery of Christ by the Cross is to somehow speak of it. But symbolic interpreting is ontologically joined to the interpreted which it somehow bears within itself and whose presentification it is. When this interpreted is the *revelatum* itself (or an element thereof), the symbolic mode of its expression is filled with its presence and visibly manifests its supernatural and

Esoterism-Exoterism: A Living Dialectic

character. When we consider symbolic forms such as plainchant, Byzantine iconography, and Romanesque or Gothic architecture, and when we compare them to profane forms (chamber music, classical painting, and civil architecture), the difference in style is so flagrant that it is recognized instantaneously and without hesitation: sacred art harbors an obvious esthetic kinship with the divine source that inspired it; it somehow participates in the *revelatum* whose direct and concrete manifestation it is. The symbolic complex of the *revelatum* is of itself like a revelation, in conformity with this saying of Christ: 'Who has seen me, has seen the Father.' Here the implicit is *de rigeur*. With their lightning-like quality and their discretion, the strongest manifestations of the Transcendent are also the briefest. But the way in which the language of doctrinal hermeneutics presents itself is quite different. Between a metaphysical and a mathematical discourse there can be no difference of tone. Sacred philosophy often speaks the same language as profane philosophy, hence the radical divergence of readings. The reason for this is simple (and I have repeated it in many different ways), even if it is not always possible to grasp its full significance: the intellect always speaks its own language, the language of its nature. In other words, it treats even supernatural things naturally; hence the impression of disrespect it sometimes gives by speaking so coldly of the most numinous realities. But it is, precisely, only at home everywhere because it is naturally nowhere. 'The intellect comes through the door,' or again 'from without', says Aristotle,[1] like 'the Stranger' of certain Platonic dialogues, the enigmatic spokesman of the paradoxical presence of Otherness in the very bosom of Sameness, of Non-Being in the bosom of Being.

This is also why this ultimate hermeneutic possibility remains at a distance from the mass of beings it illuminates or which are illuminated within it. Ontologically, it needs to have its object given to it, and so we understand why metaphysics, more than any other interpretive instance, requires revelation.[2] Only with great difficulty

---

1. *On the Generation of Animals*, II 3, 736A, 27B, 12.

2. That the metaphysical instance requires revelation does not imply that this revelation is actually given to it. The case of Greek metaphysics (Plato and Aristotle)

would the intellect gain access to an awareness of its supernatural dimensions—those dimensions by which it discovers itself to be naturally nowhere—if a supernatural Object were not given to be known by it; at least this is how it is for fallen man. Naturally superior to all the beings of visible nature, the intellect is ignorant of its own supernaturality if it does not encounter within the very order of nature a form that surpasses it and, with a single blow, returns it to its existential place, 'situating' it—this *it* which, among all other existing creatures, is nowhere. As the ultimate and supreme hermeneutic possibility, metaphysical understanding remains then in its activity at a distance from that which it illuminates; it can enter into intimacy with its Object and unite Its being with its own only by an act that renounces its own light in order to penetrate the more than luminous Darkness of faith. This is why St Dionysius the Areopagite can say: 'Blessed are the intelligences who *know* how to close their eyes.' By abolishing itself, metaphysics realizes its nature as a terminal esoterism and brings to its climax the dialectic of the open and the hidden, insofar as it is true that, with respect to the silence of the Non-Manifested, every discourse, whatever it may be, reveals the vanity of its exteriority. However the *sacrificium intellectus* is not a suicide: the annihilation of the intellect in the more than luminous Darkness of faith is with a view to its resurrection in the Light of glory, not to its pure and simple destruction. By dwelling in the 'cave of dogma', as Christ lay dead in the tomb, the intellect is reborn with Him in deifying knowledge.

---

is exemplary in this respect. It is visibly lacking in a sacred *revelatum* that would complete it (hence, in Guénon's words, its rather 'incomplete character'). This need for a revelation is explicit in the Platonist movement and is avowed especially by Proclus. With Aristotle it is perhaps expressed in his lost works—certain indications from Cicero point in that direction. Adam's case if different. We should consider that, in Paradise, this function was assumed by creation: for Adam, those natural realities that he contemplated were truly revelatory of divine transcendence (We shall return to this question in another book: *La Porte du Ciel. Fondements scripturaires de la tradition métaphysique*).

Esoterism-Exoterism: A Living Dialectic

Real Esoterism and Formal Esoterism

Up until now we have considered esoterism, according to the definition of its essence, as a living search for the interior sense of revelation. We might call this real esoterism, since it is this essence which constitutes its true reality, and since, outside of this living quest for the interiority of the divine message, esoterism is nothing and even less than nothing. From this point of view, it is set in dynamic relationship with exoterism in such a way that, in truth and in themselves, neither esoterism nor exoterism exist. Both are hermeneutic *perspectives:* what determines the nature of these perspectives is that which they look to, and the way in which they look, called 'the spirit' and 'the letter' respectively by St Paul. Now one who lives according to the Spirit is still not in full and definitive possession of this Spirit. He is in motion, in permanent conversion, tearing himself constantly away from the 'outward man' and striving to strengthen the 'inward man' (Eph. 3:16), which might be called the esoteric man, likewise named the new man by St Paul: 'put off... the old man who is corrupted,' 'be renewed in the spirit of your intellect, and put on the new man' (Eph. 4:22–24).

But we might ask: if there is only an esoterism and an exoterism dynamically coordinated with each other, should we conclude that we must reject every notion of a more formal and static distinction between the two? And if so, will we not run afoul of contradicting facts? Does not history attest to the existence of esoteric organizations recognized as such, and institutionally distinct from an officially identified exoterism?

This objection seems to call for the following remarks. First of all, whatever might be the customary language on this subject, we should acknowledge that, with the exception of the Aristotelian school in antiquity and certain societies of more than doubtful validity founded at the end of the nineteenth century and in the course of the twentieth, no organization on earth has ever characterized itself as *esoteric*. It is the historians, the sociologists, the specialists in the science of religions, or the various upholders of esoterism who have applied this term. The whole problem then is to know whether this is in good earnest, and to this it is hard to reply.

The first difficulty, which has already been raised, relates to the concept's definition: unless we are mistaken, no agreement on this subject has been forthcoming among specialists, and there is great disparity in the use of the term. Moreover, aside from scholars of the esoteric and upholders of esoterism, the majority of historians and sociologists employ the term without defining it. Since this lack of methodological rigor is as we will see the source of many ambiguities, we need to make up our mind. Suppose that, among all the possible definitions, we adhere to Guénon's, because of its strength and precision. Would our troubles be over? Certainly not. We still have to know whether this definition is well suited to the realities to which it has been applied. Who will be the judge of this suitability? The best solution would be for a member of one of the organizations so characterized to come forward and attest that he clearly recognizes what has been bracketed under this label. In certain cases this is impossible, the organizations having disappeared: not one *Fideli d'Amore*, not one Templar will ever come forward to tell us whether Guénon was right to speak of esoterism in their case. There are other cases, however, where this characterization concerns existing organizations which are therefore able to speak for themselves, either in the Christian or non-Christian worlds.

Concerning the Christian world, Freemasonry and the *Compagnonnage* are chiefly concerned, on the one hand, and on the other some all but unknown organizations, generally chivalric or Hermetic in nature, although Eastern Christianity should also be taken into consideration. As for Freemasonry, we must recognize how rare are the jurisdictions that declare themselves Guénonian, the majority having broken with the spirit of medieval Masonry, despite the efforts of a few outstanding Masons. The *Compagnonnage* seems to us practically unaware of Guénon's doctrine. But this is not so for some of the chivalric orders (lacking any data, I will say nothing about Hermetic organizations). I am convinced that the *Fraternité des Chevaliers du divin Paraclet*, in the person of Louis Charbonneau-Lassay, made itself known to Guénon in order to inform him that there still existed, in the very bosom of Catholicism, something

Esoterism-Exoterism: A Living Dialectic

conforming to his definition of an esoteric organization—a definition whose pertinence it recognized by this very fact. But was this recognition total or partial? Of this I know nothing, although I lean toward the second hypothesis†[see endnote, p85]. We are also told that other chivalric brotherhoods were more reserved in their approval, and even frankly hostile. Finally, as for the spiritual paths of Eastern Christianity, whose initiatic character Guénon himself has affirmed, their assimilation to the Guénonian model comes up against some problems, the chief one being the absence of an initiatic rite superimposed on the ordinary sacraments.

As concerns the non-Christian world (and it is impossible to consider here all the sacred manifestations that can be classified as esoteric) we will mention only Tibetan Buddhism and Sufism. In the former, it does not seem that we find anything truly in conformity with Guénon's descriptions, and I for my part am unaware of any 'Guénonian' lama. As for Sufism, we can certainly consider that Shaykh Abd al-Wahid Yahya was an authentic representative [Guénon's Islamic name. ED]—I have no doubt about this—and that he had a direct knowledge of it. I will not be so ridiculous as to contest this, although some experts deem that concrete Sufism is quite removed from the image of it he presents in his work as a whole, where it does not take up much space, Guénon preferring to express himself in the language of the *vedanta*.[1]

This will be the limit of our survey. Brief as it is, it proves in any case that quite often the search for the spiritual meaning of the sacred messages has been embodied in living communities, brotherhoods, confraternities, orders, societies, etc., in the bosom of which it has been worked with in specific ways. From this point of view, Guénon's conception of an institutional esoterism contains an incontestable truth. Notice however that, with the exception of Masonry, none of these 'initiatic organizations' exhibit the rigorous

---

1. One Islamologist has assured me that Guénon had read very few Sufi treatises: his Cairo library hardly contains any. But, he added, he none the less expounds Akbarian doctrine in a more orthodox way than Henry Corbin, who had a quite extensive knowledge of the texts. However I should allude to the question of the theophanic imaginal world about which Guénon says nothing, but which holds such an important place for Ibn Arabi.

and almost 'administrative' characteristics they have for Guénon. The facts show that, in Greek mystery cults as in Tibetan Buddhism or Sufism, affiliation with an esoteric order can be a rather tenuous bond, without very precise obligations, and may sometimes involve entire crowds.[1] Let us designate this institutional esoterism under the name formal esoterism. With it we find ourselves in the presence of a more ordinary meaning of the term. No longer is esoterism defined as a search for spiritual interiority; esoterism is the exclusion of the uninitiated, the closedness of the group and its secret nature: hence the expression 'formal esoterism', since it is the formality of a rule of belonging which separates the profane from the initiated. Clearly, such is the idea we customarily have of esoterism, an idea popularized by novels and travel accounts even more than by scholarly literature. Obviously formal esoterism does not exclude real esoterism, for which it is potentially a mode of realization.

However, the subject is not exhausted by the distinction between real (or spiritual) and formal esoterism, for this formal esoterism can in turn be viewed in two different ways. An example will make clear what we mean. What is the relationship between Sufism and Islamic palm reading, or even Islamic astrology? Each of these terms can designate both an activity and bodies of knowledge practiced within formally constituted confraternities, where a reserved learning tied to the reception of a rite is transmitted, amounting to what we ordinarily call esoterism. But neither these bodies of knowledge nor these activities have the same object: Sufism is turned wholly toward a spiritual deepening of the Koranic revelation, whereas palm reading and astrology are of use to this hermeneutic only quite indirectly and under the heading of auxiliary sciences; therefore they have only a secondary usefulness, just like all the other sacred sciences, even the 'science of letters', whereas unalloyed *tasawwuf* consists basically in the opening of the 'eye of the heart', for want of

---

1. 'When the Shaikh stayed for a few days in the country, it sometimes happened that almost the whole countryside would come to him for initiation' (Martin Lings, *A Sufi Saint of the Twentieth Century*, Berkeley: University of California Press, 1971, p102). The same phenomenon occurred at Ladakh with the Dalai Lama. As for initiations into the mystery cults, we will see about this in the last part of the book.

Esoterism-Exoterism: A Living Dialectic

which possession of any esoteric science is vain. We should, then, distinguish two kinds of formal esoterism: one, of a religious order, directly apportioned to a spiritual hermeneutic of the *revelatum*, the other, of a cosmological order, which, to be precise, encompasses not only the sciences of the macrocosm (angelology, astrology, alchemy, etc.), but also the sciences of the human microcosm (psychology, medicine, etc.).[1]

Such is the situation of esoterism in Islam, at least if we confine ourselves to the major lineages, and this conforms to the Guénonian model. But it is not so for Christianity, and the difference can be put in a few words: in the Christian religion there is no formal esoterism of the first order, at least in the sense of a general, permanent, and recognized structure. There is none, there has never been, and the whole of this book is devoted to proving this. But even before the proofs are given, one fact suffices to convince us: in this religion, we discover nothing analogous to what Sufism is for Islam, we mean a structural esoterism specifically ordered to a spiritual hermeneutic of the *revelatum*. And let no one claim that, being esoteric, this formal esoterism of the first order has left no specific trace. For, if it is necessary to be unknown and invisible in order to be esoteric, then neither Taoism, Lamaism, the mystery cults of antiquity, the Kabbalah, nor Sufism are so: the content of these forms is without doubt restricted, but their existence is known to all. Only Christianity, then, is said to have concealed in its bosom a general esoteric structure, exclusively ordered to an understanding of the *revelatum* as such and yet completely unknown to everyone. This is at once impossible and absurd. If there exists, in a revelation, a spiritual institution with which it is necessary to be affiliated in order to attain the supreme destination of the way it proposes, then this institution ought to be recognized for what it is by all who adhere to this revelation.[2]

---

1. Refer to what Titus Burckhardt has explained about this in his *An Introduction to Sufi Doctrine* (Wellingborough: Thorsons, 1976), chapter entitled 'The Branches of the Doctrine'.

2. After all, I do not see why, among today's billion Catholics, there should be none qualified for the integral deepening of Christ's message, whereas Islam counts hundreds of thousands, and Taoism about... thirty-two million!

Christ the Original Mystery

What did exist, or still exists, in Christianity is a formal esoterism of the cosmological order. We will see how it is possible to give an account of the appearance of this esoterism in the first centuries. But in no way does it alone constitute the spiritual interpretation of the *revelatum* considered in its entirety. Once again, if such were the case, it would be known. It would be altogether unlikely that no one among the Church Fathers or the Doctors of the Middle Ages, including St Bernard, St Francis of Assisi, St Thomas Aquinas, St Bonaventure, Meister Eckhart, or Nicholas of Cusa, would have mentioned it. It is conceivable that a subtle interpretation of an especially enigmatic scriptural symbol, requiring deep knowledge of Hebrew, numerology, or gematria, might be known only in a very exclusive milieu, for this understanding is not of direct importance for a full realization of the Christic message. But that the *conditio sine qua non* (according to Guénon) of this realization, namely, membership in an esoteric organization, is mentioned by none of the greatest saints or doctors, or in so obscure a way that we had to wait twenty centuries for Guénon's works to be informed of it, that is quite excessive and without example in the whole history of religions!

A Feeble Imitation: The Grail Legend

How well we know that we run afoul here of Guénon's peremptory assertion:

> There can be no doubt of the existence of Christian esoterism in the Middle Ages; proofs of all kinds are ready to hand, and denials of it due to modern incomprehension ... are impotent in face of this fact.[1]

If this involved a formal esoterism of a secondary order, it would be unobjectionable except for a few qualifications. But when Guénon

---

1. *Insights into Christian Esoterism* (Hillsdale, NY: Sophia Perennis, 2004), pp77–78.

Esoterism-Exoterism: A Living Dialectic

specifies that by Christian esoterism he means: 'the "inner" aspect of the Christian tradition,'[1] we can no longer go along with him, for a major and altogether invalidating reason: the alleged proofs have nothing essentially Christian about them. And what is this irrefutable evidence brought to light by Guénon? It lies in the Knights of the Round Table and the Knights of the Arthurian cycle of legends relating to the Holy Grail such as we find it in the works of Chrétien de Troyes, Robert de Boron, or in the *Roman de la Rose*. Now all of this data—which I am far from rejecting—is of non-Christian origin and stems from the Celtic tradition. Undoubtedly it was Christianized, although rather late, since we had to wait for the twelfth century and Robert de Boron for the Grail legend to be expressly identified with the eucharistic cup. But in its origins the legend is foreign to the revelation of Jesus Christ. All the same, we are somewhat surprised to learn that what is esoteric in Christianity are such things as the *Roman de la Rose* and other writings issuing from 'esoteric organizations', and not, for example, the *Mystical Theology* of Dionysius the Areopagite; or again, that it is the Holy Grail and not the eucharistic cup of the holy sacrifice of the Mass, which contains the divinity of Christ![2] It is comprehensible that the Holy Grail should enrich our understanding of the mystery of the Divine Blood, and we should rejoice in this knowledge; but that someone should incite us, at least if we are 'spiritually qualified', to prefer a figure of legend to a sacrosanct reality, this is very troubling. If this is the 'inner aspect' of the Christian tradition, Jesus Christ is no longer to be seen. Should he be judged foreign to this interiority? Does Celtism, then, form the hidden core, the pure spiritual essence, of this traditional form, and does Jesus Christ represent only a transitory and contingent mode of its manifestation, an exterior and on the whole exoteric shell? But then, if this is the case, how can we still speak of a *Christian* tradition?

But this is not all, for we might also ask how possible it is simply to speak about *tradition*. Using a line of argument gratuitously repeated by his numerous followers, Guénon coldly explains:

---

1. Ibid., p78.
2. This is what Guénon asserts: ibid., p79.

Christ the Original Mystery

there is no cause to wonder what the position of Christian orthodoxy, understood in the ordinary sense, might be with respect to a line of transmission outside the 'apostolic succession', such as is suggested in several versions of the Grail legend. If there is question of an initiatic hierarchy, then the religious hierarchy could not be in any way affected by its existence, which moreover it need not even acknowledge officially so to speak.[1]

As we will see, neither the history of early Christianity nor the history of the ensuing centuries, know anything of this extra-apostolic initiatic hierarchy. Besides, it is quite characteristic of Guénon to mention incontestable proofs of Christian esoterism only between approximately the twelfth century (the first Arthurian text appeared in 1135) and the fifteenth century approximately. There he finds himself, if you will, 'in familiar territory', the symbolic climate of this period agreeing with his sense of esoterism. Of the thousand previous years he tells us almost nothing, seeming not to perceive therein the least trace of esoterism, if his silence tells us anything.[2] He does not cite a single esoteric teaching from any of the Church Fathers who have explained and perpetuated the Christian tradition. Let Dante allude to the *Veltro* and the numeral DXV—that is esoteric; but let St Gregory of Nyssa lead us to the Mountain of Theognosia— that is not exciting for someone fond of hitherto undeciphered enigmas. Apparently we had to wait until the twelfth century, and to read certain versions of the Holy Grail (as interpreted in the twentieth century by Guénon) to learn of the existence of an *extra-apostolic*

---

1. Ibid., p79.
2. Assuredly, Guénon does not say that Christian esoterism was born in the Middle Ages; as we shall see, he even makes it date back to the very origins of Christianity. But, out of the vastness of Patristic literature, he has not drawn a single testimony to this esoterism. And yet St Dionysius the Areopagite, who expounds a complete doctrine of Christian initiation (cf. infra, pp 277–295) is in his eyes only a 'theologian' (in the unduly restrictive meaning he gives to this term): cf. *Man and His Becoming according to the Vedānta*, (Hillsdale, NY: Sophia Perennis, 2004), p104. In his *Insights into Christian Esoterism* (p7, n17), Guénon clearly recognizes that there are, 'particularly in the Greek Fathers…, esoteric allusions.' But this has to do with what will be later called the 'discipline of the secret'. Is this esoterism in Guénon's sense? Cf. infra, chap. 9.

Esoterism-Exoterism: A Living Dialectic

initiatic hierarchy, a possibility excluded by St Dionysius the Areopagite himself! One might well ask how, after all, Guénon reconciles the thesis of an initiatic hierarchy distinct from the apostolic hierarchy (which would therefore be exoteric) with his other thesis of a purely esoteric original Christianity... But even more, we might ask what still subsists of the idea of tradition in such a theory.

Everything that Christ taught, he taught and transmitted to the Apostles, chosen especially to receive the deposit of the *revelatum*. Undoubtedly everyone has the right to think what he likes, but the truth is that, in Christianity and outside of the apostolic transmission, it is impossible to gain access to the doctrine of Christ and to the deifying grace of filiation save by a divine freedom that can act when and as it pleases, which is obviously not the case for those extraordinary modes of revelation and initiation alluded to by Guénon, since he speaks of 'hierarchy'. There is not the least trace of any hierarchy that is both extra-apostolic and necessarily reaching back to Christ himself, not even the least hint of a trace, and we should resolutely refrain from imagining such a thing, even when trying to account for certain legends.[1]

The argument that an exoteric authority is necessarily unaware of the esoteric order is at once false and specious. It is false because the history of religions shows, to the contrary, that wherever the esoteric and exoteric orders coexist (to the extent that this categorization is valid), in Islam or in China (Taoism and Confucianism) for example, they have often entered into conflict or rivalry. Indeed, the 'authorized representatives of exoterism,' as the Guénonians say, have not hesitated to attack the most eminent representatives of esoterism (cf. al-Hallaj). A split into exclusive jurisdictions, attesting to an excessive taste for administrative distinctions, is without doubt

---

1. This does not mean there is no enigma about the Arthurian legend of the Holy Grail; quite the contrary, as university scholars endlessly attest. On the other hand, it seems obvious that Guénon has made very interesting contributions toward solving this enigma. But these derive from what we call a formal esoterism of the second order. Finally, we will see how (cf. infra, pp 277–295) in the teaching (the *didascalia*), but not in the sacramental order, we can acknowledge the existence during the first centuries of a line of teachers distinct from the line of ecclesiastical authorities. However this teaching is of strictly apostolic origin.

Christ the Original Mystery

very satisfying from the theoretical point of view, but can hardly withstand the upheavals of life and facts. It is specious, on the other hand, because it serves above all to anticipate the reactions of Christian readers intrigued to learn of the existence of so many extraordinary things in the spiritual order, which their Church, still guardian of this order, never mentions. 'Rest assured,' they are told, 'nothing is more normal than this silence, and the Church is altogether justified in ignoring these realities, since they stem from a realm no longer its own—an ignorance more 'official' than real. In fact there is no doubt that it is informed, but has not known how to deal with this realm and so intentionally abstains from pronouncing on it.' Who would not be flattered to be 'let in' on the secret of the gods and to find himself by this very fact in a position of superiority with respect to an institution before which, for two thousand years, Christians bowed their heads? Moreover, far from disputing this authority, they take credit for confirming it, but of course in its own order and provided it does not leave it. How can one not be pleased with oneself? And according to this doctrine, ignorance of an initiatic hierarchy's existence can of course no longer be just official today, since this hierarchy has entirely disappeared from a Christian tradition, which finds itself thus reduced to... the apostolic succession, to what was transmitted to it by St Peter, St James, St John, St Paul and a few others. What is left for the Christian reader is to either rest content with a tradition practically amputated from its 'inner aspect' (ever since the departure of the Rosicrucians into Asia), or turn toward the initiations of the East.

Guénon's position concerning the disappearance of Christian esoterism is ambiguous. On the one hand he clearly affirms that 'something from it subsists... as long as this traditional form remains living,' and that 'necessarily' so, for otherwise it 'would amount to saying that the "spirit" had entirely withdrawn, leaving only a dead body behind.' But on the other this esoterism subsists somehow, 'even if invisibly.' Next, making the Grail a symbol of Christian esoterism as such, he recalls what the legend teaches, namely that the Grail 'was no longer seen as it was formerly, but it is not said that it can no longer be seen;... it is always present, at least in principle, for those who are "qualified".' However, it is indeed a

Esoterism-Exoterism: A Living Dialectic

question of a possibility in principle, for since the departure of the Rosicrucians, what possibilities for 'effective initiation' do we in fact 'still find open . . . in the Western world'?[1]

Here we see how dependent Guénon is on an institutional model of esoterism: when initiatic organizations are no longer visible, there is no possibility of gaining access to the 'spirit' of the traditional form. This only makes sense if the esoteric perspective is wholly identified with the existence of some chivalric brotherhood or other. But this is not what the symbolism of the Grail seems to teach us.

If following certain indications of Guénon himself we take this symbol in its first truly Christian version, that of Robert de Boron, we will without too much difficulty grant that the Grail can be regarded as an image of the Primordial Tradition, of a primal Revelation received first by Adam and which, by way of its various guardians, came into the hands of Christ, the ultimate recipient of this deposit.[2] But we should give equal consideration to another element of the symbol: Christ is not only the recipient of the cup, since the cup itself—the Adamic Tradition—receives its true contents, the eucharistic wine, from him. It is therefore the primordial cup that receives the sacramental Blood of the new and eternal Covenant. And so this cup finds its true meaning and ultimate fulfillment when through the eucharistic Blood the Grail is vivified and becomes the source of life, an overflowing cup.[3] It is impossible to put it any more clearly: the mystery of the Holy Sacrifice of the Mass is the more than perfect realization of the primordial liturgy. But this is not all.

---

1. Op. cit., p83. What relationship can there be between a twelfth-century text concerning a change in the Grail's visibility, and the departure of the Rosicrucians 'into Asia' in 1648? Can the first foretell the second, while presenting it as an accomplished fact?

2. This is a well-known doctrine of St Augustine: 'In itself, that which today is called the *Christian religion* existed among the Ancients and has never ceased to exist from the origin of the human race until the time when Christ himself came in the flesh, and men began to call Christian the true religion which already existed beforehand' (*Retractationes*, I, XII, 3; C.S.E.L., VOL. XXXVI, p58, 12).

3. This is related to my definition of religion as an encounter between the transcendence of a revelation descending from Heaven and the cultural tradition that receives it, a tradition that comes, in the end and through many changes, from paradise.

Christ the Original Mystery

By affirming that this cup is the very one in which Joseph of Arimathea collected the blood flowing from the wounds of the crucified Christ, the legend teaches us something else.[1] Although the fact that Joseph of Arimathea and Nicodemus are both secret disciples of Jesus (John 3:2 and 19:38) might well allude to the idea of esoterism, neither should we forget that Christian exegesis, from the Fathers up until the Middle Ages, contemplating Christ asleep in death and shedding his Blood, has always seen in this the birth of the New Eve, that is to say the Church, born from the open side of the New Adam in a state of deep sleep, and receiving from him the grace of the sacraments.[2] Medieval iconography thus represents the Church kneeling before Christ on the cross and collecting his liberating Blood in a cup she raises toward him. And it is in fact she who fills this cup with Christic Blood each time she sacramentally accomplishes the mystery of the passion and death of her Founder. If, then, the journey of the Grail into the West and its arrival on the Isle of Avalon have a significance, it is clearly the Christianizing of the Celtic tradition. To it also the grace of the eucharistic Blood is communicated, to it and to all those who spring from this ancient religion, especially those knights who were its glory. They came to range themselves around the Holy Table with all the wealth of their symbols and the noble claims of their lives for honor and love, so that the 'matter of

---

1. The Gospels tell us that Joseph of Arimathea and Nicodemus received the body of Christ, embalmed it, and placed it in a tomb. That this same Joseph may also have received the eucharistic cup, confided to him by St John, this is data borrowed by Robert de Boron from a fourth century apocryphal text, *The Gospel of Nicodemus*, and which he brings forward in the *Histoire de Graal*. The word 'Graal' appears for the first time with Chrétien de Troyes, but there it designates a platter upon which is found a host, and is not connected to Joseph of Arimathea. Later, the anonymous author of the *Haut Livre du Graal* (or *Perlesvaus*) will have this Joseph be the first priest to 'accomplish the sacrifice of Our Lord's Body' (*La légende arthurienne*, Laffont, 1989, p205).

2. 'Having assumed our nature, the Word of God has not only willed to be crucified and die for our salvation; but, having yielded up the spirit, he also suffered his side to be pierced by a lance, so that the torrent of blood and water which escaped from it might come to form our holy Church, virgin and mother, unique and immaculate, the Bride of Christ, in the likeness of Eve drawn while he slept from the side of the first man' (Council of Vienne [1311–12], Denzinger, *Enchiridion Symbolorum*, 30th ed., 1955, n480).

Esoterism-Exoterism: A Living Dialectic

Britain' might receive the life-giving dew of the divine Blood. Here then, Joseph of Arimathea is an emblematic figure of the Church and, even more directly, a figure of the Christian priesthood grafting itself onto a basically chivalric tradition, because it was precisely this tradition, as exemplified by the figure of King Arthur, that was wounded, had lost its priestly dimension and languished awaiting that spiritual principle which could revive it.

The legend of the Holy Grail's function is not, then, to reveal the existence of an extra-apostolic hierarchy (besides, Joseph received the chalice from the hands of St John), nor the existence of an extra-sacramental ritual (Joseph is presented as the first priest to celebrate Mass). Its function is to teach the knights of the Celtic tradition that the fullness of time has come, that the Church is henceforth the keeper of the loftiest of mysteries, and that they have been called to participate in them. In the end, this legend is a declaration of the esoteric character of the Catholic and Apostolic Church. The 'inner aspect' of the Christian tradition, which according to Guénon signifies esoterism, is in truth the very side of Christ opened by the thrust of a lance and out of which springs forth the Church, which is the revelation of the mystery of this interiority.

Conclusion: *The Church Is Only One*

Formal esoterism, whether of the first or second order, is truly only the expression of a real esoterism, of the interior quest for the Holy Grail, of a seeking for the spiritual meaning of the *revelatum*. It is opposed to real exoterism, just as, for St Paul, the spirit is opposed to the letter, which means that in Christianity there is no formal exoterism, any more than there is an instituted esoterism. Once and for all, let us stop identifying exoterism with the visible form of the Catholic Church, as if this were something unquestionably obvious.

True, conditions imposed on revelation by its development in time and space—for the Church must be *visible*—oblige it to define itself politically and socially, and to expose itself to being secularized. No human undertaking can avoid such risks, except in the daydreams of late adolescence. Besides, the general mentality of a religious collectivity is inevitably situated at an average level and tends to become a kind of *de facto* exoterism with respect to which everything situated at a higher level of faith, knowledge, and virtue likewise becomes a kind of *de facto* esoterism. No doubt the assiduous practice of theology, for example, bound up with a similar practice of prayer, in the end engenders in a theologian's mind an understanding of dogma unknown to the profane, just as the practice of Gregorian chant awakens over time in the monk's soul a rightly incommunicable spiritual receptivity to the Word of God. And that 'godly genius' to be seen in the lives of the saints always conveys something of the incomprehensible. But both belong to one and the same Church. Peter's Church is also John's, Paul's. and the Church of the entire apostolic College, for there is only a single hierarchy, a single baptismal initiation, a single Eucharist. And this is what one text, enigmatic in origin but most clear in meaning, declares:

> There are not, then, two Assemblies [= Churches]: one exterior and the other interior. There is only one Assembly, whose exterior alone is known by many. And yet those who are of the interior do not have sacraments, Books, or secrets other than those who dwell on the exterior, but they live them and are transformed by them.[1]

To envisage the distinction between interior and exterior only under an institutional form is basically to conceive of esoterism in an exoteric manner, to want to guarantee an esoteric quality by a duly specified and recognized label. But when esoterism becomes a name, it very often ceases to be a reality. The more it is signified by marks, organizations, grades, and secret codes, the more it satisfies the outer man, flatters him, and makes access to true interiority problematic. At the same time, such an institutionalizing, with the endless multiplication of problems this entails and the precautions required (authentic affiliation, division, recognition, ritual validity, recruitment, rivalries, etc.) absorbs our energies in trifles and seriously

---

1. *Sept Instructions aux frères en saint Jean*, Arma Artis, 1986, p 85.

Esoterism-Exoterism: A Living Dialectic

dislocates the pole of the sacred. We forget that what is essential is God's own revelation, the saving gift of his Word, and his deifying grace, which requires first our humility and gratitude.

Conversely, the denial of all reserve and silence, which Guénon called 'a hatred of the secret', often goes hand in hand with the rejection and ignorance of the Spirit. In the name of the transparency and public nature of the Christian message ('we have nothing to hide'), they wipe away all trace of symbolism (in the traditional sense of the term), they break with fifteen hundred years of patristic and medieval exegesis, and they produce such a dull interpretation of Scripture and doctrine that any enthusiasm for spiritual life and understanding is nipped in the bud. And so religion either shrinks to a catalogue of sins or expands into a socializing haze. It is then that 'recognized' esoterists feel themselves justified as guardians of a superior tradition. And how do we prove them wrong if our only choice is between fraternal moralism and heavy-handed fundamentalism?†

---

† See p73. Since the first edition of this book (1997), my conjecture has been verified by the publication of several works: Stephano Salzani and Pier Luigi Zoccatelli, *Hermétisme et emblématique du Christ dans la vie et l'oeuvre de Louis Charbonneau-Lassay (1871–1946)* (Milan: Archè Edidit, 1996); Pier Luigi Zoccatelli, *Le Lièvre qui rumine. Autour de René Guénon, Louis Charbonneau-Lassay et la Fraternité du Paraclet. Avec des documents inédits* (Milan: Archè, 1999). Read especially, in *Le Lièvre qui rumine* (pp65–67), a letter from Louis Charbonneau-Lassay, which I have rediscovered in my own archives and which leaves no doubt about its author's misgivings with respect to Guénon's ideas. The study of Marie-France James (*Ésotérisme et christianisme. Autour de René Guénon* [Paris: Nouvelles Editions Latines, 1981], p303) had, moreover, already hinted about this.

II

René Guénon and Christianity:
A Critical Examination

Introduction

Direct Refutation and Indirect Refutation

WHEN GUÉNON'S THESIS is examined closely, we realize that it raises so many questions and involves so great a number of more or less interdependent elements, that it is hard to elaborate any systematic and full analysis of it. This is not surprising since a 'strong' thesis is involved here, one that touches on fundamental issues and that does so with 'simplicity and coherence'. In reading the following pages, you will discover (perhaps with astonishment) the multiplicity and complexity of the questions brought up. For want of other merits, my undertaking will be already justified if it enables a few readers to become aware of them; of course, provided that they agree to plunge alongside me into the dark wood of facts and therefore renounce, provisionally at least, the (apparent) clarity of some striking and ingeniously arranged ideas.

How, then, do we bring order to such profuse material?

We have chosen to distinguish two categories of problems: (1) those problems that Guénon's thesis, taken as center of reference, poses to whoever examines it in its agreement with the facts or with itself, and (2) those problems that result, for Guénon's thesis, from taking Christianity in itself into consideration. To some extent these two categories inevitably overlap, so great is the interweaving of these questions. This distinction is based, however, on an elementary principle of debate logic.

Actually, for any thesis whatsoever, two kinds of refutation are conceivable. With the first, with direct refutation, the thesis is considered in itself and, respectively or conjointly, either its internal contradiction (its disagreement with itself), its external contradiction (its disagreement with the facts), or even its unlikelihood is demonstrated. With the second kind, to be called indirect refutation, the thesis as such is no longer taken into account, but we consider the subject dealt with, and, explaining this subject for itself, we establish *by this means* that the thesis in question is unaware of it in its own and positive reality. The book's last part will be devoted to this indirect refutation, convinced as we are that there is nothing better for pondering the reality, insofar as it can be known, that is to say, under the circumstances, insofar as tradition and history grant us access to it. Direct refutation, by examining intrinsic problems, is certainly necessary, above all when an author enjoys as in this instance great authority: this will be dealt with in the second part. But, doing this, we should not forget that we are conceding a precondition to the thesis being refuted, a precondition that needs to be justified in itself, namely, is this thesis valid, is it truly concerned with what is involved here? In other words, a direct refutation remains, in certain respects, under the jurisdiction of the thesis to be refuted since we are admitting that it somehow poses a problem, defines the terms and sets limits. Now, for reasons that stem from the very 'mathematical' nature of his intelligence, from his distrust of the history of religions, and from the circumstances of his life and times, we are convinced that it was not granted to Guénon to 'see' what Christianity was.[1] And so, not having grasped its essence, he did not have the authority to speak in such a global and peremptory manner—which does not exclude that, on numerous particular points, he was able to communicate valuable information. Hence, to keep to a direct refutation would be insufficient and ineffective: our goal is a *displacement* of the problem posed *into its rightful place*. Without a consensus about this displacement (actually a repatriation, a recovery), we will not be understood. However, before envisioning such a recovery, and so not to be accused of being unaware of the strength either of the Guénonian thesis or the arguments advanced by some of his defenders, it is first appropriate, after

---

1. Was not Guénon implicitly recognizing this when he declared: "We must confess that we have never felt any inclination to give this subject [Christian initiation] special treatment"? *Insights into Christian Esoterism* (Hillsdale, NY: Sophia Perennis, 2004), p5.

Introduction

briefly recalling it (chap. 4), to put it directly to the test. This we will do by raising in turn three questions of unequal importance, to which Guénon has not it seems responded, or at least we have not found any response in his work: (1) Is there any likelihood in considering the revelation of Christ to be, at origin, a Jewish esoterism and, if yes, is there the least *direct and positive* proof of an exteriorisation of the Christian form as a whole? (chap. 5); (2) By admitting that this exoteric descent has indeed taken place, why, according to Guénon, has it affected the existing initiatic rites, and has it not rather entailed the elaboration of new exoteric rites? (chap. 6); and (3) Is not the possibility of such an exteriorisation of originally initiatic rites excluded by the Church, and even by Guénon's doctrine? (chap. 7).

4

Christian Esoterism According to Guénon

We have already chanced upon some elements of the general concept of esoterism proposed by Guénon. But before examining how he has applied it to Christianity, it will be useful to present it briefly as it is in itself under a more synthetic and precise form.

Recall that, according to Guénon, the majority of 'traditional forms', commonly called religions,[1] include an exterior teaching given to all and a more profound interior teaching, reserved for those who possess the qualities required to understand it. These two kinds of teaching are accompanied by two kinds of rites which communicate to those receiving them a 'spiritual influence' of non-human origin, rites by which the recipients gain an ability to effectively realize the truths communicated by theoretical teachings: exoteric (or, on occasion, 'religious') rites concerned with the individual on the one hand, and initiatic rites concerned with the 'superior states of the being' on the other.

The difference between exoteric rites (religious rites in the case of Christianity) and initiatic rites resides in a difference of ends to be attained. Religious rites offer to all the possibility of obtaining 'salvation', that is to say of knowing after death, and by various modalities, the perfection of the human state; initiatic rites offer the possibility, even in this life, of surpassing the human state and gaining access to superior (or angelic) states or even the unconditioned divine state ('deliverance'). Only in this way will the theoretical data

---

1. See the Appendix at chapter's end: 'Religion: History and Etymology'.

Christian Esoterism According to Guénon

provided by esoteric doctrine find its full significance. Initiatic rites are, then, something incomparably superior to exoteric rites, and absolutely necessary for achieving the goal of the spiritual way.

It will be appropriate to raise, however, a first difficulty resulting from Guénonian terminology: what difference and what relationship is there between the terms 'esoteric' and 'initiatic'? Is the esoteric concerned with doctrine, while the initiatic is concerned with the rites and spiritual method enabling a realization of the doctrine? This is obviously what is implied by the use just made of these terms. But, as we have seen, Guénon affirms—an oddly ignored fact—that the distinction between esoterism and exoterism does not apply to *all* traditional forms. Thus, according to him, Hinduism—a label that also has nothing traditional about it—does not present itself as two separate bodies of doctrine. Concerning metaphysical doctrine, for example, Guénon explains that in India 'all may be admitted to the teaching in all its degrees.'[1] However, there are in Hinduism, and according to Guénon himself, strictly initiatic rites (*diksha*) which are to be distinguished from the so-called rites of 'admittance' (*samskara*) administered to every follower of Hinduism. But how then do we characterize these non-initiatic (Hindu) rites? As religious rites? This is impossible, since Hinduism is not a 'religion'. As exoteric rites? This too is impossible, since the exoterism/esoterism distinction is not inherent to Hinduism. To our knowledge, Guénon provides no answers to these questions, and even at times contradicts his own set terminological rules. These difficulties with vocabulary seem to betray a difficulty in the conceptual order, which is not surprising considering the extreme diversity of rites in all religions, but at least this proves that the legendary rigor of Guénonian categories is sometimes ineffective. Guénon also recognizes, but only in the case of Hinduism, the existence of intermediate rites, at once exoteric and esoteric.[2]

After this recall of his general theory, we can now proceed to the

---

1. *Introduction to the Study of the Hindu Doctrines*, pt. 2, chap. 9, 'Esoterism and Exoterism', p112; this is why Guénon rejects the expression 'esoteric Brahmanism' used by some orientalists (*Man and His Becoming According to the Vedānta*, p16).

2. *Perspectives on Initiation* (Hillsdale, NY: Sophia Perennis, 2004), p152.

very particular situation which Guénon assigns to the doctrines and rites of Christianity in his famous article 'Christianity and Initiation' (*Insights into Christian Esoterism*, chap. 2).

At origin, and according to the intention of its founder, Christianity would have only constituted an esoterism, analogous to the one represented by the organization of the Essenes. This would involve then, although Guénon does not say so explicitly, a Jewish esoterism first, developing normally within the bosom of Judaism. The rites instituted by Christ were therefore purely initiatic and form what might be called the 'Christic initiation'. Baptism, the Eucharist and the other rites were thus superimposed over the common rites of the Jewish religion (circumcision for example), conferring a spiritual influence able to eventually lead its recipients into the 'Greater Mysteries'. Obviously, these rites were administered only to an elite of *qualified* individuals: the secret was conveyed to them only after a long series of tests. However, in spreading, this Christic esoterism had to confront a less and less religious Greco-Roman world. Having thus found itself needing to 'save what could be saved', this esoteric Christic organization decided, providentially, to proceed with a general descent of all its rites from an esoteric to an exoteric level, so not to deprive Western humanity of all spiritual influence; but, obviously, the influence by which it would benefit would thus be found limited to the realm of the individual and could only lead to 'salvation'. In this descent the rites, having become exoteric, would necessarily retain the name and the exterior form received as esoteric rites, since this form and, in certain cases, this name were instituted by Christ. What remained, then, was for the Church to produce new initiatic rites to be superimposed over the ordinary rites; and this is actually what happened, as is proven by the existence of initiatic organizations properly so-called in the Middle Ages. As to the date of this exoteric descent, it is unknown to Guénon; all that he can say is that it was 'already an established fact at the time of Constantine,' and therefore in the fourth century. Beginning with this period, Christianity having become an official religion, everything esoteric in doctrine is presented as 'dogmas' and 'mysteries', and the rites are administered publicly to all.

Such is, in broad strokes, Guénon's theory. Although widely

Christian Esoterism According to Guénon

known, it is still useful to recall it. But experience shows that ideas reputed to be the best known are not always the best understood. And it is quite unlikely that all of Guénon's readers have grasped this, at least in its consequences if not in its principles.

True, attentive readers might draw different conclusions than mine from Guénon's work, and maintain that a few discrete remarks about the present existence of a Catholic esoterism can be found, an existence never placed in doubt by Guénon. I do not, *a priori*, disregard this possibility and recognize that some passages of such a bountiful work tend in this direction. Even in this case my position would remain unchanged however, for such initiatic possibilities, subsisting within the bosom of Christianity and also in places unknown, would concern such a paltry number of people (a few hundred out of around a billion Catholics) that it would be equivalent to a pure and simple impossibility. And, besides, this is what Guénon himself declares: these initiatic possibilities 'must in fact be considered as practically inaccessible.'[1] Such is the last public formulation of his thought on this subject; it is up to us to decide.

But this is not all, nor the most important. Essentially, what has to be considered is that, in scrutinizing Guénon's texts to find confirmations of a survival of a Christian esoterism, and then drawing up an inventory of contemporary data from research into a *Catholic* initiatic organization, some continue obedient to our author's suggestions, without asking if the Guénonian model of such an organization is compatible with the nature of Christianity and, therefore, if it has some chance of being encountered within the religion of Christ? We are speaking here of a central and sufficiently present possibility so that it can be seen as an integral part of its essence; I am not speaking, then, about marginal or even episodic possibilities, the reality of which I do not deny and which bear some resemblance to the Guénonian model, but are too unusual to draw a general conclusion.

This is why, all things considered, and after reading almost everything written on the subject, I do not think that my summary of Guénon's theory is very far from the thinking of the author.

---

1. *Insights into Christian Esoterism*, p18, n32.

Appendix:
'Religion': History and Etymology

Guénon reserved the term 'religion' to designate Judaism, Christianity and Islam exclusively, which are alone in exhibiting the three elements (according to Guénon) constitutive of religion: dogma, worship and morality. To designate the genus of which religion would be only a species, he uses the expression 'traditional form'. This categorization, justified in some respects (in the case of Confucianism, for example, which is clearly one of the least religious of traditional forms) sometimes raises obstacles to its use. Thus it seems strange not to speak of the *religions* of India. Conversely, to abide by Guénon's definitions alone, I think that the term 'religion' does not strictly apply to Judaism, and perhaps not even to Islam, both being forms which seem to ignore the 'dogma' element in the precise sense of the term: to my mind, Christianity is the only still living sacred tradition which includes an explicit dogmatic system, that is an ensemble of *theological* propositions presented as being *revealed*, so that *stricto sensu* Christianity would be the only *religion*. This is the place to remark that, as I have stressed for the term 'esoterism', the concept of religion is historically determined. It seems in fact that no ancient language, not even Greek or Latin, had at its command a term which meant what the word 'religion' means for us, the meaning of which seems to have been worked out only in the early centuries of Christianity. There is no such term in Hebrew, Sanskrit or Greek, as J. Rudhardt notes in his famous work *Notions fondamentales de la Pensée religieuse et actes constitutifs du culte dans la Grèce classique* (Picard, 2nd ed., 1992), p11–5: 'Our word religion has no Greek equivalent.' *Religio* is clearly a Latin word, but for the Romans 'it indicates only an aggregate of observances, warnings, rules and prohibitions, without referring, for example, to the adoration of divinity, to mythic traditions or to the celebration of feasts' (A. Brelich, *Histoire des religions*, Encyclopedie de la Pléïade, 1970, p7). What remains now is to ask why the notion of religion is a conceptual product of Christianity. In another study I have suggested that we can see in this an effect of the radical singularity of the

Christian Esoterism According to Guénon

Christian form which, visibly distinguishing itself from the *aggregate* of all known sacred forms, specifically leads to regrouping them under one and the same general concept, with Christianity its perfect realization only to the very extent that it surpasses this concept.

As for the etymology of the term, the one ordinarily alleged (religion is that which joins together) is not at all certain from the strictly philological point of view. Hypotheses about its origin are the following: 1) *religio* comes from *relinquere* = 'to leave, to relinquish', hence the idea of 'reserve' or 'respect' in connection with the sacred—but *relinquere* would give *relictio*; 2) St Augustine (*De Civitate Dei*, x, 3) has proposed having the word *religio* derive from *reeligere* = 'to choose anew', hence the idea of a 'return to God' after the Fall—but *reeligere* would give *relectio*; Lactantius (*Divinarum Institutionum libri 7*, IV, 28) was the first to propose *religare* = 'bind back, reconnect', an often held hypothesis, which can be warranted by Lucretius' relating *religio* to *nodus* = 'knot', 'close tie' (*De natura rerum*, I, 932), which Augustine, it seems, ended up adopting (*De vera religione* LV, 113 and *Retractationes* I, 13), hence the idea of a 'binding of men to God and among themselves', or of the 'retying of an undone knot'—but *religare* would give *religatio*; 3) Cicero (*De natura deorum* II, c. 28, n72) has religion derive from *relegere* in the sense of 'reread', 'recall to mind' (but this verb can also signify 'gather anew', as we see in Ovid, *Metamorphosis* VIII, 173)—this derivation is the only philologically satisfying one and clearly leads to the substantive *religio*, and was adopted by St Isidore of Seville (*Etym.* x, *Patrilogia Latina* LXXXII, col. 392). But, for all that, do we have to completely reject the meaning of a 'bond' at once social and transcendent? Between *relegere* = 'to gather' and *religare* = 'to retie' the kinship of meaning is patent, as the *Dictionnaire étymologique de la Langue française* by Bloch-Wartburg (P.U.F., 1950) points out in connection with the word 'gather' [*cueillir*] which in the proper sense of the term means 'reunite', 'assemble' (p165). And does not 'reading' consist in a 'tying together' of signs among themselves through a meaning? This is why we think that the dominant idea to be drawn from all these hypotheses is that of the *re-establishing of a bond*; this idea refers to the Hebrew idea of a *Covenant* (*berit*), and perhaps to the Arabic *din*, which includes the idea of the creature's 'ob-ligation' with respect to its Creator. If follows that religion is somehow always secondary, that it is always a recovery, a beginning anew, a return or restoration of a broken bond, if only we strive to hear what the word itself is telling us. From this point of view *religio primordialis* would be an improper designation.

5

Jewish Esoterism Or New Covenant?

*Christianity is a Universal
Religion From Its Beginnings*

GUÉNON'S THESIS of an exoteric descent of Christianity supposes, first, a Christic way constituting at the outset simply an esoterism, for which the Jewish religion would represent, then, its normal exoteric framework, and, second, that this exteriorization was providential and somehow required by the spiritually decadent state of all pagan antiquity. The second of these assertions does not seem to be easily reconciled to the first: how are we to imagine that a Jewish esoterism, at the price of its own sacrificial exteriorization, is a proper condition to cure the spiritual decadence of an entire civilization? Would not this have to suppose the nearly universal spread of a Christic esoterism outside the normal framework of Jewish exoterism, a spread quite incompatible with its nature as an esoterism at the core of a religion? As for the first assertion, based on some data from the Islamic tradition, it is directly contradicted by the deployment of Christianity *since its birth* outside the framework of Judaism. In short: either Christianity was a Jewish *esoterism* and it could not be deployed outside its exoteric framework, or it was deployed from its origin outside this framework and was not therefore a *Jewish* esoterism. Only the second of these alternatives corresponds to the reality of some quite incontestable facts, as I will demonstrate.

Christianity's deployment outside the legal framework of Judaism did not wait for the preaching of St Paul, as is repeated only too often. It was done from the beginning, as the *Acts of the Apostles* quite plainly inform us (10:44–6). It involves a famous episode (sometimes dubbed the 'Pentecost of the Pagans') of *major* importance in the history of Christianity, and it will be good to meditate on it at length. Peter miraculously encounters the centurion Cornelius whom God has led to him. Peter speaks to him of Christ. But before he finishes preaching

> the Holy Spirit fell on all who heard the word. And the believers from among the circumcised who came with Peter were amazed, because the gift of the Holy Spirit had been poured out even on the Gentiles. For they heard them speaking in tongues and extolling God.

The 'believers from among the circumcised' were obviously Christians sprung from Judaism. They might have had the tendency to consider that the revelation of Christ was addressed to the children of Israel, but the Holy Spirit, in person, descending upon the 'goyim' constrained them to see things otherwise—this is certain. Is this not strange for an esoterism of Jewish allegiance? But stranger still is it not Guénon himself who, inexplicably, presupposes the nearly universal spread of this 'Jewish esoterism' throughout the Roman Empire, when he assures us that the primitive *Ecclesia* was induced, by its very situation, to cure the decadence of pagan antiquity? Clearly it had to be everywhere present to take on this task! After all, this presence is attested to by Christianity's first historians. Eusebius, the most important among them, informs us, with some exaggeration no doubt, that at the time of Cornelius the centurion's baptism, while Tiberius still reigned,

> the doctrine of the Savior, like rays of the sun, quickly illumined the whole world... the voice of the inspired evangelists and apostles went forth through all the world.[1]

This rapid and universal spread fulfilled the prophecy of Christ

---

1. *Church History*, L. II, c.3; English translation Rev. A.C.McGiffert (Grand Rapids: Eerdmans, 1976), p107.

Jewish Esoterism Or New Covenant?

which announced the extension of salvation to the Pagans: 'many will come from east and west and sit at table with Abraham, Isaac and Jacob in the kingdom of heaven, while the sons of the kingdom will be thrown into the outer darkness' (Matt. 8:11–2). Likewise, he gives the bread promised the sheep of Israel to the Canaanite woman (a pagan 'dog') (Matt. 15:26–8), and the 'Eucharistic' miracle of the multiplying of bread takes place significantly in pagan territory.

This is not to say, however, that original Christianity, as we will see in a moment and at greater length in the last part of this work, did not have marked esoteric features. But in this case an esoterism of a new kind is involved, which by its very nature irresistibly eludes the properly so-called form of Judaism. In other words, to the very extent that it is 'esoteric' Christianity is not Jewish, whatever might otherwise be the number and importance of elements retained from the First by the Second Covenant. For, as St Paul tells us referring to St Peter's word (to the centurion Cornelius in Acts 10:36), in Christ who 'is Lord over all...there is no distinction between Jew and Greek' (Rom. 10:12). And this surpassing of the Jewish form is not reserved for a tiny elite of Jewish initiates, for the purest of the community of Israel; it has been offered to everyone. More precisely, we should not be speaking of a 'surpassing', but of a new *rooting*. To surpass is to leave behind that form in which something was enclosed. In this sense the 'Christic initiates' would have been able to surpass the Jewish form only if they had first belonged to it. But precisely from the start this obligation was abolished in an exemplary manner, even if not understood by everyone. And this is what explains original Christianity's extraordinary power of (peaceful) expansion.

We are then quite far from what the expression 'Jewish esoterism' might possibly signify, as well as from those realities to which it might be legitimately applied. If, however, some insist on retaining it to characterize the nature of original Christianity, then it should be understood in a sense which is no longer truly Guénon's, and which would designate, more or less happily, an expression of real or intrinsic esoterism. But, in this case, if anyone agrees to see things in this way—how otherwise account for the first century spread of Christianity?—the hypothesis of an exoteric descent becomes useless. Either Christianity was a formal esoterism Jewish in essence, and its instantaneous spread to non-Jews is inexplicable, or else its very spread proves that it sprang from elsewhere, from that universal Christic center which transcends all distinctions, even those of exoterism and esoterism in the formal sense of these terms: it had no need to exteriorize in order to save the world.

All of these remarks will be verified if we turn now to Essenism, which Guénon rather names 'Essenianism' and in which he incontestably sees a Jewish esoterism. It is even the example he cites[1] to give his readers some idea of what primitive Christianity might have been, which, he declares, was 'in reality something very different from what it seems to be at present ... at least as to the ends in view of which it was established.' This is typical 'Guénonian' phrasing. But does it not provoke a certain uneasiness, for ultimately Christianity was not 'established', but founded or instituted, not by an 'anonymous' initiatic organization or some 'Unknown Superior', but by the Word Incarnate to save all men and confer on them the grace of divine sonship? As for Essenism, the Jewish esoterism in which we are bidden to see an example of original Christianity, a few remarks are imperative. First, very little was known at the time when Guénon was writing (the Dead Sea scrolls had only just been discovered), so that he is proposing to clarify the supposed enigma of Christian origins in the very doubtful light of a very real ignorance. Second, who has ever thought of Essenism as an option for the spiritual restoration of decadent antiquity. No one to my knowledge, not even Guénon—which clearly proves that, in his own eyes, Christianity is something *essentially* different and constitutes a sacred reality that the so-called Essene model by no means enables us to understand, except in its contingent and cultural aspects. Third, the considerable growth in knowledge about the Essenes, since the discovery of the Qumran documents in 1947, has established more and more clearly how profoundly their doctrines differ from those of Christianity, despite striking similarities and probable contacts. I am not denying that a study of the Essenes is valuable for a better understanding of Christian origins. But neither should it be doubted that it constitutes an exclusively Jewish organization, and even so 'purist' [*intégriste*]

---

1. *Insights into Christian Esoterism*, p4.

Jewish Esoterism Or New Covenant?

that it urges, if some of the discovered documents are to be believed and from an assuredly eschatological perspective, the extermination of all pagan nations in a kind of ultimate and symbolic war. Obviously we are at the antipodes of Christ's message. However, it is suspected that the Essenes of Qumran or Jerusalem had ties to Christian communities. But, far from Christianity being 'an Essenism which was by and large successful' (in Renan's words borrowing a polemical opinion from the *philosophes* of the eighteenth century, the inevitable Voltaire being one of them), the most recent works, such as certain archaeological findings, suggest to the contrary that there were numerous Essenes who converted to Christianity.[1]

It is true that, according to Guénon, the history of original Christianity is surrounded by an

> almost impenetrable obscurity ... an obscurity so profound that, upon reflection, it seems impossible that it should simply have been accidental, but more likely was expressly willed.[2]

This impenetrable and deliberate obscurity obviously sanctions all

---

1. 'The Rule of War' with a view to exterminating the pagans is to be found in *The Dead Sea Scrolls, A New Translation*, trans. and commentary by Michael Wise, Martin Abeqq, Jr., and Edward Cook, (San Francisco: Harper, 1996), pp150–173; likewise: *La Bible. Écrits inter-testamentaires*, Bibliothèque de la Pléiade, 1987, pp187–226 (trans. Dupont-Sommer). On the relations between Christians and Essenes, attested to by the discovery of fragments from the Gospel of Mark at Qumran: cf. the Acts of the Eichstatt Congress: *Christian in Qoumran?*, Eichstätter Studien (xxxiii), Regensberg, 1992; also a fine presentation by Brother Bonnet-Eymard in *La Contre-Réforme Catholique*, n° 294, Aug.–Sept. 1993. Some experts are today inclined to think that the term *Herodians*, utilized in the Gospels of Matthew (22:16) and Mark (3:6, 12:13) actually designate the Essenes who were perhaps numerous in agreeing to momentarily collaborate with Herod the Great in the restoration of the Temple undertaken by him. This hypothesis would explain why the Gospels mention only two (Pharisees and Sadducees) of the three sects existing in Palestine at that time according to Josephus and Philo; the third, the Essenes, having been close to St John the Baptist were only designated in an allusive manner; cf. C. Daniel, 'Les Hérodiens du Nouveau Testament sont-ils des Esséniens?', *Revue de Qoumrân*, 6, 1969, pp31–53, and Jean Daniélou, *Les manuscrits de la mer Morte et les origines de christianisme*, Édition de l'Orante, 1974, pp16–17. Carsten Peter Thiede, in *Qumrân et les Évangiles* (F.X. de Guibert, 1994), has demonstrated the presence of New Testament fragments at Qumran.

2. *Insights into Christian Esoterism*, p5.

Christ the Original Mystery

hypotheses,[1] in particular that of a general descent of Christianity, by ecclesiastic decision, into the exoteric order. In fact, as Jean Daniélou has remarked, Christianity's history is, in its beginnings, no more obscure than those of other religions;[2] it is even more examined and better known than Judaism's, Hinduism's or Islam's. Documents have been abundant and ceaselessly multiply, and can be read in quality, sometimes widely distributed publications. In addition the historical sciences, since Renan and Loisy, have made notable progress, not only in the order of knowledge, but also in the order of objectivity. Still, we should become acquainted with their results, if only by going into a public library, a step which Guénon seems to congratulate himself for never having taken.[3] Such an indifference with respect to historical information is possibly legitimate when someone intends to situate oneself on the level of principles, and therefore on a purely metaphysical level, but this should not be a substitute for competence when expressing one's opinion on the facts.

However, in the absence of an historical study of Christian origins, partly dominated around 1900 by the most narrow scientific atheism,[4] Guénon could have referred to two perfectly sure sources of information, which he has also never called into question, sources which he has even taught to be placed very much above the conjectures of an 'ignorant scholarship', but which he seems to inexplicably neglect in this instance: scripture and tradition. Taking these into account, how could the origins of Christianity seem obscure? The New Testament on the one hand, liturgical practice and the doctrinal teaching of the Church on the other provide essential and sufficient answers—even if our curiosity is not completely satisfied and many details escape us—provided of course that we have faith in them, that we call into question neither the reported facts, nor the significance given them by the new religion. Now, although Guénon

---

1. I am not even considering the numerous 'Life of Jesus' impostures.
2. *L'Eglise des premiers temps*, Seuil, 1985, p7.
3. *Comptes rendus*, Éditions Traditionnelles, 1973, p130.
4. Nevertheless it would be unjust to pass over in silence the existence of a Christian science of very high quality which, at that time, knew how to rise to the challenge cast against Church doctrine by scholarly Modernism and Renanism.

Jewish Esoterism Or New Covenant?

recognizes the first, *he implicitly denies the second*; otherwise how could he maintain that Christians, in possession of all the documents of faith, are ignorant of 'the ends in view of which it was established?' The effects of such words from the mouth of a great metaphysician are hard to describe, but the most serious is that readers take to heart the fanciful possibility of a hidden and lost Christianity, the nostalgia for which renders them deaf and blind in their own religion to the gift of himself offered them by God.

It is then excluded, *a priori,* that an authentic religion is able to silence or ignore the essential Truth about itself. To know this Truth, it is enough to open the sacred books and to listen to the word of its Magisterium.

Now, for whoever so reads the Gospels, the Acts of the Apostles, the Epistles, or inquires into the Church's teachings, something obvious leaps to their attention: Christ did indeed have the express intention of *founding* a new *Ecclesia,* a new religion, a new 'bond', a new '*Covenant*' (*berith* in Hebrew, which is translated by the Greek *diatheke* in the Septuagint, repeated by the Evangelists, and the Latin *testamentum*). The proof of this *new* Covenant is attested to by one of the most solemn moments of Christ's life, the moment which will become for the rest of time until the end of the world *the* major moment and *the* center of all Christian life. There is no question then of a chance and hard to interpret indication, the meaning of which would be intelligible only at the cost of a careful exegesis of texts. Here is what Jesus Christ declares on the eve of Good Friday:[1] 'This cup which is poured out for you is the *New Covenant* in my blood' (Luke 22:20, 1Cor. 11:25). It is at this very instant that the founding rite of the new religion was instituted and, therefore, when

---

1. It is possible that the Pascal meal, during which the Eucharist was instituted, took place not on Thursday but Tuesday. Annie Jambert has shown, in fact, that the Qumran documents reveal the existence of two calendars at the time of Christ: a traditional one followed by the Essenes, and another one of pagan origin followed by the Pharisees. With the first, the Pasch is celebrated on Tuesday evening; while the second could have occurred on any day of the week (a Friday evening during the year of Christ's death). Jesus would have followed the traditional calendar, which seems to resolve certain scriptural and historical difficulties associated with the Passion (*La date de la Cène,* Paris: Gabalda, 1957).

the declaratory act of this founding was promulgated, summarizing and fulfilling the Covenants of Noah, Abraham and Sinai. Whoever wants to know those ends for which Christianity was instituted (by the Word Incarnate!), let them interrogate this founding event and search out its meaning. Also, as a result of this event, the Christian religion is *founded anew* each time the sacrifice of the New Covenant is liturgically accomplished. Therefore this Covenant is new not only with respect to the old, otherwise it would abolish it—which is impossible—but it is intrinsically new; it is the inauguration of an eternal Covenant that transcends time and space, just as the consecratory words declare in the Roman liturgy: 'for this is the chalice of my Blood, of the new and *eternal* Covenant.' The Christian religion is thus perpetually contemporary to the act which founds it, and so its own *origin* is perpetually and actually present within it. Just here, then, is the true and original Christianity.[1]

An Examination of Proofs Alleged By Guénon: The Innovation of Nicea

If, then, Christianity never was a formally defined esoterism in the sense given to this term by Guénon, it is not surprising that there is no direct and explicit proof for an exoteric descent of the sacraments of Christian initiation, even if this descent were to be considered as providential. Guénon gives two indirect signs for this exoterization: the dogmatization of Christian doctrine beginning with the Council of Nicea in AD 325, and the admission of children, or of all postulants without an examination of their initiatic qualifications, to baptism. We shall return later to these important questions which should be studied in and of themselves. But for the time being we should

---

1. The identification of the New Covenant with the Eternal Covenant is not a Roman invention. It is found in the Epistle to the Hebrews: 'the blood of the eternal covenant' (13:20). This New Covenant, heralded by Jeremiah, is 'better' than the first (9:15). Jesus is the mediator through whom the first is fulfilled in the second (ibid.).

Jewish Esoterism Or New Covenant?

straightforwardly weigh the pertinence and demonstrative value of the two 'signs' alleged by Guénon, and this already constitutes an thick portfolio.

Asking himself about the date for the change of Christianity into an exoterism, Guénon estimates that it was

> an established fact at the time of Constantine and the Council of Nicea,' and the Council 'had only to 'sanction' it, so to speak, by inaugurating the era of 'dogmatic' formulations intended as a purely exoteric presentation of the doctrine.[1]

Hence those esoteric truths enclosed 'in clearly defined formulas' could 'only be presented as 'mysteries' in the common meaning this word has acquired.'[2] One therefore had to 'confine oneself to expressing them purely and simply as 'dogmatic' pronouncements to which the least explanation [could] never be attached.'[3] These are so many assertions which come up against serious difficulties.

The Existence of an Ante-Nicene Rule of Faith

Well before AD 325 the Church had at its disposal a 'rule of faith', also called the 'rule of truth', the existence of which is attested to at the end of the first century,[4] the Apostolic origin of which is beyond doubt. Fundamentally trinitarian, this rule of faith is expressed in definitely diverse formulations, and yet already sufficiently stereotyped and homogeneous for all Christians to make use of it as a sign of mutual recognition and as a criterium for discerning the authentic interpretation of Scripture, hence the name 'symbol' that was given to them. The contents of this rule of truth 'rendered' at the

---

1. *Insights into Christian Esoterism*, p10.
2. Ibid. p11.
3. Ibid. p13.
4. Henri Lassiat, in his work entitled *La jeunesse de l'Église: la foi au IIe* (vol. I: *Dans la mouvance de la Tradition de Rome*; vol. II: *Dans la mouvance de la Tradition d'Antioche et d'Athènes*), published by Mame in 1979, has collected all the testimonies, offered by Christian literature between AD 100 and 200, to the existence of an apostolic canon of the Christian faith. His demonstration is irrefutable.

time of baptismal initiation, is everywhere the same, as St Irenaeus informs us:

> although the languages of the world are dissimilar, yet the import of the tradition is one and the same. For the Churches which have been planted in Germany do not believe or hand down anything different, nor do those in Spain, nor those in Gaul, nor those in the East, nor those in Egypt, nor those in Libya, nor those which have been established in the central regions of the world.[1]

As for the contents themselves, St Irenaeus gives us an example in a work which had been known for a long time only by its title: *Demonstration of the Apostolic Preaching*, but an Armenian translation of which was rediscovered in 1904. In this brief apologetic and catechetical writing from the end of the second century, Irenaeus offers his readers 'exposition of the things of God,'[2] which leads him in the first place to set forth the contents of the apostolic faith, the 'canon of Tradition':

> This is the order of our faith, the foundation of [the] edifice and the support of our conduct: God, the Father, uncreated, uncontainable, invisible, one God, the Creator of all: this is the first article of our faith. And the second article: the Word of God, the Son of God, Christ Jesus our Lord, who was revealed by the prophets ... by whom all things were made, and who, in the last times, to recapitulate all things, became a man amongst men, visible and palpable, in order to abolish death, to demonstrate life, and to effect communion between God and man. And the third article: the Holy Spirit through whom the prophets prophesied and the patriarchs learned the things of God and the righteous were led in the paths of righteousness, and who, in the last times, was poured out in a new fashion upon the human race renewing man, throughout the world, to God.[3]

---

1. *Adv. Haer.*, I, 10.
2. [1] Trans. and introduction by John Behr (Crestwood, NY: St Vladimir's Seminary Press, 1997), p 39.
3. [6] Ibid., pp 43–44.

Jewish Esoterism Or New Covenant?

Now it will be useful to compare the 'Credo' of this 'popular' treatise (however highly wrought philosophically) with the account of the faith given by the very scholarly Origen in his preface to *Peri Archon* (*On First Principles*), a work coming some twenty years after the Irenaean catechesis. Origen first reminds us that, although there are certain points of divergent interpretation among Christians,

> the teaching of the Church, transmitted in orderly succession from the apostles ... is still preserved.... The holy apostles, in preaching the faith of Christ, delivered themselves with the utmost clarity on certain points which they believed to be necessary to every one, even to those who seemed somewhat dull in the investigation of divine knowledge; leaving, however, the grounds of their statements to be examined into by those who should deserve the excellent gifts of the Spirit, and who, especially by means of the Holy Spirit Himself, should obtain the gift of language, of wisdom, and of knowledge (1 Cor. 12:8): while on other subjects they merely stated the fact that things were so, keeping silence as to the manner or origin of their existence; clearly in order that the more zealous of their successors, who should be lovers of wisdom (Wis. 8:2), might have a subject of exercise on which to display the fruit of their talents.[1]

After this Origen proceeds to list 'the particular points clearly delivered in the teaching of the apostles.' These points are the following:

> First, That there is one God, who created and arranged all things, and who, when nothing existed, called all things into being ... and that this God in the last days ... sent our Lord Jesus Christ to call in the first place Israel to Himself, and in the second place the Gentiles....
> Secondly, That Jesus Christ Himself, who came [into the world], was born of the Father before all creatures; that, after He had been the servant of the Father in the creation of all things.... He in the last times, divesting Himself [of His glory], became a man,

---

1. *On First Principles,* Preface, 3. Among those points not specified by apostolic teaching, Origen indicates certain questions relating to the Holy Spirit.

Christ the Original Mystery

and was incarnate although God, and while made a man remained the God which He was ... [and] was born of a virgin and of the Holy Spirit. That this Jesus Christ was truly born, and did truly suffer, and did not endure this death common [to man] in appearance only, but did truly die; that He did truly rise from the dead; and that after His resurrection He conversed with His disciples, and was taken up [into heaven].

Then, thirdly, the apostles related that the Holy Spirit was associated in honor and dignity with the Father and the Son.[1]

We shall stop here in the transcription of Origen's text; the rest of his account of the apostolic Tradition deals with the soul's immortality, its ultimate resurrection, the affirmation of its free will, the existence of the devil, the origin and end of the world, and the existence and role of the angels.

Beneath the unfolding of this 'dogmatic preamble', it is easy to recognize the pattern of a baptismal creed identical to that of St Irenaeus, as well as to the one, very widespread in the West, which bears the name *Apostles' Creed*, and which still today must be recited at the time of Baptism. True, the form under which we profess it is not prior to the tenth century, since it began to be read, word for word, only in the *Ordo romanus* of 950. However, in the sixth century, in a sermon of St Caesarius of Arles, and, even further back, in the *Apostolic Tradition*, we find the texts of a baptismal Creed which hardly differs from today's accepted text but for a few words. Only lately identified (1916), this *Apostolic Tradition*, attributed to St Hippolytus, dates to around 215. But does it provide us with a trustworthy documentation on the liturgical practices in use at Rome in the second half of the second century? This is a disputed point and matters little to the question at hand, for, however that may be, what remains is that it is quite close indeed to the text of our present day Creed. Is it possible to go further back? Ecclesiastic science has established that, at the end of the apostolic age, there were undoubtedly two formularies in use during baptismal initiations: one short and purely trinitarian formulary, the most ancient (end of the first century),

---

1. Ibid., 4.

Jewish Esoterism Or New Covenant?

and another formulary, perhaps a little more recent (around 130), likewise trinitarian, but including besides a christological explanation. The earlier formulary is basically a brief extension of Christ's commandment in Matthew 28:19: 'Make disciples of all nations, baptizing them in the name of the Father and of the Son and of the Holy Spirit.' One formulation of this purely trinitarian Creed, which might date back to the second century, was found in the ruins of a Coptic monastery in Upper Egypt at Der Balizeh in 1907; it is to be seen on papyrus fragments (Papyrus *Crum*) dated in the seventh century. This is the text: 'I believe in God, the Father almighty, and in his only-begotten son, Christ Jesus our Lord, and in the Holy Spirit, and in the resurrection of the body, (in the) holy catholic Church.' We have to conclude, then, that contemporary research on the history of the Creed, 'far from casting doubt on the apostolic origin of its contents, has, to the contrary, quite vigorously supported it.'[1]

---

1. J. de Ghellinck, *Patristique et moyen âge*, t.1, *Les recherches sur les origines du symbole des apôtres*, Gembloux, 1949, p4.—As for what concerns the *Apostolic Tradition*, the text of the Creed is to be found in chap. 21 (*Sources Chrétiennes* 11 bis. pp84–86. M. Metzger (*Ecclesia Orans*, 5, 1988, pp241–59) has raised serious objections against attributing this text to St Hippolytus. P. Nautin, L. Bouyer and J.M. Hanssens have contested its value as witness to Roman custom and see in it rather an eastern influence (Bouyer, *Eucharist* [Notre Dame: University of Notre Dame Press, 1968] pp158–182). Moreover, at the time of his stay in Rome in 212, Origen heard a lecture by Hippolytus, who was probably a disciple of St Irenaeus, himself a disciple of St John through St Polycarp.—As for what concerns the Creed of Der Balizeh, we are translating the Greek text over the version given by Denzinger's *Enchiridion Symbolorum*, Herder, 1950, n1, p1. Some see in these papyri the remains of an ancient liturgical prayer shedding light on the 'origins of the Roman canon' (Dom Cabrol, *D.A.C.L.*, t.11–2, col. 1881–2). But new pieces of papyrus, discovered later in the same place, have proven that it was a question of a collection of prayers and not a eucharistic anaphora. Although now dated from the seventh century, this papyrus preserves very ancient elements (Roberts and Capelle, *An Early Euchologium. The Der Balyzeh enlarged and reedited*, Louvain, 1949). The word group 'in the holy catholic Church' without doubt should not be considered as an object complement of 'I believe', but as a complement of place: the 'sacred place' which is the Church, for it is 'within it' that the faith is professed. This remark is likewise valid for the creed's ending in the *Tradition apostolique* (*Source Chrétienne* 11 bis, p87, n1 of Dom Botte).

Christ the Original Mystery

The Origins of the Nicene 'Consubstantial'

Now we come to the Nicene Creed, as it was formulated by the '318 Fathers'[1] of the most famous Council in all of the Church's history. Do we have to see it as the official act of a dogmatist exoterization of the Church? The answer to this question can only be in the negative.

Without entering into detail on a question which would require an entire book, and without denying the 'novelty' of this Council—which we will return to in a moment—I will first point out that the Synod brought together at Nicea in 325 only became 'the' Council of Nicea following the Councils of Constantinople (381), Ephesus (431) and above all Chalcedon (451), which have canonically appointed it to be the major doctrinal reference and norm. It is moreover these later Councils which have progressively defined the orthodox interpretations of the Nicene formulations, to which those who subscribed to them doubtless attributed rather divergent meanings, as the post-Nicene history of Arianism proves incontestably. The adoption of these formulas, wished for by the imperial power, corresponds to Constantine's desire to pacify the Empire, were it even at the price of a compromise, and not to a desire to exoterically congeal doctrine, quite the contrary.

On the other hand, in order to credit Guénon's thesis, it would have to be admitted that Nicea inaugurates a new official presentation of the faith; but there is nothing to this. On this subject, the historians are unanimous: 'In the main, it [the Nicene Creed] marks no progress with respect to the first Christian creeds,' affirms Aloys Grillmeier, author of the most recent and the most important study devoted to the history of christological theology.[2]

Far from innovating, this Council was only reiterating the 'Creeds of the great Eastern Churches', as Amann declares.[3] Can one be more

---

1. This number 318 indicated by certain traditions—St Hilary of Poitiers for example—is probably symbolic and refers to Abraham's 318 servants (Gen. 14:14). In the history of the Christian faith, Nicea plays an 'Abrahamic' role, a role analogous to that played by the Father of the believers in biblical revelation.

2. *Christ in Christian Tradition*, vol.1, trans. John Bowden (Atlanta: John Knox Press, 1975), 2nd rev. ed, p417.

3. *Le dogme catholique dans les Pères de l'Église*, Beauchesne, 1921, p115.

Jewish Esoterism Or New Covenant?

specific and determine which Churches were involved? This question is still being debated; however, the solution which tends to prevail seems ill-suited to Guénon's assertions. Eusebius of Caesarea, an important personage at the Council, although of a rather wavering anti-Arianism, is known to have explained in a *Letter* to the faithful of his Church that the Nicene Creed is a reiteration of the one used at Caesarea. Actually, a meticulous collation of texts does not warrant such a conclusion, which Eusebius was obviously highly interested in having accepted. Present-day historians think that it was more likely a question of the baptismal Creed used in the Church of Jerusalem—which is not without interest for our subject when we realize that this Church, heir to Judeo-Christian traditions, long retained quite early liturgical customs and formulas.[1]

There is however one word which appears for the first time in the especially solemn Church text, a word which little by little will become a sign of recognition, a rallying sign for Catholic orthodoxy: it is *homoousios*, usually translated as 'consubstantial', and which can likewise be rendered as 'coessential' (from *homo* = same, and *ousios* = substance or essence).[2] It was Constantine who recommended the adoption of this term—of non-scriptural origin—with irenic intent and without doubt at the instigation of a Westerner, his counselor Ossius, bishop of Cordova, a man well-known for his holiness. This

---

1. Cf. Lorenzo Perrone, 'De Nicée à Chalcédoine', in *Les Councilles œcuméniques*, t.1. *L'Histoire*, under the direction of Giuseppe Alberigo (Paris: Cerf, 1994), pp33–7.

2. Guénon clearly distinguishes 'substance' from 'essence'. But this terminological use, justified in his doctrine, is not that of the Western tradition. It behooves us to recognize that the words *essentia* and *substantia* are, in fact, two neologisms invented by Latin writers to translate *one and the same* Greek word: *ousia*, which literally means 'being' [*étance*] and 'beingness' [*étantité*], therefore something's 'quality of reality'. *Essentia* (coined by Cicero?) on the pattern of *ousia* (by substantivisation of the present participle—absent in classical Latin—of the verb *esse* = being) had no success and was only actually used starting with Boethius (fifth–sixth century). Hence the need for Latin philosophy to propose another equivalent: this was *sub-stantia* (Seneca, *Epist* 113 §4) probably invented on the pattern of the Greek *hypostasis*, synonymous with *ousia* (*Ep. ad Haebr.* I, 3). Following Nicea, the East was led to distinguish between *ousia* to designate absolute reality (the Divine Essence) and *hypostasis* to designate the Persons. This was the cause of numerous misunderstandings for the Latins who stopped short at the equivalence: *ousia* = *hypostasis* = *substantia*. Concerning this question see *La Charité profanée*, D.D.M., pp133–46.

Christ the Original Mystery

adoption did not, however, proceed without reservations, which is easily explained once we consider the origin of a term that might seem suspect, although for differing reasons, to certain Nicene Fathers.[1]

The first evidence of it is to be found in the *Letter to Flora* (around 160), a writing of Ptolemy, a Valentinian gnostic of the Italic school, in which he declares 'that it is in the nature of the Good to engender ... beings alike and *consubstantial* to it.' This involves then a term coming from a kind of reputedly heterodox Christian 'esoterism' (although Valentinian gnosis is today the object of a reevaluation on the part of specialists). Widespread in Gnostic literature, as the citations conveyed by St Irenaeus of Lyon's *Adversus Haereses* or the *Extracts from Theodotus* composed by Clement of Alexandria testify, it is likewise present in the texts of Hermetist esoterism, particularly in the *Poimander* (second century), as well as in the writings of Plotinus and Porphyry (third century), in order to denote the soul's kinship with the divine. During this same period we find it in Origen, who was first to criticize the use that the heterodox gnosis of the 'Eastern' Valentinian Heracleon made of it, and then to have it serve quite normally as the designation for that community of essence uniting the Father and the Son.[2]

After presenting this philosophical-theological dossier, we must now consider the more properly ecclesiastical one: rightly interpreted, *homoouios* is to be met with there, although with hesitation.

---

1. On the pre-Nicene occurrences of the term *homoousios*, consult the article 'Consubstantiel' (Henri Quillet) in the *Dictionnaire Théologie Catholique*, Letouzey et Ané, t. III, col. 1610–14, which provides all needed references. The most complete study that we have read on the word's origin is that of Ephrem Boularand, S.J. in *L'Hérésie d'Arius et la 'foi' de Nicée*, t. II, Letouzey et Ané, 1972, pp 331–53. References will be found there to the texts cited.

2. *In Joa.*, I, 23, P.G., t. XIV, col. 65; and above all: *Ex libris Origenis in Epist ad Haebr.*, ibid. col.1308. Origen does not perhaps use *homoousios* in the Nicene sense of a unicity of being (but in the sense of a community of 'kind'), even though this is debatable. However, that he held to this doctrine should not be doubted, as Henri Crouzel has shown: 'Numerous texts, using all kinds of images, in forms that are dynamic rather than ontological, compel recognition that Origen is expressing the equivalent of the Nicene *homoousios*' (*Origen*, trans. A.S. Worrall [Edinburgh: T&T Clark, 1989], p 187).

Jewish Esoterism Or New Covenant?

Alluding to a debate which, around 260, had been brought before Damasus Pope of Rome by the Christians of Alexandria, Athanasius declares:

> For ancient bishops, of the Great Rome and of our city [Alexandria], some 130 years ago, wrote and censured those who said that the Son was a creature and not *consubstantial* with the Father.[1]

This text proves, then, that *homoousios* was already considered to be a mark of faith by a certain number of Churches seventy years before Nicea. It meant that the Son, like the Father, was really God: both possessed not a 'similar' *ousia* (the thesis of the homoiousians), but a single and same *ousia*, a single and same divine and absolute reality. However, this term *homoousios* could also be used to mean something rather different. In fact, besides the metaphysical and scholarly sense of identity of essence, the word likewise had a popular meaning according to which it designated a simple community of matter (which Guénon would call a community of substance): two pieces of the same bread or of the same stuff could be qualified as *homoousios*. It is by virtue of this popular usage that certain heretics, who denied the real distinction of Father and Son, used *homoousios* to indicate this non-distinction. This was perhaps the case with Paul of Samosata, (scandalous) bishop of Antioch: the Council assembled in this city in 268, at the same time that it deposed him, had, it is said, condemned the use of *homoousios*. This was certainly the case with the Sabellians. The priest Sabellius seems to have been in Rome at the beginning of the third century, the most illustrious representative of a theological school of which he was not the founder, but to which he was considered to have given much luster. According to this school, properly called monarchianism or modalism, but more recently designated under the name of Sabellianism, the Son is not other than the Father: there is only a single God, the Father, who is incarnate under the name of the Son, who

---

1. *Epist ad Afros*, 6, P.G., t. xxv, col. 1040. It seems that, in reality, only about one hundred years had elapsed between the time when Athanasius wrote (around 360) and the events that he relates.

Christ the Original Mystery

dies on the cross and who is poured forth into the Church under the name of the Holy Spirit. Thus Christ is God, but because he is the Father; the distinction of Persons is denied and, with it, the Trinity. The Sabellians, to express this non-distinction of Person, used the term *homoousios*, which thus became the rallying point and the terminological mark of the heresy. This is precisely why Arius rejected it. Being opposed to the Sabellians, he claimed for Christ a personal existence distinct from the Father, but a created existence, ontologically other than the divine *ousia* of the Father. In other words: either, with the Sabellians, Christ is God but not a Person (distinct from the Father); or, with Arius, Christ is a Person but not God, and cannot be called 'consubstantial' with the Father. After all, Arius reckons, if he is declared 'consubstantial with the Father, not only would he be made a God by essence, whereas he is (like all creatures) only God by participation, but the divine *ousia* would be divided into parts, in the manner of 'Manichee [Manes] who explains that the Son is a consubstantial part (*meros homoousion*) of the Father.'[1] Here we see that Arius, in his anti-metaphysical rationalism, conceives of consubstantiality only in the sense of a 'community of matter' (two fragments of the same loaf of bread are consubstantial), and regards its theological use as the unacceptable affirmation of a concrete division of the divine *ousia*. Such was the situation before the Council opened in 325.

Homoousios was therefore, to summarize, a current word coming from the esoteric doctrines of Gnosticism and Hermetism, used in an invalidating sense by orthodox theologians and representatives of the teaching Church, condemned by others because of the Sabellianism which it seemed to imply, and finally rejected by the Arians for the same reason, but also to avoid all risk of an ontological divinisation of the Son. And yet the Nicene fathers, after having hesitated, agreed to retain it, braving the hostility of some, breaking the

---

1. Arius, *Letter to Alexander of Alexandria* (about 320). This letter, which Arius had sent for his defense to the bishop of Alexandria, has been reproduced by Athanasius is his *De Synodis*, 16; we have read it in: Ephrem Boularand, S.J., *L'hérésie d'Arius et la 'foi' de Nicée*, t.1—L'hérésie d'Arius, Letouzey et Ané, 1972, pp49–51, which gives the Greek text of the H.G. Opitz edition, *Athanasius Werke*, III-1, Urkunde 6, pp12–3.

Jewish Esoterism Or New Covenant?

prudential indecisiveness of many, and, lastly, forever after clearing the term as an object of suspicion. Under these conditions how could anyone imagine that, for the Council, it was a question of inaugurating the exoteric era of dogmatic formulations and thus making the descent of Christian doctrine—whether ineluctable or provi-dential—official? Whatever the point of view, this theory is incongruous.

The Theological Heightening of Concepts

First let us recall what was said at the beginning about how hard it is to determine, not the later significance of the *homoousios* (as designating the divine Persons' unicity of substance), but the significance that it actually held for the fathers of Nicea: this difficulty—which stems from taking the incontestable data of post-Nicene literature into account[1]—would have obviously made no sense in the case of a formally declared and observable exteriorization. To the contrary, this difficulty and the complexity of the discussions following the adoption of the *homoousios* were nothing but quite normal, once one admits that the Council was inviting theological intelligence to an unaccustomed speculative heightening. After all, the human spirit is always slow to understand, and, if history teaches anything in this realm, it is clearly the patience of God. St Athanasius himself, a champion if there ever was one of Nicene orthodoxy betrayed some reserve about this 'consubstantial', preferring to say of the Son that he is 'the begotten of the Father's substance', and anyhow refusing to condemn as heretics those who did not happen to accept the *homoousios*, provided that they accepted its meaning and that they clung to the faith expressed in this way.[2] Where is the dogmatism in this affair?

---

1. J.N.D. Kelly, *Early Christian Doctrines* (NY: Harper and Row, 1978), pp 234–7. Kelly's work is one of the best syntheses written on Patristic theology up to Chalcedon (451).

2. *De synodis*, 41. Let me stress however that, for a group of Westerners, Ossius of Cordova and Pope Sylvester's legates, the meaning of *homoousios* as designating

It should be admitted then, and this will be my second remark, that the Nicene Fathers chose *homoousios* not to 'enclose' the faith, but to 'mark it out', to 'point it out' and signify it analogically thanks to the idea of an 'identity of substance'. Far from 'blocking' intellectual effort by subjecting it to a defined (either common or philosophical) category of Greek thought, it was more profoundly and more vigorously a question of calling for a 'metaphysical transposition' of the concept of substance (*ousia*) in line with its most ontological and even superontological meaning, for an identity of *ousia in divinis* makes sense precisely only on condition that *homoousios* is freed from its ordinary meaning of 'community of matter' or 'stuff', the one which Arian rationalism would attribute to it, as well as its narrowly 'ontic' meaning, the one which current philosophy attributes to it. And it is quite right to speak of a 'dehellinization' of dogma: the philosophical language of Middle Platonism 'spoken' by the fourth century Fathers offered them hardly any possibility of thinking about this identity of *ousia*.[1] We can see then how the *homoousios* 'worked on' theological understanding and, little by little, led it to a profound change in its mental universe. In short, and the aim of my whole argument is only to make this conclusion obvious: truly the Council has invited human understanding to an *analogical* surpassing of conceptual habits, to a veritable metaphysical conversion towards the transcendence of the trinitarian mystery, a conversion proposed to the entire Christian body, of which the religious history of humanity offers no other example, and the quickening light of which, even two thousand years later, has unceasingly supernaturalized minds. Thus, in its Nicene consecration, did the term *homoousios* recover the 'esoteric' character of its origins; it recovered it, but completed and superelevated it beyond all measure, in conformity with the rightful work of the Christian faith which is,

---

the unity of substance was not in doubt. The essential texts relative to the Arian crisis (Arius, Athanasius, Eunomius and Basil) have been published by B. Sesboüé and B. Meunier in: *Dieu peut-il avoir un Fils? Le débat trinitaire du IVe siècle* (Paris: Cerf, 1993).

1. B. Lonergan, S.J., 'The Dehellinization of Dogma', *Theological Studies*, t. XXVIII, 1967, pp344–5; likewise: B. de Margerie, *La Trinité chrétienne dans l'histoire*, Beauchesne, 1975.

Jewish Esoterism Or New Covenant?

in imitation of its Master, to assume to perfection all human nobility. And we possess a clear testimony of this invitation to a spiritual and interiorizing uplifting of knowledge, that offered by Eusebius of Caesarea in the already mentioned *Letter* which he addresses to the people of his dioceses. In presenting them with an introduction to *homoousios* in the Creed and leading them to accept it, is he telling them to bow down and obey without understanding? No, he appeals to their sense of esoteric doctrines: 'To place oneself in the spirit of such mysteries,' he explains in connection with the procession of the Son from the substance of the Father and the term *homoousios*, 'it is fitting to make an appeal to the *divine and secret words*.'[1]

The Council did not intend to proceed to any imprisonment of doctrine within a dogmatic yoke; it only wanted to irrevocably determine in which direction our understanding should be oriented in order to be *theological*. Even today, anyone can certainly refuse, like Arius, to let oneself be 'oriented'; anyone can refuse, by speculative habit, to let oneself be dispossessed of one's own philosophic knowledge and refuse to effect the 'renewal of the intellect' spoken of by St Paul (Rom. 12:2). We should, however, enter into a conceptual 'metamorphosis' (ibid.). Otherwise, if revelation should ever only wisely repeat the 'truths' that a certain philosophy would have settled on once and for all, what is the good of revelation? Perhaps God also has a plan for us to learn something that we would not have known: what metaphysics can claim to measure out to God his right to speak, what metaphysician can forbid the Holy Spirit to express himself as he will? And what other testimony of his will do we have than the one given us by the Church in its magisterial function? Or should we declare, like the Socinians in their *Rakow Catechism* (1605): 'The dogma of the Trinity is contrary to reason. It is absurd to think that, by the will of God, who is reason and loves his creatures, men should believe something incomprehensible and useless

---

1. *Epist ad Caes.*, 72B–C. This letter has been preserved for us by Athanasius in his *De decretis Nicaenae synodi*, and is recopied next by the historians Socrates and Theodoret (fifth century). It constitutes the only direct document that we have on the Council of Nicea. I am not ignoring that this letter is a *pro domo* plea and Eusebius' orthodoxy is doubtful. But what is decisive is that a bishop publicly justifies a change to the Creed by advancing the esoteric nature of the truths expressed.

to the moral life, and therefore to salvation'?[1] How can we not see in the work of the first four ecumenical Councils (traditionally compared to the four evangelists) the work of the One whom Christ had promised to send his Church so to 'teach it all things' (John 14:26) and, most particularly, so to 'teach it *what must be said*' (Luke 12:12)? It is in this way that a 'Third Testament' is written, that of the divine Paraclete, which might be called the *Theological Testament* of Christian dogma, which, even independently of its content, is, insofar as a religious phenomenon, something unique in the body of known religions.

The great innovation of the Nicene Council is not, then, for having *formulated* faith. It is not even for having been a council, for, without going back to the Council of Jerusalem spoken about in the Acts of the Apostles (15), the conciliar (or synodal) practice of the Church was constant from the end of the second century. This Church then had a 'rich experimentation' during the third century with what an assembly of bishops and doctors is, according to 'rather diversified conciliar typologies'.[2] But this innovation, and the incomparable authority with which Nicea is invested with respect to preceding synods, comes from having reunited, for the first time, not just all bishops, but bishops of the whole Church: this is why it deserves with good reason the ecumenical title. By making manifest in this way the universality of its faith, the Church was sanctioning no esoteric descent of doctrine. Quite the contrary, by recalling the traditional faith, it strove to avert the peril of a radical exteriorisation that triumphant Arianism spread to doctrine by reducing it to a rationalizing monotheism. This strongly exteriorizing nature of Arianism manifested not only in the theological order, but also in the liturgical and sacramental orders, since it rejected the rule of the secret in baptismal and eucharistic celebrations: St Athanasius testifies to this rejection, reproaching Arians for wanting to represent the holy mysteries before catechumens or even pagans.[3] The Council

---

1. Cited in H. de Lubac, *La Foi chrétienne*, p 11; cf. Kant's analogous doctrine in *Religion Within the Limits of Reason Alone*, 3rd part, 2nd section, Remark, Ak., vi.
2. L. Perrone, *Les Counciles oecuméniques*, t. 1, *L'Histoire*, p 21.
3. *Apologia contra Arianos*, ii, P.G., t. xxv, col. 265–9.

also reacted against this and—which should be likewise food for thought—imposed much more severe conditions for admittance of neophytes to baptism and of the baptized to the other sacraments, especially to priestly and episcopal ordination.[1]

Nicene 'Dogmatism'

Guénon's thesis not only asserts that Nicea marks the official inauguration of Christian exoterism, it also specifies that this 'descent' was made obvious by the appearance of 'dogmatic formulations'. The term dogma is understood here in its modern and, one might say, most common 'free-thinking' sense. But such a significance applied to the Nicene Creed, and even to the Councils coming after it, constitutes a veritable anachronism. And it is now appropriate to shed some light on this.

Dogmas and Dogma: A Brief History of a Word

During the New Testament period, that is around the first century, the word *dogma* had, in the Greek language of revelation, two principal meanings: the juridic sense of decree (Luke 2:1) which has a tendency to be overshadowed, and the more frequent sense of *opinion*. Usually, even in Latin, one speaks of the 'dogmas of the Stoics' (*stoicorum dogmata*). This meaning is the most widespread in antiquity and up until the end of the Middle Ages; it designates a thesis or a doctrine recognized as characteristic of a philosophical school (that of Diogenes Laertes for example).

---

1. *Dictionnaire de Théologie Catholique*, t. xi, col. 409; also: *Les Counciles oecumeniques*, Cerf, 1994, t. ii, *Les Décrets*, vol. 1: *De Nicée à Latran V*, pp36-57, canons i to xix.—By way of example and to establish certain ideas, look at Canon 3: 'The great Synod has stringently forbidden any bishop, presbyter, deacon, or any one of the clergy whatever, to have a *subintroducta* dwelling with him, except only a mother, or sister, or aunt, or such persons only as are beyond all suspicion.'

Christ the Original Mystery

The first evidence of *dogma*, in the sense of a conciliar decree, but without an explicit doctrinal specification, is to be met with in the *Acts of the Apostles* (16:4) where it designates the decisions of the Council of Jerusalem: 'As they went on their way through the cities, they delivered to them for observance the decisions (*dogmata*) which had been reached by the apostles and the elders who were at Jerusalem.' The doctrinal sense (without complete exclusion of the juridical sense) appears in the *Epistle of Barnabas*, who tells us that 'the *dogmata* ('maxims' or 'precepts') of the Lord are three in number (hope, justice, and love).'[1] Likewise the *Didache* enjoins us to follow the 'dogma' of the Gospel.[2] Even more clearly doctrinal, St Ignatius of Antioch counsels us to 'stand firm in the teachings (*en tois dogmasin*) of the Lord and of the Apostles.'[3] For Clement of Alexandria and Origen the term designates the whole body of Christian teachings.[4] In the fourth century and above all in the fifth, its meaning is specialized and begins to be applied to the 'sole truths which are the object of faith, and which are clearly distinguished from the laws or obligations taught by Christian revelation.'[5] But this still only involves a 'neutral' mode of designation, without the term's later connotations. Although the term is basically applied to the *truths* of faith, and not to disciplinary obligations, it also serves to designate heretical theses; 'false dogmas' are spoken of intentionally. Surely, it should not be denied that Christian revelation expressed itself at the time in a certain number of 'dogmas', the body of which constituted a formulary received by all, and, besides, this is self-evident. However, it must be concluded that 'it is only in the eighteenth century that church documents employ the word in its strict modern sense; still, they speak of dogmas or of *such* a dogma, not *about* dogma, as has been done since the nineteenth

---

1. *Letter of the pseudo-Barnabas*, I, 6; *The Apostolic Fathers*, trans. F.X. Glimm, J.M.F. Marique, G.G. Walsh (Washington, D.C.: Catholic University of America, 1962), p191.
2. XI, 3; ibid., p180. This involves an evangelical precept which enjoins us to welcome an apostle as we would the Lord.
3. *Letter to the Magnesians*, XIII, 1; ibid., p100.
4. Origen, *On First Principles*, IV, 1; P.G., t. XI, col. 344.
5. E. Dublanchy, article 'Dogma', *D.T.C.*, t. IV, col. 1574–5.

Jewish Esoterism Or New Covenant?

century.'[1] Thus, and although the importance and sharpness of terminological discussions in the course of the early centuries cannot be doubted, it should be observed that accentuation of the limiting and constraining character of definitions called precisely 'dogmatic' is something quite late in the history of western Christianity. Besides, let us not forget that, during the period of 'triumphant dogmatism, in the nineteenth century, and even after the first Vatican Council and the proclamation of papal infallibility, we see remarkable efforts by major theologians to work out a concept of dogma which does not purely and simply identify the transcendent contents of sacred truths with the authorized formulations established for them by church tradition.[2] Is the situation of the Church so very different in this respect from that of Oriental traditions? The *Vedanta*, for example, has its 'dogmas' consisting of the five hundred fifty-five sayings of *Vedanta*—or *Brahma Sutra*—expressed by the sage Badarayana: now, to read them, these formidably concise sentences do not seem any more readily understandable than Christian dogmatic formulas. Doubtless, they were intended to be commented upon—like the articles of the Creed. But the five traditionally recognized commentaries (Shankara, Ramanuja, Nimbarka, Madhva, and Vallabha) often show even stronger divergencies than the commentaries of the various theological schools![3]

So, from the first, the existence of a 'rule of faith', of a 'canon of truth', as well as the semantic evolution of the word 'dogma' in

---

1. Yves Congar, *La foi et la théologie* (Paris: Desclée, 1962), p 55; this book is very instructive.

2. Cardinal Newman and those theses set forth in *An Essay on the Development of Christian Doctrine* (1845) come to mind. He distinguishes the 'episcopal tradition' which, from the first, defines those fundamental articles forming the deposit of faith, and the 'prophetic tradition' which is an inspired hermeneutics of this deposit (the 'mind of the Holy Spirit', Rom. 9:27): a multiform work of the living Church, but surprisingly faithful beneath apparent change. The Rev. Léonce de Grandmaison speaks of the 'elasticity of dogma' in *Le dogme chrétien. Sa nature, ses formules, son développement* (Beauchesne, 1928), pp 1–65.

3. The *Vedanta Sutras* with Sankara's commentaries have been translated into English by George Thibaut: *The Vedanta-Sutras of Badarayana with the Commentary of Shankara*, in two parts, Dover Publications, NY (first editions: 1896, vol. XXXIV and XXXVIII of 'The Sacred Books of the East', edited by Max Müller). On the

Christ the Original Mystery

the course of time—ignorance of this evolution is the source of deep confusion—does not enable us to credit the Guénon thesis of a Nicene Church officially imposing an exoteric dogmatism on the people of the Mediterranean. To these two reasons must be joined a third of no less importance: the Church has never dogmatized of its own free will or by a taste for authority, but under the pressure of events and in an attempt to avert or render impossible heretical interpretations of the apostolic faith. The Church does not decide, because an idea might have come to it and to adapt its message to the growing mass of the faithful, to produce a vulgarized and sufficiently brief—although paradoxical—formulation so to be remembered by all: such an idea does not correspond to the facts. However, this is what Guénon proposes, even associating the 'exteriorisation' of doctrine with the intervention of temporal power in the presentation of the faith.

The Arian Crisis and the Authority of the Magisterium

It was in fact the emperor Constantine who, in 325, assembled the Council of Nicea and who participated consultatively in its deliberations (not in its decisions), but without presiding over it. We readily imagine, then, that the Church, protected at last by imperial power, enters into a time of peace; but at the price, or so we think, of a submission to the political and social order and its necessities: Christianity becomes an 'official religion'. The reality is quite different. True, the Emperor Constantine first imposed the 'faith' of Nicea on the Church, exiling some recalcitrant bishops. But, three years later, at the very moment when the intractable Athanasius, hardly thirty years old, assumed the throne of Alexandria, succeeding the venerated Alexander, Constantine, without doubt under the influence of

---

five chief commentaries, cf. *L'Inde classique. Manuel des études indiennes*, by Louis Renou and Jean Filliozat, t.II, with cooperation of Paul Demiéville, Olivier Lacombe, Pierre Meile, École Française d'Extreme-Orient, 1953; new edition 1985 (agent: Adrien Maisonneuve): §§1392–1420.

Jewish Esoterism Or New Covenant?

his half-sister Constantia, is 'completely turned around';[1] he recalls all the Arian bishops from exile and resumes relations with Arius (doubtless after 333). For about fifty years, with the exception of the brief reign of Julian the Apostate who wanted to restore Paganism, all the emperors, probably anxious to keep the peace,[2] will support the anti-Niceans, will impose Arian bishops and will exile Pope Liberius and oblige him to sign a dubious profession of faith (that of the Council of Sirmium of 358). As for Athanasius, he of exemplary destiny, he will be driven five times from his episcopal throne and will spend more than seventeen years in exile. Under such conditions, where is the 'official doctrine' of the Church? Where are the formulations imposed on the body of a supposedly obedient Christianity? The Nicene faith, far from being 'vulgarized', is to the contrary persecuted (Pope Liberius was forcibly removed by the emperor); it goes into hiding, it takes refuge in the desert, in silence, or on the margins of the empire. This situation will endure at least until the end of the fourth century. In its whole length and breadth, Christianity—pope included—is subjected to an almost triumphant Arianism. Even after Constantinople (381), entire peoples will remain Arian: the Visigoths until the baptism of Clovis at the end of the fifth century, the Lombards until the middle of the seventh century. As can be seen, the danger from Arianism was not an empty threat, nor was it a legitimate interpretation of the faith that a more 'metaphysical' Magisterium could have integrated 'painlessly'.[3] Neither the imperial power, nor the Arian hierarchs asked this Magisterium its advice or were even disposed to take it into account. Had Heaven let heresy

---

1. Henri-Irénée Marrou, *L'Église de l'antiquité tardive*, Seuil, 'Points', p 44.
2. This concern for appeasement was already Constantine's who, before Nicea, wrote both to Arius and to Alexander, bishop of Alexandria, beseeching them to agree just as 'philosophers themselves will agree on an opinion *(dogma)*' despite their divergences (Eusebius, *Vita Constantina*, II, 71).
3. Some thinkers maintain that the heresies of Sabellius (the Son is not other than the Father) and Arius (the Son is not God) are legitimate interpretations of revelation, interpretations that a truly metaphysical and less dogmatically circumscribed Magisterium would have known how to integrate without problem. But the historical truth is exactly the opposite. It was Sabellius and Arius who reduced the trinitarian mystery to just one of its dimensions, and who show themselves incapable of combining apparently antinomic perspectives. And it is the Magisterium,

definitively triumph over the orthodox faith, it would have been the end of Christianity, which would have been transformed into a 'theism of Christic hue'.

It was therefore inevitable—and Guénon was not wrong on this point—that, in emerging from such a crisis, something changed in the presentation of the faith: the formulas which express it and to which the Church commits its authority, and therefore God's authority, are made more precise, more declarative; all historians have noticed it. But this was so in order to remain faithful to the apostles, and St Athanasius jeered at those who, at the third 'council' of Sirmium, in 359, wanted to impose a *dated Creed*. This progress in the explanation of dogma without doubt presents some drawbacks: you cannot win on every front. Thus, passing judgment on certain theologians of the second or third centuries, whose language is lacking in the same precision, will be conducive, in the following centuries, to suspecting the orthodoxy of their faith; this is chiefly the case with Origen. Now, when an expression of faith does not include those elements required to avert a future heresy, we should not conclude that it cleaves to this heresy or that it does not subscribe to the later more precise formulation. Yet, however this may be, no one will deny that these new precisions, restricting the chances for heretical interpretations, are only made necessary by the advent of the latter. These precisions are never the fruit of a despotic urge to dot every i. Some argue that it would have been better to leave the articles of trinitarian faith in a 'holy indeterminacy', and that, in making precise the ontological relationships of the Son with the Father, we are petrifying a super-rational mystery and making its difficulty more glaring. Such a consideration is not devoid of truth, but, in this case,

---

faithful to the catholic Tradition, which ultimately knew how to produce, according to the analogy of faith, a synthesis between sometimes divergent but equally acceptable formulations. H.I. Marrou (op. cit., p274) shows this excellently, mentioning in particular the Catecheses of St John Chrysostom recently discovered on Mt. Athos. Here we actually see the illustrious doctor explain how we ought to avoid Sabellius and Arius at the same time, and doing this with the help of an accepted formula (consubstantial), as well as with the help of a disputed formula (similarity of substance): *Huit catéchèses baptismales inédites*, I, 21–2; S.C. 50, ed. Wenger, 1958, pp119-20.

Jewish Esoterism Or New Covenant?

it does not apply. For orthodoxy did not have a choice and could not do otherwise. It was not orthodoxy that sought to dot the i's; to the contrary, the traditional faith's greatest champions did not want 'dogmas' of such depth to be made so dangerously precise: this is so for Peter, Alexander and Athanasius who succeeded each other on the throne of Alexandria.[1] It was the heretics (*hairesis* signifies choice and exclusion) who wished to introduce into the faith conceptual precisions apt for rendering its meaning perfectly explicit and unequivocal; it was Arius, the ascetic priest, nourished by Greek philosophy, whose mind was endowed with great conceptual clarity, who wanted to make plain, once and for all, the metaphysical relationships of the Father and the Son by turning them into rational diagrams of a vigorous simplicity—but, obviously, by leaving aside all scriptural data not in accord with these diagrams. And it is to the point that some of his (dissident) disciples, the Anomians, were accused of transforming 'theology into technology' for their systematic use of Aristotelian dialectic.[2] But we should not be fooled by the resolutely philosophical nature of Arian theology: Arius, and those who followed him, also sought the approbation of the Christian people. They were not 'marginal' intellectuals smitten with esoterism and reserved doctrines. Arius, among other writings, composed a poem, *Thalia* (the *Banquet*) in which he set forth his theology under a popular form. Better still: he wrote songs 'for voyagers on the sea, gristmill work, and journeys by land; ...it was by the pleasure that he made them find in these melodies that he drew the most ignorant people to his own impiety.'[3] He also preached this teaching to the parishioners of the church of Baucalis, in the seaport quarter of Alexandria. It was these parishioners, and not the recognized

---

1. L. Duchesne, *Histoire ancienne de l'Église*, Fontemoingt Éditeur, 1908, t. II, pp 138–9.

2. Theodoret of Cyr, *Histoire de fables hérétiques*, IV, 3; P.G., t. LXXXIII, col. 420. Likewise Gregory of Nyssa, *Against Eunomius*, XII; P.G., t. XLV, col. 906–7.

3. Philostorgius, *Historie ecclésiastique*, II, 2; Grieschischen Christlichen Scriftsteller, t. 21, p 13. The text from this disciple of Eunomius, an arianizing dissident, is only known through the fragments cited by Photius: cf. Boularand, *L'Hérésie d'Arius*, t. 1, p 54. Arius died, we are told, 'in the latrines', in 336, just before he was to make his official reentry into the Church of Alexandria: cf. Duchesne, *op. cit.*, p 104.

theologians, who, outraged by this doctrine, appealed to their bishop about it: such is the historical origin of the conflict that would shake all Christianity until the end of the century and beyond. At least it proves that the 'faith' defined at Nicea had not been 'inaugurated' by the Council, but was traditionally held by the Christian people. Finally, in order to take an accurate measure of this theologico-metaphysical debate, we should recognize the thousands of deaths which ensued, the massacres and persecutions between 367 and 378, for example, directed against the Niceans (both clergy and faithful) in Egypt under the Arian emperor Valens.

The 'fault' of the Arian crisis, and the frightful series of woes it brought, should not be imputed, then, to the rigidity and narrow-mindedness of a Magisterium dogged in its exoteric formalism. The official Magisterium, the institutional Church, 'Rome' if you like, was in no condition to either effectively resist heresy or to victoriously combat it since this heresy was supported by the imperial power which, *de facto,* played the role of Pope (this is what has been rightly called caesaro-papism). Therefore it was not a nearly ruined hierarchic and visible Authority that saved the faith; it was a few puissant individuals who, here and there, arose and not only rejected Arianism, but even the deceiving compromises and accommodations held out to them, without for all that falling into the ultra-Niceanism of a Lucifer of Cagliari who, unlike St Athanasius, refused to pardon repenting Arian bishops, asserting that they had lost all sacerdotal power. Such are the true facts. And how can we deny that the Holy Spirit spoke in the Athanasii, Hilaries, Ambroses, Basils, and Gregories rather than in the Eusebiuses, whether of Caesarea or Nicomedia? We have to conclude, then, that the Catholic Tradition did what it had to do under the guidance of the Holy Spirit: for want of the dogmatic prism whose facets it knew how to cut according to the angles willed by Divine Wisdom, for want of that reflected light which emanated from it, Catholic doctrine would have been extinguished long ago.

And so we recognize in the dogmas crystallizations of revelation's formless light. But these crystallizations do not lock in revealed truth like a chest locks away gold, or like a nutshell encloses its nut. They constitute a presentation guaranteed by the Spirit; as much as

Jewish Esoterism Or New Covenant?

it can be seen, they enable this truth to be seen, according to the most appropriate mode *both* as to the nature of the object of faith to be made known *and* as to the nature of the knowing subject. They are a 'doctrinal icon' offered to the theological gaze; they condense and crystallize the revelatory light according to the form traced by the Wisdom of the Spirit immanent to the Church, not to imprison or stupefy the intelligence, but, like a semantic matrix, to orient and guide it in its contemplative delving. Far from forbidding or blocking metaphysical commentary, dogmatic forms summon forth this intelligence and set it free within its most sanctifying space.

On the Immutability of Dogmatic Formulations

By distinguishing the dogmatic content from the canonical form given it by the Church, I do not mean to lend credence to any motive for continuously questioning this form, as is the custom nowadays. To the contrary, I believe that the canonical form fixed by the Church is in fact—if not by rights—the sole means of gaining access to a certain and objective understanding of its contents, insofar as this is possible. This is why, in some respects, Pope John XXIII's declaration concerning Catholic doctrine in his discourse at the opening of the Second Vatican Council (Oct. 11, 1962) seems ill-considered; he affirms without further ado: 'It is important that this certain and immutable doctrine be studied and expounded according to the methods demanded by this present set of circumstances. The substance of the ancient doctrine of the deposit of faith is one thing, and the way in which it is presented is another.'[1] These are ill-considered proposals because, beneath a classical appearance, they introduce a revolutionary principle. The distinction of the substance of the faith from the forms which express it is traditional. Theologians speak of the *substantial* immutability of dogma; by right, the Church retains the power, if need be, to modify their form, even though previously

---

1. *Documents secrets du Concile. Ière Session*, texts collected by Carlo Falconi, Éditions du Rocher, 1965, p16; I am unaware of the Latin original.

Christ the Original Mystery

and solemnly defined—although in fact this has never happened. But still it needs must intend to do so and express the intention publicly. Now, Pope John XXIII explicitly affirms the opposite: 'The salient point of the Council is not the discussion of such or such a fundamental doctrinal theme of the Church.' The Council wishes to be pastoral and not dogmatic.[1] We should logically conclude then that, in the eyes of the Pope, to meddle with the form of the dogmas is not answerable to dogmatics: this is an amazing lack of awareness of the *philosophical* problems posed by the relationships between form and essence.[2] For it should be clear that the distinction between the form and substance of a dogma should not be envisaged, *quoad nos*, that is to say from the viewpoint of human understanding, in such a way that we *actually separate* the substance of the deposit of faith from the formulation with which it has been 'clothed'. Besides, the image of 'putting on clothes' is debatable. Dogmatic formulation is not a garment in which the Church dresses the naked truth of dogma, like a little girl dresses and undresses her doll. Dogmatic formulation, willed and therefore guaranteed by the Holy Spirit, is a *sign of orientation* for theological understanding, it defines the mode according to which Divine Wisdom wants to give us access to the mystery as such, because It alone knows what is good for us, and because we are thus assured, not of *seeing* the mystery in its essence—this would exceed the ordinary capacity of the intellect—but at least of looking in the right direction. Lacking this sign of orientation, this symbol of faith, we either do not know where to look, or, which is more serious, we do not look in the right direction and we theologize (or 'metaphysicize') over an object which is, in reality, not the one about which we think we are speaking. With respect to these dogmatic symbols, all that we can do is interpret them theologically, which is to say understand them first and then explain them according to the needs of the times and audience. But it is not possible to formulate them to suit what one might think a more profound

---

1. Ibid.
2. I have shown in *Le mystère du signe* (pp156–161), contrary to Saussure's theory, that a sign is not a two-sided (signifying/signified), but a *one-sided* entity; this point is decisive for all that concerns the philosophical problems of language.

Jewish Esoterism Or New Covenant?

understanding, which, besides, under pain of being arbitrary—and therefore illegitimate— should have no other point of departure than the canonical formulation itself.

Obviously, this does not mean that dogmatic formulations descend from Heaven completely formed. Just like the body of Christ which is drawn from the human substance of Mary, the dogmatic formulations are drawn from human cultures and Greek culture in particular. They are marked, then, with a certain contingence and are offshoots of *philosophy* which is, formally speaking, a Greek thing. Without doubt, some might deem that another speculative language would have been better adapted: the language of the *vedānta* for example. But it must be observed that such was not the opinion of God, since it was God himself who became incarnate in a place where and a time when the Abrahamic revelation was knit together with the Greek philosophic tradition, and John's decision to name the Son *Logos* is an unimpeachable witness to this. We will have to conclude—God knowing full well what he is doing—that no other language was more apt for expressing the truths of the faith than that of the philosophic tradition. On the other hand, by assuming certain elements of this tradition, the Christian faith has consecrated them and rendered them canonical. Hence these cultural forms, although contingent in some respects (everything said *thusly*, for this very reason might be said *otherwise*), acquires a normative fixity. I recognize that these speculative forms were first—and the history of their hesitant elaboration confirms it—ways of understanding among other equally possible or even temporarily held but finally rejected ways. Why be surprised at this? The history of God is written with men and human words. The dogmatic elaboration of Christian doctrine is sometimes represented as a *directed* history. From some hidden center, more or less unknown Superiors, knowing what must be said and how to say it, act from inside information and each time make decisions imposed by the cyclical moment. This view is imaginary and only satisfies our taste for 'esoteric machinations'. In reality, leaving aside the rather rare cases when the Holy Spirit 'speaks by the prophets', men, be they bishops or popes, *a priori* do not know what to say in response to questions posed, nor how to say it. They only know, in all certitude, what has been directly taught by Christ or by the Apostles to whom the deposit of the whole revelation had been confided and who therefore possess complete dogmatic knowledge. But the mode according to which this knowledge is communicated always includes its share of the implicit, since, by definition, no form exhausts its object. As a consequence, when this implicit share is no longer understood and when misunderstandings arise, the need to have to explain with authority those contested and still latent points from the deposit of the faith will present itself. The Church opens, then, an inquiry, striving to understand the *common*, that is to say the universal or catholic, faith, and to express it with the help of the resources of human cultures, at least those of which it has an experience.

There is then an historical genesis of conciliar formulations: 'ways of understanding' at first, they become 'canonical modes of explanation', but God does not dictate to the council Fathers what they should decide. In the same way, anyone who, from without, might have observed Mary's pregnancy and the formation of the child in her womb would have seen nothing but what is natural: a development similar to that of all human pregnancies; and yet it was the fruit of the Holy Spirit. Having once appeared, this man Jesus, similar to men in everything, was nevertheless unique: the New Adam, his humanity becomes normative and revelatory. So, *mutatis mutandis*, are conciliar decisions. And this is why, in their very form, they should be regarded as *practically* immutable.

To summarize: in dogmatic matters we need to distinguish the *mystery* in itself, which ultimately leads us back to such or such an 'aspect' of Divine Reality, the dogmatic *formulation*, elaborated by the Church, which contemplates the mystery according to that human mode of expression willed by the Holy Spirit, and the *interpretation* developed by the theological intelligence on the consecrated ground of its dogmatic formulation. Without doubt, there is a share of interpretation in every formulation, since it is of human origin. But this share is minimal to the very extent that its choice by the ecclesial Magisterium, as a dogmatic form, tears it away from its cultural contingency, from its rootedness in the soil of a particular language, confers on it a kind of semantic virginity, and, finally, by consecrating it, transfigures it.

Jewish Esoterism Or New Covenant?

Dogmatic Mystery and Baptismal Mystery

'Mystery' in Ante-Nicene Literature

Truly no one, according to Guénon, has ever sought to give 'the least explanation' for the Church's dogmatic formulations; this is why truths thus defined are transformed into 'mysteries in the commonly accepted sense of this word.' The first statement, dealt out peremptorily, leaves one aghast: what then were the theologians, the Church Fathers, and the spiritual doctors or geniuses doing for two thousand years, and is it enough to ignore them for them to cease to exist? As for the second, with respect to 'mystery', it raises no fewer difficulties. We of course suppose that Guénon is alluding here to expressions such as 'mystery of the Trinity' or 'mystery of the Incarnation'. But whatever may be the scorn that this judgment seems to manifest with respect to such venerable formulas, he betrays a surprising misunderstanding of the history of the word 'mystery' in Christianity. Undeniably in current language, and without doubt already among the Greeks, this word may designate nothing other than a hidden truth, or even something apparently incomprehensible, which is, moreover, quite normal. In any case, and without setting aside these perfectly legitimate meanings, it is certainly not the so-called 'dogmatic' presentation of revelation after Nicea which has led to characterizing the truths of faith as mysteries. I will outline a history of this word in the last part of this work. For the moment, let us simply recall that *mysterion* is an integral part of New Testament language (21 times in St Paul, 4 times in the Apocalypse, and 3 times in the Synoptics in a parallel passage). And it is Christ himself who declares to his disciples: 'To you it is given to know the mysteries of the kingdom of heaven; but to them it is not given' (Matt. 13:11, Mark 4:11, Luke 8:10). And St Paul specifies that he teaches 'the wisdom of God *in a mystery*, which is hidden' (1 Cor. 2:7). As we will see, the term is likewise present in later Christian literature, but I will indicate a few occurrences right now.

Christ the Original Mystery

St Ignatius of Antioch provides one of the first, which is also the first post-Lucan attestation of Mary's virginity. He writes in one of his letters: 'Now the virginity of Mary was hidden from the prince of this world, as was also her offspring, and the death of the Lord; three *mysteries* of renown, which were wrought in silence by God.'[1] This text proves that at the end of the first century, three hundred years before the Council of Nicea, the virginity of Mary, the Incarnation, and the Redemption were considered 'mysteries'. Now, if St Ignatius is deemed unrepresentative of a truly initiatic spirit, I will cite Origen who speaks of the 'mystery of the Incarnation' (*to mysterion tes ensomatoseos*).[2] True, the import of Origen's *mysterion* is disputed; a term which not only designates the veil of obscurity (or incomprehensibility) masking the truths of the faith—although this sense is by no means excluded—but also and above all the very being and substance of the sacred truth considered in itself in its deifying power.[3] Moreover, we must not forget that the Greek *mystèrion* is most often translated, in the only surviving Latin versions of Origen's text, by the word *sacramentum* (we will come back to this); hence some translations do not hesitate to translate *sacramentum* as 'sacrament', understood in the sense of a sacred reality. The connotation of obscurity should not be set aside for, as Origen tells us, Scripture encloses 'ineffable mysteries, too great to find a human expression or to be heard by mortal ear.'[4] We will return to this text in a moment in connection with the vexed question of the 'veil of the Temple'. For now let me stress that the mysterious character of scriptural teachings is tied in, for Origen, with the *inexpressible* nature of revealed truths, not with their intrinsic incomprehensibility. In another passage, this superabundance of the mysteries appears in a still more striking way: he compares the reading of

---

1. Letter to the Ephesians, 19:1.
2. *Commentary on St John*, VI, 34 (§ 172).
3. Marguerite Harl, *Origène et la fonction révélatrice du Verbe incarné*, Seuil, 1958, p143. Harl thinks that for Origen the term *mysterion* most often retains its sense of veiling. Also read: H.U. von Balthasar, 'Le *Mystèrion* d'Origène', *Recherches de Sciences Religieuses*, XXVI, 1936, pp513–569 and XXVIII, 1937, pp38–64; republished under the title *Parole et mystère chez Origène* (Geneva: Ad Solem, 1998).
4. *Homilies on Joshua*, XXIII, 4.

Jewish Esoterism Or New Covenant?

Scripture to a 'little ship' which, having quit the reassuring shore, sails off onto the high seas and dares to navigate 'in so vast an ocean of the mysteries' (*vastum mysteriorum pelagus*).[1]

These few citations are, I think, enough to show that the indissociably mysterious and mysterial character of Christian revelation is not the sole property of the Constantinian era. But they also, and quite logically, testify in favor of its at once esoteric and exoteric nature. Is this not most especially what St Ignatius means when he speaks so magnificently of the 'mysteries of renown, which were wrought in silence by God'? Uniting the secret of silence with the brightness of proclamation, the Christian mystery realizes the paradox of an esoterism that intends to address itself to the multitude; we stressed this at the beginning of the chapter and must now say a few words about it.

The Argument of Baptism

That the New Covenant presents the characteristics of a veritable esoterism—but of an intrinsic or essential esoterism—is what is thrown into relief by the very teachings of Christ. On the one hand, he stresses the interiorization of faith and our relationship to God, as well as the surpassing of exterior forms and the prescriptions of the Mosaic law; on the other hand, some of his teachings have been given in secret and covered, for a time, with an obligation for silence (John 4:21–24; Matt. 9:36, 13:10–13; Mark 4:34, 7:36, etc.). But he also proclaims that there is 'not any thing secret that shall not be made manifest, nor hidden, that shall not be known and come abroad' (Luke 8:17). And even more: what he has himself taught in secret—and therefore such a teaching has indeed been given—ought to be proclaimed before the entire world: 'Nothing is covered that shall not be revealed: nor hid, that shall not be known. That which I tell you in the dark, speak ye in the light: and that which you hear in the ear, preach ye upon the housetops!' (Matt. 10:26–27);

---

1. *Homilies on Genesis*, IX, 1.

and likewise in Luke (12:3): 'For whatsoever things you have spoken in darkness, shall be published in the light: and that which you have spoken in the ear in the chambers, shall be preached on the housetops.' Christ does not therefore institute a formal esoterism, whatever might be the necessary reserve imposed by circumstances or the diversity of the audience. He does so neither in the matter of doctrine, nor in the matter of rites; as St John says: 'He is truly the *Savior of the world (soter tou kosmou)*' (John 4:42), and not just guru to a few 'initiates'. All men have been called to drink the blood of the New Covenant: 'drink ye all of this' (Matt. 26:27), even though it is true that few heard and responded to this appeal to the multitude (Matt. 22:14). Christianity's specificity and proper vocation is to seek to communicate the interiorizing virtue of Christic grace to the greatest number: does not *Ekklesia,* that is to say Church, come from *ekkaleo* which means 'to call abroad'?

This is why Guénon's argument of baptism offered to all, and to children in particular, proves nothing as to the esoteric or exoteric nature of the rite. 'A rite,' Guénon states, 'conferred upon new-born infants, without any means being employed to determine their qualifications, could not have the character and value of an initiation, even if this were to be reduced to a mere virtuality.'[1] Pedobaptism, or the baptism of children, is thus considered to be the historically dated sign of the exteriorization of the sacraments. It might be asked if this argument does not pose a difficult metaphysical problem, since the circumstantial exterior has been set up as a criterium for the essential interior. But, besides, it comes up against a decisive objection already raised by recognized Guénonians; I am thinking, in particular, of Jean Tourniac who has underscored with pertinence[2] that, according to the Acts of the Apostles, Baptism was administered, on the very day of Pentecost, to a crowd of three thousand persons which certainly included children, since St Peter proclaims: 'For the promise is to you, *and to your children,* and to all that are far off, whomsoever the Lord our God shall call' (Acts 2:37–41).

---

1. *Insights into Christian Esoterism,* p15.
2. *Propos sur René Guénon,* Dervy, 1973, pp55–58. I will soon show that initiation to the pagan mysteries was quite regularly conferred on children.

Jewish Esoterism Or New Covenant?

In doing this, the newly-born Church was only obeying the commandment of Christ, who told his displeased disciples to bring the 'children' to him to be touched: 'Suffer children to come to me, and forbid them not: for of such is the kingdom of God' (Luke 18:16). And also: 'Whosoever shall receive this child in my name, receiveth me; and whosoever shall receive me, receiveth him that sent me' (Luke 9:48). And finally: 'See that you despise not one of these little ones: for I say to you, that their angels in heaven always see the face of my Father who is in heaven' (Matt. 18:10).

If children are then baptized on the day of Pentecost, and if such a practice denotes the exoteric nature of Baptism, just when does the disappearance of its originally initiatic character (according to Guénon himself) occur? It might be conceded, along with many theologians and Church Fathers, that Christian baptism is founded on Christ's baptism. In any case, the obligation to baptize is expressly formulated by the commandment given before the Ascension: 'Go therefore: make disciples of all nations; baptizing them in the name of the Father, and of the Son, and of the Holy Ghost (Matt. 28:19). We see the problem: how do we assign to Guénon's thesis about an exoteric descent of baptism a date between Ascension and Pentecost? Does this make the least sense? Some no doubt will hope to avoid this difficulty by supposing two kinds of baptisms succeeding each other in time: the first of an initiatic nature, the other of an exoteric nature, both with the same name. But, far from resolving the difficulty, this hypothesis only reinforces it; for it must be admitted then that, if one wants to remain at all cost faithful to Guénon's doctrine, it was on *that very day* when the Apostles received the fullness of the Holy Spirit, that is to say the perfection of initiatic grace, the day when they issued from the Cenacle to announce the Good News in a miraculously universal language, and that it was on this same day, by conferring baptism on children, and even on non-Jews, that they also proceeded to the exoteric descent of a previously initiatic rite: this is the height of absurdity.[1]

The only solution in sight to remedy this situation or at least mitigate it, if one holds fast to maintaining the alternative 'either esoterism or exoterism', would be to suppose that, *from the beginning*, a duality of initiatic rites and 'religious' (in the sense that this term has for Guénon) rites has existed in Christianity. With the baptism spoken about in Acts being 'evidently' of an exoteric nature, it would then be necessary to frame the hypothesis of another baptism, this one initiatic, to which will be eventually given the name 'baptism in the Spirit', exoteric baptism being only 'in water'. Certain scriptural indications might seem to go in this direction (we will however see that there is nothing to this). But, however it may be, if this duality is admitted, the thesis of exteriorization which thereby becomes useless has to be abandoned. Besides, two renowned Guénonians have indeed favored such a 'solution', perceiving that the thesis of their master was in reality unsupportable. Of these two, Jean Reyor and Michel Vâlsan, I will now speak.

1. Did Guénon perceive the extreme difficulty of his thesis, in which, let us recall, the destiny of Christianity as a whole, and therefore the eternal destiny of those thousands of Christian readers who will be convinced of its truth, is at stake? On this question, Jean Tourniac cites some excerpts from letters Guénon addressed to him in 1950 (op. cit., pp 57–8); at least they prove the embarrassment of their author before the scriptural data alluded to by his correspondent. Further, Guénon seems to ignore the baptism of the centurion Cornelius by St Peter—an event which the Prince of Apostles himself connects to the events on Pentecost (Acts 15:8)—since he attributes the exteriorization of the rite to the activity of St Paul who spread Christianity 'outside the Judaic milieu' (p 57). But it is Peter who, at the Council of Jerusalem, decides in favor of the baptism of the uncircumcised: 'Brethren, you know, that *in former days* God made choice among us, that by my mouth the Gentiles should hear the word of the gospel, and believe (Acts 15:7). Remember it is neither Peter nor Paul who have proceeded to this so-called 'exteriorization', but the Holy Spirit himself! It is quite significant to observe that, before the difficulties of making his theoretical construct agree with the scriptural data contradicting it, Guénon by no means thought of abandoning it. He wrote to Jean Tourniac: 'what is strange is that, the more one seeks to examine all of that up close, the more one discovers unexpected complications!' (op. cit., p 58). But this is not strange: in every domain, things are only simple when seen from afar. But complexity is not complication. The 'unexpected' complications that he discovers result above all from his own way of seeing things. He seeks to rediscover, at all costs, in Christianity a model perhaps legitimate elsewhere, but which, here, does not apply. Not that baptism poses any problem: newly born Christianity is a living and multiple reality, not the easily diagramed unfolding of a metaphysical theorem. But the solution to these problems is *first* a taking into account of (and a fidelity to) Church doctrine (Why dissemble by not saying what is *essential?*) and not in his suspicion or in his setting it aside, as if the Church had wanted to hide something which only Guénon's 'initiatic' perspicacity would be able to decipher.

Jewish Esoterism Or New Covenant?

The Torn Veil

Of Jean Reyor I will say nothing except that he himself has informed me of his divergence, on this point, from Guénon's position during an interview. As for Michel Vâlsan, he has expounded at length on all aspects of the question in his answers to the study of Marco Pallis published in *Études Traditionnelles,* under the title 'Le voile du Temple', a study in which he interprets the tearing of the Temple veil at the death of Christ as signifying the abolition of the separation, in Christianity, between esoterism and exoterism.[1] Michel Vâlsan rejects this interpretation and thinks that

> there are two lines of transmission of spiritual influences, one purely initiatic, the other simply religious, which go back to the same source, and that the ordinary sacraments, in their sacred institution, have been somehow modeled on the form of the original rites which were purely initiatic by nature and which have remained such, but in a strictly esoteric order.[2]

What should we think about this?

---

1. *Études Traditionnelles,* n° 384–385 (pp155–176), 386 (pp55–66); July–Dec. 1964 and March–April 1965. Michel Vâlsan, 'L'initiation chrétienne'—réponse à Marco Pallis, *Études Traditionnelles,* n° 389–390 (pp148–184), May–Aug. 1965. The triple n° 406–407–408, March–Aug. 1968 contains moreover a dossier entitled: *La question de l'Initiation chrétienne,* including 'Notes supplémentaires sur l'initiation chrétienne' by Marco Pallis (pp116–141), and 'Mise au point' by Michel Vâlsan (pp142–152), as well as 'Études et documents d'hésychasme' (pp153–179). [For English translations of the Pallis articles, cf. 'The Veil of the Temple: A Study of Christian Initiation', *Sophia. The Journal of Traditional Studies,* vol. 5, num. 1, Summer 1999, pp113–145 (reprinted from *The Sword of Gnosis,* Jacob Needleman [ed.], Boston: Arkana, 1986), and 'Supplementary Notes on Christian Initiation', *Sophia,* vol 6, num. 2, Summer 2000, pp37–70 TR.]

2. *Études Traditionnelles,* 389–390, p175. As we see, here there is no longer any exoterization; the initiatic rites remain initiatic 'in the strictly initiatic order,' while the Church proceeds with the (early or late?) making of exoteric rites (the 'ordinary' sacraments) modeled on the first which accounts for the formal similarity of the (supposed) two kinds of rite. This hypothesis, fabricated for the needs of the case, obviously has nothing to do with that of Guénon, which Michel Vâlsan, by a strange blindness, refused to admit ('Mise au point', 406–408, p150) when Marco Pallis

Christ the Original Mystery

First we have to recognize that, distinct from every other consideration, the significance attributed by Marco Pallis to the tearing of the Temple veil is self-evident, or else nothing means anything. By definition, the tearing of a veil separating two realms symbolizes the end of this separation and the revelation of the mystery hidden by this veil; this is why Marco Pallis was completely justified in making an emblematic argument in his remarks.[1] To the extent that the distinction between esoterism and exoterism can be identified with those between the spirit and the letter, reality and appearance, there is no Christian authority who has not seen in this event the passage from an exterior to an interior worship, from the shadow of mystery to the light of revelation, from a prophetic figurative heralding to the saving accomplishment in truth; the earlier worship no longer has any place, the earlier sacrifice has lapsed as to its own form, since what it represented in image has arrived in its perfect form: priest and sacrificial victim are only one.

Contrary to this, however, Michel Vâlsan asserts that there were two veils in the Temple, and that it was the more exterior one that had been torn; the other, more interior veil continues to mark the separation, then, between the two 'religious' and initiatic realms.

On this contested question, I will say this:

In the Temple, there was in fact an exterior veil called *masak* in Hebrew, separating the court from the Holy Place (where the ordinary liturgies took place), and an interior veil called *paroketh*, separating the Holy of Holies from the Holy Place (where, it seems,

---

pointed out this incontestable divergence (ibid., p120). Vâlsan's thesis is, in certain respects, more plausible than that of Guénon, but yet it does not escape every contradiction: if original Christianity had known two kinds of rite, how can it be seen as a 'Jewish esoterism'?—which Vâlsan maintains contrary to all logic: 'when the Christic way occupied in Judaism the *normal position* of an initiatic way within a general traditional framework....' (p149) What would then be the use of exoteric Christian rites? And if Christianity were only an initiatic Jewish way, how could it have experienced such a universal diffusion originally? One always comes up against the same insurmountable difficulties.

1. Pallis has let it be understood that he was inspired by a critique elaborated by Frithjof Schuon, a critique published twenty years later in the *Dossier H* dedicated to Guénon (Lausanne: L'Age d'Homme, 1984) [English edition in press: *René Guénon: Some Observations* (Hillsdale, NY: Sophia Perennis, 2004.)]

Jewish Esoterism Or New Covenant?

the high priest penetrated only once a year). The Greek biblical version called the 'Septuagint' does not terminologically distinguish between these two veils, making use of the same word *kataphétasma* to designate them. Flavius Josephus, who left an admiring description of the first veil, the only one visible from without, does the same.[1] None of the evangelists specify which veil was torn at Christ's death: they speak only of the 'the veil'. From this mention of the veil in the singular doctors and commentators have drawn different conclusions: some, like St Jerome,[2] followed by St Thomas Aquinas,[3] deem it could only be the exterior veil, the tearing of which alone was visible and had therefore the value of a sign for all; the others think that the mention of the veil without any other detail proves that it could only be the interior veil, the most important from the spiritual point of view.[4] This opinion is shared by some recent exegetes: 'in all likelihood the evangelists are thinking of the curtain to be found before the Holy of Holies, for the exterior curtain would have had too little significance.'[5] But, by strictly adhering to the positive data of the Gospel text, it is impossible to give a verdict.[6]

However, it is important to consider the Epistle to the Hebrews. Whether it is from St Paul or one of his disciples, its canonicity is

---

1. *The Jewish Wars*, V, v, 4–5: 'Before it was a Babylonian curtain ... where blue, purple, scarlet and fine flax were mixed with such art that it could not be seen without admiration, representing the four elements' (scarlet = fire, fine flax = earth, blue = air, purple = the sea). Also to be seen there was 'the whole order of the heavens.'
2. *Epist. CXX, ad Hedibiam*, P.L., t. XII, col. 992.
3. *Summa theologiae*, IA IIAE, q. 102, a 4.
4. For example: Cornelius a Lapide, in his monumental *Commentaria in Scripturam Sacram*, the edition procured by Auguste Crampon, Vivès, 1863, t. XV, *Commentaria in Matthaeum*, cap. XXVIII, 51, p633, which provides a brief patristic dossier. Jean Maldonnat, is his *Commentarii in quatuor Evangelistas*, edition procured by Conrad Martin, Moguntiae (= Mayence), 1853, t. 1, pp477–478, distinguishes several interpretations among the Fathers and Doctors (a sign of 'desecration', announcement of the dispersal of the Jews, etc.). These various interpretations do not seem contradictory to him: 'the tearing of the veil is the sign of some great mysteries.'
5. *Theologisches Wörterbuch zum neuen Testament*, von G. Kittel, Kohlhammer, Stuttgart, bd. III, 1967, 'katapesma im N.T.', pp631–632.
6. S. Legasse, 'Les voiles du Temple de Jerusalem', *Revue biblique* 87, 1980, pp560–589; cf. also *Dictionnaire encyclopedique de la Bible*, Brepols, 1987, pp1343–1344.

incontestable: it forms a part of Holy Scripture. This epistle mentions the veil of the Temple in three places: 6:19, 9:3 and 10:20. The first mention: this hope 'which we have as an anchor of the soul, sure and firm, and which entereth in even within the veil (*eis to esoterion tou katapesmatos*); where the forerunner Jesus is entered for us, made a high priest for ever according to the order of Melchisedek.' The second veil is obviously the one being dealt with here, which the second mention, that describes the interior layout of the earthly Temple—a description of archetypal rather than historical value—specifies in the following way: 'After the second veil [but the first veil is not mentioned!] comes the tabernacle [= the tent] which is called the holy of holies' where 'the high priest enters once a year' (Heb. 9:3, 7). 'But Christ, being come an high priest of the good things to come, by a greater and more perfect tabernacle not made with hand . . . entered once for all into the Holies, having obtained eternal redemption' (Heb. 9:11–12). 'The mediator of the *new testament*' (Heb. 9:15), 'Jesus is not entered into the holies made with hands, the patterns of the true: but into heaven itself' (Heb. 9:24). According to the express will of the crucified Son, we have been 'sanctified by the oblation of the body of Jesus Christ once' (Heb. 10:10). 'Having therefore, brethren, a *confidence in the entering into the Holies* by the blood of Christ; a *new* and living way which he hath dedicated for us *through the veil* [third mention], that is to say, his flesh' (Heb. 10:19–20). As may be seen, these texts do not speak of a tearing of the veil expressly. However, in reading them, it is nearly impossible not to think of it, even if the last citation is hard to interpret. Anyhow, there is certainly signified, in the clearing of the second veil, a free access to the loftiest mysteries, which confirms—at the very least for a reader of Guénon—the mention of Melchisedek placed in direct rapport with the clearing of the veil, Melchisedek whose name characterizes the Christic priesthood: by the sacrifice of his blood, Christ, the eternal high priest, has opened to us the Holy of Holies. But the traversing of the interior veil does not only refer to the curtain of the sanctuary; it more generally signifies the traversing of corporeal appearances, the veil of the flesh, and entry into the heavenly liturgy. The relationship between the traversing of the veil and the traversing of the flesh could, it is true, lead us back to the first

Jewish Esoterism Or New Covenant?

veil, since Flavius Josephus has informed us that is was decorated with a representation of the entire corporeal world, and, in particular, with a representation of the four elements inherent to all flesh. However, it is not excluded that the second veil had likewise borne such a symbolic decoration, or had an analogous symbolism, since Flavius Josephus tells us that it was 'made of the same material.' However that may be, what remains is that, by linking membership in the priesthood of Melchisedek with the clearing of the second veil, the epistle designates Christ's priesthood as the supreme priesthood, thereby identifying it with the highest 'initiatic hierarchy'.

Hence, whether the tearing affected the first or the second veil, the meaning remains the same: it is the abolishing of a separation between two orders, one exterior and the other interior. Basing himself on Origen, for whom it was, probably, the first veil that had been torn so that the second veil became visible, Michel Vâlsan concluded from this that, according to the great Alexandrian himself, the distinction between exoterism and esoterism has been preserved.[1] But the text of Origen cited by Vâlsan does not have the 'Guénonian' significance attributed to it. For Origen, what remains veiled and hidden in the Holy of Holies is the perfect and definitive knowledge of the divine mystery, that which can be granted only at the end of the spiritual way when 'I will know even as I am known', according to St Paul's formula (1 Cor. 13:12), whereas 'at present I know in part.' It is precisely to this text of St Paul that Origen alludes in the passage cited:

> if we 'knew' not 'in part only', if, from this flesh, Christ had revealed all to his beloved disciples, both curtains would have had to be torn, both exterior and interior. But since we still have to ceaselessly progress in knowledge, only the exterior veil was torn 'from top to bottom'; thus 'when perfect knowledge shall come', and when all mysteries shall be unveiled, the second curtain likewise will be raised, and we will be able to see what is hidden behind, namely, the true ark of the covenant and its

---

1. *Études Traditionnelles*, n° 389–390, May–Aug. 1965, pp154–155.

Christ the Original Mystery

veritable aspect; and the true cherubim, and the veritable propitiatory, and the manna collected in golden vessels.[1]

In reading this text, we clearly see that the preservation of the second veil by no means signifies, for Origen, the preservation of a formal esoterism, that is to say the preservation of a certain order of knowledge reserved for a few. It only signifies the imperfect character of every knowledge, including esoteric knowledge, when the supreme degree of 'face to face' (1 Cor. 13:12) gnosis has not been attained. Vâlsan's argumentation would make sense only if access to esoterism would necessarily imply access to such a knowledge; whereas, in fact, since, according to Origen, the second veil signifies the veiling, here below, of the supreme degree of gnosis, of entry into the beatific vision, of union with Absolute Reality ('the *true* ark of the covenant', that is to say not the historical ark, but the Reality of which it was the sacred manifestation), the tearing of this veil would signify that the Parousia, the total Presence (this is the meaning in Greek of the word *parousia*) of God within all people, would be realized. But what esoterist, including Guénon and Vâlsan, has ever claimed that initiation and esoterism would give access effectively and *ipso facto* to the ultimate gnosis? For the great majority of initiates, whatever their traditional affiliation, the ultimate mysteries remain equally veiled; they also dwell on this side of the ultimate veil, they also know 'in a mirror' (1 Cor. 13:12). Nor has esoterism drawn aside the second veil; to the contrary, *it shows it*, it causes it to be seen, it reveals that all is symbol and prophecy, and not letter only, that all is anagogy, which especially the exoterist has a tendency to ignore.

---

1. *Commentarium in Mattaeum, Sermo* 138, Klostermann et Benz, Greichischen Christlichen Schrifsteller, t. 11, pp 284–286. In this text, the passages in single quotes are from St Paul. Let us recall that at the time of Christ the Holy of Holies was empty: the second veil did not, then, hide the ark of the covenant (which, according to one tradition, was taken away at the burning of the Temple, in 586, by Jeremiah, who buried it in a secret grotto of Mount Nebo), nor the propitiatory, the cherubim or the manna. Origen was not ignorant of the disappearance of these supports for the *Shekhina;* but he accommodates himself to the description of the Holy of Holies, likewise ideal, given us by the Epistle to the Hebrews (9:3–5), except on one point: he does not speak of 'the golden altar for perfumes' which the Epistle places strangely in the Holy of Holies, whereas it was situated, it seems, in the Holies.

Jewish Esoterism Or New Covenant?

Besides, has not Guénon often stressed that the term *yogi* or *sufi* could be applied, in all rigor, only to someone who has attained the supreme realization?

The fact, then, that the second veil may not have been torn (if one opts, along with Origen, for this solution and accepts his interpretation) should not militate against the thesis of Marco Pallis. To the contrary, this thesis is found to be confirmed, since the tearing of the first veil makes the second veil visible, which means that esoterism is henceforth revealed *as such* to the crowds. Here we discover that the exoteric point of view is produced from an ignorance, or a misunderstanding of revelation's esoteric dimension. This ignorance is, henceforth, no longer possible. True, someone could object that, formally speaking, this revelation of the mystery by its very veiling was already realized by the exterior veil which showed to all, by its very existence, that there was something of the hidden in the Temple. This is incontestable. But, as I have stressed, there is no pure exoterism; every revelation is already a process of interiorization, which the first veil marking the separation of the profane from the sacred symbolizes; then again, the existence of a second veil refutes beforehand an 'exoteric' conception of esoterism, according to which the esoteric is identified with the *occulted visible,* the 'mysterious' in the common sense of the term. The existence of the two veils is thus in harmony with the theses that I have developed on the nature of the esoteric and the exoteric, which are processes of interiorization or exteriorization, not statically defined regions. To enter into the esoteric is not to *see* what the exoteric has hidden away, it is to understand that we must plunge into the mystery of God. It is precisely to this exoteric conception of the esoteric that Christianity has come to put an end to. By revealing the mysteries, it makes it obvious that the esoteric knowledge of revelation demands a complete conversion of the spiritual gaze; were everything open and betrayed to the curiosity of all, the essential would still be misunderstood. So it is with the body of Christ, abandoned to the stares of all, stretched out before the world, transpierced right to the heart, and yet who retains, invisible, the secret of his divine Resurrection.

This is not, for all that, to say that Origen denies any idea of a reserved teaching, very far from it; he even quite clearly affirms its

Christ the Original Mystery

existence, but by no means identifies it with the mysteries of the Holy of Holies. Thus, following a text whose beginning we have cited already, there are, in Scripture, ineffable mysteries

> greater than either the human word is able to utter or the mortal sense of hearing to hear; things that ... cannot be explained worthily and wholly. ... I do not know if they are explained fully and completely even by the holy apostles themselves I did not say that they may not be fully known, but they may not be fully explained. For it is certain these things were known and completely apprehended by the one who 'was snatched up to the third heaven'.... Paul knows and comprehends all things in the Spirit, but he was not been permitted to make this known to people.... But he probably spoke those things to those who were longer walking as humans (1 Cor. 15:9). He spoke them to Timothy, to Luke, and to the other disciples whom he knew to be capable of ineffable mysteries.[1]

The ineffable mysteries as being the object of a teaching, even if reserved, should not then be identified with those mysteries that remain under the 'second veil', and that cannot be the *object* of a teaching in the ordinary sense of the term, that is to say of a theoretical statement, since it is exclusively then a question of their perfect realization. If Christ had not revealed them 'in the flesh', this is because they do not belong to the order of formulation, and not because they involve a reserved teaching. As for mysteries that do involve a reserved teaching, their formally esoteric character is quite relative—for all authentic esoterism, as I have maintained—since Origen's just cited text ends with a prayer in which he begs God to grant, to him and to all Christians who hear his sermon, the grace of a plenary gnosis of the scriptural mysteries. Remember that this text where, for a Guénonian, the distinction of esoteric from exoteric is formally attested to, this text is a sermon preached to an audience of 'all-comers',[2] which renders somewhat 'surreal' the remark of Michel

---

1. *Hom. on Jos.*, XXIII, 4; Origen, *Homilies on Joshua*, trans. B. J. Bruce (Washington, DC: Catholic University of America Press, 2002), p202.
2. Henri Crouzel, op. cit., p114.

Jewish Esoterism Or New Covenant?

Vâlsan on the prudence that Origen had to observe in his declarations on esoterism, mindful of 'ecclesiastic censure',[1] refers to a much later time. In reality, as Marguerite Harl[2] has recalled, Origen does not formally distinguish two categories of Christian, but degrees of knowledge that everyone is called to traverse, even if everyone does not do so. The terms designating these degrees have a symbolic or, if preferred, an emblematic rather than a technical significance: the same person can belong, under different rapports, to several 'spiritual types' at once, and no one is excluded, *by nature*, from supreme gnosis.[3]

Nevertheless, for Origen, to be 'incapable' (Matt. 3:11, in connection with John the Baptist) or to be 'unworthy' (of untying the strap of Christ's sandal) as John has written (3:11) is not the same thing. For it is possible to become capable without being worthy of it; it is also possible to be worthy, yet without being capable. If graces have been bestowed according to our interest and not only 'in proportion to faith' (Rom. 12:6), this would be a manner of acting for a God who loves men, as in sometimes denying someone an aptitude he would be worthy of, because he foresaw the harm that presumption and the ensuing haughtiness would cause.' And Origen concludes:

> However much we may advance, there are stills things left behind not yet understood, since ... 'when a man has finished, then he

---

1. Michel Vâlsan, 'L'initiation chrétienne', *Études Traditionnelles*, n° 389–390, p165. To affirm the existence, for Origen, of two classes of Christian, Vâlsan is basing himself on a study by Jules Lebreton.

2. *Origène et la fonction révélatrice du Verbe incarné*, Seuil, 1958, pp264–266.

3. Origen dedicates one of the longest chapters of the *Treatise on First Principles* (III, 1), to refuting the doctrine of Valentinus' disciples, according to whom the spiritual destiny of a soul is determined by its 'hylic' (or 'choïc' = earthy), 'psychic' or 'pneumatic' nature. According to Origen, beyond individual differences, human nature is one in each person who, being free, is responsible for either his salvation or his loss, as well as for the degree of knowledge to which his love of God gives access. Origen, moreover, distinguishes (according to 1 Cor. 12:8–9) not two but three degrees of knowledge: faith, gnosis (the perfection of faith) and wisdom which knows in the Son, the Wisdom of the Father. However, with respect to the beatific vision, these three degrees are almost nothing (*Homilies on Exodus*, III, 1). Likewise see Crouzel, op. cit., pp112–116, the best current synthesis on Origen.

begins, and when he has ceased, he shall be at a loss (Eccles. 18:6).[1]

For Origen, the profound opposition is not then between categories of believers, the simple and the perfect, but between those who hear and do nothing and those capable of passing from power to act: 'All have the possibility of becoming children of God; only some of them change this possibility into reality.'[2] And this is precisely what—eschatologically—the preservation of the veil before the Holy of Holies signifies, that veil which will only disappear on the day of the apocatastasis, when Christ will be all in all.

This whole doctrine is summarized by St Thomas, with his customary clarity, not in the ever-quoted text of the *Summa Theologiae*,[3] but in his *Commentary on the Gospel of St Matthew*, where we read the following text: 'These two veils would signify a double veiling: the most interior veil would signify the veiling of the heavenly mysteries, when his glory will have appeared. The other, more exterior veil would signify the veiling of the mysteries relative to the Church. Hence the more exterior was torn and the other not so to signify that, in the death of Christ, the mysteries relative to the Church became manifest; but the other veil was not torn because the celestial arcana remain as yet veiled.' This veil, St Thomas explains citing St Paul (2 Cor. 3:16), will only be raised at the end of time, at the moment of the conversion of the Jews.[4]

---

1. *Com. in Joan.*, VI, (180–181, 183); Origen, *Commentary on the Gospel according to John*, vol. 1, trans. R.E. Heine (Washington, DC: Catholic University of American Press, 1993), pp 219–220.
2. Marguerite Harl, *Origène et la fonction révélatrice du Verbe incarné*, p 264.
3. III, q.102, a. 4, ad. 4°.
4. *S. Thomae Aquinitatis in evangelia S. Matthaei et S. Joannis commentaria*, t.1, ed. II, Taurinensis, Eq. Petri Marietti, Roma, 1912, c. XXVII, p 391.

Jewish Esoterism Or New Covenant?

The Eschatological Economy of Christianity

To close this debate, perhaps it would be appropriate to meditate not only on the tearing of the Temple veil, but also and above all on the death of Christ which is its cause. What, then, might this death signify as to the question that preoccupies us? The answer is given by Christ himself who teaches us that, in death, his body is *'the body given for all'* (*to soma mou to hyper hymon didomenon*, literally: the body of me for you being given—Luke 22:19). Now what is the body of Christ, if not first the very body of revelation, revelation made body: 'Who has seen me has seen the Father.' A synthesis of all revelation, the body of Christ becomes, in the Passion, the body given, the body abandoned: everything revealable, everything, of the mystery of God, which is teachable to some degree, communicable, everything is delivered up, abandoned 'for us', into our hands like the corpse of Jesus into the hands of his Mother. Even more: this body has been 'bled to death'; the true immolated lamb, he has given all of his blood, right down to his transpierced heart: *he has kept nothing for himself*. Thus, it is not only the exterior form of the body of revelation, it is also its most intimate secret represented by the blood shed 'for you and for many', which is disocculted, uncovered; and not only uncovered and transpierced, but even exposed and stretched out in its nakedness, and raised aloft on the cross in the sight of all until the end of the world. Now who will deny that the blood symbolizes the initiatic mysteries? The death of Christ constitutes, then, a unique and decisive event *completely* changing the 'economy' of tradition. Clearly, it has the significance of a rupture with the ancient and universal economy which divided the degrees of sacred knowledge and participation in divine grace according to the distinction of exoteric and esoteric orders. To tell the truth, and this remark is important, this rupture is an anticipated realization of what will be perfectly accomplished only at the end of time, when the distinction of interior and exterior will definitively cease. This is why Origen or Thomas refer the tearing of the second veil to humanity's eschatological horizon. This is, as I will perhaps explain on another occasion, in conformity with the function of Christianity, the prophetic anticipation and therefore *imperfect* realization, 'in image', of the religion of the new 'Aeon', or 'future Age', since that is, from the 'cyclical' point of view, the *raison d'être* of Christianity in the sum of religious forms. This complete change in the economy of tradition is *signified* explicitly by the tearing of the veil and *realized* by the death of Christ. It is inscribed in the very nature of the New Covenant. With respect to the Parousia, or total and universal Presence of the divine Word in every creature and every creature in the divine Word, the distinction between esoterism and exoterism no longer makes any sense. And so this New Covenant is, as I have stated, eschatological in its very substance; it is formed by the echo of the future Age prophetically reverberating in the today of post-Pascal time.

Thus, it is by very virtue of the privilege of its cyclic function that the Christian religion 'ignores' the formal separation between esoterism and exoterism. This 'ignorance' flows from its very essence, insofar as it realizes, during the eschatological wait, the anticipatory image of the religion of the second coming. But it is only an image of it, which means that, although in its very form it has to reflect beforehand the parousial disappearance of the two realms of every traditional economy, it also has to continue to distinguish them, no longer as formal structures of its charismatic economy, but as the ever pregnant effect of the nature of things. This is not then, as has sometimes been said, because as a way of love Christianity feels repugnance for such an institutional distinction, but because Christianity is set between the first Testament, of which it is the unveiling, and the last Testament, of which it is the veiling and the prophetic figure.

I think we have passed in review the chief difficulties expressly raised by Guénon's thesis of a general exoteric descent of Christianity at a date unspecified, but officially sanctioned by the Council of Nicea. Since this thesis first includes assertions relative to the history of Christianity, it was appropriate to likewise proceed with its examination from a historical point of view, without for all that neglecting considerations of a more theoretical or metaphysical nature.

Jewish Esoterism Or New Covenant?

These conclusions are to be summarized in the following way:

1) Christianity has never been a Jewish esoterism (in the formal sense of the term), but has presented itself from the beginning, from Christ's incarnation (the elder Simeon, the Magi), as a revelation destined for the salvation of the nations;

2) there is no direct proof of a general descent of the teachings and the rites into the exoteric order, and the indirect proofs advanced by Guénon do not have the significance attributed to them;

3) the nature of the Christian religion, and the function which flows from it, is to realize, by anticipation and in figure, the erasing of the formal separation between the two realms.

However, two appended questions remain to be examined, one logico-historical in nature and the other doctrinal.

6

Sacraments and Sacramentals

EVEN IF one accepted Guénon's thesis of a descent of rites into the exoteric order, unlikely though it be, one would still have to explain a point which no one, to my knowledge, has ever raised despite its obviousness (even so it is not unrelated to some of Vâlsan's just referred to declarations). This point is the following: if the Christic *Ecclesia* had been constrained, by the spiritual decadence of Antiquity, to transform itself into a universal 'religion', why did it not go ahead and produce new rites, rites of an exclusively exoteric nature, since it was impossible to modify the seven sacraments instituted by Christ? Thus, the sevenfold sacraments would have retained their original nature, and they would have not been obliged—an hypothesis nevertheless devoid of the least historical basis—to create wholly new esoteric rites not instituted by Christ. Surely, this was the *only solution imaginable*, the only logical hypothesis: that Guénon has not said why this solution did not prevail is truly incomprehensible.

This solution, or an analogous one, should be imperative especially since Christian doctrine has always distinguished, at least practically if not theoretically, *two* categories of rites in its liturgical life, called 'sacraments' and 'sacramentals' by theology. Without doubt this distinction was *formulated* at a late date. In the West the doctrine of the seven sacraments explicitly made its appearance only in the twelfth century in Peter Lombard's *Book of Sentences*.[1] However, although it does not figure—and does not have to figure—explicitly in Scripture, this doctrine should be regarded as 'of the faith' and going back to Christ himself. Moreover, there exists a hard

Sacraments and Sacramentals

to deny positive proof: not only is this doctrine accepted and taught in the Latin Church, but it is also recognized in the Greek Church and the array of Orthodox Churches as expressing their own faith; and—an even more decisive proof—it is also acknowledged by the Coptic, Jacobite and Armenian Churches, which have been separate from the Roman Church since the fifth century, that is to say at a time when no writings had attested to the doctrine of the seven sacraments. Whatever the reasons for this silence which has sometimes been attributed to the 'discipline of the secret'—which I will deal with in the third part of this book—we should recognize in the doctrine of the seven sacraments an illustration of the traditional adage *lex orandi, lex credendi,* that is to say: the law of prayer (and therefore of liturgical practice) gives proof of the rule of faith.

Sacramentals are, for example: prayer, the invocation of the Name of Jesus, the Sign of the Cross, blessings, candles, liturgical or spiritual reading of Holy Scripture, monastic consecration, etc. The sacrament/sacramental distinction does not exactly overlap, then, the esoterism/exoterism distinction—which is not at all surprising since such a *formally constituted* distinction is foreign to Christianity. Nevertheless, these sacramentals, since they existed from the start, sometimes even imported from Judaism, could have provided ritual forms, from either Christic (or apostolic) institution or practice, for the composing of exoteric rites. One obvious example of such a possibility is the 'baptism of John' in water: is this not something like an exoteric rite of purification (analogous to Essene baptism?) with respect to the 'baptism in water and in Spirit' instituted by Christ? Another no less obvious example is that of the 'agapes' celebrated by the first Christians: is this not as if a preparation and exoteric figure for the eucharistic sacrifice which, besides, accompanied them without being confused with them?

---

1. *The Book of Sentences,* 1, IV, dist. II, c. 1: the *Book of Sentences* (*IV Libri Sententiarum*) of Peter Lombard (c. 1152), in which are set forth and discussed in a systematic and orderly way the opinions (sentences) of the Fathers and Doctors relative to the theological teachings of Sacred Scripture, was, from the thirteenth to the fourteenth century in Europe, *the* textbook and *the* manual for baccalaureate students in theology.

Christ the Original Mystery

Let us pause a moment over this second case, a case more easily summarized than the first which, historically, poses more complex problems.

Two kinds of 'ritual banquet' must be distinguished then in Church practice during the first four centuries. Generally, the name *agape* ('charity' in Greek) is given to the first: it is a fraternal meal sacralized by the reciting of blessings partially borrowed from Jewish ritual. The second is named *eucharist* ('thanksgiving' in Greek): it is the ritual and sacrificial actualization of the death and resurrection of Christ giving his Body to be eaten under the species of bread and his Blood to be drunk under the species of wine. Now, as it happens, these terms are interchangeable: the *Didache* ('Teaching' or 'Doctrine' in Greek) calls the agapes 'eucharist',[1] while St Ignatius of Antioch speaks of 'doing the *agape*' for accomplishing the sacrifice of the Mass.[2] But these terminological reversals are rare and, in any case, the kinds of rites, whatever their names, have never been confused. Only the Eucharist is considered as a 'mystery' in the sense of the Greek mysteries, and it alone is within the province of what Christianity began to call *initiation*. Specifically, these agapes, this 'minor eucharist' to speak as does Father J.P. Audet who, in his work on the *Didache*, quite logically calls the sacramental Supper a 'major eucharist',[3] clearly form a part of the Christian ritual and only the baptized can participate.[4] They seem to be a survival of exoteric Jewish ritual in the liturgical practice of early Christianity: this is precisely what is shown in a comparative study of the texts.[5] These two forms, the one exoteric and the other initiatic, of the 'ritual banquet' of Christ were

---

1. *Didache*, IX, 2; the complete title is: *The Doctrine of the Lord Transmitted to the Nations by the Twelve Apostles*. Discovered in 1873, this text goes back, without doubt, to the year 70.
2. *Epistle to the Smyrnians*, VIII, 1–2; this epistle dates from about the year 100.
3. *La Didachè, Instruction des Apôtres*, Études Bibliques, 1958, p372 ff. The very well thought out study of Father Audet has, in particular, established that chapters IX and X of the *Didache* are concerned with the agape, while chapter XIV is concerned with the Eucharist.
4. *Didache*, IX, 4.
5. W. Rordorf, 'La *Didachè*', in *L'Eucharistie des premiers chrétiens*, Beauchesne, collection 'Le Point Théologique', 1976, pp15–22.

Sacraments and Sacramentals

often celebrated one after another: the *agape* and then the Eucharist. After the fourth century the *agape disappeared,* even though it has subsisted here or there, right down to our day, as a feeble echo in the distribution of blessed bread at the end of Mass. It is probable that some of the *agape* prayers have been integrated at this moment into the eucharistic celebration; we are therefore witness to an initiatic retrieval of exoteric ritual elements. But, and it is important to stress, contrary to what Guénon's thesis would have us anticipate, no eucharistic prayer has been, at this moment, transformed into a 'mealtime prayer'.[1] If anyone thinks the material from the *Didache* a little too indecisive, let them study the question in an author incontestably favorable to 'esoterism', Clement of Alexandria. There we find the same distinction formulated clearly between what Clement calls 'sacred repast' and the Eucharist, even more clearly than with St Ignatius of Antioch.[2] The conclusions would be the same for Tertullian, a contemporary of Clement, and Origen, his disciple and successor.[3] It would be necessary to bring in a third kind of repast here, one that might be called an ordinary meal. It is not to be confused with the *agape,* but is itself also sanctified by the eucharistic banquet, as it is still so today in Christian families and also monasteries, since a simple lay person is not allowed to eat at the table of a monk or nun. Perhaps it is this extension of sacralization to all meals, combined with the progressive effacement of Judeo-Christian elements, that has contributed to the disappearance of the *agape.*

Without doubt, examples could be multiplied or those already mentioned could be explained more amply.[4] However, what I have said will suffice for grasping the importance, for Guénon's thesis, of the coexistence of the two categories of rites in original Christianity. But Guénon does not speak of them. Surely, if the Church had had

---

1. W. Rordorf, op. cit., p15.
2. *The Instructor,* II, 61, 1; cf. A. Méhat, 'Clément d'Alexandrie', in *L'Eucharistie des premiers chrétiens,* p110.
3. Ibid., p110, n44.
4. The case of baptism—or baptisms—alone would require a separate work. On this subject, I will cite, among others, the book by Kilian McDonnell and George T. Montague, *Christian Initiation and Baptism in the Holy Spirit* (Collegeville, MN: Liturgical Press, 1991). I will return to this book in the last part of this study.

to conceal its initiatic rites and present only 'religious' rites to the body of the faithful, there was no need to have baptism and the Eucharist 'descend' from the esoteric to the exoteric level, since there were already rites of a less lofty order than the cardinal sacraments, but sufficiently similar to these sacraments to be considered as their analogue 'on the outside'. How then is its possible that these analogous and prefigurative rites have disappeared and the spiritual authorities have judged it preferable to have the most sacrosanct rites 'descend' into the exterior order?

Here we are at the limits of the conceivable. When anyone strives to account for the facts, they are obliged, in order to remain faithful to Guénon's doctrine, to juggle a host of highly improbable and nearly indefinite hypotheses. Are not such difficulties simply 'artifacts' produced by the theory itself when someone wants to apply it to Christian realities? And can one escape from them otherwise than by modifying the nature of Christianity to the point of making it unrecognizable and as if a stranger to itself? Thus, I have heard it said to Christian Guénonians that baptism, by virtue of its exoteric nature, was nothing but a rite of psychic admission to the religious form, which, in fact, follows logically from Guénon's thesis, but has no relation to the doctrine of St Paul and the Church who teach that the baptized, ransomed and washed in the blood of Christ, actually become the temple of the trinitary life which henceforth dwells within it. This is perhaps not the truth of Guénon, but it is the truth of God.

7

The Nature of the Sacraments is Immutable

On the Nature of the Sacraments

THE LAST POINT involves an objection of principle raised against the 'exoteric descent' of the sacraments thesis: it is a priori impossible, it is said, to modify the nature of the sacraments which are of divine institution, whatever secondary modifications they are subject to in the course of history. The objection is in fact decisive, and is also in conformity with the teachings of the most classical theology. However, to this objection Guénon has countered with an exception which will be good to examine first.

The 'permanence of the initiatic character,' he declares,

> applies to the human beings who possess it and not to the action of the spiritual influence or to the rites that are intended to serve its vehicle; it is absolutely unjustified to transfer this notion from one to the other, which amounts in the end to attributing to it an altogether different significance, and we are certain that we have never ourselves said anything that could provoke such a conclusion.[1]

Even though a little difficult in construction—and however it may be for his last assertion, to which I will return by way of conclusion—Guénon's text seems clear enough: the initiatic character is without doubt something permanent for anyone who receives initiation, but

---

1. *Insights into Christian Esoterism* (Hillsdale, NY: Sophia Perennis, 2004), p 8.

neither for the initiatic rite itself nor for the grace that it communicates is there this same permanence.

And yet this answer is nevertheless obscure when an attempt is made to specify its terms. Observe first how the objection does not lie with the permanence of the initiatic *character,* but with the permanence of the initiatic *nature* of the rite. Accordingly, the alteration implicitly effected by Guénon would only be justified if the notion of permanence could be logically applied only to the character—and not the nature—of a rite in such a way that to speak of initiatic permanence would be necessarily and *ipso facto* to speak of the permanence of the character conferred by the rite. This would entail that the rite's nature or essence should not be qualified as permanent, in other words a rite is not initiatic (or is exoteric) by nature, but only in its effects. This is rightly inconceivable unless—another possibility—the rite's effect is independent of its nature, so that a rite of initiatic nature can produce, permanently, non-initiatic effects—which is no less inconceivable, since a nature is only known through its operations. True, someone might object with the well-known adage: he who can do more can do less; and from this we could conclude: nothing prevents the Church from restricting the effects of an initiatic rite to the exoteric order. But the difficulty increases: not only, as I will show, is such a modification strictly impossible (the Church does not do whatever it likes), but it should even be recognized that there is, between esoterism and exoterism, only a difference of degree (of more or less) or a difference of… nature, precisely. Without doubt, for Guénon at least, a difference in nature is involved. Nevertheless, it is obvious that what might modify or restrict the *effects* of sacramental grace is to be found on the side of the receptacle, not on the side of whoever is its steward.[1] Finally, I will not conceal the fact that Guénon's conception of a Church

---

1. At least it is true as soon as it is a question of *sacramental* grace—which is precisely the case—and as soon as it is distinguished from its *effects*—as should be done—: the Church's function is to *bestow* this grace, not *measure* it out. Such is my argument's essential point. I will show that the Church restricts or extends the application of grace (according to what it judges necessary), but it cannot modify the nature of *what* it has a mission to transmit. It is not the same for the sacramentals over which the Church is master: the Church institutes them and measures out

The Nature of the Sacraments is Immutable

manipulating the sacraments seems to betray the author's disputable taste for the 'manipulation of spiritual influences'. Granted, however, Guénon is somewhat loath to speak of a permanence of a rite's initiatic nature to the extent that the term 'permanence' evokes the idea of something that 'remains in', but it is not easy to say *in what* this nature would remain, even though the question has been examined by theologians.[1] This is why, rather than permanence, I will speak of the *immutability* of a rite's nature.

On the Sacramental Character

Another series of question should be now raised concerning the notion of character. In what sense does Guénon understand it? In the general sense of 'distinguishing sign', of 'proper quality', in which case this term could be very well applied to the nature of a rite and designate what *characterizes* it? Or is he using it in the precise sense given to it by Catholic theology, which I will explain in a moment? If this is the case, it would be absolutely obvious that the permanence of initiatic *character* can only be applied to the rite's recipient: it will be granted much more readily that this involves the very definition of the notion of *character*. But that presumes nothing as to the immutability of the rite's *nature:* that one sense is true by no means prevents the other from being equally true.

A few indications make me think that Guénon uses the term

---

the grace that they can produce according to the dispositions of the subject: the sacraments act *ex opere operato,* 'by virtue of the work effected', whereas the sacramentals act *ex opere operantis,* 'by virtue of the work of the one effecting the work'. This does not mean that a sacrament sanctifies us automatically, but that it produces its own grace independently of whatever the subject will do with it, provided that he not set an obstacle in its way. — The parable of the 'unfaithful steward' shows that God has agreed to a reduction of conditions for the application of sacramental grace.

1. The medieval doctors said at first that the sacraments *contained* grace like a jar contains perfume. But this metaphor presents some drawbacks, as St Thomas notes (*Summa Theologiae,* III, q.62, a.3): it ignores how the sacrament belongs to the genus of the *sign.*

'character' in the theological sense, or at least in an closely allied sense. First there is the just cited text; otherwise, as I have stated, what would stop it from being applied to the rite itself and from speaking about the immutable character of its nature. But there is also a passage from *Perspectives on Initiation* in which Guénon, speaking of the 'permanent character' that initiation confers on anyone who receives it, points out that such a permanent character is likewise conferred by 'certain religious rites', which he enumerates in a note: it is baptism, confirmation and Holy Orders that present such an analogy with initiatic rites that they could be regarded as an 'exoteric transposition' of the latter.[1]

Therefore, a few words must be said about the theological significance of this term according to Catholic doctrine, since it is clearly from this doctrine that Guénon has borrowed it (whereas he never uses the term 'grace', for which he substitutes 'spiritual influence').[2]

In the first sense, the word 'character', which comes from the Greek *karakter*, signifies 'imprint' or 'mark' (cf. 'printer's mark'); hence, in the derived and general sense, the meaning of 'distinguishing sign' and therefore of 'proper' or 'essential quality'. From this first sense is likewise derived the very precise meaning conferred on this term by Catholic theology. It makes use of it, in fact, following Scripture (2 Cor. 1:21), to designate the 'mark', the 'seal' (*sphragis* in Greek), the *indelible* 'spiritual sign' that the three sacraments imprint *in the soul* of those who receive them, and which, for this reason, cannot be repeated. This notion has been formulated, after St Augustine, to account for the fact that, according to the ordinary and constant practice of the Church, repenting heretics were not rebaptized, although the heresy had impeded the supernatural effects of baptismal grace: what had they received, then, in order for this same grace to become active, once heresy was abjured, without a repetition of the sacrament however necessary for its operation? Clearly, we would have to suppose the permanence in their being of

---

1. *Perspectives on Initiation* (Hillsdale, NY: Sophia Perennis, 2004), pp107–108.
2. I will rely chiefly on the treatise *On the Sacraments* of St Thomas Aquinas in the *Summa Theologiae*, III, q. 60–65, and on the notes and commentaries by Father Roguet: D.D.B., 1951.

The Nature of the Sacraments is Immutable

a 'something' conferred by the rite, something which, the obstacles having been raised, could become the instrumental cause of the effects of grace. It is this 'something' that St Augustine designates by the term 'character'. Now what about the mysterious nature of this 'something' (that St Thomas regards as a supernatural power conferred on the soul's natural powers, and that other theologians regard as a mark immediately imprinted in the soul's substance and interiorly disposing to the supernatural order)? Opinions vary, but the best authors agree in seeing in it the image (the 'seal') of Christ imprinted in the soul of the baptized.[1] We understand why this seal should be distinguished from sacramental grace properly speaking, since its function is to direct the soul to become a sharer in the priesthood of Jesus Christ, and therefore of making possible the sacramental work that this priesthood accomplishes.

Such is the basic reason for the permanence of the sacramental character, and it is a singularly ignored reason. The sacraments, St Thomas teaches, produce two effects in man: on the one hand they heal us of sin and lead us to the glory of deification, on the other hand they render us ministers of the sacramental order, either as recipients or bestowers, and make us members of the Church. The first effect is the very work of grace, the second is a result of the imprinted character.

> The faithful are deputed to a twofold end. First and principally to the enjoyment of glory. And for this purpose they are marked with the seal of grace.... Secondly, each of the faithful is deputed

---

1. St Augustine, *Contra epistulam Parmeniani*, L. II, c.13, n29; P.L., t. XLIII, col. 71. The Greek Fathers do not use *karakter* but *sphragis*, which means 'seal' (*sigillum*), as I have said, with the sense of 'imprint' then, but also 'confirmation'. The rabbis spoke of circumcision as of a seal (*hotam* in Hebrew): cf. Gedaliahu Guy Stroumsa, *Savoir et Salut* (Paris: Cerf, 1993), p 278. For St Paul (Rom. 4:11) the sign (*semeion*) of circumcision is, with Abraham, a seal (*sphragis*) confirming the justice of his faith; in 2 Tim. 2:19, the invocation of the Name of the Lord imprints a seal in the human being; while in 2 Cor. 1:22 or Eph. 1:13 and 4:30, the *sphragis* is im-printed by the Holy Spirit: it is in fact the Holy Spirit who realizes the image of Christ within us. Quite logically, in the earliest texts (Clement, *2 Cor.* VII, 6; etc.) *sphragis* serves to designate that baptism bestowed in the Name of the Trinity which initiates us into *theosis* or 'deification'.

Christ the Original Mystery

to receive, or to bestow on others, things pertaining to the worship of God. And this, properly speaking, is the purpose of the sacramental character.[1]

Thus, the sacramental character is nothing but a certain sharing of

> Christ's faithful... in His Priesthood; in the sense that as Christ has the full power of a spiritual priesthood, so His faithful are likened to Him by sharing a certain spiritual power with regard to the sacraments and to things pertaining to Divine worship.... Now Christ's Priesthood is eternal, according to Ps. 109:4: 'Thou art a priest for ever, according to the order of Melchisedek.' Consequently, every sanctification wrought by His Priesthood, is perpetual, enduring as long as the thing sanctified endures.... Since, therefore, the subject of a character is the soul as to its intellective part, where faith resides... it is clear that, the intellect being perpetual and incorruptible, a character cannot be blotted out from the soul.[2]

And if only three sacraments confer a character, this is because the Melchisidekian priesthood of Christ includes three functions: that of King, into which we are configured by the baptismal character; that of Prophet, into which we are configured by the chrismatic (the unction of the chrism of confirmation) character, and that of Sovereign Priest, into which we are configured by the character of Holy Orders.[3]

---

1. *Summa Theologiae,* III, q. 63, a. 3.
2. *Summa Theologiae,* III, q. 63, a. 5. Recall that this doctrine is in perfect conformity with the teaching of the Church, especially of St Peter who, in his first epistle, ascribes to the people of the baptized a 'royal priesthood' (1 Pt. 2:5–9, and also Apoc. 1:6, 5:10, and 20:6). This title 'royal priesthood' is not to be understood in a metaphorical sense, but corresponds to an objective determination of the baptized, as shown by St Thomas, and is found to be well established theologically. Undeniably, a certain accentuation of the presbyterial priesthood, in the course of modern times, confronted by a laity divested of any function in the Church, has almost entirely obscured what is a revealed truth. Alas, the laity's 'promotion to the priesthood' has been carried out today to the detriment of the unique sacred character of the presbyterial function.
3. *D. T. C.,* t. II, col. 1705.

The Nature of the Sacraments is Immutable

According to Catholic doctrine, this is what character is, and this is what it cannot but be: the seal of Christ's Priesthood imprinted in the soul of the baptized and endowing it with the power to participate, as subject or as actor, in its priestly operation. Obviously the Church has no power over the Christic Priesthood, the primary instrument of which is the humanity of Jesus. This Priesthood is not, moreover, a character in Christ, but designates the essential and permanent actuality of his redemptive Passion. And character is an equally permanent participation in this same redemptive Passion, under the form of an indelible imprint entitling someone to perform 'sacerdotally'. Character is, then, the effect of a sacrament, an effect which becomes in its turn a cause of sacramental grace, but a secondary instrumental (and not an efficient) cause: it does not produce it out of itself, but makes its operation possible in the soul that it has consecrated.

In Itself, Sacramental Grace Is Not Susceptible To More Or Less

This is, however, only a matter of a participation. Although the Church can change nothing of the Christic priesthood's essence, is it the same for a sacramental participation in this priesthood? Could this Church, on its own and for reasons of opportunity of the kind mentioned by Guénon (the spiritual rescue of pagan antiquity), have reduced the extent of this participation and have made the sacrament produce only exoteric effects?

This curious theory—which creates a problem at the very core of Guénon's thought—is explicitly excluded by Catholic doctrine, for the good and simple reason that sacramental grace is immutable in its own nature and, as such, always communicated to the being who receives it, provided that he set no obstacle in its way, since it is precisely this grace that Jesus Christ wanted to communicate when he instituted the sacrament destined to produce it.

Explanations of the different kinds of grace and the nature of the sacraments will not be useful. But, as for grace, an actual and an habitual grace are first distinguished. Actual grace is a divine gift actually bestowed transiently on the soul to help in its operations (a help in trials, an inspiration, etc.). Habitual grace is a divine gift communicated to the soul's substance which perfects the being that receives it 'in an *immediate and permanent* manner',[1] with a view to its sanctification; such a permanently acquired disposition is, what is called in philosophy, a *habitus* (a Latin word meaning 'manner of being acquired'), hence the term 'habitual' grace. By this grace the Holy Spirit comes to dwell substantially in the human being. The chief effect of habitual grace is what theologians call *justification*, or deification,[2] or even sanctification: hence the term *sanctifying grace* which is given to the principal effect of habitual grace.

But what about this sanctifying grace considered objectively in itself or in its end? 'Thus envisaged,' St Thomas answers, 'it is obvious that sanctifying grace cannot be greater or less, since, of its nature, grace joins man to the Highest Good, which is God.' It is subject to variation only with relation to the subject within whom it resides.[3]

Now, this habitual grace, that God infuses in the soul so to produce sanctifying grace, can be communicated according to different modes, either directly and interiorly without any mediation—for 'the Spirit blows where he will'—or with the help of exterior means. It is certain, then, that the primary effect of a sacrament is to produce in the soul this sanctifying grace or grace of justification; it should be distinguished from the second effect which is to produce a sacramental grace properly speaking (*what* the sacrament signifies), and from the third effect which is, for certain sacraments, a

---

1. J. Berthier, *Abérgé de théologie dogmatique et morale*, (Lyon: Vitte, 1927), n701.
2. Cf. Mgr. Louis Laneau's treatise, *De la déification des hommes*, trans. Jean-Claude Chenêt (Geneva: Éditions Ad Solem, 1994): a work unique in the Latin literature of the Catholic Church.
3. *Summa Theologiae*, I–II, q.112, a.4; St Thomas teaches the same doctrine when he declares that grace is a form (this is its immutable essence) which has its achieved (or complete) being in the human being within whom it subsists; now, 'since the soul as long as it is a wayfarer is changeable in respect of the free-will, it results that grace is in the soul in a changeable manner': grace's 'manner', not grace 'in itself' (*Summa Theologiae*, III, q.63, a.5, *ad primum*).

The Nature of the Sacraments is Immutable

character. Obviously, the order attributed to these effects has no 'chronological' significance, but rather indicates their relative importance. As for the necessity of a sensory mediation for communicating grace (a conditional necessity which does not restrain divine freedom), it principally results from the corporeal nature of the human being and is basically brought back to the raison d'être for the Incarnation: although the divinity of Jesus is the source of sanctifying grace, the dead and resurrected humanity of Christ is the primary mediation, the primary instrument of sacramental grace, and therefore, in a certain manner, the primary Sacrament. The seven sacraments, properly speaking, are the seven fundamental modes according to which grace is applied and communicated to us, grace which, by virtue of the hypostatic union, springs forth from the Pasch of our Christ: the sacramental sevenfold is the redemptive incarnation of Jesus Christ made operatively present for all, whether in space or in time.

In terms of what I have just explained, we see that, in these seven fundamental modes, we must distinguish two elements: an interior element, the sacramental grace proper to each one of them and which specifies them (if there are seven sacraments, this is because each one is necessary and all of them sufficient), and, on the other hand, an exterior element composed of a sensible 'matter (water, bread, etc.) and a 'form' (generally words). The interior and invisible element is what theology names the *res*, the 'thing', the 'reality' communicated by the rite. The exterior and visible element is what theology names the *sacramentum* in the strict sense of the term, that is to say the *sacred sign*, the rite as concrete symbol. Although, strictly speaking, sacramental grace should be called 'thing' (*res*) and not *sacramentum*, that is because this term implies the idea of a visible sign; now grace is not a sign since it is invisible and should not 'signify', being itself the reality signified, being *what* the *sacramentum* as such, the sacred sign, signifies.[1] However, *character* can be considered as *res-et-sacramentum*, as reality signified *and* as sacred sign: on the one hand it is a seal imprinted, a mark, and on the other this mark renders really and immediately effective the presence of sacramental grace in the human subject who does not pose an obstacle to it. Thus it is said in theology that character *requires* grace.

Christ the Original Mystery

Guénon's Thesis Is Triply Unacceptable

After this brief recall of some more or less classical notions about the different kinds of grace and the structure of the sacraments, we can attempt a response to the questions posed by Guénon's thesis. This response will be articulated in three points: the first relates to the divine institution of the sacraments, the second to their validity, and the third to their way of working.

The Institution of the Sacraments

With respect to the first point, the question to be posed is the following: if it is admitted that the sevenfold sacraments have been instituted by Jesus Christ, what follows from those changes that the Church has the freedom to bring about? Guénon's thesis is based on the idea that the exterior form (the 'matter' and 'form' of the Scholastics), having been fixed by Christ, is impossible to modify; otherwise everyone would and should see that the same rite is no longer involved. The only element that the Church can modify is the interior element, the *res*, the reality of grace signified by the *sacramentum* as such (the *sacramentum tantum* of the Scholastics). But this is quite exactly contrary to the truth.

Let me first stress the strange duplicity Guénon's thesis imparts to a Church otherwise reputed to be the sole traditional authority in the West. A minimum of honesty would demand that a sacred institution, which modifies so completely the nature of the rites it is charged with administering, signal this modification by a correlative

---

1. Neither is the term 'thing' without drawbacks. It in fact leads us to think of the being of grace as a substantial reality which is hardly to be conceived of otherwise than as the *gift of a participation* of the human order in the divine order. It is justified however, allowance being made for the fact that, under the influence of St Augustine, all that exists is divided into two categories: signs and things; but grace is not a sign.

The Nature of the Sacraments is Immutable

change in their exterior form. Otherwise, and whatever may be certain secondary changes occurring in the administration of the rites—changes to which Guénon attributes an undue significance (I will return to this)—nothing would betray such a change. And besides, unless I be mistaken, we would have had to wait two thousand years and for the contingencies which have given rise to the writing of 'Christianity and Initiation' to be informed: the disproportion between the two events borders on absurdity.

Likewise, I will pass over another disastrous consequence of this thesis: the 'providential faking' of appearances which it supposes destroys the analogical correspondence between exterior signs and signified realities, thus ruining at once the basis for the whole symbolic order and the work of the *Logos*. For, if the *Logos* incarnate has chosen such or such a visible element to signify and to give the gift of such or such a spiritual reality, this is because it was the most appropriate; thus for baptism: *all* exterior constituent elements of this rite signify a new birth in God, which is even initiation, but, according to Guénon, producing nothing but a psychic incorporation into a religious organization, whereas the surest definition of sacrament is *a sign that does what it signifies*.

Now we come to the question of institution. By faith we have to believe that Jesus Christ has instituted the seven sacraments. This is incontestable for baptism and the eucharist, as is recognized by the Protestants. Scripture, in fact, indubitably establishes what should be the matter and form of these two sacraments. About them it can be affirmed without the least hesitation that the material signs and the ritual words have been fixed by Christ. And yet, however fixed they might be, matter and form allow for some variations: the water of baptism is, in principle, composed of water blessed to this end, but one can use, in case of need, ordinary blessed water, or even natural water, and, whatever the water may be, apply it by immersion, sprinkling or infusion; as to the words, they differ for Latins and Greeks.[1] The question posed is, then, upon what does the divine

---

1. Latins: 'I baptize you in the Name of the Father and of the Son and of the Holy Spirit'; Greeks: 'The servant of Christ, N..., is baptized in the Name of the Father and of the Son and of the Holy Spirit.'

institution turn, which is not only *de fide* but about which we should not have the least doubt, just as I have outlined with my demonstration in the chapter on the sacraments and sacramentals; for here, more than in any other realm, tradition has shown. Now, specifically, ecclesiastical tradition informs us that, not only has the exterior element varied somewhat in some of its non-essential parts, there where it had been fixed by Christ, but that it might even be varied in its essential parts, where this element does not seem to have been determined by Christ: in particular, this is the case with ordination formulas which are completely different for Greeks and Latins. It is clear in the first case, as theologians teach, that secondary variations are only possible on condition of not impairing the essential significance of the instituted formula. This possibility, be it noted, averts all risk of a magical conception of ritual efficacy which would be attached to the literalness of the words, or even the language used.[1] But the same explanation is valid in the second case: provided that *the sense willed by Christ* is clearly signified in its *identity*, the formulas which express it, where Christ has not fixed them, can be entirely different according to the letter.

The conclusion thrust upon us is therefore the following: far from the Church having no power over the exterior forms of the sacraments, she can to the contrary modify them, in terms of circumstances and needs, but provided that the rite's essence is not altered. As a result, wherever the question posed is: upon what does the divine institution of the sacraments turn? The only possible reply is: on the interior element, the nature proper to sacramental grace that the rite is charged with conveying. Wherever the question is not posed—for baptism and the eucharist—it is obvious that the divine institution turns at once on both elements. Thus, *what* Christ has certainly instituted, and *that over which*, as a consequence, the Church has no power is *that which He has willed* to institute, *that*

---

1. St Thomas explains that, although certain words are required for a sacrament's validity, it is by reason of their sense and not of their sound: 'No matter in what language this sense is expressed, the sacrament is complete' (*Summa Theologiae*, III, q.60, ad 1um). As for a rite's validity, St Thomas has seen no theological obstacle to the use of a vernacular language for the celebration of the Mass.

The Nature of the Sacraments is Immutable

which He has had the *intention* of doing by instituting the sacrament, this is, one might say, the objective *intent* constituting the sacrament's immutable and incorruptible essence, or again, since a sacrament is a sign, its essential significance objectively considered is 'the sacramental being properly speaking', to phrase it like John of St Thomas.[1] This whole doctrine is summarized in this text from the Council of Trent:

> this power has ever been in the Church, that, in the dispensation of the sacraments, *their substance being untouched*, it may ordain, —or change, what things soever it may judge most expedient, for the profit of those who receive, or for the veneration of the said sacraments, according to the difference of circumstances, times, and places.[2]

On this substance, that is on this fundamental reality, all the Fathers, all the Doctors, all theologians of the East and West, all the councils agree; the Church has no authority, and can in no instance modify its nature in any way whatsoever. Whoever thinks otherwise about this subject is guilty of major heresy and outside ecclesial communion. Such is the pure and unvarnished truth.

Furthermore, from the principle of the immediate divine institution of the sacraments, as to their substance, proceeds this second consequence, likewise recognized by all Christian Churches: the Church does not have the power to institute new sacraments.

A last question could still be raised. As immutable and determined as it might be in its nature and substance by reason of its immediate divine institution, a sacramental being is none the less unfinished in itself: it is completed and finished only in the being who receives the sacrament and within whom it bears fruit, for grace is a reality in becoming which is ontologically accomplished only in the one whom it leads to sanctification. But, as St Thomas explains with precision, this nowhere contradicts the immutability of the sacramental nature. It is necessary to conclude:

---

1. *D. T. C.*, t. xiv, article 'Sacraments', col. 533 and 576.
2. Session xxi, chap. ii; *Les Counciles oecuméniques: Les décrets* (Paris: Cerf, 1994), t. ii, p 1477.

Christ the Original Mystery

the sacraments render permanent, continue, and apply the sanctifying action of Christ. The structure of their being and their activity is therefore in conformity with the structure and the activity of the God-Man.[1]

The Validity of the Sacraments

We can now broach the second point, that of validity. Seeing that the Christian sacraments, as to their essence, can be only what Jesus Christ has *willed* them to be, the only question to be posed is that of their *validity,* a term which designates the characteristic that a rite should possess to effectively realize in our soul what it signifies. As we see, validity is not concerned with the essence of the rite, but with its existence: Is such a rite effectively accomplished valid, is its existence as a sacrament in conformity with its essence, that is to say with *what* Jesus Christ has *willed* it to be?[2] To pose the question of a rite's validity is to pose, then, the question of the conditions for validity. Now, as I have shown, what in a sacrament is subject to condition cannot be the interior and essential element as such. This element being of divine origin, its own nature has no other condition than that of the Divine Will. God willing specifically that such or such a grace be conferred by such or such a sacramental rite, and His will

---

1. A.M. Roguet, *Traité des Sacrements* of St Thomas Aquinas, op. cit., p209.
2. Licitness and validity are not to be confused: the episcopal consecrations accomplished by Mgr. Lefèbvre were illicit, but their validity is not in doubt. The distinction of licitness and validity is tied to the distinction of hierarchies or *jurisdiction* and *order*. The Church is a sacred society. Insofar as it is a society, it has its laws and its proper authorities which define ecclesiastic discipline, the highest authority being, for Catholics, the Pope who possess the power of supreme *jurisdiction;* this power is exercised in the highest degree over the constitution of the episcopal college, the first element of an ecclesial society. Insofar as it is sacred, this society has for a raison d'être the actualization of the sacramental *order,* which is hierarchical since grace descends from the Head, Christ (this is why this grace is called 'capital grace'), to the ministers ordained for its transmission (bishops, priests and deacons) and charged with communicating it to the Christian people. From the viewpoint of the hierarchy of order, the bishop of Rome has no other powers than

The Nature of the Sacraments is Immutable

being immutable, when the sacramental rite is regularly accomplished, grace is conferred. The only element which can be opposed to the communication of sacramental grace is therefore the exterior element; only in this connection can we speak about conditions of validity. This element—which we should qualify as exterior lacking a better term—is composed at once by the 'matter' and the 'form' of the sacrament: thus, in the sacrament of the Eucharist, the matter is the bread and wine, the form is the words of consecration (but it is not always easy to identify what is the matter and what is the form in a sacrament, and this distinction should not be made a hard and fast one). Since one function of this exterior element is to *signify* the interior and invisible element, clearly the conditions for a rite's validity will be concerned with the aptitude possessed by form and matter to adequately signify that reality that ought to be communicated. Beyond even the conformity of the *sacramentum* to the rules fixed by the Church, the basic principle is that matter and form should be sufficiently *declarative* of the nature of sacramental grace.[1]

---

those of no matter what other bishop; and the same for the cardinals (bishops) and archbishops. A cardinal who is not a bishop (Lubac, Balthasar, Congar, etc.) obviously does not have a bishop's powers of order. Even lay cardinals are possible: this was the case with Mazarin and would have been the case with Maritain. In the just mentioned cases, it is clear that the title of cardinal is hardly more than an honorific distinction, whereas in principle the cardinals constitute the clergy of the dioceses of Rome charged with helping the Pope administer his dioceses; this is why, as in every clergy, there are cardinal-bishops, cardinal-priests and cardinal-deacons (the three degrees of the hierarchy of order). What is authorized by the hierarchy of jurisdiction is licit; what is accomplished according to the hierarchy of order is valid. In his dioceses, the bishop is at once the head of the hierarchy of order and the head of the hierarchy of jurisdiction, since he is the only one to possess the fullness of sacerdotal powers (only he can confer the sacraments of holy orders, confirmation and penance—he can delegate the last two) and every sacrament is licitly administered in his dioceses only with his authorization. The Pope possesses the supreme power of jurisdiction only because he is bishop of the Church of Rome, which is the 'mother and teacher' of all the Churches.

1. This principle, which rests on the nature of things, should be able to help resolve the debate over the validity of the new rite of the Mass: it seems to me that the *Novus Ordo*, strictly respected, undoubtedly expresses the sacrificial nature of the liturgical action, although less adequately than the old rite.

Christ the Original Mystery

The conformity of the signifying elements to the realities signified does not by itself, however, assure a sacrament's validity. In fact, a rite is not only a succession of words and gestures putting a matter to work in conformity with a recognized ritual. It is not enough for these gestures to be executed, words pronounced, matter consecrated for the sacrament to be validly accomplished and sacramental grace produced. Otherwise, as the Fathers say, an actor performing the rite of baptismal initiation on a theater stage would really baptize. A sacrament also supposes a minister of the sacrament and a subject to whom the sacrament is administered. The work of the sacrament's two actors, minister and subject, obviously requires the respect of certain conditions for its validity, the first of which is that the one is not the other: no one can baptize himself.[1] On the other hand, and from the side of the minister, he has to be validly ordained or authorized by the Church to administer the rite. Not because one should not give what has not been received, as some believe, since to the contrary a non-baptized person can validly administer baptism. But it must be understood that the sacrament's minister acts, not personally in giving what he has—which would hardly make any sense—but in accomplishing the sacerdotal work confided by Christ to the Church, a work which is to communicate to the faithful the grace of His redemptive Passion. Only the Church is, then, directly appointed for the administration of the sacraments, or, on occasion, authorizes someone to administer independently of an ordination properly speaking. Exterior elements (words, gestures, matter) do not, then, produce sacramental grace by themselves; it is the power endowed by the Church's sacerdotal deputation on a minister, a power which mysteriously vivifies the formal elements and materials and transforms them into secondary instruments of divine grace. By this, let us stress anew, every magical conception of ritual activity that would have the sacramental power reside in the words, gestures or matter as such is set aside.

---

1. One might draw from this that, in the case of marriage, where the spouses are the ministers—and not the priest who ecclesially ratifies their consent—who administer it to themselves. We could conclude, then, that each spouse is the minister of the sacrament for the other.

The Nature of the Sacraments is Immutable

But is this all? Surely not. It is not enough that a minister is regularly ordained or legitimately authorized by the Church in order for sacramental acts to be valid: a priest entering a bakery and saying 'This is my body' over the breads does not consecrate. Besides a regularly deputed 'sacerdotal' power, a second condition is required in the minister: intention. This requirement is well known, but perhaps not always well understood. Thus it has been objected that, with the validity of the rite requiring the minister's intention, the nature of the rite would depend on the nature of this intention: if the minister were to modify this intention without changing the visible form, the nature of the effects produced by the rite would be likewise modified. This objection is unacceptable, but it brings up a rather surprising doctrinal point. And in fact, contrary to what might be believed, the intention dealt with here by no means makes the sacrament dependent on the minister's subjectivity, but just the opposite: it makes the minister's subjectivity dependent on the sacrament's objectivity. To grasp this we have to consider the raison d'être of this condition: if the minister's intention is required, this is because he is not a passive instrument, a kind of pure means for manufacturing the supernatural, but a true actor forming an integral part of the ritual act. This is why an *objective* intention is mentioned here, an intention that does not involve a minster's personal adherence to the sacramental work, in such a way that he would be interiorly fixed in a spiritual state exactly corresponding to the exteriorly accomplished sacramental mystery. If this state occurs in a minister, so much the better; but it is not a required condition. The intention required clearly depends on the minister as to its intentional form, since it is an act of his will, not as to its content, as to *what* the minister wills. What is required is for the minister to have an objective will to realize what the *sacramentum* signifies objectively, and, in an even more general way, according to the classical formula, to have 'the will to do what the Church does when it accomplishes this rite.' This formula is the only decisive one because it frees the minister from all scruples of conscience: if subjective intention were required, one moment of distraction during sacramental activity, the raising of a doubt, or even a lessening in the intensity of faith would be enough to invalidate the rite. This is why it should be held with complete certainty that a minister who has personally lost the faith nevertheless accomplishes the rite validly, provided that he objectively rely on the faith of the Church, according to the principle: *fides Ecclesiae supplet* ('the faith of the Church supplies for deficiencies'). And one last point to be raised: is relying on the Church a condition for validity, when this very Church rightly or wrongly gives the impression of having lost the faith? Now here is something most surprising: the Catholic Church in no way imposes as a condition for validity that the minister have the intention of doing what the Catholic Church is doing at the present time—which might on occasion give rise to doubts in the soul of the minister—but that he have the intention of doing what the *Church of Jesus Christ* does. Such is the Catholic doctrine.[1]

Here we rediscover the theme of Christ's sacramental will, a theme so insistently stressed in the previous pages and now we understand why. It is this will that is the norm; it is with this will that the minister ought to be united, objectively and formally, by intention, even if he otherwise finds himself invincibly ignorant of this will's content and the specific nature of the grace conferred. It has to be finally concluded, then, that neither the minister, nor the Church whose deputy he is have the least power over this grace. They can only administer or not administer it, and that is all.

The conditions for validity on the side of the subject remain to be examined. This question would lead us too far afield if treated exhaustively, for each sacrament requires its own conditions for validity on the part of the subject who receives it. I will just say that the same holds true for the subject as well as for the minister: the subject is also an actor, an integral and constituent part of the sacramental act, and not a simple passive recipient. The principal condition required, proper to all the sacraments, is neither a state of grace, nor even a faith explicitly known and professed (since a heretic can validly receive baptism), but here as well it is the intention of receiving the sacrament that the Church specifically wishes to confer; the subject has to will that the sacramental work that the Church of Christ wishes to accomplish be accomplished in him. We are therefore dealing with an objective consciously formulated intention (no

1. *D.T.C.*, t. VII, col. 2272.

The Nature of the Sacraments is Immutable

adult can be baptized against his will), but this in no way requires an explicit and complete understanding of the nature of the grace communicated. As before, the principle *fides Ecclesiae supplet* is valid.

Such are the conditions for the validity of the sacraments; they amount to three: observance of the divinely and ecclesially established ritual forms, the legitimacy of the minister and the conformity of his intention, and the adequately intentional disposition of the recipient.[1] These conditions being fulfilled, the sacrament is valid and necessarily produces its effect which is thus deposited in the soul of the recipient. We are then led to the third indicated point: after the divine institution and the conditions for validity, we will conclude by saying something about 'operation'.

The Operative Mode of the Sacraments

Here we touch on the well known question of the *ex opere operato* mentioned already at the beginning. This formula, which does not

---

1. The question of the qualification required of the recipient (they vary according to the sacraments) does not necessarily concern their validity, but can concern their licitness or 'fruitfulness: thus a masculine qualification is required for the validity of Holy Orders; but the absence of certain physical infirmities that would render sacerdotal work difficult or impossible is only required for licitness. Guénon maintains that religious rites require no qualification. If, by qualification, the possession of certain individual bodily or psychic capacities is understood, Guénon is right: no one is excluded from the grace of Christ for lack of particular aptitudes; to the contrary, Christ has come for the one-eyed, the lame, the stutterer, the hunchbacked, the blind, the deaf, the paralytic and all the sick. But if by qualifications we understand the dispositions of heart and body required for the reception of a rite, then all the sacraments very much require certain qualifications, lacking which they will be fruitless, even if sacramental grace has indeed been conferred. And this is quite especially true for rites which consecrate a particular vocation, either religious or conjugal. It is moreover curious to observe how Jacob, after his struggle with the angel, was lame (Gen. 32:32), and how Moses had difficulty speaking (and perhaps stuttered: Ex. 4:10). Yet, according to Guénon, two major disqualifications for initiation are involved here; the second instance prohibits 'the correct pronunciation' of the Divine Name (*Perspectives on Initiation*, p101). But to Moses was revealed the *Tetragrammaton*... And Jesus teaches: 'It is better for thee to enter lame into life everlasting, than having two feet, to be cast into the hell of unquenchable fire' (Mark 9:44).

seem to be prior to the thirteenth century, has given rise to many reflections, not all of which are acceptable to Catholic theology; this is why it is good to define its meaning as much as possible. Let us recall that this Latin expression, somewhat 'rude' in construction, is broken down in this way: *ex,* a preposition followed by the ablative, indicates cause or origin, and signifies 'from', 'out of', 'by virtue of'; *opere,* the ablative of *opus,* signifies 'work'; *operato,* a participle of the verb *operor* (which always has an active sense), should be taken here in a passive sense and signifies 'operated'. Literally translated, then, it reads: 'by virtue of the work operated'. This theological precision takes on its real meaning only when compared to this other formula: *ex opere operantis. Operantis* is the genitive of the present participle, *operans,* and signifies 'of the one operating'. The entire expression is therefore translated: 'by virtue of the work of the one operating,' or even 'of the one who operates,' it being understood that the one operating is either the minister, the subject or both at once. These precisions assumed, we see that the *ex opere operato* signifies that a sacrament does not act by virtue of the one who operates (the one operating is not the cause of sacramental grace, and neither personal qualities, defects or degree of sanctity have any power over the production of grace), but it acts solely by virtue of the sacramental act accomplished.

Should we deduce from this that the one operating, especially the subject, plays no role in the fruitfulness of sacramental grace? Obviously not. Without the efforts of the one who cooperates with grace, grace would bear no fruit. Should we likewise deduce from this that Christ is not the true giver of grace, and that it is no longer the virtue of His redemptive grace that acts in the sacrament? Surely not. Grace acts first by virtue of the Supreme Operator, Jesus Christ dead and risen from the dead; in this sense one could just as well say that the sacrament acts *ex opere Operantis,* provided that we understand by this the person of the Incarnate Son. But this is not the question, which is decided by the following notions: (1) Christ always and permanently operates the work of His grace; (2) He has instituted seven sacraments through which this grace is communicated to us; (3) insofar as these sacraments consist in so many ritual operations accomplished by men (the ministers) and the effects of which are

The Nature of the Sacraments is Immutable

communicated to others (the subjects). Hence there is this question: since the means for applying the grace of Christ have been confided to us, when are we certain that this applied work has indeed been effected? For grace is an invisible reality: neither the 'visible' sanctity of the minister, nor a visible sanctification (spectacular gifts and charisms) can assure us of its presence. After all, do not forget that God can produce sanctifying grace, accompanied on occasion by the most extraordinary gifts, in whom He wishes and as He wishes. It is therefore necessary that the Church, instituted by Christ to be steward of His grace, be in possession of a complete certainty about the accomplishment of its mission. Now, as for its operations and actions, man can acquire complete certainty only about the very factuality of the fact accomplished, and not about its nature, its truth, its well-foundedness, efficacy or fruitfulness. Caesar, for example, could always ask himself if he was right or wrong to want to cross the Rubicon, if this act has indeed the significance that he attributes to it, if it would have the effects that he expected, and so forth; but whatever the truth and consequences of this act, one thing (in the human order) is absolutely clear: if the act is accomplished, it is accomplished, and nothing can undo it. Consequently, as for whatever pertains to the sacramental act, the only complete certainty to be obtained in this matter is that is has or has not been accomplished. Here, however, a difference from ordinary acts, the significance or truth of which are always relative, presents itself; to the contrary, faith attests that the significance or truth of sacramental acts has been determined by the very will of God. Hence, the certainty that the Church can obtain on the subject of accomplishing a sacramental act—lacking which it would be forever deprived of any assurance concerning the accomplishment of its work of grace—is in itself enough to likewise vouch for its intrinsic truth. Now the conditions which guarantee the efficacy of this accomplishment are known: these are the conditions for validity. As a consequence and with these conditions being fulfilled, the truth of the sacrament is realized solely by virtue of its accomplishment.

Such is the significance of the *ex opere operato:* if the sacrament has been validly accomplished (this is the *opus operatum*), sacramental grace, the *res* proper to the *sacramentum,* has been actually conferred, just as sacraments include character. There is nothing magical here, as Luther and numerous Protestant theologians claim, accusing the Catholics of believing in an 'automatic sanctification' which would dispense with all personal effort. In reality, this objection discloses a complete misunderstanding of the sacramental order and its objectivity, which is clearly also a misunderstanding of Christianity's very nature the essence of which is to be, as we will see in the last part of the book, a sacramentarian religion. Finally, it is a certain misunderstanding of the mystery of the Incarnation, for the objectivity of the sacramental order is a direct consequence of the objectivity of Christ's incarnation, which it prolongs in time and the virtue of which it communicates. Thus, whoever receives a sacrament is 'consecrated' or 'sacramentalized' by it, but he does not for all that become a saint.

Basically, the doctrine of the *opus operatum* flows from the very definition of a sacrament as from an efficacious sign that produces what it signifies. This is why certain recent theologians[1] have ranked the sacraments in the category of *performed* expressions [*énoncés performatifs*]. By this, modern linguistics designates expressions that produce what they express by the very fact of expressing it, and so are not confined to stating a fact (stated or descriptive expressions); for example: 'I promise to...' The baptismal formula is clearly performative: 'I baptize you...' The difference however, this being a matter of sacramental signs, is that a mysterious and transcendent operation is involved in the process of their realization, which is obviously not the case for ordinary performative expressions.

All these considerations converge to bring to light the impossibility of Guénon's thesis concerning an essential change in the nature of sacramental grace. The sole 'measure' of this grace, as to its fruitfulness, is the possibilities of those who receive it:

> the same sacrament [say the theologians] produces *ex opere operato* an equivalent grace in those who are equivalently disposed: grace is proportional to the dispositions of the subject.[2]

---

1. Louis Chauvet, *Symbole et sacrament* (Paris: Cerf:, 1988).
2. *D.T.C.*, t. xiv, col. 626.

The Nature of the Sacraments is Immutable

And if the particular minister of a sacrament does not, of himself, have the power to 'measure' the grace communicated, neither is the minister general of the sacramental order—the Church—any more capable of doing so. A sacrament does not act by virtue of the Church's decisions, but by the operative virtue of its own significance; no authority in the world has any power over that.

Conclusion: *The Sacramental Order Is Incorruptible*

Now we see in broad daylight the intrinsic independence and incorruptibility of the Christian sacramental order. This order can be annulled if the will of Christ that has instituted is not respected; it cannot be modified or degraded in any way: it is what it ought to be, or it is not.

How do we explain the enormity of the error committed by Guénon? It is so much more difficult to account for it since, for Freemasonry, he himself had set aside the possibility for such a modification in the nature of its rites. Has he not written:

> even where an initiatic organization is in fact involved, the members have no power to change its forms at whim or to alter them in their essentials. This does not exclude certain possibilities of adaptation to circumstances, but these are much rather imposed on individuals than willed by them, and they are circumscribed by the need not to injure the means that ensure the conservation and transmission of the spiritual influence of which the organization in question is the repository. If this condition is not met, the result will be a veritable rupture with the tradition and the organization will thereby lose its 'regularity'.[1]

Why would what is true of a particular initiatic organization—the 'exterior' corruption of which is only too obvious—not apply to the initiatic organization that was the Church in the words of Guénon

---

1. *Perspectives on Initiation*, p35.

Christ the Original Mystery

himself? If there is no contradiction here, is there not at least a real difficulty?

And yet I am unable to quiet a suspicion that has grown all through my analysis: what is there in common between the content of Guénon's theses and the reality of the Christian sacraments? The response clearly seems to be: nothing or almost nothing. Without doubt, Guénon speaks of rites, and sacraments might be ranked in this general category. But it becomes apparent, to whoever studies the ritual of various religions objectively, that they exhibit only rather exterior similarities to Christian sacramentality. Guénon was aware of this, since he recognized that the word *sacrament* 'designates something the exact equivalent of which is not found elsewhere.'[1] He does not draw any conclusion from this remark and forthwith classifies these Christian sacraments in the category of *samskara*, that is to say 'rites of "admission" [or better of integration] to a traditional community':[2] this is not completely false, but it is extraordinarily limiting and insupportably reductive. It is here that, with good reason, we could speak of someone who sees things only 'from without'!

To see things 'from within', we need no recourse to considerations that are hard to establish; it is enough to become aware of the Scriptures and Christian tradition. And the following observation is drawn from this: although many religions have developed a (quantitatively) important and finely detailed ritual complex beyond all common measure with that of Christianity, none—to my knowledge—have elaborated a doctrine and sacramental theology comparable to those about which I have just given some idea. What is to be met with elsewhere, in return, (especially in the Hindu writings) are considerations of a cosmological nature relative to the symbolic forms and structures set to work by the ritual—considerations which are, it seems, much less developed in Christianity. The reason is simple: in Christianity, the Body of Christ functions as the macrocosm, but summarizing and surpassing it. This is why the doctrine of the sacraments can concentrate on grace

---

1. Ibid., p153.
2. Ibid.

The Nature of the Sacraments is Immutable

and its supernatural being and develop a theology of divine operation in the sacramental acts, a theology without equivalent.[1]

Whoever accepts to follow me into this book's last part will be even more persuaded of this.

---

1. The chapter that F. Chenique has devoted to initiation in *Sagesse chrétienne et mystique orientale* (Paris: Dervy, 1996), p506–515 (in the composition of which I have partially collaborated) does not exactly express my point of view.

III

Christianity in Its Mystery

Introduction

The Christian Religion Speaks of Itself

BROACHING the indirect refutation of Guénon's theses relative to Christianity, I will attempt to proceed with a displacement of what is involved, which amounts to restoring Christianity to its proper place and to cease subjecting it to demands foreign to its nature. We have seen how, at the end of my reflections on the sacraments, the need for such an endeavor was thrust upon me and must now be undertaken.

But, to situate Christianity in its rightful place, is to consider it first from the point of view of its true 'hermeneutic site'. To begin with I should stress: 'every revelation includes a certain understanding of itself, which is the mode by which it presents itself to us. . . . To this hermeneutic we *have* to be attentive.' Lacking this and supposing we were speaking about Christianity, we would in reality be speaking about something else. This signifies that it is also with the help of its own light that a religion should be illumined, and not only with the help of the intellect in general. In other words, the mode of expression assumed by the *revelatum* to manifest itself to men—and which is the work of the Holy Spirit—also determines the mode of understanding under which it might best be grasped; the mode of understanding of the revealed Object is basically only the reflection, in the intellective mirror, of its mode of expression; it is the Object which quickens the intellect and yields to it the keys of Its own intelligibility.

Without doubt, among the formal elements assumed by the *revelatum*, we encounter many susceptible to a universal interpretation because they have been borrowed from humanity's universal tradition. This is chiefly the case with symbolic elements. Each one of these elements can always be extracted from the religious context

Christ the Original Mystery

into which it has been inserted and viewed as to its archetypal significance. In this respect, it clearly seems that Guénon's work is truly irreplaceable; and anyway, who says forms of expression, says cosmic forms: now the world is one and the same for all. However, and since the original Fall, the manifestation of created forms is no longer the unique Book of divine revelation that Adam had as a mission to spell out. Each tradition selects from among these created forms so to create its own cultural synthesis, in which the elements used acquire a new significance in conformity with the spirit of this culture. And this is even more for a religion such as Christianity, a religion more strongly 'centered' than any other around its unifying and transcendent principle, Jesus Christ. As a result, all the formal elements of this religion have been semantically transformed by the relationship which they henceforth maintain with the unique center of the *revelatum*.

If anyone would like to know, then, Christianity's hermeneutic site, it would be appropriate to first take into consideration the general figure that the sum total of its formal elements delineates. It is this that will provide the global vision, the inspiring 'idea' out of which this religion might be appreciated and understood. Certainly, such a comprehension cannot but be brought about from structures and concepts appropriate to the intellect, which is to be neither ignored nor rejected. The role of *a priori* categories of thought and the importance theoretical knowledge should not, then, be eliminated here. But, in this undertaking, the intellect should also take into account formal 'suggestions' which come from its object and which amount to a veritable esthetic of religious forms, or, if preferable, a kind of phenomenology. For the formal style of a religion, the style of its language, symbols and ritual gestures, more than the analysis of some of its constituent elements, is revelatory of its essence and wordlessly communicates an intuition of it to the intellect. And it is the intuition of this essence thus perceived—with the risks of subjectivism that this includes—which should guide the work of the intellect.

But this is not all. A religion not only includes formal elements delineating its spiritual physiognomy in an implicit and connotative way. It also includes explicit words, in which is expressed, in a quite

Introduction

denotative way, the consciousness that it has of itself, and which provides the keys for it to be understood aright. We have to lend the greatest attention to this express declarations, and strive at first to mark them out so to learn from the religion itself what it has to say about its own essence. Such is the object of this last part: no longer to answer an argument with another argument, but to seek out the evidence for the consciousness that the Church has had of the nature of its message and take heed.

However, this should not involve taking into account all of the elements just spoken of: they are too numerous and a list could not even be truly drawn up. Nor will the distinction just mentioned between connotative and denotative elements help to organize so vast a material: both are so closely intermingled that it would be vain to want to separate them, or we would, then, be exposed to frequent repetitions. This is why it seems wiser and more convenient, leaving aside the majority of the properly symbolic formal elements, to chiefly hold to a study of the language used by the Church to say its message, as well as to an examination of the arrangements adopted to administer the grace that God has confided to the Church as a deposit. Whether implicit or explicit, connotative or denotative, these elements of Christian discourse or ecclesial sacramentality seem the most apt for guiding us toward that understanding which revelation offers of itself, either directly or indirectly.

Nevertheless, to enter into this understanding, it is not enough to take into account some terms to be met with in the New Testament or in paleo-Christian literature, whether they relate to the expression of doctrine or are concerned with certain disciplinary arrangements in the administration of the sacraments. We still have to rediscover the meaning that they had when the Church (the Apostles and their successors) chose them from among others, and what was the Church's intention. Moreover, these terms are known: they are essentially those of Scripture and therefore ours as well. But this is precisely the reason why we no longer understand them, or, rather, no longer perceive them: two thousand years of use has made them somewhat transparent, obliterating their most singular and most life-giving significance. This is why recourse to history proves useful, if not indispensable. Surely, I am not expecting from historical science the truth about our faith, which should not be at the mercy of the most recent publication. And, besides, it is all too certain that this science has given proof of many a misunderstanding when studying phenomena foreign to the modern mentality.

And yet we clearly have to recognize that many things have changed since the beginning of the twentieth century in this domain, especially in the study of scriptural vocabulary and narration. There is here as if a providential compensation for the ravages of time. As much as I reject the conclusions of modern exegesis when it is used to cut up the sacred texts into shreds of disparate origin, to deny their traditional authenticity, and even, which is rightly a sacrilege and criminal, to put in doubt the truth of Christ's words, which is then presented as a catechetical construct of the primitive community, I also highly value present day efforts when they focus solely on *reading* the text and scrutinizing it with all the learned resources and analytical methods elaborated by the textual sciences. Doubtless, such a way of approaching Holy Scripture is dispensable for whoever has faith in the Word of God and reads it in light of Church doctrine. But it is not forbidden to scrutinize its formulation and to acquire a more fecund understanding of it once the text itself is respected, respected as the primary datum and absolutely irreducible basis for all interpretation. In this respect, there is no doubt for me that the best of modern exegesis pursues and develops the labor of reading so admirably inaugurated by the Origens and Augustines and somewhat forgotten to the benefit of a too exclusively theological use of Scripture, as if the Word of God had no other use than to shore up the conclusions of the dogmaticians.[1]

---

1. Once again, I am not impugning any course when it forms a part of tradition and has borne fruit. That Scripture also serves to stand security for theological conclusions is not only useful for theology, but even for Scripture itself, which is by essence theological, 'God-the-Word', and which thus reveals this essence (something that the best modern exegesis has a tendency to forget). But it cannot be reduced to this function, as if Scripture no longer had anything else to teach us than what is theologically formulated. Thus it was maintained, for example, that 'Whoever rejects the *Summa Theologica* to rest content with the authority of Scripture and the traditions of the Fathers, will not acquire a true knowledge of theology and

Introduction

This reading method has been employed likewise in ecclesiastic literature with results I think fruitful. Rather than to judge an author, or even a body of documentary texts relating to a given question, with formally constituted doctrinal categories—which has led to notable misinterpretations (in the evaluations brought to bear on Origen, for example, or Meister Eckhart)—but to strive instead to enter into the text's manners of speaking by an attentive and meticulous study of its vocabulary and narrative strategy, and without suspecting its orthodoxy *a priori,* such is one of the necessary ways to attain to understanding a text 'up close' and as it is in itself.[1] This is also the one that I am following here and which I have previously employed in connection with the words 'rule of faith', 'dogma' and 'consubstantial'.

Nevertheless, it is significant to observe that Guénon, who has written an introduction to the *study* of Hindu doctrines (and not directly to these doctrines themselves), did not think that he had to

---

will not sufficiently understand what Scripture and the Fathers are teaching us; neither will his faith be solid, nor his spirit vigorous. To the contrary, whoever chooses St. Thomas as sole guide, will benefit at the same time from all the wisdom of prior ages.' (Cardinal Satolli, *De Trinitate,* prologus, pII; approvingly cited by Dom Paul' Renaudin, abbot of Clairvaux, in an article devoted to 'The theology of St. Cyril of Alexandria according to St. Thomas', published in *Revue thomiste,* 1910, pp171–184).

1. Doubtless, another two ways should be added to this way: a scholarly knowledge of the historical circumstances of the text's production on the one hand, and, on the other, a comprehension of its meaning with respect to objective Truth, this third way being the most essential. In other words, to understand a text we need to know: why it has been written (historical circumstances), what it actually means (textological analysis), and if what it says is true or false (philosophical or theological comprehension). Today this philosophical or theological requirement is universally misunderstood; yet it is indispensable, since a text generally intends to tell what it is about and should be independently appreciated, then, for this objective aim. If in this work, however, we do not take into account the dogmatic requirement in the first place, this is because I consider it in principle as taken for granted and beyond discussion: I am addressing readers who *a priori* hold to the entirety of the Church's perpetual and infallible doctrine, that is to 'what has been believed everywhere, always, and by all,' according to St. Vincent of Lerins' beautiful definition (*'quod ubique, quod semper, quod omnibus creditum est,' Commonitorium,* 2; Rouët de Journel, *Enchiridion patristicum,* n2168, (Fribourg en Brisgau: Herder and Co., 1932), p686.

Christ the Original Mystery

write an introduction to the study of Christian doctrines. He was in fact aware of the mental reform demanded by the study of Hinduism if it were rid of certain western preconceptions and relocated to its own hermeneutic site; no one has pressed more effectively for this displacement and repatriation. But he never asked if a similar effort might be required for Christianity. Born in a Christian country, without doubt he was convinced that he had a direct knowledge of the most ordinary aspects of this religion. As for the other aspects—Guénon could not have been unaware that they were as distant, in time, from the modern mentality as eastern doctrines were in space; he thought he only needed the categories of his own doctrine to understand them: initiatic organizations, esoterism, etc., which are however not those of Christianity. And, when dealing with these properly Christian categories, he was often content to understand them in the most banal and ordinary sense. Very fastidious about terminology when the East was involved, he uncritically accepted the use made by his contemporaries of the words philosophy, dogma, mystery, mysticism and many others.

I certainly do not have the intention of writing that introduction to the study of Christianity that Guénon was unable to give us. But I do think that I can contribute to it by gathering evidence where the awareness that ecclesial Tradition had of the nature of its message and rites is confirmed.

Among all the evidence, whether implicit or explicit, provided by the message of revelation, like that of ecclesiastical literature, it seems necessary to go straight to what is essential, since, as I have mentioned, it is now no longer a question of rectifying the views of an author on some more or less secondary points, but of entering into an understanding of the very essence of the Christian *revelatum* such as it offers itself to be seen and heard. Now there is *one* term of scriptural and paleo-Christian terminology in which is summarized the entirety of the Gospel message, a term which we have already encountered in a few texts, but which I have not yet broached for itself: this is the word *mystery;* it is this which forms the central theme of this last part.

In a first chapter (8), essentially devoted to mystery under its doctrinal aspect, we will study the history of the word and the

Introduction

thing in a series of articles which will lead us from the New Testament to the fourth century Fathers. Here I will foster a constant preoccupation to situate the Christian 'mystery' with respect to the Jewish and Hellenistic contexts in which it developed. And we will likewise see what is to be thought about the existence of *secret traditions* in early Christianity, as well as their contents, chiefly with Clement of Alexandria and Origen. Next, I will recall in a second chapter (9) the traditional teaching of the Church in connection with the three rites of *Christian initiation*, and bring up the question of the 'discipline of the secret'. Finally, in the third and last chapter (10), I will attempt to characterize the nature of the *mystical way*, first by searching out the meaning of this term throughout its history, and then I will turn to the teachings of the mystics themselves, at least some of them: thus we will be able to established that we are clearly dealing with an integral way.

8

Mystery and Doctrine

The Mystery of 'Christianity'

Dom Odo Casel, in a justly famous book published in 1932 (*The Mystery of Christian Worship*) wrote:

> Christianity is not a 'religion' nor a confession in the way the last three hundred years would have understood the word: a system of more or less dogmatically certain truths to be accepted and confessed, and of moral commands to be observed or at least accorded recognition. Both elements belong, of course, to Christianity, intellectual structure and moral laws but neither exhausts its essence. [Nor, he adds, is Christianity] a matter of religious sentiment, a more or less emotionally toned attitude.... St Paul thinks of Christianity, the good news, as 'a mystery'. But not merely in the sense of a hidden, mysterious teaching about things of God, as sense [specifies Dom Casel] the word already bore in the philosophy of late antiquity.' [For St Paul] '*mysterium*' means first of all a *deed of God's*, the execution of an everlasting plan of His through an act which proceeds from His eternity, realized in time and the world, and returning once more to Him its goal in eternity.[1]

Dom Casel was probably unaware of Guénon who was unaware of Dom Casel. Nevertheless it might be said that these lines from Casel constitute a kind of response to Guénon's theses on the Christian

---

1. *The Mystery of Christian Worship*, (New York: Crossroad/Herder & Herder, 1997), p9.

Mystery and Doctrine

religion. Perhaps some points would be debatable, points on which contemporary scholarship has concluded in a different direction, in particular for everything touching on the certain Jewish origin of the Christian mystery-complex. Without doubt it is also necessary to object to Casel's underestimation of theology's role, supposing that it is not just a simple reservation, on his part, with respect to the excesses of the triumphing neo-Thomism at that time. However it may be, it should not be denied that there is something incontestably true in Casel's thesis, something that contrasts with the ordinary way of presenting the Christian form and that, quite simply, reveals its essence. In reading his most celebrated work, we become convinced that a truly initiatic sense of the Christian religion is being attested to here, not in an evasive and partial manner, but according to an avowed and integral mode. That such a mystery-based awareness of the nature of Christianity—an awareness which has not remained a dead letter, but which has given birth around the Abbey of Maria-Laach to a powerful liturgical movement, the primary intentions of which have been, alas, slowly deployed[1]—that such an awareness is manifest within the bosom of the Catholic Church in the teachings of a famous and recognized Benedictine, in a most open and decisive

---

1. Dom Casel's work has been quite negatively evaluated in Didier Bonneterre's book (*Le Mouvement liturgique*, Éditions Fideliter, 1980, pp 44–45), which deems that Dom Casel has destroyed the Tridentine doctrine on the Sacrifice of the Mass (the author refers to the twelfth session of the Council of Trent, but the 'twenty-second' should be read). This accusation is tendentious. Dom Casel cites a good part of what is essential in the Tridentine text on the true and real visible sacrifice that is the Mass (*The Mystery of Christian Worship*, pp 40–41) and comments on it excellently. That said, it must be recognized that, in separating the decree on the Eucharist (thirteenth session) from the decree on the sacrifice of the Mass (twenty-second session), the Council has not facilitated the task of those theologians who strive to show the unity of sacrament and sacrificial liturgy. It would be just to recognize this, as does Father Joseph de Ste Marie, O.C.D., in his admirable (but not too well known) book: *L'Eucharistie–Salut du Monde*, Éditions D.M.M., 1982, pp 282–283. That there is a difficulty, if not an impasse here is proven by the size of Marcel Lépin's book (*L'idée du Sacrifice de la messe d'après théologiens depuis les origines jusqu'à nos jours*, Beauchesne, 1926) which had to have no less than 815 octavo pages to explain the subject. On the going astray of the liturgical movement read the testimony of Father Louis Bouyer in *Le métier de théologien*, Éditions France-Empire, 1979, pp 49–80.

Christ the Original Mystery

way, at the beginning of the twentieth century, this is what the pure Guénonian doctrine was absolutely unable to anticipate.

However, what Dom Casel has so vigorously brought to light[1] is in perfect conformity with the letter as well as with the spirit of revelation and by no means constitutes an innovation. Simply to consider the name by the help of which the new religion was designated is enough to show this: I mean the word 'Christianity'.

As we know, the name 'Christian' was bestowed for the first time at Antioch, about 40, on the disciples of Jesus of Nazareth (Acts 11:26)—perhaps by the Roman authorities, since the Jews designated them rather by the name of 'Nazaraeans', and since, among themselves, the disciples called themselves 'saints', 'brothers' or 'disciples'.[2] *Christianos* derives from *Christos,* a term by which the hellenized Jews translated, in the Septuagint, the Hebrew *machiah,* which likewise could be transcribed under the Greco-Latin form *messias,* from which we obtain the English 'messiah'. The Hebrew *machiah* signifies 'anointed', 'consecrated by unction', or again and quite precisely: 'the one who has been marked by unction with a view to exercising a sacred function', as with David who is the 'Anointed' or the 'Messiah of the Lord'. After the Babylonian exile, the sacred kinship having disappeared, it is the High Priest who becomes head of the community. He also is a 'messiah', adorned with the unction by

---

1. Dom Casel maintained that the *philological* (not *theological*) source of the vocabulary of the mysteries in St Paul is to be found in the Hellenistic literature of the Mystery cults. Contemporary scholarship has established, to the contrary, that St Paul and the apostolic Church were inspired by the Greek vocabulary of the Septuagint, as well as by Jewish apocalyptic writings. The proof seems irrefutable (cf. G. Bornkamm, *Theogisches Wörterbuch,* t.IV, s. v. *mysterion,* pp 800–834). Dom J. Dupont points out, for example, that St Paul never speaks of the 'opening' or the 'transmitting' of the mysteries, which stems from the technical terminology of the pagan cults, but of a 'revelation' (*apocalypsis*) of the mysteries; cf. '*Gnosis*'; *La connaissance religieuse dans les épîtres de S. Paul* (Paris: Gabalda, 1949), p 200, n1.

2. Pirot-Clamer, *La Sainte Bible,* Letouzey et Ané, t. XI, 1949, pp 169–170; in the same sense: X. Léon-Dufor, *Dictionnaire du Nouveau Testament,* 2nd ed. (Paris: Seuil, 1975), s.v. 'chrétien', p 165. But the knowledgeable Father Spicq, O.P., deems this attribution impossible; he translates verse 11:26 of Acts in this way: 'For the first time at Antioch, the disciples officially took the title of Christian.' (Cf. 'What the title Christian means', in *Théologie morale du Nouveau Testament* (Paris: Gabalda, 1965), t.1, pp 407–416.

Mystery and Doctrine

which God ordained that Aaron the High Priest be consecrated (Ex. 29:7). Priestly anointing is therefore a real sign of the sacred function: the individual nature is as if effaced under the oil poured out, and ritually identified with the divine action whose support it is here below. This identification of being with function is realized to perfection in Christ's person, the Anointed One par excellence. But what is to be said about this?

Without doubt, this signifies that Jesus of Nazareth is indeed the One who is to come, the 'Desired of the eternal hills'. But, if he fulfils the messianic hope of the Jewish people, this is because he incommensurably surpasses it. He is *the* Christ because, in him, divine action ontologically becomes a sacramental Mystery, becomes the effusive being of Divine Grace.

If we consider the work of Christ, as revealed in the Gospels, we see that it includes first a being, second a teaching, and third an action. This being is, in fact, a work: it is the incarnation by which the Person of the Word unites his Divine Nature to a human nature, through the operation of the Holy Spirit. The first work of Jesus Christ is *to be*, to be there, among us: 'I am.' An act of being by which is introduced into our world the grace of the hypostatic union: Jesus is the very incarnation of grace. From this grace-being flows on the one hand a theological teaching, relative to the knowledge of God (essentially the Trinity), and, on the other, a moral and spiritual teaching (essentially the love of God and neighbor). Insofar as the work of Jesus founds and constitutes the New Covenant, the new religion destined to remain permanently among men, the first form of this work has been accomplished: the redemptive incarnation has taken place and has been completed by the Ascension. It can therefore serve as the designation for this religion (which, from this point of view, might have been called 'incarnationism'). As for the second form of the work, its permanence is assured by memory and tradition for the theological aspect (in this respect the new religion might have been called 'unitrinitarism'), and, for the moral and spiritual aspect, by the practice of the commandments (in this respect the new religion might have been called 'theophilia' or 'caritatism').

But more important and more essential than the work of teaching is the work of Christic action, since it is this that restores humanity to the divine friendship. All the prophets have spoken, no one else has accomplished the act of his own sacrifice 'for the glory of God and the salvation of the world.' Here priest, victim, and sacrificial act are only one. Here the contents of the message is the messenger himself. And this is why Christ is the preeminent priest, because in him, consecrated being and sacerdotal act are identified and are really only one. Thus this third aspect of the work of Jesus of Nazareth can serve to designate the New Covenant in what is most specific to it. And in fact how does the Christic deed, the sum total of all the acts accomplished by Christ, which are founded in the ultimate act of the Cross, how can this deed remain in time, unless by realizing it as well and in its own way, a kind of identification between its being and its acting, that is to say by being, in its specific essence, nothing but rituality or sacramentality, for the rite, so admirably said by Guénon to be the fixation of a deed, is in fact the only mode by which the permanent actuality of an act accomplished once for all can subsist. And this is why the new religion is not a 'Jesusism' (which, beyond the human nature of the One so named, would refer to the personal nature of the Word Incarnate), but a 'christianity', that is, if rightly translated, an 'unctionism' (which refers to a function). From standpoint, Christianity is not a religious reality, a sacred form that would accomplish the distinct ritual acts of its inherent being, but it is, in its essence, rituality or sacramentality in act. And so Christians were well named: not only because they were disciples of Christ, keeping his word and his commandments, but also because they were 'anointed' and sacramentally identified with the unction received. St Cyril of Jerusalem teaches nothing else to the newly confirmed: 'Once privileged to receive the holy Chrisma, you are called Christians.'[1] At the beginning of the same catechesis he even declares:

> As 'partakers of Christ', therefore, you are rightly called 'Christs', i.e., 'anointed ones': it was of you that God said: 'Touch not my Christs' (Ps. 104:15).[2]

---

1. *Mystagogical Lectures*, 3, 5; *The Works of Saint Cyril of Jerusalem*, vol. 2, trans. L.P. McCauley and A.A. Stephenson (Washington, DC: Catholic University of American Press, 1970), p172.

2. Ibid., 3,1; p168.

Mystery and Doctrine

And likewise with St Augustine: 'We are to be joyful and give thanks that we are not only become Christians, but Christ.'[1] The name of Christian to which baptism entitles us (the pouring of water *and* the holy oil) does not, then, signify a belonging to a religious organization called 'Christianity': it designates the *sacramental state* conferred on the very being of the baptized. To be in a state of sacramentality, such is the nature of a 'Christian', of the 'anointed'. This is what St Peter means in his first epistle when he declares that Christians have become a 'royal priesthood' (2:9). Having received the priestly unction, they are by this even dedicated to divine worship.

This doctrine, as we have seen, has been likewise taught by St Thomas Aquinas, who explains that sacraments have two ends: to confer heavenly glory upon us on the one hand, and on the other we are 'deputed to receive, or to bestow on others, things pertaining to the worship of God. And this, properly speaking, is the purpose of the sacramental *character* [the indelible seal conferred by baptism, confirmation and holy orders].[2] Now the whole rite of the Christian religion is derived from Christ's priesthood. Consequently, it is clear that the sacramental character is specially the "Christic character",[3] to whose character the faithful are likened by reason of the sacramental *characters*, which are nothing else than certain participations in Christ's Priesthood, flowing from Christ himself.'[4]

---

1. *Tract. in Joan.*, XXI, 8; cited from Dom Casel, *The Mystery of Christian Worship*, p14.
2. On the notion of sacramental *character*, see above, pp159–163.
3. I so translate *character Christi*, literally the 'character of Christ'; but Christ is not *marked* by a character since, to the contrary, it is he who *marks* the faithful. Therefore we have to understand *character Christi* as signifying: the character 'Christ': it is Christ who is the *character* by which the faithful are marked, and who impresses his image within them.
4. *Summa Theologiae*, III, q.63, a.3. This is also why Christ's priesthood is 'according to the order of Melchisedek', as the Epistle to the Hebrews (5:6, 7:1–18) informs us. Why is this priesthood superior to that of Aaron? Because Melchisedek is 'without genealogy' (*agenealogètos*, Heb. 7:3). To enter into the priestly Melchisedekian order is to enter into a priesthood not transmitted by birth, like the priesthood of Aaron which belongs to the tribe of Levi and requires a Jewish mother. In other words, the Christian priesthood is not tied to a *cast*, is not connected with a transmission by blood, but with a transmission by the Holy Spirit. Here we are in a cultural realm quite different from that of the brahmans in Hinduism, which is only

Christ the Original Mystery

To say 'Christianity' is therefore to say 'unctionism', 'the religion of unction', or even 'the religion of consecration'. In its specific, formal essence, Christianity is a 'sacramentalism', if I might dare use this neologism. And just as the whole Christic deed, all the acts accomplished by Jesus of Nazareth on this earth, is summarized and founded in the ultimate act of his redemptive Passion, so all rites and all sacraments, by which the permanent actuality of the Christic deed is assured until the end of the world, are summarized and founded in the ultimate rite of the sacrificial Memorial of his Passion. In short, this signifies that Christianity is identified with the ritual action of the Divine Liturgy. From this point of view, that of its formal specificity, it is perfectly just to say, with Dom Casel, that Christianity is a mystery religion by essence, since Mystery can be defined as That which, in the Divine Work (the Mystery of salvation) comes to inform and configure human action so that it becomes a sacramental anamnesis, forming in this way an initiatic community separated from the world of profane action.[1] And, in fact, the participation of the faithful in this ritual configuration in act truly and very really *initiates* them into the very Life of God and sacramentally

---

explained if we admit that the Christic priesthood rightly constitutes the supreme form of the universal priesthood. Assuredly, it is still a form and not the very essence of priesthood (which refers us back to the trinitarian mystery). This is why this priesthood is named 'according to the order of Melchisedek', that is to say most exactly (from the Hebrew *'al-dibrati*) 'in the manner of', 'according to the Melchisedekian type': Christ is not a member of an order at the head of which would be Melchisedek; but, to the contrary, it is Melchisedek who is 'in the likeness of the Son of God' (*aphômoiômenos*—a hapax—*tô uiô tou théou*, Heb. 7:3; a patristic dossier on this question will be found in J. Tourniac, *Melkitsedeq ou la Tradition primordiale*, Albin Michel, 1983). And, for anyone accepting the Guénonian interpretation concerning the 'King of Salem', the form of the Christian priesthood would have to be considered as being a manifestation of the 'Agarthic' priesthood as such. However, I should add that, even though the 'Melchisedekian' priesthood of Christ is without genealogy, independent of both 'race' (Heb. 7:6) and blood, its operative power nevertheless resides in the Blood of the crucified Word. But this is no longer that blood transmitted by nature, it is the Blood poured forth and communicated by the Spirit. Blood is still, then, the vehicle of the Covenant. Through the shedding of his Blood, Jesus Christ the Jew makes of the community of believers the new Israel, for 'salvation comes from the Jews' (John 4:22).

1. O. Casel, op. cit., pp 53–54.

Mystery and Doctrine

unites them with his redemptive action. This is why the mention of '*Mysterium fidei*', inserted by the Church at a very early date into the scriptural formula of eucharistic consecration, should be understood only in the sense of the miracle of transubstantiation to which faith alone enables us to gain access, but more profoundly as designating the '*mysterium*-object' that constitutes what is essential for the Christian faith, the 'grace-laden *sacramentum* in which the entire (objective) faith, the whole divine order of salvation is comprised.'[1]

By everything I have just explained, we see what initiatic sense it is appropriate to attribute to the designation of the new religion as a 'Christianity'.[2] If we are to take this designation seriously, we will have to conclude that the religion so named, the New Covenant in the Blood of Christ, constitutes the preeminent *Mysterion*.

We have grasped Christianity, then, according to its specific form, namely according to the ritual and sacramental action by which its

---

1. J. A. Jungmann, *The Mass of the Roman Rite, its Origins and Development*, vol. 2 (New York: Benziger Brothers, 1955), p201. To be specific: it is not the consecrated wine in as much as 'object' that constitutes the *mysterium fidei*, but the act of the eucharistic sacrifice in its entirety seen in its objective reality, an act from which the transubstantiated bread and wine cannot be detached. After all, it must be granted that the Eucharist was celebrated from the Church's origins (on the day after Pentecost), and before any of the Gospels were written. Hence the consecratory formula used by the Church is prior to the evangelic and Pauline accounts of the eucharistic institution. It was necessarily transmitted orally and dates back, Tradition says, to St Peter.

2. Although *christianos* (= Christian) is mentioned for the first time in the Acts of the Apostles (11:26), the term *christianismos* (= Christianity) is hardly less ancient, since its first known mention dates back to St Ignatius of Antioch and is to be read in a letter that he wrote to the Christians of the Church of Magnesia (*Magn.*, x, 1 and 3). The term is opposed there to 'Judaism' (*joudaïsmos*), which indicates a clear awareness of the difference between the two religions, contrary to the theses which would make of original Christianity a simple esoteric form of Judaism, and which thus attests to such a tendency among some Christians. 'It is absurd to profess Christ Jesus, and to Judaize. For *Christianity* did not embrace *Judaism*, but *Judaism Christianity*, that so every tongue which believeth might be gathered together to God.' This letter was, without doubt, drafted within the first years of the year 100, which proves that *Christianity* was already in use at that time. As for *Judaism*, 'it was already standard at least since the Maccabean period' (2 *Macc.*, 11, 21, etc.; S. C. 10, p105), that is to say about 200 BC. We likewise encounter *joudaïsmos* in St Paul: Gal. 1:13–14.

Christ the Original Mystery

realizes its existence, by which it is rendered historically and concretely present among us. The Church is essentially liturgy, and this is why the temple where this liturgy, this *mysterion*, unfolds is also called a 'church': the place of passage, the place of Pascha, the place of approach and of the way which leads us from without to within, from loss to salvation, from the servitude of sin to the deliverance of love. And yet, however central and essential it may be, ritual activity does not exhaust the totality of Christ's mystery: Christ is not only *Way*, he is also *Truth* and *Life*. On the one hand, entry into his mystery requires a conversion and an adherence to a *body of truths* (the articles of the Creed), to a doctrine which, from the start, is necessarily proposed to the intellect; on the other hand, the realization of the *mysterion* can only have for an end the interior transformation of the Christian and his accession to the spiritual life. The Christian disciple thus proceeds from the mystery-truth to the mystery-life through the grace of the mystery-way. Curiously, the history of the word *mysterion* in the Christianity of the first centuries seems to illustrate this process, since, over the course of three hundred years (until the beginning of the fourth century), it had an almost exclusively doctrinal sense; next it was applied as a designation for the Christian sacraments, before serving to characterize, under the adjectival form *mystikos*, supernatural knowledge and the realities which are its object. Without doubt this evolution is not linear and it would be good to strongly nuance this outline. Nevertheless, its validity on the whole is incontestable, as is recognized by numerous scholars.[1] It is this evolution, then, which will dictate the succession of my last three chapters, the first devoted to the doctrine of the mysteries, the second to sacramental initiation, and the last one t the mystical life. However, I do not want it thought that I am according to this semantic evolution the value of a verification, through their historical development, of determinations implicitly contained in the concept of *mysterion*. This (Hegelian) view is not completely

---

1. Especially Louis Bouyer in his book *The Christian Mystery, From Pagan Myth to Christian Mysticism*, trans. Illtyd Trethowan (Edinburgh, Scotland: T & T Clark, 1990; certain conclusions of this masterly and intriguing synthesis, concerning neoplatonism in particular, seem arguable.

Mystery and Doctrine

false. But neither should we neglect certain 'contingencies' which have contributed to this evolution. In particular, we have to take into account the fact that the origin of the word *mysterion* is neither Jewish nor Christian, but pagan, and that the exclusively ritual-related use that the Greeks made of it prohibited the Christians from first applying it to the sacraments. At least it is probable to suppose this if we want to explain why this application was so late and only occurred at the beginning of the fourth century. After all, the Christians were most vividly aware of the abyss which separated the mystery cults from the rites of the New Covenant. This is why, before broaching a study of the doctrinal *mysterion* in Christianity, we need to study the cultic *mysterion* in paganism, otherwise we would be inclined to see in the awareness of this difference only a manifestation of a feeling of superiority proper to every religion. As we will see, there is nothing to this.

The 'Mysteries' of Paganism

Obviously this is not a matter of exhaustively treating a subject (the nature of the mystery cults and their influence on Christianity) which would fill several volumes. The question of relationships between the pagan mysteries and Pauline doctrine alone has given rise to an immense literature.[1] But, as I have already stressed, contemporary science has found that the notion of *mysterion*, such as it appears in the New Testament, is theologically of Jewish origin. It is the Old Testament use of the word *mysterion* in the Septuagint version which authorized the Synoptics to take it up again. This is also the use made of it by 'Jewish apocalyptic', an expression by which is designated the body of (canonical or apocryphal) texts which appeared in quantity between 200 BC and AD 100, and which claim

---

1. Whoever wishes to be informed about the historiography relative to the question of the Greek mysteries in St, Paul, the *Dictionnaire Apologétique de la Foi Catholique*, with its article 'Les mystères païens et saint Paul' (col. 984–1014), offers a quite complete panorama (up until 1913, its date of publication).

Christ the Original Mystery

to reveal (*apocalupsis* = unveiling) the secrets of the heavenly world and its eventual future manifestation. This Jewish apocalyptic constitutes a dominant current at the time of Christ[1] and St Paul knew it very well. As for the *mysterion* of the Septuagint, it appears in the late books of the Old Testament (Tobit, Judith, Wisdom, Sirac, Daniel and 2 Maccabees) to translate the Aramaic *râz* or the Hebrew *sôd* which designate a 'secret thing'.[2]

Nevertheless, as certain as the Old Testament affiliation for *mysterion* may be, the question of a Greek term borrowed from Hellenistic culture remains, a term which should therefore show some affinity of meaning with the Semitic terms for which it was substituted: hence the need for a brief historical glance over the meaning of the word and the realities that it designated.

Etymology and Vocabulary

Contrary to common opinion, the etymology of this word is obscure. *Mysterion* (to be pronounced *musterion*, the *y* being used in Latin to transcribe the Greek *u*) is composed of the radical *mus-* and the suffix *-terion*. This radical has often been made to derive from the verb *muo* = 'I close the lips'.[3] Many specialists now think a 'folk etymology' is involved.[4] More likely it should be related to the verb *mueo*, which will later signify 'to initiate into the mysteries'; as this verb also takes a contracted form *muo*, it might appear to be identical with the verb *muo*, but in reality it is nothing of the sort: such, in particular, is the opinion of Fr Festugière, an expert Hellenist if there

---

1. Cf. Cardinal Jean Daniélou, *The Theology of Jewish Christianity*, trans. J.A. Baker (London: Darton, Longman & Todd, 1964) p118 ff.

2. *Vocabulaire de théologie biblique*, dir., X. Léon Dufour (Paris: Cerf, 1977), p807, who points out that *râz* and *sôd* 'figure side by side in the texts of Qumran.'

3. Henri Estienne, for example, in his monumental *Thesarus Linguae Latinae* (1572), republished by Firmin-Didot (1842–46); and G. Bornkamm, in Kittel, *Theologisches Wörterbuch zum Neuen Testament*, Stuttgart, 1933, etc., t. IV, pp809–10.

4. Walter Burkert, *Ancient Mystery Cults* (Cambridge, MA: Harvard, 1987), p137, n36.

Mystery and Doctrine

ever was one.[1] However it may be, 'the verbal root *my(s)-* seems to be attested in Mycenian Greek, possibly for the initiation of an official.'[2] As for the suffix *-terion*, it frequently serves to designate the place relative to the action or the state signified by the radical with which it is associated; thus: *baptisterion* = bathing-room (baptistry), *telesterion* = building for initiations, *chreterion* = oracular chamber, *monasterion* = dwelling for solitaries (monastery), etc. Is this what we are dealing with here? It is not impossible: an inscription was found at Sardis in which *musterion* indicates a 'hall of the mystes', but in other inscriptions it designates a 'ritual banquet' or even 'the secret revealed by the divinity' (epitaph of an Eleusinian hierophant).[3] Most often, however, the word is in the plural (*musteria*) and designates 'festivals in Mycenaean as well as in later Greek.'[4] Just as frequently as *musteria*, *mustes* (= the myste) designates the 'initiate', the one who has received initiation, but equally the 'initiator'. As for *mueo*, it is less frequent and is hardly used except in the passive form, *muesthai* with the infinitive (= to be initiated, to receive initiation), hence *mustes*. Likewise note, as belonging to the same family, the adjective *mustikos* which, then, literally means 'initiatic', 'secret', or 'relative to the mysteries': e.g., *ta mustika* = the sacred realities or the secrets. Finally there is *muesis*, which signifies 'initiation'.

To this word family derived from *mus*, another one should be added which forms a competing line and is built up from another radical, namely: *tel-*, which are evidently confronted with in *telos*, the 'goal', the 'end', the 'term'; hence the idea of perfection, accomplishment, completion. The sense is, however, less exclusively initiatic than for the words of the *musterion family*. *Telein* (with the infinitive) therefore signifies 'to initiate', but also 'to accomplish' or 'to celebrate'; *telete* (*teletai* in the plural) designates 'initiation', but also 'feast' or 'rite'; *telestes*, the 'initiation priest'; etc.[5]

---

1. *Le monde gréco-romain au temps de Notre-Seigneur*, Bloud et Gay, 1935, t.II, p169.
2. Burkert, op. cit., p8. Mycenian is an archaic form of Classical Greek, inscriptions of which were discovered at Mycenae (about 800 BC).
3. Festugière, op. cit., pp168–169.
4. Burkert, op. cit., p8.
5. Ibid., p9.

Christ the Original Mystery

One last semantic remark: when I say that *muesis* or *telete* signify initiation, I only mean to conform to the usage of the Latins, in particular to Cicero who has played an important role in the construction of the philosophical and mystery-related vocabulary of Latin. It is in this way that the words *initia* (the 'sacred realities'), *initiatio* ('initiation') and *initiare* ('to initiate') were chosen to translate *musteria*, *muesis* and *muein*, setting forever the initiatic vocabulary for Latin Christianity and all the West. Let me stress that, although in Greek the idea of *telos*, of end or completion, has served as the designation for initiation; in Latin it is the idea of start and beginning, or even the idea of 'going into', of 'penetrating into something': *initium* and *in-ire*.

We have studied the word *musterion* (which I will henceforth write *mysterion*), but what about the thing itself? As I stated at the beginning, it is out of the question to treat such a complex matter in a few pages. It will be enough to raise some rather surprising points for whoever, on this subject, holds to the image generally given to it by esoteric literature, and, for the remainder, I will refer to already cited works.[1]

Aristotle, in a famous formula which will be returned to by Dionysius the Areopagite in particular, informs us that 'in the mysteries it is more a question of experiencing (*pathein*) than of knowing (*mathein*).'[2] This formula, the importance of which should not be exaggerated given its author, shows that in the pagan mysteries the doctrinal part is secondary, or even non-existent, with respect to 'religious life'. When one broaches the study of Greek religion, what is striking is the difficulty at having any precise idea of what a Greek believed. If we consider the manifestations of the public cults, that is to say the 'religion of a city', many historians think that mythological

---

1. An ample bibliography is to be found at the end of Burkert's book.
2. This precious testimony of the young Aristotle (Fragment 15) has been preserved for us by Synesius of Cyrene (*Dion.*, 48A); cf. N. Turchi, *Fontes Historiae Mysteriorum Aevi Hellenistici*, Roma, 1930, n° 83, p53. It is impossible to translate into French [or English] the play on words between *pathein* and *mathein*. It turns up again with Dionysius the Areopagite in his *Divine Names* (II, 9; P.G., t.III, col. 648B): 'not only learning but also experiencing the divine things (*ou monon mathôn alla pathôn ta théia*).

Mystery and Doctrine

teachings play only a quite minor role, and perhaps not even any role.[1] On the other hand, what seems clear is that these exterior cults (agrarian, familial and civic) could not satisfy the truly spiritual needs inherent to human nature.[2] Hence the need for a more interior rituality able to provoke an extraordinary experience putting the initiate in a more or less direct contact with the divine. Such seems to me to be the function of the 'mystery cults'. Their history is long and complex, it assumes more and more diversified forms to the extent that it approaches its end (the fifth century of our era).[3] The immense reputation which they enjoyed and the impressive aura surrounding them certainly resulted, at least in part, from the contrast that they offered with a particularly 'exoteric' civil religion. That said, those features which ordinarily characterize the *musteria* in western imagination have become less and less relevant to the very extent that our knowledge of them progresses.

---

1. Mythology and philosophy, the work of poets and philosophers, concern only the cultivated part of the population. 'This work of organization and unification... hardly influenced religion properly so called, the one expressed in the cults' (F. Vian, 'Grèce archaïque et classique', *Histoire des religions*, Pléiade, t.I, p538). The same judgement from the reverend Festugière: 'Nothing is more confused, more complex, harder to analyze... than the relationships between myth and rite among the Greeks. There are tales—those of Homer—which are pure fabulation and have nothing to do with religion.' But, obviously, the personages of the gods and goddesses, above all under the statuary form, play an important role (*Études de religion grecque et hellénistique*, Vrin, 1972, pp234–235).

2. The fundamental separation of the 'race of men' from the 'race of the gods' (Pindar) 'is at the base of Greek morality; man should neither aspire to become a god nor act like one, otherwise he would be guilty of immoderation, the most serious of crimes... Between man and God, communion is no longer involved', but only 'contractual relationships' (Vian, op. cit., p503); 'the majority of official manifestations seem devoid of a true religious spirit' (ibid., p524).

3. It is thought that the Eleusinian Mysteries were inaugurated in the fifteenth century BC; cf. G.E. Mylonas, *Eleusis and the Eleusinian Mysteries*, Princeton, 1961, p41. But it is certain that they experienced a heightened importance on the basis of a new organization from the sixth century BC—which confirms what Guénon has said about this pivotal date.

Christ the Original Mystery

General Characteristics of the Pagan Mysteries

The secret is the first specific point; it corresponds to what I have called formal esoterism. Now, although the majority of the *mysteria* were covered by an obligation to silence, all secret rites were not *mysteria*, such as the individual practice of magic. Some, like the reverend Festugière, think that the connotation of esoterism in the *mysteria* is, in reality, 'evanescent';[1] thus *mysteria* can designate public festivals organized by a city, like the 'Great Mysteries' of Athens.[2] Nevertheless, it is certain that, quite often, the rule imposes being silent about what happens at the time of initiation. This silence was symbolized by a wooden basket, which was confided to the initiate and which he had to keep, the *cista mystica*. On the whole, this secret has been respected. This is why we should not speak, like F. Cumont, of a 'shipwreck' of the literature of the mysteries, for the simple reason that this literature never existed. The *mysteria* were *arrheta*, 'unspeakable', because speech was powerless to express them, and not because they had to be hidden.[3] In short, the obligation to veil was itself only the symbol of their properly ineffable nature, at least if we view things in the most favorable light.

The second point to detain us concerns the communal or social aspect of the question. We readily imagine that the existence of Antiquity's *mysteria* should be accompanied by the existence corresponding initiatic organizations. It seems that this is a mistake. It has to be noted from the outset that initiation to the mysteries was, in general, by no means reserved for a small number of duly qualified adepts. In reality, as Herodotus informs us with respect to the Eleusinian Mysteries: 'Whoever of the Athenians and the other Greeks wishes, is initiated.'[4] On the other hand, anyone initiated to one god can turn to other gods and receive as many initiations as he

---

1. *Le monde gréco-romain au temps de Notre-Seigneur,* p169.
2. Burkert, op. cit., pp8–11.
3. Ibid., p69.
4. *Histories,* VIII, 65; Burkert, op. cit., pp10–11. Likewise: 'the characteristic of the mysteries which interests us here (the Great Mysteries of Athens organized each year at Eleusis) is that they are always open to all Greeks (women and slaves included).

Mystery and Doctrine

judges good.¹ Doubtless, they join a *thiase*, a form of community (*koinon*) which reminds us of an initiatic organization as defined by Guénon, but one quits it a little like one quits a club after being admitted to it.² The inscriptions left concerning the Bacchic Mysteries, show that a quite public search for honors was often involved.³ There was, moreover, no general term to designate initiates to a particular mystery cult: it is modern scholars who speaks of 'Dionysiacs', 'Eleusinians', 'Mithraics', etc. Finally, and this feature does not agree with the Guénonian conception, children were admitted to receive initiation without any problem. Thus, a Roman funeral stele of the fourth century informs us (in Greek) that the deceased, dead at seven years old, 'had already been made a priest of all the gods: first of Bona Dea, then of the Mother of the Gods and of Dionysus Kathegemon'.⁴ In the Bacchic Mysteries, these initiations of children 'frequently appear... even at Eleusis there was a 'child from the hearth' initiated at each festival.'⁵ As we see, a Greek initiate would not have understood it when the initiatic nature of a

---

The only condition for admittance indicated, by the hierophant of Eleusis' 'proclamation', is the use of the Greek language and the absence of that stain of murder, which is just as disqualifying for all religious acts' (Louis Gernet and André Boulanger, *Le genie grec dans la religion*, Albin Michel, 1970, p270). The number of Eleusinian initiates (many were foreigners) seems to have been considerable. Herodotus speaks of a procession of thirty thousand people (ibid., p271). To qualify such public rites as 'great mysteries' would be no doubt surprising to a reader of Guénon. And yet it is a fact. Devoted to Demeter, the Eleusinian Mysteries constituted the 'greater mysteries'. The 'lesser mysteries' were those of Agra (a suburb of Athens), into which it was necessary to be initiated first to gain access (after a minimum delay of seven months) to those of Eleusis (ibid., p275). To refer the latter to the obtaining of the divine state and the former to the obtaining of the primordial state is without support in archeological data: the texts speak only of a 'sharing of the gods' dwelling-place' (cf. *Phaedo*, 69c).

1. Burkert, op. cit., p49, speaks of 'the almost tedious multiplication of priesthoods and initiations... between AD 360 and 390.'

2. On the *thiases*, cf. Aristotle, *Nichomachian Ethics*, VIII, 1160A 15–25; Festugière, *Études de religion grecque et hellénistique*, pp15–18.

3. Burkert, op. cit., p41; the liturgies of the mysteries (meals, processions, etc.) were costly and an occasion to display one's wealth.

4. Ibid., p28.

5. Ibid., p52; the same testimony in Plutarch's *De Iside* (32, 364E) which informs us that Klea was 'consecrated' by 'father and mother' to the Egyptian gods.

Christ the Original Mystery

rite, baptism for example, is denied under the pretext that it is administered to a child.

It seems necessary to conclude that, in general, there has never existed, and taking into account the extreme diversity of situations, any 'mystery communities'.[1] What, in some respects, comes close to this is the existence of initiatic functions vested in certain aristocratic family lineages (the Eumolpides for example), which would assure a certain permanence of the institution through time.[2] If something of the mystery initiations of antiquity, in Greece or in Italy, beyond the fifth century, it is without doubt in the bosom of a few very ancient families.[3] Likewise we should admit that the members of the 'clergy' who assured the functioning of the mysteries constituted a group rather stable in space and time. But it is not the same for 'lay' initiates. In brief, there was nothing similar in the pagan mysteries to what early Christianity called an *Ekklesia*. This term, which dates back to the Septugint but which will be ultimately rejected by the Jews for the sake of *synagoge* (its synonym), is derived from a Greek verb which means 'to call', 'to con-voke', that is 'to assemble by voice' (*ek-kaleo*): it is the Word of God which creates an *Ekklesia*.[4] This *Ekklésia* subsists by itself across time and space. It encompasses not only a clergy of initiators, but also the assembly of all the initiated that it forms into a single Body perfectly complete in itself and independent of civil society. Such a reality 'has no equivalent in pagan religion', even Reitzenstein had to acknowledge this.[5] To which should be added care for the poor, an economic mutual assistance, and a moral enhancement (the condemnation of homosexuality, prostitution and the exposure of infants) about which the pagan world had no idea.[6]

---

1. *Mysteriengemeinden;* a concept invented by Reitzenstein (1927). It has been abandoned today (Burkert, op. cit., pp30 and 114.
2. Burkert, p34.
3. Cf. Alexandre de Danann, *La mémoire du sang,* Archè, Milano, 1990.
4. *Ekklesia,* in koine Greek, designates a political assembly of the people.
5. Burkert, p51.
6. Antiquity practiced this mode of 'birth control': the unwanted new-born were exposed in public places (public squares, crossroads, etc.) provided for this end and abandoned until they died or were taken in.

Mystery and Doctrine

The third point concerns the relationship of the mysteries to theological doctrine. As already indicated, this relationship is extremely problematic. Here also, it is Christianity which has taught us to consider that the community of initiates is united not only by a common rite, but even by an adherence to a single transcendent truth, the proclamation of which is required at the time of (baptismal) initiation. There was nothing like it in any of the Greek mysteries, not even in the Mithraic Mysteries, which did seem, however, to come nearer than others to an initiatic organization such as 'Masonry for example'.[1] Plato already deplored, in *Letter VII* (333E), that the fraternity that joins the initiates to the mysteries, whether mystes or epoptes (the ultimate degree of initiation) are involved, was not based on the unity of a true philosophic doctrine. And Aristotle, as we have seen, affirms that those who are initiated do not have to *learn* something but *experience* a certain 'lived' something. The meaning of this formula should certainly not be strained: it puts the accent on revelatory experience rather than dispensing with the existence of some kind of knowledge.[2] Nevertheless, we know that the mysteries, especially those of Eleusis, contained a 'revelation' presented under the form of three distinct rites: the *dromena*, the *legomena*, and the *deiknumena*. The *dromena* were the liturgical dramas, the mythological scenarios of which were probably evocative of the soul's posthumous destiny. The *legomena* accompanied the *dromena*. If *dromena* signified '(things) done' (cf. epics [Fr. *chansons de 'gestes'*, literally 'deed-songs']), *legomena* signified '(things) said', words pronounced. But can we consider them to be the expression of a teaching? This *legomena* comprised 'perhaps mythological commentaries and genealogies.'[3] Most certainly they also consisted of

---

1. Burkert, p 41. Still, it is right to ask if there is a Masonic doctrine, since this organization imposes no other dogma than that of an especially accommodating and speculatively rather inconsistent 'humanism'.

2. Robert Brachet, in an original and well-documented work, *L'Âme religieuse de jeune Aristote*, Éditions Saint-Paul, 1990, pp 80–87, sees this fragment as an indirect disclosure of the Philosopher, revealing the profoundly religious nature of his soul.

3. Francis Vian, 'Grèce archaïque et classique', *Histoire de religions*, t. 1, p 556. The most recent histories have a tendency to reevaluate the (relative) importance of *legomena* in initiation, which earlier histories considered to be very weak. Their function in the whole complex remains, however, quite modest. Without doubt it

Christ the Original Mystery

sacred words, brief and elliptical invocations which were designated by the name of *sunthema* (*sunthemata* in the plural), that is 'passwords', or even by the name of *sumbola*, literally the 'symbols'. Thus Plutarch writes, with respect to those (Epicurius and his disciples) who deny the soul's immortality: 'this is a doctrine by which they hinder you from believing the teachings of our fathers as well as the mystical formulas (*mystika symbola*) of the cult of Dionysus, the knowledge of which we others share.'[1] As for the *deiknumena* (the term signifies '[things] shown'), this is a question of sacred objects, the *hiéra*, of portable size (they were carried in procession by the priestesses), the sight of which should provoke a 'revelation', an 'illumination' for an epopte (whose name signified 'one who has seen'). We are ignorant of the nature of these objects. In any case, they are what constitute the essential and supreme moment of initiation.

As we see, if we keep to what can be known with some certainty of the mystery liturgies, the communication of a secret and transcendent doctrine holds little or no place. This is also, as Burkert says, because 'ritual does not need explicit theology to be effective'; and he adds that there is 'not the slightest evidence to support Reitzenstein's assertion that mystery communities were held together by fixed forms of a Credo.'[2] Once more we are measuring here the gap which separates the celebration of the pagan mysteries from the celebration of the Christian mysteries.

---

likewise has to be admitted that changes have intervened over the course of time, especially under the influence of Orphism that introduced written texts into the mysteries, there where originally only ritual and the mythic word came into play

1. *Consolation for his wife* (*Consolatio ad uxorum*, Plan. 23), 10, 611e; edited and translated by Jean Hani: Plutarque, *Œuvres morales*, t. VIII, Traités 42–45, Les Belles Lettres, 1980, p197. This knowledgeable Hellenist specifies in a note (ibid., p256) that here *mystika symbola* would not be designating 'sacred objects used for initiation and which the initiate would preserve as a souvenir. It is rather a question of formulas which accompanied the unfolding initiatic ritual, and therefore of the *synthemata*. He adds that, among the Pythagoreans, it is customary to designate precepts and teachings by the name of *symbola*; just as Christians have applied the name *symbolon* as a designation for the *Credo*; cf *Le Mystère du signe*, pp43–47.

2. Op. cit., p46. He is alluding to the work—famous in its time—of R. Reitzenstein: *Die hellenistichen Mysterienreligionen nach ihrer Grundgedanken und Wirkungen*, 3rd ed., 1927, p23. Many historians have concluded in the same vein as Burkert;

Mystery and Doctrine

This is not to say that we have to exclude, for all that, the idea that the mystery rituals worked with an implicit theology which, outside of the liturgical celebrations, might form the object of a doctrinal teaching. However, it needs stating that this doctrine had either nothing very fixed about it, or was being more or less confused with *philosophy*, entertaining complex relationships of complicity and rivalry with this discipline. Thus Plato the philosopher denounces the 'soothsayers [who] go to rich men's doors and make them believe that they... have accumulated a treasure of power,' and who, invoking 'a bushel of books of Musaeus and Orpheus' promise to redeem the injustices committed in this life 'by means of sacrifices... and also [by] special rites for the defunct, which they call initiations.'[1] The 'modernity' of Plato's remarks will be readily appreciated. Conversely, the discourse that he has Diotima, a priestess of Mantinea, hold in the *Symposium* is a veritable mystagogy. It is also certain that to those who complain that 'the "craftsmen" of private mysteries just take the money but do not lead their clients to "knowledge",' some more discreet mystagogues recommend calling upon philosophy to provide more revealing explanations.[2] One inscription in Rome's central Mithraeum, which offers an astronomical interpretation of the bull sacrifice, designates this science by the name *philosophia interna*, that is 'esoteric philosophy'.[3] But we had to wait for Plutarch (50–125) for a metaphysical interpretation, evidently in the lineage of Platonism, of the mystery liturgies to

---

thus Gernet and Boulanger write: as for the question 'of knowing if there is a teaching dispensed by the mysteries... here the response can only be decidedly negative' (*La génie grec dans la religion*, p 275). With respect to the eschatological doctrines implicitly taught in the Eleusinian Mysteries, J. Rudhardt writes: 'A panegyrist of the Mysteries, Isocrates enumerates the advantages that they promise with significant imprecision: Eleusis was not possessed of an eschatology as rigorously elaborated as the myths mentioned by Plato' (*Notions fondamentales de la Pensée religieuse et actes constitutifs du culte dans la Grèce Classique*, Picard, 2nd ed., 1992, p 119).

1. *Republic*, II, 364B–365A; trans. Paul Shorey, *Plato, The Collected Dialogues* (Princeton, NJ: Princeton University Press, 1961), pp 611–612. [Shorey translates *teleateasin* as 'functions'. The *initiations* of the French text is retained here.]
2. This is what the *Deverni Papyrus* tells us; cf. Burkert, op. cit., p 72.
3. Ibid., p 84.

Christ the Original Mystery

appear.¹ But to what extent does this interpretation correspond to the implicit theology of the mysteries? This is a difficult question; and as for what concerns the Mysteries of Isis and Osiris, Jean Hani thinks the relationship problematic: it is a Greek (Plutarch) who is thinking over an Egyptian myth.² However, it has also happened that one Numenius of Apamea (a Greek philosopher of the second century AD) had had the feeling of having 'betrayed the secret of Eleusis through philosophy.'³ In short, here we are dealing with what I have called a speculative hermeneutic, and the question of its relationship to the findings yielded by the archaeology of the mysteries clearly might have not exactly the meaning that the histories envision. For the symbols of the mystery liturgies also have an *intrinsic* significance: that it may not be perceived by those who accomplish them is not enough to make it invalid. Is this not what Macrobius seems to indicate when he declares that

> the mysteries themselves are hidden in the tunnels of a figurative expression, in such a way that, even for initiates, the nature of such realities cannot be presented nakedly, but there is only an elite who are in the know, by means of a wisdom-filled interpretation, while the rest are satisfied with venerating the mystery, protected from banality by these figurative expressions.⁴

However that may be, we should not doubt that, between the second and fifth centuries, a philosophic effort was to be witnessed, especially among the Neoplatonists,—undoubtedly in the hope of taking up the challenge of an unexpected and *despised* rival (Christianity)— to endow the philosophic way with a dimension of ritual and mystery (Proclus for instance), or, conversely, to confer a philosophic truth on the theurgy of the mysteries (Iamblicus for instance, who composed his treatise *On the Egyptian Mysteries* to respond to the 'anti-theurgist' critics of his teacher Porphyry). On this point my

---

1. Cf. Jean Hani, *La religion égyptienne dans la pensé de Plutarque*, Les Belles Lettres, 1976.
2. Ibid., pp 228–232.
3. Burkert, p 85, who refers to Macrobius, *Commentary on the 'Dream of Scipio'*, I, 19, where this fragment from Numenius is to be found.
4. *'Dream of Scipio'*, I, 2, 17 ff; Burkert, p 79.

Mystery and Doctrine

conclusion is: in their properly liturgical accomplishment, no metaphysical teaching was included in the pagan mysteries, or, in any case, that part was miniscule; but their symbolism has given rise to, lately if we bear in mind their two-thousand-year duration, an explicit theology that can be called 'esoteric philosophy' *(philosophia interna)*, and that, by virtue of its nature as a pure speculative hermeneutic, could be neither secret nor even less inexpressible. We will see in a moment how far we are from the Christian theological order.

The fourth point to broach concerns what Burkert calls the 'extraordinary experience', in other words: what effects does a mystery initiation produce in the initiate's soul? As before, I will keep to what is strictly necessary, to what seems essential from the Christian point of view.

That they did produce an effect, that they were the occasion of an 'extraordinary experience' as suggested by Aristotle's formula, should be undeniable. Dom Casel recognized this explicitly. He writes to a correspondent:

> You say that the pagan mysteries bestow only an 'illusion', while the Christian mysteries procure the reality. For my part I would prefer to say that the pagan mysteries indeed bestow a reality, but that this reality remains a prisoner to cosmic forces.[1]

This remark, as we will see, is in perfect agreement with St Paul's teaching. It is also confirmed by the growing importance of theurgy, and even magic, in the mysteries. But was it only that? In fact, the difficulty of appreciating the nature of the effects produced by mystery initiations is not just recent. Proclus already admitted it at a time (about 450) when, certainly, the Eleusinian Mysteries had been gone for fifty years, but when some initiates well known to him were still alive. He writes:

> That the myths on the other hand also have an influence over the common herd is proven by the initiations. For the latter, making use of myths to enclose the truth about the gods, are for souls, in

---

1. Letter to B.R. of October 31, 1944. Cf. *The Mystery of Christian Worship*, p 61.

a manner unknowable and divine to us, causes of a community of affect (*sym-pathéia*) for what concerns the rites accomplished (*dromena*). So that, among those initiated, some without doubt remain stricken with stupor, filled as they are with supernatural terror, but others enter into a communion of disposition with the sacred symbols, and, having gone out of themselves, are entirely fixed in the gods and penetrated with the divine.[1]

In the *sym-patheia* of Proclus we can recognize the *pathein* of Aristotle: this 'community of affect' is sometimes interpreted as a kind of hebetude, sometimes as a form of exaltation, if not ecstasy, by which one communicates with the deity, but a deity of a secondary order (the 'gods'), quite far from union with the transcendent One. Without doubt, this is the reason why Proclus ranks initiates with the 'common heard', which will surprise more than one modern reader.

To summarize, the most common characteristic of the archaeological data is that initiation assures a good posthumous destiny, whereas those who have not received it will only know an inert state or frightful torments after death. And this is almost all that anyone can say about it. A good deal of latitude is needed to see in all this something which recalls, even distantly, the distinction between salvation and deliverance.

Pagan Mysteries and Christian Sacraments

Finally, one last point remains to be examined to close this inquiry. Many historians of the nineteenth century—and some from the

---

1. *Commentarire sur la 'République'*, (Kroll, II, 108, 18–24), 16th Dissertation; translation and notes by J. A. Festugière, Vrin-C.N.R.S., 1970, t.III, pp 51–52. Proclus had been instructed, moreover, in theurgy by Asclepigeneia, the daughter of Plutarch of Athens (not to be confused with the famous Plutarch of Chernea cited previously), and grand-daughter of the 'great Nestorios', an Eleusinian hierophant (cf. Marinus, *La vie de Proclus*, 28, in: Proclus, *Commentaire sur le Parménide*, translation and notes by A. Ed. Chaignet, 1900, t.I, p 32) who could, we are told, make it rain, evoke Hecate, perform wonderful healings, etc.

Mystery and Doctrine

twentieth—have thought that baptism and the eucharist were only a return to and an imitation of mystery liturgies. But what about today? Is it still possible to see in the rites of the pagan cults the models for the Christian sacraments?

First let us recall that the pagan intellectuals themselves often reproached the Christians for having plagiarized rites of the mystery liturgies: Celsus for instance, an anti-Christian philosopher who, around 170, wrote a *Discourse on Truth,* a good part of which Origen has preserved for us in his refutation of it (*Contra Celsum*). In this Greek's eyes there is nothing original in Christianity: its doctrine and morality are, as to what is essential, poorly understood Plato; other teachings come from the Mithraic Mysteries, the Egyptian myths of Typhon, Horus and Osiris, the Kabiric Mysteries, and, obviously, Jewish tradition.[1] At the end of the fourth century, Faustus, a Manichean who combatted St Augustine, attacked Christians in this way:

> The sacrifices you change into love-feasts, the idols into martyrs, to whom you pray as they do to their idols.... You keep the same holidays as the Gentiles; for example, the calends and the solstices....[2]

In short, the Christians are thieves and plagiarizers (an accusation that Christians, such as St Clement of Alexandria and Dionysius the Areopagite, send back to the Greeks). But modern scholarship does not confirm the judgment of these intellectuals—which all pagans did not share however, many to the contrary being struck by the unheard of (and therefore unacceptable) nature of the Christian message; hence the persecutions. I will mention the case of the two essential sacraments: baptism and the eucharist.

As for what concerns the bath of spiritual regeneration that is the baptismal rite, certainly a number of mystery liturgies seem to present us with its equivalent: they include a rite of lustration, by water or other elements, which symbolizes a death followed by a

---

1. *Against Celsus,* VI, 1–VII, 58; cf. chiefly: Pierre de Labriolle, *La réaction païenne. Étude sur la polémique antichrétienne du Ier au VIe siècle,* L'Artisan du Livre, 1950, pp 118 ff., pp 450–451, etc.

2. St Augustine, *Contra Faustum,* XX, 4 (P.L., t. XLII, col. 370); Labriolle, p 45.

Christ the Original Mystery

rebirth. In connection with the Isiac Mysteries, the only text 'in the first person' that we have of an initiation account is cited in the *Metamorphoses*, of Apuleius,[1] an initiation which ought to be received 'as the equivalent of a voluntary death and a freely granted salvation.'[2] 'I approached the frontier of death, I set foot on the threshold of Persephone, I journeyed through all the elements and came back, I saw at midnight the sun sparkling in white light, I came close to the gods of the upper and the nether world and adored them near at hand.' Likewise, the sacrifice of the taurobolium, practised in the cults of Cybele and Attis (about the second century AD) can be seen as a kind of baptism. Prudentius, a Christian writer from the end of the fourth century, describes this spectacular, if not repugnant rite. The initiate descends into a ditch covered by planks pierced with holes upon which a bull, whose blood he receives, is immolated:

> He offers his head to the defilement of this torrent which sullies his clothing and his entire body. He holds out his face, cheeks, lips, nostrils, even his tongue, until he is wholly soaked with blood; he then issues from the ditch and everyone greets and worships him closely.[3]

Nevertheless, under these easily registered exterior similarities, today the differences appear much greater than was imagined. They are essentially related to the nature of what is accomplished, which, in Christianity, is bound up with the death and resurrection of Christ, in which the Christian initiate very really participates, the essence of the baptismal rite consisting precisely in a dying and being reborn with Christ, as St Paul states. But *there is nothing of the like in the pagan myths and mysteries*: many are the gods and goddesses to die and be reborn, but no God incarnate dies and is risen while making of this Passover the sacrament of the death and resurrection of the initiates. This is why Burkert concludes:

---

1. XI, 23, 6–8; Burkert, p97.
2. *Metamorphoses*, XI, 21, 1. The other name (not devoid of humor) for this philosophico-initiatic fiction is *The Golden Ass*. Apuleius, a Neo-Platonist of the second century AD., was accused of having used magic to marry a rich widow.
3. *Peristephanon*, X, 1011, seq.; Labriolle, p348, n5.

Mystery and Doctrine

To sum up, there is a dynamic paradox of death and life in all the mysteries ... but there is nothing as explicit and resounding as the passages in the New Testament ... concerning dying with Christ and spiritual rebirth.[1]

As to the form of the baptismal rite, which derives, beyond any doubt, from a Jewish practice (with borrowings of some secondary elements from the pagan mysteries), we have to admit that 'there is hardly any evidence for baptism in pagan mysteries, though this has often been claimed.'[2] Here, as in so many other realms, a metaphysical precision and a spiritual depth are projected onto the sacrality of the ancients which, it needs must be declared, have only made their appearance with Christ.

As much now needs to be said about the eucharistic sacrifice. There surely exists, in the majority of mystery celebrations, ritual meals during which are consumed, among other things, the flesh of sacrificed animals. After all, this is an altogether universal fact of the history of religions. And besides, certain Christian writers of the first centuries have themselves stressed the similarities between the sacred feasts of the pagans and the eucharistic ritual. This is the case with St Justin, 'philosopher and martyr', in relation to the cult of Mithra. As we know, this divinity of Indo-Iranian origin invaded the West (with the exception of Greece) in the first century AD. and at that time gave birth to a mystery cult whose prodigious success, in Renan's words, was on the point of counterbalancing that of Christianity. From Italy to England, the map of Mithraic sanctuaries covers Europe. The essential act of the cult is accomplished by Mithras sacrificing the bull (tauroctony). The commemoration of Mithras Tauroctone was celebrated in the course of a sacred meal in which

---

1. Burkert, p101. On this topic let us recall the outcome arrived at by Wahib Atallah, which he has recorded in his doctoral thesis: *Adonis dans la littérature et l'art grec*, Paris, 1966. Despite the assertions of some historians, he has found, prior to Christianity, no text enabling us to interpret a return of Adonis to the earth, after his death and infernal sojourn, as a resurrection. It is indeed necessary to agree, the Pascal event represents, among the totality of ancient cultures, something altogether new.

2. Burkert, ibid.

Christ the Original Mystery

bread and water were offered. St Justin sees there a diabolic imitation of the Christian rite:

> Here, in the mysteries of Mithra, the wicked devils have imitated commanding the same thing to be done. For, that bread and a cup of water are placed with certain incantations in the mystic rites of one who is being initiated.[1]

This is not all. We find in the Mithraeum of St Prisca, at Rome, a Latin inscription which reads: '*et nos servasti... sanguine fuso*', that is: 'you preserved us ... by shedding the blood.' At mid-sentence is to be found an illegible word; the reading first proposed: *eternali*, 'eternal (blood), has been ultimately rejected.'[2]

But we see the differences as to the theological essence of the rite: they are radical. First, what about the 'salvation' brought by the bull's shed blood? If we translate *servasti* by 'you have preserved', 'kept', rather than by 'saved', this is precisely to avoid all ambiguity: it is in fact impossible to attribute to the Mithaic feast—the sacramental nature of which is quite dubious[3]—a properly spiritual significance, surpassing the cosmological level. Essentially, the shed blood assures the vivification of earthly existence. On the other hand, this blood is not that of a god; Mithras neither dies, nor is resurrected. Moreover, in a general way, whether the cult of Mithras or other cults are involved, in the majority of sacred meals—if not even in all cases—it is never a question of 'eating the god'.[4] Finally, the characteristic simplicity and poverty of the eucharist should be added, whereas the sacred banquets of paganism were very expensive and consumed a great quantity of food and drink.

---

1. *I Apologia*, LXVI.
2. Burkert, pp111–112.
3. Mircea Eliade, in *A History of Religious Ideas*, vol. 2, trans. W.R. Trask (Chicago: University of Chicago Press, 1982), p328, leans rather toward 'ritual banquets common in the imperial era.' I have become aware of Robert Turcan's work: *Mithra et le mithriacisme* (Les Belles Lettres, 1993) too late to be able to take it into account, but a cursory reading seems to confirm my conclusions.
4. Burkert, p111, refutes this thesis chiefly supported by J.G. Fraser in his famous *Golden Bough*.

Mystery and Doctrine

Perhaps we can grasp here what is most specific to the Christian difference. A moment ago I asked about the extraordinary experience that the mystery cults procured for their adepts. This experience should not be doubted, insofar as it is not excluded that it was accompanied by the support of a powerful visual and auditory production. Several participants, Plutarch and the just cited Proclus, describe for us the frenzy and 'divine possession' that seizes the initiate. But can we speak of a mystical ravishing, analogous to the one that certain Christian or Hindu (*samadhi*) experiences take into account? The data to warrant this is lacking. And so Burkert can conclude: 'No ecstasy in the full sense can be credited to Eleusis, and even less to the cult of Isis or Mithras.'[1] But what seems certain, abiding by the texts remaining from early Christian literature, is that it is not the absence of all extraordinary, or even spectacular experience (the Apostles, issuing from the Upper Room, after the fire of Pentecost, seemed drunken, and the charisms subsequent to the reception of baptism are well known), but it is its on the whole secondary character in the actual experience of the baptismal and eucharistic liturgies: for the Christian initiate, the essential is elsewhere. Hence the sometimes modest appearance of the sacramental liturgies, in any case beyond any common measure with those of the pagan liturgies. What is realized, in the sacramental operation, is of another order: beyond a 'psychic experience', the Christian initiates were aware of gaining access to an ontologically spiritual ('pneumatic') level, of which the natural individual (the 'psychic man' of St Paul) would have no direct perception, an access which is accomplished in an entitative and interior participation in the saving work of Christ. There is here—however favorably one is disposed to interpret it—something that seems foreign to the mystery experience of paganism.

---

1. Burkert, p113.

Christ the Original Mystery

The Theological 'Mysterion' in the New Testament

In the Gospels

Everything that I have unfolded here basically has but a single end: to restore to the Christian reader of our time the understanding of the Word of faith. If we could hear the Gospel texts with the cultural soul of a hellenized Christian of the first centuries, many of the difficulties that we come up against would quite simply not exist, for frequently they only consist in a loss of meaning. One patent example of such a loss is the term *mysterion,* as is proven by some of Guénon's texts that I have quoted on this subject, and according to which, when Antiquity speaks about 'mysteries', it is speaking about 'esoterism', but when Christianity uses this same term, it inaugurates the era of exoteric formulations and doctrinal lack of intelligence. Now there is here a glaring misreading which it is good to be aware of and measure its gravity.

When the evangelists chose, in imitation of the Septuagint, the term *mysterion* to translate what Jesus Christ named *raz* in Aramean (*sod* in Hebrew), they knew quite well the meaning that this word had received in pagan culture.[1] Assuredly it was subject, like other terms that have become canonical, to a profound modification, unknown to that culture. This is even, here, a general law of the Christian process of inculturation, that is of the process by which Christian revelation is inserted into a preexisting cultural tradition: by assuming its forms, it tears them away from their first setting and gives them a new meaning. However the innovation itself will only

---

1. The existence of the pagan mysteries is mentioned in the *Book of Wisdom* in two places (14:15 and 14:23) to denounce their profoundly immoral nature: 'celebrating infanticide initiations or hidden mysteries, or furious orgies in strange solemnities.' The *Book of Wisdom* (called *Wisdom of Solomon* in the original Greek, but this is a literary fiction) dates from the first half of the first century BC.

Mystery and Doctrine

be understood by those to whom it is addressed provided that the former meaning lends itself to this transformation. It is this former meaning that I have just shown. Therefore, it is to this that we have to refer if we are to grasp the connotations that the use of the word *mysterion* implied for the early Christians, because it is *out of* this meaning the Christian transformation is wrought. The result of all this is that, to understand the New Testament's *mysterion* in its original meaning, it is appropriate to not start with the significance conferred on it by modern languages. Not that this meaning is false, or improper. But a characteristic and even, the truth to tell, altogether essential note is lacking to it, the note of a 'sacred reality'.

When we read in St Mark (4:11): 'he said to them: to you it is given to know the *mysterion*[1] of the kingdom of God: but to them that are *without*, all things are done in parables,' this involves not just the revelation of a secret, and even less the enunciation of an incomprehensible truth, but first and foremost the communication of an altogether transcendent and properly unheard of Reality to the disciples, a truly theological Reality, the reception of which distinguishes by this very fact those who receive it from those 'without' (*exo*). The mystery of the Kingdom is mentioned by Christ in connection with the parable of the Sower: it constitutes the key to its interpretation. Now this parable is itself the hermeneutic key for evangelic preaching and therefore of the Christic Word, which somehow makes of

---

1. This is the only place in the Gospels where *mysterion* is in the singular. In the parallel passages of Matthew (13:11) and Luke (8:10), we read *ta mysteria:* 'the mysteries of the Kingdom' ('of heaven' in Matthew, 'of God' in Luke). Father Carmignac in *Le Mirage de l'eschatologie* (Letouzey et Ané, 1979, pp 26–27), prefers to speak here of 'Reign' rather than 'Kingdom'. But he maintains that *mysterion* must be translated by 'mystery' (and not by 'secret' as A.J. Festugière does in his translation of *La Bonne Nouvelle de Jésus-Christ selon Marc* (Paris: Cerf, 1992), p19; the reason being that at Qumran the Aramean *raz* is employed 'with a profoundly theological significance.' As for the use of the singular of this term, Louis Bouyer thinks—and rightly so—that its origin must be attributed to Jesus himself: it is Jesus who effects this transition from the plural of Jewish apocalyptic (the mysteries) to the unique mystery where everything is united and revealed (*The Christian Mystery*, p95). St Paul returns to this usage, as we will see: he employs *mysterion* in the singular and sometimes without even a noun complement, designating in this way the Mystery par excellence.

this parable the major parable of the Gospel as such. A parable is, in fact, a 'speech form' composed into a symbolic story which has for its object the teaching of the theological, spiritual or moral truths of revelation. Now, we find that, among all the parables, it is the one which has for its object, not truths of faith, but the word (Fr. *parole*) itself in the act of its evangelic proclamation. The parable of the Sower is therefore the parable of the word (Fr. *parole*) which is itself always of a 'parabolic' nature.[1] We see the importance that must be attributed to this, and why it is on precisely this occasion that Christ, in order to summarize the totality of his Good News, speaks of the *mysterion* of the Kingdom. I have proposed to examine what Christian tradition has to say about itself, in what light it situates its own message. With the evangelic mention of the *mysterion*, we are undoubtedly in the presence of such an indication: no longer does it fall within the domain of kerygma as such, but within the domain of a metakerygmatic instance, or even, if you like, of the hermeneutic order.

Mysterion is, then, the vocable by which Jesus typifies the entirety of his teaching's content, insofar as this content is not solely composed of a body of knowledge, but is identified with the very Reality that this knowledge reveals, for here the Word is a Being and an Act: Jesus Christ himself effecting our salvation. This is precisely what *mysterion* signifies, and the reason for Christ's use of it: a Word, and therefore an understanding, which is also, and inseparably, a Being and an Act. This is why, to the question: Is an esoteric teaching in the sense of a formal esoterism involved here? the response can only be nuanced. On the one hand, the parable informs us that the Word is given to everyone since it is sown everywhere, on the rocks and among the thorns, as well as in the good earth. But on the other hand, only those into whose interiority the Word has entered, enter into the most essential interiority of this Word, into the mysteriousness and mystery of its interiority. Now to these Christ indubitably

---

1. This is what Christ himself teaches to his disciples: 'Are you ignorant of this parable [of the Sower]? And how shall you know all parables?' (Mark 4:13). As for the relationship of parable to word [Fr. *parole*], it is all the more evident as the latter is only a phonetic alteration of the former: *parabola > parole*.

Mystery and Doctrine

communicates a reserved or, if you like, secret teaching. This secret is the one spoken about in the Gospel of St John, if one agrees to see this Gospel in its entirety as a revelatory echo of the ineffable dialogue that the Father and Son exchange in eternity and that John heard when his head rested on the Savior's breast. It is to this dialogue that Matthew and Luke allude when they teach that: 'no one knoweth the Son, but the Father: neither doth any one know the Father, but the Son, and he to whom it shall please the Son to reveal him' (Matt. 11:27). In this sense, I subscribe to the thesis of Father Bouyer when he declares:

> we have to accept, perhaps even more emphatically than Jeremias did himself, his conclusion that Jesus, in addition to his public teaching to the crowds, had also another, private to the Twelve and perhaps some other trusted disciples.[1]

It will be observed, however, that, in St Mark, Jesus does not oppose to those 'without' the especially designated category of those 'within', as if it were a question of two kinds of formally and statically constituted listeners. It is actually the reception of the manifested Word—and not a formal categorization—which differentiates the disciples from 'those without', because the proclamation of the message already forms an integral part of the Kingdom.[2] It is the very gift of this mystery, that is the unheard of revelation of the Son of God's salvific undertaking. Here we rediscover Casel's conception of the *mysterion* according to which it is identical to what Christians of the East call 'economy', the expression and revelation of 'theology' in time.[3]

---

1. *The Christian Mystery*, p 114.
2. Is there a 'secret gospel' of Mark? Morton Smith has discovered a letter mentioning such a gospel, a letter which he thinks attributable to Clement of Alexandria; cf. *Clement of Alexandria and a Secret Gospel of Mark,* Cambridge, Mass., 1973. This attribution has been disputed: Gedaliahu Guy Stroumsa, *Savoir et Salut,* Cerf, p 139.
3. In Greek the work 'economy' (*oikonomia*) is from the same root as the word 'house' (*oïka*): economy is the law of the house. Now, as we will see, for Origen the teaching of the mystery is the one given 'in the house'.

Christ the Original Mystery

With St Paul

With St Paul we encounter the most frequent use of *mysterion* (twenty-one times), without any doubt, those uses which are the most related to the language of the pagan mysteries. This is all the more surprising because St Paul, Apostle to the Gentiles, that is the *Goyim,* is chiefly addressing the pagans: he thus runs the risk of promoting confusions. But, precisely, the *mysterion* that Christ has given him as a mission to reveal is that the pagans are inheritors of salvation:

> I am made a minister according to the dispensation of God, which is given me towards you, that I may fulfil the word of God: the *mysterion* which hath been hidden from ages and generations, but now is manifested to his saints, to whom God would make known the riches of the glory of this *mysterion* among the Gentiles, which is Christ in you, [and] the hope of glory.[1]

Likewise, and more fully, he specifies in Ephesians (3:3–9):

> According to revelation, the *mysterion* has been made known to me, as I have written above in a few words; as you reading, may understand my knowledge in the mystery of Christ, which in other generations was not known to the sons of men, as it is now revealed to his holy apostles and prophets in the Spirit: that the Gentiles should be fellow heirs, and of the same body, and co-partners of his promise in Christ Jesus, by the gospel: of which I am made a minister.... To me, the least of all the saints, is given this grace, to preach among the Gentiles, the unsearchable riches of Christ, and to enlighten all men, that they may see what is the economy of the *mysterion* which hath been hidden from eternity in God, who created all things.[2]

---

1. Col. 1:25–27, according to Father Prat's translation (*The Theology of Saint Paul*, trans. John L. Stoddard (Westminster, MD: The Newman Bookshop, 1926–1927), vol. II, p 6. 'Christ in you' and 'the hope of glory' constitute two aspects of the *mysterion*: it is given for now *and* it will be completed in glory.

2. Prat, ibid., p 6; notice the relationship between economy and mystery.

Mystery and Doctrine

It is impossible to affirm more clearly that the revelation of the *mysterion* of Christ is, quite exactly, that of its *intrinsic universality*.

For the mystery hidden to the generations is not only that the pagan nations are henceforth admitted to salvation, in such a way that the preaching to the Gentiles would constitute the very definition of this mystery and would exhaust it by realizing it. The hidden and now revealed, the confirmed and made known mystery is Christ himself viewed in his intrinsic nature as universal Redeemer. That Christ is the Messiah promised to Israel, this mystery was in no way hidden from the previous generations: he was, to the contrary, known about and hoped for. But that this Messiah is *in reality* the Savior of the entire world as St John says (4:42), that is something, it seems, which has never appeared in the annals of human history.

As we see, *mysterion* here, as elsewhere in the Gospels, does not signify 'secret', 'occult' or 'hidden' at least chiefly; in the first place it designates a transcendent reality which can, without doubt, be the object of a veiling, but which can also be the object of a revelation, without losing, for all that, its name *mysterion*.[1] In other words, it is still necessary to go even further than we have until now, or, in any case, we need to be a little more explicit than we have been, if, as St Paul asks, we wish to appreciate 'the knowledge [that he has] of the *mysterion* of Christ,' a significant and singular formula.

The universality of the Christic revelation is not, for St Paul, an accidental fact of the knowledge of Christ. It represents, to the contrary, an essential and central truth: it is *the* mystery par excellence, it is the very essence of Christian revelation: to have knowledge of Christian revelation is to understand that. Now such a *mysterion* is not only hidden by a scriptural (Old Testament) silence; that the Scriptures have not spoken about it only constitutes, on the whole, an accidental and somehow contingent veiling. But it is hidden 'in the silence of the eternal ages', that is within God himself, in the heart of his Essence. This is what St Paul declares most solemnly in the final doxology of the *Epistle to the Romans* (16:25–26):

---

1. Father Prat is not of this opinion: *mysterion* signifying 'secret' for him, this secret has ceased to be one 'since it has now been revealed' (ibid., p383). Attentively read, St Paul's text does not seem to authorize, *stricto sensu*, such an interpretation.

Christ the Original Mystery

> [Glory] to him that is able to establish you,
> according to my gospel,
> and the preaching of Jesus Christ,
> the revelation of the *mystery*
> enveloped with silence for eternal ages,
> and now is made manifest by the scriptures of the prophets
> according to the precept of the eternal God.

Thus the 'Silence' in which this *mysterion* has been enveloped is the 'Abyss' of the Divine Essence; this is what St Paul suggests when he defines the nature of his preaching (1 Cor. 2:6–10):

> Howbeit we speak wisdom among the perfect: yet not the wisdom of this world, neither of the princes of this world that come to nought; but we speak the wisdom of God in a *mysterion*, a wisdom which is hidden, which God ordained before the world, unto our glory.... But to us God hath revealed them, by this Spirit. For the Spirit searcheth all things, yea, the abysses of God.

Do we need to be reminded that the two terms 'Silence' (*Sige*) and 'Abyss' (*Bathys*) designate, among the Alexandrians, what Guénon calls Non-Being?[1] However that may be, it is clear that the revelation of the universality of salvation in Christ is viewed by St Paul as the 'economic' expression of a 'theological' Reality. On this subject, notice once more the proximity of the words *mysterion* and *oikonomia* in the Pauline text. St Paul declares—as we have seen—that to him, 'the least', has been entrusted the task of showing 'what is the *economy of the mystery*' (Eph. 3:9); and already in 1 Corinthians (4:1), he asks that we look on the disciples as '*economes* [stewards] *of the mysteries* of Christ'.

The universality of the proclamation (*kerygma*) of the *mysterion* does not, then, basically correspond to a desire for proselytism, to a need that the apostle Paul would have experienced to see everyone 'be like him' through a kind of hegemonic will to eliminate differences. Even less are we dealing with an extrinsic or quasi-accidental claim of the 'Christianity is a universalist religion' type. But what St

---

1. *The Multiple States of the Being*, (Ghent, NY: Sophia Perennis, 2001), p 41, n10.

Mystery and Doctrine

Paul tells us is that he has become aware of the true dimension of this Christic *mysterion*, of its true nature. And there is here something so extraordinary, so unheard of, that Saul the hellenized Jew, an expert among the experts of the religious sciences, was shaken from top to bottom, thrown to the ground with light, and filled with a stupefying revelation: if the kerygma of Christ Jesus is 'for all men', this is because in this Christ resides the *mysterion* of the *religio universalis*, the secret of the universal Covenant of all things with all things and with God. In him, those who were 'afar off' have been 'made nigh', for it is he who has made of the two worlds only one 'breaking down the middle wall' separating them (Eph. 2:13–15), so that in him 'there is neither Jew nor Greek, neither bond nor free, neither male nor female' (Gal. 3:28). And this *religio universalis*, this universal covenant to which everyone is called, flows from the very nature of Christ, and constitutes the very essence of his *function* in the universal history of salvation. If it is by Christ that it has pleased God to lead all things to him, 'reconciling all things unto himself, making peace through the blood of his cross, both as to the things that are on earth, and the things that are in heaven' (Col. 1:19–20), this is because 'in him dwelleth all the fullness (*pleroma*) of the Godhead corporeally' (Col. 2:9). That is 'the *mysterion* which hath been hidden from ages and generations, but now is manifested,' the *mysterion* of which Paul is the minister (Col. 1:25–26) and whose mission it is to make it known. It is the mystery of the One

> Who is the icon of the invisible God,
> the firstborn of every creature,
> for in him were all things created
> in heaven and on earth,
> visible and invisible,
> whether thrones, or dominations, or principalities, or powers:
> all things were created by him and for him.
> And he is before all, and by him all things subsist. (Col. 1:15–17)

At once theological and economic, as we see, the Pauline *mysterion* has hardly any relationship with the *mysterion* of the mystery cults. It is situated on a metaphysical level without any equivalent in the religious forms of paganism.

Christ the Original Mystery

One last point worthy of mention: although Paul uses *mysterion* to name that knowledge, received by revelation, of the transcendent and operative reality of Christ, he employs no other term from the vocabulary of the pagan mysteries. We find in him neither *telete* or *muesis* (initiation), neither *telesmenos* nor *mustes* (initiate), nor *hierophantes* (initiator), nor *epopteia* (contemplation).[1] In short, outside of *mysterion,* the ritual and liturgical terminology of the mystery cults is absent in St Paul, as elsewhere in the body of the New Testament. In return, with him as in the other apostolic writings, *mysterion* takes on an essentially doctrinal significance which is itself absent from pagan literature. As for those reasons which allow the absence of cult terminology in the New Testament texts to be explained, there is nothing fortuitous here: this can only involve an express will affirming the awareness that the apostles have of the radical novelty of the Christian sacraments with respect to a still very much alive pagan rituality. Three centuries later things will no longer be the same. But we also have to take into account the deep-rootedness of Christian rituality in Jewish sacrality: it is in 'the organization of worship' that 'Jewish Christianity has made its deepest and most enduring mark on the Christian Church.'[2]

The Triple 'Mysterion' of Christian Doctrine

Up until now we have not encountered, in the canon of Scripture, any text in which *mysterion* or *mysteria* (the mysteries) would designate 'incomprehensible doctrines'. Neither will we encounter this in the writings left by Christian tradition during the three following centuries. In return, and in the lineage of Paul and Mark, we find an abundance of passages in which these terms have an almost exclusively *doctrinal* significance. Here we have a distinctive mark of

---

1. Prat, op. cit., p389.
2. Jean Daniélou, *The Theology of Jewish Christianity*, trans. and ed. John A. Baker (London: Darton, Longman & Todd, 1964), p315.

Mystery and Doctrine

nascent Christianity. I have said how modest was the place of teaching in the mystery cults, which were often reduced to a sometimes spectacular, but ever meticulous and engrossing ritualism. The converted 'barbarians' were only too inclined to see religious life and the new obligations imposed on them only under the form of a certainly different, but just as engrossing ritualism. And they do so insofar as this is, in fact, all that a change of cult in antiquity demanded, a change which never required the rejection of one theology for another. This is why the Church, since its origins and save for exceptions, was led to accentuate the importance of teaching the doctrine of the faith and the intellectual adherence that this demanded. It is to the point that this distinctive trait has been turned into ridicule by Christianity's adversaries. Tertullian relates that, at the end of the second century, a wild-beast tamer exhibited a caricature of Christ in the streets of Carthage, representing him *book in hand*.[1] This association of a book with Christ, which can be observed on the mosaics and sarcophagi of the fourth and fifth centuries, is to be found in all Christian iconography, Byzantine and Medieval in particular. The interrogations of persecuted Christians, who carry the treasure of the Gospels and St Paul's letters with them in a coffer, also testify to this.[2]

Here we have a first specification of the Christian doctrinal *mysterion*, namely the *mysterion* of the Scriptures: an open mystery since reading is enough to become aware of it, and yet a closed mystery, because it is not enough to know how to read to understand what is being said. It is also necessary to know of what and Whom the Book speaks. Hence the importance of the second specification of this doctrinal *mysterion* to be considered now, which is constituted by the enunciation of the doctrine of faith, which the *Apostles Creed*

---

1. *Apology*, xvi. Involved is a representation of an 'ass-headed' Christ. Here is the passage: 'a certain vile man who was wont to hire himself out to cheat the wild beasts... exhibited a picture with this inscription: *The God of the Christians, born of an ass* (*Deus Christianorum onochoetes*). He had the ears of an ass, was hoofed in one foot, carried a book, and wore a toga.'

2. 'L'Écriture au service de la catéchèse' by Yves-Marie Duval, in *Le monde latin antique et la Bible,* under the direction of Jacques Fontaine and Charles Piétri, Beauchesne, 1985, p 263.

Christ the Original Mystery

summarizes and which Christ has taught to his disciples, but which is not explicitly revealed in the Scriptures.

To grasp the importance of this doctrine of faith (the 'canon' or the 'rule of truth'), I first need to stress a de facto situation that Christians were immediately aware of and that accounts for many facts of Church history. This situation has been brought to light by the work of historians interested in what, in English, is called the problem of Christianity's *self-definition:* how have the Christians seen themselves and how have they been distinguished from others? This question is essential for the last part of my research. Now the most obvious trait of this care for identification,[1] is that 'no known mode of identifying ethnic and religious groups' could serve Christians in expressing their specificity:[2] neither ethnic origin (they are neither 'Greeks, Jews or barbarians'), nor language, nor their place of residence (they inhabit 'Greek as well as barbarian cities' the various languages of which they speak), nor way of life (they follow 'the customs of the natives in respect to clothing and food'), nor their political behavior ('as citizens, they share in all things with others').[3] All that can be said of the 'religion' of the Christians is that it is a *mysterion* that could never be learned 'from any mortal'.[4] Only doctrine remains, a doctrine which will enable Christians to identify each other and to be distinguished from non-Christians. As G.G. Stroumsa notes, 'All frontiers—and a collectivity as new and fragile as primitive Christianity felt an urgent need to lay out such frontiers—have to be of an *ideological* nature, namely categorical options relative to religious truth.'[5] Although the term ideology

---

1. I say 'identification' and not 'identity' because the first Christians had no doubt about the latter: they knew who they were and named themselves in conformity with their essence: *christianoi*. But this involves knowing what consequences flow from this essential identity for Christian existence and how it might be formally signified.

2. Guy Stroumsa, *Savoir et Salut,* p175. The author refers to R.A. Markus, 'The Problem of Self-Definition: from Sect to Church', in Sanders (ed.), *Jewish and Christian Self-Definition,* vol. 1, pp1–15, 217–219.

3. All quotes in parentheses are drawn from an anonymous writing of the second century entitled *To Diognetus,* v, 2–4.

4. Ibid., IV, 6.

5. *Savoir et Salut,* p175.

Mystery and Doctrine

is misplaced here—he should have spoken of doctrine or theology—this remark is most accurate. This is precisely why heresies are inevitable, and why they were so numerous right from the beginnings of the new religion, a phenomenon rather unique in the history of ancient religions. If 'there must be also heresies', according to the word of St Paul (1 Cor. 11:19), this is because they testify *a contrario* that Christianity is first a doctrine of truth: 'it is the very quality of its search for truth, the lofty nobility of its quest, which has divided Christianity into sects.' Thus, for an Origen, by virtue of its existence as doctrine 'Christianity is no different than any other veridic branch of knowledge, such as philosophy or medicine.'[1]

Here we rediscover the fundamental importance of the 'rule of faith', that is the doctrinal *canon* by which Christians are united across time and space: hence the name *Symbol* that this canon receives—the word *sym-bolon* signifying 'con-junction' etymologically. With this *Symbol* Christians are mutually united and identified, and they basically have no other 'password', no other 'sign of recognition'.

As for the expression 'rule of faith', or other such similar ones, that are to be met with in the Church literature of the first centuries, I will first point out that it does not designate 'a formal principle, a criterium for religious truth distinct from truth itself, from the teaching of *what* is transmitted. The rule of piety and truth is not the authority of the ministers as such, it is what is kept and transmitted by them.'[2] On the other hand, neither does this 'rule' form a system of propositions which are logically deduced from each other; it enunciates 'dogmas' that are so many 'theological facts', which could not be established deductively and which the Christian understanding should 'hold as one', should gather together to form the whole of a doctrinal corpus. The *Symbol of Faith* [Creed] is, then a 'symbol'

---

1. Ibid., Stroumsa is without doubt alluding to a text from *Contra Celsum* (v, 61) in which Origen replies to the accusations of Celsus by stressing that, comparable to Christianity, philosophy and medicine recognized a multiplicity of sects.

2. Cardinal Congar, *La Tradition et les traditions*, t.1: *Essai historique*, Fayard, 1960, p 45.

Christ the Original Mystery

(or conjunction) not only extrinsically because it gathers together Christians scattered throughout the world, but also intrinsically because it is itself the assemblage, the composition of fundamental axioms defining in a necessary and sufficient way the doctrinal identity card of Christian revelation. It is not, then, an *explanation* of this revelation, a metaphysical working out of its theoretical intelligibility—this would be the work of speculative theology which exercises a veritable magisterium of gnosis—but it is a *defining formulation* of it, or, if preferred, a determinative formulation: it tells *what is to be believed*, by a kind of 'theological positivism' which is situated exactly at the interface between pure 'logic' and the opaqueness of the pure *revelatum*. And that is why this doctrinal icon (Christian dogmatics) clearly constitutes a *mysterion*. No other religion, I think, has been officially identified in this way with such a *Symbol of Faith*.

However, the *mysterion* of Scripture and the *mysterion* of the Canon of truth are not enough to constitute the integral Christian doctrinal Mystery. For it is not enough to know the Word of God and about what and Whom it speaks; the relationship between the scriptural mystery and the mystery of faith must also be made intelligible, as much as it can be, which requires that the believer possess some intellectual keys as much exegetical as theological in nature: exegetical to explain how the Scripture can speak *in this way* about its Divine Object, and theological (basically: trinitarian theology, Christology, and soteriology) to work out an understanding of the Object of faith, namely, precisely in what and Whom one believes, and to verify that such an Object has indeed been actually designated by Scripture—going from Scripture to faith and from faith to Scripture.

Now this third specification of the *mysterion* is presented with somewhat different characteristics. If the first *mysterion* is accessible to all and if the second is so to the baptized believer, the third seems to be much more secret and reserved. Recall here St Mark's previously cited text (and the parallel synoptic passages): Christ himself teaches that knowledge of the *mysterion* involves the interpretation of his teaching 'in parables'. In fact, as Origen indicates, 'the Evangelists kept secret the explanation which Jesus gave of the greater

Mystery and Doctrine

number of the parables,'[1] so that the interpretation of these parables is no less esoteric than that of the Apocalypse, that is of the revelations made to John in which are hidden 'ineffable mysteries'![2]

We are, then, in the presence of a much debated theme of the existence of secret traditions in the first centuries of Christianity. Some will perhaps be surprised to see me combine this theme with that of the rule of faith: how can I rank under the same term of *mysterion* the dogmatic formulary of the Christian faith openly proclaimed and the secret hermeneutics of the parables?

I am nevertheless only conforming to the usage of the Church Fathers. The difficulty is not in proving it—evidence abounds. It resides rather in extremely complex historical data, a complexity which happens to amplify certain modern ways of seeing things (and sometimes of not seeing things). The data is complex because it overlaps and intermingles, to the very extent that a single datum needs to be appreciated in terms of various demands, which themselves imply certain perhaps debatable, and rarely debated, preconceptions. Thus we hear talk of 'tradition', 'secret', 'apostolic origin', 'rule of truth', 'discipline of the secret', 'gnosis', 'mysteries of Scripture', 'doctrinal' or 'sacramental esoterism', 'Jewish apocalyptic', etc. And all these categories are brought into historical discourse as if they were self-evident and as if it was enough to utter them to classify religious phenomena, and even to explain them. Without doubt these expressions often correspond to incontestable facts, but the qualification of these facts obviously stems from the preconceived ideas of the historian, which are those of the cultural milieu in which he is formed.

On the other hand, it has to be stressed that a single historical datum can serve for attesting to the existence of varied and even contradictory religious themes, which makes the stating of these themes rather difficult and dooms it to be taken back.

---

1. *Com. Mth.*, XIV, 2; cited by J. Daniélou, *Gospel Message and Hellenistic Culture*, trans. 2nd ed., John A. Baker (London: Darton, Longman & Todd, 1973), p 455.

2. *First Principles*, IV, 2, 3; trans. R. A. Greer, *Origen* (New York: Paulist Press, 1979), p 495.

Christ the Original Mystery

Finally, neither should the existence of these secret traditions be represented after the image offered of them by modern and contemporary occultism, which is quite strongly marked by Romantic occultism. For modern esoterism, if there were secret traditions, this is necessarily because their contents were incompatible with the official doctrine known to all; both the doctrine of faith and the hermeneutic of scriptural arcana should not be equally qualified with *mysterion*. But, in reality, neither was the doctrine of faith as open as is claimed (I will even show that it was covered by the discipline of the secret for several centuries), nor was the hermeneutic tradition as closed as might be supposed. The distinctions posed, at the beginning of this work, between real and essential esoterism and formal and accidental esoterism should, it seems, allow for a more nuanced and more exact appreciation of the facts.

Having made these remarks, we can proceed with an examination of these more or less secret traditions, communicated by Christ to a few apostles. It is a question, as I have stated, on the basis of St Mark's text, of teachings coming directly from the Word Incarnate, and dealing at once with the theology of the doctrinal Canon and with the exegesis of scriptural symbols.

As to the first point, for which there is no positive evidence, we are on the whole reduced to hypotheses, and yet to me its existence is not in doubt. Certainly, it is hard to imagine Christ in the role of a teacher of philosophy. Nevertheless, it is impossible that he may not have given, to those who could make use of them, some speculative keys good for intellectually 'situating' the sacred dogmas of the *revelatum*. It is impossible because there was no knowledge to be received according to the general conceptions of a receiving subject, and because it was therefore necessary for Christ to endow his disciples with 'metaphysical' notions enabling them to *rightly* comprehend the truths that he had to reveal to them, the most essential of which would clearly upset their mental habits: as with the Trinity or the Incarnation. Certain of the data from the Gospel of John seems to imply such a 'metaphysics', for example when Christ speaks of the 'true vine' or the 'true bread'—which presupposes a Platonic conception of the real (at least in a broad sense). Even more clearly, the designation of the Son as *Logos* plainly constitutes a metaphysical

Mystery and Doctrine

interpretation of the Second Person of the Trinity, the origin of which, in my opinion and which is bound to make the credentialed exegetes smile, can only be Christ. But we can equally consider other facts which impose similar conjectures. I wish to speak of the first battle against the heresies of Gnosticism, traces of which we already find in St John and St Paul, and the most complete exposé of which is *Against the Heresies* by St Irenaeus. Now, what is striking above all in this great work—and which has perhaps not been sufficiently stressed—is that St Irenaeus combats Gnosticism essentially on the terrain of cosmology and metaphysics, because Gnosticism is first a cosmological and metaphysical heresy by nature: it recognizes (almost) the same scriptural texts as the great Church, but it interprets them with a very different doctrine of the world and the divine. Why, then, combat this interpretation (which is not always devoid of plausibility) if apostolic Tradition was not itself the retainer of a doctrine on the world and God? There is—at least on some major and decisive points—a cosmological and metaphysical orthodoxy incompatible with the speculative hermeneutic of Gnosticism. That is what the work of Irenaeus proves, with he himself affirming on each page of his vast treatise that this orthodoxy is of apostolic origin, which means that it comes, for what is essential, from Christ himself.

Concerning the second point—the tradition of scriptural hermeneutics coming from Christ—we can go beyond conjecture and maintain that we have some positive evidence for it, both in the New Testament and in the Church literature of the first centuries. That there was such a hermeneutic tradition is not at all surprising; it is rather its absence that would be inexplicable. On the one hand Christ is a Jew who reads Scripture (Luke 4:16) and who has been apprised of the Rabbinic exegesis, and therefore of the science of symbols that it uses. On the other, he is himself the source of a new Scripture, either directly (as in the teaching of the parables), or indirectly by everything that the evangelists and apostles have written about him. Now the inventing and the composing of the parables—as well as their interpretation—suppose a knowledge of the procedures of symbolic expression (sometimes quite precise) of the Machalist tradition (the Hebrew *machal* signifies 'proverb', 'enigma', and 'parable') within the domain of which the parables of Christ fall. A remark equally valid for the interpretation of all Scripture (old and new). True, recognition of the veritable Referent of Scripture does not, properly speaking, belong to the scientific order, but depends on the revelation that Jesus has made of it, that it is enunciated in the Canon of truth (the *Credo*) and held by faith. However, although the Referent has changed, or rather has been revealed ('It is I who speak the Scriptures'), the scriptural signifier is itself always the same, the text of the Scriptures (the *First Testament*) remains. Therefore its procedures of expression and the meanings assigned to them by the hermeneutic science of Jewish tradition also remains: Scripture 'spoke' before the coming of Christ. True, this 'speech' was veiled and has been henceforth unveiled. But precisely to the extent that the Christic Referent has not been arbitrarily imposed on the scriptural signifier, to the extent that, on the contrary, It *fulfills* the Scriptures, the textual signifier must have had this new referential aim potentially contained within itself, even and above all there where it does not seem to explicitly indicate It (that is there where it is not formally a question of the Messiah). The new hermeneutic should explain, then, how the signs of the text, beside their traditional meaning, were bearers of a more profound but indecipherable significance before the Referent, which they secretly aimed at, appeared. That such a deepening is possible, revealing an implicit and unnoticed sense, should not surprise anyone: a symbol always has a potential plurality of meanings, or, rather, *is* a potential plurality of meanings, a plurality which, as I have shown in *Le mystère du signe*, does not by any means contradict its unity of meaning. Thus the Christic hermeneutic prolongs the Rabbinic tradition of hermeneutic science only to transform it by fulfilling it. And the pilgrims to Emmaus were surely the beneficiaries of this renewed hermeneutic science: 'And beginning at Moses and all the prophets, he interpreted to them in all the scriptures, the things that were concerning him' (Luke 24:27). How are we to suppose that this science did not represent for the Apostles and first Christians a most precious deposit which they transmitted with the greatest care?

True, Christian antiquity has left us no treatise on such a science, without doubt for the reason, as we will see in greater detail, that it

Mystery and Doctrine

constituted a relatively reserved knowledge. But despite everything we find something like a general outline of it in Origen's *Treatise on First Principles,* and later something like a beginning realization in St Augustine's *De doctrina christiana.* But there is no doubt that it was present among the apostles themselves. The *Gospel of St John* and above all his *Apocalypse* are irrefutable witnesses to it: they utilize the most precise and most technical of symbols, such as that of numbers, showing by this that cosmological and arithmological symbolism were part of the language of revelation.[1] On the other hand Christian iconography and Patristic literature employ it everywhere, and first the Ante-nicene literature, so auspiciously studied by Cardinal Daniélou. This employ is not, moreover, always implicit and the existence of a common symbolism is not to be inferred just from observing recurrent interpretations in scattered writings; it is also sometimes explicitly affirmed, when, for example, the exegesis proposed is said to go back to Christ himself, or at least to the apostles.[2]

Such are the three components of the Christian doctrinal *mysterion*, the three domains to which the term *mysterion* was actually applied: (1) Scripture, the ocean of the mysteries, (2) the Canon of truth, the mystery of faith, and (3) the interpretation of Scripture and the understanding of the faith, the mystery of gnosis. The first mystery can be referred to the Father, the second to the Son-Logos,

---

1. It might be asked if the famous *Key of Meliton of Sardis,* a kind of dictionary of biblical and Christian symbols, does not constitute a witness to this hermeneutic tradition. St Meliton of Sardis lived toward the middle of the second century. Through Eusebius (*Ecclesiatical History,* 1. IV, c. XXVI) we know that he is the author of a lost work entitled *The Key.* In 1855 the learned Cardinal Pitra published a medieval Latin manuscript which he identified, wrongly it seems, as being the lost *Key.* This text has been published by Jean-Pierre Laurant: *Symbolisme et Écriture—Le Cardinal Pitra et la 'Clef de Méliton de Sardes',* preface by Emile Poulat, trans. Francis Bertin (Paris: Cerf, 1988). J.P. Laurant's introduction provides unpublished information on the existence in France, in the bosom of the nineteenth century Church, of a current, at once scholarly, traditional, and symbolist, which strove to combat *in depth* invasive Modernism. But the bias of 'enlightened' Catholic opinion went with the historical critical method which triumphed in the person of Mgr. Duchesne, the adversary of Pitra.

2. This is the case with the parable of the Good Samaritan: concerning the exegesis that he gives for it, Origen tells us that it comes from Christ (*Hom. in Luc.,* 34).

Christ the Original Mystery

knowledge of the Father, and the third to the Holy Spirit, the preeminent Hermeneute, the One who causes the Word of the Father to be heard and who illumines it: and it is, in fact, through this mystery of gnosis that the mysteries of Scripture and faith are united.

However, such a *mysterion* poses a particular problem. The science of speculative hermeneutics like that of sacred hermeneutics is not, strictly speaking, a revelation and should not posses the value and authority of a revealed truth. It is a recovery of a tradition that it transforms and renews, but the symbolic and conceptual elements of which existed previously. And, doubtless, we even need to take into consideration other cultural traditions than those of Rabbinism. Being very probably trilingual, as many Jews at that time spoke Aramean, read Hebrew and understood Greek, the universal language of the Mediterranean basin, Christ could draw from Hellenistic as well as Jewish culture those elements needed for the teaching of his doctrine.[1] This is what we will now examine.

---

1. On this subject read, in the book by Jacqueline Genot-Bismuth (*Un homme nommé Salut—Genèse d'une hérésie à Jérusalem*, F. X. de Guibert, 1995) the chapter entitled 'Diaspora et cosmopolitisme' in which she shows what was the real situation in Jerusalem at the time of Christ from the linguistic point of view: 'We should treat as a false debate the question of knowing what was *the* language spoken by Jesus. The reality was a plurilingualism in all its registers and levels' (p23). As for a knowledge of Hebrew, the *Talmud* informs us that there was at that time in Jerusalem four hundred and eighty synagogues, each one provided with a school where they learned to read the *Torah* (p171). The author speaks of a 'massive teaching of reading and writing to every strata of the population, even the most common', but supposes (after John 7:15) that Jesus did not know how to read (p164). This is an error. John is only saying that the Jews were surprised that a man, who had not been to a synagogue school knew precisely how to read: 'How does this man know letters, having never learned?' After all, the 'science of letters' is not limited solely to the alphabet learned at school. Besides, St Luke (4:16–20) attests that Jesus knew how to read and customarily read Scripture in the synagogue of Nazareth on the day of the Sabbath. John's text clearly signifies that, although Jesus possesses the science of letters, just like the best rabbis (it should be supposed that he had learned to read from his mother), he endows this science with a content that comes directly from his Father: 'My doctrine is not mine, but his that sent me' (John 7:16).

Mystery and Doctrine

The Christian Mystery and the Esoteric Traditions of Rabbinism

Christian patristic literature is rich in commentaries on the Scriptures. And before that the New Testament writings, chiefly St John and St Paul, also employed exegetical traditions. From where might they have come if not from the Jewish culture in which Christ and his apostles were steeped? Christ's care at distancing himself from these traditions of Rabbinic exegesis proves both their existence and the knowledge that he had of them. On this subject some speak of a *Jewish apocalyptic* which seems to be concerned with that portion of the literature called 'intertestamental', and one will not be surprised that the *Apocalypse* of John—which stems from this literary form— utilizes symbolic procedures. But, in the first place, the existence of several esoteric currents in the Judaism of this period must be mentioned (I spoke about it in the second part). The Christian writers knew these doctrines (written or oral) and they resumed many of their teachings, many of their exegetical traditions, having somehow become more or less canonical modes of interpretation good for illuminating the mysteries of Scripture.[1] This resumption is all the more certain as this science of symbols—which involves a cosmology and an anthropology—although esoteric, is none the less rather openly present in the most varied milieux. Let us not imagine a Jewish esoterism whose doctrine, following the conceptions of Romantic occultism, would be the apanage of self-enclosed secret organizations. To the contrary, it has been established that, at the time of Christ, esoterism subsisted in the bosom of Rabbinic Judaism and in close connection with it; it is moreover a question of an

---

1. Certainly, it does not seem that the Jewish exegetical tradition had at its command a veritable 'hermeneutic code' of the kind represented by *The Key of Meliton of Sardis*. But 'the behavior of the texts produced (by this exegesis) gives the appearance of a certain number of constants' (Michel Tardieu, *Codex de Berlin—Écrits gnostiques* [Paris: Cerf, 1983], p9). It is the same for every true body of symbolism. To the extent that it is alive, scriptural hermeneutics excludes a simple 'lexical' deciphering.

esoterism whose origins are very ancient[1] and which is ordered around two subjects: (1) the knowledge of the mystery of creation through the interpretation of the book of *Genesis* (*Bereshit*), and (2) the revelation of the secrets of the spiritual ascension of the soul through the interpretation of the 'chariot' (*Merkabah*) vision the description of which is given by Ezechiel (1:1–28).

We find traces of this esoterism in the *Mishna*, that over the centuries transmitted the teaching of the oral *Torah* relative to an understanding of the written *Torah* (the biblical text), a teaching put in writing around AD 200, at a time when the rabbis, after the destruction of the Temple in AD 70, reorganized Judaism.[2] This *Mishna* (the word signifies 'repetition', 'study') was next integrated with the *Gemara*, that is with the commentaries elicited by the *Mishna* at the time of *public* discussions, around 500, into the vast compilation of the *Talmud*. Now the *Mishna*, the vehicle for the esoteric tradition of Israel, is qualified as *mistorin* by the rabbis, who thus Hebraisize the Greek *mysterion*,[3] whereas, in post-Talmudic literature, it will receive the name *kabbalah*,[4] a term that rightly signifies 'tradition' and is a translation of the Greek *paradosis*. Under these conditions it is significant to observe that, in two thirds of the instances where Origen uses the word *paradosis*, he is referring to ancient or rabbinic Jewish traditions.[5] This incontestably proves the fecundity of Jewish thought and its specific terminology for the great Alexandrian's exegetical practice. After all, Origen had

---

1. Gershom Scholem, *Jewish Gnosticism, Merkabah Mysticism and Talmudic Tradition,* New York, 1960; likewise, from the same author: *Origins of the Jewish Kabbalah,* trans. A. Arkush (Princeton, NJ: The Jewish Publication Society, Princeton University Press, 1987) pp18 and 24–33.

2. The collection was made by Juda the Saint (135–200) from some written traditions, but above all from the traditions of the *tannaim*, the 'repeaters', who, between 10 and 200, learned the *Mishna* by heart so to assure its transmission; cf, X. Léon-Dufour, *Dictionnaire du Nouveau Testament,* Cerf, 'Mishna'.

3. G.G. Stroumsa, op. cit., p140.

4. Ibid., p140, n67, who refers to G. Scholem's article 'Kabbalah', *Encyclopedia Judaica,* 10, pp489f. In the *Talmud, Kabbalah* designates the books of the Bible other than the Pentateuch, but still not esoteric tradition.

5. This is the result of a study by R.P.C. Hanson, *Origen's Doctrine of Tradition,* London, 1954, p73.

Mystery and Doctrine

acquired a direct and living knowledge of both exoteric and esoteric rabbinic traditions, thanks to his numerous contacts with converted Jews and rabbi friends.[1]

Such is the principal source from which the first Christian exegesis drew its science of sacred symbolism. Without doubt, elements borrowed from various Hellenistic currents and conveyed by the Greek language should be added: Pythagorism, Platonism and Stoicism.[2] But this science, esoteric science if you prefer, is only concerned with the most indispensable philosophic notions or even Scripture's symbolic modes of expression;[3] it should not be concerned with determining its Referent: it possibly teaches us to know how Scripture speaks, not about what—and above all about Whom—it speaks. This is why Christianity denies the exegetical esoterism of the rabbis when it implies cosmological theses contrary to its doctrine, and, in a general way, because it remains as yet on the *outside* of Scripture and does not allow access to its Christic Referent. It is not Moses who penetrates into the Promised Land, it is Joshua who bears the name of Jesus:[4] he is his precursive figure. Origen is a good witness to this denial. Thus he rejects, in connection with John the Baptist being identified with Elijah, the thesis of transmigration (metemsomatosis) about which he states that, for the Jerusalem Jews, it was 'derived from the tradition of their fathers and in no way alien to their esoteric teaching (*he en aporrhetois didaska-*

---

1. The reference work in this matter is N. De Lange's *Origen and the Jews. Studies in Jewish-Christian Relations in Third Century Palestine* (Cambridge: Cambridge Oriental Publications 25, 1976); cf. Crouzel, *Origen,* trans. A. S. Worrall (San Francisco: Harper & Row, 1989), p13.

2. Jean Pépin's book *Mythe et allégorie* (Aubier, 1958) provides some evidence of this: pp221–246 for Jewish exegesis, pp250–252 for St Paul's, and pp265–272 for Clement of Alexandria's. For Origen's borrowings from pagan symbolism, see M. Borret's introduction to his translation of *Homélies sur le Lévitique,* Sources Chrétiennes 286.

3. For example, the symbolic significance of Hebrew names, a realm in which Origen enjoyed a high reputation. According to St Jerome, he would have continued, for the New Testament, the *Book of Hebrew Names* that Philo had drawn up for the Old Testament: *Liber de nominibus hebraicis,* Praefatio, P. L., t. XXIII, col. 771–772. Philo is himself reliant on Jewish exegesis.

4. In Hebrew and Greek Joshua and Jesus are the same name: *Yehoschoua, Ieosus.*

lia).'[1] This is because, in order to enter into an understanding of the Gospels, especially St John's in which 'ineffable mysteries are hidden', the 'key of gnosis' (Luke 11:52) is needed, which the scribes possessed, in Christ's very own words, but which they did not use to enter into the mystery of Christ.[2] Beyond the fleshly and the psychic senses, the gnosis of the truly spiritual sense of the Scriptures, the one which lifts the veil by which Scripture is covered according to St Paul (2 Cor. 3:16), is the knowledge of Christ:

> The splendor of the coming of Christ, by illuminating the Law of Moses with the radiance of truth, removed that veil which had been placed over the letter, and laid open for all who believe in Him the 'good things' [Heb. 10:1] that were hidden covered within.[3]

As Cardinal de Lubac has shown in his study on Origen's exegesis, the third sense of Scripture does not, then, derive from rabbinic Judaism or Philonian exegesis which knew only *two* senses; it is rightly Christian and is to be identified with the very revelation of Christianity, that is not only with the mystery of Christ, but also with the mystery of the Church.[4]

This manner of situating the Christian doctrinal *mysterion* in its relationship with ancient and rabbinic Judaism and the esoterism that it conveys is not only so with Origen. It is already so with the apostles, and even, when considered attentively, St John the Baptist, who was, quite certainly, rather close to the Essenes (without however being one of them). At the time that they were alive Christ, St John the Baptist, the apostles, St Paul, the presbyters and the first Christians in general necessarily had numerous contacts with the sages of Israel, the cosmological ideas and the hermeneutic lore that circulated in Palestine. Was not Nicodemus, 'a master in Israel'

---

1. *Com. in Joan*, VI, 73 (in connection with John 1:21); op. cit., vol. I, p189. Some experts nevertheless deem that metemsomatosis only appeared in Judaism with the eighth century of our era.
2. Origen, *First Principles*, IV, 2, 3 (K. 310 and 311); Greer, p181-182.
3. Ibid., IV, 1, 6 (K 302); Greer, p176.
4. Lubac, *Histoire et Esprit—L'intelligence de l'Écriture d'après Origène*, Aubier, 1950, p160 and all of chapter IV.

Mystery and Doctrine

(John 3:1–14), to whom Jesus revealed—at night—one of his most mysterious teachings, one of these sages? Early Christianity was profoundly imbued with this culture, that is indisputable. But for all that its doctrine should not be reduced to this. A priori, the teaching revealed by the Incarnate Word possessed, in Christian eyes, an authority beyond all common measure with that of any human or angelic tradition. This is what Judeo-Christianity—or rather judaizing Christianity—had a vivid awareness of and which it did not cease repeating under all its forms.[1]

The example of what historians call 'Jewish apocalyptic' will succeed in convincing us. According to a thesis vigorously supported by Cardinal Daniélou, it is necessary to see in this Jewish apocalyptic the contents of that 'secret gnosis' spoken about by

---

1. Jacqueline Genot-Bismuth recalls (op. cit., pp192–196; cf. supra n96) the importance the esoterism of the *Merkaba*, that is of the vision of the *Chariot* with which the book of Ezechiel opens. As I have said, this vision constitutes, along with the first chapters of Genesis *(Bereshit)*, two major themes of Jewish esoterism. The vision of the *Merkaba* gave rise, she states, at the end of the Second Temple (first century BC), to 'a veritable Jewish gnosis', which was combatted by the Pharisees who opposed its mystical prophetism with the cult of Scripture. Now the author quite correctly remarks that the inaugural declaration of Christ, at the beginning of St John's Gospel ('you will see heaven open and the angels of God ascending and descending *upon* the Son of Man' 1:51), combines references to Ezechiel ('the heavens were opened,' 1:1; eighty-seven occurrences of 'Son of Man') with a reference to Genesis and Jacob's ladder (the degrees of the real), a ladder with which Jesus identifies himself. She concludes: 'John's account makes of Jesus an incontestable mystic of the *Merkaba*... an adept of that very ancient Jewish gnosis' (p195). It might be added that he effects a synthesis of the eschatological esoterism of the world's end with the cosmological esoterism of the world's creation. But he can only do this because he surpasses both of them. Christ is neither an adept of anyone nor of any esoteric tradition: he is *the* Son of Man because he is *the* Son of God (John 1:49). — Another scriptural datum might be brought up here, so much the more significant as it is implicit: it is a question of the Sermon on the Mount in *Matthew* (5:1–8:1). It has been established that the Gospel presents this major event as the exact counterpart of the Sinai revelation to Moses, with the difference that Moses transmits what he has received from God, while Jesus explicitly marks his authority over the Mosaic Law by speaking in the first person: 'and I say to you' (5:22); cf. Vincent Mora, *La symbolique de la création dans l'Évangile de Matthieu* (Paris: Cerf, 1991), pp45–47; unfortunately this work plays fast and loose with the most absurd hypotheses of exegetic modernism.

Christ the Original Mystery

Clement of Alexandria and many others.[1] As a result 'in this gnostic tradition ... it is a question of something other than the official tradition contained in the rule of faith, the Creed.'[2] This thesis seems to be true only in part.[3] Certainly it is Jewish apocalyptic which provides the cosmological setting and the anthropological structure that the description of the soul's voyage in its spiritual ascension toward the divine throne implies. Combined within it is, in fact, the cosmological esoterism of the *Bereshit* and the angelological esoterism of the *Merkaba*. In short, this involves a description of the degrees of manifested reality and of the superior states to which a human being can gain access, as well as of the spiritual hierarchies which he is called to become identified with (at least in a certain manner). These categories borrowed from the Guénonian vocabulary allow for a convenient formulation of the data provided by Daniélou, data that should be incontestable. It is indeed in this mental universe—we too often forget—that Christ, the apostles and the first Christians lived. And it is out of this that they spoke or to this that they referred, either implicitly or explicitly, especially when they spoke of an ascension through the heavens (2 Cor. 12:2–3). Let us go further. It is to this angelological cosmology that St Paul sometimes applies the name *gnosis:* 'Although I be rude in speech, yet not in gnosis', he declares in 2 Corinthians 11:6, precisely before bringing up his spiritual ascension: 'I know a man in Christ ... such a one was caught up to the third heaven ... and heard ineffable words' (2 Cor. 12:2, 4).

However, two reservations impose themselves. First of all it happens, as St Paul says, that 'this gnosis puffs up.' To know the angelic hierarchies, their degrees and their names, to possess the science of

---

1. J. Daniélou, *The Theology of Jewish Christianity*, trans. and ed. John A. Baker (London: Darton, Longman & Todd, 1964), pp173–204, for the Judeo-Christian apocalyptic; *Gospel Message and Hellenistic Culture,* pp445–500, especially 453, for the gnosis of Clement and Origen; likewise: 'Les Traditions secrètes des Apôtres', *Eranos Jahrbuch,* 1962, pp199–215.

2. 'Les Traditions secrètes des Apôtres', p200.

3. It has been, moreover, contested by André Méhat and some other specialists of Clement of Alexandria: cf. *Études sur les 'Stromates' de Clément d'Alexandrie* (Paris: Seuil, 1966), p425, n19. It needs to be added that this identification of gnosis with apocalyptic represents, after all, only one aspect of the learned Jesuit's thought.

Mystery and Doctrine

symbolic forms, and even to be sometimes able to manipulate certain celestial influences thanks to a kind of theurgy is not necessarily an evil for those who have mastery over themselves; but it is also a risk, the risk of pride and the risk of losing oneself in the indefiniteness of cosmological data. The very existence of heretical gnosis shows that this danger is not vain, for a luxuriance of angelic or 'divine' entities are deployed there—'for there be gods many, and lords many' (1 Cor. 8:5)—as well as a supercharged and confused symbolism which denotes a loss of the sense of what is essential and a straying into the realm of intermediate Powers. On the other hand, if gnosis should be reduced to this cosmology, it would draw its upholders into completely misunderstanding the transcendence of the Christic reality. This is quite obviously what St Paul had in mind and what he would have us grasp when he evokes the *mystery* of Christ. This whole 'mythology', this luxuriant symbolism, which some identify with true esoterism, all of that is, for St Paul, still secondary, *exterior*, compared to Christ and his teachings (summarized in the *Credo*). Without doubt such an assertion will seem insupportable for many modern esoterists in whose eyes the verses of the *Nicean Creed* are all too familiar banalities, whereas Judaizing esoterism seems to disclose well nigh inaccessible treasures of the 'high science'. Now this was also probably the conviction of a majority of St Paul's contemporaries. Hence the need for the apostle to forcefully mark the transcendence of the Christic message by opposing it precisely to the cosmological considerations of Jewish angelology and apocalyptic. Here we have, to my mind, the whole meaning of the teachings in the *Epistle to the Colossians* (1:16–18) and the reason for which he enumerates each category of angel: for Christ is the 'First-Born' of creation, by whom and in whom everything was created, *including the angelic hierarchies*, and who therefore contains and summarizes them in himself.

Here we are at a most important moment when the very essence of Christian revelation is at stake. As we see, it is by no means a question for St Paul, as is too easily believed by today's Christian, of rejecting esoterism as such, nor even its teachings, by aggressively opposing it with the 'democratic' virtues of a simplifying and egalitarian exoterism, but rather of having the Colossians (and many a

Christ the Original Mystery

Christian) understand that, both the clearly esoteric intention with which they approach the study of this most mysterious angelology and the *theurgic and eschatological hopes* that they place in it, should be brought back to the mystery of Christ in whom is to be discovered the treasures of supreme gnosis and sovereign power. This is what he declares in Ephesians (1:17–23) in a most solemn manner:

> That the God of our Lord Jesus Christ,
> the Father of glory,
> may give unto you the spirit of wisdom and of revelation (*apocalypsis*),
> in the knowledge of him:
> The eyes of your heart enlightened,
> that you may know what the hope is of the glory of his inheritance in the saints.
> And what is the exceeding greatness of his power towards us, who believe
> according to the operation of the might of his power,
> which he wrought in Christ,
> raising him up from the dead,
> and setting him on his right hand in the heavenly places.
> Above all principality, and power, and virtue, and dominion,
> and every name that is named,
> not only in this world, but also in that which is to come.
> And he hath subjected all things under his feet,
> and hath made him head over all the church,
> which is his body,
> and the fullness of him who is filled all in all.

A formal and 'visible' esoterism is not without merit. As St Clement of Alexandria and Origen have said, it awakens the sense of spiritual interiority within us, points to mystery, and leads us to seek the depths hidden beneath the apparent simplicity of doctrine, for want of which the believer runs the risk of remaining on the outside of the faith to which he clings. From this point of view, there are some differences between Christians according to the degree of their comprehension (which has, moreover, nothing to do with their degree of knowledge). But, nevertheless, it is still the same faith and the same

Mystery and Doctrine

dogmas. And this is that 'having of gnosis', according to St Paul's expression, not the one that 'puffs up', but the one that 'manifests its fragrance in us' (2 Cor. 2:14): not only for entering into the possession of reserved doctrines, as Daniélou maintains, but for understanding the unsuspected depths of the Church's faith in a new light. 'O the depth of the riches of the wisdom and of the gnosis of God (*gnosis tou Theou*)!' St Paul exclaims in his *Epistle to the Romans* (11:33).[1]

The result of these analyses is that, if there was in Christianity something that might possibly be regarded as formally esoteric doctrines, this especially concerns the science of sacred symbols and the elements of the world (the *stoikeia tou kosmou*, Gal. 4:3 and 9), as well as the cosmological degrees (the heavens and the angelic orders) involved with this science. This science is chiefly of Jewish origin, its teaching is the object of a reserved transmission, if only because of its technical nature. It equally includes speculations bound up with a knowledge of the Hebrew tongue and the symbolism of its writing.

But does this esoterism subsist? I am inclined to think that it did not disappear with the Constantinian peace, and that it has even perdured until our own day. A depository of the antique science of symbolic forms—the sensible forms of sacred architecture, iconography and music, as well as the language forms of Holy Scripture—this knowledge has not ceased to be transmitted, either within various craft brotherhoods (builders, image-makers, weavers, etc.), or in organizations of a more intellectual nature, chiefly in the monasteries. How, without this, do we explain the unity of Christian symbolic language, no treatise of which exists however—at least to my knowledge—whereas it is everywhere employed in a most precise way?[2]

---

1. Irenaeus concludes in this sense. Far from rejecting gnosis, he thinks that it consists in 'bringing out the meaning of those things which have been spoken in parables, and accommodating them to the doctrine of truth' (*Against the Heresies*, I, 10, 3).

2. This is not the place to prove the precision of this language. In this realm consult the works of Jean Hani: they are the clearest and surest guides to be found. *Le langage de l'image au Moyen Âge* (Le Léopard d'Or, 1982) has been studied in an extremely probing way by François Garnier. On the other hand, we find survivals of

Christ the Original Mystery

Of course, although being of Jewish—but also Hellenistic— origin, these keys do not remain any less Christian in their applications, just like the understanding that they procure and to which they have been subordinated. In this respect we should not have the least doubt. What is quite certain, among the ecclesiastic writers of the first age, including the New Testament writers, is that all the promises of a supreme and truly esoteric knowledge heralded by the traditions and books of the Jews and pagans when they speak of mystery, hidden science, revelation, or illumination, these promises are held and fulfilled by Christ come in the flesh.

Secret Traditions in Clement of Alexandria

Cardinal Daniélou's thesis basically rests upon a dual identification: the secret traditions of Clement and Origen are identical to gnosis about which the latter so often speaks (without ever saying in just exactly what it consists), and gnosis is itself identical to Jewish apocalyptic. This thesis seems to be insupportable. If Jewish apocalyptic or, in a general way, the hermeneutic esoterism of the *Bereshit* and the *Merkaba* indeed constitutes a aspect of the secret traditions covered by the term gnosis (as we have seen with St Paul), this is far from exhausting its meaning. Above and beyond a formal and in

---

the sacred sciences in modern times. I do not see how it would be possible otherwise to account for the data provided by Mgr. Devoucoux's *Études d'Archéologie traditionnelle* (republished with: Edme Thomas, *Histoire de l'antique cité d'Autun*, Arché, Milano, 1992) which show the relationship between the numerological value of biblical names in Hebrew and the dimensions of churches. Likewise a reading of Luc Barmont's study on *L'ésoterisme d'Albert Dürer* (Paris: Éditions Traditionnelles, 1947) or Nicolas Boon's exegetical meditations (published by Monique André-Gillois: *Au cœur de l'Écriture,* Paris: Dervy, 1987) thrusts upon us the conviction that certain hermeneutic keys have not been lost (Nicholas Boon was a Catholic priest). Besides, notice how the *Institution arithmétique* of Bœthius (Les Belles Lettres, 1995), a remarkable adaptation of the *Introduction arithmétique* of Nicomachus of Gerasa (Vrin, 1978), teaches the medieval monks and builders the Pythagorian science of numbers.

Mystery and Doctrine

some manner technical esoterism, the gnosis of Clement and Origen, if it is really the supreme science, the *gnosis Theou* spoken about by St Paul necessarily designates something incomparably more lofty, something the secret and ineffable character of which no longer stems from a more or less conventional rule of silence, but from the very impotence of all human speech.

I have stressed the quite vivid awareness that St Paul has of the transcendence of the mystery of Christ with respect to the order of the mysteries of Jewish gnosis. We can see in this awareness the expression of his convert's enthusiasm; it is also and above all the reflection of an experience, a experience of a completely new and unimaginable reality beyond all common measure with what he had experienced until then. Such an awareness is equally to be found again, as we will discover, in Clement and Origen, and is marked, in the hermeneutic realm, by the appearance of a new sense of Scripture that Jewish exegesis, it seems, had not known. Cardinal de Lubac maintains in particular that, as strong as Philo of Alexandria's influence might have been on Origen,[1] it does not however take into account his doctrine relative to the third sense of Scripture, the spiritual sense, for the two senses (allegorical and moral) that Philo sometimes distinguishes beyond the historical sense, are situated, for Origen, at the same ontological level:

> There is no threefold sense to be found in Philo. There is nothing in his work nor in the work of anybody else outside of the Christian tradition that truly corresponds to Origen's third sense, his mystical or spiritual sense. There could not possibly have been like this to be found in any of them, since there was nothing in their consciousness that resembled the regenerative newness of the Christian fact.[2]

Here we have, I believe, the key to the attitude of the Fathers with respect to their Jewish or pagan sources, so that true gnosis should

---

1. Cf. Jean Daniélou, *Origen*, trans. Walter Mitchell (New York: Sheed & Ward, 1955), pp178–191. Philo's influence on Clement seems to be less obvious.

2. Lubac, *Medieval Exegesis*, vol. 1 (Grand Rapids, MI: Eerdmans, 1998), pp147–148; Lubac is of the opinion, contrary to Wolfson and other experts, that Philo has

Christ the Original Mystery

be identified neither with Rabbinic esoterism, nor with Hellenistic philosophy. It might be good, however, to introduce here a major and moreover obvious distinction. Christianity does not have with Hellenism the same relationship as it does with Judaism: the first relationship is cultural, the second is spiritual and religious; the first is concerned with a doctrinal formulation of the faith, the second with the very substance of the *revelatum*. It is, then, the God of the Jews, the God of Abraham, Isaac, and Jacob who is being expressed in the language of Plato.

This situation was, after all, already that of the Hellenized Jews of Alexandria and, from this point of view, Christian philosophers and theologians had illustrious models before their eyes to authorize their own course. The best known of these Jews nourished with Greek philosophy is precisely Philo the Jew, also called 'of Alexandria' (20 BC – AD 50). He probably did not know Hebrew, read the Bible only in the Septuagint version (considered to be inspired), and moved with ease in the language of Platonism. But he is profoundly Jewish and very cognizant of the esoteric hermeneutics of the rabbis. But—perhaps under the influence of Plato's philosophy and surely by fidelity to his Jewish faith—he had an acute sense of the transcendence of God and clearly affirms that what there is of the most lofty in the order of knowledge does not stem from a contemplation of the created world, but from an apprehension of Divine Being in itself, insofar as this is possible. Thus neither for him, for him first of all!, should true 'gnosis' be identified with apocalyptic alone. It surpasses all creation and even every formulation—which has led Philo to lay the foundation for all later negative theology.

Philo takes up not only Greek philosophical language, however, but also combines it with that of the mystery cults (as does Plato himself). Here we rediscover the general theme of my study, and, more precisely, Clement of Alexandria who, he as well, takes up the

---

not elaborated a *doctrine* of threefold sense, whereas Origen has formulated and established it with much vigor and precision. For Crouzel, it is more a question, with Origen, of a hermeneutic theory than of a true exegetical practice: *Origen*, pp79–80.

Mystery and Doctrine

language of the mysteries (into which he had perhaps been initiated before his conversion). Philo expresses himself in this way:

> there exists a more perfect and better purified intellect, an intellect initiated into the greater mysteries, which is not confined to acquiring knowledge of the Cause from created things, like one discovers a permanent substance from its shadow, but which, beyond the created, perceives a very clear image of the Uncreated, in such a way that, thanks to the latter, it perceives the Uncreated and its shadow at the same time, that is the *Logos* and the sensible world together as a whole.[1]

Bréhier summarizes this by declaring that the lesser mysteries 'which constitute the first degree of initiation are related to the powers and the greater are related to the first being.'[2] And, to be precise, what, for Philo, purifies the intellect and confers on it the supreme initiation to the gnosis of God in his Being is revelation, in this case, as the continuation of the text explains, the illumination that Moses received from God himself.

This is then what was, for a Jewish philosopher, the source and the content of the loftiest knowledge, namely the *Logos,* the more or less divine intermediary between God in himself and the human intellect. What is valid for Philo is a fortiori valid for a Christian philosopher such as Clement of Alexandria. Although he presents Christ as having taught to some disciples a secret tradition of gnosis, this is certainly not with the intention of making the Word Incarnate the source of a knowledge that the apostles might easily find elsewhere, in the various schools of Jewish esoterism, and which, to sum up, deals with relatively secondary questions.

It is necessary to admit, therefore, that in Clement the tradition of gnosis covers teachings of a varied nature, with the doctrines

---

1. *Allegories on the Laws,* liber III, c. XXXIII, n100. Clement utilizes the same language: 'O truly sacred mysteries! O stainless light! My way is lighted with torches, and I survey the heavens and God; I become holy whilst I am initiated. The Lord is the hierophant, and seals while illuminating him who is initiated' (*Exhortation to the Heathen,* XII, 120).

2. See *Les idées philosophiques et religieuses de Philon d'Alexandrie,* Vrin, 1950, p 245.

belonging to Jewish apocalyptic representing only one part, and certainly not the most important part.¹ We find with him, moreover, a text which has a rather Philonian ring to it and which clearly shows how he conceives of the highest degree of initiatic knowledge, the degree which, among the pagans, the term *epopty* (*epopteia,* literally: 'supreme vision') designates. 'The Mosaic philosophy,' he writes, 'is accordingly divided into four parts (or aspects or genres): the first is historic, the second is specially called the legislative, which two properly belong to moral doctrine, the third is the liturgical (hierurgical) part, which already corresponds to natural science; and the fourth, above all others, is the theological part, epopty, which Plato predicates of the truly great mysteries, and that Aristotle calls metaphysics';² to the theological or epoptic part he also connects the 'dialectics according to Plato, which is a science apt for discovering the significance of beings.'³ Such is, then, the level on which the epoptic science is situated: it is theological or metaphysical and not cosmological in nature, even if it sometimes happens—I will give an example—that natural philosophy is also qualified as gnostic.

Turning now to those texts where Clement affirms the existence of a secret tradition of gnosis, we will see my conclusions confirmed and made precise.

Clement comments on a verse from Colossians (1:26) in which St Paul evokes 'the mystery which has been hidden from ages and generations, but now is manifested to his saints.' These mysteries, says Clement, 'hidden until the apostles' have been 'transmitted by them

---

1. André Méhat distinguishes nine aspects in Clementine gnosis: 'gnosis, understanding of Scripture', 'the gnosis of time', 'gnosis as philosophy', 'the gnosis of God and his Son', 'the mystery of creation', 'the gnosis of intelligibles and spirits', 'the knowledge of human things', 'eschatology and gnosis', and 'gnosis and charity' (*Études sur les 'Stromates',* pp 421–488).

2. As we know (cf. chap. 1, p12, n3), Clement is the first witness to the use of 'the esoterics' (*ta esoterika*) to designate one of the two classes of Aristotle's writings. It is therefore normal that he would see in his 'metaphysical' (*ta meta physika*) treatises the equivalent of the epoptic science.

3. *I Strom.,* c. XXVIII, 176, 1–3; I have not followed the Caster translation of 'Sources Chrétiennes', n° 30, p 173.

Mystery and Doctrine

as they have received them from the Lord.'[1] They are therefore of Christic origin. But what do they deal with? Chiefly with the interpretation of the parables;[2] and here we rediscover a well-known theme which seems to provide a most sure indication about the object of Christian esoterism during the earliest period. This interpretation, having come from Christ, was transmitted to Clement by a line of teachers some of whose names he has given:

> these teachers, preserving the tradition of the blessed doctrine derived directly from the holy apostles, Peter, James, John, and Paul, the sons receiving it from the father (but few were like the fathers), came by God's will to us also to deposit those ancestral and apostolic seeds.[3]

Save for the rarest of exceptions, an oral transmission is involved: 'The Lord ... allowed us to communicate of those divine mysteries, and of that holy light, to 'those who are able to receive them' (Matt. 19:11). He did not certainly disclose to the many what did not belong to the many; but to the few to whom He knew that they belonged, who were capable of receiving and being moulded according to them. But ineffable things [*aporrheta*] are entrusted to speech, not to writing, as is the case with God. But the mysteries are delivered mystically [*mystikos*], so that what is in the mouth of the initiator may be in the mouth of the initiated; rather not in his voice, but in his mind.'[4] Clement does not ignore that Jesus has announced that everything would be revealed; but, according to him, this does not mean that gnosis will be given to all: 'True, the Lord has told us: 'What ye hear in the ear, proclaim upon the houses'; bidding them receive the secret traditions of the true gnosis, and expound them aloft and conspicuously; and as we have heard in the ear, so to deliver them to whom it is requisite; but not enjoining us to

---

1. *V Strom.*, c. X, 61, 1. On the secret traditions in Clement, read the commentary that A. Le Boulluec has devoted, in the fifth Stromata, to chapters IX (59) to XII (88), regrouped under the title 'L'ésotérisme'; cf. Sources Chrétiennes 279, pp 217–290.
2. *VI Strom.*, c. xv, 126–128.
3. *I Strom.*, c. I, 11, 3.
4. *I Strom.*, c. 1, 13, 2.

communicate to all without distinction, what is said to them in parables.'¹ This explanation might seem embarrassed, and even 'sophistic'. Yet it will be understood if we see here, not a will to unjustly keep aloof from the mass of believers, but a pedagogic care (Clement was a professor) to adapt the teaching to the listener and the fear of profaning the highest truths. Nevertheless, it can be admitted that Clement's attitude on this point had evolved: I will give one testimony of this at chapter's end. But for the moment, I will cite a text which seems to attest to a rather broad diffusion of gnosis among believers of the first hour. This involves a fragment from the *Hypotyposes* (a lost work of Clement) that can be read in the *Church History* of Eusebius. In this passage, which probably dates from the last period of his life, Clement declares: 'The Lord after his resurrection imparted gnosis to James the Just and to John and Peter, and they imparted it to the rest of the apostles, and the rest of the apostles to the seventy, of whom Barnabas was one.'² This fragment is interesting, not only by the mention of Barnabas—without doubt due to an *Epistle* attributed to him and which Clement considered to be inspired—but also by mention of the seventy, an expression which is perhaps alluding to a text in the *Gospel of Saint Luke* (10:1) where we learn that, beside the twelve, Jesus 'appointed also other seventy-two [disciples]. And he sent them... before his face.' Thus we see that the secret tradition of gnosis was communicated to the entirety of the apostolic church and not only to a quite small custodial group.

Can we go further and, contrary to Daniélou (and some others), maintain that the gnosis spoken about by Clement is not to be situated outside of the official doctrine of the Church? I believe it, as Bossuet believed it, even if it is necessary to maintain that it is not to be literally identified with the formulation of this official doctrine (the baptismal Creed for example), since it is the theological and spiritual interpretation of it. The idea of a necessarily heterodox gnosis—seeing that the teaching is hidden from the vulgar and that it is reserved for a spiritual elite who alone are able to withstand its revelation—above all betrays the Romantic imaginings that inspired

---

1. *1 Strom.*, c. XII, 56, 2.
2. Fragment 13: *Church History*, II, 1, 4.

Mystery and Doctrine

it. Far from answering the question posed (What is gnosis for Clement?), it inextricably multiplies the difficulties. In return, things become more simple if we admit that the word 'gnosis', having once recognized the legitimate variations of its use, designates, in its essence, a *state of spiritual knowledge.* Obviously, this does not exclude that the word can also designate a grouping of some metaphysical principles (which, then, are equally concerned with 'physics', that is with Nature and the natures or essences of things): if this gnosis is, in fact, the object of a communication, it clearly needs to be formulated and is, hence, able to be formulated, at least to some extent. But the error would be to think that these principles constitute an autonomous doctrinal corpus which would be superimposed on the common doctrine. In reality, they are hermeneutic keys enabling us to enter into a truly profound and interior understanding of the common faith of the Church, which remains the norm and reference for every properly Christian speculative course. Otherwise, if, for Clement, the understanding of the faith could be abandoned to its inspirations alone and follow only the demands of its theoretical imagination, I do not see why he would be so careful to distinguish orthodox gnosis from heterodox ones.

Many of Clement's texts confirm my just outlined definition. Thus, it happens that he speaks of a 'physics' or of a 'gnostic physiology', that is of a 'gnostic science of nature'. This 'physics' has hardly any relationship with the science that our contemporaries call by this name. In particular, it teaches to discern the intelligible archetypes present in sensible realities, not only with a view to contemplating the Invisible out of the sensible, but also to know how to make these physical realities adequately serve in the celebration and liturgical presentification of divine realities, that Clement names 'hierurgy' (= 'sacred action') and which, according to him (as we have seen), implies a 'natural science'. Here we rediscover the science of symbols and everything that I have indicated concerning the traditional sciences and their function in the constitution of liturgical forms. But this whole physiological gnosis should be standardized by the rule of truth:

Christ the Original Mystery

It is necessary for us to gain access to the true gnostic science of nature [*gnostike phsiologia*], receiving initiation into the lesser mysteries before the greater; so that nothing may be in the way of the truly divine declaration of sacred things... the science of nature, then, or rather epoptic illumination, as contained in the gnostic tradition according to the rule of the truth [*he kata ton tes aletheias kanona gnostikes paradoseos physiologia, mallon de epopteia*].[1]

This is a remarkable text since it conjoins three major themes of my study: initiation to the mysteries, the tradition of gnosis, and lastly the rule of faith. In this way we understand the authentic sense that cosmological esoterism can have: although it is dependent on the lesser mysteries (as in Philo), this is to introduce us to metaphysical esoterism, to the greater mysteries of epoptic theology, that is to the contemplation of the mysteries of faith that the rule of faith has given us to be believed. There is no gnosis without fidelity to Church doctrine. This is why gnosis is itself 'ecclesiatic': explaining that true gnosis consists in the interpretation of Scripture, he specifies that he is speaking of an interpretation 'in conformity with ecclesiastic gnosis [*kata ten ekklesiastiken lego gnosin*].'[2]

Clement's constant reference to Church doctrine—he uses the expressions 'rule of faith', 'rule of tradition', 'ecclesiastic rule'[3] indiscriminately—is basically identical to that of Irenaeus who declares that the 'pneumatic', who according to St Paul (1 Cor. 2:15) 'is judged by no man,' is the one to whom the Spirit of God 'furnishes the gnosis of truth';

> it is a true knowledge which consists in the doctrine of the apostles, and the ancient constitution [*systema*] of the Church throughout all the world, and the distinctive manifestation of the body of Christ according to the successions of the bishops, by

---

1. *IV Strom.*, c. I, 3, 1–2.
2. *VII Strom.*, c. XVI, 103, 6.
3. See the citations in: Damien Van den Eyden, *Les normes de l'enseignement chrétien dans la littérature des trois premiers siècles*, Gembloux and Paris, 1933, pp299–300.

Mystery and Doctrine

which they have handed down that Church which exists in every place, and has come even unto us, being guarded and preserved... a lawful and diligent exposition in harmony with the Scriptures... and lastly the pre-eminent gift of love.[1]

If gnosis is such, so also is the gnostic. The gnostic is not so much someone privileged, having received a secret teaching, but someone endowed with a truly spiritual comprehension, that is someone whose indispensable intellectual capacities will not lead him to a scorning of the virtues (Clement above all dreads and combats 'licentious gnosis') and to freeing himself from Church dogma. Besides, in the bosom of the Church, it has a necessary teaching function. Asking himself about the nature of 'gnostic souls', Clement first sees souls possessed of contemplation (*theoria*), next souls who obey the precepts, and finally souls capable of instructing men in goodness.[2] Now the contents of *theoria* (knowledge and contemplation) is the Christic tradition, it is the vision of Christ and his mystery, handed over to us by the canon of truth and which is the key to the Scriptures.[3] Thus we are sent back to St Mark's verse (4:11) on the teaching of Christ handing over to the apostles the interior sense of the parables, but also to St Luke (24:25–27) who relates how, opening the intellective hearts of the Emmaus pilgrims, Christ 'expounded to them in all the scriptures, the things that were concerning him.'[4] The loftiest gnosis has been henceforth opened by the resurrection of Christ, since, in the manifestation of his glorious Body (anticipated at the Transfiguration), is revealed the mysteries of cosmic eschatology, when the flesh of the world will be assumed

---

1. *Against the Heresies*, IV, 33, 7–8.
2. *VII Strom.*, c. III, 13, 1.
3. This point has been forcefully stressed by Walther Wölker, *Der wahre Gnostiker nach Clemens Alexandrinus*, Berlin-Leipzig, 1952. pp363–364.
4. Many of the Gnostic writings proclaim a teaching that Christ would have given to his disciples after the resurrection. Orthodox gnosis also lay claim, for some of its doctrines, to such an origin. Thus Irenaeus declares: 'If any one read the Scriptures in the way just shown—for thus it was that the Lord discoursed with the disciples after His resurrection from the dead, proving to them from the Scriptures themselves 'that Christ must suffer, and enter into His glory'—the disciple will be perfected' (*Against the Heresies*, IV, 26, 1).

Christ the Original Mystery

into the Spirit and when the new heaven and the new earth will appear.

As for the precepts to which the true gnostic is obedient and as for the virtues that he practices, they are summarized in the three theological virtues of St Paul: 'Gnosis,' Clement says, 'is raised on the foundation of the holy triad: faith, hope, and love.'[1] I have just said: no gnosis without fidelity to Church doctrine; now I have to say: no gnostic without love, and, vice versa, no love of God without knowledge; no precedence between the two, but mutual conditioning because gnosis like love is a mode for the realization of the One. Even more, it might be said, one is the *secret* of the other, one leads to the other as to the revelation of its mystery. All these considerations seem to have been gathered together in the following text, or are at the very least subjacent to it:

> It is not, then, without reason that we commanded boys to kiss their relations, holding them by the ears; indicating this, that the feeling of love is engendered by hearing. And 'God', who is known to those who love, 'is love' (1 John 4:8), as 'God', who by instruction is communicated to the faithful, 'is faithful' (Matt. 11:27); and we must be allied to Him by divine love: so that by like we may see like, hearing the word of truth guilelessly and purely.[2]

Such is, it seems, the conception of Christian esoterism to be found in Clement of Alexandria. It is in conformity with the general doctrine of the Fathers, bearing in mind the native genius of its author, and is to be identified with the idea of an apostolic tradition. Among the writers of that period this apostolic tradition is, in fact *oral*, comes from Christ, precedes the Scriptures and is prolonged in the Church. Were there no apostolic writings, it would be enough to follow the order of the tradition fixed by the apostles and 'handed down by to those to whom they entrusted the communities,' Irenaeus tells

---

1. *IV Strom.*, c. VII, 54, 1.
2. *V Strom.*, c. I, 13, 1. I cannot, alas, expatiate on this subject as I would like. Please refer to the magistral synthesis that Méhat has presented on 'gnosis and charity' in his *Études sur les 'Stromates'*, Seuil, pp 475–488.

Mystery and Doctrine

us.[1] This *paradosis* of the Church contains a principal and normative part: the rule of faith or of truth, for which the Nicean Creed will provide one formulary among others (even though clothed with an unequalled authority); 'but other things are equally "transmitted": elements of discipline or rules of behavior, customs, worshiping or liturgical customs above all, examples or ways of acting.'[2] And, I will add, exegetical ways of knowing. Some of these secondary (or rather 'seconding') elements might be the object of a teaching more reserved than others and might constitute an esoterism in the more formal sense of the term. All of Clement's expressions where explicit evidence of an esoterism in principle is thought to be found—for good or ill—should be read in the light of those distinctions addressed in this book's first part. What Clement wishes to communicate to his reader—for, after all, these texts have been written for the Christians or pagans of his time (not for the occultism enthusiasts of our own) and they could be read publicly—is essentially a 'spirit of esoterism', which might just as well be called a 'sense of the Spirit'. Without doubt pearls should not be cast before swine. Without doubt there are things which cannot be spoken about before the profane because they are sacrosanct. And there are still other things which are not easily mentioned, even in front of the baptized, either because they might perplex them, or because they are in themselves hard to grasp. And it is the same today. But, as for essentials, it is the same doctrine which is given to all those desiring it, received here in the obscurity of faith, deepened by some until an angel-like gnosis. We learn at least one thing from the climate of esoterism to be drawn from Clement's work, we the offspring of a democratic, ideologically egalitarian age in which everyone has a right to everything, and it is this: the Truth is infinitely holy and we have to labor to render ourselves worthy to understand it, if just with our natural reason. Yes, the Truth is precious, even priceless, and I am speaking of the simple truth such as can be communicated to everyone and conceived of by their understanding. To peddle and vulgarize it is also to

---

1. Yves Congar, *La Tradition et les traditions—Essai historique*, Arthème Fayard, 1960, p 49, who is summarizing Irenaeus, *Against the Heresies*, III, 4, 1.
2. Congar, op. cit., p 45.

profane and prostitute: hence our prodigious indifference with respect to doctrine, even revealed doctrine. Faced with the present insignificance of a data-gathering where everything is equal to everything, Clement's esoterism is of the most extreme urgency, the most pressing necessity. But faced with the least chance of a hearing and of conversion, he allows for the generous gift of the most secret mysteries. Let us listen once more to St Clement of Alexandria:

> Far from the gnostic jealousy! It is for this that he goes so far as to ask if it is less good to give to someone unworthy than to deny someone who is worthy, and, in the great love that inspires him, he exposes himself to the risk of communicating the divine gnosis not only to those who have appropriate dispositions, but even to the unworthy who earnestly ask for it; and that, not because of a mere request (for he does not seek to give a good appearance), but because he considers the perseverance in a course which is at the same time an exercise preparatory to faith.[1]

Esoterism and Knowledge in Origen

The work of Origen, Clement's successor to the *Didaskaleion* of Alexandria,[2] offers us a substantially identical teaching, paired however with a more explicit and philosophically more worked out theology.

Earlier,[3] I recalled the importance of rabbinic exegesis in Origen's work, an importance solidly established by modern scholarship.[4]

---

1. *Extracts from the prophets* (*Eclogae propheticae*), fragment 27, 7–28. The *Eclogae* are collections of texts assembled by Clement with a view to his personal work. It is not impossible that there may be recorded therein the teachings of his teacher, Pantanaeus, whose missionary travels had led to India (Daniélou, *Gospel Message and Hellenistic Culture*, pp 454–455, 461.
2. Was the Didascalion of Alexandria an official Church institution or a private catechetical school? The question has been debated. The 'succession' of the didascales (doctors) should not be understood perhaps *stricto sensu*.
3. Cf. above, p 241, n1.
4. Crouzel, *Origen*, p 13 and G.G. Stroumsa, *Savoir et Salut*, p 141.

Mystery and Doctrine

On this subject we have seen Origen speak of secret traditions. Likewise he has a good knowledge of Philonian exegesis, as well as of Old Testament apocrypha.[1] But does he, in his setting forth of Christian doctrine, return to the practice of that formal esotericism exemplified in Judaism? Some scholars, and not a minority of them, have been convinced of it. Thus Father Lebreton deplores the distinction, in Origen, of two kinds of Christians: the simple faithful, led by faith, and the perfect or 'disciples' who have acquired *gnosis*, a term which, in Origen's vocabulary, essentially designates supernatural knowledge and 'is rarely applied to a knowledge of the natural or scientific order';[2] he even judges this distinction 'unsettling' because it ends up presenting the truths of faith as 'a salutary lie'.[3] More recently G. G. Stroumsa (with other intentions) has maintained an identical position. Not only, for Origen, 'should the Christian truth not fall into pagan hands,' but there exists besides with him 'another level of esotericism'; in fact it is 'also through the very interior of the Christian community that a line passes separating initiates from non-initiates, who do not receive the teaching of the truth in its totality.'[4]

Such a way of expressing oneself gives rise to many difficulties. From the very first, one will have trouble finding a single text in the Christian literature of this period in which the baptized are qualified as 'non-initiates'. Quite the contrary—and even though we had to wait until the fourth century for the vocabulary of the pagan mysteries to serve as a designation for the sacraments—Origen is precisely one of the first to name baptism a *telete*, that is an 'initiation'.[5] Obviously, it could be that the terms initiate and non-initiate have only a vague significance under Stroumsa's pen. It would have been better

---

1. Daniélou, *Origen*, pp 139–173.
2. Crouzel, *Origène et la 'connaissance mystique'*, D.D.B., 1961, p 395. What is essential to my documentation has been drawn from this fundamental work.
3. 'Les degrés de la connaissance d'arpès Origène', *Recherches de sciences religieuses*, 1922, t. XII, p 295.
4. *Savoir et Salut*, pp 133–134.
5. *Against Celsus*, III, 59. The same remark is to be made for the word *mysterion*. In the majority of Origen's works, it is presented with one or another of the meanings that I have already marked out; either properly technical when it designates the pagan mysteries, or properly theological when it designates divine realities or the redemptive work of Christ. This is quite exactly its meaning for St Paul. It chiefly

Christ the Original Mystery

to refrain from using them so as not to promote a false reading. In any case, we clearly see that everything turns on the distinction between formal esoterism and real esoterism, and that, lacking a rigorous theory of this distinction, such as I have tried to work out, texts can be made to support the most contradictory theses.[1]

The point to start with, the one which governs all of Origen's conceptions in the matter of exegesis, of revelations, of hidden or open teachings is, I believe, the one which distinguishes three stages, or three degrees, in the unveiling of divine realities, which obviously implies a veiling for the first two degrees, and therefore, to be consistent, two levels of esoterism, the definitive unveiling being attained only at the third stage. I have already outlined this doctrine in connection with the two Temple veils.[2] It has been taken up again by St Ambrose and is deep structure of all medieval thought. Origen draws this 'triple gradation' from a verse in the *Epistle to the Hebrews* (10:1): 'For the law having a *shadow* of the good things to come, not

---

involves, then, a noetic sense. However, it is also with Origen that we see the sacramental or cultic sense of *mysterion* and the adjective *mystikos* appear (Crouzel, *Origène et la 'connaissance mystique'*, p 29): baptism in particular is qualified by *mysterion*, the prayer consecrating the baptismal water is called 'mystical invocation', and 'mystagogy' the teaching of Christ about this rite. Finally Purgatory, the 'eschatological baptism of fire', is the *mysterion* which will purify us at the time of the Resurrection

1. As much needs to be said about those who characterize as esoterism, in the formal sense of the term, the practice current in the philosophical Schools of the time, which consists in distinguishing two kinds of listener: one composed of all comers, and the other of chosen disciples to whom the teacher speaks heart to heart and who he invites to pose questions. This was the case with Plotinus (Porphyry, *Life of Plotinus*, 3; cf. Plotinus, *Ennéades*, Les Belles Lettres, t. I, pp 3–4). Clement proceeded in the same way (Méhat, *Études sur les 'Stromates'*, p 490) and Origen likewise, as Eusebius reports in his *Church History* (VI, 15). Already Aristotle, as we have seen, distinguished two kinds of teachings and two kinds of writings: his *Metaphysics* and his *Physics* belong to a class of texts that his School will call the *esoterics*. This practice is in fact universal and rests on the nature of things and not on the will to communicate a mysterious and secret doctrine: what is there of the esoteric, in the formal sense of the term, in Aristotle's considerations on local movement? But they are not within the compass of all minds. Read what H.I. Marrou says on the two levels of philosophic teaching in his *A History of Education in Antiquity*, trans. George Lamb (New York: Sheed & Ward, 1956), pp 206–210.

2. Cf. above, pp 139–148.

Mystery and Doctrine

the very *image* of the *realities*; by the selfsame sacrifices which they offer continually every year, can never make the comers thereunto perfect.' The Christian goes, then, from the *shadow*, the Old Testament, to the *image* (*eikon*), the New Testament, which will lead to the *realities* (*pragmata*) of the knowledge of the 'future Age'. The Law of Moses gives the shadow, the 'temporal Gospel' gives the image of the 'divine realities, the mysteries which will be contemplated in, what Origen calls (according to *Apocalypse* 14:6), the 'eternal Gospel', that is the perfect knowledge of beatitude.'[1]

Failing to recognize this general doctrine of the three levels of knowledge, one will come up against a multitude of apparently contradictory texts, one will not come to the end of trying to provide a coherent interpretation for them, and one will find how to justify the most opposite of readings. As I have noted, great scholars, like Father Lebreton, have been deceived by it, at least for a time.[2] It is also because it is hard not to project modern ways of seeing things on ancient texts, and even more difficult to escape that persistent set of problems of which we have a direct experience. In an age marked by egalitarian and democratic ideology, a Christian will be inclined to have only unacceptable scorn for every hierarchic doctrine of the degrees of knowledge. At the same time, he will picture every esoterism to himself in the manner of nineteenth-century Romantic reconstructions, or even according to models provided by some contemporary organizations the structure and style of which, elaborated in the eighteenth century, chiefly reflect the quite modern ideology of the 'Enlightenment'. And the believing historian will ask: what does all this have to do with the truth of Christ? He will be inclined, then, to be suspicious of authors whose language unfortunately recalls that of the least Christian esoteric organizations of that

---

1. Crouzel, *Origen,* p112. As Crouzel has shown, there is in Origen a return to the terminology of a famous passage in *Letter VII* of Plato (342 AB), brilliantly interpreted and integrated with the Christian dialectic (*Origène et la 'connaissance mystique'.* pp 213–215). This return to the Platonic text is to be found in *Against Celsus,* VI, 9.

2. In 1923, in the article cited, Lebreton denounces Origen's 'aristocratism'; in 1938, in volume two of Fliche and Martin's *Histoire de l'Église,* he no longer sees there anything but a 'danger' (p 277).

Christ the Original Mystery

time: has not Christ praised the simplicity of ignorant and mocked the pseudo-wisdom of the learned? Conversely, the esoterism enthusiast will be prompt to annex some famous names and enlist them under his banner, above all if they enjoy a reputation as near-heretics like, lo and behold, Origen. These are so many misreadings. The truth is that there is no formal esoterism in Origen, whatever the texts one believes able to cite in this respect, but only this dialectical conversion by which the Spirit draws us from the shadow toward the image and from image to eternal reality, that incessant Pascha which leads us from Moses to the visible Christ of the temporal Gospel and from Christ to the Divine Word of the eternal Good News.

It is at this supreme degree that the most reserved knowledge is to be found. But, before bringing this up, a rather difficult question needs to be framed: was there, for Origen, an ultimate level of knowledge, a kind of radical esoterism which would reserve in God something absolutely unknowable to any creature? The answer is not easy to give.

One thing is certain: for Origen, the Word Incarnate is the synthesis of all the mysteries and contains all of them within itself: 'for Christ is formed of visible realities and hidden realities,'[1] and, as Crouzel notes, 'he totalizes the science of the two worlds,' within him is the truth 'beyond shadow or figure,' he is 'the preeminent Mystery'.[2] But Christ is not only a man in whom the beings and degrees of all creation are summarized and illuminated, he is also the Divine Word in whom the knowledge of God the Father is illumined. The fundamental mystery is therefore the mystery of the Trinity.[3] And, within the Trinity, the mystery of mysteries is that of the generation of the Word. Utilizing the symbolism of the Temple's ultimate sanctuary, whose 'door is closed so that no one may see the High Priest eat the bread in the Holy of Holies',[4] Origen sees in this rite the image of Christ who, in the bosom of the Father, eats the bread of his eternal engendering, the engendering of knowledge by which he has

---

1. *Com. in Matth.*, x, 6; Sources Chrétiennes 162, p159.
2. *Origène et la 'connaissance mystique'*, p72.
3. *Hom. in Num.*, xii, 1; Sources Chrétiennes 29, p237.
4. *Hom. in Ezech.*, xiv, 2–3; Sources Chrétiennes 352, p441.

Mystery and Doctrine

been established in 'the unceasing contemplation of the depths of the Father.'[1] And without doubt as much can be said about the Person of the Holy Spirit. This is why we have to admit that an integral knowledge of the trinitarian relationships will always elude the creature: 'the bread that the Son receives from the Father, he eats alone.'[2]

And yet 'God is not unknowable in himself,'[3] provided that we accept to enter into the knowledge given to us by the Son, through whom God is precisely Knowledge and Truth; also provided that God give us the grace of an interior illumination, for 'no one has perfect knowledge[4] of the Father, but the Son, and he to whom it shall please the Son to reveal him' (Matt. 11:27). And this is true not only of the attributes of God, but also of the created realities and mysteries of the visible world the key to which Christ contains within himself. As for the divine attributes, we know them by analogy, thanks to the scriptural 'names'. To Celsus who asserts that 'no descriptions by words or expressions can show the attributes of God', Origen replies that God cannot, in fact, be directly named by his own qualities, which, besides, is also true for many natural things; how for example, asks Origen, do we differentiate between the sweetness of dates and figs with words? But, when Scripture speaks of God it can be '*indicating* something of his attributes to *guide* the listener and have him understand some one of God's attributes, to the extent that it is accessible to human nature.'[5]

As for intelligible realities and the mysteries of creation, they are known through revelation and supernatural illumination equally. For, beside the bread that the *Logos* eats alone, there is the bread that he shares with creatures, both angelic and human. Otherwise we would know nothing but corporeal and visible realities. Our mind 'is shut in by the fetters of flesh and blood . . . although, in comparison with our bodily nature, it is esteemed to be far superior'; also, when

---

1. *Com. in Joan.*, II, 18; op. cit., vol. 1, p 99.
2. Crouzel, op. cit., p 91; equally in the treatise *On First Principles:* 'only God the Father with his Only Begotten Son and the Holy Spirit holds knowledge not only of what he created but also of himself' (IV, 4, 10; *Origen*, p 216).
3. Ibid., p 93.
4. Cf. my remarks on 'epignosis' in La charitée profanée, p 391.
5. *Against Celsus*, VI, 65.

Christ the Original Mystery

'it nevertheless strives to attain incorporeal things (the intelligible realities) and search for an intuition of them, it hardly obtains a spark or the light of a lamp.'[1] To the contrary, when the soul has

> clearly beheld the beauty and fairness of the Word of God, it falls deeply in love with His loveliness beauty and receives from the Word Himself a certain dart and wound of love.... If, then, a man can so extend his thinking as to ponder and consider the beauty and the grace of all the things that have been created in the Word,[2] the very charm of them will so smite him, the grandeur of their brightness will so pierce him as with a chosen dart—as says the prophet (Isaiah 49:2)—that he will suffer from the dart Himself a saving salutary wound, and will be kindled with the blessed fire of His love.[3]

And so, delivered from our fleshly prison, we will

> enjoy with Christ Jesus the rest proper to blessedness, contemplating through all things the wholly living Word. By him we shall be nourished, in him understand manifold wisdom and be modeled by the Truth-in-itself, having our minds enlightened by the true and unceasing light of knowledge, that we might gaze upon what is to be naturally seen in that light with eyes illuminated by the Lord's commandments.[4]

Is this knowledge absolutely forbidden to us here below? If it has been granted, it was only to rare contemplatives in any case: without doubt to St John, for 'John, by reclining on the *Logos* and resting on more mystical things, was reclining in the bosom of the *Logos,* analogous also to the *Logos* being in the bosom of the Father';[5] evidently to St Paul, who was transported into some 'heaven' and heard

---

1. *On First Principles,* I, 1, 6.
2. The creation of the prototypes in the Word.
3. Origen, *The Song of Songs, Commentary and Homilies,* trans. R.P. Lawson (New York: Newman Press, 1957). pp 29–30.Prologue 2, 17; Sources Chrétiennes 375, pp103–105.
4. *Exhortatio ad martyrium,* XLVII. [This translation differs in a few details from the Greer translation, op. cit., p76. TR.]
5. *Com. in Joan.* XXXII, 20 (13); Sources Chrétiennes 385, pp299–301.

Mystery and Doctrine

'ineffable words' which he was forbidden to repeat (2 Cor. 12:4). With the mention of 'ineffable words' we have come expressly to those texts of Origen which seem to attest to the existence of a secret tradition or a reserved teaching, the one being almost equivalent to the other since, if there is teaching, there is a transmission.

On this topic an initial observation imposes itself: although it is true that, with Origen, we find the existence of secret traditions proper to the Rabbinic exegesis of Scripture affirmed—I have given some examples[1]—it is no less certain that, for him, Christian 'esotericism' is essentially different from Rabbinic esoterism: the secret knowledge to which the doctrine of Christ ought to lead is bestowed directly on the soul by God himself and not by a human teacher: 'Let us take, for example, St Paul's teaching to Timothy: Timothy receives suggestions from St Paul and goes himself to the source from whence Paul has come; he draws from and becomes Paul's equal.'[2] Thus the adjective *aporrhetos* (secret), sometimes under the *aporrheta* (secret doctrines) form, does not have the same meaning when Judaism and Christianity are involved: characterizing a formally and 'technically' esoteric teaching in the first case, while, in the second, it designates a knowledge so interior and so secret that it evades human formulation.

What is obvious is that Origen possesses the 'sense of the secret' in the highest degree: the mysteries of the Gospel are so lofty that they can only be taught 'in the silence of the house'. Innumerable texts affirm this. After all, Origen is only being in conformity to the saying of Christ who commands not to 'cast pearls before swine,' a saying which he has commented on abundantly. And there is, in fact, peril in speaking in front of those who are incapable of understanding because they are fleshly and 'walk according to man', and not according to God like Timothy, to whom Paul was able to transmit all gnosis. There is danger both for the truth itself and for man: a poorly understood truth can be *homicide*, for 'the same foods that nourish the good choke the bad; what is life for pious souls is death

---

1. Cf. above, p240, n5.
2. *Fragm. in 1 Cor.*, XI; *Journal of Theological Studies*, London, IX, p240 (cf. Crouzel, op. cit., p116).

Christ the Original Mystery

for impious ones.'[1] This is why 'the mysteries of God are ever hidden under some veils for the sake of listeners who are still children'[2] and should not be handed over to the profane crowds,[3] nor even committed to writing when it is a question of certain points such as the descent of souls into the body or some aspects of eschatological doctrine without doubt relative to the apocatastasis.[4]

Nevertheless, the truly heavenly mysteries are all beyond writing and even speech; this is why they can be revealed to only a small number, to those capable of understanding what is beyond words:

> But if we say that some know that which is beyond what is written, we do not mean that these things can be known to the majority. They are known to John.... The 'words that cannot be spoken' (2 Cor. 12:4) which Paul has learned are also 'beyond that which is written,' (1 Cor. 4:6), if indeed men have spoken the things that have been written.[5]

It has to be admitted, then, that the teaching given to the crowd of beginners cannot be the same as the one fitting for the perfect. Thus Isaac, who symbolizes the Divine Word, 'sows barley in the Law [an allusion to Genesis 26:12], but wheat in the Gospels. He provides the one food for the perfect and spiritual, the other for the inexperienced and natural.'[6] And in the same way, those who rest content with the science of the incarnate Christ possess only the science of the 'first principles of Christ' (Heb. 6:1),[7] while those who ascend toward the Divine Word gain access to the science spoken about 'among the perfect' as St Paul declares (1 Cor. 2:6–8).

You see, therefore [Origen explains], how this most learned priest [Paul] when he is within, among the perfect ones as in the

---

1. *Hom. in Jud.*, v, 6; Sources Chrétiennes 389, p145.
2. *Hom. in Ezech.*, I, 3; Sources Chrétiennes 352, p53.
3. *Against Celsus*, v, 29; Sources Chrétiennes 147, p89.
4. Ibid., vi, 26; Sources Chrétiennes 147, pp243–245.
5. *Com. in Joan.*, xiii, 33–34; op. cit., vol. 2, p75.
6. *Hom. in Gen.*, xii, 5; Origen, *Homilies on Genesis and Exodus*, trans. R.E. Heine (Washington, DC: Catholic University of America, 1982), p181.
7. Ibid., vii, 4; Origen... p132.

Mystery and Doctrine

'holy of holies', uses one robe of doctrine, but when he 'goes out' to those who are not capable he changes the robe of the word and teaches lesser things.[1]

Whereas the crowd sees Christ only in 'the plain of the literal sense', to a quite small number of the perfect the Lord reveals his Thaboric Transfiguration, to those who follow him 'on the heights of the most lofty and sublime intellect, which contains the words of wisdom hidden in a mystery.'[2]

And yet, if anyone wants to understand these texts (and many others that I could have cited) according to their most genuine sense, it will be seen that they express no other doctrine than the one I have tried to formulate in the beginning of this work. The almost excessive insistence by which Origen underscores the existence of several degrees of understanding, and the difference that separates the letter from the spirit, should not be valid proof of a formal esoterism. A formal, in some manner technical esoterism can only be discrete, it can make it known 'without' that there are reserved teachings 'within' only in an allusive way and as if in passing. Why, one wonders, does Origen speak of them, to the contrary, on every occasion and in all circumstances in a most overt and pressing way? There is only a single answer possible for this question, which is that he intends to invite the greatest number to enter into the most interior sense of the Scripture. Are we to imagine an 'initiate', in the technical sense of the term, who, not only in his learned commentaries, but even in his public preaching, everywhere proclaims that he is an 'initiate', that he is in possession of a transcendent science, but that he cannot reveal it to the crowds of those who hear him because they are by nature inept at understanding? He would quite quickly risk hearing the response: If this is so, what good is it to speak to us about it? Go, take your bragging elsewhere! By definition, a formal esoterism (the existence of which I do not deny, even with Origen) can only be unperceived, even though its presence is

---

1. *Hom. in Lev.*, IV, 6; Origen, *Homilies on Leviticus 1–16*, trans. G.W. Barkley (Washington, DC: Catholic University of America Press, 1990), p185.

2. *Against Celsus*, VI, 77; G.C.S., vol. II, p149 (this text has not been retained as authentic in the Borret edition of *Sources Chrétiennes*).

suspected: thus, in contemplating a cathedral, we see the beauty of the building, not the science of numbers and proportions that presided over its construction.

Here, then, something else is involved. What proves it, besides Origen's significant insistence on bringing to light the mysterious nature of revelation, is both his most steady and urgent thinking on the truth of perfect knowledge, and his embarrassment and hesitations as to what he must say and what he must remain silent about.

On perfect and ultimate knowledge, that is on total and not a partial, in-a-mirror gnosis, Origen's doctrine is constant: this knowledge belongs to the 'future age', when Christ will be all in all.[1] Also, as Father Crouzel shows, the concept of 'perfection' or 'perfect knowledge' is, for Origen, a 'concept-limit: it indicates a direction rather than a state.'[2] The case of St Paul is exemplary in this respect:

> When St Paul declares: it is not that I have already attained or am already perfect (Phil. 3:12), in writing that he is gazing on the summits of celestial perfection. But when he affirms: we who are perfect are thus minded (Phil. 3:15), he is only considering a degree of human perfection. [And in fact] Paul and those who are like him are said to be perfect in comparison with others; but no human being can be called or be perfect in comparison to the highest knowledge or to the perfection that exists among the heavenly orders.[3]

No less significant is Origen's embarrassment concerning what he must say or be silent about as to mysterious teachings. The difficulty that we have in attributing or not to the great Alexandrian the thesis of a secret doctrine is only the reflection of the difficulty that he himself struggles with insofar as he is a Christian preacher. For on the one hand Christ has said: cast not pearls before swine, and on the other he has commanded: all that you hear in the darkness, tell it in the light (Matt. 10:27):

---

1. For example: *Com. in Joan.*, XIII, 10; Sources Chrétiennes 222, p 63.
2. *Origène et la 'connaissance mystique'*, p 483.
3. *Com. in Rom.*, x, 10; Origen, *Commentary on the Epistle to the Romans*, Books 6–10, trans. T. P. Scheck (Washington DC: Cath. Univ. of America Press, 2002), p 276.

Mystery and Doctrine

'For he commands them, since they are enlightened [by the Holy Spirit] and, for this reason said to be in the light, to proclaim the difficult and unclear mysteries which have been delivered to them [the disciples] in secret and in the hearing of only a few, to everyone who is made light.'[1]

Numerous are those passages where Origen declares his hesitation: 'all of that should have been hidden, a public exhibition of it avoided; but the heretics have forced us to manifest what should be concealed.'[2] In the opinion of the scholars, he has never expressed himself with more intensity than in the *Dialogues with Heraclides*:

> For the sake of the worthy, I want to speak so as not to be guilty of defrauding of the Word those able to hear it. Because of the unworthy I hesitate to speak ... so as not to throw holy things to the dogs and cast pearls before swine. It was for Jesus alone to know how to distinguish among his hearers between those without and those within.... I hesitate to put off speaking, and when I do speak I change my mind again. What is it I really want? To treat the matter in a way that heals the souls of my hearers.[3]

Faced with these texts, the occasionally held thesis of a double truth, one for the ignorant and that would be found in the *Homilies* or certain *Commentaries,* the other for the learned that have been delivered in the treatise *On First Principles,* does not hold together and is based on passages drawn from works that they specifically should not be reading![4] Besides, it seems that Origen has clearly explained himself on that in his greatest work the *Against Celsus*. Celsus was a pagan Platonist of the second century (he lived around seventy years

---

1. *Com. in Joan.,* II, 28 (174); op. cit., vol. 1, p141.
2. *Hom. in Ezech.,* I, 3; Sources Chrétiennes 352, p51. Likewise: 'I do not know if it appropriate to unveil so profound a mystery and explain it to the crowd, to a crowd that comes so rarely to hear the word of God, and who, when they have heard soon go away, without continuing to meditate any longer' (*Hom. in Num.,* XIII, 7; Sources Chrétiennes 29, p275).
3. *Dialogue with Heraclides,* 15; *Origen, Treatise on the Passover and Dialogue of Origen with Heraclides and his Fellow Bishops on the Father, the Son and the Soul,* trans. R.J. Daly (New York: Paulist Press, 1992), p69.
4. Cf. Crouzel's demonstration, op. cit., pp165–166.

Christ the Original Mystery

before Origen who was born around 185) and a resolute adversary of Christianity, against which he reacted in a very 'Guénonian' manner; 'in short,' he declares, 'the doctrine of the Christians is a secret doctrine, and to preserve it they put on an indomitable constancy'; but, contrary to Plato, who knew that one should keep quiet in public on the essentials, the Christians wish to teach this secret doctrine to all believers.

Origen responds in this way: Celsus

> calls *our doctrine secret*, we must confute him on this point also, since almost the entire world is better acquainted with what Christians preach than with the favorite opinions of philosophers. For who is ignorant of the statement that Jesus was born of a virgin, and that he was crucified, and that his resurrection is an article of faith among many, and that a general judgment is announced to come.... And yet the mystery of the resurrection, not being understood, is made a subject of ridicule among unbelievers. In these circumstances, to speak of the Christian doctrine as a secret system, is altogether absurd. But that there should be certain doctrines, not made known to the multitude, which are [revealed] after the exoteric ones have been taught, is not a peculiarity of Christianity alone, but also of philosophic systems, in which certain truths are exoteric and others esoteric.[1]

As we know, this esoterism is chiefly composed of the exegesis that Christ has given of his parables:

> If you come to the books written after the time of Jesus [= the Gospels], you will find that those multitudes of believers who hear the parables are, as it were, without and worthy only of exoteric doctrines, while the disciples learn in private the explanation of the parables. For, privately, to His own disciples did Jesus open up all things [Mark 4:34], esteeming above the multitudes those who desired to know His wisdom. And He

---

1. *Against Celsus*, I, 7.

Mystery and Doctrine

promises to those who believe upon Him to send them wise men and scribes' [Matt. 23:34].[1]

This is why the Christians, the defenders of Christ, knew better than the pagan philosophers what must be said and what must be kept quiet:

> Jesus, who was greater than all these, conversed with His disciples in private, and especially in their sacred retreats, concerning the Gospel of God; but the words which He uttered have not been preserved, because it appeared to the evangelists that they could not be adequately conveyed to the multitude in writing or in speech... they [the disciples] saw better than Plato (by means of the intelligence which they received by the grace of God), what things were to be committed to writing, and how this was to be done, and what was by no means to be written to the multitude, and what was to be expressed in words, and what was not to be so conveyed.[2]

As for this doctrine of Jesus Christ, it is the very doctrine of the Church, and Origen quite clearly affirms this: in the Church is to be found 'the holy place' where dwells 'perfect faith and love from a pure heart and good conscience' (1 Tim. 1:5);

> one who remains among these *in the Church* let him know that he stand 'in a holy place'.[3] That is the first condition for an access to the truly esoteric doctrines of the Christian faith: 'Who are they 'who sow'? They are those who bring forth the word of God in the Church. Therefore, let teachers [*doctores*] hear lest perhaps they trust the words of God to 'a contaminated' soul, to 'a harlot' soul, to an unfaithful soul, lest perhaps they cast 'a holy thing to

---

1. Ibid., III, 46.
2. Ibid., VI, 6.
3. *Hom. in Lev.,* v, 3; *Origen,* op. cit, p95. Gaston Bardy notes [in the *Sources Chrétiennes* edition], 'few have been more attached than Origen to the motto: *sentire cum Ecclesia* (to think with the Church),' and he cites numerous passages that attest to Origen's will to remain faithful to what he calls the 'ecclesiastic kerygma' (the treatise *On First Principles,* Preface, 3–10; K. 12–16 for example); cf. *D. T. C.,* t. XI, col. 1509–1510.

the dogs and pearls before swine'; but let them choose clean souls, 'virgins in the simplicity of faith which is in Christ' [2 Cor. 11:13]; let them commit to them secret mysteries; let them speak to them the word of God and the secrets of the faith [*arcana fidei*] that 'Christ may be formed' in them through faith.[1]

We see that to fidelity to apostolic dogmas is joined another no less important condition: conversion of the moral life. These two conditions alone enable us to enter 'into the dwelling', there where Christ delivers his most reserved teaching. According to Origen, this is what Christ's reply of 'come and see' (John 1:38) meant, when asked by Andrew and John where he dwelled: 'Come' is action and the apostles are still without; 'see' is contemplation 'which follows the conversion of the moral life' and which 'occurs in the house of Jesus.'[2] Yet more vividly, in his famous *Conversation with Heraclides*, Origen tells us what should be understood by exoterism and esoterism:

This being outside or coming into the house has a mystical meaning (1 Cor. 5:12). Whoever sins is outside. This is why those outside must be spoken to in parables, in case they might be able to leave the outside and come inside. The coming into the house has a mystical meaning. Whoever enters Jesus' house is his true disciple. He comes in *by thinking with the Church, by living according to the Church.* Being within and the without are spiritual realities.[3] Thus, 'every now and then particles of light are shed upon the deeper mysteries' for beginners, deeper than a simple moral interpretation, so that 'some small sparks of spiritual understanding [of Scripture] might be cast into their minds': 'there would be no desire, if that which is desirable be utterly unknown.'[4]

However—and we will conclude with this very beautiful text— to enter into the interiority of the Christic dwelling, this is also to gain access to the mystery of one's own interiority:

1. *Hom. in Lev.*, XII, 7; Origen, op. cit., p230.
2. *Comm in Joan.*, II, 36; op. cit., vol. 1, p154.
3. *Dialogue with Heraclides*, 15; op. cit., p69 (my emphasis).
4. *Com. in Cant.*, II, 8, 35; op. cit., pp157–158.

Mystery and Doctrine

Therefore, you also attempt, O hearer, to have your own well and your own spring, so that you too, when you take up a book of Scriptures, may begin even from your own understanding to bring forth some meaning, and in accordance with those things which you have learned in the church, you too attempt to drink from the fountain of your own abilities. You have the nature of 'living water' [Gen. 26:19] within you. There are within you perennial veins and streams flowing with rational understanding, if only they have not been filled with earth and rubbish.... You too, therefore, cleanse your natural ability that sometime also you may drink from your own springs and may draw 'living water' from your wells. For if you have received the word of God in yourself, if you have accepted 'the living water from Jesus and have accepted it faithfully, 'a fountain of water springing up into life eternal' [John 4:14] will arise in you.[1]

That is what a Catholic priest preached *publicly* to all-comers of Caesarea's faithful at the end of the third century, a priest who was, along with St Augustine and St Thomas Aquinas, the greatest genius of Christian thought and without doubt the most prolific author of universal history, and who humbly declared:

I hope to be a man of the Church [*vir ecclesiasticus*]. I hope to be addressed not by the name of some heresiarch, but by the name of Christ. I hope to have his name, which is blessed upon the earth. I desire, both in deed and in thought, both to be and be called Christian.[2]

Even more radically, commenting on Christ's injunction in Matt. 5:30 — 'if thy right hand scandalize thee, cut it off and cast it from thee' — he submitted himself to any sanctions that might strike him:

I who seem to be a right hand to you and am named a presbyter and seem to preach the word of God, if I should do anything against the teaching of the Church and the rule of the Gospel, so

---

1. *Hom. in Gen.*, XII, 5; op. cit., pp 183–184.
2. *Hom in Luc.*, XVI, 6; *Origen, Homilies on Luke, Fragments on Luke*, trans. J. T. Lienhard, S.J. (Washington, DC: Catholic University of America, 1996), pp 67–68.

Christ the Original Mystery

that I create a stumbling block for you the Church, may the whole Church in one accord, acting in concert, cut me off and fling me, their right hand away. 'For it is expedient for you,' the Church, to enter into the kingdom of heaven without me, your hand, which, by doing evil, prepared a stumbling block, than with me 'to go to Gehenna.'[1]

Origen is known to have experienced martyrdom during the persecution of Decius and died, four years later, in 254, as a consequence of tortures endured for the Catholic faith.

Clement of Alexandria and Origen are far from being the only ones to extol what Father Crouzel calls a 'tradition of esoterism', namely 'the idea of a more profound understanding of what has been given to all, the Bible'; it should even be affirmed that, in reality, this esoterism 'is that of all spiritual Christians.'[2] Numerous authors could be cited, such as, among the most orthodox, St Basil of Caesarea, St Gregory Nazianzus or St Gregory of Nyssa, who will be found again in the next chapter. And, if we address ourselves to St Dionysius the Areopagite, evidence of this spiritual esoterism betrays itself on every line, that is in which a formally declared and manifest esoterism ought not to be taken 'literally' (precisely), but interpreted as the *symbol* of the mystical sense of revelation and an invitation, an appeal, to penetrate into its deifying interiority.

Such is the 'mysterious' nature of Christian doctrine. It would be fitting to have it grasped in some of its principal aspects and to give some texts to be read in which it is expressed most exemplarily: nothing in fact replaces a direct contact with the living Tradition, and nothing can give a more patent idea of what the spirit of this Tradition was, which, I repeat, was not the apanage of the Alexandrians, but clearly 'a universal practice in the Church from the third to the fifth century.'[3]

---

1. *Hom. in Jos.*, VII, 6; op, cit., p82. The two just cited texts were brought together by H.U. von Balthasar to serve as an epigraph for his Origen anthology: *Spirit and Fire*, t.1, *L'Ame*, (Paris: Cerf, 1959), p9.
2. *Origène et la 'connaissance mystique'*, p165.
3. Louis Bouyer, *The Christian Mystery*, trans. Illtyd Trethowan (Edinburgh: T & T Clark, 1990), p159.

Mystery and Doctrine

*Doctrinal Esoterism
of the First Centuries*

Christ Taught the Doctrine
of the Faith to the Apostles Orally

I have to conclude now and give a plausible idea of what I have called doctrinal esoterism. The question posed was the following: was there, in the beginnings of Christianity, an institutionally recognized distinction, *in the bosom of the Church,* between an exoteric teaching given to all, and an esoteric teaching formally reserved to a few, secretly transmitted since Christ and constituting a doctrine other than the commonly held one? To this precise question the answer can only be negative. One exception will be made, however, for everything answerable to an esoterism of a rather cosmological nature, originally either chiefly Rabbinic, in the case of certain exegetical practices, or more broadly Judeo-Hellenistic or Mediterranean when the elaboration of the sacred forms of the liturgy is involved, an elaboration which works with, in submission to the data of Tradition and Scripture, all the sacred sciences, not only the sciences of visual and sonic forms (architecture, painting, sculpture, music, sacred chant, etc.), but even the sciences related to time and space: thus the formation of the liturgical year (both temporal and sanctoral) could not have been effected without a rather considerable know-how. How do we account for such an elaboration (which has ended up affecting Europe, a part of Africa and the western fringe of Asia) without presupposing the existence of exact knowledge about the symbolic properties of different moments of the annual cycle, transmitted within monastic communities in touch with craft confraternities?[1] As a specialized knowledge, but a

---

1. This transmission was not only oral. There exists, for example, texts debating the date of the Easter festival that show what might be, at that period, the 'science of time'; cf. *Homilies pascales,* I, II, and III, Sources Chrétiennes 27, 36, and 48.

Christ the Original Mystery

knowledge ordered to ecclesial ends, it can be legitimately admitted that it constituted a kind of formal esoterism. This is not, for all that, a formal esoterism which might introduce into the Church a general division between two categories of believer. It would be ridiculous to maintain that, in the eyes of the Christian community, a member of a builders' confraternity, a specialist in ecclesiatic computation, and even an expert in Jewish apocalyptic, were considered, *by that very fact,* as belonging to a category of the faithful superior to the one that embraces a desert hermit lacking any 'initiation' other than that of his baptism.

It does not follow that every notion of esoterism is inapplicable to the teaching of Christian doctrine during the first centuries—if it is at least thought necessary to use this term—but provided that it is seen, then, as designating a 'spirit of esoterism' and not an institutional esoterism. If I insist on this point, this is certainly not by an impassioned rejection of all formal esoterism, as is sometimes the case in the works and studies devoted to this question: I deny the existence of such an esoterism—for which Guénon has provided the most theoretical model[1]—because the factual truth imposes it, except to consider that not only I, but even Clement, Origen and others were *all* ignorant of such an esoterism, since the esoteric doctrines that I have spoken of would not have corresponded to it. In reality, we find that the Christian religion invites the multitude of believers to aspire to the most perfect gifts, that is to enter into the mystery of Christ which is the gift of filial adoption for all those who, baptized in his blood, are 'born of God': *salvation* in Jesus Christ is the grace of deification.[2] There is no line of the New Testament that does not go in this direction. Such is the ultimate finality of the Church's doctrine. Can there be a second one, superior to that? No.

---

1. This model is, it seems, applied as such only to speculative Masonry and, properly speaking, is not to be met with in any other religion.
2. Guénon's distinction between salvation and deliverance has its interest. But how can Guénon claim that, each time it is a question of salvation, it is exclusively a question of what he himself envisages under this term? This is a point that I have never understood. Is Guénon the absolute master of labeling? Should the vocabulary of all time submit to his jurisdiction? Should words used two thousand years before him have the same meaning as the one that he has been pleased to assign them?

Mystery and Doctrine

And is this finality offered to everyone? Yes. This is what decides the question: there should not be, and there never was, in the Church, with regard to the ultimate completion of revelation, two categories of believer. But this does not mean that there were no reserved teachings. To understand this, we have to return to the teaching of Christ.

The first order of (real) esoterism is constituted by the knowledge of the 'mysteries of the Kingdom' that Jesus Christ teaches to his disciples in secret by explaining the parables. This involves an esoterism which distinguishes, among the hearers of the Word, the disciples and the crowd, that is, basically, those who belong to the Church, the baptized (this is the teaching given 'in the House'), and those without, the non-baptized. This does not involve, then, a division between two categories of Christians, but between Christians and non-Christians. If one holds to this, here we have a formal esoterism, and the Church, the *House of God*, should be legitimately seen as an initiatic institution. Such is the conclusion which is imposed by the scriptural data and which we will rediscover, in the next chapter, when I speak of the discipline of the secret and the catechumenate. This esoterism rests on the fact that the Christic *revelatum* is entirely a mystery.

The Keys of Gnosis Were Only Entrusted to Four Disciples

Nevertheless—and here we are broaching the second order of real esoterism—we have to admit, according to the data of the Christian Tradition, especially attested to by St Clement of Alexandria,[1] that Christ has given to a few apostles a reserved teaching that Clement

For him there is no doubt: whenever anyone speaks of salvation, it involves a posthumous preservation in an individual state. What, then, does the name *Jesus* (= Salvation) mean, at the invocation of which every knee bends, not only on earth and in hell, but even in Heaven?

1. Evidently, for the majority of historians, the express declarations of Clement are legends or fables designed to vouch for his teaching. This interpretation is objectively insupportable.

designates by the name of gnosis. These apostles are Peter, James, and John, to whom he adjoins Paul; that is, the three witnesses of the Transfiguration and the beneficiary of the illumination of Damascus.

Note well that this gnosis was entrusted to them, not to be kept secret and to be transmitted only to a small college of initiates, but to be taught to all the disciples of Christ. This is what Clement says: 'The Lord after his resurrection imparted gnosis to James the Just and to John and Peter, and they imparted it to the rest of the apostles, and the rest of the apostles to the seventy, of whom Barnabas was one.'[1]

Now, what is the content of this gnosis and why give it to a few chosen apostles and not to all, when these four guardians have, they themselves, necessarily received the mission to transmit it to the whole of the apostolic College, and even beyond, otherwise they would not have done so? And let us not forget that this gnosis has actually reached Clement, since he speaks of it, and that it was transmitted to him as coming from Christ according to the chain of intermediaries that he points out to us.

This is my conjecture.

What Christ has taught to all the apostles, in other words the 'mysteries of the Kingdom,' or again *that which* is spoken about in the parables, is, synthetically expressed, the rule of faith, the canon of truth that the baptismal Creed summarizes in twelve propositions, but that encompasses the sum total of Christian doctrine: the trinitarian mystery, incarnation, redemption, the sacraments, the structure of the Church and the first principles of its liturgy, etc. That this doctrine might have been reserved I will demonstrate in the following chapter. But anyone can see that it is not to be found as such or explicitly formulated in the Gospels, not even in the entirety of the New Testament: it has been necessarily transmitted, then, orally. Finally, that it expresses that which is spoken about in the parables, only this is acceptable when we realize that this doctrine alone illuminates the Scriptures and gives them their meaning. This is not only valid for the New Testament, but also for the Old,

1. Cf. above, p254, n2.

Mystery and Doctrine

for, in the Scriptures, everything looks to Christ in whom resides the completeness of the truths of faith.

The apostolic doctrine is, then, of Christic origin. It is not the result of a relatively late elaboration wrought from scriptural data, as claimed by many Modernist critics, a thesis which seems unintelligible: I do not see how it was possible to deduce the Christian doctrinal corpus from the text of the Scriptures; from one to the other there is a hiatus, a humanly insurmountable break in continuity. And moreover the same critics, or at least their rationalist ancestors (Voltaire and his ilk), have not failed to speak ironically about the fragile support that Scripture offers dogmas, ignoring without doubt that it is the truth of the doctrine of the faith that determines the meaning of Scripture, not the reverse: faith (the doctrine of faith) comes *ex auditu* (from hearing = from oral tradition) and not *ex visu* (from sight = from reading). In the light of the trinitarian mystery, the Scripture's teachings on the Father, Son, and Spirit are illuminated and make sense; without this illumination, the same teachings might sanction the most divergent theological constructions, as proven by the history of the heresies, each one of which can refer to a Gospel verse. Besides, reason suffices to show that it could not be otherwise: the meaning of no text is determined on the basis of its intrinsic significance, and, to know what it is saying, it is first necessary to know what it is speaking about.[1] The principle '*scriptura sola interpres ipsius*' is *philosophically* false: Scripture is neither the only, nor the first, interpreter of itself.

---

1. This is what I have demonstrated in *Le mystère du signe*, which we have to refer to once more. Present-day catechesis too often forgets this philosophic truth. I am certainly not saying that Scripture is not the source of faith. Of this faith it is the first *signifier*. Just as a sign is a *signifier* that looks to a *referent* by means of a *sense*, so Scripture is the sacred and immutable signifier in its textual concreteness that looks to the theo-christic referent which the doctrine of faith (Church dogma) expresses by means of the sense that a reading of it produces, a reading conjointly exegetical and theological. And just as the knowledge of a sign presupposes a knowledge of its significance, so the knowledge of faith can only start from a doctrine of truth, abstractly expressed and objectively conceived. Is this to say, then, that Scripture serves but to verify *a posteriori* the conformity of abstractly expressed doctrine to the culturally dated presentation of it offered by Scripture? This would be derisive. Doctrinal knowledge, of a mental nature, goes to Scripture as to its vivifying source,

Christ the Original Mystery

As we see, it is the very existence of a doctrine of faith, of a canon of truth, attested to from the beginning, which would be inexplicable if the historical genesis of this *unanimous and universal* doctrine had to be explained from Scripture alone: therefore it could only have come from Christ. However, the simple teaching of this doctrine of faith is, by itself, insufficient to assure its proper transmission. Without doubt it is necessary to express those truths making up the *revelatum,* the sum total of the dogmas that determine the meaning of the Scriptures in general and the parables in particular, but a human understanding will only receive this doctrinal deposit correctly if it is able to comprehend it in its authentic significance and possess a sure apprehension of it. In other words, it is not enough to express that about which Scripture is speaking; it is also necessary to explain, both how Scripture can be related to such an object (exegesis), and how such an Object is 'possible,' that is to say what is, with respect to the intellect's demands, the intrinsic significance of such an Object (theology). Otherwise, the human understanding will indeed receive the dogmatic statements, but, having at its disposal neither the exegetical keys that would show their relationship to Scripture, nor the speculative (metaphysical and theological) keys that make their assimilation by our intellect possible. It will only be able to transmit them as such as an erratic deposit, without a relationship to the Word of God or to the human intellect (pure fideism), and the doctrine of faith would rapidly vanish. Unless this understanding forges for itself the needed exegetical as well as theological keys, the dogmatic statements will be progressively altered in their most essential truth: every heresy derives either from a poor reading of Scripture, or from a poor grasp of apostolic doctrine. These exegetical and theological keys (that is, the science of symbols and metaphysics)

---

because this Scripture is the most direct and the most concrete testimony that we have of the very Word of God: God is really present in Scripture, not in his substance (which is reserved to the Eucharist), but in his form (since Scripture is a formal reality, and not a substance like bread and wine); as for dogmatic expression, God is only intentionally present there, and not 'in reality'. The outcome of these precisions, I note in passing, is that Christianity, contrary to an all too widespread opinion, is not a 'religion of the Book' but a religion of the Word made flesh.

Mystery and Doctrine

constitute, to my mind, the gnosis that Christ taught to those few apostles capable of receiving it.[1]

This is because Christ, in fact, to accomplish his task of founding the Church,[2] had only two or three years and twelve men at his disposal. Although he taught the revealed doctrine to the Twelve, he gave the keys of gnosis to only four of them; while, for Paul, we have to concede an extraordinary mode of teaching. These four are not chosen to receive a revelation that would relativize the deposit entrusted to the Twelve, nor should these four, as a consequence, communicate it only to a few, in such a way that a two-tiered ecclesial structure would be set in place, one exoteric and the other esoteric.[3] But the keys of gnosis were entrusted to them to open, thanks to these keys, the mind of the apostles and then of all the disciples, and have them enter into a true understanding of the mysteries of the Kingdom each time that the need presented itself. They were not to be like those scribes or lawyers spoken about by Christ: 'Woe to you lawyers, for you have taken away the key of gnosis: you yourselves

---

1. This is also what St Irenaeus means when he attacks the 'gnosis falsely so-called,' which implies the existence of a true gnosis. In connection with the rule of truth, of which Irenaeus gives us one of the most ancient formulations (*Against the Heresies*, I, 10; cf. above, chap. 5, n15), Father Adelin Rousseau specifies in the Commentary of his superb edition (Sources Chrétiennes 163, p135): 'If there is a false 'gnosis'... there is also an authentic 'gnosis' that is situated at the interior of the faith'; it consists 'in explaining the Scriptures... and more especially the parables in light of the rule of truth.'

2. It is often said—and I too say—that Christ came to found a religion. Although legitimate, this manner of speaking is somewhat inexact, and Christ has never expressed himself in this way. He did speak of establishing a new Covenant in his blood, of founding an *Ecclesia*, which is rather different: there are several religions, there is only one *Ecclesia*. This point begs to be developed.

3. This is the place to recall that there are not two *Ecclesia*, one Peter's and the other John's: this distinction is without explicit support in Tradition. Moreover, it would be interesting to know the date of its first appearance: it might well be that it is quite recent. St Paul warns us (1 Cor. 1:12): 'Every one of you saith: I indeed am of Paul; and I am of Apollo; and I am of Cephas; and I of Christ. Is Christ divided?' On the other hand, let us not forget that to Peter—displeasing as it is to the supporters of the so-called esoteric Church of John—gnosis was also given, according to Clement who knew better than us, This does not mean that John does not represent, in the bosom of the unique Church of Peter, the function of the highest spiritual knowledge, the preeminent magisterium of gnosis, as is highlighted by his Gospel.

have not entered in, and those that were entering in, you have hindered' (Luke 11:52). With the help of these keys, they should, to the contrary, respond to demands for intelligibility, explain the revealed deposit to the apostles and disciples, by 'giving a reason', as St Peter says (1 Pt. 3:15), and by 'joining gnosis to virtue' just as he recommends in his second epistle (1:5). In other words, each time that an apostle or disciple meets with a difficulty or an uncertainty in comprehending the *revelatum*, he will have recourse to the theological or exegetical competence of Peter, James, John and later Paul. In this way a magisterium of gnosis is formed, that is a doctrinal magisterium: all the disciples possess the *revelatum*, all do not equally possess its science *(gnosis)*, for all have not the same intellectual qualifications and all have not received the same charisms.

It is not without significance that the last word of this gnosis was given after the Resurrection to the three witnesses of the Transfiguration. The Transfiguration is the revelation of the already intrinsically glorious nature of the Body of Christ, a revelation kept secret until the Resurrection (Mark 9:9). In this revelation, the three witnesses see realized in Jesus the transcendent union of the exterior *Torah* (Moses) and the interior *Torah* (Elijah), to the very extent that the opaqueness of the God-Man's flesh is changed to transparency and its luminous reality revealed: here are reconciled exterior and interior, visible and invisible, exoteric and esoteric. And that is supreme knowledge, that which perceives the immanence of the relative in the transcendence of the Absolute. In itself, this Knowledge is actually real only in the Word Incarnate. The three witnesses, and St Paul, have only had a glimpse of its blinding light, soon covered by the Cloud. But this experience sufficed to leave in their souls an ineffaceable burning, it sufficed to open the eye of the hearts within them for receiving the keys of gnosis that Christ was going to entrust to them. And this is what St Peter teaches when he evokes the memory of the Transfiguration experience in his second epistle. Of this experience of Christ's 'majesty', he was one of the 'eyewitnesses' (1:16); 'eyewitness' is a translation of the Greek *epoptes*, literally: 'onlooker' or 'one who sees into', which is used to designate that initiate who has reached the highest degree of the knowledge of the mysteries: it is the Taboric vision that makes of Peter, James and John

Mystery and Doctrine

epoptes of divine gnosis. Next, recollecting the voice of the Father proclaiming: 'This is my beloved Son in whom I am well pleased,' he affirms: 'And this voice we heard brought from heaven, when we were with him in the holy mount. And we have the more firm prophetical word: whereunto you do well to attend, as to a light that shineth in a dark place, until the day dawn, and the day star arise in your hearts' (1:18–19).

Transmissible gnosis is, then, distinct from the 'arising of the day star' in a disciple's heart, since this arising is the end and completion of gnosis. Tranmissible, it is taught with human words and deals with the 'prophetical word' (that is with the Scriptures and the Gospel) a 'more firm' possession of which it makes possible; in other words, it assures the orthodox hermeneutic of this word. This is why St Peter declares immediately after the just cited text: 'Understanding this first, that no prophecy of scripture is made by private interpretation' (1:20). Therefore this gnosis does not have as its goal the communicating of a revelation distinct from the common doctrine, but the enabling of a 'more firm' possession of it and the controlling of the 'in Church' interpretation of the prophetical word. It should then, with time, be taught in itself as also coming from Christ to those who are able to receive it and who will pursue the work of the magisterium inaugurated by the four apostles. It is only reserved by reason of its intrinsic difficulty. Moreover, this is what distinguishes its real esoterism from the formal esoterism of the cosmological sciences. These sciences require too particular and too specialized a learning for a knowledge of them to be ever broadly disseminated, but they offer no insurmountable speculative difficulties: to know them, it is enough to learn and practice them. In return, it is not enough to learn the gnostic science in order to understand it, it is also necessary to be able to intuitively perceive the meaning of the realities and principles which are, nevertheless, the most simple and the most universal that exist. Moreover, this is why they can be, *in principle*, communicated to every believing intellect. But this science of gnosis remains secret and forbidden for those not having faith, since it has for an aim precisely the enabling of the human soul to welcome this faith with understanding. As we see, gnosis, that forms the object of a specific teaching, is not transmitted for itself, but in order to illuminate the *revelatum;* it is ordered to faith and only has its end within it. Hence its interdiction to non-believers: what good is it to give the keys to someone who has nothing to open? Without doubt this is the reason why Clement reveals almost nothing *in writing* (readable by all) of this gnosis, but which he declares to be situated in the line of church tradition, and which can be, then, only a hermeneutic of the common faith.

The Doctrinal Magisterium in Christian Tradition

That this doctrinal magisterium does not constitute a formal and institutional esoterism, an organization hierarchically superposed to the ecclesiastic hierarchy, this is what the image that Daniélou presents of the *didascalia* at Alexandria highlights.[1] The reality of what he calls 'the lineage of *didascaloi* gnostics' from the beginning to the fourth century should not be denied, even if this lineage does not present the characteristics of a formal continuity that has been attributed to it. On the other hand, it is certain, at least with Origen, that the doctrinal magisterium sometimes appears to be a 'rival' of the ecclesiastic magisterium, and that the true *didascalos,* the teacher of gnosis, the one who has received an illumination of the heart in order to penetrate the 'hidden mysteries' of Scripture (*secreta mysteria*) and the 'arcana of faith' (*arcana fidei*),[2] is given as the model that the church hierarchy (bishops, priests, and deacons) should strive to imitate:

---

1. Cf. *Origen*, pp 45–51. The Greek *didaskaleion* ('didascalion' when transliterated into English) signifies 'School'; 'didascalia' *(didaskalia)* designates teaching in general. At the head of a *didascalion* is to be found a *didascalos* or 'Master of the School'. The existence of a didascalion (of a catechetical and theological School) at Alexandria is presented by Eusebius of Caesarea as a church institution dating back to the beginning. It should rather be a question of a 'semi-institution', that will only become official precisely with Origen.

2. *Hom. in Lev.,* XII, 7; op. cit., p 230.

Mystery and Doctrine

From this I think it is one thing for the priests to perform their office, another thing to be instructed and prepared in all things. For anyone can perform the religious ministry, but few there are who are adorned with morals, instructed in doctrine, educated in wisdom, very well adapted to communicate the truth of things and who expound the wisdom of the faith, not omitting the ornament of understandings.[1]

However, if 'the Church, as Origen sees it, is the hierarchy of the faithful in their various degrees of holiness grouped round the spiritual master, rather than the ecclesiastical community grouped round its bishop,'[2] this is precisely because 'spiritual hierarchy' does not assume an institutional form. In return, when it does happen to assume such a form, then it also risks not being worthy of the function that it claims to exercise, and, in this sense, it is, just as much as the sacerdotal hierarchy, the object of Origen's severe criticisms: 'Often it happens that someone who has a base and vile mind and loves earthly things occupies a high station in the priesthood or a *doctor's chair*, while someone who is so spiritual and free of an earthly way of living that he judges all and is judged by nothing, holds the rank of a lower official or is even left in the crowd.'[3] The degrees of true gnosis rarely correspond to the degrees of the hierarchy, whether it be sacerdotal or doctrinal. And it was to this disparity that Origen was unable to resign himself. Basically, he suffered from seeing that deacons, priests, bishops, monks, and doctors were rarely saints.

However, at the beginning of the third century, a change occurs of which Origen is the most striking example: the doctrinal magisterium tends to be more and more the appanage of the ecclesiastic magisterium. If Origen, who incontestably exercises a recognized

---

1. Ibid., vi, 6; p126.
2. Daniélou, op. cit., p48; this assertion demands some nuancing, for Origen's ecclesiology is fundamentally orthodox just the same: he is known to be one of the first witnesses of the adage: outside the Church, no salvation (*Hom. in Jos.*, III, 5), a formula that for him, as for St Cyprian, *concerned the schismatics and not the non-Christians.*
3. *Hom. in Num.*, II, 1; Sources Chrétiennes 29, p83.

doctrinal magisterium at Alexandria, is ordained priest (against the will of the local ordinary!), without doubt this is because it seems more and more unacceptable for a layman to preach in the churches.[1] This means that, in the end, the need had been felt for an ecclesial guarantee for a doctrinal magisterium the intrinsic competency of which was more and more difficult to recognize. Origen is, moreover, favorable to this evolution and in no way contests the sacerdotal hierarchy its right to teach doctrine: 'for him, the office of doctor belongs to the bishops and priests.'[2] He only deplores that this function is not fulfilled well.

Such an evolution is obviously governed by circumstance. When, in apostolic times, the guardians of gnosis were only three or four, it was not hard to recognize them: all the faithful knew who to address to ask for light. It was no longer the same when the number of the faithful grew and the need for being taught multiplied. It was also clearly necessary to multiply the guardians of a gnosis found to be thus exposed to falling into unworthy or inexpert hands (Clement had already deplored this), at the same time it became more difficult to preserve its secret character.

Besides, this secrecy does not offer only advantages. A common doctrine, universally shared and recognized, is difficult to alter: each person, at every moment, can be assured of his own orthodoxy by consulting the orthodoxy of the whole Church. But, while a doctrine is being transmitted secretly, we can be led astray by anyone who claims to reveal it to us, having by definition no means of verifying its authenticity; as for the supposed Christic origin of this teaching, one is then in a situation like the three blind men of Compiègne (as

---

1. The bishop of Alexandria, Demetrius, having learned that at Caesarea Origen, still a layman, had been invited by Theoctistus, the local bishop, to pronounce a homily, protested vigorously: 'Such a thing was never heard of before, neither has it hitherto taken place, that laymen should preach in the presence of bishops.' To which Theoctistus and other bishops replied by citing numerous cases to the contrary (Eusebius of Caesarea, *Church History*, VI, xix, 16–19); it is possible, however, that the reply of Theoctistus is subsequent to the facts charged by Demetrius (cf. Crouzel, *Origen*, p15).

2. D. Van den Eyden, *Les normes de l'enseignement chrétiens aux trois premiers siècles*, p233.

Mystery and Doctrine

recounted in an old French tale) to whom a practical joker had declared, aloud, that he would hand over to one of them an *écu* to pay the innkeeper: each one believed in good faith that one of the other two had received it. These remarks are not unconnected to the multiplication of gnostic sects at that time and their claim to hold the secret teachings of Christ; very numerous are the texts making a case for such claims.[1]

This is why it was inevitable that certain teachings which were transmitted in secret, apart from the profane world of the pagans, ended up being the object of a public and even solemn teaching on the part of the only instituted hierarchy, the Church, whose visibility is an essential characteristic, for it should be always *recognizable*. This was already the reason that Origen gave for justifying his own exegetic work:

> But even now the heterodox, with a pretense of gnosis, are rising up against the holy Church of Christ and are bringing compositions in many books, announcing an interpretation of the texts both of the Gospels and of the apostles. If we are *silent* and do not set the true and sound teachings down in opposition to them, they will prevail over inquisitive souls [by providing them with] foods that are forbidden and are truly unclean and abominable; [this is why, if some one] who is able intercede in a genuine manner on behalf of the teaching of the Church and reprove those who pursue the gnosis falsely so-called, [he ought to] take a stand against the heretical fabrications by adducing in opposition the sublimity of the Gospel message.[2]

So much the more this task, which was until then that of the teachers of doctrine, was imposed on the church hierarchy that henceforth assumed not only the function of guarding and communicating the

---

1. This is especially the case with the so-called *Gospel of Thomas* that is a spurious relatively late one (fourth century), 'indiscreetly apocryphal by its artificial composition' (J. Doresse, *L'Évangile de Thomas,* Le Rocher, 1988, p71). Obviously this spurious Gospel contains elements anterior (second century?) to its composition, but nothing that precedes our canonical gospels.

2. *Com. in Joan.,* v, 8; Origen, *Commentary on the Gospel according to John,* vol. 1, p166.

revealed deposit—which it had always done—but even of specifying in what sense the terminological keys most suitable for this purpose should be interpreted and defined if necessary.

It was not, then, a cosmological esoterism that was disocculted at this time. The sacred sciences that accompany the revelation and allow for its inscription in the forms and substances of the corporeal world continued to be transmitted in the bosom of craft confraternities, as well as in the monasteries for the more difficult and more abstract parts of these sciences, which, after all, assures their subordination to the demands of the *revelatum,* and therefore to the authority of the Church. If this cosmological esoterism remains rather secret, despite the development of the new faith and the growth in the number of the faithful, this is surely by reason of the quite technical nature of the knowledge and practices that go into it, knowledge and practices that require an extreme specialization, but it is also because it touches on the revealed faith in a much less essential way, and because, by that very fact, it is at a lower risk of being concerned with heretical deviations. Without doubt, there will come a time (ours) when the corruption of sacred forms will seem to border on heresy, when the art of piety and inspiration, for want of science, will betray its function as mediator of orthodoxy—even though the pure doctrine of the faith, insofar as being received and guarded by the intellect, is a stranger to the vicissitudes of its sensory manifestations and so remains incorruptible. But, in the fourth century, we are far from such a degeneration and ecclesiatic authority does not have a good reason to manifest itself publicly in a realm where the essentials of the faith are not at stake.[1]

---

1. Such a manifestation of ecclesiastic authority will occur later, at the time of the famous quarrel of the icons (or images), in the seventh and eighth centuries. However, what was targeted then was not so much the theological validity of the *procedures* and science of pictorial art, as the validity of its content: the iconoclasts were not opposed to a non-figurative art, but rejected every 'portrait' of God. —One of the causes for the decadence of sacred art (at least in architecture) might have been the disappearance of operative Masonry and its replacement by speculative Masonry at the beginning of the eighteenth century: this change, that is clearly registered in the line of the ideology of progress, has had the most disastrous consequences in the West.

Mystery and Doctrine

To the contrary, the properly doctrinal esoterism, the magisterium of gnosis, is itself directly concerned with the canon of truth, the authorized hermeneutic of which it is. When the falsifications of this hermeneutic were multiplied, provoking a disarray of 'inquisitive' minds, as Origen expresses it, it became necessary to *emerge from silence* and publicly define the orthodox modes for understanding the *revelatum*. This is why they more and more resorted to use of synods and local councils. Finally, in the serious and generalized crises, as with Arianism, that are *theological* crises, the Church had to be brought together ecumenically and solemnly define such or such a speculative key as a criterion for orthodoxy: 'consubstantial', 'essence and hypostasis', 'hypostatic union of the two natures', etc.

Once these keys were publicly defined by the Church, their Christic origin risked being lost from view and some will be inclined to see them as innovations of the Magisterium.[1] And yet this is erroneous. True, Christ had probably never used such terms in the teaching of gnosis that he gave to a few disciples. But, being hermeneutic in nature, as I have ceaselessly repeated—and as every metaphysics is in reality—, such a teaching requires, not the repetition of unchanging formulas committed to memory, but, *based on these unchanged and unchangeable formulas,* an intellect in the act of understanding, which is always effected with the help of its own speculative means, that is with the help of its own cultural tradition; it is therefore always in the act of reinterpretation. To interpret is to reinterpret, and this by definition (understanding either is or is not an act). The hermeneutic task being permanent—whatever its object[2]—is effected, when a question of the mystery of Christ, under the guidance of the Holy Spirit who alone can ready the theological intelligence to accomplish it. This is why Christ announces to the apostles that the Spirit will teach them all things:

---

1. Thus St Cyril of Jerusalem, in his *Catecheses* (around AD 350), never uses 'consubstantial', which the Council of Nicea had imposed however twenty-five years earlier (without doubt because it is not in Scripture).

2. A book, a theorem, a doctrine, a song, etc., do not *exist* outside of the act which thinks about and interprets them.

Christ the Original Mystery

not because he will reveal new things, but because he will permanently give to the apostles and their successors an understanding of what Christ has revealed. The Master of hermeneutics is the Holy Spirit.

And yet, if with time the magisterium of orthodox gnosis, of the science of the *revelatum,* is more and more assumed by the Church, especially at the time of the major dogmatic councils, it does not follow that the charismatic *didascalia* disappeared completely. The coexistence of these two magisteria is, moreover, in conformity with the nature of things, for the episcopal authorities—even the Pope— do not necessarily possess the required intellectual qualifications; this is why, on a few major occasions, the bishops had to be present at a theological council, as we see all through the history of the Church and right down to our own days: there is nothing unusual here.[1] But what tends to be effaced, then, is an awareness of the esoteric nature of this theological tradition and of its primarily Christic origin. And this is precisely what Clement and Origen were so vehemently opposed to: what they strove to revive, to the very extent that they were aware of its threatened disappearance, was a 'spirit of esoterism' proper for safeguarding the *sacred* character of theologic gnosis, that St Thomas Aquinas will call the *doctrina sacra* or *scientia divina,* and which will be called theology later; for it is sacred not only in its object, but also, in some respects, in its cognitive mode, all theological speculation being, of itself, adoration and prayer, and not a simple exercise of profane reason—although it might be reduced to that. It has, then, an intrinsically *mystical* character, as St Dionysius the Areopagite has striven to teach.

The irregular case of the Dionysian writings rightly represents one of the remanifestations of the magisterium of gnosis that has never disappeared from the Church. The symbolism of its quasi-apostolic presentation is as important as the thoroughly Platonic inspiration of its intellectual language or as the 'esoterico-hymnic' style of its expression. This symbolism affirms in fact the traditional nature of a teaching revealed more than four hundred years after the

---

1. This does not mean that the counselors in theology are necessarily at the top of their form. as for certain *periti* of the last Council.

Mystery and Doctrine

death of its saintly author—and which was up until then transmitted in secret—at the same time that it revives an awareness of the 'sacral' character of Christian truth.[1] The importance of this revelation to the destiny of Christian theology, at least in the West, is rightly incalculable.

✠   ✠   ✠

It seems to me that I have provided a plausible idea of what might be called 'doctrinal esoterism' in the Christianity of the first centuries. I have striven to take historical, cultural and patristic data into account, but also the demands imposed by the Christian faith on every conception of this kind. Without doubt some will be reluctant to concede that it continues to be the same for modern theology: how can we still recognize any mark of esoterism in it? If it were a question of formal esoterism, they would be only too right; but, I repeat, such an esoterism has never prevailed in sacred science. If it is a question of real esoterism, that is of an effort to gain access to a more profound, truly transforming and necessarily hardly propagated understanding of the faith, then it could be said that such an esoterism has never ceased being practiced, whatever the term used to designate it. Besides, the duality of an ecclesiastical magisterium and a theological magisterium has by no means been abolished today. Significantly, this theological magisterium has no hierarchical status in Church institutions. No theologian, not even St Thomas Aquinas, can be qualified as the 'official theologian' of the Church (contrary to what is repeated here and there), in the sense that his work would possess a dogmatic value as to the Catholic faith.[2] There is no doctrinal 'power' in the theologian, like there is a

---

1. I deal more particularly with the Dionysian *theologia* in *Lumières de la théologie mystique* (Lausanne: Éditions L'Âge d'Homme, 2002), pp 17–177.

2. Cf. St Thomas, *Summa Theologiae*, II–II, q.10, a.12: 'the very doctrine of catholic doctors derives its authority from the Church. Hence we ought to abide by the authority of the Church rather than by that of an Augustine or a Jerome or of any doctor whatever.'

power of orders in the sacerdotal priesthood. But, conversely, every believer who teaches the doctrine of the Church is infallible.[1]

Some will perhaps object that the theological work has lost not only its esoteric character, but also its traditional character. Is it not, each time, the product of an individual who, with the help of the resources of his cultural formation, comes to a new presentation of revealed doctrine? This objection arises from a unilateral idea of tradition, that is not repetition, but a hermeneutic recovery. What is fixed and immutable is obviously Scripture and the apostolic revelation; what is fixed and irreformable is the doctrine of the Church that explains the dogmatic tradition over time (chiefly the Councils). But what should be ceaselessly recovered and reactualized with the help of the present conditions of intelligibility, with the help of the theologian's culture and the needs of his time, is an understanding of the faith, in itself (in the irreformable formulation of its dogmatic tradition)[2] and in its relationship to Scripture. Theological understanding is, then, truly traditional to the precise extent that it invents neither its object, nor the 'loci' where it can be found, nor

---

1. In a footnote of *Perspectives on Initiation* Guénon is surprised that, in Catholicism, infallibility is 'concentrated entirely' in the papal function alone (p284, n7). Actually this would be quite surprising; but it is not so. Theology distinguishes active infallibility that belongs, according to the promise of Christ, to the Church, and therefore to the Pope when he speaks in the name of the whole Church and to the bishops in union with the Pope on the one hand, and, on the other, the passive infallibility that belongs to the priests and the faithful insofar as they teach the doctrine of the Church: 'Thus normally the whole Church is infallible, for she is enlightened and united by one sole spirit of truth' (Mgr. Bartmann, *Précis de théologie dogmatique* [Mulhouse: Éd. Salvatot, 1938], t.1, p57); let me specify here that 'the whole Church' means here the sum total of Christians and not just the magisterial Church.

2. Please refer to what I have said on the difference between dogmatic *formulation* and theological *interpretation* (cf. above, chap. 5, art. 3, sect. 3). The dogmatic tradition has been constituted once and for all in its principle that is the revealed deposit, which I have called here the *revelatum*; but it is not so in its formulation that is constituted in the course of *Church history* which is the very locus of its being explicitly defined according to the needs of the time. From this point of view, the history of the Church is not less a bearer of theology than the apostolic *revelatum*, with the express reservation that the latter remains the principle and basis, while the former is only its development and consequence: the fruit also bears a revelation about the nature of a tree.

Mystery and Doctrine

the spirit in which it labors, that is if it aims, not at modifying by one iota the revealed deposit (the apostles and the Councils), but in making possible a faithful and present-day assimilation of it. It is no different for any other living tradition.[1] And so the *opus theologicum* is clearly a work of gnosis, the effect of which is, as St Peter teaches, to 'make firm' the received faith, not to transmit higher truths that ignore the common doctrine.

In concluding this long chapter, it would be best to cite this text from St Clement of Alexandria in which is to be found summarized what is essential to my remarks:

> Faith is, so to speak, an elementary and abridged gnosis of things necessary [to salvation]. Gnosis is a strong and firm demonstration of what is received by faith, built upon faith by the Lord's teaching, conveying [the soul] on to a state of steadfastness and intellectual understanding.[2]

---

1. The theological labor does not consist in a reworking of the doctrine of the faith, but in its reappropriation by the intellect of today's people. Alas, it behooves us to recognize that many so-called theologians, in the name of what they suppose to be the needs of contemporary thought (chiefly the needs of science) proceed with a *substantial* modification of the faith. Such is the case with Father Martelet who, rejecting the dogma of Original Sin (contrary to the 'laws' of evolutionism), has been led closer and closer to a complete recasting of the dogmatic corpus (more radical than that of Teilhard de Chardin). The ideas of this Father have been warmly welcomed (given the reputation for seriousness and moderation enjoyed by their author) in a major portion of the French clergy, that is therefore found to be in a situation of implicit heresy. Nevertheless there are also theological syntheses of a great intellectual quality and an irreproachable orthodoxy, that of Father Nicolas for example.

2. *VII Strom.*, c. X, 57, 3.

9

Sacramental Initiation & the Discipline of the Arcane

Introduction:
A Manifest Esoterization

THE QUESTIONS that we turn to now arise from what must be called sacramental and liturgical esoterism. The distinction between the theological and the liturgical is not without inconvenience, since, as I have stressed, the Christian *mysterion* is indissociably dogmatic and ritual, and since Christian authors do not, in their works, separate the truth taught by Christ from his redemptive action, the theology of economy. It is, however, indispensable for a clear explanation, insofar as the problems raised by the theological *mysterion* are not to be presented *historically* in the same way as those problems raised by the sacramental *mysterion*. In dealing with the former, I asked: was there, inside the Church during the early centuries, a institutional distinction between an exoteric teaching given to all and an esoteric one reserved to a few and transmitted secretly since Christ? My answer was that, granted the existence of a real and as if natural esoterism, we would be dealing with a formal esoterism. But, as we will now see, it is altogether the same for the sacraments of Christian initiation, which seem to exhibit some traces of formal esoterism. And yet here too the subject is complex and the historical data does not all go in the same direction. I

Sacramental Initiation & the Discipline of the Arcane

want to reflect on what has been called the 'discipline of the arcane', a contentious issue among historians, but one not impossible to reach some certainty over.

However, before asking if, yes or no, the Church has indeed *instituted* such a discipline between the end of the second century and the beginning of the sixth, we have to inquire about the advent of a change in the Church's sacramental terminology. This change of vocabulary occurred during the fourth century (the century of 'Nicea' and 'Constantinople'), and manifests a (relative) break with the language of the time just surveyed. It is also no less significant, for the present subject, than the question of the Christian 'arcanum', for it pleads in favor of a kind of 'general esoterization' of the sacramental rites, of the doctrine that accompanies them and of the liturgy that puts them into practice. And it behooves us to observe that this *manifest* esoterization happened at the very moment when Guénon declares the exoterization of *visible* Christianity to have been 'accomplished'.[1] There is a hard to explain paradox here, given that, at the time when Guénon wrote his books, works on these questions were available and, had he read them, this might have led to a revision of his thinking.[2] However that may be for this particular point, what remains is that, for anyone in search of data that attests to the Church's self-awareness, such an evolution of terminology is especially important.

---

1. *Insights into Christian Esoterism*, pp 9–11.
2. It might be asked whether Guénon, who particularly respected the 'official' data that a Tradition provides about itself, was not somehow a victim of the way in which certain authorized historians of Catholicism presented the 'arcanum' question, namely as a purely pedagogical practice, or even an invention of Protestant and German scholarship. Reading Mgr. Batiffol, for example, his conviction about the exoteric nature of the sacraments is found to be reinforced. Nevertheless, he would have been able to take into account the fact that the institution of the catechumenate flourished above all in the fourth and fifth centuries and by no means at the beginning as he asserts (ibid. p 15).

Christ the Original Mystery

Mysteries, Sacraments, and Initiation

We have seen that the term *mysterion* takes on, in the language of Christian revelation, a new meaning that develops and completes the one conferred on it by the Greek Bible. Christ, the apostles, and Church writers, for three centuries, used it to designate what was most central and essential in *revealed* doctrine (Scripture and the oral teaching of Christ to the Twelve). That is its first meaning. A second meaning appears then at the beginning of the fourth century, undoubtedly because in this period there occurred a major event in the history of Christianity: the mass conversion of the pagans, within the Roman empire as well as outside it (the Sassanid empire, Armenia, the Caucasus, Arabia, Ethiopia, Germany, etc.).[1] These conversions were not the result of a concerted politics of evangelization decided upon by the hierarchy: they were the fruit of a spontaneous explosion of the faith; missionary politics will come later (the seventh century). These pagans, at least those of Greek and Latin culture (and without doubt also a majority of the others), were profoundly religious people, who often had a knowledge (direct or indirect) of the mystery cults: for them the word *mysterion*, or rather the plural *mysteria*, designated ritual action and especially sacred liturgies. There was no term in their vocabulary more appropriate for naming the new rites and liturgies into which they were going to be initiated. There is nothing surprising, then, if the Greek speaking catechists used it in their teaching with a new sense, but one situated in the perspective opened by its New Testament use and a quite normal extension of it: in short we pass from theological mystery to the mystery of sacramental economy, from the science of the divine Trinity to the science of the redemptive activity of the Son incarnate, to whom has been entrusted the economy of grace. A third meaning of *mysterion*, and more especially of one of its derivatives: the adjective *mystikos*, will be imposed correlatively to characterize the

---

1. Henri-Irénée Marrou, *L'Église de l'antiquité tardive*, Seuil, pp 67–68.

Sacramental Initiation & the Discipline of the Arcane

spiritual fruit of participation in the holy mysteries of the Christian sacraments and liturgical worship: to this will be devoted the next and last chapter of this book.[1]

This new use of the plural *mysteria*, which does not abolish its doctrinal use, was accompanied by an importation into sacramental language of the vocabulary of pagan esoterism which, up until then and with the sole exception of *mysterion*, had remained foreign to it. Without doubt, among authors like Clement of Alexandria, we find numerous instances of this vocabulary, but it was not being applied to the rites. The text of the *Exhortation to the Heathen* that I have cited[2] makes liberal use of the lexicon of the mysteries, but we should see there a symbolic description of the beatific vision rather than the concrete evocation of a baptismal liturgy. Only with the fourth century is the practice of designating baptism by the term 'initiation' (*telete*) and the baptized by the term 'initiates' (*muetoi*) is universally established. Had the writers forgotten the pagan origin of these terms? By no means. An author such as St Gregory of Nazianzus was fully aware of this origin and the risks of confusion that might occur. In a homily evoking Christ's baptism, the prototype of the baptism of Christians, he cries out:

> Again it is my Jesus and again a mystery that we celebrate, but a mystery which is not misleading or indecent, for it does not derive from the folly of the Hellenes and their intoxication (for that is what I call what they consider holy things...), but from a supreme and divine mystery, akin to the splendors of heaven.

And then he enumerates the mysteries of Eleusis, Bacchus, and Mithras, etc., even the Orphic initiations.[3] However, we perceive

---

1. As previously indicated, here we are following Father Bouyer who has given a clear analysis of this evolution; cf. *The Christian Mystery*, p171.

2. Cf. above, p251, n1. It even seems that, with Clement, there is no cultic use of *mysterion*. Also recall that Origen (cf. above, p148, n1) is one of the first to apply the term 'initiation' (*telete*) to baptism, just as it is with him that 'we see the sacramental value' of *mysterion* appear, but generally bound up with the spiritual exegesis of Scripture, and not designating a rite per se; cf. Crouzel, *Origéne et la 'connaissance mystique'*, p26, n5.

3. *Orationes*, 39, 1; P.G., t. xxxvii, col. 336A (Bouyer, op. cit., p167).

that this mention of the pagan mysteries is already wholly rhetorical: it is more an oratorical effect than an actual warning. At the time that he pronounced these words (around AD 380) the Eleusinian mysteries had nearly disappeared.[1] They are hardly a still to be feared rival to the Christian mysteries, and this is undoubtedly one of the reasons why Church writers no longer hesitated to introduce into their teachings on the sacraments and the liturgy—essential themes of catechesis—the vocabulary of pagan esoterism, the only one worthy of the grandeur of Christian ritual.[2]

One terminological point, however, has still to be made precise: the history of the word *sacramentum*. When I say that the vocabulary of the mysteries begins to be applied to the catechesis of the sacraments, I seem to be presupposing that the term sacrament, like the thing designated, were known at that time; this is not altogether true. Certainly, the seven fundamental rites communicating sanctifying grace form part of the apostolic revelation. But, with the Latins, they were not necessarily designated by the word *sacramentum*. It might even be doubted that there was a general and specific concept for these rites at the time. Not that they are to be confused with other rites; I repeat, in practice the 'seven-fold sacraments' existed from the beginning, as is incontestably proven by the fact that the various Christian Churches, even those separating from the Church of Rome at a quite early date (the Coptic, Jacobite and Armenian Churches, etc.) and the Greek Church have recognized in the doctrine of the sevenfold sacraments, explicitly formulated by the Latins in the twelfth-thirteenth centuries, their own immemorial belief.[3] But, during the first three centuries, it was precisely a practice whose theory would only be developed over time. Therefore, lacking a definition for 'sacrament in general', the literature of that time could

---

1. Renato da Ponte, in his introduction to *Écrits sur la maçonnerie* by Julius Evola (trans. Ph. Baillet, Pardès, 1987, p13, n14) vouches for the present-day survival of pagan initiations (especially the Mithraic), which is not impossible, but this should not invalidate the fact of their visible disappearance from the year AD 400.

2. These remarks are valid for St Augustine, who hardly granted any importance to the pagan mysteries; cf. *La Cité de Dieu*, Bibliothèque Augustinienne, 33, liv. I–V, complementary notes, Desclée De Brouwer, p785.

3. Mgr. Bartmann, *Précis de théologie dogmatique*, t.II, p206.

Sacramental Initiation & the Discipline of the Arcane

not provide us with either a technically formed sacramental vocabulary, or a kind of more or less exhaustive list of the sacraments.

On the other hand, the Latin word *sacramentum* was not exclusively applied to what we call a 'sacrament' today, but was chosen by Christian writers of the Latin tongue to translate the Greek *mysterion*. This point of view is of major importance, and it should never be forgotten that the Latin *sacramentum* is nothing but the Greek *mysterion*.

The Latin versions of the New Testament Books that were in circulation quite early (around AD 50), especially the Book of Pauline epistles, provide the first evidence of such a translation. Two centuries later, St Jerome will be content to revise, sometimes superficially, that old and generally very faithful Latin text.[1] Outside of the Old Testament, it is in the epistles of Paul (Eph. 1:9, 3:3, 5:32; Col. 1:27; 1 Tim. 3:16) and in St John's Apocalypse (1:20, 17:7) that we find *sacramentum* translating *mysterion;* in an exception to these occurrences, the Greek *mysterion* is simply Latinized (an not translated) into *mysterium*. A famous example of a possible mistranslation is provided by Ephesians 5:32, where, in speaking of the union of Christ and his Church, St Paul cries out: *'sacramentum hoc magnum est'*, which one might attempt to translate as: great is this sacrament (by applying it to the union of man and woman which he had just been dealing with), while it should be translated: great is this *mystery*, the mystery, that is the sacred operation by which Christ and the Church enter into synergy, or again by which the Church initiatically cooperates with Christ's redemptive activity.

We know the prodigious success of *sacramentum*, which would become the *proper* designation for the Christian faith's cardinal rites,

---

1. It is probable that St Jerome did not revise all New Testament books: Acts, Paul, the Catholic epistles and the Apocalypse seem to have been revised by one of his Bethlehem disciples, Rufinus the Syrian. It is also not always easy to know, when confronted with the manuscripts (some date back perhaps to the time of St Jerome), whether we are dealing with an 'Old Latin' lately revised by their owners according to the Jerome's Vulgate, or with a Vulgate that has retained a good portion of the 'Old Latin'; cf. J. Gribomont, 'Les plus anciennes traductions latines', in *Le monde latin antique et la Bible,* under the direction of Jacques Fontaine and Charles Piétri (Paris: Beauchesne, 1985), p 61.

so proper that there is no equivalent, not even *mysterion* for which it was at the start one among other possible translations, and which has itself kept a plurality of meanings. Among these possible translations for *mysterion*, mention should be principally made of the substantive *arcanum* ('secret', 'mystery'), or its adjectival forms: *res arcana* (a 'secret thing'), or again *arcana sacra* (the 'sacred mysteries'), etc.; this term is in fact encountered in the better writers as equivalent to *mysterion*, and therefore this one might have been chosen. However, there is a meaning in *sacramentum* not to be found as clearly expressed in *arcanum*, a meaning that hardly indicates an idea of concealment or secrecy, and this meaning is 'sacred act'. This is why it might be supposed that the Latin *sacramentum* has contributed to drawing the Greek *mysterion* (of which it was only a translation at first) toward a more clearly sacramental usage, and has influenced, then, the passage from doctrinal to ritual mystery dealt with in the present chapter.

What was the primary sense of *sacramentum?* The term was borrowed from judicial language: it designated the sum of money deposited in the hands of the pontiffs by the parties pleading in a trial: the stakes of the losing party was *consecrated* to the service of the gods; it also designated the 'oath' (the common derivation of *sacramentum*) that the Roman soldier pronounced and through which he *consecrated* his military commitment before the gods. In both cases, then, the separating of a thing or a person from the profane order and their union with a sacred order is involved. In the instance of the *sacramentum militiae* (= 'military oath') this consecration was at times attested to by a sign, the *fidei signaculum*, the sign of (sworn) faith. All of these terms and the ideas that they express have played a major role in the development of sacramental doctrine.[1]

---

1. The history of the word *sacramentum* has been thoroughly studied. Its essentials are to be found in the *D.T.C.*, t. xiv, col. 485–495 (the 'Sacrement' article) which summarizes the classic work of J. de Ghellinck, E. de Backer and J. Poukens: *Pour l'histoire du mot 'sacramentum'*—vol. 1: *Les anténicéens*, Louvain, 1924. Additionally, the Christians were not alone in transposing the *sacramentum militiae* from the military domain into a properly speaking religious one. The Romans themselves encompassed 'at times a whole world of mysterious things under this term, relegating the precise reality that had justified its use somewhat to

Sacramental Initiation & the Discipline of the Arcane

And so the connotations that predestine the pagan *sacramentum* to serve as the proper name for the Christian sacraments are more easily seen. Nevertheless, what remains is that it translates the Greek *mysterion* and that it conveys its central meaning of a 'divine reality invisibly present and acting in a human form by language or gesture.' This 'esoteric' dimension is always of great import in the use Christian writers make of this term, and therefore in the Church's consciousness. Even when *sacramentum* will be reserved for an exclusive designation of the sacraments (in general), it will retain its mystery connotation.

This is quite clearly the case with Tertullian, one of the first writers of Latin Christianity (he was born in Carthage around 155). If he applies *sacramentum* to Baptism, this is because he compares this rite to the 'military oath' by which the baptized enlists as a soldier of Christ. Now, for the Romans, this military oath constitutes a true *initiation*. This is why, with Tertullian, *sacramentum* explicitly takes on the meaning of a 'rite of initiation to a mystery'; it designates, then, the Eucharist as well as Baptism. It can also be applied to the interior reality that the rite communicates and can directly signify the mystery, the secret thing, or even prophecy, as well as the Creed: thus Tertullian explains that there is no other unity among the churches if not 'the one tradition of the selfsame sacrament.'[1] We are still quite far, then, from the specific sense that the term will receive later. This is what the literature of that time (in St Cyprian of Carthage for example) and the following century verifies. The instances when *sacramentum* is applied to Baptism and the Eucharist are quite rare and is, most often, only a question of their visible

---

the background' (Dom Bernard Capelle, *Bulletin de théologie ancienne et médiévale*, t. I, pp154–155). Also, the adepts of the Cult of Mithra likened the Mithraic confraternity to a 'holy militia': 'When the neophyte joined he was compelled to take an oath *(sacramentum)* similar to the one required of recruits in the army' (F. Cumont, *The oriental religions in Roman paganism*, Chicago: Open Court Publishing Company; [etc., etc.] 1911, p xix). Here, then, *sacramentum* incontestably takes on the meaning of initiation (cf. P. Batiffol, *Études d'histoire et de théologie positive*, Lecoffre, 1907, p 13).

1. *Prescription Against Heretics*, xx, 8. For other references, cf. *D.T.C.*, t. xiv, col. 489.

form: here *sacramentum* is the 'sensible sign'.[1] A little later, with Lactantius (around AD 300), the *sacramentum-mysterium* is still omnipresent: in his works it is generally only a question of the *sacramentum veritatis* (the doctrine of faith), of the *mysterium sacramenti*, the 'mystery of the sacrament', that is the mystery of revelation *(sacramentum = revelatum)* which causes us to know the *sacramentum Dei*, the 'sacrament (or mystery) of God', as well as the *sacramentum hominis et mundi*, the 'sacrament (or mystery) of man and the world'.[2] Although the sacrament-mystery continues to predominate with St Hilary of Poitiers (died 367), although he often speaks of the sensible sacrament-sign, figure and symbol, yet with him we begin to find explicit and formal occurrences of the sacrament-rite, productive of sanctifying grace, a tendency fully ratified in the work of St Ambrose (died 397).[3] Starting with the fifth century, the term's meaning is definitively fixed and its study no longer of direct concern here.

Now we come to what is the principal object of the present article, namely the proofs for what we have called a general esoterization of the sacramental vocabulary.

One of the first to have applied the term *mysterion* as a designation for Baptism is St Athanasius in his treatise *Against the Arians*.[4] During the same period, we find a similar usage in Eusebius of Caesarea, and later in Theodoret of Cyr among many others. This use of the term, in the plural more often than the singular, is likewise related to the Eucharist.[5] Special mention should be made of St Cyril of Jerusalem and his famous catechetical teachings, certainly for their beauty, but also for the frequency of mysterial vocabulary. In the *Procatechesis*, the 'preface' to his *Baptismal Catecheses* (themselves preparatory to the rite of Baptism), he exhorts the future baptized: 'Prepare your own heart to receive instruction for communion

---

1. This is why, when the sacramental doctrine will be fully developed—already with St Augustine—*sacramentum* will be opposed to *res*, as the symbolic signifier to the thing signified.
2. D. T. C., t. xiv, col. 491.
3. Ibid., col. 493–494.
4. P.G., t. xxvi, col. 236.
5. See the references in Bouyer, *The Christian Mystery*, pp 160–171.

Sacramental Initiation & the Discipline of the Arcane

in the sacred mysteries. Pray more earnestly that God will make you worthy of these heavenly and immortal mysteries.'[1] In a catechesis extemporized at Jerusalem, he expresses himself in this way:

> Disciples of the New Testament and partakers of the mysteries of Christ, as yet by calling only, but ere long by grace also, make you a new heart.... *Come for the mystical Seal,* that ye may be easily recognized by the Master.[2]

Note that *mystical* is to be understood here as the adjective of *mystery* and not in the seventeenth century sense. Equally significant is the use by Cyril of the term *mystagogia* to designate the post-baptismal teaching given to the 'myst', that is to the initiate, and to be found in the pagan Plutarch, for example, in the sense of an initiation to the mysteries; thus the saint declares:

> These daily mystagogical catecheses, and new instructions, which are the announcements of new truths, are profitable... most of all to you, who have been renewed from an old state to a new.[3]

This term, which does not however have a scriptural guarantee, is to be found again in Basil of Caesarea, Gregory of Nazianzus, Gregory of Nyssa, and John Chrysostom.[4]

Along with *mysterion* and *mystagogia,* the entire initiation terminology is also introduced into the sacramental vocabulary, beginning with *telete* and the words belonging to the same family. Already, in the most comprehensive liturgical compilation of Christian antiquity, the *Apostolic Constitutions* (fourth century, but attributed

---

1. *Procatechesis,* 16; Bouyer, op. cit., p160.
2. First Catechesis, I, 1–2.
3. *Second Mystagogical Catechesis,* 20, 1. *Mystagogia* literally signifies: introduction (from *ago:* 'I conduct', 'I lead') to the mystery, that is: initiation.

References in Bouyer, op. cit. p161. Likewise note the occurrences provided by St John Chrysostom's *Three Baptismal Catecheses* (published 1990, in French); the holy bishop avows, for example, that, if he did not have other pressing matters, he would have broached 'more ardently the explanation of the high *mystical* realities' of Baptism and direct his hearers 'with a greater security toward this redoubtable initiation (*mystagogia*)', he would introduce them into 'the sanctuary itself' and show them 'the Holy of Holies with all that is to be found there: not a golden vase containing manna, but the Body of the Lord... not a sheep without blemish that had been

Christ the Original Mystery

to St Clement of Rome), we can read the text of this benediction pronounced by the bishop over the catechumens: 'O God Almighty.... Vouchsafe them an holy initiation, and unite them to Thy holy Church, and make them partakers of Thy divine mysteries, through Christ, who is our hope, and who died for them.'[1] We have marked out in Origen the first evidence of such a designation for Baptism. Eusebius of Caesarea likewise adopts it.[2] St Basil of Caesarea, because of his great reputation for orthodoxy, is an especially valuable witness. For him, not only is Baptism an initiation (*teleios*), but it is a perfect initiation, conferred when the various stages of this initiatic course that is the catechumenate has been crossed:

> then, in fact, since one has put on the Son of God, one has been judged worthy to accede to the perfect initiation (*teleios bathmos*) and Baptism is received 'in the name of the Father,' our Lord Jesus Christ himself giving the power to become children of God.[3]

With St John Chrysostom we encounter *telete* in several places. Let us cite this text drawn from the *Eight Baptismal Catecheses* (unedited) published by H.I. Marrou in 1958:

---

slaughtered, but the Lamb of God who has been sacrificed in a *mystical* sacrifice the sight of which is redoubtable to the angels themselves' (*Catechesis II*; Sources Chrétiennes 366, pp169–171). Notice how at this period, as still today with the Orthodox, *baptismal* initiation includes three rites: Baptism, Chrismation (or Confirmation) and the Eucharist. In the strictest sense, this is what the verb *mystagogo* signifies for the Fathers: to initiate into the three mysteries; hence the substantive *oi mystagogoumenoi* = 'those who have been initiated' (*Catechesis I*, 3; Sources Chrétiennes 366, p119). Conversely, the catechumens who are thus distinguished from the category of the faithful (the *pistoi*), are as yet *amuetoi*, 'non-initiates' (*Catechesis II*, 8; ibid., p195).

1. VIII, 6, 13. This book VIII has St Hippolytus of Rome's *Apostolic Tradition* as its source.
2. *De laudibus Constantini, Proemium*; P.G., t. xx, col. 1317.
3. *On Baptism*, I, 2, 24; Sources Chrétiennes 357, p177. Baptism for St Basil is indeed given in the Name of the three Persons of the Trinity; but he disengages the significance proper to each of them: 'having received Baptism in the Name of the Holy Spirit, we are born from above; having been born, then we are baptized in the Name of the Son, we have put on Christ; having put on the new man created according to God, we have been baptized in the Name of the Father and proclaimed children of God' (I, 3, 1; ibid., p191).

Sacramental Initiation & the Discipline of the Arcane

When the priest pronounces over the interested party: 'Such or such a one is baptized in the Name of the Father and of the Son and of the Holy Spirit,' he plunges the head three times into the water and raises it, by this mystical initiation disposing the subject (*dia tes mystikes tautes teletes*) to receive the visitation of the Holy Spirit.[1]

Such is the language with which the Church speaks about its sacraments in the fourth century. Not only are baptismal rites in the restricted sense of this term involved, as we have noted in passing, but also Confirmation (Chrismation) and eucharistic Communion, which is not an initiation in the sense of a beginning (like Baptism), but in the terminal sense of perfection and fulfillment. This is what St Basil of Caesarea indicates in his treatise *On Baptism:* 'whoever is born anew thanks to holy Baptism should be nourished henceforth by participating in the divine mysteries.'[2] We find the same language in St Cyril of Jerusalem: 'Even of itself the teaching of the Blessed Paul [relating the institution of the eucharistic rite, 1 Cor. 11:23] is sufficient to give you a full assurance concerning those Divine Mysteries, of which having been deemed worthy, you are become of the same body and blood with Christ.' Having described all the rites of the Mass (with the exception of the consecration),[3] he comes to the communion rite: 'After this you hear the chanter inviting you with a sacred melody to the communion of the Holy Mysteries, and saying, O taste and see that the Lord is good.'[4]

To conclude, we will mention a Syriac homily of the fifth century, probably by Narsi, a doctor of the Church of Edessa, a homily that recovers the extraordinary atmosphere of the primitive liturgies. Narsi speaks to us of the invocation of the Holy Spirit (epiclesis) so

---

1. *Cat. II*, 26; Sources Chrétiennes 50, p147.
2. III, chapter title; Sources Chrétiennes 357, p191.
3. These mystagogical catecheses are stenographies of an oral teaching (their attribution to Cyril has been disputed); perhaps the stenographer has observed the discipline of the arcane on the subject of the consecratory rite. Likewise, in the text of the eucharistic anaphora of Adi and Mari (Syria, third century), the absence of the consecratory rite can be explained in this way.
4. *Cat. IV,* 1 and *Cat. V,* 20.

Christ the Original Mystery

that he descend upon the bread and wine and transform them into the Body and Blood of Christ:

> O marvel, that, whereas He is the Spirit with which everything is filled, until the earth-born commands He does not approach! O gift, which, though given from the beginning, is not received until a son of dust makes entreaty! He is the Spirit, with all and in all, in the height and the depth: and He is hidden and concealed, and the priest points Him out by his words. . . . His power lights down upon the visible table, and bestows power upon the bread and wine to give life. His power strengthens the hand of the priest that it may take hold of His power; and feeble flesh is not burned up by His blaze.
>
> A corporeal being takes hold with his hands of the Spirit in the Bread; and he lifts up his gaze towards the height and then breaks it. He breaks the Bread and then casts [it] into the Wine, and he signs and says: 'In the name of the Father and the Son and the Spirit, an equal nature.
>
> With the name of the Divinity, three hypostases, he completes his words; and as one dead he raises the Mystery, as a symbol of the verity. In verity did the Lord of the Mystery rise from the midst of the tomb; and without doubt the Mystery acquires the power of life.[1]

Before these texts and so many others that could be cited, who will maintain that there might be a mystery greater than the eucharistic sacrifice, an initiation more lofty than the one that makes us partakers of the divine nature, according to St Peter's teaching? And who can doubt that the Church, during the five or six hundred years covered by these citations, had the most vivid awareness of the true nature of what was at stake? To those who might object that this

---

1. *Homily 21:* 'On the mysteries of the Church and on Baptism', *The Liturgical Homilies*, trans. R. H. Connolly, vol. VIII, *Cambridge Texts and Studies* (Cambridge: Cambridge University Press, 1916) pp 58–59. This rite of commixtion has been kept in the Roman Mass. — 'though given from the beginning [*créé*, 'created', in the French text]' does not mean that the Holy Spirit is a creature, but that He exists, proceeding from the Father, forever.

Sacramental Initiation & the Discipline of the Arcane

awareness, this 'spirit of esoterism', no longer exists today, I reply that, if this is true, it is without doubt regrettable, but not enough to change the nature of sacramental realities, as we have shown. But yet is it certain that such an awareness has entirely disappeared? The sacramental vocabulary has not in fact changed so much since those distant times. Undeniably, we are alas often witness to the invasion of baptismal and eucharistic liturgies by the most bothersome—and the least spiritual—'democratic' ideology; still, here and there, and especially in certain monastic communities, there are wholly beautiful and most dignified liturgical celebrations. But, once this upsetting, sad and so often decried decadence is acknowledged, what remains is that the Church continues to speak of sacramental *mysteries*: chapter II of the conciliar constitution on the Sacred Liturgy is entitled *De sacrosancto Eucharistiae mysterio* ('Of the Sacrosanct Mystery of the Eucharist'), and repeats this term in many places. As for the baptismal rite (chapter III, §64), the obligation of the catechumenate has been restored for adult baptisms: 'By this means the time of the catechumenate, which is intended as a period of suitable instruction, may be sanctified by sacred rites to be celebrated at successive intervals of time.' Still more significantly, the term 'initiation' is uttered, and in an especially explicit context, as anyone can judge: 'In mission lands it is found that some of the peoples already make use of initiation rites. Elements from these (*illa etiam elementa initiationis*), when capable of being adapted to Christian ritual, may be admitted along with those already found in Christian tradition (*quae in traditione christiana habentur*)' (§65). As for the confirmation rite: it 'is to be revised and the intimate connection which this sacrament has with the whole of Christian initiation *(cum tota initiatione christiana)* is to be more clearly set forth' (§71); 'the *whole* of Christian initiation,' that is not only Baptism, but also the Eucharist—this is going in the direction of the Church's most ancient traditions.

These are only words, some will say, to which they might be tempted to apply the conclusion formulated by G. Bardy: after the fifth century, 'they will continue to say that the baptized are initiated, but here this word has lost its proper meaning.'[1] The whole question

---

1. *Encyclopedia Catholicisme*, article 'Arcane', t. I, col. 765.

Christ the Original Mystery

turns, then, on just what this 'proper meaning' is, and whether the term should necessarily refer to the Masonic-Occultist model that Bardy probably had in mind and that he projected on the mysterial realities of Pagan-Christian antiquity. As for me, I think that this term, to the contrary, acquires its true meaning with Baptism: the expression 'Christian initiation' has not been unduly preserved down to our own time and has actually become the official designation for the three main rites of the Church and the teaching that accompanies them, for there is none better suited. The only problem would be to restore a certain 'spirit of esoterism', that is, quite simply, the sense of the sacred. In this respect, how can we not agree with this remark of Father Louis Bouyer's: with the fourth century

> the influx of recent converts with more or less sufficient (or insufficient) formation led the clergy, naturally enough, to emphasize, tangibly, as it were, the respect due to the sacred rites.... [But] the recent abandonment among us of such precautions has shown all too quickly what an evaporation of faith results from it, through a failure to recognize, in the actions of the Constantinian clergy, a simple proof of pastoral good sense, to which only armchair liturgists could remain blind.[1]

The Discipline of the Arcane

Significance and History of the Expression

This expression is the translation of a Latin formula (*disciplina arcani*) coined in the seventeenth century. *Arcanum* signifies 'secret', 'mystery', and is to be met with frequently in Christian literature as equivalent to *mysterion* (in the plural: *arcana* = *mysteria*); thus, by *arcana verba*, the Vulgate translates the 'secret words' heard by St Paul in his rapture (2 Cor. 12:4). *Disciplina* is, in Church Latin, the

---

1. Bouyer, op. cit., p164.

Sacramental Initiation & the Discipline of the Arcane

dedicated term for designating the Church-imposed rules insofar as it is an instituted society ('canon law'), rules concerned with the circumstances and conditions of administering the sacraments for example. This discipline can vary with time: Tertullian already opposed the mutability of the *disciplina* to the stability of the *regula fidei*. 'Discipline of the arcane' therefore designates a 'law which, in the early centuries, obliged the faithful and clergy to never speak openly of the faith and worship before the catechumens and the infidel.'[1] All historians agree in observing that this law has never been the object of an express declaration by Church authority: it seems to be found in no council canon whatsoever.[2] Nevertheless, it is impossible to doubt its existence, so that it might be less a question of a law properly speaking than an extremely widespread even though not always observed practice. In the expression *disciplina arcani*, 'arcane' is more important than 'discipline'.

That the question raised by the existence of the Christian arcane differs from the one raised by a secret tradition of gnosis dating back to Christ is obvious. We are no longer dealing with a knowledge that, by its very nature, should not be received by all, although no one would be excluded from it by virtue of a formal rule;[3] we are now dealing with an explicit interdict concerning a certain category of believer, the catechumens, regarding the ceremonies of Christian worship as well as sacramental doctrine. The reason for the 'secret'

---

1. Batiffol, *Études d'histoire et de théologie positive*, p13.
2. With the exception of the Council of Laodicea (circa 450?), in its canon 46 which forbids the public recitation of the *Credo* (*D.T.C.*, t. II, col. 1082). The existence of this council is problematic.
3. It is the same for gnosis as for sanctity: everyone has been called, but few minds possess this contemplative and penetrating quality that enables one to understand the revealed truths with a depth and rectitude that vivifies them and makes them worthy of adoration. About intellects devoid of gnosis it might be said: 'seeing they may see, and not perceive; and hearing they may hear, and not understand them' (Mark 4:12). This gnostic quality is obviously without any direct rapport with intellectual acumen or learnedness. A modern example of a truly gnostic although somewhat 'unlearned' intelligence is St Theresa of the Child Jesus; an ancient example of an incontestably gnostic intelligence (and immensely learned) although not the intelligence of a (recognized) saint is Origen. Augustine and Thomas Aquinas unite learning and gnosis with sanctity.

Christ the Original Mystery

no longer resides in the presence, or absence, of a natural quality of contemplation proper to the *intellectus fidei,* but in the sacramental situation of the faithful. The 'secret' of the tradition of gnosis is basically inexpressible and should not be the object of a formal institution. The 'secret' of the catechumenal arcane is concerned with access to liturgical forms of worship and with those words formally attached to them: it can be the object of a disciplinary rule. Nothing bears, then, a closer resemblance to a formal esoterism of the Guénonian type than the catechumenal arcane, with this difference however: in this case it is the *Ecclesia* of the baptized in its entirety that constitutes the initiatic organization, while exoterism would be reduced to the category of the catechumens—which no longer corresponds to Guénon's conception. To conform to this conception, it would in fact be necessary for the catechumens to belong to a constituted exoterism, with its practices and rites; but it is impossible to imagine what exoterism might be involved here. Judaism or the pagan religions could not fulfill this function: the latter, because the immense majority of the catechumens were of pagan origin and ignorant of all Jewish religion; the former, because the catechumenate required their decisive rejection. With the arcane we indeed have an esoterism, but no longer any exoterism. And, we repeat, this baptismal esoterism is most manifest in the fourth and fifth centuries, that is at the very time when Guénon situates its definitive disappearance.[1]

Before offering some texts in which the *disciplina arcani* is attested to, we have to first say something about this expression's history.[2]

---

1. In his dissertation *Die Arkandisziplin in der alten Kirche* (Heidelberg, 1956), H. Clasen has shown that 'the century after the Council of Nicea represents the acme of the ecclesial arcane'; cited from G.G. Stroumsa, *Savoir et Salut,* p130, n9. This conclusion is common to all historians.

2. We are principally relying on the documentation provided by Mgr. Batiffol, article 'Arcane' of the *D.T.C.,* t. 1, col. 1738–1758; this article is somewhat dated (1903) and its point of view on the arcane (for him purely pedagogical in nature) is insupportable and is, besides, no longer supported by historians. But, as for what concerns the history of the formula and the debates that it provoked, from the seventeenth to the nineteenth centuries, he is the only one to have supplied, in French, a truly complete exposé. Add to this the article 'Arcane' by E. Vacandard

Sacramental Initiation & the Discipline of the Arcane

At the beginning of the seventeenth century, the notion of a discipline of the arcane had been the stakes in a debate between Catholics and Protestants on the origin of the sevenfold sacraments. The Protestants rejected this doctrine of the sevenfold sacraments, taught by the Council of Trent but, according to them, without basis in Scripture. The Catholic disputants answered quite often by imputing the silence of Scripture on the sacraments to a need to hide certain doctrinal points from the uninitiated and, of course, from unbelievers. Melchior Cano in 1563, St Robert Bellarmine in 1599, and many others, asserted, in connection with the Eucharist for example, that its true nature could not be publicly exhibited. To the Protestants, who relied on some of St Augustine's texts to deny transubstantiation, Cardinal Duperron answered that these were 'popular sermons during which all kinds of people were present, the initiated as well as the uninitiated, baptized as well as catechumens, pagans or unbelievers, which Africa was quite full of at the time, among whom it was not permissible to disclose the secret of the sacraments.'[1] Protestant scholars did not entirely reject the existence, in the Fathers, of an obligation for silence, but they denied that it was of apostolic origin, seeing therein, to the contrary, a contamination of the pure evangelical doctrine by the mystery cults of paganism. The first to have formulated this opinion, which was to have a considerable success with non-Catholic historians and

---

of the *D.H. G.E.* (Baudrillart), t. III, col. 1497–1513 (1924): it rectifies Batiffol's conclusions by relying on F.X. de Funk, *Das Alter der Arkanddisziplin*, in *Kirchengeschichtliche Abhandlungen und Untersuchungen*, Paderborn, 1907, t. III, pp 42–55. Funk shows that if the arcane was simply pedagogical, it would be hard to understand why it would be concerned with the Apostles' Creed and baptismal theology, the knowledge of which would have had to precede, pedagogically, the reception of the sacrament. That this teaching was revealed to neophytes only after Baptism proves that the reason for the arcane was of a mysterial nature. In *Savoir et Salut* ('*Paradosis.* Esoteric traditions in the early Christian centuries', pp 127–143), Stroumsa has presented the most recent synthesis (some of his conclusions are debatable: cf. above, p 276).

1. *Traité de l'eucharistie*, 1622, I, 8; *D.T.C.*, t. I, col. 1739. Denis Pétau, one of the most learned Jesuits of the seventeenth century (at eighteen he corresponded in Greek with the Protestant Casaubon), is of the same opinion: *Dogmata theologica* (1644), II, Praef. 5.

Christ the Original Mystery

persist up to the middle of the twentieth century, was Isaac Casaubon, in a work published in London in 1614.[1] However, it was necessary to await the years 1675–1680, and the works of the Protestant Jean Daillé, to see the appearance of the expression *disciplina arcani*, an expression that will prevail in both camps as the best possible formulation; at the same time he presents a more satisfying conception of it, since he sees in this arcane a means to 'arouse in the mind of the catechumens a respect and intense desire for the sacraments';[2] however he denies that this discipline dates back to Christ.

The Catholic theologians recovered this formula for themselves, but by asserting that this rule of silence was indeed instituted by Christ. This was chiefly the work of the canon Schelstratus, a former prefect of the Vatican Library. In a series of treatises (contested by Protestant scholarship) he maintains that the arcane, instituted by Christ (and first by Moses), covered 'the dogma of the Trinity, the dogma and rite of the Mass and sacraments ... the cult of the saints, transubstantiation, etc.'[3] The thesis of Schelstratus enjoyed great prestige and was almost official in Catholic theology until the end of the nineteenth century.

Such is, in brief, the question's history. We also see that the Catholic Church of modern times was by no means an enemy of a certain esoterism, that it even recognized its existence during the first five or six centuries and reclaimed it as its own.

---

1. *De rebus sacris et ecclesiasticis exercitationes XVI; D.T.C.*, ibid., col. 174. This thesis, as we have seen, has been almost abandoned. But illustrious scholars have shared it in the course of the centuries: Renan, Reitzenstein, Loisy, and the all too famous 'French citizen' Dupuis, who declared that the formula for the exclusion of the catechumens, pronounced by the deacon before the Offertory of the Mass, had been borrowed by Christians 'from the ancient pagans, just like they have borrowed all the rest'; *Abrégé de l'origine de tous les cultes*, chez H. Agasse, Paris, An VI de la République, p482. Not lacking in erudition, this is an obsessional and tedious anti-Christian work.

2. *De usu Patrem ad ea definienda religionis capita, quae sunt hodie controversa*, Geneva; *D.T.C.*, t. I, col. 1740–1741.

3. *D.T.C.*, ibid., col. 1741. The treatises of Schelstratus are: *Antiquitas illustrata circa concilia, etc.*, Anvers, 1678; *Commentatio de Antiocheno concilio*, Rome, 1685.

Sacramental Initiation & the Discipline of the Arcane

Arcane and Catechumenate

Entering the quick of the subject from now on, I will first ask: why the need for a rule of silence? Often the reply is that the discipline of the arcane was tied to the institution of the catechumenate, that is to the obligation for a time of doctrinal and even ritual preparation, more or less long, before receiving baptismal initiation. This institution, it has been said, was not in force from the beginning, since, as we have seen, the Acts of the Apostles mentions baptisms that we can think of as being administered without catechumenal preparation. This is why, around 1900, it was maintained that the arcane did not date back beyond 300: 'In the second and even the third centuries, an esoteric teaching did not yet exist in the Church; the discipline of the secret was unknown to Catholics.' This assertion of the Abbé Bareille[1] would be hardly acceptable today.

All historians agree in recognizing that, without doubt, the existence of an institutional catechumenate, in the precise sense of the term, is hardly attested to before the beginning of the third century. It is around 200, in fact, that catechetical schools (the 'didascalia') are set up and the catechumenate is organized into two stages marked by special rites (exorcisms, the laying on of hands, and signings): first there were the 'listening' (*audientes*) catechumens, subject to a remote preparation of three years maximum, and then the catechumens 'to be baptized', the *baptizandi*, also called the 'elect' (the candidates for baptism were designated by vote) or the 'competent' (*competentes*), and, among the Greeks the 'future illumined' (*photizomenoi*), subject to a near preparation during the time of Lent. In addition, the newly baptized, the 'neophytes' (or 'new plants') received a second catechesis after their baptism, often called a 'mystagogical catechesis'.[2]

---

1. *D.T.C.*, t. II, col. 1979; article 'Catechumenate'.
2. Beside the already mentioned works and dictionary articles, we have consulted: A.G. Martimort (*et alia*), Introduction à la liturgie (Paris: Desclée et Cie, 1961), pp 515–528; likewise, Jean Daniélou, *L'Église des premiers temps—Des origines à la fin du IIIe siècle* (Paris: Seuil, 1963), pp 77–82 and 169–176. The bibliography on the subject is immense. Useful information will be found in the already mentioned work by K. McDonnell and G.T. Montague), *Baptême dans l'Esprit et initiation*

Christ the Original Mystery

However, since the apostolic age, and aside from the first years of Christian preaching when a discourse by Peter or Paul was enough 'plunge the enthused crowds into the waters of Baptism,'[1] baptism was always preceded by a period (for adults obviously) of preparation and instruction comprised of the two just mentioned phases: a distant preparation followed by an immediate preparation in the course of which those to be baptized fasted for some days. Now, during this catechumenate, whether embryonic or developed, the prohibition from participating in the mysteries of Christianity seems to have been always observed. Without doubt we inevitably come up against the problem that I have often raised: a total silence, by definition, should not be attested to by a text. Whoever says that he is keeping quiet has already said too much. This is why, if he is content to make it known that *such or such* a rite and *such or such* a doctrine should remain secret and that it is not permitted to disclose them, the writer should be resigned to the compromise and 'disclosure', however miniscule, of that which he does not have the right to reveal and thus make possible its identification. This is quite exactly what happened, as the church literature of that time testifies. But there is still another reason that favored a semi-unveiling and rendered useless a strict observation of the *disciplina arcani*: the rites and doctrines covered had absolutely nothing 'magical' about them. It had nothing to do with keeping the handling of spiritual influences, which would have been dangerous in unskilled

---

chrétienne, (Paris: Desclée De Brouwer, 1993, even though its subject essentially deals with the question of charisms. Documents on baptismal initiation, starting with the third century, are rather numerous and quite informative. They show that usages have varied according to time and place. These variations even affect elements held to be essential. In the *Apostolic Tradition* of St Hippolytus, the oldest text (215) with respect to liturgical institutions (it describes, perhaps, the ritual practice of the decade after 150), the formula: 'I baptize you...' or 'Be baptized in the Name of the Father and of the Son and of the Holy Spirit,' is not mentioned. But this is a text reconstituted from late versions in various Semitic languages, and its attribution to St Hippolytus is disputed as well. This text seems to reflect, not the Roman liturgy of the second century, but the needs of its author (Bouyer, *Eucharist* [Notre Dame, Indiana: University of Notre Dame Press, 1968], pp158–191).

1. A. Hamman, *La vie quotidienne des premiers chrétiens*, 1971, p 221; likewise: G. Bardy, *L' Église à la fin du Ier siècle*, Bloud et Gay, 1932, p 54.

Sacramental Initiation & the Discipline of the Arcane

hands, away from the curiosity of a possible sorcerer's apprentice. In reality, the Christian arcane was in compliance with a dual need: subjectively, the mind of the catechumen had to be awakened to an awareness of the transcendent nature of the mysteries in which he was going to participate; objectively, the truths to be known can be *really* understood only in the light of faith, that alone confers baptism. Faith is a gift of God and it is precisely this gift that the one to be baptized asks to receive when he presents himself at the doors of the church. The first question posed is in fact the following: 'What do you ask of the Church?'; and the answer is: 'Faith'. That is the positive reason for the discipline of silence, and for the dismissal of the catechumens before the Offertory, or before the recitation of the Nicean Creed, when its use was introduced (around 450) into the Sunday Mass. Insofar as they have not received sanctifying grace, insofar as they have not been marked with the seal of Christ's priesthood, they can neither liturgically confess 'the sacred text of the symbol [Creed] which came under the *disciplina arcani*,'[1] nor contemplate the visible form of its holy mysteries, nor welcome within themselves the truth that they enclose, for, hearing, they would not understand, and, seeing, they would not perceive. Even more than a profanation, it would be something useless and a dead letter.

Such is the principle. However, its application raises some difficulties. To publicly confess the Symbol of the Apostles (and later the *Credo* of Nicea) at the time of baptismal initiation, to recite it next with fellow initiates at the time of the eucharistic liturgy immediately following Baptism, it obviously had to be learned. The prohibition, for the non-baptized, from knowing its content could only have been relative then: complete for an unbeliever or a 'hearing' catechumen, it was lifted for the 'elect', 'those to be illuminated'. This is why, in the weeks preceding initiation, the catechists (lay doctors, priests or even bishops) proceeded to what would be called the *Traditio Symboli*, that is the 'transmission' of the *Credo*, each article of which was pronounced *orally*, commented on and repeated in such

---

1. J.A. Jungmann, *The Mass of the Roman Rite* (New York: Benziger Brothers, 1951), vol. 1, p 479.

Christ the Original Mystery

a way that each one to be baptized would learn it by heart. Somewhat later the 'tradition' of the Lord's Prayer would be added, and then, somewhat later still, around 550, and chiefly at Rome, the 'tradition' of the Gospels, that is to say the handing over of the Book of the Gospels to those to be baptized.[1] After the tradition of the Symbol came, on the eve of baptism, or a little before the immersion, the *Redditio Symboli,* a rendering (or restitution) of the Symbol. This was the first act of the future neophyte: aloud, before his fellow Christians, he proclaimed the Catholic faith. As for the rendering of the *Pater,* it seems to have followed the reception of baptism: having become children of God by grace, the neophytes could truly call Him 'Father'.[2] Not only were the handing down and rendering of the Creed and the *Pater* done orally, but to speak of them before the uninitiated ('hearing' catechumens or pagans) or to set down their texts in writing was expressly prohibited.

To today's confirmed esoterist it seems most unlikely that the Creed and the Lord's Prayer—so banal and anodyne have they become—were once the focus of a secret tradition. And yet, as will be shown, it is a well-proven fact whose traces have not entirely vanished. For my part, I attribute the greatest importance to this as a most irrefutable witness to what the Church saw as truly esoteric. No one can deny, after everything I have explained and recalled, that baptismal initiation is linked, to a degree unheard of in pagan initiations, with the possession of a knowledge, that is with a gnosis, and that the content of this gnosis is, in the end and synthetically

---

1. This addition occurred at the moment when the *Credo* of Nicea-Constantinople had been substituted for the Symbol of the Apostles as baptismal creed, to be explained by the generalization of child baptisms that made lengthy catechetical instructions impossible, instructions that could be provided later by a reading of the Christian scriptures; cf. Martimort, *Introduction à la liturgie,* pp 524–525. St Augustine explains why the *Traditio Symboli* came before the 'tradition' of the Our Father: knowledge of the One in whom we believe (*Credo*) ought to precede the formulation of the requests addressed to Him (*Pater*); cf. *Sermon LVII,* 1, 1; P.L., t. xxxviii, col. 377.

2. A post-baptismal rendering of the Lord's Prayer is indicated in the *Apostolic Constitutions* (vii, 44; P.G., t. i, col. 1045). St Cyril of Jerusalem explained the *Pater* only after initiation and participation in the pascal Mass (*The Fifth Mystagogical Catechesis,* 11–18).

Sacramental Initiation & the Discipline of the Arcane

expressed, the Catholic *Credo*. That the upholders of esoterism will agree with their adversaries in rejecting such a conclusion is, alas, only too foreseeable.[1] But, if this is so, it is because both have been blind to the true significance of the treasure in their hands. To the latter I would say: do not seek without what you already possess, remain within; to the former: do not remain outside, sin not against the Holy Spirit, enter into the depths of the mystery, and to everyone: know at last the gift of God.

We come now to an examination of Church literature.

The Arcane in the Texts From the Second to the Fourth Centuries

Of the testimonies giving evidence in favor of the Christian arcane, those of St Irenaeus and St Justin are sometimes set aside. The latter, in fact, criticizes the practice of the secret that the heretical gnosis was fond of and that it would bestow only by means of a 'high price'.[2] However, I believe that Irenaeus rejected, not the arcane itself, but the extravagant triviality of the so-called secrets of pseudo-gnosis and its associated 'money-grubbing', to which he opposes a disinterested search for the true mysteries of revelation, illuminated by the rule of truth and with the awareness of our smallness before God's infinite grandeur: it only convinces us that 'we have need of *receiving*

---

1. The attitude indicated here is quite well represented by G.G. Stroumsa's already mentioned book, *Savoir et Salut*. Interesting for the pieces of information that it communicates about rabbinic esoterism, its '*Paradosis*' chapter is ultimately deceiving about Christianity because devoid of a theoretical elaboration of the notion of esoterism as such. Stroumsa speaks of it as if it is a self-evident cultural category to be treated identically in every context. In reality, he is only speaking of a formal esoterism of the rabbinic kind, the continuation of which he, like Daniélou, sees in the 'secret traditions' of the first three centuries. After that, gnosis would disappear in favor of either mystical experience or the cult of the saints, with esoteric knowledge becoming 'the appanage of isolated groups of persecuted heretics' (p143), and with 'no trace of esoteric doctrine' in Dionysius the Areopagite (p142). These views are only supported at the price of a (quite exoteric) misunderstanding about the nature of Christianity.

2. *Against the Heresies*, I, 4, 3.

Christ the Original Mystery

knowledge of God's mysteries.'[1] As for St Justin, he does not seem to keep silent about the rites of the Eucharist, since he quite clearly exhibits them at the end of his *First Apology* (around 150). However, far from denying it, the texts seems to suggest the existence of a separation between those who have not received baptism, to whom is dispensed a more or less long pre-baptismal catechesis, and those who have received the regenerating 'immersion' called 'illumination' (*photismos*). It is only then that, 'after having been washed and joined to us, we lead him into the place where those who we call brothers are gathered.' Then come the prayers in common, Scripture readings and the 'Memoires of the Apostles', the sacrificial eucharist and communion.[2] As for the fact that Justin speaks openly, but very briefly, of the eucharistic mystery, this is sufficiently explained by the nature of his writing: it involves defending before the imperial authorities—it is an *Apology*—the reputation of Christians who, at that time, were accused, among other horrors, of giving themselves up to monstrous orgies in the course of secret banquets where those initiated to the Christian mysteries had to kill a child and drink its blood.[3] If the eucharistic liturgy had been public, such accusations would have been impossible.

Such must also be said about those later texts (around 215) where Tertullian refutes the same slander.[4] How, he asks the slanderers, can you know what happens in our mysteries 'since, by virtue of their very nature, all mysteries require a commitment to silence (*cum vel*

---

1. Ibid., II, 2, 3. Irenaeus does not say much regarding the sacraments, but he does still associate the reception of the 'rule of truth' (the syntagma 'rule of faith' is absent from *Against the Heresies*) with baptismal initiation (ibid. I, 9, 4). Thus the 'rule of truth' spoken of in *Against the Heresies* can be identified with the 'rule of faith' about which he speaks in his *Demonstration of the Apostolic Preaching* (cf. supra, p108, n3).

2. *Apology I*, 61–67: cf. *La philosophie passe au Christ: L'œuvre de Justin*, D.D.B., trans. Pautigny and Archambault, revised and produced 1982, pp 89–95.

3. Cf. what the Christian Minucius Felix relates (around 195) in his *Octavius*, IX, 6; in De Labriolle's *La réaction païenne*, p91.

4. *The Apology*, VII; cf. Tertullian and St Augustine, *Œuvres choises*, under the direction of D. Nisard, 1845, pp 13–14. This slander was quite widespread and the Latin rhetor Fronton, tutor of Marcus Aurelius (a persecutor of Christians), to whom Minucius Felix attributes it, was not the only one to spread it: thirty years

Sacramental Initiation & the Discipline of the Arcane

ex forma omnibus mysteriis fides silentii debeatur)', and all the more so if crimes abominable to justice, both human and divine, are involved. To these declarations from *The Apology* attesting to the arcane of the Christian mysteries must be added certain passages from *On Baptism*,[1] a work contemporaneous to the *Apostolic Tradition* of St Hippolytus: they prove that there reigned at the beginning of the third century, at Carthage as at Rome, the practice of the catechumenate and therefore of the arcane that is inseparable from it. Tertullian also reproaches the heretics, especially the 'Gnostics' (probably the disciples of Marcion), for admitting the uninitiated to the celebration of the mysteries, whether they be heathens [the *Ethnici*] or catechumens:

> I must not omit an account of the conduct also of the heretics— how frivolous it is, how worldly, how merely human, without seriousness, without authority, without discipline [*disciplina*], as suits their creed. To begin with, it is doubtful who is a catechumen, and who a believer; they have all access alike, they hear alike, they pray alike—even heathens, if any such happen to come among them. 'That which is holy [*sanctum* = the Eucharist] they will cast to the dogs, and their pearls,' although (to be sure) they are not real ones, 'they will fling to the swine.' Simplicity they will have to consist in the overthrow of discipline, attention to which on our part they call affectation.[2]

This is why neither heretics nor the unbaptized can receive the *tradition sacramenti*, the tradition of the 'sacrament'[3]—by which

---

after Justin's *Apology*, 'the whole empire resounded with the same imputations' (Vacandard, article 'arcane', *D.H.G.E.*, col. 1507). We encounter identical accusations at Alexandria, Antioch, Lyon, Vienne (in Gaul), and finally Carthage as we see with Tertullian (who, however, is perhaps copying Minucius Felix).

1. *On Baptism*, 20.
2. *The Prescription against Heretics*, 41. The 'pearls to the swine' refers to Matt. 7:6. The same reproach of breaching the eucharistic arcane has been likewise addressed to the Marcionites by St Epiphanius: *Haer.*, XLII, 3; P.G., t. XLI, col. 733. Here we have an important indication about what heretics and orthodox consider to be esoteric: the cosmological teachings of Hellenized Judaism were esoteric to the former, while the liturgy of the sacraments was so to the latter.
3. *The Prescription against Heretics*, 20, 7, 8.

Christ the Original Mystery

Tertullian understands 'the sum total of the truths of salvation and the mysteries of the faith'[1]—since it is the unity of the rule of faith that marks Church unity.[2] He is, moreover, adverse to infant baptism ('let them become Christians when they have become able to know Christ')[3]—which precisely supposes the existence of pedobaptism, but which intensifies the rigor of the catechumenal discipline and, therefore, the rigor of the arcane. That, for him, this arcane indeed corresponds to an ecclesiastic rule is what he explicitly asserts when he asks himself how to reconcile the Pauline *precept* (1 Tim. 1:2) of continual prayer with the Gospel *precept* (Matt. 6:5–6) of what he calls 'secret prayer' (*praecepta secrete orandi*). Basically he replies that the precept remains, but necessity has the force of law, as proven by the Apostles' example who, imprisoned, prayed before their jailers, or the example of St Paul celebrating the Eucharist on the boat that took him away to Rome 'in the presence of all.'[4] This remark is important because it clearly shows what the Christian arcane is and how it differs from the arcane of the mystery cults: among Christians, there is no magical superstition about the secret, about a precept for silence accompanied by threats for those who would transgress it. Secrecy and silence are in harmony with the majesty of the mystery accomplished, but are in no way the guardians of this mystery: it is not reserved to a few, all have been called to it.

Origen was born around twenty-five years after Tertullian. He also is an irrefutable witness to the discipline of the catechumenal arcane. In one of his homilies—of which only a Latin version remains—commenting on the texts of Leviticus on the priesthood, he recalls that, for the Christians, Christ is the true Pontiff who has reconciled all men through the sacrifice of his blood, and exclaims: 'Hear what the Word of God is telling you: This is my blood, shed for you unto remission of sins. When one has been penetrated with the

---

1. McDonnell and Montague, *Baptême dans l'Esprit et initiation chrétienne*, p108.
2. *The Prescription against Heretics*, 20, 7, 8.
3. *On Baptism*, 18.
4. *On Prayer*, 1 and 24; Tertullian is alluding to an episode in Acts (28:35) the meaning of which is disputed: is it a simple meal or the Eucharist? He himself sees there a eucharist, the public nature of which demands an explanation.

Sacramental Initiation & the Discipline of the Arcane

mysteries, one knows the flesh and the blood of the Word of God. We linger not over what is known by the initiated and cannot be disclosed to the ignorant.'[1] 'Initiated' translates the Latin *scientibus*, that is: those who know, the gnostics. The true meaning of the eucharistic mystery is, then, placed under the law of the arcane. And we will see proof of this arcane borne out in the following century.

Starting with 300, in fact, the institution of the catechumenate is everywhere attested to; it flourishes precisely at the moment when the Council of Nicea (325) is assembled and when—in the midst of some difficulties, as we have seen—its trinitarian doctrine is imposed. The fourth and fifth centuries are, then, the major periods of the catechumenate, those periods in which proofs of the Christian arcane are the most numerous and the most precise, and not periods of a definitive exteriorisation. Like Tertullian and St Epiphanius against the 'Gnostics', St Athanasius, the champion of Nicene orthodoxy, reproaches the Arians[2] for transgressing the precept of the secret:

> the Arians [he writes] are not ashamed to parade the sacred mysteries before catechumens, and worse than that, even before heathens; whereas, they ought to attend to what is written, 'It is good to keep close the secret of a king' [Tobit 12:7], and to the Lord's precept, 'Give not that which is holy unto the dogs, neither cast ye your pearls before swine.' We ought not then to parade the holy mysteries before the uninitiated (*amuetoi*), lest the heathen in their ignorance deride them, and the catechumens be offended by knowing them in this way.[3]

St Cyril of Jerusalem has left us the most beautiful catecheses of Christian antiquity. Taken stenographically by a listener, it is composed of two groups: the first is intended for the *photizomenoi*, for those to be illuminated (the *illuminandi*), and essentially deals with the various articles of the *Credo*, the second (the *Mystagogical Catecheses*) successively unfolds the significance of the three rites of

---

1. *Homilies on Leviticus*, IX, 10. [The French version of the text is used here. TR]
2. *Apologia contra Arianos*, 11; P.G., t. xxv, col. 269.
3. Recall that Leo XIII named St Athanasius a 'Doctor of the Church'.

Christ the Original Mystery

Christian initiation: Baptism, Confirmation and the Eucharist. The *Catecheses for those to be illuminated* has as its object what Cyril himself calls 'gnosis', theological knowledge; it consists, as previously mentioned, in a commentary on the *Credo,* and it is covered by the arcane: 'When the lecture is delivered,' St Cyril declares,

> if a catechumen [not as yet being one of 'those to be illuminated'] ask you what the teachers have said, tell nothing to him that is without. For we deliver to thee a mystery.... Guard the secret for Him who gives the reward.... But you are now standing on the border of the mystery: take heed, pray, not to let slip a single word fraudulently.[1]

And, in fact, the stenographer himself has respected the discipline of the arcane. When it is said that these catecheses deal with the different articles of the *Credo,* it should be added that the text of the Symbol of faith does not appear as such and *in extenso* therein. However, St Cyril speaks quite explicitly of a *formulary* of the Christian faith:

> Since all cannot read the Scriptures, some being hindered as to the knowledge of them by want of learning, and others by a want of leisure, in order that the soul may not perish from ignorance, we comprise the whole doctrine of the Faith in a few lines.[2]

Besides, it is possible to reconstitute, out of the elements of the *Credo* scattered through the stenography and from the titles of various catecheses (are they Cyril's?), precisely what the Jerusalem *Credo* was at that time.[3] This *Credo* had to be learned 'by heart' and could not be put in writing.[4] The Trinity could not be spoken of openly in the presence of catechumens, no more than the other dogmatic mysteries or the true nature of the sacraments of initiation. And

---

1. *Procatechesis* (a preliminary discourse to the *Baptismal Cathecheses*), 12; P.G., t. xxxiii, col. 332 A.
2. *Fifth Baptismal Catechesis,* c. 12; P.G., t. xxxiii, col. 520 B.
3. Cyril follows the order of the articles in the *Apostles' Creed*, except for baptism and the remission of sins which are treated at the beginning (Catecheses 1 to 2). On the problems posed by this reconstitution (Dom Touttée, 1700) and the date of this *Credo* (it does not include the *homoousios*), cf. *D.T.C.,* t. iii, col. 2539–2542.
4. *Fifth Catechesis,* c. 12; P.G., t. xxxiii, col. 521.

Sacramental Initiation & the Discipline of the Arcane

even when they had been received, Cyril continues to observe a certain silence about their form.[1]

A Star Witness: St Basil of Caesarea

Such is the practice of the Church of Jerusalem around 348.[2] And altogether identical practices are also to be found in the Latin West. But first special mention must be accorded to St Basil the Great, bishop of Caesarea, older brother of St Gregory of Nyssa and friend of St Gregory Nazianzus. He is in fact one of the major witnesses to the Christian arcane, some have even asserted: 'the only one'.[3] A major witness because he affirms in a most explicit way the apostolic origin for the 'discipline of the arcane'.

It is not unimportant that, in his *Treatise on the Holy Spirit*, St Basil[4] sets forth his teaching on this point, to prove the ancientness

---

1. *Sixth Catechesis*, 29, col. 529; *Sixteenth*, 26, col. 596; *Eighteenth*, 32, etc.; *D. T. C.*, col. 2561.

2. Liturgical practice at Jerusalem at the end of the fourth century is well enough known, not only through St Cyril, but also through other documents, one of which is an astonishing 'travel journal' (the *Peregrinatio*) by a Gallo-Roman lady named Etheria (or Egeria, or perhaps Sylvia), who quite meticulously describes what she observed. This document was discovered in Italy in an Arezzo manuscript around 1889. On the subject of the *redditio Symboli* rite by which those to be baptized 'render up' to the bishop the Symbol that they have received, she recounts the episcopal address that followed this *redditio*. To those who are still only catechumens, the bishop declares that they have been instructed in the truths of the faith, according to the Scriptures and the Symbol, insofar as a catechumen can be instructed: 'but about a more lofty mystery, namely baptism itself, nothing can be said to you who are still catechumens about the most secret mysteries' (translated from the Latin text published as an appendix by L. Duchesne, *Origines du culte chrétien*, Ernest Thorin, editor, 1889, p 498).

3. 'A single writer, who had seen the catechetical arcane in force around him, wanted to see in this an institution comparable to the discipline imagined by Schelstratus. Such was St Basil' (Batiffol, *D. T. C.*, t. I, col. 1756). This is an improbable thesis!

4. On the life of St Basil of Caesarea and his spiritual physiognomy, the foremost work is Dom Robert Pouchet's *Basile le Grand et son univers d'amis d'après sa correspondance. Une stratégie de communion*, Studia Ephemerides Augustinianum 36, Institutum Patristicum 'Augustinianum', Roma, 1992.

of the trinitarian formulas, right after he speaks about its tradition, the *paradosis*. I have already stressed the privileged relationship between the notions of esoterism and tradition in Origen.[1]

As is customary with Church writers, the word 'tradition' assumes, for St Basil, a dual meaning: an active sense of 'transmission' (this is the case when one speaks, for example, of the 'tradition of the Symbol'), and a passive sense of 'that which has been transmitted'. In both cases tradition has been distinguished from Scripture, most often as that which is secret from that which is public and proclaimed. What has been proclaimed, the 'proclamations', this is what Basil designates by the Greek term *kerygma* (plural: *kerygmata*). To designate the generally secret teachings of tradition, the 'doctrines', he uses the term *dogma* (plural: *dogmata*). Thus we have two pairs of terms (tradition/Scripture, proclamation/doctrine) that do not altogether coincide, to the extent that tradition does not only transmit *dogmata*, but also *kerygmata*. Anyhow, the teaching (*didaskalia*) of the Church encompasses both.[2] However it is for this rather complex question, the 'dogmas' (= the doctrines) themselves are observed to be almost always the object of a secret transmission. Thus, the word which, for Guénon (and some others) bears the manifest stamp of a massive exteriorisation, designates to the contrary for Basil the most reserved teachings.

Here, then, is what one of the principal Fathers of the Church declares:

> Of the beliefs and practices, whether generally accepted or publicly enjoined which are preserved in the Church, some we possess derived from written teaching; others we have received delivered to us 'in a mystery' (*en mysterio*) by the tradition of the apostles; and both of these in relation to true religion have the same force. And these no one will gainsay—no one, at all events, who is even moderately versed in the institutions of the Church.

---

1. Cf. above, p240, n5.
2. On all of this, cf. Benoît Pruche, in his introduction to Saint Basil of Caesarea's *Sur le Saint-Esprit*, text, translation and notes by Pruche, 2nd edition entirely recast; *Sources chrétiennes* 17 bis, pp139–141.

Sacramental Initiation & the Discipline of the Arcane

To reject the secret doctrines is to offend against 'the Gospel in its very vitals' and to empty the proclamations of their meaning.

For instance [at the time of the baptismal initiation] ... who has taught us in writing to sign with the sign of the cross those who have trusted in the name of our Lord Jesus Christ? What writing has taught us to turn to the East at the prayer? Which of the saints has left us in writing the words of the invocation at the displaying of the bread of the Eucharist and the cup of blessing? For we are not, as is well known, content with what the apostle or the Gospel has recorded, but both in preface and conclusion we add other words as being of great importance to the validity of the ministry, and these we derive from unwritten teaching.[1] Moreover we bless the water of baptism and the oil of the chrism, and besides this the catechumen who is being baptized. On what written authority do we do this? Is not our authority silent and mystical tradition? Nay, by what written word is the anointing of oil itself taught? And whence comes the custom of baptizing thrice? And as to the other customs of baptism from what Scripture do we derive the renunciation of Satan and his angels? Does not this come from that unpublished and secret teaching which our fathers guarded in a silence out of the reach of curious meddling and inquisitive investigation? Well had they learnt the lesson that the awful dignity of the mysteries is best preserved by silence. What the uninitiated [*amuetoi*] are not even allowed to contemplate [*epopteuein*] was hardly likely to be publicly paraded about in written documents.[2]

Moses had already separated the profane from the Levites and the High Priest who, alone, once a year, could contemplate 'the Holy of

---

1. Notice that the text respects the arcane and does not transcribe these words. But we have a rather precise idea of them through what has come down to us in the liturgy of St Basil, a liturgy still practiced in the Orthodox Church. The apostle involved is St Paul who, in relating the words of the consecration, *transmits* what he has *received from the Lord* (1 Cor. 11:23–27). This is thought to involve the most ancient 'recital of the eucharistic institution' (Spring 55). 'Gospel' refers to Matt. 26:26–29, Mark 14:22–25, Luke 22:14–20.

2. *On the Holy Spirit*, xxvii, 66.

Christ the Original Mystery

Holies with fright', knowing well 'that contempt stretches to the trite and to what everyone has access to.'

> In the same manner the Apostles and Fathers who laid down laws for the Church from the beginning thus guarded the awful dignity of the mysteries in secrecy and silence, for what is bruited abroad random among the common folk is no mystery at all. This is the reason for our tradition of unwritten precepts and practices, that the high knowledge [*gnosis*] of our doctrines [*dogmata*] may not become neglected and contemned by the multitude through familiarity. Doctrine [*dogma*] and proclamation [*kerygma*] are two distinct things; the former is observed in silence; the latter is proclaimed to all the world. One form of this silence is the obscurity employed in Scripture, which makes the meaning of 'dogmas' difficult to be understood.[1]

It does not seem that St John Chrysostom (born between 344 and 354) provides as firm and explicit a teaching on the apostolic origin of the arcane.[2] But he has put in practice the rule of silence and says so without ambiguity. In a homily preached at Antioch he recalls 'the word pronounced by those who initiated you (the 'mystagogues'),' then he hesitates:

> I want to speak clearly, but I dare not because of the uninitiated: they make the task of commenting [on Scripture] difficult, compelling us either not to speak clearly or declare to them the ineffable mysteries. Nevertheless, as I may be able, I will speak as through a veil.

What is this word then? The continuation of the text will inform us: it is the *Credo*, the baptismal Symbol:

> Thus, after the enunciation [at the time of the Symbol's *traditio* and the *redditio*] of those mystical and dreadsome words, and the

---

1. Ibid.
2. On this question, one of his recent commentators refers to Batiffol's works; cf. A. Piedagnel, *Trois catéchèses baptismales de S. Jean Chrysostome*, Sources chrétiennes 366, 1990, pp226–227, n. 20: 'the catechetical convention [of the arcane] is not prior to the fourth century.' An opinion belied by the texts that we have collected.

august canons of the dogmas which have come down from heaven, this also we add at the end when we are about to baptize, bidding them say, *I believe in the resurrection of the dead,* and upon this faith we are baptized.[1]

Not only does the arcane cover the *Credo*, it also covers the Lord's Prayer: if we pardon those who have offended us, says the holy bishop, 'we will be able... to approach this sacred, awe-inspiring table and pronounce with confidence those words associated with the prayer. The initiated know what is to be said.'[2]

The Arcane From the Fourth Century Onward

Faced with so many testimonies, we begin to better understand perhaps why I have always maintained that Christianity's secret gnosis was synthetically contained in the rule of truth, the ecclesial canon of the Christian faith. And perhaps we begin to better understand why this canon received the name '*Symbol*', which, let us recall, signifies 'sign of communion' in Greek, since it is clearly that sign by which all the Churches of Christ are united, because within it they recognize their unique and unifying doctrine. And perhaps it will be easier, then, to accept the idea, so often expressed here, of the rightly doctrinal, theological nature of the Christian identity. A symbol of knowledge, unity, and identity, the *Credo* is all of that, and this is why it is a 'password' gaining the one to be initiated entry into the sacred Temple of the Christic *Ecclesia* and there to be united with all those who commune in the same baptismal gnosis.

One of Tertullian's texts already contains a significant indication of this function of the *Symbol*. In his treatise *The Prescription against Heretics*, he passes in review 'the apostolic churches, in which the very thrones of the apostles are still preeminent in their places.' From these he comes to the Church of Rome:

---

1. *In 1 Cor.*, Homily XL; P.G., t. LXI, col. 347.
2. *Saint John Chrysostom, Homilies on Genesis,* Homily 27 (25), trans. R.C. Hill [Washington, DC: Catholic University of America, 1990], p181.

Christ the Original Mystery

How happy is its church, on which apostles poured forth all their doctrine along with their blood.... United (*contesseratis*) with the Church of Africa, she acknowledges only one God, Creator of the universe, and Christ Jesus born of the Virgin Mary, the Son of God the Creator; and the Resurrection of the flesh; the law and the prophets she unites in one volume with the writings of evangelists and apostles, from which she drinks in her faith. This she seals (*signat*) with water, arrays with the Holy Spirit, feeds with the Eucharist.

Now the adjective *contesseratus* (with the ablative plural), which Tertullian uses to express the bond that unites the Churches of Africa with the Church of Rome, has a very precise meaning. It refers to the practice of the '*tesserae* of hospitality', which the Greeks specifically designated by the term *symbolon*, that is to say the earthenware token, a portion of which is possessed by each of the contracting or allied parties, or even to a 'password', to a verbal sign of recognition by which the initiated might be recognized among themselves and which is formed here by the rule of baptismal faith.[1]

But, clearer than Tertullian, we encounter with St Ambrose, a western contemporary of St John Chrysostom, an undeniable proof of the secret character of the baptismal Symbol. We have the good fortune to possess, just like the eastern Fathers that I have cited, a stenography for a session of a *traditio Symboli* in the course of which the Bishop of Milan (around 385) teaches and transmits the *Symbol* to those to be baptized (this stenography has, besides, faithfully recorded the imperfections of spoken language). In this catechesis, having come down to us under the title *Explanation of the Symbol* (*Explanation Symboli*), St Ambrose declares:

---

1. *De Praescriptione*, xxxvi, 1 and 3–5. On the meaning of the words *symbolon* and *tessera* cf. my book *Le mystère du signe*, pp 17–20 [also cf. *The Secret of the Christian Way* (Albany: SUNY Press, 2001), pp 61–67 TR]. Numerous *tesserae* of hospitality in pottery can be seen in the Gallo-Roman museum of Grand in the Vosges. — We recognize in the faith 'sealed with water', 'arrayed with the Holy Spirit' and 'fed with the Eucharist' the three stages of Christian initiation: Baptism, Confirmation and Communion.

Sacramental Initiation & the Discipline of the Arcane

> Now this I desire you to be warned of, that the Symbol is not to be written down.... Wherefore? So we have received, that it is not to be written down. But what then? to be remembered.... Say over the Symbol to yourself inwardly, — yes, I say, by all means inwardly. Why? Lest you form a habit, and when you are accustomed to saying it over aloud where there are some of the faithful, you come to saying it among catechumens or heretics.[1]

And in fact the stenographer has respected this prohibition, being content, when St Ambrose pronounces the article of the Creed that he will comment on, with indicating the first and the last word, hence Dom Botte's conclusion in connection with the discipline of the arcane: 'This does not then involve a fiction, but a regulation still in force.'[2] For St Ambrose, as well as for St John Chrysostom (and many other Fathers), neither should the Lord's Prayer be recited in the presence of catechumens: 'take care,' he says, 'not to imprudently divulge the mysteries of the Symbol and the Lord's Prayer.'[3]

Numerous texts from St Augustine can be cited to prove either the existence of the catechumenate and the dismissal of the uninitiated before the sacrifice of the Mass, or the distress of a preacher who, in public, cannot unveil the mysteries of eucharistic communion. Thus, preaching about St John's text (6:56): 'my flesh is meat indeed: and my blood is drink indeed,' he declares for the benefit of the uninitiated: 'This has been veiled to you, but, if you wish, it will be revealed. Submit your name for baptism ... and you will understand the meaning of these words.'[4] On the other hand, the famous beginning of his instruction to the catechumens is known:

> Receive, my children, the Rule of Faith, which is called the Symbol. And when you have received it, write it in your heart, and be daily saying it to yourselves.... The Creed no man writes so as not to expose it to be read by profane eyes. Engrave it, then,

---

1. *Explanatio*, 9; *Des Sacrements. Des Mystères*, ed. Dom Botte, Sources chrétiennes 25, pp 57–59. [The translation used here is that of Dom R.H. Connolly (*Texts and Studies*, vol. x: London: Cambridge University Press, 1967, pp 26–7 TR.]
2. Ibid. p 22 of the introduction.
3. *On Cain and Abel*, I, 9, 37; P.L., t. XIV, col. 335A.
4. *Sermon CXXXII*, 1; P.L., t. XXXVIII, col. 734.

Christ the Original Mystery

deeply in your memory, if you do not want to forget what you learned with such a noble ardor.[1]

To conclude, let us recall two well known testimonies of the Christian arcane; they are of unequal authority, but both are quite significant. The first is a text of St Innocent I, who was Pope from 401 to 417. In a letter of March 19, 416, he replies to Decentius, Bishop of Gubio, who had come to Rome to learn what rites should be observed in the 'mysteries to be consecrated as well as in the arcana to be accomplished.' The Pope speaks in veiled terms. He specifies, in connection with a new question, that, at Mass, the *peace* should be given 'not before the accomplishment of all these things about which I should not speak openly.' Concerning the rites of baptism, he mentions the *consignation* of children by the bishop (with the Holy Chrism), but he is silent about its formula: 'as to the words, I cannot pronounce them for fear of seeming to want to say more than the answer demands.' And he concludes in this way: 'for the rest, since it is not permitted to put it in writing, we will be able to speak of it when you come and question us.'[2] As the majority of historians have stressed, such a document, emanating from the Roman magisterium, is rare. But, for all that, it should not be considered singular: to the contrary it exhibits the marks of an established custom.

The second text comes from Sozomen, a Greek speaking Palestinian historian, who, around 440, wrote an *Ecclesiastical History*. Relating the history of the Council of Nicea, he comes to the *Credo*: 'pious friends, who understood such matters' had dissuaded him from transcribing a text that only the 'initiated and mystagogues' have the right to recite and hear, and that should not fall into the hands of the uninitiated.[3] Without doubt, many other historians of the same period have also respected the arcane of the Symbol. Nevertheless, this is clearly not the individual fancy of some marginal historian, but he himself is only following a rule, assuredly not absolute, yet well known and everywhere present.

---

1. *Sermo ad catechumenos de Symbolo,* I, 1; P.L., t. XI, col. 627.
2. Cited in Latin by Batiffol, *D. T. C.,* t. I, col. 1756.
3. *Ecclesiastical History,* I, chap. XX; P.G., t. LXVII, col. 920.

Sacramental Initiation & the Discipline of the Arcane

After the fifth century, it becomes difficult to find hard evidence for the rule of the arcane. It is thought that this is because it had lost its raison d'etre, since the catechumenate, from which is was inseparable, disappeared little by little with the increasing rarity of adult baptism.

Must we see, in the generalization of child baptism and the rule of the arcane's obliteration, obvious signs of the disappearance of Christian esoterism? I will return in a moment to the question of child baptism, but as for the rule of the arcane, my entire study has endeavored to show that Christian esoterism is not exactly and fundamentally bound up with the institution of the catechumenate's existence. For all that, the catechumenate itself can be considered in a narrow sense and a broad sense. In the narrow sense, as previously stated, it is hardly detectable before 200 or after 500. In the broad sense, it is already to be seen around 140 and its transformations are to be observed well after the sixth century. Moreover, it has never totally disappeared and, as we have seen, the last Council has asked for the reestablishment of adult baptism. As for the dismissal of the catechumens before the Creed, its practice continued in the West, under certain circumstances (provided for by the Missel), until the twelfth and thirteenth centuries. The deacon proclaimed: Let the catechumens withdraw! If someone is a catechumen, let him withdraw! Let all catechumens go outside! 'This manner of dismissal was used in the cathedrals... until the very end of the Middle Ages within the Mass on the days during Lent.'[1] In the Christian East, the dismissal formula is still in force.

Arcane and Esoterism

More or less strict, more or less observed, the arcane itself has never been presented as an absolute discipline, nor as a simple pedagogical

---

1. J.A. Jungmann, *The Mass of the Roman Rite*, vol. 1 (New York: Benziger Brothers, Inc., 1951), p 479. The Latin formula, among other similar ones, was the following: *Catechumeni recedant. Si quis catechumenus est, recedat. Omnes catechumeni exeant foras.*

Christ the Original Mystery

arrangement as some historians, Mgr. Batiffol for one, have maintained. Its significance, besides the respect due to things that are truly holy, is theological in nature. 'Only baptismal illumination initiated one into those mysteries reserved in this way, inaccessible (in fact, really so), without being secret for all that.' Such is the conclusion of a study (unpublished) by G. Hocquard on the *disciplina arcani*, a conclusion that seems to be in exact agreement with my own.[1] And so we should speak of a real arcane and a formal arcane. The real arcane corresponds to the intrinsically mysterial nature of the Christian faith. In the beginning, this arcane was observed in some manner, both because of its very transcendence and the small number of those who welcomed it. The first Churches were domestic Churches. The new faith spread in the bosom of a few families. No need, then, for any other barrier than that of private life to protect the mystery. And when these families grouped themselves into small local communities (those 'Churches' addressed by St Paul), they were still preserved from profane intrusion by the hostility they encountered in their places of origin: hostility from Jewish society, both in Palestine and in the Empire, then hostility from the Roman State and persecutions, for Christianity was the only expressly illicit religion in all of Antiquity.[2] 'Catacomb Christianity' could only be quite reserved in its liturgical manifestations. But, when peace and the freedom to worship came, and when the pagans, by a miracle unique in the history of religions, came forward *en masse* to ask for baptism, then the need for an examination of candidates for initiation became apparent, then requirements for precautions and verifications were imposed. And the response to these requirements were the catechumenate and the appearance of a formal arcane, or

---

1. Cited by H.I. Marrou, *A History of Education in Antiquity*, p445, n2.
2. There does not seem to have been a positive law prohibiting the Christian cult, the formula for which would have been: Christians are not allowed to exist (*non licet esse christianos*). This thesis, based on Tertullian has been abandoned today. But there was one usage, a custom created by jurisprudence. It was 'the *nomen christianum*, the Christian name, that was condemned, even in the absence of any crime or misdemeanor of the political order or common law: basically, the misdemeanor was the existence of an illicit religion' cf. Claude Lepelley, *L'Empire romain et le christianisme* (Paris: Flammarion, 1969), p110.

Sacramental Initiation & the Discipline of the Arcane

rather, a formal accentuation of the real arcane. During Christianity's earliest period, the members of the Christian communities never, in their specifically Christian activities, mingled with the profane. With the spread of the message throughout the ancient world, contacts with the paganism in which those to be baptized were steeped multiplied. No longer was it only families that received the faith,[1] these were individuals undertaking a personal course and who, having come from pagan surroundings and being more and more ignorant of biblical tradition, brought with them ways of seeing, thinking, and feeling that could not, as such, be integrated into their new religious life and so, with respect to this life, the *marking* of a spiritual break was needed. This need was so much the more urgent as Christianity, during this long period of antiquity, did not reject the cultural formation of Greco-Roman Hellenism. For centuries, the education of Christian youth occurred in the schools of paganism, where the models, teachers, and manuals of Classical knowledge were accepted as being a preeminent knowledge,[2] and yet a *profane* knowledge, a knowledge basically ignorant of man's supernatural destiny. It was in this climate that the need for a formal accentuation of the arcane made its appearance. But, once the world of antiquity had been Christianized little by little (both in breadth and in depth), this need to formally mark breaks and separations was discarded for the sake of another, more essentially Christian distinction to which we will now turn.

Christianity presents in fact a distinction, if not a separation, inherent to its very structure: the distinction between the natural and supernatural orders. This distinction does not exist under this form in any other religion. By 'natural order' must be understood not so much the order of 'nature', of the created cosmos (which is rather seen to be revelatory of God, theophanic), as that of the

---

1. This was in fact a characteristic feature of early Christianity, a feature which 'was essentially a continuation of the Jewish tradition' (cf. Marrou, *A History of Education in Antiquity*, p314).

2. This subject has been studied in a remarkable way by H.I. Marrou: cf. op. cit., pp318–329. Besides, matters transpired similarly in the Middle Ages: the manuals of grammar, logic and arithmetic, the rhetorical models, the astronomical treatises, etc., are those of Greco-Latin paganism.

human world, society. Christianity does not include a sacred language, sacred social or political institutions, whatever might have been the efforts to realize a 'Christendom' in the course of history. The Gospel was made to be translated and was so from the beginning. Far from being a lack or weakness, this absence of a sacred language betokens the transcendence of the Christian message; the form of which is everywhere because its content is nowhere. 'My kingdom is not of this world.' If it does not have any original language, this is because its language has no origin: it is the language of the Spirit, 'and thou knowest not whence he cometh, and whither he goeth.' Thus, deprived of a culture of its own and without being bound in principle to any set human world, Christianity is, as to its sacred essence, in a heterogeneous relationship with respect to every social order whose profane character it can only structurally accentuate and over which it—necessarily—superimposes itself. In other words, and properly speaking, Christianity is devoid of exoterism, even if, by force of circumstance, it in some way assumes such an appearance. This is why there should not be any Christian esoterism either, in the formal and technical sense of this term, that is any constituted spiritual form, embracing the whole of Christian revelation and within which this revelation would exclusively have access to its loftiest and most inward understanding. There should not be any such form and, in fact, *none exists*. There exist, or have existed, *particular* Christian esoterisms, proper to such or such a social activity or function. And again, such formally esoteric organizations arose essentially in the Middle Ages, that is precisely at a time when Christianity attempted to *exoterically* organize society into a Christendom. But, even then, there was nothing for Christianity in general what Sufism is for Islam. This is, we repeat, a striking fact the importance of which should not be exaggerated. Lutheranism undoubtedly in this respect constitutes as if an exacerbation of the nature/supernature tension that arose at a time when the equilibrating factors developed in the Middle Ages lost their efficacy: this distinction becomes an opposition, the religious person withdraws into transcendence and inwardness, but an inwardness lived with an individual awareness and no longer the spiritual inwardness of an intellect contemplating truth—whereas the natural and social domain, emancipated from all

Sacramental Initiation & the Discipline of the Arcane

ordering to the sacred, can freely involve itself in a search for material efficacy, or, using the same logic, identify the religious with the political (something never done in the Middle Ages[1]).

Nevertheless, as blurred as the marks of a formal esoterism might be in Catholicism, they have not, however, entirely disappeared. Leaving aside everything that stems from the monastic institution which, in many respects, somewhat fulfills the function of an 'esoterism'—which does not imply, as we will see, that religious profession constitutes an initiation rite—we would like to mention two liturgical practices that seem to represent authentic survivals of the discipline of the arcane: the recitation in silence of the canon of the Mass, and the recitation of the Lord's Prayer, *in secreto,* on certain occasions or in certain parts of the monastic office. As concerns the Lord's Prayer, we know that catechumens could not hear it, which perhaps explains 'the custom of saying it with lowered voice in certain rites';[2] this is the case, for example, at the time of the rite of absolution, after a funeral Mass, as well as in the recitation of the monastic office: at all the 'Hours', except for Lauds and Vespers, only the first words and the last part of the Our Father are said, 'so that all respond: *but deliver us from evil.*'[3] As to the silence in which the Canon is recited, between the *Sanctus* chant and the final Amen exclaimed by the people, its raison d'etre and even its antiquity have been the object of numerous discussions. But, all things considered, I think it impossible not to see in this the need for respect imposed by the greatness of the mystery accomplished.[4]

☩ ☩ ☩

Such is the data I wanted to present on the subject of this famous 'discipline of the arcane' the importance of which many modern

---

1. These reflections should be developed in detail, but that would take us too far from the topic at hand.
2. Martimort et alii, *Introduction à la liturgie,* Desclée et Cie, p136.
3. *The Rule of Saint Benedict,* chap. 13, is where the first evidence of this practice is to be found.
4. See Appendix 1, *On the Canon of the Mass Recited in Silence,* p379.

historians have striven to minimize, something in which they see no more than a cultural curiosity to be conveniently forgotten, while I have endeavored to show its strength, antiquity and duration. Understandably, this is not only a question of proving the existence of a kind of 'formal esoterism' within the Church—hardly ever mentioned by Guénon—which flourished at the very moment when, according to him, the definitive exteriorization of the sacraments, the liturgy and doctrine occurred. More profoundly, it is a question of attempting to revive, among today's Christians, a certain 'spirit of esoterism', that is to say the sense of sacred mystery *and* of transcendent interiority. For 'the kingdom of heaven is like unto a treasure hidden in a field. Which a man having found, *hid it*, and for joy thereof goeth, and selleth all that he hath, and buyeth that field' (Matt. 13:44).

Sacramental Doctrine

After what was explained in the previous article, there should be no doubt that the Church did have a most sure awareness of the mysterial nature of the sacraments of Christian initiation. However, some might be inclined to ask if, besides the liturgical and disciplinary forms attested to by this awareness, there are not other forms to which a quite different awareness seems to attest, either from the beginning, or in the course of history; in particular, some might deem the truth of my assertions invalid for the present-day Church, the sacramental practice of which has been profoundly altered.

To answer these objections exhaustively would require a complete study of all forms assumed by the conferring of the sacraments from the beginning to our own day. This task far exceeds my own abilities. But one thing is certain: the accidental forms of the conferring of the sacraments have known hundreds of variations in the course of Church history. Some quite rare variations have sometimes even affected these forms in what is essential to them.[1] And yet one thing

---

1. See above, chap. 7, art. 4, sect. 1, pp{PP#}

Sacramental Initiation & the Discipline of the Arcane

has never varied: this is the Church's sacramental doctrine, that is the theological definition of what the Church intends to do when it administers the sacraments entrusted to it by Christ. And this point is decisive, although it is never taken into consideration in the debates mentioned here.

Contrary to the Guénonian thesis, we have established that the Church has no power to modify the *nature* of the sacraments. But some might still retort that this does not prove their initiatic value, if anyone especially thinks—along with Michel Vâlsan—that they have never had any: the immutability of their nature only proves that they remain today what they were of old, simple exoteric rites.

But this thesis becomes much more difficult to support if the just presented facts concerning the discipline of the arcane are taken into consideration: these facts quite clearly situate the sacraments in the esoteric, or rather mysterial order[1]—the term 'esoterism' having never been part of the Christian vocabulary. It might still be objected that this only involves disciplinary arrangements for the conferring of the sacraments and not necessarily revelatory as to their nature. It is not enough that a rite is administered with the exterior forms of an initiation for its initiated nature to be thereby guaranteed. This is why we need to finally approach the very nature of the sacraments of Christian initiation (Baptism, Confirmation, and Eucharist) if the debate is to be settled. Obviously this nature can be known only by means of Church-proclaimed definitions. To whomever would deny this point, to whomever would maintain that the Church can really do something other than it declares it accomplishes, we have nothing to reply; this argument disqualifies anyone who uses it and is unworthy of any refutation.

---

1. 'Mysterial' does not exist in Greek, where we find only *mystikos* as an adjective of *mysterion* = 'relative to the mysteries', that is most often 'relative to the sacraments'; *mystikos* should then be translated by 'sacramental' and not by 'mystical' which makes it liable to mistranslation, given its semantic evolution. However, to stay close to the Greek connotations, some authors have had recourse to the neologism 'mysterial'; this is the case with Henri de Lubac, in *Corpus mysticum*, pp 56–57, or again with Jean Daniélou in *Platonisme et théologie mystique*, p 21: 'Lastly, *mysterial* expressions of the *mystical* life reappeared' [my italics], that is: Gregory of Nyssa used *sacramental* expressions to describe the stages of the *spiritual* life.

Now the doctrine of the Church concerning the sacraments, especially the sacrament of Baptism, can only be the one taught to it by Christ, either directly or through the apostles, the guardians of this teaching. And in fact, despite some secondary variations, the Church has always taught the same doctrine on the nature of Baptism.

The Baptismal Catechesis of Jesus Christ

This doctrine defines the baptismal rite as a death and a new birth. Christ himself taught this to Nicodemus (John 3:1 ff.) and provides the norm of truth on this point, a norm with which no ecclesiastical authority would be in disagreement, save to destroy this very authority. And so it would be appropriate to consider most attentively this baptismal catechesis given, *at night*, by Jesus Christ:

> And there was a man of the Pharisees,
> named Nicodemus, a ruler of the Jews.
> This man came to Jesus by night, and said to him:
> 'Rabbi, we know that thou art come a teacher from God;
> for no man can do these signs which thou dost,
> unless God be with him.'
> Jesus answered, and said to him:
> 'Amen, amen I say to thee,
> unless a man be born from above,
> he cannot see the kingdom of God.'
> Nicodemus saith to him:
> 'How can a man be born when he is old?
> Can he enter a second time into his mother's womb, and be born again?'
> Jesus answered:
> 'Amen, amen I say to thee,
> unless a man be born again of water and the Spirit,
> he cannot enter into the kingdom of God.
> That which is born of the flesh, is flesh;
> and that which is born of the Spirit, is spirit.

Sacramental Initiation & the Discipline of the Arcane

Wonder not, that I said to thee,
you must be born again.
The wind breatheth where it will;
and thou hearest its voice,
but thou knowest not whence it cometh, and whither it goeth:
so is every one that is born of the Spirit.'[1]

The baptismal rite, then, effects two births that are only one: the birth by water *and* Spirit, both being as if the two aspects of being born from above. Jesus, in fact, begins by expressing the primary condition for 'seeing the kingdom of God':[2] the receiving of a heavenly birth, to be 'born of God' as this same St John teaches in his gospel's prologue: 'He has given the power to become children of God to those who believe in his name, who are born, not of blood, nor of the will of the flesh, nor of the will of man, but of God.' Nicodemus asks, how is such a birth possible? Jesus replies with the dual birth of water and Spirit: it alone enables us to not only 'see' but also to 'enter into the kingdom of God'. For this dual birth, being born of water represents its negative and purifying face; being born of the Spirit represents its positive and illuminating face. Through water the disciple of Christ dies to his erstwhile and natural state, the one marked by the seal of Original Sin. Water, in fact, universally signifies purification and death. But what water? According to the constant teaching of the Church of yesterday and today, this water is the one whose saving epiphanies are celebrated, on the night of Pascha, at the moment of the blessing of the baptismal waters, according to mankind's true metaphysical history: a cosmic liturgy that joins the

---

1. The baptismal character of this teaching has been contested by a few exegetes. If the mention of water is suppressed, the text remains altogether intelligible and can be read as a purely spiritual teaching, without any sacramental significance. This is also why these same exegetes think that the mention of water was added later to the original text. However, *all* manuscripts of this gospel include the formula 'born of *water* and the Spirit' (without article: *gennethe ex hydatos kai pneumatos*); an allusion to baptism is therefore incontestable. Notice that *gennethe anothen*, 'born from above' could also be translated: 'born anew', *anothen* having two meanings—which refers to the theme of a 'new birth'.

2. With the mention in verse 5, this is the sole occurrence of the syntagma 'kingdom of God' in the Gospel of John; its importance can thus be appreciated.

waters of Genesis to the sign of Jonah in passing through the waters of the Flood and the opened waves of the Red Sea under the mighty breath of the Spirit. For every Christian is thus someone 'saved from the waters', a Noah,[1] a Moses and a Jonah, since the waters in which he has been plunged and buried (in Greek *baptizein* means 'to plunge') are the waters of the death of Christ, already anticipated in the waters of his own baptism by John in the Jordan. There the Spirit had descended upon him, just as at the beginning of the world it brooded over the primordial waters, and just as, at the moment of the incarnation, it overshadowed the immaculate waters of Mary, that pure creature unique since the beginning of time. By this is accomplished both the regeneration of the cosmic elements and the regeneration of being, by this is begotten a new creature and a new creation, by this is effected the salvation of the world:

> For God so loved the world,
> as to give his only begotten Son;
> that whosoever believeth in him, may not perish,
> but may have life everlasting.
> For God sent not his Son into the world,
> to judge the world,
> but that the world may be saved by him.
> (John 3:16–17)

Such is the 'second birth', after the human and natural birth that the will of the flesh produces.

As can be seen, we are quite far from any social rite of integration to a religious collectivity, a characteristic, according to Guénon, of all exoteric rites, and to which he has reduced Baptism.[2] And yet it is true that, in some respects, it should be granted that the effects of this second birth are also concerned with the individual order and the regeneration of the psychic elements. And this is, moreover,

---

1. 'Baptism,' St Peter declares (1 Pt. 3:20–21), 'is the counter-figure [the *antitypos*, that is to say the reality] of Noah's ark [the figure, the *typos*] that saves you now, you as well.'

2. *Perspectives on Initiation*, pp152–158. It is self-evident that baptism is also a rite of affiliation with a community: the Church; but it is a sacred and supernatural community identified with the Mystical Body of Christ.

Sacramental Initiation & the Discipline of the Arcane

most likely the case for the baptism of John: 'I myself,' he says, 'baptize with water' (John 1:26); and we know that his is a baptism of penitence.

But it cannot only be a question of that, for, as St Peter tells us (1 Pt. 3:21), baptism is 'not the putting away of the filth of the flesh, but the examination of a good conscience towards God by the resurrection of Jesus Christ': not only a regeneration of the 'flesh', that is of the psycho-corporeal elements of the individuality, but an interior and rightly spiritual transformation. These waters of purifying and regenerative death are, in fact, waters of fire. 'I myself,' says John the Baptist, 'indeed baptize you in the water unto conversion, but he that shall come after me, is mightier than I . . . he shall baptize you in the Holy Spirit and fire' (Matt. 3:11). This water of fire in which Christ's disciples are plunged is the water changed into wine for the wedding-feast at Cana, it is blood, liquid fire, shed on the Cross, which has 'washed us from our sins' (Apoc. 1:5), the 'Blood of the Lamb' in which the elect have 'washed their robes, and made them white' (Apoc. 7:14). This is why, at the time of the blessing of the baptismal waters, the newly lit pascal candle is plunged three times into the water so that the Spirit might penetrate into its substance, just as it made the Marian substance fruitful, thus forming therein the blood of Christ. Then the priest breathes in the form of the letter Ψ on the blessed water which has become an animic water (Ψ = Psi, the initial letter of the Greek word *psykhe*, 'soul'), and which is thus truly transformed into the 'water of life eternal'. Plunged into this water of living Fire, we can say with St Paul:

> Know you not that all we, who are baptized in Christ Jesus, are baptized in his death? For we are buried together with him by baptism into death; that as Christ is risen from the dead by the glory of the Father, so we also may walk in newness of life' (Rom. 6:3–4).

The tomb from which Christ arose is the cradle of our 'third birth'. And of those who have been purified by the divine blood it must be said that a properly divine life has been communicated to them. Into the purified substance of their soul-become-baptismal-water, the fire of the Divine Pneuma can descend, so that, henceforth, a truly spiritual blood courses within them. They are, then, born from above, begotten of the Spirit, and have become spirit: no longer psychic but pneumatic, no longer earthly but heavenly. We are not the one saying this, it is Jesus Christ himself: 'That which is born of the flesh, is flesh; and that which is born of the Pneuma, is pneuma.' The 'third birth'—which is only one with the second, the transcendent and interior dimension of which it is its true principle. There is in fact only one baptism, as proclaimed by all the faithful at Mass: not 'a baptism', but 'one, *sole* baptism'. It is the rule of faith that imposes this. There is not a baptism of water *and* a baptism of the Spirit, but one of 'water and Spirit', at the same time and inseparably. This affirmation is not the result of a belated will to reduce everything to the exoteric order, it is the result of the specific nature of Christian baptism, of a baptism that *is* Jesus Christ, which is to be distinguished from all other baptisms, especially the baptism of John.[1]

This is why there is no need to speak of a 'baptism in the Spirit' distinct from sacramental baptism. True, in the beginning, charisms were a part of the manifestations that normally followed the reception of the sacrament, which has no longer been the case for quite some time. The merit of today's charismatic movements is to remind us that this descent of the Spirit should also transform us body and soul, and produce within us those effects that herald our resurrected state. This does not involve, however, a new rite, but only a new manifestation of that baptismal grace conferred once for all at the time of initiation, or, more exactly, the manifestation of new effects of the grace received. The fruitfulness of baptism is, as we have seen, still a function of the spiritual dispositions of the one receiving it. It goes the same here for the heretic as for anyone: received grace—he has been truly baptized—encountering within him the obstacle of heresy cannot bear its fruits; so within anyone the work of initiation, accomplished once for all, subsists in its permanent actuality under the form of a 'seal', of that 'character' by which one is ineffaceably marked, but its effects are developed only insofar as the baptized accepts letting himself be transformed by this work and cooperates with it.

---

1. Cf. Appendix 2: *The Degrees of Salvation*, p384.

Sacramental Initiation & the Discipline of the Arcane

The Seal of Sin and the Seal of Baptism

We have just considered the doctrine of the baptismal seal that refutes, I believe, the thesis of a plurality of baptisms, at the same time that it accounts for data that might possibly justify this thesis. But let us pause to search out its significance. Might not this notion of *sphragis* (= 'seal' in Greek) that casts such a decisive light on the problem of the *effects* of baptism likewise help clarify even more the *nature* of baptism? Access will be gained to this more profound significance, I think, if not only baptism itself is regarded as a seal, but also that which baptism heals and comes to erase *by substituting itself for it,* namely, original sin. If baptism is in fact a seal, this is because that to which it brings a remedy is somehow also one. But baptism is not reducible to an erasure of sin, as if it were to be defined in a purely negative way, simply effacing itself in the restoration of a pure nature. Baptism adds something else; surely it repairs wounded nature and erases original sin, but by applying to the wound a supernatural remedy that tranforms it into a source of grace.

To consider original sin as a seal will be acceptable if one first remembers that original sin and personal or actual sin are not to be confused: no infant at birth has committed the sin of Adam, nor the least sinful act; original sin, say the theologians, is a sin of nature.[1] Does this mean that, since it is not a sin in act, it might be considered to be a sin 'in potentiality', or even the possibility of committing sins in general? Certainly not: if a particular sin is involved, one does not see for what sin original sin would constitute a potential state; and, if the possibility of sin in general is involved, it resides in human freedom and is not to be identified with original sin. Thus, the potential to sin was in Adam before he accomplished his sin; it is to identified

---

1. This doctrine presupposes a distinction between person and nature. Adam's sin is a personal one (an act of his person) the consequence of which is to wound the integrity of a nature for which he was responsible. He then transmits to his descendants a ruined nature. Our nature being the means and the mode of our relationship to the world, it is offered to our person as a field to be worked, an image to be rendered into likeness, an instrument upon which the person should play, but a discordant instrument. If the person becomes involved in this discord, obeying the deviant orientations of his nature, he commits a personal sin.

Christ the Original Mystery

with his freedom, and it is the very person of Adam that sins. But, once accomplished, this original and personal act marks nature with a humanly indelible seal, the function of which is to *dispose* this nature to disorder, that is to place it in an actual *relationship* with diabolical forces for the accomplishment of every particular sinful act. Original sin within us is not, then, the general and indeterminate possibility for sinning (implied by our freedom), but it is a steadfast orientation of our nature to deny the supernatural end to which God's love summons us; in short, it is a *habitus*. The seal of baptism imparts a remedy to the reality of this orientation toward 'inferior states', substituting for it the reality of an orientation toward 'superior states', that is to say by establishing a real *relationship* between the human being and heavenly states, the holy angels and God, with the activity of whom the human being can henceforth enter into a supernatural synergy through the mediation of Jesus Christ. The effects of wounded nature remain, and the faithful, although baptized, continue to transmit to their descendants this impaired nature, marked by the seal of sin. But the seal of baptism introduces them into the sacramental order and confers on these natural effects of sin the power to eventually become an occasion for grace and a path to sanctity; thus suffering too becomes such an occasion. Baptism does not magically heal nature by reestablishing it purely and simply in its first state. It would be wrong to speak of the 'restoration of the primordial state' as if human history had not taken place. This static and cosmological vision does not correspond to reality, which is that man has been engaged in a struggle, an effort, a task. Simply put (!), baptism grants us (in a completely gratuitous way) participation in a divine work; it appoints us, as we have said, to a supernatural mode of living and existing. This supernatural mode realized by the sacramental order is not a provisional means for attaining a stable state of perfect nature; it is our new and permanent manner of being as long as our earthly pilgrimage lasts, and in this way we have been formed into members of the royal priesthood of Jesus Christ.[1]

---

1. Recall that the dogma of original sin obliges us to believe two things: on the one hand, we have lost the integrity of our nature, and, on the other, we contract, from our conception, a fault that we have not committed, but for which we are

Sacramental Initiation & the Discipline of the Arcane

These remarks likewise enable us to answer at greater depth certain questions posed by the notion—and experience—of a 'baptism in the Spirit'. The thesis of a 'new baptismal rite' should be set aside not only, as I have said, because it is contrary to the Rule of truth, the Symbol of faith, but even in the sense of seeing a passage to the actual state of a baptismal grace, having remained 'in potency' until then, in this new baptism. Baptismal grace is not a potential grace to be progressively actualized in the course of the baptized's spiritual development. Such an idea would lead us to speak of a 'virtual baptism' each time that the (unique) reception of baptismal grace was not accompanied by charismatic manifestations visibly attesting to the coming of the Spirit. Now there is no virtual baptism, a rather hapless expression: either baptism is conferred, or it is not. And if conferred, it is so as to the sacramental work accomplished, according to the perfection of its sacramental act: nothing more can be given.[1] But, what is in potency—because in becoming—is the baptized himself with respect to the spiritual possibilities of his nature.

---

culpable. This truth is hard to hold. However, this can be understood if we allow that our nature not only has the task of developing itself along the line of its natural orientations, but is likewise pledged to entering into a relationship with supernatural life. This is even its most profound ontological duty. To deny the original fault that marks us, is to deny that man has a supernatural destiny and to enclose him in a purely natural one. To maintain the tradition of this dogma is to teach man that he bears within himself the seal, the mark, the *negative trace* of a deep-seated duty of being oriented to the supernatural life. Original sin is the memory within us of a first and lost grace; its ontological depth and mystery are only revealed by the redemptive annihilation of Jesus Christ: only the seal of baptism reveals the seal of sin by which our nature has been historically marked. Thus the guilt, inherited because of primal sin and the unity of human nature, is not a personal guilt, but a guilt inherent to the Adamic origin of our nature. We do not have to answer for an uncommitted fault before God, but for our fallen nature and what we have done with respect to its spiritual destiny. As for the lot of those who have died without baptism, especially infants, let us recall that, according to the *Shepherd* of Hermas, written during the apostolic period, the Apostles 'descended into Hell' to baptize the just who died without the 'seal' of Christ (*Similitudes,* IX, 16).

1. Guénon distinguishes a virtual and an effective initiation: 'Virtual initiation is therefore initiation understood in the strictest sense of the word, that is, as an "entering" or a "beginning"' (*Perspectives on Initiation,* p193); as for effective initiation, it is the realization of the way for which virtual initiation is the point of departure. As stressed, this doctrine makes complete sense only in Latin, where *initium* in

Christ the Original Mystery

Undoubtedly it is hard, *in concreto*, to distinguish the spiritual perfecting of nature from the workings of grace. It is within nature that grace acts as an invisible force imperceptible in its effects. Even more, without a nature to transform, one could not speak of a working of grace. But, *in abstracto*, one should not and cannot distinguish between the potentialities of the natural order and the permanent actuality of sacramental grace.[1] Concretely, certain charismatic events can be experienced, in the life of the baptized, as a new baptism, a 'baptism in the Spirit'. None the less what remains is that a single baptism, a single rite of initiation, and a single seal has been bestowed. If anyone insists on retaining the expression 'baptism in the Spirit', it must then be specified that here the term has a symbolic sense. This does not mean that a 'true baptism' is not involved, in the sense that by these words we understand a 'true immersion', a 'true plunge', since that is the literal meaning of *baptismos* in Greek. But, if understood in the technical sense of a sacramental rite, the expression is unacceptable and rightly heretical. Basically this question is simple enough and should not come up for discussion.[2]

Having made these remarks, we can now return to the correspondence pointed out between the seal of baptism and the seal of original sin. More than a correspondence, an identity is involved here, for, if the seal of sin is a wound in the integrity of human nature, by which it is open to an invasion of the powers from below and ends up dying from, it is this same opening that Christ, mortally

---

fact means 'entry', 'beginning'; it would seem incongruous to a Greek, for whom initiation is *telete*, a term that conjures up ideas of perfection, completion. Is it not also curious that initiation 'in the strictest sense of the word' is qualified as 'virtual', which would make effective initiation only an initiation in the broadest sense of the word? Especially since Guénon is one of those who most insist on the ineffaceable—and thus quite real and effective—nature of initiatic 'character'. 'Virtual' initiation is of itself perfectly 'effective'; it is only virtual with respect to the spiritual development of the initiate who receives it without implementing it, who does not develop the *virtue* of what he has received. One could then speak of the virtualities of an initiation received, but it seems troublesome to speak of a virtual initiation.

1. Cf. Appendix 3, *Operative Habitus and Entitative Habitus*, p385.
2. Cf. Appendix 4, *Saint Symeon the New Theologian and Baptism in the Spirit*, p386.

Sacramental Initiation & the Discipline of the Arcane

wounded in the integrity of his nature by this same sin, converts into an opening to grace and to the infusion of the powers from above. He can effect this conversion because his death is not suffered like that of a child of Adam (the irrecusable law of our nature), but willed and accomplished as the most dazzling act of his glory. Henceforth, this is the cause of death changed into a source of life, this the heart engulfed with darkness now transpierced with light, this is the funeral dirge of exile become a triumphal hymn and cry of love: return, prodigal son, the Father's forgiveness is upon you!

Baptism thus reveals its most obvious significance: the sacrament of our birth from above, it makes us children of God, confers on us the grace of adoption and introduces us into the mystery of our deification, as the *Catechism of the Catholic Church* reminds us: 'The Spirit heals and transforms those who receive him by conforming them to the Son of God. The fruit of the sacramental life is that the Spirit of adoption *deifies*[1] the faithful by uniting them in a living union with the only Son, the Savior.'[2]

But that is not all, and the text from St John cited at the beginning includes an even more extraordinary declaration of Christ, at least if we abide by the data of our common experience. What limits does Jesus assign to our baptismal regeneration? To tell the truth, he indeed seems to assign none. What does he say of anyone reborn of the Spirit? That 'he is spirit'. And what about anyone who is spirit? What is their mode of existence? How is it presented? In a quite strange way: we hear its voice, but, like a breath of wind, we do not know from whence it comes or where it wants to go. According to Christ, such is the state of the baptized. What is to be said if not that, in his interior reality, the baptized has surpassed 'name-and-form' and has become a 'noble traveler', a 'cherubinic wanderer', someone who Christian hermetism called symbolically a 'Rose-Cross'?

However, if this exegesis is exact, if we have read St John's text clearly, it will be understood that, in reality, it is not the 'Rose-Cross'

---

1. The word *deificet* is footnoted in the Latin text with a reference to 2 Peter 1:4 ('partakers in the divine nature'). *Deificit* has been supplanted in the English text by its footnote. ED

2. §1129.

state that enables us to glimpse what a baptized person is, but clearly the reverse: it is the baptized state that represents the truth for which the Rose-Cross state is a symbolic designation. This state consists in a sacramental participation in Christ's resurrection: 'Buried with him in baptism, in whom also you are risen again', St Paul tells us (Col. 2:12), which means that, like the resurrected Christ, the baptized are not altogether of this world. Not only have they been cleansed of the original fault, but they have even received the pledge of their deification and the infusion of a never to be extinguished light. And St Irenaeus affirms most expressly that this is a *de fide* teaching: by faith, such

> as the elders, the disciples of the apostles, have handed down to us... we know that this baptism is the seal of eternal life and rebirth unto God, that we may no longer be sons of mortal men, but of the children the eternal and everlasting God.[1]

Dionysian Theology and Christian Initiation

An 'Archetypal and Mysterial' Doctrine of the Sacraments

The Church has always taught, according to both Tradition and Scripture, that baptismal initiation both purifies us of the Adamic fault (and of all sins committed before its reception) and confers on us the grace of divine sonship. Innumerable testimonies to this doctrine, from the beginning down to our own day, could be cited. But recalling a few aspects of St Dionysius the Areopagite's sacramental doctrine will suffice. This author's work, the mysterial character of which is recognized by all, will provide an answer to certain objections raised by Guénon against the initiatic nature of baptism.

---

1. *On the Preaching of the Apostles,* 4; Behr, p42.

Sacramental Initiation & the Discipline of the Arcane

We know that the text in which Denys sets forth his sacramental doctrine, the *Ecclesiastical Hierarchy,* is the very one that makes it most difficult to attribute the *corpus areopagiticum* to the Denys converted by St Paul (Acts 17:34). In fact, it takes into account the description of a liturgy, involving instituted rites and the unfolding of ceremonies, that does not correspond to what we know of the liturgical practice of the apostolic age and is only to be found at a later period. And yet this—which is undeniable—is not enough, in my opinion, to discredit the apostolic character of the work, but only proves that it was 'up-dated' in some of its parts to take into account the state of the liturgy at the moment when it was made public. As for its basis and prime inspiration, nothing stands in the way of its dating back to Denys of the Areopagus, not even the Neoplatonic language with which it was clothed in the fifth century and the use of which was appointed as quite proper for having its meaning understood. The *corpus* should be seen, then, as the fixation of a Dionysian tradition reserved up until that time, with an eye it its divulgence at a crucial moment in the Church's history. Concerning the sacramental liturgy, its intention is clear: to manifest the mysterial nature of the Church's sacraments, not as a new revelation, but, to the contrary, as the constant teaching of the most ancient Tradition. For that, the rites spoken of would have to be immediately recognizable (hence their up-dating), and, on the other hand, they would have to be presented in a prototypical and as if timeless manner. This is why the description of the sacraments in the *Ecclesiastical Hierarchy* is at once precise, assuring quite trustworthy identifications, and yet devoid of any indication apt to situate them historically or geographically. Here we have a positively undeniable fact: whereas the liturgico-canonical texts of the second, third and fourth centuries include numerous details about time and place, the Dionysian *corpus* has intentionally stripped its liturgical settings of any particular detail, so to abide with the essence of the rites. As René Roques states, the formulas of Denys 'remain hopelessly vague.'[1] And that is even a revealing key. That said, we can now broach an explanation of Dionysian doctrine.

1. *L'univers dionysien,* Aubier, 1954 (republished by Cerf), p 26.

Christ the Original Mystery

His vocabulary is that of Greek esoterism; the 'sacraments' are designated by the term *telete* which rightly means 'initiation', and which is applied indiscriminately to every 'hierarchical activity', that is every act relating to an active participation in a *sacred order*, whether it is the celestial hierarchy (the sacred order formed by the angels), the ecclesiastical hierarchy (the sacred order made up of the Church's priestly functions), or the hierarchy of the faithful. Every 'hierarchical' activity, being sacred, is by that very fact a rite, and aptly receives the name *telete*, which might therefore be more exactly rendered as 'initiatic liturgy' rather than as 'sacrament', since it goes beyond the limits of the sevenfold sacraments.

Notice, in passing, how the perfect realization of Christianity seen as a 'sacramentalism', or even as a 'liturgism', can be seen in this doctrine, as suggested at the beginning of chapter eight. The order of all creatures, from heavenly to earthly, has been structured like an immense symphony of sacramental functions, and the activity of each of these creatures, insofar as it appertains to this order and insofar as it forms this order by its very activity, is by nature liturgical—a cosmic liturgy, as Hans Urs von Balthasar has called it in connection with St Maximus the Confessor, a disciple of Denys, but even more so a liturgical Cosmos. The Dionysian universe truly *is* liturgy.[1]

Beside *telete*, we also find *teleiosis*, '(initiation to) perfecting', *muesis*, 'initiation' (sometimes with a nuance of doctrinal illumination),

---

1. *L'univers dionysien. Structure hiérarchiques du monde selon le Pseudo-Denys*, by René Roques is the best overall study available in French. To this must be added the nine chapters of the second part of *Structures théologiques: de la gnose à Richard de Saint-Victor* (P.U.F., 1962, pp 63–242) where the same author studies particular points raised by the Dionysian question, which, to our mind, is almost the same line of questioning. An edition and a truly scientific translation of the text of Denys is lacking in French—except for the *Hiérarchie céleste* in 'Sources Chrétiennes' (introduction by Roques and a new translation by de Gandillac). [The French translations used by Jean Borella differ somewhat from Colm Luibhéid's English version. This is why, rather than reproduce this version, the work's French version is used. TR.] Hans Urs von Balthasar, in the *Glory of the Lord*, vol. 2, *Studies in theological style: clerical styles* (trans. Andrew Louth, Francis McDonagh and Brian McNeil; ed. John Riches [San Francisco: Ignatius Press; New York: Crossroad, 1984]), pp 144–210), has written the most profound pages that we have read on Denys.

Sacramental Initiation & the Discipline of the Arcane

mystagogia, and other terms which stem from that mysterial vocabulary very much present, not only in the Neoplatonism of the fourth and fifth centuries, but also, as indicated, in many ecclesiastical texts and in the greatest writers, St Gregory of Nyssa in particular.[1] It is the Church's own vocabulary.

This profusion of terms might make us doubt if we are indeed, with Denys, in the presence of the sacraments as traditionally recognized by the Church. Recall that the doctrine of the sevenfold sacraments has been 'officially' held only since the twelfth century, and therefore that it would not be encountered as such in Denys, who lists, among the number of sacramental liturgies, rites such as monastic consecration, that will be defined later as sacramentals. However, and this is worthy of note, the most critical historians have, in this regard, no hesitation. Despite the very 'archetypal' way in which Denys speaks, 'the rites are described with enough precision for us to recognize in them the sacraments of the Church, just as, for example, in the *Apostolic Constitutions* or in the *Homilies* of Cyril of Jerusalem and Theodore of Mopsuesta.'[2] In particular, we can identify with complete certainty the three major sacraments of Christian initiation: Baptism, Confirmation and the Eucharist.[3]

The Three Stages of the Way and the Three Degrees of the Hierarchy

As we know, all spiritual progress in Denys is effected according to three basic stages that he terms 'purification', 'illumination', and 'perfection' or 'union'. But this sequence, which will become a guiding theme of Western Christianity's mystical doctrine, is, for Denys, inseparable from hierarchical activity, that is from the ministerial degrees of this hierarchy and from the sacramental liturgies that it is

---

1. Cardinal Daniélou has elucidated this point remarkably well in *Platonisme et théologie mystique. Doctrine spirituelle de saint Grégoire de Nysse*, Aubier, 1953, pp 17–45 and 178–190.
2. Roques, *L'univers dionysien*, p 336.
3. The other 'sacraments' are priestly and monastic consecrations, and funeral rites.

Christ the Original Mystery

charged with performing. For there are three factors to be considered, namely, the sacraments, the ministers and the faithful; 'every hierarchy is divided into three parts: the most divine sacraments, those beings who, living in God, know these sacraments and become their initiators, and finally those that they sacredly initiate.'[1] Thus we see, contrary to certain regrettable developments occurring in modern times, Denys does not imagine a mystical life independent of the sacramental life in the bosom of the Church: 'there is no divinisation outside of the framework willed by God.'[2]

The term 'divinisation' or 'deification' (*theosis*) should not be surprising. It in fact designates the proper finality assigned by Denys to the sacramental activity of the hierarchy, whatever the sacrament being considered, a finality, moreover, that cannot be obtained without love of God: 'the proper object of our hierarchy is to assimilate us to and unite us as much as possible with God. But, as the Holy Scriptures teach, we will succeed only through charitable love.'[3] Doubtless, some today are accustomed to considering, since Guénon, that the Christian sacraments can have no other goal but salvation, which, for them, signifies precisely a *post mortem* perpetuation of the individuality, exclusive of all participation in the Divine Nature. Such is not the teaching of Denys who declares, in a most formal way: 'our salvation is only possible through our deification. And to be deified is to be likened to God and to be united with him as much as is possible for us. The goal of every hierarchy consists, then, in this continuous love of God and the divine mysteries that produce in us the unifying presence of God himself.'[4]

Although deification constitutes the goal of every hierarchical activity, each degree of this activity plays, however, its own role

---

1. *Ecclesiastical Hierarchy*, v, 1 (501A).
2. Roques, op. cit., p 92.
3. *Ecclesiastical Hierarchy*, II, 1 (392A). The word *theosis* is unknown to the Greek pagan world, it belongs solely to Christian literature; its first use is to be witnessed with Gregory of Nazianzus: *Oratio XXI* (fifth theological), 28 (P.G., t. xxxv, col. 665 B–C), except for considering the texts of Denys as earlier. But however that may be, it is Denys who is the great doctor of deification. Cf. Bouyer, *The Christian Mystery*, p 227–228.
4. *Ecclesiastical Hierarchy*, I, 3 (376A),

Sacramental Initiation & the Discipline of the Arcane

according to its nature, whether it involves the sacraments, those who initiate or those who are initiated, and always with reference to the triple work of purification, illumination and perfection: 'Thus, since hierarchical order implies that some be purified and others purify, that some be illuminated and others illuminate, that some are perfected and others accomplish this perfecting initiation, each one will imitate God in the mode appropriate to its function.'[1] Theoretically, Denys should be led to distinguish three sacraments (of purification, illumination and perfection), three orders of those who initiate, respectively appointed to confer each one of these sacraments, and three orders of the initiated in accordance with the sacraments received. And, in fact, among those who initiate he distinguishes bishops vested with the work of perfection and union, priests set aside for the work of illumination, and the ministers to whom is assigned the work of purification. Likewise, among the initiated, he distinguishes consecrated monks, the holy people of the baptized and the not yet initiated order of the purified. But it is obviously impossible to sort out the sacraments in this way, it being understood that the order of the purified includes the catechumens, who have not received any sacrament, while Baptism itself confers not only purification, but also illumination, and while Confirmation is ordered to union and perfection, just like the Eucharist to which it [union] belongs by right however. It is the same for the monastic consecration to which no exclusiveness of the grace of perfection and union should be attributed, since this grace is conferred by the Eucharist as well as by Confirmation, two sacraments that non-monks can receive. Without any doubt, there is a problem here in the Dionysian synthesis, but we should also understand it as a will not to subject the living practice of the Church to the rigidity of a theoretical diagram.

On the other hand, we will have to guard against forgetting that the orders of those initiating and those being initiated, these too, have nothing systematic about them. Each initiator, in fact, confers purity, light and unity at once, and each of the initiated, according to

---

1. *Celestial Hierarchy*, III, 2 (165 C). Cf. Appendix 5, *The Three Stages of the Mystical Way and the Three Parts of Philosophy*, p387.

his measure, according to his *analogia*¹ says Denys, that is according to a certain 'proportion' which defines his nature, participates at once in these truly divine workings: 'each spirit, heavenly or human, has its own set of primary, middle and lower orders and powers that are manifested to the extent of its capacity,' so that, according to the 'hierarchical illuminations' received, 'each one, insofar as it is enabled and is able, becomes a participant in that purification beyond all purity, that superabundant light, that perfection preceding all perfecting initiations.'² And, in the last analysis, it is actually

> the beatitude of God ... uncontaminated by any dissimilarity, full of an eternal light, a light perfect and lacking no perfection' that 'is absolute purity, light and perfection, by itself primary source and principle of every perfecting initiation, beyond purification and light, the cause of every hierarchy, and yet separated by transcendence from every sacred thing.³

There is, then, no air-tight compartmentalizing between hierarchical functions, nor irrevocable shutting up of beings in their immutably fixed individual natures. Human beings are on the way to perfection in proportion to the *love* that bears them toward the trinitarian Thearchy: when minds, to whom God 'has at first communicated only a modest glimmer,' having 'tasted of the light ... and desire more,' God then 'illuminates them prodigiously, because they have loved much (Luke 7:47).'⁴ This is even a rather remarkable feature of the spiritual anthropology of Denys as he never takes into account the typology of Valentinian gnosticism which ranks men into three categories: the 'hylics' (in whom matter [= *hyle* in Greek] predominates), psychics, and pneumatics; the first doomed to damnation, the second destined to salvation if they choose gnosis, or to damnation if they refuse it, the third being saved 'by nature'.⁵

---

1. *Ecclesiastical Hierarchy*, III, 3 (400 B). Cf. my book *Penser l'analogie* (Geneva: Ad Solem, 2000), pp 127–132.
2. *Celestial Hierarchy*, x, 3 (273 C).
3. Ibid., III, 2 (165 C)
4. *The Divine Names*, IV, 5 (700D–701A).
5. Cf. the *Extracts from Theodotus* collected by Clement of Alexandria (56, 3; *Sources chrétiennes* 23, pp 173–175). About Theodotus nothing is known, except that

Sacramental Initiation & the Discipline of the Arcane

Whatever the true significance of this thesis, it is a fact that Denys has not alluded to it, even though warranted by certain Pauline formulations in 1 Corinthians.

Thus, for the initiating hierarchy, there is, in reality, only the one and selfsame deifying work accomplished in this perfecting and unitive initiation, but one which requires, for its completion, that everything in the soul rendering it unlike God be eliminated—this is purification—and that the mind be filled with the divine truth—this is illumination. This is why anyone who purifies participates both in the work of illumination and in deifying perfection, but in his own way and only in his own way; and the same for anyone who illuminates. Better put: insofar as he (the minister of Baptism) purifies, he also illumines and deifies, because then he is acting in union with the entire hierarchy and participates in all of its work; and the same for anyone who illuminates: insofar as he reveals divine secrets to minds participates in the sacrament of union and cooperates in the work of the supreme hierarchy. But not otherwise; that is the minister of a inferior rank should not exercise, in the proper sense of the term, those functions under the jurisdiction of a superior rank, for precisely then he would be disobedient, and, by introducing disorder into what is the preeminent sacred order, he would sunder the unity in which he participates for the completeness of hierarchical acts: 'it is impossible for those inferior to trespass on the functions of those superior,' whereas those superior can exercise those functions usually delegated to their subordinates.[1]

---

he was a disciple of Valentinus. That which is saved or lost 'by nature' is the pneumatic *element* or the hylic *element*: 'to pneumatikon physei sozomenon', 'to hylikon phusei apollutai.' Can the personal human being be identified with an element that predominates in it? This is a question debated among the specialists of Valentinian gnosis. The thesis of 'necessitating nature seems to correspond to a hardening of Valentinus' true doctrine: cf. Simone Pétrement, *Le Dieu séparé* (Paris: Cerf, 1984), p 275.

1. *Ecclesiastical Hierarchy*, v, 7 (508 c).

Christ the Original Mystery

The Hierarchy of Initiators and the Hierarchy of the Initiated

If we consider distinctions within the hierarchy of initiators, we see that it is entirely dependent on the function of bishop, who Denys calls nothing but 'hierarch' and who possesses the supreme sacramental power, or, as it will be phrased later, the fullness of the priesthood.[1] This doctrine is, after all, perfectly orthodox. No less worthy of remark is that, according to Denys, the head of the initiatic hierarchy excludes no one from the grace of which he is the guardian; here again, Denys is faithful to Church tradition. To continue: by almost literally quoting St Paul's teaching on the universal saving will of God (1 Tim. 2:4), he writes:

> The high priest (the bishop), who desires that all men, each for their part, be saved by acquiring likeness to God, and that they all gain access to the knowledge (*epignosis*) of the true, announces to all the veritable good news, namely that God has mercy on the Earth's inhabitants by virtue of his own natural goodness, that, in his love for mankind, he has deigned to come down to us, and, by uniting with us, conforms us to himself as does fire all those granted union, to the extent of our ability to receive deification.[2]

The two other degrees of the initiatic hierarchy, the priests (whom Denys calls *hiereus,* like the pagans, and not *presbyteros*) and the ministers, that is to say the deacons (whom he calls *leiturgos* = leiturge, and not *diakonos*), are in close subordination to the bishop and co-operate as much as possible in realizing the universality of the good news in its deifying work. Thus, the priests can assist the bishop with the sacrament of the altar, and the ministers accomplish their work of purification, not only by conferring baptism on the catechumens, but also by fulfilling their office as door-keepers, that

---

1. Did Denys recognize a *jurisdictional* power above the bishops? He calls St Peter 'chief of the disciples'; it is he who receives Matthias 'among the number of the bishops' (*Ecclesiastical Hierarchy,* v, 3; 512 D). Peter is 'the chief summit and eldest among the theologians and the most perfect among the initiators' (*Divine Names,* III, 2; 681 C–D). Cf. Roques, op. cit., pp181–182, n1.

2. *Ecclesiastical Hierarchy,* II, 2 (393 A).

Sacramental Initiation & the Discipline of the Arcane

is by having the 'profane' leave at the time of the celebration of the eucharistic sacrifice, and by standing 'close to the sanctuary doors to keep them closed.'

As for the hierarchy of the initiated, we have seen that, as with all Dionysian hierarchies, it is comprised of three degrees, the lowest of which, the degree of the purified, is itself subdivided into three classes that are, in order of increasing dignity: the class of catechumens (who are going to receive baptismal initiation), the class of 'energumenes' or 'possessed' (superior to the catechumens because baptized, but having fallen under demonic control), and the class of penitents (initiates on the return path).[1] A characteristic of this lowest degree of the hierarchy is that its members are 'held apart from sacred activities and the sacramental operations',[2] either because, not being baptized, they do not have the right to such, or because they have lost it. This is, then, a negative but by no means negligible characteristic, since, despite everything, they form part of the ecclesiastical hierarchy from which only complete non-Christians are excluded. The second degree is formed by the baptized; they participate in the sacred operations, receive the sacrament of perfecting unction and can commune in Christ's Body and Blood: 'this order,' says Denys repeating an expression of St Peter (1 Pt. 2:9), 'I call the holy people.'[3] Finally, the order of perfect initiates is that of the 'holy legion of monks' or again 'servants'.[4] The monastic consecration confers on them the grace of perfection and union. What distinguishes them from the initiates of second rank is this: 'many acts

---

1. Ibid., III, 2 (425C).
2. Ibid., VI, 1 (529D).
3. Ibid., VI, 1 (532D).
4. Ibid., VI, 1 (532D). Is there a difference between monks and servants? 'Some,' says Denys, 'are called servants (*therapeutes*), others monks (*monachos*) because of the service (*therapeia*) and the pure worship they render to God, and because of their undivided and single life that unifies them in a recollection excluding all distraction, so to be led to the deiform *monad* and to the perfection of divine love' (Ibid., 532D–533A). The category of Therapeutes comes from Philo of Alexandria and constitutes an enigma of history (cf. Emile Brehier, *Les idées philosophiques et religieuses de Philon d'Alexandrie,* Vrin, 1950, p321). Marginal for Philo (Are they Jewish monks?), they are, for Denys, completely integrated into the ecclesial structure.

Christ the Original Mystery

accomplished by the middle order, although not condemnable, are absolutely forbidden to the monks who have been marked by the One', and who, by this very fact, 'have the duty to be one with the One' and 'to be recollected into a holy monad.'[1] Monks should not, however, be set in opposition to the baptized, since there is not two but three categories of initiate, and since there is a greater difference between the purified unbaptized and the baptized, than between the baptized and monks. Nevertheless, the monk is also a servant. Even though, insofar as he is a monk, that is insofar as he is unified (has renounced every inner division), the initiate has attained to 'perfect philosophy',[2] insofar as a servant he remains subject, like the baptized of which he is only, in short, the full realization, to the hierarchy of initiators and, therefore, to the priestly hierarchy, which he is never permitted to judge or even less condemn. Denys strongly insists on this point in his letter to Demophilus, someone initiated to the third rank [a deacon], who had ill treated a priest too prompt, in his opinion, to give absolution: 'Divine law does not allow for a priest to be corrected by the ministers, the rank of whom is superior to yours, nor by the servants who belong to the same rank as yourself, even if they give the appearance of treating the divine mysteries in an impious way.' The place for the servants 'is at the doors of the sanctuary. There they receive the holy mysteries and there they stand, not like sentries, but by reason of their hierarchical rank and the quality of their knowledge (*epignosis*) by which they are related more to the holy people than to the priestly orders.'[3] Furthermore, as Christ himself revealed to his friend Carpos (who wished the damnation of two sinners) in the course of a vision related significantly by Denys: 'I now am the one you must strike. Here I am, ready once again to suffer for the salvation of man and I would do it joyfully if in this way I could keep other men from sin.'[4] By these astonishing words we measure what separates the Dionysian idea of a

1. *Ecclesiastical Hierarchy*, VI, 3 (533 D–536 A).
2. Ibid.
3. *Letter Eight* (1089 A).
4. *Letter Eight* (1100 C). In 2 Tim. 4:13, St Paul mentions the name of Carpos with whom he had left a cloak now needed in his prison at Rome, and he asks Timothy to bring it to him from Troas. Nothing is known about this man. Denys presents

Sacramental Initiation & the Discipline of the Arcane

perfect initiate from the one filled with pride, conceit and callousness that too many sworn esoterists believe should be adopted. In short, according to Denys the monk is a man of interiority and not that 'exteriority' implied by every initiating function in the ecclesial hierarchy: a man of transcendent solitude in the very bosom of the sacral community.[1]

Nevertheless, in reading Denys, we have the feeling that he situates all things in an archetypal light, which makes us sometimes wonder if he is speaking about an historically identifiable monasticism, of a fixed practice of the Church (the Syrian Church has been mentioned), or even if he is not rather describing, through the image of the monastic state, the spiritual state of someone who has realized his interior unity thanks to his union with the One who is perfectly One. Such is the impression imposed, even though we cannot disregard the quite precise analysis of those details concerning the ritual of the consecration of monks given by Denys. But it is rightly this alliance between the exactness of ecclesial data (somewhat 'detemporalized') and the permanent essentialization of the realities evoked that confers on this enigmatic work an incomparable tone, 'an idiom which no-one has ever used before him or since.' His language has issued 'from an inward commitment to the divine character of God and all his saving revelations. The Christian *disciplina*

---

him as a holy priest (he was perhaps bishop of Troas) with a purified mind. Having visited him 'in Crete', he gleans from the mouth of Carpos this account of a vision sent him by God to reprove him for having been angry with two sinners of his church. This feature is one of those that (fictitiously?) situate the Dionysian *corpus* in the apostolic period.

1. In other words, the degrees of sanctity by themselves do not constitute degrees of priestly hierarchy. Whatever his spiritual state, a monk does not possess the powers of a priest: 'the order of monks does not have the task of leading others, but... established within itself in a holy unity, it is placed under the guidance of the priestly orders' (*Ecclesiastical Hierarchy*, [533C]). However, the converse is not altogether true, in the sense that Denys seems to be unaware of the doctrine of *opus operatum*, and that, for him, initiators only have the power of sanctification by reason of their own sanctity: the priestly functions require the possession of degrees of sanctity implied in sacramental works. This point begs to be carefully fathomed, and probably stems from the intention of Denys not to emerge from an archetypal vision of things—as will be seen in a moment—that is a vision in which the interior reality of beings is in perfect agreement with the exterior functions that they exercise.

arcani and the Hellenistic mystery-language provide only a philological and aesthetic tool for this unique creation of theological form. For this Denys needs both the atemporal and what belongs to all time.' This is why he 'withdraws from all doctrinal polemic', and, 'from the viewpoint of timeless *theoria*', proceeds to an 'ecclesiastical celebration of the divine mysteries in a supratemporal form [which] is what we mean by liturgy.' It is, then, not only cosmology that is liturgy, it is also theology, as Hans Urs von Balthasar concludes at the end of the beautiful text just cited.[1]

After initiators and initiated, we come now to a Dionysian presentation of the sacraments of Christian initiation.

The Sacraments of Initiation: Baptism (of Adults and Children)

The first three sacraments of Christian initiation, in conformity with the unanimous doctrine of Church writers, are Baptism, Confirmation, and the Eucharist. These sacraments, let us recall, while remaining distinct, were often conferred at a single time and were considered, as we have seen, to be part of the baptismal rites. True, the rite of post-baptismal unction is not required for being able to participate in the rite of communion. Without doubt, this is one of the reasons why Denys studies the Eucharist before Confirmation and just after Baptism which, for him, is necessary for receiving the Body of Christ. On the other hand, although Denys relates the eucharistic rite to union and perfection, and although the baptismal rite is related to purification, yet it must not be forgotten, as has been said, that Baptism is also an illumination and that Confirmation likewise includes the grace of union and perfection. As for monastic initiation, the rites of which are akin to baptismal rites, it consecrates a special state of life within the initiate community and endows its recipients with the grace of leading the most perfect existence there is, without being able to say, for all that, that it confers something more than the Eucharist.

---

1. *Glory of the Lord,* vol. 2, *Studies in Theological Style: Clerical Styles,* pp152–153.

Sacramental Initiation & the Discipline of the Arcane

We will begin with Baptism. Quite classically, Denys considers it to be a purification *(catharsis)*. However, the two terms with the help of which he designates it are those of 'divine birth' (*theogenesia* = theogenesis) and 'illumination' (*photisma*). These two terms do not have altogether the same significance: the second, illumination, views Baptism in its immediate effect, the first considers it in its entitative workings, that is insofar as it establishes the baptized in a new state of being, a hierarchical and divine state. Denys is quite clear on this topic, and bases himself on the principle that, in order to act, it is necessary to be; hence, in order to act divinely, it is necessary to be established in a divine mode of subsistence:[1]

> To be deified is to give birth to God within oneself; consequently, no one would understand, and still less put into practice, the truths received from God if he had not been first granted a divine subsistence. Do we not, on the human level, first need to subsist before acting according to our faculties?[2]

This divine subsistence is properly a Christic grace. As Roques has remarked,[3] the texts of the *Ecclesiastical Hierarchy* devoted to Baptism are, of all the *corpus*, those where the mention of 'Christ' (and not only 'Jesus' that Denys generally uses in the rest of his work) recurs most often. It is Christ's redemptive incarnation that makes our own theogenesis possible. It is he who has first led the attack on Satan. This is why it can be said of the new initiate, who has

> vanquished all the works and all the substances that create obstacles to his deification, by dying to sin through baptism, that he mystically shares in the very death of Christ.[4]

To be baptized is to become a soldier of Christ:

---

1. Here subsistence designates a state of being, a manner of existing, and not properly what enables a continuance in existence, as in the expression: means of subsistence. The Greek term used by Denys is *hyparxis* (the noun for *hyparkhein* = to subsist) that is to be found with the same meaning in Proclus.
2. *Ecclesiastical Hierarchy*, 392 B.
3. *L'univers dionysien*, pp 248–249.
4. *Ecclesiastical Hierarchy*, 404 A.

the initiate has been summoned to those pious battles that he will henceforth undertake under Christ's leadership.... Christ himself having descended into the lists with the combatants to defend their freedom and guarantee their victory.[1]

To enter this legion and receive the grace of divine subsistence, it is first necessary to desire it, next to approach 'one of the initiated' who, becoming the sponsor of the catechumen, will lead him before the bishop and be in charge of his instruction, on the duration of which Denys says nothing. The rather complex rites of initiation will follow: imposition of hands, inscribing of the postulant's name, exorcism, a stripping bare, renouncing of Satan, profession of faith, pre-baptismal unction, triple immersion, and new clothing.[2]

> To the one who proceeds thus, Divine Blessedness grants a share of itself, it imprints within him as if the *seal* of its own Light, making him a man of God, receiving him into the community of those who have earned deification and who form a sacred assembly.[3]

And so we are led to the question, a decisive one from the Guénonian point of view, of the baptism of infants.[4] The description of baptismal initiation given by Denys—and which we have amputated from these two latter rites (confirmation and the eucharist)—seems exclusively appropriate to adult baptism. But does it explicitly set aside the case of infant baptism? And if not, does it at least specify that in this case it is no longer possible to speak of initiation and deification? Neither for one nor the other. Denys thoughtfully examines this question and responds—along with the totality of Christian tradition—: yes, baptism is the initiation by which the initial grace

---

1. Ibid., 401D–404A.
2. Ibid., 393B–396D. These rites are 'essentially those of the Syrian liturgy' (Roques, *Structures théologiques*, p184).
3. *Ecclesiastical Hierarchy*, 400C–400D.
4. According to Guénon 'the fact that infants are baptized as soon as possible' and the absence of 'rigorous precautions' in view of the conferring of the sacrament 'can only be explained by a radical change in the very concept of baptism, a change following which it was considered to be an indispensable condition of "salvation".' (*Insights into Christian Esoterism*, p15).

Sacramental Initiation & the Discipline of the Arcane

of divine birth is conferred on us; yes, infants should be admitted to it. A reply so much more significant in that it comes from 'Denys', for it compels us to recognize that, since the apostolic beginnings (if this work is from St Paul's convert), or, anyhow, at the end of the fifth century (if judged by the appearance date of the Dionysian *corpus* and if we bear in mind the degree of development of some of the church institutions mentioned), baptism was incontestably considered to be an initiation, and incontestably administered to infants; and this in a treatise written by the most esoterist of all Christian authors!

However, in the doctrine of Denys, this pedobaptism might not be self-evident. Already, in his dealings with adult baptism, we perceive the concern that he has to respond to certain criticisms on the part of pagans, inclined to find the baptismal rites rather extravagant, or even altogether indecent:

> This so to say symbolic initiation of the sacred birth of God within us contains nothing inappropriate or profane; it does not even contain any sensory image.... By its sacred instructions, [it] impresses on the initiate the precepts of a holy life, at the same time that, through the symbolic purification of the water, it teaches in a more bodily fashion to be purified of all malice.[1]

But, even if this initiation was not inappropriate for adults, was it not ridiculous for infants? As for them, how can we speak of an illumination of the intellect?

> What seems to earn the ridicule of the impious is that infants too, although incapable of understanding the divine mysteries, are nevertheless admitted to the sacrament that gives birth to God in their soul, as well as to the most sacred symbols of thearchic communion [the eucharist]; the hierarchs [the bishops] can be seen teaching the divine mysteries to someone incapable of understanding them, of handing over the sacred traditions in vain to someone who does not comprehend them. What lends

---

1. *Ecclesiastical Hierarchy*, 397 A–B. Likewise, on the propriety of ritual symbols, cf. 401 C, 404 B, etc.

itself to even more laughter is that others [the sponsors] pronounce, in place of the infants, ritual abjurations and sacred promises.[1]

To these objections Denys first replies that, in any case, many of the sacred mysteries revealed in baptism are only fully understood by the angels, or even by God alone. But we ought to obey 'what, on this point, our holy initiators, themselves *initiated into the earliest traditions,* have transmitted to us.'[2] Now, the most ancient tradition teaches that a Christian education is everything: raised up 'according to holy precepts, children will acquire habits of holiness.' This is why

> our divine mentors judged it good to admit children to the sacraments, provided that the child's natural parents.... entrusted him to some good teacher, himself initiated into the sacred mysteries, someone who might complete his religious instruction as a spiritual father and guarantor of his salvation.

Moreover the guarantor, that is the sponsor, 'is not himself initiated into the divine secrets in the child's stead,' but, by his mouth, 'it is the child himself who promises and commits himself.' Admitted in this way 'to participation in the sacred symbols,' the child can be nourished by them and 'pass his entire life in unfaltering contemplation of the divine mysteries.'[3] To the contrary, lacking this baptismal initiation and the grace that it confers (the divine subsistence), neither the adolescent nor the mature individual would be able to produce a 'hierarchical act' and lead a properly holy life.

Once again we see everything that separates Dionysian esoterism from Guénonian esoterism. For the Christian, this does not involve the forming of an elite of rare initiates each of whom would pursue, deep within an occult organization, his own 'spiritual realization', while the crowds of exoterists would have to rest content, *post mortem,* with being preserved in an individual human state (at best!); it does involve forming a *holy people,* an entrance of all men into the

---

1. Ibid., 565 D.
2. Ibid., 568 A.
3. Ibid., 568 B–568 C. Cf. Appendix 6, *Infant Baptism in the Church Fathers,* p 389.

Sacramental Initiation & the Discipline of the Arcane

assembly of the saints, into the Christic *Ekklesia,* within which to be saved is to be sacramentally deified. As stressed, it is altogether significant that Denys has chosen to remind us, at the beginning of his chapter on Baptism, of that major text of St Paul in which is proclaimed God's universal saving will; and it is no less significant that he closes this introductory paragraph by mentioning St John's text on the power of becoming children of God given by Christ to those who are born of God: from universal salvation to baptismal deification, such is the declared orientation of this Dionysian catechesis. And the rightful place that Denys assigns to the deification process is the hierarchical order, that is the Church, outside of which there is no salvation, in other words outside of which there is no other saving place, no other hierarchical order of an exoteric nature. Surely, baptismal initiation introduces a separation between the profane order and the sacred one, but, within this sacred order, there is not the least trace in Denys of a distinction between an exoteric sacramentality and an esoteric rituality.

A word remains to be said on the two other initiation rites of the faithful.

Confirmation and the Eucharist: Perfect Initiation

The first point to consider is that Denys, faithful to Church practice, does not separate the reception of these two rites from the conferral of baptism. In fact, baptismal initiation includes, immediately after the triple immersion and the putting on of new clothing by the baptized, an anointing with 'perfumed oil' (*muron* in Greek), to be distinguished from simple oil (*eilon*) used by the bishop for the pre-baptismal anointing of the catechumens,[1] and, lastly, the reception of the eucharist during the course of the Mass:

> The consecration by oil agreeably perfumes the initiate with a sweet odor, for the holy perfection of the birth of God within

---

1. A perfumed oil (*muron*) is not only used for confirmation, but also for the consecration of the baptismal waters (*Ecclesiastical Hierarchy,* 396c).

them unites the initiates with the hierarchical Spirit.... Once all these rites have been accomplished, the hierarch invites the one whose *initiation is now complete* to the most holy eucharist and so admits him to communion in the mysteries that ought to perfect him.[1]

This is an important text because it clearly expresses the situation of confirmation with respect to baptism and the situation of these two sacraments with respect to the eucharist.

As for rites that initiate in the proper sense of the term, that is those that make someone 'enter into' a new state of being by conferring a definitive mark, there are only two: the rite of immersion and the rite of anointing that completes the previous one and perfects it:[2] with these two rites, as the italicized passage in the text above specifies, initiation is complete. In this sense the eucharist, the sacrament of union, is not an initiation rite; but it is an initiatic rite insofar as it makes us really participate, in a temporary and renewable way, in the very reality of the One: with this rite, dare we say, it is the One himself who enters into us, it is God who is somehow 'initiated into man'. And so confirmation and the eucharist are both sacraments of perfection and union, and in certain respects their dignity is equal:

> the holy liturgical rite [of anointing] is set so high, it has such a power that it is used for the hierarchical consecrations ... its dignity is equal and its power is identical to [the power and dignity] of the holy mysteries of communion.[3]

And yet the sacrament of the eucharist also enjoys an intrinsic primacy:

> since I have referred to holy communion, it would be a sacrilege to pass it by and honor it above some other function of the

---

1. Ibid., 404C–404D.
2. The Catholic term 'confirmation' is therefore as appropriate as the Orthodox 'chrismation'. The second indicates the matter of the sacrament, an anointing with Holy Chrism; the first stresses its significance as a complement and completion of baptismal initiation.
3. Ibid., 476C.

Sacramental Initiation & the Discipline of the Arcane

hierarchy. It is indeed, according to my celebrated teacher, *the sacrament of sacraments.*[1]

If we then attempt to characterize each one of these rites often joined together by Denys in one same celebration without however confusing them, things could be presented in the following way. The sacrament of anointing is a sacrament of perfection and union insofar as it crowns and perfects all the other hierarchical rites, whereas the sacrament of the eucharist is the sacrament of perfection and union because it contains within itself the One who is One and Perfect and because it unites us with him. The first confers perfection and union as to sacramental operations, the second as to the sacramental reality communicated. Accentuating the formulas somewhat, it might even be asked if it is appropriate to distinguish here between perfection and union, which are, however, generally conjoined by Denys. And in fact I think that, with him, anointing is more clearly ordered to perfection (in the active sense of the term) than to union, whereas the eucharist is more clearly ordered to union (in the active sense) than to perfection. Or put another way: anointing unites because it perfects, whereas the eucharist perfects because it unites. This is a dual characterization that should be related to the trinitary Person more especially 'committed' to each one of these initiations, namely the Holy Spirit for confirmation and Christ Jesus for the eucharist. For the Spirit is perfect Workmanship, and the Son-Logos is the unique work, the Sole-Reality known and communicated. And here we likewise rediscover baptism, which is the grace of divine filiation in Jesus that the Holy Spirit makes fruitful within us and elevates us to the perfection of deified activity.

In connection with the sacrament of perfumed oil, Denys writes:

> the holy oil is used moreover for all liturgical consecrations, thus clearly showing that, according to the word of Scripture, the One who effects every consecration remains identical to himself through all the workings of his thearchic Goodness. This is why the most divine consecration of the holy oil perfects within us the gratuitous and sanctifying gift of God's holy birth. [Only the

---

1. Ibid., 424c.

Christ the Original Mystery

death of Jesus has communicated the grace of this birth to us]: To deify us Jesus himself, by the most sublime and most divine of humiliations, has consented to die on the cross, wresting from the ancient pit of destructive death whoever, according to the mysterious expression of Scripture, has been baptized into his death, causing them to be reborn in God for Eternity. [And, to signify this regenerative death] into the sacrificial baptistery the hierarch pours the holy oil in drops in the form of a cross.

Thus the sacrament of anointing is not to be separated from the sacrament of birth: 'by very sacredly initiating us into the sacrament, thanks to which God is born in us, we are infused with the thearchic Spirit by the sanctifying anointing of the holy oils.' For

> the very One who, under a human figure, has received the consecration of the thearchic Spirit [an allusion to the descent of the Holy Spirit on Jesus at the time of his baptism], all while preserving the essence of his divinity unchanged, he himself sees to the effusion of the Holy Spirit within us.[1]

Accomplishing all things, leading all things to their completion and unity, the Holy Spirit is infused and poured forth in all the hierarchical workings by the infusing of his sacred ointment. Likewise the only Son communicates the perfection of his Unity by the dividing of his Body and Blood distributed to the many. This theme of Unity poured forth and communicated governs the sum total of the chapter that Denys dedicates to the eucharist. There are few texts of the *corpus* where mention of the One reoccurs so often, almost on every line: the mystery of the One that can change the multiplicity of those to whom the One is given through love. Having called to mind the rite of consecration of the bread and wine, Denys comes to the communion:

> The bread had been covered and undivided: he [the bishop] uncovers it and divides it into numerous parts; likewise he shares the one cup among all participants, multiplying and thus distributing the One symbolically, which constitutes the most

---

1. Ibid., 484A–C.

Sacramental Initiation & the Discipline of the Arcane

holy working of the liturgy.... By offering Jesus Christ to our eyes, [the bishop] is showing us perceptibly and as if in an image what constitutes the very life of our mind; he reveals how Christ emerged from his mysterious divine sanctuary to assume, through love of man, a human shape, to be incarnate without being mixed in any way; how he has descended processively, but without change, from his natural oneness down to the level of our divisibility, [so that we can] be one with his most divine life' and 'truly enter into communion with God and with the divine mysteries.[1]

And, as previously stated, insofar as it unifies the sacrament of the eucharist confers their perfection on the hierarchy's rites. The goal of every rite is to 'gather into divine conformity what is, with us, divided'; this is why there is necessarily a sacrament the specific character of which is to realize this deifying union, which will then be the unifying center of all other sacraments, the 'high point of each rite' that 'realizes by its divine operation the spiritual unification of anyone who receives the sacrament.' Thus, 'each sacrament is imperfect in the sense that it does not complete our communion with the One', whereas the goal and 'high point' of each rite is a participation 'in the mysteries'. It is this point that the eucharist attains and realizes. 'Also the priestly science has clearly attributed to *communion* a name that signifies in all truth the very essence of its operation.'[2] In short, the eucharist is as if the essence of all the other sacraments.

The Degrees of Contemplation and Monastic Initiation

We will not accompany Denys in the unfolding of his chapter, a chapter entirely devoted to describing the different ceremonies of the Mass (the Mass of the Catechumens and the Mass of the Faithful). We will only take note of two features in his doctrine.

---

1. Ibid., 444A–C.
2. Ibid., 424D–425A.

Christ the Original Mystery

The first concerns the forms of union realized by the eucharist, the second the degrees of this union.

As to the forms of union, there are three to be noted. In realizing union with the One, the eucharist not only unifies the intelligent creature with its Creator, it also unifies it with itself: 'it is impossible to gather oneself together to attain to the One, or to participate in a peaceful union with the One, if someone remains divided from himself.' This is why, 'through knowledge of the One', we can succeed in 'gathering ourselves and unifying ourselves in a truly divine fashion.'[1] On the other hand, having been united in the One with ourselves, we will also be united with the host of the faithful united to him. Actually, desires and passions not only divide us within ourselves, they also separate us from each other. But, 'by assuring the salvation of our almost entirely fallen essence, [the thearchic Goodness] will deliver the secret abode of our souls from accursed passions and evil defilements.'[2] Thus purified and illuminated, we can take part in the memorial of the 'divine work' and the 'divine sacrifices . . . divinely wrought by Jesus . . . for the salvation of mankind with the agreement of the most holy Father and in the Holy Spirit.'[3] It is because the catechumens have not yet been purified and illuminated that they are excluded from the synaxis. The union of the faithful is so strong and so interior that it would be ruined by the physical presence of an element incapable of receiving within itself the unifying power of the One. In return, the Church's liturgical practice shows that the entire ecclesiastical hierarchy is gathered around the eucharistic Center, from the hierarch to the last of the faithful, in a unanimous celebration. All the rites of the divine liturgy converge to realize the spiritual unity of the synaxis; such is the case with the 'sacred chants' that 'attune us to the divine chants [the angelic hymns]' and 'bring us into accord not only with divine realities, but with ourselves and each other in such a way that we form but one unique and homogeneous choir of a sacred people.'[4] Also

---

1. Ibid., 437 A.
2. Ibid., 441 B.
3. Ibid., 441 C.
4. Ibid., 432 A.

Sacramental Initiation & the Discipline of the Arcane

'all the sacred orders, reunited according to their hierarchy, after having taken part together in the communion of the most divine mysteries, conclude the ceremony with a holy thanksgiving.'[1]

And yet, as strong as the unity of the members of the synaxis might be, it does admit of degrees in the eucharistic participation in the unity of the One. Here we have to distinguish the 'imperfect'[2] from those who have access to a more lofty contemplation. Must we see in the latter, as Roques supposes,[3] the 'perfect orders' of the ecclesiastical hierarchy and, therefore, beyond the initiating orders, those initiates having received the monastic consecration? We do not think so. It seems in fact quite remarkable that, in the text presently before us,[4] Denys does not specifically use the expression 'the perfect' to characterize those who, in eucharistic contemplation, are to be distinguished from those he calls the 'imperfect'. Who are the 'imperfect' then? They are the 'newly initiated', the neophytes, those who have indeed received the two sacramental initiations (baptism and confirmation) and have partaken of the eucharistic meal, but who are only beginners in the initiatic way of the sacraments. The distinction between these two categories is not, then, of a sacramental (or more generally ritual) nature, but points to a difference in spiritual maturity: both have received the same sacraments, and have communed with the same bread and the same chalice. But the former are the 'newly initiated' who still see in the eucharistic liturgy only a succession of symbols. 'Coming down to their level,' writes Denys, 'I will say that the variegated composition of the sacred symbols, as external as they might seem, is far from devoid of significance for their understanding.' In particular they will understand 'that by becoming truly accustomed to approaching the divine mysteries, they will truly deserve to be assimilated to and enter into communion with them.'[5]

The second category of contemplatives therefore encompasses all

---

1. Ibid., 445B.
2. Ibid., 428C; 'But let us leave these signs to the imperfect...'
3. *L'univers dionysien*, p261.
4. *Ecclesiastical Hierarchy*, 428A–C.
5. Ibid., 428A–B.

Christ the Original Mystery

those whose personal capacity and long familiarity with the liturgical mysteries have rendered them fit to pass from the perceptible to the intelligible. Whereas 'the chief preoccupation [of the imperfect] remains as yet their own purification... to those who have entered into the illuminative and unitive phase, the mystery of union offers a more lofty intelligible meaning,' a meaning no longer 'cathartic' and 'moral', but truly 'theocentric'.[1] They have learned how to pass from the signs to the archetypes that are their causes:

> in thinking about holy communion, let us go back from effects to causes and, thanks to the light that Jesus bestows, we will be able to harmoniously contemplate the intelligible realities whose brightness manifests the blessed beauty of the original patterns— that are even beyond understanding. Yourself, o holy sacrament, the most divine of all the sacraments, lift those enigmatic veils that envelop you with their symbols, clearly reveal yourself to our gaze and fill the eyes of our mind with a unifying and unveiled light![2]

If this interpretation is correct, it follows that we should not purely and simply identify the highest spiritual degree with the monastic order. But then, it will be asked, what difference is there between these just mentioned high contemplatives and those monks who, in the *hierarchy* of initiates, occupy the degree that Denys designates this time as the degree of the 'perfect'? My opinion is that, between the former and the latter, it is a difference between a spiritual state considered in itself and a 'state of life', a mode of existence which corresponds 'in principle' to that spiritual state, which manifests it visibly *in* the Church and which is, moreover, consecrated by a specific rite. The function of the monk is, then, to represent ecclesially what, in itself, is an interior, formless and transcendent state, and to confer on it a place and a form in the sum total of hierarchical activities: a quite real function required by the needs of a resolutely hierarchico-liturgical vision. However, do not forget, as I have stressed, that this vision is also resolutely archetypal, which means that the

---

1. Roques, *L'univers dionysien*, p262.
2. *Ecclesiastical Hierarchy*, 428 C.

Sacramental Initiation & the Discipline of the Arcane

monastic state, far from exclusively designating the spiritual elite of initiates, constitutes, for the whole Church, the recognized symbol of a contemplative state not necessarily consecrated by a special rite, and which can pertain to others beside the 'therapeutae'.

If this were not so, monastic initiation would have to be presented as a rite *superior* to baptismal initiation, to chrismal initiation and even to the communion rite in which—Denys explicitly affirms this—the imperfect participate. But it is not so. Far from being considered as the supreme sacrament for initiates—which Guénon would call initiation into the Greater Mysteries—monastic consecration is, for Denys, a *secondary rite* not even within the bishop's competence, but the priest's: this is why 'the sacred institutions grant [to monks] a perfecting grace' and 'judge them worthy of a certain consecratory invocation not pertaining to the hierarch (who intervenes only to confer priestly ordinations), but to the holy sacrificers entrusted with this secondary rite of the hierarchical liturgy.'[1]

Conclusion: *A Certain Spirit of Esoterism*

We have now finished dealing with the sacraments of Christian initiation, as well as a related one dealing with the Church's awareness of their esoteric or rather mysterial nature. We have sought out the principal testimonies of ecclesiastical Tradition witnessing to such an awareness: New Testament texts, the Church Fathers, liturgical institutions, pastoral discipline and magisterial decisions. We think that we have demonstrated the reality of such a self-awareness of the Church in the course of the first six centuries, that is up until a date when it is truly no longer possible to doubt the continuity of the sacramental liturgy and its doctrine with ours, notwithstanding the secondary formal variations the conferring of these rites has known.[2]

---

1. Ibid., 533A. Cf. Appendix 7, *The Nature of Monastic Consecration According to Catholic Doctrine*, p389.

2. From its beginnings the Church has known baptism by infusion (immersion being the general usage). The *Didache* (c.100) declares: 'If you have no running

Christ the Original Mystery

This is why it was useful to close this study with the testimony of the Dionysian *corpus,* for, whatever its antiquity might be, it is a fact that it appeared publicly around 530 with stylistic, liturgical and ecclesiastical characteristics that make it truly difficult to date it back to the end of the first century, even if one concedes that these books 'were not unknown to the first Fathers, who transmitted them from hand to hand as expressing an esoteric doctrine for use by the more advanced disciples', as Mgr. Darboy writes in 1845 in his introduction to *Œuvres de saint Denys.*[1] Made public in this way, and despite some soon expressed doubts, the Church has not disavowed them and recognizes its teaching therein. But, although the late manifestation of this work testifies in favor of the continuity of sacramental tradition down to ourselves, its supposed antiquity testifies in favor of the primitive character of this tradition, at least indirectly, since it was able to be presented in the sixth century, *without an outright denial,* as being of apostolic origin.[2] To even suppose that there was, not fraud, but a symbolic representation, it would still mean that this representation had to be acceptable and not in contradiction with what was known of the early sacramental tradition, and this was already a lot, as is clearly proven by many texts by ecclesiastical writers between 200 and 500, or again and above all as do compilations as venerable and venerated as the *Apostolic Constitutions,* which present numerous parallels to the liturgical data of Denys. It is therefore absolutely impossible to question the identity of the sacraments of Christian initiation from the beginning to the sixth century and from the sixth century to our own day, just as it is absolutely impossible to find the least trace of major initiatic rites other than

---

water, baptize in other water.'... But, if you have neither, pour water three times on the head "in the Name of the Father, Son, and Holy Spirit."' (vii, 3); cf. Acts 16:33.

1. Typographie Augustinienne, 1982, pcxxx.

2. The Dionysian *corpus* was produced, in 532 at Constantinople, by moderate Monophysites to support their thesis in a debate that set them in opposition to orthodox doctrine. Hypatius of Ephesus, the leader of the Catholic bishops, rejected these writings as apocryphal. However they were quite rapidly accepted and several Popes confirmed their authenticity, without for all that making all doubts disappear. Today it is conceded that the Christology of Denys is substantially Chalcedonian. The Council of Chalcedon, in 451, defined the union of divine and human natures in the single person (= hypostasis) of the Son.

Sacramental Initiation & the Discipline of the Arcane

the three sacraments of Christian initiation, not taking into account specific rites of priestly initiation, the study of which would add nothing to our thesis. That a text as openly and integrally esoterist as the Dionysian *corpus,* without contest the most resolutely esoterist of all Christian literature, says nothing, in the matter of sacraments (and sacramentals), but what the Church has known and taught for ever, this should be enough both to spoil Guénon's thesis and to compel its abandonment by anyone with objectivity.

But, having done this, we ought to equally pursue another goal. The abandonment of Guénon's thesis should not go so far as to reject that 'spirit of esoterism' conveyed by his thesis. And we clearly recognize how problematic such an assertion is today. Nevertheless, if this study proves one thing, it is precisely the importance and even the omnipresence of this spirit of esoterism—which is, in many respects, only one with the sense of the sacred and mystery—in the Church of the first six or seven centuries. Now this is a factual given entirely rejected by what there is of the 'modern' in present-day Christianity. Our own time has surely known a powerful movement of interest in the Fathers, and patristic science has made, for a century, truly gigantic progress. But what does this return to the Fathers serve? Quite often it only serves to reduce dogmatics to dust by stressing either the divergences between authors, or the many difficulties raised at the *reception* of conciliar definitions; moreover it seems to justify the most surprising revolutions in liturgical practice, in the name of the variety of customs revealed by the texts. In short, some go to seek in the Fathers reasons to put in question, and therefore to reject, the Church's traditional teaching; but to take them as teachers, to learn from them just what the Christian is, how we ought to understand and live, that is something that hardly crosses the minds of our contemporaries. And when, as an exception, it occurs to them to retain out of patristic teaching something besides arguments in favor of doctrinal and liturgical relativism, this recovery is never concerned with spiritual exegesis—something expressly disqualified—and even less with the sense of 'the secret' and mystery, in which is seen henceforth no more than a dated curiosity, an archaism devoid of the least theological value, and regrettably anti-egalitarian as well.

There is, then, little chance for my plea for the restoration of a certain spirit of esoterism to be heard. And yet for at least seven hundred years, and even, to a lesser degree, right up to the middle of the twentieth century, the greatest saints and intellectual geniuses have believed, almost unanimously, with the Church itself, that a sense of the secret was necessary for an in depth understanding of Christ's message. To deprive Christians of it is to deprive them of a precious means for gaining access to a truly interior and transforming relationship with the Divine Mystery, and also quite often makes a spiritual awakening impossible.

It is precisely about this awakening of spiritual awareness in the Christian soul that I will now speak. Rather recently, theology has given it the name 'mysticism', a term out of which Guénon has created a foil for the initiatic way. I will nevertheless retain this label that a use of three centuries has made indispensable, and define it as the living science of the Christic mystery, a science that the Holy Spirit teaches in secret to the faithful soul.

Appendix I:
On the Silently Recited Canon of the Mass
(cf. n4, p337)

Is the Latin custom of silently reciting the canon of the Mass evidence of a sacramental esoterism? This question of the 'silence of the canon', or, according to a more ancient formula, the 'silence of the mysteries', in the words of a fine specialist like Louis Bouyer, 'itself is the most obscure mystery of perhaps the whole of the history of the liturgy' (*Eucharist—Theology and Spirituality of the Eucharistic Prayer,* [Notre Dame: University of Notre Dame Press, 1968] p366). This custom, considered to be immemorial by many of the eminent liturgists from the seventeenth to the eighteenth centuries, such as Mabillon, Martène, Valmont, and Le Brun, codified by the Roman Missel (the first express evidence: the Roman Ordinary num. II, end of the eighth century, in Frankish lands; cf. Joseph A. Jungmann,

Sacramental Initiation & the Discipline of the Arcane

Missarum Sollemnia—Explication génetique de la Messe romaine, t. III, Aubier, 1954, pp 9, 39), and confirmed by the Council of Trent which anathematized those who assert that the canon *should* be recited aloud and in the vernacular (*Session XXII, can.* 9), was not *perhaps* the custom of the early Church, neither at Rome, nor in the East, nor in Gaul (according to some ancient historians and a majority of modern ones). However, firm conclusions in one direction or another are hard to establish, as is brought out by Bouyer's study (op. cit., pp. 366–379). Beyond the absence of well established data in favor of this silence, modern historians impress upon us that the eastern anaphoras like the Roman canon—which certainly, let us recall, dates back to the highest antiquity, even before the so-called 'Saint Hippolytus' canon (Bouyer, op. cit., p 252)—have been 'obviously' composed to be proclaimed, even chanted (like the blessings of the synagogal liturgy of the pascal meal), and that there was no reason to celebrate the canon in silence before an assembly of initiates from which the uninitiated (*amuetoi*), that is the catechumens, were excluded (A. G. Martimort, *L'Église en prière—Introduction à la liturgie,* Desclée & Cie, 1961, p 385). The need for silence would have been introduced only after the disappearance of the catechumenate, when anyone could enter a church. Other historians ask if we must apply an idea of esoterism to the silence of the canon, if this custom might not come from an excessive development of choral singing (in the East as in the West) which would constrain the celebrant to lower his voice during the performing of the *Sanctus* and the hymns that prolong it (this is Bouyer's thesis, op. cit., pp 375–376). To tell the truth, this reason is not convincing, for it might just as well be the excessive development of choral singing, which sometimes (the twelfth century) lasted from the *Sanctus* to the *Pater* (Jungmann, t. III, p 50), came about precisely from the need to offer some sustenance to the piety of the faithful during the celebrant's silence. This is, I think, the only plausible hypothesis.

However this may be, the distinction between a real and a formal esoterism (cf. chap. 3, article 4) seemed likely for clarifying somewhat this vexed question: (1) ecclesiastical tradition has always considered the eucharistic sacrifice as 'the' pre-eminent mystery of the faith (*mysterium fidei*); (2) this real esoterism is sometimes—but not always—expressed by means of a formal esoterism; (3) the necessity for a formal esoterism (silence) is accentuated to the extent that liturgical worship is addressed to more and more numerous populations.

As for the first point, it would be useless to provide evidence: I have spoken about it sufficiently. As for the second and third points, we will examine some data that seems, in some instances, to attest to a proclaimed canon.

First we have to account for the (just pointed out) fact that the great 'blessings' (*berakoth*) of the Jewish liturgy were chanted or psalmodized; now (as is supposed) it is according to this liturgy that the first Mass, on Holy Thursday, had been celebrated by Christ: the inference is that it was the same for the apostolic liturgy, which reinstated some elements of the Hebrew pascal liturgy. Next I will mention the testimony of Eusebius of Caesarea (*Ecclesiatical History*, VII, 9, 4) that quotes a letter from St Denys of Alexandria (third century) involving one of the faithful who, for lack of being validly baptized, had improperly 'heard the eucharist'. Likewise St Caesarius of Arles (sixth century) speaks of "hearing and seeing the consecration of the Body and Blood" (*Serm. append. Aug. CCLXXI*, 2; cited by Battiffol, *Leçons sur la messe*, Gabalda, 1927, p211). As counter-proof we can assert (Bouyer, op. cit., p374) that those authors most inclined to stress the esoteric nature of the eucharistic sacrifice, such as St. John Chrysostom, St Denys the Areopagite (*Ecclesiastical Hierarchy*, 3, 2; 425D) and St Maximus the Confessor, seem totally unaware of a silent canon.

In an opposite direction now, a decision by the emperor Justinian on March 26, 565 is often referred to, a decision intending to impose a canon said aloud: 'by this the people assisting at the Mass might pray with understanding and not afterwards uselessly answer *Amen* to ratify what was done at the altar in the name of the entire Church' (R.P. Louis Thomassin, *Traité de l'Office divin dans ses rapports avec l'Oraison mentale*, 1686, republished at Ligugé, 1884, p105). But Father Thomassin, who draws from this an argument in favor of the antiquity of a silent canon, read this text in a late Latin version. The original Greek text (Justinian was an emperor of Byzantium) is less convincing: the obligation to proclaim aloud perhaps does not

Sacramental Initiation & the Discipline of the Arcane

pertain to the canon (E. Bishop, 'Silent Recitals in the Mass of the Faithful', Bouyer, p369). More decisive are the testimonies provided by the already cited letter (p332, n2) of Pope Innocent I (416), as well as by the seventeenth homily of the Nestorian Narsai (510). Pope Innocent speaks in veiled terms of the offertory and the canon, evoking 'the custom observed by the Church of Rome in the mysteries to be consecrated and the secret rites to be accomplished [*agendis arcanis*],' mysteries that 'I should not reveal [*aperire*]' (quoted by Batiffol, op. cit., p208). As for Narsai, who belonged to the Syrian Church, he expresses himself in this way: 'let the orant [= the priest celebrant] pray with his heart and not with his tongue!'; but 'at the end of the prayer [of the canon] the priest raises his voice so to be heard by the people' (*Sur l'exposition des mystères*, Homily 17, trans. Ph. Gignoux, in: *L'initiation chrétienne*, D.D.B., 1980, p224 and p233). Above all what is striking, in these and certain other testimonies, is the absence of the least indication that an innovation is involved here, which can only be explained if we concede that the custom of a silent canon had been long 'maintained'. Is this not what is implied in this passage from St Ambrose in his *De Mysteriis* (55; c. 390): 'the mystery ought to remain sealed up with you, that it be not violated by the deeds of an evil life and pollution of chastity, that it be not made known to you, for whom it is not fitting, nor by garrulous talkativeness it be spread abroad among unbelievers' (*L'initiation chrétienne*, p83)? In any case, this is what appeared in the first strictly incontestable proof in the 'rubrics' (= directions marked in red—*ruber* in Latin—in the missals on the manner of celebrating) of the Roman Ordinary II at the end of the eighth century. It mentions the following: *surgit solus pontifex et tacite intrat in canonem* (P.L., t. LXXVIII, 974A), which reinstates the Ordinary I rubric (seventh century), but adds the adverb *tacite*; this means: 'only the Pontiff stands again (while everyone else is bowing to chant the *Sanctus*) and enters into the canon in silence.' Is this *tacite* to be interpreted as an innovation? Or should the novelty of this mention in the Missel's rubrics be understood rather as a necessary reminder about a custom no longer sufficiently adhered to? However that may be, henceforth the silence of the canon is an established fact—but perhaps not everywhere present nor everywhere

Christ the Original Mystery

observed in the same way: not an absolute silence, but a recitation in a low voice might be involved here. As for the significance attributed to it, it is clearly that of an arcanum. Thus, in the ninth century, Pope Nicholas I replies to the Bulgarians who have asked him for a Missel (brought to them by the bishops that he sends into their country) by specifying that 'this kind of book should not be communicated to any of the laity' (Nicholas I, *Responsum ad consul. Bulgar.*, P.L., t. CXIX, 1008). About the same time the use of an iconostase wall separating the sanctuary from the nave is called for (or makes its appearance) in the Byzantine Church, whereas earlier they were separated by a low wall. Some historians, such as Cardinal Bona (seventeenth century), will wonder if the first Roman custom was not the chanted canon. But a host of experts will devote their efforts rather to combatting the Jansenist (and sometimes Gallican) clergy and scholars who, here or there, wanted to institute a canon recited aloud and in the vernacular; an historical account of the question can be read in Dom Guéranger's *Institutions liturgiques* (Paris: Débecourt, 1841), t. II, pp. 170–204. A fine presentation on the esoterism of the silent canon can be found in one of the eighteenth century's liturgist monuments, the *Instructions sur le rituel*, written by Mgr. A.L. Joly de Choin, Bishop of Toulouse, in 1748 (Besançon: chez Petit, 1819), t. I, pp. 274–281. After having referred to the authority of St. Ambrose on safeguarding the mysteries, he writes: 'the chief reason for silence during the priest's recitation of the canon of the Mass is drawn from the sublimity of the eucharistic mystery, and from the very profundity of the consecration or canon prayers' (p 278).

To conclude I will cite a text from the Abbé Bergier summarizing the common opinion of theologians up to the end of the eighteenth century. Nicolas-Sylvestre Bergier, born in 1718 in the Vosges, dead at Versailles in 1790, confessor to the Count of Provence, a pious and learned canon, an intractable adversary of the 'philosophes', 'the best apologist of his time' (J. de Viguerie, *Histoire et dictionnaire du temps des Lumières*, 'Bouquins', 1995, p 754), drew up, for the *Encyclopédie méthodique*, published, according to the order of subject matter by Panckoucke from 1782 to 1832 (166 volumes with plates), a *Théologie* or *Dictionnaire de théologie*, one of the first of its kind, and many times re-edited up until the end of the nineteenth century. In volume III (1790), for the article 'Secret of the mysteries', he begins by affirming that 'the discipline of the secret... dates from the time of the Apostles' and he concludes that the custom of reciting the Canon of the Mass in silence stems from this discipline: 'those who do not wish to conform to it seem akin to Protestants, and like them, if they were the masters, they would perhaps decide that it was necessary to celebrate Mass in the vernacular, and that the simple Faithful might consecrate the Eucharist with the Priest. The Council of Trent has proscribed this fanaticism, it has anathematized those who dare criticize the custom established in the Roman Church of uttering in a low voice a part of the Canon and the words of Consecration, *Sess.* 22, C.9' (*Théologie*, t. III, p484). We had to wait for the post-Conciliar liturgical revolution to see all these principles questioned again, not only by some historians, but also by pastors.

I think I can conclude that, although this early custom does not seem to be everywhere the same, yet one is right to see the silence of the canon as an ancient and perhaps immemorial custom. Moreover, we should attribute to it the significance of an arcane, not in the sense of an absolute arcane, which has never existed in Christianity, whereas it is to be met with in the pagan mysteries, but in the sense of a circumstantial esoterism, such as we have defined it, its need imposed by the spiritual pedagogy of the sacramental mysteries as a sign of their transcendence.

Appendix II:
The Degrees of Salvation
(cf. n1, p344)

In certain respects one might relate baptism in water and Spirit to the two finalities that Guénon assigns to spiritual realization, namely, the restoration of the primordial state on the one hand, and 'final deliverance' or the divine state on the other; especially since, as we have seen, the baptismal liturgy included—and still includes in the Orthodox Church—not only the conferral of baptism, but also the conferral of chrismation and communion. The first element of baptism, water, would thus be related to the restoration of the adamic state, while the second 'element', Spirit, would be related to the realization of the 'superior states' of the being (the spiritual hierarchies) and the 'ultimate state'. Doubtless, this relationship should not be forced, but it might as well be mentioned that Guénon's distinction is not without analogy in Christian tradition, provided that we admit the one and only goal of salvation includes these two degrees. In fact, the Fathers sometimes distinguish between a 'return to (the earthly) paradise' and entry into the 'kingdom of heaven'. Here is what Dom Anselm Stolz has written on this topic: 'For the Ancients' paradise and the kingdom of heaven were 'two different places. According to them, insofar as the redemptive work restored our union with God broken of old by Adam, the way of sanctification led first to paradise. But, since the grace of Christ has far surpassed it, it could not be the final abode of the redeemed.' For St Ambrose paradise is

> as if the subsoil of the kingdom, the base upon which the kingdom of heaven properly speaking has been built aloft; it is the lower region from which the elect, each according to his merit, will ascend to heaven's loftier regions (*Théologie de la mystique,* Chévetogne, 1947, p75).

According to St Ambrose, Christ's promise to the good thief signifies that "he will reach the kingdom from paradise, and not paradise from the kingdom" (*Ep.* 71, 8; P.L., t. VII, col. 1222B). Irenaeus even distinguishes three posthumous places: the New Jerusalem, paradise and the kingdom, according to the degrees of perfection attained (*Ad. Haer.*, V, 36, 1–2). Origen likewise distinguishes paradise, a kind of 'school for souls', from the 'kingdom of heaven' (*On First Principles,* II, 11, 6–7). But it is only one and the same sacramental baptism that offers the chance to gain access to these different posthumous states. When the Fathers mention another baptism, the baptism of fire spoken of by John the Baptist, it is a question of purgatorial fire—a torment for the imperfect and a heavenly dew for the perfect.

Appendix III:
Operative Habitus and Entitative Habitus
(cf. n 2, p 348)

Sanctifying grace, says theology, is a habitus. Now, according to philosophy, a habitus, which is a permanent disposition acquired by a faculty of the soul rendering it capable of effecting a specified work, is a *potential* state intermediate between pure potentiality and an act properly speaking. Thus, mathematics is a purely potential state in a mind unaware of it (but which *can* learn it, unlike a block of wood); it is in a habitus-state in an intellect that has the know-how without exercising it; it is in act in an intellect in the course of exercising this know-how (for example in the intellect of a professor when he gives a mathematics course). A habitus is therefore a quality received in a faculty, perfecting it *with an eye to a specified work*. A habitus is then, according to philosophical analysis, always *operative:* to know how to swim or ride a bicycle is a habitus. Grace is also clearly a habitus (a received and perfecting quality), but of a kind unknown to philosophy since it is not a quality of the soul that it first perfects, but the soul's very *being;* hence the term *entitative habitus*. In other words, sanctifying grace, or habitual grace conferred by a sacrament, does not descend into such or such a power of the soul to enable it to accomplish such or such an action, it descends into the being of that person who it establishes in a *new state*, the state of partaking of the divine nature. This is, says St Thomas—and St Paul (2 Cor. 5:17)—a 'new (*ex nihilo*) creation': 'in the nature of the soul does [man] participate in the Divine Nature, after the manner of a likeness, through a certain regeneration or re-creation' (*Summa Theologiae*, I-II, q. 110, a. 4); 'grace is said to be created inasmuch as men are created with reference to it, i.e. are given a new being out of nothing" (ibid., a. 2, reply to objection 3). This is why grace 'cannot properly be called a habit because it is not immediately directed to an act but to a certain spiritual existence' (*De Veritate*, q. 27, a. 2, ad 7), which St Thomas specifies as being a participation in Divine *Beauty* (*Summa Theologiae*, I-II, q. 110, a. 2). This is also why sanctifying grace, the grace of baptism for example, does not produce a virtue in the soul (ibid., a. 3), and therefore should not be something virtual. But, of course, an operative habitus can also flow—mediately—from this entitative habitus.

Appendix IV:
St Symeon the New Theologian and Baptism in the Spirit
(cf. n 3, p348)

St Symeon seems to maintain that there are two baptisms: a sacramental baptism and a baptism in the Spirit (accompanied by the gift of tears): 'In the first baptism, water symbolizes tears and the oil of chrismation prefigures the inner anointing of the Spirit. But the second baptism is no longer a type of the truth, but the truth itself' (*Symeon the New Theologian. The Practical and Theological Chapters and the Three Discourses* [Kalamazoo, Michigan: Cistercian Publications, 1982] p 42). However, I do not think that St Symeon was envisioning two distinct rites (the second of which would have been conferred by Heaven itself); he speaks only of the full mystical realization of the truth of the sacrament received. It transpires here as with Christ who speaks of the '*true* vine', or '*true* bread', or '*true* light'. From the standpoint of ultimate reality, the palpable and corporeal vine is only a symbol of the heavenly Vine that alone realizes the perfection of every vine's essence. The instances of baptism and the vine are not in all points identical, since baptism is a sacred act and not a thing. In such an act essence coincides with existence. This is why it effects our salvation: it is truly something of the heavenly in the earthly. But the truth of baptism can also be considered from the standpoint of the baptized who should actively *become* what he or she *is*: 'He has given the power to *become* children of God to those who have been *born* of God,' that is who have received baptism. Some modern exegetes and theologians do not understand how someone can become what one is, and yet this is a major key of human destiny: by being actively identified with our essence, we gain access to the *freedom of the children of God.*

Sacramental Initiation & the Discipline of the Arcane

Appendix V:
*The Three Stages
of the Mystical Way and
the Three Parts of Philosophy*
(cf. n 2, p 355)

The purification-illumination-perfection sequence is not without ties to the Neoplatonic tradition. And it is to be found again, with notable variants, in Origen and Gregory of Nyssa (Daniélou, *Platonisme et théologie mystique,* pp 17–23). Hugo Koch (cf. Roques, *L'univers dionysien,* p 98, n 2) has set the formulas of Denys in parallel with numerous Neoplatonic texts; 'but none of the texts cited present the systematic rigor of the Dionysian texts' (Rocques, ibid.). A relationship could likewise be established with the philosophic threefold curriculum found, from Plutarch on, in middle Platonism (an expression that designates the dominant interpretation of Plato in the first and second centuries); this curriculum distinguishes *'praktike'* (or 'ethics'), 'physics', and 'theology' (or 'metaphysics' and even 'epoptic'): cf. P. Hadot, *Qu'est-ce que la philosophie antique?,* Folio, 1995, p 238. Ethics is directed to the soul's purification, physics to the knowledge of incorporeal natures and causes (and therefore to the illumination of the intellect) and theology to the contemplation of God: insofar as an epoptic, theology (or metaphysics) 'is, as in the mysteries, the goal of initiation" (Hadot, op. cit., p 238). This interpretation is especially developed with Origen, who borrows it from Philo and who relates ethics to *Proverbs,* physics to *Ecclesiastes* and epoptic to the *Song of Songs.* Evagrius returns to it (*Practikos,* §1): 'Christianity is the dogma of Christ our Savior. It is composed of *praktike,* of the contemplation of the physical world and of the contemplation of God' (*The Praktikos and Chapters on Prayer,* trans. J.E. Bamberger [Kalamazoo, Michigan: Cistercian Publications, 1981], p 15). Hadot is surprised (op. cit., p 375) that physics is related to the 'kingdom of heaven', to be distinguished, following Origen, from the 'kingdom of God' which is related to theology (*Praktikos,* §§ 2 and 3). But there is nothing very surprising here. 'Heaven' can obviously designate and encompass all that surpasses the human world: from this point of view there is no difference between the 'kingdom of heaven' and the 'kingdom of God' (besides, this is the opinion of all the modern exegetes: cf. Carmignac, *Le miracle de l'eschatologie*, Letouzey et Ané, 1979, p 20). However, it is equally certain that the 'heavens' (always pluralized in Hebrew) designate God (unnameable in Himself) only metaphorically. In the proper sense, the heavens designate the superior degrees of creation and therefore the angelic hierarchies and the world of created essences, that is the world of cosmological principles, and therefore the 'site' of true physical science.

Appendix VI:
Infant Baptism in the Church Fathers
(cf. n 3, p 366)

It is the most Platonic of the Fathers who provide the firmest authority in favor of pedobaptism: Clement, Origen, St Ambrose, St Augustine, etc. Tertullian laments pedobaptism, but specifically testifies to its practice around 170. As for St Irenaeus, he declares: 'For He came to save all through means of Himself—all, I say, who through Him are born again to God: infants, and children, and boys, and youths, and old men" (*Against the Heresies*, II, 22, 4). And St Gregory Nazianzus teaches that it is better to be sanctified without knowledge than to die without the seal of Christian initiation (*Orat.*, XL, 17, 28; P.G., t. XXXVI, col. 380). On this question, cf. *D.T.C.*, t. II, col. 192–196. Perhaps it will be asked why the initiation of infants to the *Christian* mysteries was apt to provoke the mockery of a pagan Greek, whereas it raised no difficulty, as we have seen, within the framework of the Eleusinian and other mysteries. The answer is likely to be sought on the side of the very *theological* nature of Christian initiation (attested to by the Creed), while the doctrinal side of the pagan mysteries clearly seems to have been, if not non-existent (the tendency today is to reevaluate the importance of the *legomena*), at least quite limited, and, anyhow, having nothing in common with the knowledge of Scripture and revealed doctrine required for baptism.

Sacramental Initiation & the Discipline of the Arcane

Appendix VII:
The Nature of Monastic Consecration According to Catholic Doctrine
(cf. n1, p375)

Should we see in the monastic consecration, as some of Guénon's readers have suggested, *the* initiatic rite not to be found, according to them, in the sacramental order? As for this hypothesis, I will grant that the monastic consecration actually offers some analogies to an initiation, if simply the communication of a grace with a view to a certain state of life is meant by this. However, such a solution corresponds neither to the (quite vague) description of this 'secondary' rite given by Denys, nor, as I am about to show, the Church's idea of it.

If by initiatic rite is meant, according to the definition of Guénon himself, the transmission of a 'spiritual influence' by an initiator, who is its keeper, to a recipient, who is indelibly marked by it, it has to be stated clearly, at the risk of some surprise, that there is no such thing in the consecration spoken of by Denys, nor in what the Church calls rather the 'profession of the evangelical counsels'.

As for Denys, it has to be pointed out that there is a problem with his doctrine here. Denys does not, in fact, respect the principle which, according to him, presides over the organization and life of the entire hierarchical order, angelic as well as ecclesiastic: every more lofty order confers on the order immediately below it the gifts that it has itself received and that, in the end, reascend to the superessential Thearchy (which, be it noted in passing, replicate in sacramental mode the Plotinian figure of a hierarchy of hypostases emanating from the One). Now, this principle is only partially corroborated in the ecclesiastical hierarchy: the bishop confers initiations, baptismal initiations for example, that, theoretically, should be conferred by lower mediations, those 'ministers' who, as the last echelon of the initiating triad, should likewise consecrate monks, the first degree of the triad of the initiated. Denys, who says nothing on the relationships of the orders among themselves, probably had to temper his principles to account for the liturgical practice of the Church (cf. Rocques, *L'univers dionysien,* pp. 196–199).

As for the 'profession of the evangelical counsels', we need to know that, traditionally, the 'way of the precepts', which is valid for all the faithful, is distinguished from the 'way of the counsels' (poverty, chastity and obedience among others), also called the 'way of perfection'. This distinction is drawn from the teaching of Christ to the rich young man: 'if you would enter into life, keep the precepts (*serva mandata,* keep the commandments)'; 'if you would be perfect, go sell what you have, and give it to the poor, and you will have treasure in heaven, and come follow me' (Matt. 19:17–21). The term 'perfect' or 'perfection', taken up again by the entire Christian tradition, is therefore to be understood in a quasi-technical sense—this is precisely what Denys does when he speaks of the 'perfect'. This term, which designates more a category of disciple than a spiritual state, is the object of numerous theological analyses (cf. *D.T.C.,* t. XII, art. 'Perfection', col. 1219–1251).

Monastic profession consists in publicly committing oneself by a vow to practice the evangelical counsels, a commitment that established the professed in a state of perfection, that is not in a perfection definitively possessed, but in a form of life, a condition of existence, ecclesially recognized and defined by the obligation to tend towards evangelical perfection itself and the state of perfection: someone can be perfect without being in a state of perfection, and vice versa (*Summa Theologiae,* II–II, q. 184, a. 4). This does not involve, then, an 'acquired or communicated (*exercendae*) perfection, like the episcopate,' but 'a school where someone tends to acquire (*acquirendae*) it' (*D.T.C.,* t. XIII, art. 'Religieux', col. 2158).

The profession of the evangelical counsels is a rite, a sacramental, but not a rite of transmission. It is the vow itself, the fact of professing the counsels, which, under certain circumstances, have a sacramental value. The Church, in the person of the bishop or the superior of the monastic house in which the profession is made, ratifies the commitment, receives it and blesses the habit that the professed will wear. Furthermore, through the liturgy by which it surrounds the profession and the accompanying eucharistic celebration, the Church shows that it considers this profession as a true and

Sacramental Initiation & the Discipline of the Arcane

real consecration (cf. Second Vatican Council, *Dogmatic Constitution on the Church* [*Lumen Gentium*], 45). But here the one who consecrates is the one who is consecrated, not an initiator who confers the grace of the monastic state on the professed.

There is also a rite for the 'consecration of virgins' of very ancient origin, restored to honor since the Second Vatican Council. This rite, which is reserved for women, should not be confused with religious profession. It follows the latter for a professed who makes a vow in a set 'religion': the Benedictine, Carmelite or Franciscan 'religion', for example. But it can also be independent of all entry into a house: this is the case for virgins consecrated 'in the world', who do not belong to a 'religion' and live outside a monastery or convent. The consecration of virgins includes a vow that the person pronounces kneeling before a seated bishop, her hands in those of the hierarch; a consecratory blessing comes next. In general, the identity of virgins consecrated 'in the world' is unknown to the secular world in which they live.

In itself, profession can be related to the sacrament of baptism, which is presupposed and a prolongation of which it is: the professed 'have dedicated their entire lives to the service of God, and this constitutes a special consecration, which is deeply rooted in that of baptism and expresses it more fully' (ibid., *Decree on the Adaptation and Renewal of Religious Life* [*Perfectae Caritatis*], 5). This relationship between baptism and profession is traditional: a very ancient ritual declares that profession 'is a second baptism' (cited by O. Casel, 'Die Mönchenweihe bei St. Benedikt', *Jahrbuch für Liturgiewissenschaft*, Münster, Aschendorf, t. 5, 1925, p34). We find the same teaching in St. Thomas Aquinas who justly cites with support drawn from the *Lives of the (Desert) Fathers*, VI, 9: 'By entering religion one receives the same grace as by being baptized' (*Summa Theologiae*, II–II, q. 189, a. 3, ad 3), by which should be understood, it seems, the remission of temporal punishment due to sin (a plenary indulgence). And so we see that the sacramental virtue of the monastic profession flows from the grace received at baptism, of which it is a specification relative to a particular state of life. It is baptism, therefore, that constitutes the chief and necessary rite of Christian initiation in the proper sense of the term, and we rediscover, with religious profession, what I have already explained in connection with other states of life, such as those of the craftsmen and knights, but with this difference: a state of evangelical perfection is involved, and not a social and secular function.

Michel Vâlsan had supported the hypothesis that I am contesting, seeing in the Hesychast blessing an instance of an initiatic and supra-sacramental rite (in Guénon's sense): *Études Traditionnelles*, n° 406–408, March–August, 1968, 'Études et Documents d'Hésychasme', pp153–179. In this article, I think that Michel Vâlsan unduly enlists Mgr. Scrima's text upon which he claims to base his conclusions. In connection with the aforesaid blessing, Mgr. Scrima in fact declares:

> we are, essentially, in a world other than that of an esoteric doctrine protecting, by a secret initiation, its 'universal truth' against the psychics and hylics. This distinction, itself exterior, between esoteric and exoteric, is devoid of meaning here.

One could not be clearer. Vâlsan does indeed cite this passage (p164), but does not draw from it its implied consequences (Mgr. Scrima's article was drawn from the review *Istina*, nos. 3 and 4, 1958, 'L'avènement philocalique dans l'Orthodoxie roumaine').

We will be all the more convinced of the falsity of this hypothesis once we realize that the monastic consecration confers no permanent *character* (no more than the Hesychast blessing), which should be the case, however, according to Guénon. We know, in fact, that the Catholic Church has always defined, beside modalities for entrance into religion, modalities for leaving, and this not just for temporary professions, which is self-evident, but also for perpetual professions: a religious, provided that he or she has followed the prescriptions arranged by the Church for 'leaving religion' (secularization), is relieved of his or her vows and obligations, as if the monastic consecration had never taken place; obviously priest-religious are not relieved of their priestly obligations. The baptismal, chrismatic or priestly character itself remains indelible.

Such is the clear and rigorous concept of the monastic state in the Catholic Church. And it only confirms the conclusions of our study. But, surely, we would be the last to deny that monasticism is

Sacramental Initiation & the Discipline of the Arcane

the pre-eminent place, if there is any, where Christianity's pure mysterial tradition is kept alive, at least there where the modern spirit has not triumphed. That, however, is another story, a story that in no way invalidates what I have just explained.

10

The Mystical Way

*Introduction: Listening
to the Christian Word*

OFTEN AMONG GUÉNON'S READERS, and with Guénon himself, we encounter reflections of this kind:

[If in Catholicism] the deposit of tradition has remained intact, which is in itself much, it is doubtful whether its deeper meaning is fully understood, even by a restricted elite, which, if it existed, would doubtless show itself either in action or in influence, neither of which, in fact, is anywhere to be seen.[1]

In other words, if there were still true Christians in the Catholic Church, that is a spiritual elite who had integrally actualized this tradition's loftiest possibilities (which only subsist in a latent state any longer), we should be able to be observe this exteriorly. Now this, we are told, is something not to be observed.

Such an argument seems surprising: not because it supposes a certain relationship between an interior reality and an exterior situation, which I grant, but because it supposes, for whoever uses it, the ability to make this observation and even to have a complete knowledge (cf. 'anywhere') of the aforesaid situation. This is a somewhat exorbitant claim, given the immensity of a Church that today numbers a billion followers. True, Guénon had recognized in another work: 'we lay no claim to an exhaustive knowledge of the present

---

1. *The Crisis of the Modern World* (Hillsdale, NY: Sophia Perennis, 2004), pp 63–64.

The Mystical Way

organization of the Catholic church.'[1] But this reservation (of a rather formal nature) is not sufficient: it would not only be necessary that the observer have a complete knowledge, but also be able to *appreciate* the indications and signs observed. Here we return to the question that began this book: Is the Guénonian hermeneutic in harmony with the nature of Christian revelation? I do not deny that the tree can only be judged by its fruits; but the fruits themselves—who should be tasting them?

This question seems to be especially pertinent, involving as it does the mystical way and what Guénon says about it. Not that I am *a priori* denying him the right to judge matters as he has done. Besides, if he were to be denied this right, it would be quite easy to retort that nothing is more legitimate than to denounce confusions and assign each thing its rightful place: which I concede. But still, is this indeed the case? To validly distinguish the initiatic way from the mystical way, this means one needs to have an actual knowledge of *both,* and to base the judgments brought forth in their regard on factors reasonably apt to be appreciated by every sufficiently intelligent reader of good faith. Otherwise the reader is reduced to whatever more or less blind confidence the author's reputation inspires in him.

Now, the only objectively appreciable elements in this matter are the texts of the mystics themselves, or the words they have uttered, whereas their interior reality and the 'degree of realization' to which they have attained are strictly unobservable and known only to God; they cannot, then, be brought into the debate. True, a second factor of appreciation might be considered, namely, the authorized judgment that religious Tradition gives on the person and work of saint and mystic; however, this judgment being that of the Church, it is expressed in this Church's categories, which makes comparative appreciations problematic. This data should not be neglected, but obviously the text themselves should hold first place.

If we turn now to Guénon to ascertain which texts he claims to marshal in support of his theses, we discover that he cites *none.* He has, however, devoted a certain number of pages to the question of

---

1. *Spiritual Authority and Temporal Power* (Hillsdale, NY: Sophia Perennis, 2004), p20, n8.

mysticism, and has never hesitated to refer to them at need. He has even made a case for the sole objective criterium that we have recognized—the language of the mystics—to judge the nature of the mystical way; but he has been content with characterizing this language in a general (and, as we will see, very inexact) way, without providing *one line of text*—which is certainly somewhat surprising. As for names, I have found two and will come back to them: Anne-Catherine Emmerich and St John of the Cross. Without doubt mention might also be made of Louis-Claude de Saint-Martin, who Guénon classifies as a mystic, but, given his quite marginal situation from the Catholic Church's point of view, nothing will be said about him.

In view of these scant results, the mysticism or mystics spoken of by Guénon have a precise outline, or even existence, only within his discourse. This is why, if we truly want to know about this way called the 'science of the saints' or 'holy sapience' in the seventeenth century, if we want to be able to possibly taste within it the revelatory fruits of the Christian tree enlivened by sacramental grace, we must heed the words of the mystics themselves. Throughout this book it has been my most steadfast care to have the voice of Christianity, such as it is in itself, be heard, and this is still so now, at the end of these endeavors. After all, what other method is there for putting everything in its proper place, and without exposing the gift of God in those souls that He has gratified with His knowledge to misunderstanding?

However, before letting some of these known or almost unknown mystics speak, we need to restore the very term 'mystic' to its authentic meaning, the one conferred on it by Christian tradition. This meaning is embedded in the evolution of the Christian term *mysterion*, an evolution retraced in the two previous chapters. At first exclusively reserved to designate the contents of Christian doctrine, this term next served to name the sacramental actions that the Church accomplished in its liturgy. Now we will see expressed, from the fourth century to modern times, its most inward meaning: here mystery is identical to the essence of spiritual *life*.

The Mystical Way

What the Fathers Understood by 'Mystical'

In the first and pagan Greek sense, *mystikos* is an adjective derived from the verb *mueo* (= 'to initiate to the mysteries'); it therefore signifies 'relative to the mysteries', or again and literally 'initiatic'. Such is the philological data.[1] The Christian writers were heir to this terminological tradition even though modifying it somewhat, as we have seen, adding a doctrinal content to it that it did not have. But, however it may be with this point, if we want to understand what they meant by qualifying something as mystical, we have to, at least temporarily, cease taking the term exclusively in accord with its accepted meaning since the seventeenth century.

We have met with proofs of this first meaning in the two previous chapters: 'mystical' qualifies then either what is relative to the mystery of Christ, especially in Scripture, or what stems from the mysteries of the liturgy and sacramental realities. Let us turn to some occurrences of these two uses.

Scripture in its two Testaments is speaking of Christ. It speaks of Him secretly in the first Testament and openly in the second, but yet not in such a way that it would exhaust its Divine Object who, even though revealed, remains hidden in His most profound mystery. Also, to have the sense of Scripture is to know that the Reality in question, the Referent toward which it points, is always beyond the words it employs and even the things and events mentioned: everything has been given, but the gift itself remains hidden if we refuse to enter into its invisible interiority. It is this invitation to the inner voyage that the word 'mystical' indicates each time that it is applied either to the realities or events spoken of by Scripture, or to the manner in which we read it; the sense of Scripture is mystical because the Object made known is itself mystical. In other words, what is esoteric in Christianity is Christ Himself; along with the One who relates all things to Him (the Holy Spirit), *He constitutes Christian*

---

1. Cf. above: pp 202, 307, 339 n1, etc.

Christ the Original Mystery

esoterism properly speaking. An esoterism 'in broad daylight' ('who has seen me has seen the Father'), the esoterism of Christ exposed naked on the Cross, opened right to the heart, His blood shed on the world, and yet eternally transcendent, beyond space and time, beyond the angelic heavens and every creature.

As a result, a good translation of 'mystical' would consist in translating it precisely by 'esoteric', obviously understood in its real and essential sense, wherein the spirit of interiority and the interiority of the Spirit are conjoined, and not in the formal and somewhat 'occultizing' sense. But this also means that a good translation of 'esoteric' would be 'mystical', in the sense that we are trying to catch a glimpse of here.

Thus Origen, in Greek or in the Latin of his translator Rufinus, speaks of 'mystical reason', 'mystical interpretation' and 'mystical understanding', alluding to the 'secrets' (*arcana*) of Scripture that can be fathomed only by 'ascending from the historical account to the mystical and allegorical understanding of the spiritual meaning.'[1] Likewise the adverb *mystikos* (mystically) could often be translated by such turns of phrase as 'beneath symbols laden with mysteries' or 'with the intention of expressing mysteries'; in a general way, this is the meaning of the expressions 'to name, say, teach, cry out, understand and prophesy *mystically*.'[2] Doubtless what has happened is that the secret things spoken of by Scripture, those about which the Apostle John had a revelation when he rested on the heart of Jesus, have themselves been designated as 'mystical realities' (*ta mystika*) or rather 'more mystical' (*mystikotera*).[3] But on the whole it clearly seems that, with Origen, the adjective *mystikos* and the corresponding adverb describe a mode of knowledge rather than the realities sought for by this knowledge.

The tradition of the *sensus mysticus,* inaugurated chiefly by Origen, colors the whole history of Christian exegesis. Cultivated by all the Fathers and Doctors (to several degrees), we have to wait for

---

1. *Homilies on Genesis and Exodus,* II, 1; op. cit., p72. Lubac, *Medieval Exegesis,* vol. 2 (Grand Rapids: Eerdmans, 2000) pp89–98, provides other instances.
2. Crouzel, *Origène et la connaissance mystique,* p28.
3. *Com in Jo.,* XXXII, 20; G.C.S. IV, p461.

The Mystical Way

Luther to see it rejected under the pretext that this 'mystical theology', from Origen to Gerson in passing through Denys, 'Platonizes more than it Christianizes.'[1]

Let me stress, however, that it would be an error to see only an exegetical procedure in this *sensus mysticus*.[2] The mystical intellect spoken of by Origen is in fact an overall attitude, an orientation of the entire being raised up in the light of the Spirit. This was already the case for Clement of Alexandria who also evoked the need to possess a 'mystical sense' for understanding the most difficult words of the Gospel; thus, when Christ declares that He is the 'true Bread': 'Be it noted,' says Clement, 'the mystical sense of bread' (*to mystikon tou artou parasemeioteon*).[3] For him, as for many writers of the early centuries, this 'mystical Bread' is that of the Scriptures in which the *Logos* is bestowed as food and drink on minds purified and illuminated by baptism. Eusebius of Caesarea explains: 'By receiving the evangelical Scriptures, you see the entire doctrine of our Savior according to what He has said, not of the flesh that He had taken, but of His mystical body and blood' (*peri de tou mystikou somatos te kai haimatos*).[4] And we have the same teaching in St Basil of Caesarea, St Ambrose, St Jerome, St Augustine, 'and many others.'[5]

We rediscover the same theme, on the verge of the main Patristic tradition, in Evagrius Pontus. Recalling the biblical episode (Gen.

---

1. *Werke*, Weimar edition, t. VI, pp 561–562; cited by M. de Certeau, *La Fable mystique* (Paris: Gallimard, 1982), p 130.

2. This point takes into account certain differences between specialists. The learned Father Robert Javelet thought that de Lubac had emphasized to excess the quadruple character of medieval exegesis: the historical, allegorical, moral (also called tropological) and anagogical senses (according to the accepted medieval formula). For Origen (the first to have developed a theory of the various scriptural senses—before the Kabbalah, it is said) there were three of them, relative to the three parts of man: body, soul and spirit. As for anagogy, Javelet says: 'This is not a fourth scriptural sense, although it often follows history, allegory and tropology on paper (and even in distich!).' It designate the transcendent principle of 'the divinization of souls' ('Au XIIe siècle, l'Écriture sainte servante de la mystique?', *Revue des Sciences Religieuses*, t. XXXVII, 1963, p 358, n 59).

3. *The Instructor*, I, c. 6, 46.

4. *Ecclesiastical Theology*, I, 3, c. 12; P.G., t. XXIV, col. 1021 B.

5. Henri de Lubac, *Corpus mysticum. L'Eucharistie et l'Église au moyen âge*, 1949, p 17.

Christ the Original Mystery

18:2–7) which recounts the visit of three mysterious personages to Abraham near the oak of Mambre, he speaks of the 'mystical table' that Abraham 'prepared for the friends that had made their appearance at midday.'[1] But all cannot sit down at this mystical table of the Divine Word to eat the offered food, 'for all are not capable of understanding the mystical sense (*ten mystikoteran dianoian*) of Scripture'; to gain access to this ultimate sense, this Scripture has to be understood 'in an intelligible and spiritual way.'[2]

The theme of the mystical table of Scripture, or of the mystical bread that is Christ's living Word, enables us to pass to the sacramental uses of *mystikos*, just as we have passed from the doctrinal *mysterion* to the *mysteria* of the saving rites and liturgies. Also, in connection with the 'flesh of the *Logos*', it is not always easy to tell if an author is speaking of Scripture (words as the carnal vesture of meaning) or the body of the incarnate Word. But incontestably with time the syntagma 'Mystical Body' more and more comes to designate, as we will see, the eucharistic bread.

For the moment, we will recall some uses in which *mystikos* might be translated as 'sacramental' or relative to the sacramental order. Eusebius, for example, speaking of the eucharist, calls it a 'mystical liturgy',[3] and Theodoret of Cyr, a 'mystical hierurgy'.[4] Likewise, in St Gregory of Nazianzus we again find that 'mystical table' already encountered in his pupil Evagrius Pontus, but rightly applied here to the altar where the eucharistic sacrifice is celebrated.[5] The work of St Gregory of Nyssa offers no less rich a harvest. In him the sacraments are called 'mystical symbols' (*ta mystika symbola*),[6] and the sacramental rites in which one participates are 'the mystical practices' (*ta mystika ethe*).[7] And those who have been regenerated have been so 'by this mystical economy' (*dia tes*

---

1. *Scholies aux Proverbes*, 189, 9; *Sources chrétiennes* 340, p 283.
2. Ibid., 250–251; p 347. Louis Bouyer inexactly asserts (*The Christian Mystery*, p 179) that Evagrius does not use *mystikos*.
3. *Life of Constantine*, IV, 71 and 75.
4. *Epist. 146* and *Hist. rel.*, XIII; Schultz, vol. IV, p 1260 and vol. III, p 1208.
5. *Orat.*, 40; P.G., t. XXXVI, col. 404A.
6. *Against Eunomius*, XI; P.G., t. XLV, col. 881A.
7. Ibid., col. 877D.

The Mystical Way

mystikes tautes oikononmias) that is baptism.[1] In his commentary on the *Song of Songs* he does not hesitate to call baptism a 'mystical kiss': 'after the soul has been distanced from its attachment to evil, it desires to draw its mouth close to the source of light by a mystical kiss (*mystikou philematos*): this restores its beauty.'[2]

I will stop here, for nothing further will be gained by multiplying citations. What is striking in these texts is that, as just now in connection with its hermeneutic use, the adjective *mystikos* should not be seen as a simple substitute for 'sacramental'. Not only does it denote the major rites of the Church, it also connotes something more and refers, like *sensus mysticus*, to a kind of 'spiritual experience', and therefore to something purely interior that is, at once, both an actual transformation of the being and a sure knowledge of this state: 'We are thus,' declares Father Bouyer, who I am following here, 'at the fringe, and even in the midst, of the third and final stage in the meaning of μυστικοσ [*mystikos*], that in which we shall see the word applied directly to the most intimate experience of the Christian faithful, to the revelations made and the gifts granted.'[3]

However this third sense is still not, or not altogether, the one that will appear in the seventeenth century with the noun 'the mystical'. Or, if someone keeps speaking of the mysticism of the Fathers—which is perfectly legitimate—we must not forget then that, for them, this mysticism was *never* separated from the doctrinal mystery of the contents of Scripture, nor from the mystery of grace at work in the sacraments. Not that these authors cared about anticipating such a dissociation—that would be a *modern* way of seeing things—but quite simply because they had no idea of it. Mystical life or, if preferred, spiritual life is, for them, the sacramental grace living within us and illuminating our intelligence with faith's mysteries.

---

1. *Oratio catechetica*, XXXIV, 4; P.G., t. XLV, col. 860.

2. *In Cantica cant.*, homilia XI; P.G., t. XLIV, col. 1001B. I cite Jean Daniélou's translation, *Platonisme et théologie mystique—Doctrine spirituelle de saint Grégoire de Nysse*, Aubier, 1954, p20.

3. *The Christian Mystery*, p171. We know that Guénon rejects the notion of experience applied to the initiatic way. Would it be better to speak of an 'effective taking possession of spiritual states'? This formula seems to have something unfortunately 'proprietary' about it.

Christ the Original Mystery

Without doubt we had to wait for St Augustine's *Confessions*, and even more our own time, for a certain 'psychologization' (at least in appearance) of the mystical life to be manifested: the soul seems to lead a spiritual adventure 'in solitude', detached from its sacramental and scriptural sources; and even if, in reality, it is always dependent on them as its productive cause, everything transpires as if, in its living manifestations, it could ignore them. We will return to this point, but it would be fitting to say something about it to forestall possible misunderstandings at the very moment of broaching the spiritual meaning of *mystikos*. Except for the enigmatic Areopagite, the first author in whom the properly spiritual sense of *mystikos* appeared is, I believe, Origen. In his *Commentary on St John*, he evokes the direct knowledge, without mediation of symbols, that the angels have of God, 'for they have a high priest of the order of Melchizedech [Christ] as leader of the saving worship for those who need both the mystical and secret contemplation' (*tes mystikes kai aporretou theorias*).[1] Origen is also the first to have had the genius to interpret the dialogue between Sulamith and her Beloved (in the *Song of Songs*) as a mystical description of the soul's vicissitudes in seeking its God—which, for him, does not exclude the traditional interpretation, recovered from Judaism, that sees in the bride a figure of the Church, the new Israel. By inaugurating this exegesis and developing it throughout his work, Origen was led to formulate the array of themes that will characterize mystical theology down to our own time. And let us not forget that it would be wrong to only consider here the theme of a 'nuptial mysticism' that some would like to oppose to a 'mysticism of the essence'.[2] For Origen, as for the great mystical doctors who succeed him, the search for God by the soul is the fruit of sacramental grace and is realized according to a mode that I call *ontonoetic*, and not only in response to certain psychological vicissitudes.[3] For union is knowledge (Origen bases himself on

---

1. XIII, (146); op. cit., vol. 2, p99. Likewise: 'the ineffable and mystical contemplations' (*aporreta kai mystika theoremata*), ibid., 1, 30; *Sources chrétiennes* 120, p162.
2. Some have even spoken, in connection with nuptial mysticism, of a *Nonnenmysik*, that is of a 'nun-mysticism'!
3. Psychological events are not, however, either absent or condemnable: 'Often,' states Origen, 'I have perceived the Bridegroom drawing near... then suddenly he

The Mystical Way

'Adam knew his wife Eve' [Gen. 6:1]), and knowledge (*gnosis*) realizes the union of the knowing being and the Being known.[1]

If Origen founds the Christian doctrine of mystical theology, it is with St Gregory of Nyssa, however, that the adjective *mystikos* assumes its most specifically 'mystical' meaning. This is because, with him, the doctrine of *theoria*, that is contemplation, was to experience a systematic development essentially based on the examples of Moses and St Paul, both of whom embody the model of contemplative ascension. The syntagma *theoria mystike* is to be found, in particular, at the beginning of his *Commentary on the Song of Songs* to designate the mystery hidden therein: what is being dealt with in this love poem is 'mystical contemplation',[2] that is 'the contemplation of the mystery in its timeless substance'; however, this *theoria* differs from other contemplations by degree and not by its nature: 'liturgical *theoria*, scriptural *theoria* and mystical *theoria* are ultimately various aspects of one same reality.'[3] With St Macarius the Egyptian (today called the Pseudo-Macarius), whose writings are situated within St Gregory of Nyssa's sphere of influence, we encounter another syntagma that will also prove to be highly successful, the syntagma 'mystical union' (*mystike synousia, unio* or *unitio mystica*).[4] By the end of the fourth century, the vocabulary and themes of Christian mysticism are in place.

And yet we should not conclude this rapid overview without mentioning the unique importance that the appearance of the

---

has withdrawn.... I long, therefore, for Him to come again, and sometimes he does so. Then, when... I lay hold of him, he slips away once more... until in Truth I hold him' (*Song of Songs*, Homily One, 7; op.cit., p280). Was Origen speaking of himself here?

1. Crouzel, *Origène et la 'connaissance mystique'*, pp496–523.

2. *Homily 1*; P.G., t. XLV, col. 765A. Daniélou (*Platonisme et théologie mystique*, p182, n1) points out that *mystike* might refer here to spiritual exegesis rather than to contemplative experience, contrary to Bouyer (*The Christian Mystery*, p177).

3. Daniélou, op. cit., p163.

4. *Second Homily*; P.G., t. XXXIV, col. 416D. Bouyer, op. cit., p178. Perhaps it is a question of writings attributed to a 'blessed' (*makarios* in Greek), since in other respects St Macarius the Egyptian, who was a highly reputed desert monk, is known for no literary activity. The syntagma 'mystical union' is, among others, to be met with in St Cyril of Alexandria, *In Joannem*, P.G., t. LXXIII, col. 161, 1045, 1048, etc.

Christ the Original Mystery

Dionysian corpus at the end of the fifth century or the beginning of the sixth assumes for this evolution. Its author will be considered the preeminent mystical doctor, and, in fact, no work makes such a use of this term or presents so masterful a synthesis. As with St Gregory of Nyssa, and beyond the varied meanings that I have marked out, Denys applies the adjective *mystikos* to the designation of the loftiest realities and to the supreme mode of knowledge, which is in fact an 'unknowing': thus he describes Moses who, 'freed from the objects and the very organs of contemplation, penetrates into the truly mystical Darkness of unknowing.' What is this 'truly mystical' Darkness (or Cloud)? Is it the very Object of 'mystical theology'? True, this phrase is to be read in the short treatise[1] on which Denys has bestowed this title, inventing by the same stroke an expression which, a thousand years later, will give birth to the French noun *la mystique*.[2] But precisely this theology, the mention of which is strangely absent from the treatise (except for its title), is not an expressible science, a discourse *on* something, a theology *of* the mystical; here *theologia* designates a knowledge by unknowing, not then a knowledge *of* something, but a pure knowledge that is without Object, that is knowledge of Nothing.[3] This Nothing is the Darkness, the Cloud into which Moses entered; 'truly mystical' because it embodies the truth of the Divine Mystery, and because it is only one with the apprehended knowledge of it, or rather with the unknowing in which the theologizing intelligence is finally established when *all* knowledge is stripped away. Here we glimpse how mystical theology designates the very (unassignable) place where the theologizing intellect and its theological Object are indistinguishable: a 'secret', inexpressible place, neither here nor there, a mode without mode, and yet a presentiment of it transits the soul at each moment of its quest for God.

---

1. §2, col. 1001 A; Gandillac p178 (modified translation: Roques, *Hiérarchie Céleste*, S. C. 58, p XXXIV).
2. [In French *la mystique* can denote either the study of mysticism or mystical theology. The latter is intended here TR.]
3. Cf. our study of the Dionysian *theologia* in *Lumières de la théologie mystique* (Lausanne: L'Age d'Homme, 2002).

The Mystical Way

With the mention of the Cloud of unknowing we are obviously led to the goal of the mystical way, or at the very least to what we can discern of it at present. Since we can go no further in the discursive order, it will be undoubtedly useful to cast a glance over the road traveled and to regain, in a synthetic view, the various teachings provided by this brief history of *mystikos*.

The Nature of Mystical Contemplation

'Mystical' is that which relates to the Christian mystery according to its threefold but inseparable sacramental, scriptural, and spiritual dimension. Or again, what there is of the mystical is that by which (or in which) the sacraments, scripture and the spiritual life are reunited and are only one. If the third element appears later on, or less clearly, this is not, then, because it was first excluded or ignored, but rather because it is so naturally implied by the designation of Christian revelation as a 'mystery' that the need to stress it was not at first felt. Nevertheless, the use of the adjective *mystikos* would not have been imposed if it were only a question of denoting what related to the liturgical mysteries or the secrets of the Divine Word. This is because the adjective in fact speaks of the essence, while the noun speaks of the subject, the thing, the subsistent being. And, if it was only a question of signifying things or (hidden, invisible) realities, *mysteria* would have sufficed. *Mystikos*, insofar as an adjective qualifying a noun, expresses something more, a common character belonging to the essence of the realities qualified, a common character made known by the very thing that it states. In fact, to state the quality of an entity, by attributing this quality to it, is to reveal its nature. Thus *mystikos* is related to a *knowledge* of the *essence* of mysterious things.

'Mystical' should not denote just a 'sacramental thing' or the secret referents spoken of by Scripture, or the hermeneutic discourse that designates these secrets. It should also denote a certain state of

Christ the Original Mystery

knowledge in the very being of anyone entering into these mysteries and into whom these mysteries have entered. What about the state of knowledge then?

Since knowledge is involved, this state requires a certain self-awareness.[1] Assuredly, we can qualify as mystical the ordinarily unfelt effects of sacramental grace in a soul, in the sense that this term connotes the ideas of 'secret', 'hidden', and 'invisible'. And certainly, in the eyes of God and in itself, the soul of a baptized newborn is filled with the Holy Spirit's presence, although it does not seem to have any awareness of it. From this point of view, all of the baptized might be said to be in a state of mystical knowledge. Although this formulation is objectively acceptable, subjectively it is otherwise, because then reference to this effective spiritual awareness, this sense of the supernatural implied by the adjective *mystikos* would be lacking.

Baptized adults, save for exceptions, obviously know that they have received this sacrament, know that they have communed, know that Scripture speaks of mysterious realities, and might even have a very elaborate theological conception of them. Such a knowledge should be called psychological when it stems from the simple existence within us of an awareness that accompanies all of our personal experience; it might possibly be called speculative when formed into a science. But it is still not mystical to the extent that, as a simple expression of the knowledge characteristic of every human mind, it reveals no ability to know ourselves even unawares, it gives rise to the appearance, or rather opening, of no new organ of inward perception. Now, if a knowledge is mystical, this is because it is secret and mysterious, as are those mystical realities whose presence our intelligence has been invited, through faith, to surmise. In short, the term 'mystical' is employed by the sacred authors only with a view to calling our understanding to a self-heightening, a transposition of its

---

1. This does not rule out that this mystical awareness leads to a 'superconsciousness' or even a transcendent 'unconsciousness', an 'infinite ignorance' (Evagrius Ponticus): entry into the more than luminous Darkness. 'It is from knowing that we must gain access to unknowing. Then our knowing will be transformed into a divine unknowing' (Eckhart, Pfeiffer, p15; cf. Emile Zum Brunn, 'Un homme qui pâtit Dieu', in *Voici Maître Eckhart*, Jérôme Millon, 1994, p269).

The Mystical Way

gaze, orienting it toward the presence of what can not be seen and for which our ordinary experience of the world offers no models. Not that a simple word by itself possesses such a power; but, by indicating to our mind that it is confronted by a reality beyond any natural experience and that can only be welcomed by faith, it warns our intellect to suspend its customary activity and the natural direction of its noetic focus, silently inviting it to lend an ear, to listen for what it has never heard, and yet it bears within itself an inexpressible anticipation of it.

Are all the baptized capable of this effort? In principle, yes: by virtue of the grace received and the profound nature of our spirit. To be intelligent, whether we know it or not, is to desire to see God. In other respects, this heightening toward supernatural knowledge has no relationship to mental power or the degree of culture; otherwise Voltaire, Renan, Loisy, or Sartre would have been mystics, and it could not be said that Therese of Lisieux, who read little, was the greatest saint of modern times.[1] Anyhow, the Church Fathers ceaselessly invite all disciples of Christ to this effort. Commenting on the word of the apostle: 'For you are all the children of God by faith, in Christ Jesus. For as many of you as have been baptized in Christ, have put on Christ' (Gal. 3:26–27), Clement of Alexandria writes: 'some are not then "gnostics", while others would be "psychics"; in the *Logos* ... all are equal, all "pneumatics" in the Lord's eyes.'[2] But, obviously, this in-principle capability can be impeded by accidental limitations stemming at once from the individual psychism and the conditions of our existence or circumstances of our lives.

Now it might be asked if the advent of a spiritual awareness is always experienced as an inner upheaval, marked by extraordinary events in the psyche, and if—another question—it introduces a rupture into the life of the spirit, a radical discontinuity, the psychic events of which would be as if a sign and proof.

---

1. To be explicit: simplicity of spirit and modest culture do not mean stupidity. The modern *intelligentsia* should even ask themselves, in view of their works, if foolishness does not grow apace with learning.
2. *Christ the Educator,* bk. 1, chap. 6, 31, 2 (New York: Fathers of the Church, Inc., 1954), p31.

Christ the Original Mystery

As for the first question, the Fathers never speak of it, neither to inform us of their own experiences, nor to inform their listeners or readers about what they might experience on their spiritual path. This is why many modern theologians and historians, confronted with this general silence, have wondered if these Fathers had truly known 'mystical states'. St Augustine himself, an apparent exception in this respect, describes in his 'ecstasy at Ostia', not so much an extraordinary (yet certainly real) personal event, as an exemplary ascension of a soul climbing through the degrees of creation toward God who is at once within and above it. In this way he Christianizes an objective scheme of Platonic origin, offering it to his readers as an 'experimental' verification.

I do not deny, then, that psychological experiences occurred in the spiritual life of the Fathers. But the occurrence of these events is one thing, and the awakening, in the intellect, of a mystical sense that becomes a permanent quality—a *habitus*—of the intellective gaze is another. According to individual temperaments, this opening of the spiritual eye might possibly be accompanied by an inner upheaval, but this should not be the same as a proof that birth to the Spirit clearly constitutes a complete break with respect to the preexisting intellectual order. In other words, the second question is independent of the first one—and conversely, for extraordinary events can occur in a soul without it having access to a true spiritual awareness.

The reply to this second question (break or continuity in the order of spiritual intelligence) would require weighty explanations, but a few remarks will suffice. First, we must distinguish between the birth of spiritual awareness and the highest degrees of the mystical way. As for these degrees, I think that the 'ecstasy' (and therefore break) or 'enstasy' (and therefore continuity) alternative, seen as inevitable by many, is actually not very relevant and by no means has considered the texts—especially those of Denys, but also Gregory of Nyssa and Augustine—which tell us that the 'summit' of *theologia* is at once a complete going out of oneself and an entry into our most intimate and most profound truth. However that may be, this is not what I am referring to when I mention the springing up in the soul of the *sensus mysticus;* we are here on a much more modest level, the only level on which this question can be posed: at the summit it is all

The Mystical Way

too obvious that conceptual distinctions no longer apply. Now, where this elementary level is involved, I think that the teaching of the Fathers tends to favor a certain continuity (as to the truth of the intellect) that can be experienced, at the psychic level, as a change. Surely the awakening of the mystical sense is a 'novelty', but it is not presented as an intellective break. Otherwise how could it be connected inseparably with the very life of faith, that is with knowledge of the Scriptures and sacramental practice? In an article entitled 'Connaissance religieuse et connaissance mystique chez saint Augustin dans les *Confessions*',[1] Pierre Blanchard writes significantly: for St Augustine

> eternal life is within us: we discover it with the light of faith by interiorization.... *Metaphysical and religious knowledge, without change of nature, is transfigured and deepened into mystical knowledge.*

And, if St Augustine burns to communicate this experience to the faithful, this is because he is convinced that all are called to it. Now this metaphysical knowledge that is also religious ('the intellectual perception of the truth [for Augustine] was religious and his religious experience was intellectual'),[2] this knowledge, transfigured by grace and deepened by the exercise of a daily practice of prayer, is that which the Greek Fathers call *gnosis,* and which is in a certain manner nothing but the *life* of faith in the intellective soul. Here the paradox of a voluntary faith-adherence of the intellect to the *revelatum* and a faith-gift of the Holy Spirit infused by baptism is clarified. Baptismal initiation communicates precisely to the intellect in its act of adherence a *virtus gnostica,* a virtue of gnosis that lifts it higher and enables it to enter into a certain connaturality with the divine mysteries. 'The ontological perfection of our intellectual faculty,' writes Dom Stolze, 'not only inclines it to give its assent to dogma.

---

1. In *Recherches augustiniennes,* vol. II (Hommage au P. Fulbert Cayré), 1962, pp 311–312; in this citation, the italics are the author's.
2. Dom Cuthbert Butler, *Western Mysticism, The teaching of S.S. Augustine, Gregory and Bernard on Contemplation and Contemplative Life* (London: Constable, 1951), p 206.

Christ the Original Mystery

In addition, it confers on it a spontaneous and, in a certain sense, unfathomable knowledge of the "divinity" of dogmatic truths that are manifested without intermediary to divinized reason.' The soul is found to be then, he says, in 'a certain nearness to the Beatific Vision. . . . Here the simple faithful become then, in the sense of the ancient authors, gnostics and mystics.'[1]

Thus the gift of faith and religious practice (prayer, liturgy and Scripture)—combined with love of neighbor—little by little form within us a gnostic habitus, a deepening contemplative state that communicates to us the 'sense of Christ', or rather a sense of the Mystery that is Christ. Faith given and faith exercised confer this contemplative state, if not on every soul, at least on anyone who in their sacred practice faithfully uphold the spiritual intention of 'gathering all these things in [their] heart' (Luke 2:19). Having been gathered into the heart, the *mysteria* deposit therein a perfume that suffuses the soul, as do flower petals a sachet. This perfume—the work of the good odor of Christ that is the Holy Spirit—scents our spirit and opens within it a sense of the supernatural, a contemplative ability, which is an *adorative* quality of intellection that intellection is astonished to find to be its own. Break or continuity? The answer must be: break for the profane intelligence, but continuity for the sanctified intelligence that has received the grace of the *virtus gnostica:* having gained access to adorative intellection, it perceives that it has thus recovered, in some manner, the use of the 'spirit of life' that God the Creator opened in our face at the origin of time.

---

1. *Théologie de la mystique,* pp190–192. 'We ought to reconquer the paradisal tongue to be able to adequately express the mystical experience', ibid., p193, n1. Thus does a Benedictine professor of dogmatic theology at the pontifical College of Saint Anselm at Rome, in 1936, express himself. This admirable little book merits republication.

The Mystical Way

From Adjective to Noun

From the Fifth to the Tenth Century: The Heritage of the Fathers

The subsequent evolution of the word *mystical* (and the thing itself) has not altered very profoundly the nature of contemplation as just described. But it has introduced modifications that have changed its appearance, at the risk of disfiguring it, at least for anyone who looks at things from without. It is this change in the 'packaging' that might justify, in some respects, the judgments that Guénon has brought to bear on *the* mystical, or rather on mysticism. And this is why we should now take this into account.

The Christianity that was progressively established in the West inherited, as we know, only a part of ecclesiastical culture, that which comes from St Ambrose, St Jerome, St Augustine, Boethius and some others. We had to wait for the translations of Hilduin and then John Scotus Eriugena, in the ninth century, for Denys to be known in Europe. Origen and St Gregory of Nyssa arrived only in the twelfth century. True, the essentials of the spiritual doctrine of the Greek Fathers and eastern monasticism is transmitted to the monks of the West thanks to St John Cassian and St Gregory the Great. But it is not altogether the same for vocabulary, especially for the adjective *mysticus* (a Latin transcription of *mystikos*), since the authors in whom its properly spiritual sense is registered most clearly—this is the case in the highest degree with the Areopagite—only arrive at the end of the ninth or the beginning of the tenth century. And besides, even then, this sense does not seem to prevail, as we will see.

This is because its richest meaning remains the one that connects *mysticus* to *mysterium*, either as a designation of sacramental and liturgical realities, or as a designation of the transcendent secrets of the Word of God; in this respect *mysticus (-a, -um)*, or *mystice* (mystically) almost always qualify a certain way of surpassing the visible or the literal toward the invisible and the spiritual. In St Augustine,

Christ the Original Mystery

for example, *mysticus* does not seem to be a part of the vocabulary of contemplative experience, but most often refers, above all under the adverbial form, to spiritual exegesis.[1] We understand then why, insofar as the referent of the mystery is only attained through a 'mystical' exegesis, it receives the very character of this exegesis and is found to be qualified in its turn as 'mystical' according to a semantic transfer common to all languages. Such is the case with the heavenly Church, mystically spoken of in the New Testament when naming the earthly Church, and which, by this fact, has been called *Ecclesia mystica*.[2] Of this Church, says St Ambrose, Christ is the 'mystical Head',[3] and, Bede the Venerable will say later, Christians are its 'mystical members'.[4]

John Scotus, called Erigena, provides a good example of these uses of *mysticus* and *mystice*.[5] These terms first qualify a certain understanding of Scripture, the *intellectus mysticus*,[6] and, most specifically, a reading of the *Law* of Moses, that is of the Old Testament, that enables the announcement of New Testament revelations to be seen in this 'shadow'.[7] Moreover, they can be applied, as we have seen, to things or beings that are the object of a mystical interpretation: thus John Scotus speaks, in connection with the golden candlestick glimpsed by the prophet Zacharias (4:2)—interpreted as a figure of Christ and the Church—of the 'mystical candlestick of the Church'.[8] Similarly the Jewish Pascal lambs announce Christ: 'It is

---

1. *The City of God*, xv, 1. Likewise *Genesis in the Literal Sense*, IX, XII, 20 (*significatio mystica*); 22 (*mysticum*); etc.

2. *Sermo* 2 52; P.L., t. XXXVIII, col. 1175. We are quite close to the notion of 'Mystical Body' that will however only appear later, as we will see.

3. *In Psalm.* 118, Sermon 20; P.L., t. XV, col. 1483 D.

4. *In Samuelem*, III, 9; P.L., t. XCI, col. 657 B.

5. I have studied the comparative meanings of *symbolum* and *mysterium* for John Scotus in *Le mystère du signe*, pp 47–54.

6. *Homily on the Prologue of John*, XXIII; S.C. 151, p 316. This syntagma is in the plural: the 'mystical senses' (*intellectus mystici*).

7. *Commentary on the Gospel of John*, I, 25; S.C. 180, p 114. Likewise: ibid., I, 30 (*doctrinae mysticae*, p 160; *mystice*, p 162); IV, 6 (p 308); etc.

8. *Homily on the Prologue of John*, XXIII (p 314). Likewise: *Periphyseon* (*The Division of Nature*), II (P.L., t. CXXI, 564 B), trans. I.P. Sheldon-Williams, revised John J. O'Meara (Washington DC: Dumbarton Oaks, 1987), pp 166–167. John Scotus identifies the seven branches of the candlestick with the seven gifts of the Holy Spirit;

The Mystical Way

He, the mystical Lamb, the only one, the unique one.'[1] As for the names attributed by the Gospels to the Precursor, these are 'mystical names' that must be explained.[2]

On the other hand, *mysticus* can qualify everything relative to the sacramental and liturgical rites. Following Denys, he considers that 'the chief symbols of the New Testament are the three *teletai*, that is the three mystical rites' of baptism, communion and chrismation.[3] Here we see the equivalence that I have pointed out many times functioning fully, the equivalence between 'initiatic' (*telete* = initiation) and 'mystical'.

Finally, we might expect to find, with this disciple of the Areopagite, a clearly spiritual significance for *mysticus* or *mystice*, especially thanks to the theme of 'mystical theology'. In fact, and probably being inspired by Maximus, John Scotus speaks of the one who, by

> this simple theological science...is elevated to the divine infinite...in its perfection and mystery: it is as if starting out from the intellect of Christ, he were to be mystically (*mystice*) elevated to his divinity.[4]

This elevation clearly leads to what John Scotus calls, along with the Greeks, *theologia*, that is to the highest contemplation of the divine mystery.[5] But everything still transpires as if this *theologia*, because it designates so high a degree of knowledge, could receive no qualifier. This is exactly the opposite of what will happen in the seventeenth

---

Homily on the Prologue of John, XXIII (p314). Likewise: *Periphyseon* (*The Division of Nature*), II (P.L., t. CXXI, 564B), trans. I.P. Sheldon-Williams, revised John J. O'Meara (Washington DC: Dumbarton Oaks, 1987), pp166–167. John Scotus identifies the seven branches of the candlestick with the seven gifts of the Holy Spirit; this symbolism comes from St Maximus the Confessor: *Questions à Thalassios*, LXIII, (P.G., t. XC, 665A); intro. by Jean Claude Larchet, trans. and notes by Emmanuel Ponsoye, Les Éditions de l'Ancre, 1992, p292 ff.

1. *Commentary on the Gospel of John*, I, 31; p176 (311A).
2. Ibid., I, 28; p144 (305B).
3. Ibid., I, 30; p163 (308C).
4. Ibid., I, 33; p189 (312D).
5. *Homily on the Prologue of John*, XIV, 16 (291C); 'this lofty contemplation of the divine nature that the Greeks name 'theology': no intelligence should venture beyond it' (p273).

century when we will see, in the syntagma 'mystical theology', the adjective absorb the noun: then they will speak of 'the mystical',[1] 'theology' being at first understood, then definitely obliterated. True, in the meantime, *theologia* lost its exclusively contemplative significance, coming to designate only sacred doctrine as scientifically elaborated, becoming therefore improper as a designation for supreme gnosis.

However, it is not only the evolution of *theologia* that has led to this usage, it is also the evolution of *mysticus,* not insofar as it qualifies a scriptural mode of interpretation, since even up until our own day we continue to speak of a mystical sense of the Divine Word, but as applied to the sacramental rites and the mysterious realities formed by them. Cardinal de Lubac has recounted this history in his famous work: *Corpus mysticum. L'Eucharistie et l'Église au Moyen Âge.* A word or two must be said about this.

From the Eleventh to the Thirteenth Century: From the Eucharistic to the Ecclesial Sense

Between the ninth century, that of John Scotus, and the thirteenth, the expression *corpus mysticum* loses its first, properly eucharistic sense,[2] to acquire a second exclusively ecclesial one. This at first purely eucharistic significance is, for us, a rather surprising fact, since we are accustomed to understand by 'mystical body' the sum total of Christians mysteriously united with Christ in the Church. And yet this fact is quite broadly attested to in the ninth and tenth centuries; it is only continuing the grand tradition that connects *mysticum* to *mysterium*. Now the Eucharist is the 'sacrament of sacraments', or in Greek the 'mystery of mysteries': to it, then, is applied preeminently the quality 'mystical'. A 'mystical food' and a 'mystical

---

1. [This discussion is germane to the French usage of *la mystique* which has no one word English equivalent TR.]
2. A hundred or so examples of this eucharistic sense will be found in *Corpus mysticum,* Aubier, 2nd ed., 1949, pp 23–66.

The Mystical Way

drink' served on a 'mystical table' for a 'mystical supper', it constitutes a 'divine mystagogy'. *Corpus* is certainly in competition with *caro*, 'flesh', and texts speaking of *caro mystica* are not lacking. However, Christ himself has said: 'This is my Body.' On the other hand, St Paul speaks of the Church as being the Body of Christ. This is why, since the beginning, the theology of the Church is inseparable from the theology of the Eucharist, as the word *communio—synaxis* in Greek—proves, that designates the assembled Church as well as the participation of the faithful in the eucharistic meal: the Church forms the Eucharist which forms the Church. To treat of the Church is to treat of the sacrifice of the Mass and vice versa. This profoundly traditional vision will fade away only at the end of the Middle Ages, to make room for an ecclesiological reflection separated from its sacramental fulfillment (something not foreign to the Protestant Reform).

In this perspective, ninth century authors were led to make a case for the three forms of the *Corpus Christi* which must then be distinguished by appropriate qualifiers. Thus Paschasius Radbertus will speak, in a famous text, first of the Body that is the *Ecclesia*, next of the *Corpus mysticum*, of the 'true flesh of Christ consecrated each day by the Holy Spirit for the life of the world', and finally of the *Corpus natum de Maria virgine*, of the 'Body born of the Virgin Mary.'[1] The eucharistic Body has been qualified as mystical because it is hidden, secret and invisible, not because it should be purely 'ideal'. After all, it is clearly a question of three forms of a single and unique Body, a unity that has never been lost sight of, a unity that confers on the vision of the Church-community of the faithful an admirable strength and coherence whose active principle and ever-living heart is the Eucharist.

However, this terminological situation tends to be changed, starting with the eleventh century, under the effect of two factors. First of all and undoubtedly by a more and more defined development in a worship of the Eucharist seen and contemplated for itself as the

---

1. *Liber de corpore et sanguine Domini*, VII; P.L., t. CXX, col. 1284–1286. Lubac, op. cit., p 40. I have meditated on these three forms of the Christic Body in *The Sense of the Supernatural* (Edinburgh: T & T Clark, 1998).

Christ the Original Mystery

visible Body of Jesus Christ,[1] theologians became accustomed to speak no longer of the *sacramentum Corporis* or of the *mysterium Corporis*, but, quite simply, of the *Corpus*.[2] Hence, this 'form' of the Body of Christ having become *the* Body, the need to distinguish it by a particular qualifier was attenuated. Numerous are the texts in which the eucharistic Body and the ecclesial Body are designated, in the same sentence, by one and the same 'Body of Christ' syntagma.[3] But, if it is the consecrated Host that is the *visible* Body of Christ, the Church should then be envisaged as the invisible Body, the Body that can not be *shown*, but only *signified* and mysteriously—that is to say mystically—realized by communion with the eucharistic Body. Thus are we led to designate the Church as the Mystical Body.

To this factor may be added a second that interacts with the first. This is the time (the eleventh century) when certain heresies make their appearance, especially that of Berengarius of Tours, who denied (or attenuated) the reality of the eucharistic presence. In response the Church doctors were led to stress this reality by qualifying the eucharistic Body as *true*, '*verum Corpus*'. With respect to this *verum Corpus* (cf. the fourteenth century hymn still sung today: *Ave verum Corpus*), the mystical nature, that is the 'mystically signified' nature, of the ecclesial Body becomes still more tenuous: the eucharistic Body receives this qualification in a definitive manner.

The first evidence of this can be noticed, it seems, in a work by Master Simon, a very poorly known theologian of the twelfth century, who declares: 'In the sacrament of the altar there are two things: namely, the true Body of Christ, and, what is signified thanks to it, his Mystical Body, that is to say the Church'; the true Body 'is

---

1. The worship of 'Jesus-the-Host' ended up, in the twelfth century, changing the liturgy by the introduction of the elevation of the Host at the consecration, and, in the thirteenth, by the celebration of an adoration of the Blessed Sacrament detached from the Mass. These practices, by promoting a worship of the 'sacred thing', have caused the sense of liturgical *action*, of the true and real sacrifice, to become somewhat lost. The post-conciliar reform only accentuated this tendency, and has made possible a total disappearance of the *liturgical sense* (Masses facing the people and bereft of ritual).

2. Lubac, op. cit., p 95.

3. Ibid., p 97.

The Mystical Way

hidden under the species', and the Mystical Body 'is signified.'[1] Starting with this date (*circa* 1150), this usage tends to become imposed as the *proper sense* of the expression. Around 1230 it has become fixed and will be made official, in 1302, by Pope Boniface VIII, in his Bull *Unam Sanctam:* 'A single and holy Church ... that represents a single Mystical Body, the head of which is Christ.'[2]

From the Fourteenth to the Sixteenth Century: Mystical and the Mystical

Such a terminological usage obviously contributes to a modifying of Catholic ecclesiology and to causing it to lose sight of the ontological relationship that unites the Church to the sacrament of Communion, with all the consequences that this entails, both for the *Ecclesia* which tends to become identified with the priestly hierarchy, and for the eucharistic sacrament which tends to become isolated from the sacrificial liturgy and the ecclesial community.[3] But no less are the effects on the meaning of 'mystical'. What almost entirely disappears is its relationship to the *mysteries* of the liturgy and sacraments. As for its use in hermeneutics, it is maintained and enlarged but also find itself threatened by this very extension. It comes to designate no longer exactly a mode of interpretation *of Scripture* (and, on occasion, a quality of those referents denoted by this interpretation), but, in a general way, every sensory or present reality in the world of common experience that is the object of a metaphysical or spiritual transposition.

More and more in the fifteenth and sixteenth centuries we hear of the 'mystical rose', of the 'mystical garden' or 'orchard', of the

---

1. Ibid., p119.
2. Ibid., p13.
3. Thus, at the Council of Trent, the doctrine on transubstantiation and the real presence is expounded in chapter v of Session XIII (Oct. 11, 1551), and the doctrine on the sacrificial liturgy of the Mass at Session XXII (Sept. 17, 1562). And yet it is a question of one and the same Eucharist. This strain will be heavy with theological difficulties.

'mystical wine-press', the 'mystical voyage', the 'mystical Gospel', etc.[1] So wide-spread a use of the adjective 'mystical'—which, until then, had remained semantically subordinate to the noun that it qualified—ended up by conferring on it a kind of independence and forming it into a general category: *the* 'mystical'.[2] The hermeneutic sense itself, if it remains at all, becomes somehow secondary with respect to an essence *of* the mystical that is, *de facto,* posited in itself, in its own reality, and no longer as what is specifically relative to the Christic *mysterion.*[3] Formed thus into a category, the mystical, whether it is called such or not, opens up a new realm of knowledge, a new 'epistemic' field, that is a new series of inquiries. In effect, insofar as it was simply an adjective attributed to a noun to qualify it, 'mystical' was in the position of a clarifying notion (as happens with every attributive judgment: it makes the subject explicit): to attribute to something a mystical quality is to indicate in what sense this thing should be understood. To the contrary, when 'mystical' arrives at the status of a noun, 'the mystical', it demands in turn to be defined and qualified: what is the mystical? how do we situate its essence?

The answer to this question might be sought in many directions. Insofar as the adjective was connected to the Christic *mysterion, a priori* we know where the secret of this essence is to be found, even if we were truly incapable of penetrating it: it was between the hands of the Word Incarnate, whose *mysterion* was nothing but the salvific doing of it. But once this connection was broken, some were led to

---

1. The term is even extended to the scientific realm: in his *Traité des coniques—*known only thanks to Leibniz—Pascal had called a figure composed of six straight lines a 'mystical hexagram' (*Œuvres complètes,* ed, J. Mesnard (Paris: Desclée De Brouwer, 1990), t. II, p1103 for the text and p1129 for the figure).

2. 'By being made more complex and precise, these practices have gathered adjectives within a suitable compass'; cf. Michel de Certeau, *La Fable mystique,* Gallimard, 1982, p104. Debatable because of its Structuralism, this book gathers much data and presents stimulating views; we are in only partial agreement with the analyses. [The author differentiates the new use which takes the 'masculine' definite article (*le mystique*), from the earlier use taking the 'feminine' article (*la mystique*). TR]

3. The adjective taken nominally (*the* mystical/*le mystique*) made its appearance in the seventeenth century: 'Corbinelli is shaped entirely by the mystical' writes Madame de Sévigné (Sept. 11, 1689).

The Mystical Way

locate its residence, later, in everything that seemed to imply being put in touch with a superior and invisible order of realities, be it Rosicrucianism, alchemy or the occult sciences.[1] Thus the sense of 'extraordinary spiritual knowledge' prevailed over all the other senses of the word, seeing that a transcendent and hidden reality can only appear to an extremely lofty secret and inward knowledge. Now there was such a tradition of knowledge in the Church for quite a while: with St Denys the Areopagite it had received the name of *theologia mystica, theologia* being understood here in the strong sense of a properly divine state of knowledge. This is why the noun 'the mystical' could have arisen only under the mighty patronage of the venerable Doctor and can only be appreciated in reference to his doctrine. It seems, in fact, that the first instance of it is provided by the following passage from Pierre Charron's famous work, *De la Sagesse* (end of the sixteenth century): 'Theology, even the mystical [= *la mystique*], teaches us that, to prepare our soul well for God and the impress of the Holy Spirit, it is necessary to empty it, drown it.'[2] Beginning with him the term is circulated and little by little becomes current usage. In 1640, Sandt speaks of a 'natural mystique', and Surin writes, in 1661, a treatise (unpublished): *De La mystique*.[3] Concurrently, the adjective also begins to be used nominally to designate, often with a critical nuance, anyone who has attained, or seeks to attain such a state of knowing (or unknowing): thus with Thomas of Jesus who, with respect to the *Theologia germanica*, speaks of the 'errors of the Beghards and other Mystics included in this mediocre work.'[4] At century's end, Boileau will conjure up one who,

---

1. In 1513 Josse Clichtove composed a *De mystica numerorum significatione*, H.C. Agrippa spoke of 'mystical figures' (1533), F. Patrizzi wrote a *Mystica Aegyptorum philosophia* (1591), etc.; cf. Certeau, p132.
2. *De la Sagesse*, II, 2; cited following Littré, *Dictionnaire de la Langue française*, s. v. Charron died in 1603. The definitive edition was procured by his disciple, La Rochemaillet, in 1604.
3. Certeau, op. cit., p149.
4. Cited by Jean Orcibal, *La rencontre de Carmel thérésien avec les mystiques du Nord*, P.U.F., 1959, p195. Chapter XII in my book *Lumière de la théologie mystique* (Lausanne: L'Age d'Homme, 2002) is devoted to the *Theologia germanica*, which is not at all a mediocre work.

Christ the Original Mystery

...an insolent mystic and tranquil fanatic
in the midst of sins,
of a more perfect love thinks to have
the happy gift
and, in the arms of a demon, believes himself
God-possessed.[1]

The 'quarrel of pure Love' occupied many minds at that time in France and Europe, the 'mystical' became a topic of conversation, and Fénelon's condemnation was not far off, the consequences of which will be felt down to our own time.

Under the Patronage of St Denys the Areopagite

However that may be, the importance of a Dionysian patronage in the birth of the mystical should be stressed. This alone is enough to refute Guénon's image of an entirely exoteric and purely psychological mysticism. True, the word is new, as just shown following many others. Neither St Teresa of Avila, nor St John of the Cross use it to designate what they, along with all of tradition, call 'contemplation' and 'spiritual life'. They only make use of 'mystical' with reference to Denys and, in this case, speak of 'mystical theology', which they identify with contemplation by unknowing in the Darkness: 'Contemplation,' declares St John of the Cross,

> consequently, by which the intellect has a higher knowledge of God, is called mystical theology, meaning the *secret wisdom of*

---

1. *Épitre XII*, 87–90; *Œuvres poétique*, Hachette, 1912, p183. This is the same judgment of Leibniz with respect to Angelus Silesius: 'Here and there among the mystics are to found some extraordinarily audacious thoughts... bordering on impiety' (*Opera omnia*, Geneva, 1768, t. VI, p56: letter 43, to Placidus); cf. E. Susini, *Angelus Silesius*, P.U.F., 1964, t. I, pp8–9, n2. At the beginning of the nineteenth century, in Germany and chiefly under the influence of Franz von Baader, a rehabilitation of the mystics occurred (Eckhart, Boehme); cf. E. Benz, *Les sources mystiques de la philosophie allemande*, Vrin, 1968, pp11–26.

The Mystical Way

God. For this wisdom is secret to the very intellect that receives it. St Denys on this account refers to contemplation as a ray of darkness.[1]

To be more precise however, as hidden as it may be, this theology is no less delightful to the understanding and constitutes a true *science*:

> The sweet and living knowledge she says He taught her is mystical theology, that secret knowledge of God which spiritual persons call contemplation. This knowledge is very delightful because it is a knowledge through love. Love is the master of this knowledge and that which makes it wholly agreeable. Since God communicates this knowledge and understanding in the love with which He communicates Himself to the soul, it is very delightful to the intellect, since it is a knowledge belonging to the intellect.'[2]

But here St John of the Cross is only the heir and echo of an uninterrupted Dionysian tradition that is especially accentuated at the dawn of modern times. Since John Scotus Eriugena the influence of Denys in the West has never weakened. It spreads up to the eleventh and twelfth centuries, then becomes important for St Albert the Great, St Thomas Aquinas, St Bonaventure, Thomas Gallus, and even preponderant for Meister Eckhart and the Flemish Rhinelanders. Combined with the influence of the latter authors, chiefly thanks to Tauler translated into Latin and Castillian (1551) and disseminated in Spain, it saturates Teresa's spirituality and above all St John's.[3] Denys was also declared 'prince of Platonists' by Marsilio Ficino, and 'prince of theologians' by Nicholas of Cusa. One century later, this reputation was only growing: he was officially designated as 'the greatest of theologians' and 'the prince of Christian theology';

---

1. *Ascent of Mount Carmel*, II, 8; *Coll. Works of St John of the Cross*, tr. Kavanaugh and Rodriguez (Washington DC: ICS Publications, 1973), p128. My italics.

2. *The Spiritual Canticle* B, Stanza 27, 5; op. cit., p518.

3. We say it again and again: Eckhart's gnostic type of spirituality should not be set in opposition to St John of the Cross' devotional type of spirituality. J. Orcibal has *demonstrated* (*Saint Jean de la Croix et les mystiques rhéno-flamands* (Paris: Desclée De Brouwer, 1966), what knowledge the Spanish mystic had of the Rhineland mystic, whose condemnation was seen to be concerned only with the Beghards (p135), and whose name was perhaps not unknown to him.

Christ the Original Mystery

'to be authorized it was necessary to resemble him', and St Bernard himself 'is only the second Denys of our France', declared Léon de Saint-Jean in 1661.[1] Let us go further. This importance of Denys is not only a concern of theologians and other ecclesiastics, it overflows to the cultured public at large. Just consider this extraordinary fact: 'from 1580 to 1630, there was a new edition of the Dionysian *corpus* a year'![2] To this should be added the editions and re-editions of the most famous commentaries, as well as the publication of numerous translations.[3]

All of this data must be kept in mind to gain a somewhat exact idea about what is meant, during this time, when anyone speaks of 'mystical', and not reduce its content to the image of it offered by some 'seers' at the end of the nineteenth century. It is clearly a question, as so admirably formulated by St John of the Cross, of a 'secret and delightful knowledge of God,' a definition that will be taken up again, or spontaneously rediscovered, by the majority of seventeenth century mystical authors. For Dom Augustine Baker, it is *Holy Wisdom, Sancta Sophia* who teaches the 'ways of contemplative prayer.'[4] For the blind Carmelite Jean de Saint-Samson, as well as for the learned Pierre de Bérulle, it is the 'science of the saints': 'a science not of memory but the spirit, not of study but prayer' and which 'renders spiritual its rightful owner.'[5] It enables us to attain to the *Chrétien intérieur*[6] and discover divine knowledge in the secrecy of

---

1. Certeau, op. cit., p142.
2. These unbelievable figures (by comparison, from 1943 to 1996, there is only *one* edition of the *Œuvres complètes,* reissued in 1980, and two editions of the *Hiérarchie céleste,* in 1958 and 1970) were supplied by P. Cochois, 'Bérulle et le Pseudo-Denys', *Revue de l'Histoire des Religions,* t. CLIX, 1961, p176; Certeau, p141. [Denys fares no better in twentieth century English editions. A volume of his complete works will only be published in 1987 by the Paulist Press 'Classics of Western Spirituality' series TR.]
3. Certeau, op. cit., pp140–141.
4. *Holy Wisdom* was written around 1633 and published, after the death of its author (1641), at Douai in 1657.
5. Cited following Joseph Beaude, *La Mystique,* Cerf, 1990, pp9–12.
6. The title given in 1661 by Father Louis d'Argentan to a compilation of manuscripts of a famous Normand mystic, Jean de Bernières, dead in 1659. This layman founded the Hermitage of Caen and was spiritual director to numerous religious.

The Mystical Way

our souls. Such a knowledge is none other than the gnosis spoken of so much by the Fathers, and this is what Fénelon had understood perfectly. Hence his wish to set forth the whole of mystical doctrine, identical to pure love, with the help of St Clement of Alexandria, in a book titled *Le Gnostique*,[1] an account of the great Alexandrian's doctrine supported by citations. He was clearly aware of the novelty of the terms 'the mystical' or 'a mystic', but he affirms: 'The reader will conclude therefore of necessity that the gnostic is nothing else but the perfect Christian; and I myself will also conclude that the perfect Christian is the passive man of the modern mystics; because it is certain that St Clement's gnostic, and the passive man of the mystics of these last centuries, are only two names given to one and the same thing.'[2] This is what a prince of the Church, the tutor of the Duke of Burgundy, a great writer and somewhat of a theologian thinks of the mystical, someone who had been condemned by Rome only with much reticence and under pressure from the French court.

It is to be acknowledged that there are many reasons to qualify as esoteric a way that defines itself as the 'secret science of God', 'Divine Sapience', and which tends, not to multiply extraordinary phenomena, but base itself in a naked and silent knowledge of the unique Divine Essence at the core of the trinity of Its hypostases. Once apprised of the fact that this secret science is accompanied, not rarely, by a 'formal esoterism', the various manifestations of which would require an attentive study, we ought to be even more convinced. During this period, between the fifteenth and the sixteenth centuries, numerous groups, fraternities and confraternities are constituted and reconstituted, groups such as the *Fraternité des Chevaliers du divin Paraclet*, the Cenacle of Meaux assembled

---

1. *Le Gnostique de saint Clément d'Alexandrie*, an unpublished opuscule, first published with an introduction by Dudon, Beauchesne, 1930. This text, written in 1694, could not appear. The review *La Place Royale*, n° 37, Oct. 1996, has republished Fénelon's text (pp 48–102), without Dudon's introduction or notes.

2. Op. cit., p166. Fénelon relates 'the gnostic as distinguished from the just' to 'St Paul's spiritual man', to the 'deiform contemplative of St Denys', to the solitaries of Cassian', to the 'sublime men who, St Augustine says, are taught by God alone', 'to blessed John of the Cross', and 'to the contemplative of St Francis de Sales': 'the gist of the thing is the same' (p165).

around Mgr. Guillaume Briçonnet, the local bishop,[1] or again the *Compagnie de Saint-Sacrement* in 1630, from which certain associations have issued, such as the *Aa*, that is to say the *Assemblée des Amis (de Dieu)* [Assembly of the Friends (of God)] a secret society that was at the origins of the *Congrégation du Saint-Esprit*.[2]

The Nineteenth Century: The Appearance of 'Mysticism'

All too briefly told, such are the facts that enable us to restore to the mystical its true significance. One last stage of terminological evolution is yet to be considered: that signaling the appearance of the masculine noun *'le mysticisme'*, a term Guénon will prefer to designate the mystical way as understood in its general form. This term is, however, rather recent (in 1880 Littré still considered it a neologism). Its use is, however, registered at the end of the eighteenth century, at a moment when the broad current of 'mystical' Europe shone with its finest lights. 'Mysticism' is not, moreover, devoid of a pejorative connotation.[3] In France, it made its appearance at the beginning of

---

1. Briçonnet was not without connection to the *Fraternité du Paraclet*.
2. In *René Guénon et les destins de la Franc-Maçonnerie*, Ed. de l'œuvre, p35, Denys Roman alludes to the A.A., that he interprets: 'Anonymous Associations', which seems hardly acceptable. The expression 'the friends of God' has a scriptural basis in John 15:15, and a technical meaning in the vocabulary of Christian spirituality, in Tauler for example (cf. B. Gorceix, *Amis de Dieu en Allemagne au siècle de Maître Eckhart*, Albin Michel, 1984). I have mentioned this in my article on the *Theologia germanica*. I am therefore siding with Rouquette's opinion in his articles 'A.A.' and 'Congrégations secrètes' for the *Dictionnaire de Spiritualité*. I believe that, like the Cenacle of Meaux, the Aa is included in the movement which, subsequent to the Council of Trent, aimed at reforming the Church in the direction of holiness and poverty (cf. Y. Poutet and J. Roubert, *Les 'Assemblées' secrètes des XVIIᵉ-XVIIIᵉ siècles en relation avec l'Aa de Lyon*, Plaisance, 1968; likewise: Joseph Michel, *Aux origines de la Congrégation du Saint-Esprit: l'influence de l'Aa sur Claude François Poullart des Places*, Beauchesne, 1992. Father Bruno Lanteri, who played an important role, in Italy in the fight against the ideas of the French Revolution, was a member of the Aa (cf. Paolo Calliari, O.M.V., *1789. Révolte contre Dieu*, D.M.M., 1986, p6).
3. Around 1788, Kant characterized as *mysticism* the illusion that claims to know something of the metaphysical Ideas by means of the symbols that are supposed to

The Mystical Way

the nineteenth century in surroundings foreign to the Church. It designated a mental attitude inclined to seek for true reality by being in contact with the invisible, the hidden, the supernatural (in the vague sense). And so one of the first occurrences of the term is to be met with in 1804, under the pen of Benjamin Constant, to characterize Plato's philosophy.[1] Schlegel, in 1819, used it in a work dedicated to St Bernard in which 'the true love of God' is opposed to 'false mysticism'.[2] Victor Cousin will see in it the last of the four systems to which the human mind successively clings: according to him, throughout its history it proceeds from materialism to idealism, from idealism to skepticism, and finally from skepticism to mysticism, which, by reaction, can bring it back to materialist sensualism, and so forth.[3] During the nineteenth century, the term is used more and more broadly in the very diverse realms of the novel, medicine, psychology, occultism, spiritism, and everything that touches on paranormal phenomena. Philosophy itself, at the end of the nineteenth century and the beginning of the twentieth, will make some use of it, as with William James and Henri Bergson (in *The Two Sources of Morality and Religion*). As for the Church, it will adopt this word only with reticence, precisely because it is not Christian in origin.[4] What it designates, as mentioned, is a somewhat exalted turn of mind that believes itself able to commune with the divine through a sentiment of interior fusion. As such, mysticism can exist everywhere, since it has been reduced to a rightly psychological attitude:

---

represent them (*Critique of Practical Reason*, AK, v). For Kant the symbol is nothing but an allegory.

1. *Journal intime*, cited by Robert, *Dict. analogique de la langue française*, s.v.
2. *Von der wahren Liebe Gottes und dem falschen Mysticismus*, in the review *Œlzweige*, Vienna, 1819.
3. *Histoire de la philosophie*, II, 9th lesson (according to Lalande). Ravaisson summarizes in this way: 'What he means by mystical systems is that they are obviously those to which all Christian theology belongs, wherein one is believed able to concede a direct communication between God and man' (*La philosophie en France au XIXe siècle*, in *De l'habitude*, Fayard, 1984, p71).
4. The *D.T.C.* ignores 'mysticism'. The *Dictionnaire de philosophie* by Elie Blanc (Lethielleux, 1906), and Christian in perspective, distinguishes mysticism, filled with extravagances, from *la mystique*, the 'part of theology that has as its object the supernatural relationship of the soul with God' (col. 868).

there is nothing specifically Christian about it. It forms part of the study of religious phenomena in the general and vaguest sense of this term. This is why theologians will intentionally speak, and without the least reservation, of natural mysticism with respect to Hinduism, Buddhism, Sufism, Neoplatonism, pantheism, Gnosticism, etc.; whatever be the impropriety of a term that can be just as well applied to spiritist and Theosophical doctrines. To tell the truth, its meaning has become so vague that it now only seems to denote anything that escapes, by deep unyielding imprecision, the grasp of reason.

This is why it gradually disappeared from the Christian vocabulary. Around 1930, Father J. Maréchal spoke again of 'Christian mysticism' [*mysticisme chrétien*],[1] although he used the expression 'Christian mysticism' [*mystique chrétienne*] more readily. *Today the term 'mystical' has been fully reestablished, as can be seen in Father Bouyer's quite forceful synthesis*: The Christian Mystery.

Retraced in this way, the evolution of the vocabulary certainly attests to a correlative evolution of the mystical way itself—this is incontestable. However, it must be observed that this evolution is not necessarily a confirmation of Guénon's views on the subject. This is what we now have to examine.

Break or Continuity in the Mystical Tradition

A Certain Psychologization of the Mystical Life

All historians who have retraced the Western history of Christian mysticism [*la mystique*] have been struck by the change in spiritual style initiated around 1350, a change that will be truly completed

---

1. *Études sur la psychologie des mystiques*, D.D.B., 1938, t. I, p171. Please note that, when found in opposition, *la 'mystique'* is Christian and *le 'mysticisme'* non-Christian; for example: 'Since non-Christian mysticism *(le mysticisme)* is interjected here solely as a term for comparison with Christian mysticism [*la mystique*]....' (p249).

The Mystical Way

only at the dawn of the seventeenth century. This being the case, certain authors, both lay and ecclesiastic, are loath to designate by the same term 'mystical' spiritual manifestations as seemingly distant from each other as those of an Origen commenting on the *Song of Songs* and a Thomas à Kempis writing the *Imitation of Christ*. The difference would be even more marked if we turned to St Teresa of Avila and St John of the Cross: there is nothing equivalent in the previous literature. And the model that they have presented is so compelling that it has imposed itself as the preeminent form of the mystical life. This change was not only apparent to the historian's eyes. The contemporaries of Ruysbroeck the Admirable (died 1381) themselves began to speak of a *Devotio Moderna* in connection with his doctrine and the major spiritual movement to which it gave rise.[1] Ruysbroeck himself was, in some respects, a disciple of Meister Eckhart; there is nothing surprising, then, if certain features of this *Devotio Moderna* are rediscovered among such avowed Eckhartians as Suso and Tauler: it contributes in this way to the spread of the Meister's doctrine in post-medieval Europe.[2]

This change can be characterized, quite summarily,[3] as a psychologization of spirituality: the mystical life is studied and appreciated

---

1. Some of the most characteristic marks of the *Devotio Moderna* are previous to Ruysbroeck. Following the Franciscans, it made its appearance already among the Beguines (Hadewijch of Antwerp I and II, for example): hence the devotion to the Infant Jesus and the humanity of Christ. It is in a Beguine setting (there were two hundred thousand of them in Germany during Eckhart's time) that the most extraordinary phenomena occurred around 1250: visions, levitations, changes in bodily form, resurrections, etc.; cf. J.-B. Porion's introduction to *Hadewijch d'Anvers* (Paris: Seuil, 1954), p15. Several Beguines have been canonized.

2. Modern scholarship has established that the spread of Eckhart's teaching ('the greatest mystic of the Middle Ages') was unhindered by the 1329 condemnation, only made public in the diocese of Cologne. This spread was chiefly assured, starting with Cologne, by a compilation of Flemish-Rhineland works, several sermons of Eckhart among them, published in 1543 under the name of Johannes Tauler and entitled *Institutiones*. This compilation seems to be attributable to St Peter Canisius. It had 'a great success ... that would continue until the decline of the seventeenth century' (L. Cognet, *La Spiritualité moderne*, t.1 — *L'essor: 1500–1650*, Aubier, 1966, p53). The *Institutions of Tauler* were still being published in 1909 (Tralin, Libraire-Edit.).

3. 'Summarily' with respect to the immensity of the subject: 'Not even taking unpublished works into account, the number of authors (between 1500 and 1650)

Christ the Original Mystery

in terms of the effects produced in a mystic's soul. The description and the critical science of these states reaches, in St Teresa of Avila, a rare mastery, a mastery that presupposes on her part an uncommon intellectual discernment, and, in reality, an extremely lucid *spiritual awareness*. But ultimately, attention seems to turn away from dogmatic realities and liturgical mysteries to concentrate principally on what occurs in the soul itself. Correlatively, a nearly exclusive importance is accorded to Christ's humanity: psychologization of the mystical life and the humanization of Christic worship evidently going hand in hand. As we know, Guénon will see in this proof that the mystical way does not surpass the level of the individuality (we will return to this in a moment).

Now some remarks are called for here. What is new in the history of Christian spirituality is not the consideration of Christ in his humanity, since, without the humanity of the Word, there would be no Christianity. To my knowledge, no Church Father, no orthodox spiritual writer has ever seen in this humanity an obstacle on the way that leads to God, *Christ in his incarnation being himself this way;* and 'who has seen me has seen the Father.'[1] What is relatively new is the attraction to the most particularized, the most individualized aspects of this humanity, we might even say the most anecdotal aspects: accentuated is everything belonging to the psycho-corporeal 'real-life' experiences of the God-Man, to his most historically fixed manifestations, and even the most biologically conspicuous; and we know that, in this respect, a cultus like that of the Sacred Heart will assume aberrant forms at the end of the nineteenth century.

---

whose works have come down to us defies all estimation' (L. Cognet, op. cit., p9). This is a fact that should never be lost sight of by anyone who, in a few lines, might think himself capable of dismissing a Catholic mystical tradition about which he is almost totally ignorant.

1. The alternative: either the humanity or the divinity of Christ, betrays a complete misunderstanding of the mystery of Jesus: 'devotion to the humanity of Christ and to the sacraments, for Eckhart as well as for Suso, is not a concession by a speculative mystic—for them there was no good reason to make an abstraction of it to grasp it in its purity; these contemplatives are not condescending metaphysicians, anxious not to mislead the ordinary faithful.... The two aspects—devotion and simple gaze—both uphold and call for one another among the Rhineland mystics' (J.-B. Porion, *Hadewijch d'Anvers*, p18, n18).

The Mystical Way

Everything is sacrificed to the suggestive power of an imagery bordering on the pathological.[1] This reduction of the holy humanity of Christ to its most contingent aspects was effected to the detriment, not of its divine dimension—as if there were no other choice than: either humanity or divinity—but to the detriment of its *theological* meaning. What risks being lost sight of here is the *theological* truth of the Christic humanity: Christ as the New Adam, that is the pre-eminent theomorphic creature, the one within whom shines the god-like nature of True Man, the paradigmatic synthesis of the entire universe within which God contemplates his own beauty. But this theological truth of the True Man finally realized in the humanity of Jesus Christ has been lost sight of by the partisans of mystical (and even pseudo-mystical) naturalism, as well as the partisans of an essentialist supernaturalism that perceives in the humanity of the Savior no more than a means for beginners, a means that should be disregarded by the more advanced. These two attitudes are, in fact, correlative and both stem from a weakening of the very sense of the redemptive Incarnation as constituting the central *Mysterion* of Christianity.

Here is to be seen the whole importance of my previously presented analyses. That the mystical life is understood as the very life of the Christic mystery within us, a mystery inseparably scriptural and liturgical, that is to say dogmatic and ecclesial, and that the Body of Christ is precisely the site where all of these sacred realities are tied together, this is not one possible concept among others, it is the most central and most necessary truth of Christianity. This Body of Christ is, identically, the Body born of the Virgin, the ecclesial Body and the eucharistic Body.[2] As long as a living awareness of this one Body under its different modes is maintained, the spiritual life is ignorant of such reductive alternatives as 'either humanity or divinity'.

---

1. *The Crucified Christ* of the 'Issenheim Retable' (painted by Matthias Grünewald around 1515) is an inspired testimony of this exacerbated naturalism that hems in the truth of the Spirit in the anatomical exactness of a corpse—but not without a great dramatic power.

2. This point has been developed in *The Sense of the Supernatural* (Edinburgh, Scotland: T & T Clark, 1998), pp 69–96.

Christ the Original Mystery

But when the organic bond, the 'mysterial nexus' uniting the spiritual life of the Christian to his dogmatic and liturgical life becomes undone, the theological references informing this life and giving it its meaning also give way. To orient contemplation and nourish it, what remains is the Body of Christ in its most formal objectivity. Also the soul, by a kind of compensatory disequilibrium, experiences the need, so to rediscover a sacred center of attraction, to turn to the most 'realistic' representations of this body, those representations that most immediately attest to its presence.

Aristotelianism Has Weakened the 'Gnostic Virtue' of the Intellect

As for the reasons that have brought about this loosening of the mysterial nexus, they are not easy to determine. Undoubtedly they are to be sought for in the economic and social changes that favored, during this period, the development of individualism: the progressive disappearance of feudal ties and the birth of urban and middle class communities. This has been described many times. But such causes are, however, too general to directly account for the very particular phenomenon that we are studying. Other, more specific causes must be added, the chief one seeming to be the arrival of Aristotelianism (due to the Arabs) in a culture which, until then, had remained wholly Platonic under the influence of St Augustine. One effect of taking Aristotle into account was an in-depth change in the system of medieval intellectuality by imposing a new noetic, that is a new model of the cognitive process. To treat of this appropriately would require another book, so I will limit myself to a few indispensable remarks. There is, in Plato, no analysis of the cognitive process: for him, what is important is to know if what one knows is truly real. Aristotle, to the contrary, masterfully analyzes the act of knowing. He sees there a process of abstraction: the intelligible form is abstracted, disengaged from the thing known by the intellect, and its form is imprinted on our mind. It is by the mediation of this form, abstracted from a thing, namely the concept, that we know a

The Mystical Way

thing; whereas, for Plato, true knowledge is basically an intuitive participation of the intellect in the essence of the object known. The two doctrines do not completely exclude each other, but one can pretend to ignore the other and think itself sufficient.[1] And so, for a noetic that wants to be exclusively Aristotelian: it is found to be in the position of someone who would study the nutritive process by only analyzing the structure of the digestive organs and their functioning in assimilating food, deliberately neglecting the taste that it has for the one eating it—a comparison so much the more apt since knowledge, like nutrition, is an assimilating process.

Methodologically, this 'neglect' is justified. Transformed into a negation of principle, it becomes dangerous, for it goes for known truths as it does for food: it is by taste and savor that both have a relationship with the personal being who knows and eats. This savor that our knowledge has, and by which it ceases to be purely factual, objective and exterior, is communicated to us in what we have called the semantic experience:[2] a key notion that seems to be absent (at least explicitly) from Aristotle's noetic. It is a key, in fact, since it gives us access to *sapiential* knowledge, and therefore to a *savory* knowledge; *sapientia* (wisdom) is derived from *sapere*, signifying 'to taste' in Latin. By revealing the sapiential dimension implicit in every *science*, that dimension in which the interiority of the known being begins to open itself to the interiority of the knowing being, this experience defines the very place where knowing and being cease to be perceived as foreign to one another. Where mystical knowledge is involved, we can gauge its importance as well as the

---

1. For numerous Thomists, to be a Platonist is a defect, a sign of intellectual weakness. Concerning Bérulle, the founder of the Oratory and the French school of spirituality, Maritain assures us that he was 'something quite redoubtable, a mystical and confused Platonist'; he sees in him a victim of the 'prestige' accorded to 'Pseudo-Denys and his hierarchies' (*Approches sans entraves*, Fayard, 1973, p 512). For Maritain, as for Gilson (*Le Thomisme*, Vrin, 1942, pp 193 ff.), the prestige of Denys consists only in his usurping of the rank of Paul's disciple. The intrinsic value of his doctrine (where intellectual confusion and an unconscious pantheism reign) is all for nought; a somewhat unflattering judgment on the discernment of those—St Thomas himself among them!—who see there one of the highest expressions of Christian theology.

2. Cf. supra, chap. 2, art. 4.

dangers to which our forgetting about it exposes us. And, of these dangers, we discern three chief ones.

First, by accentuating and solidifying with time, despite the admirable equilibrium of Thomas' synthesis, the Aristotelian noetic leads, contrary to the wish of its partisans, to the Nominalist reaction—from which its implicit Platonism preserved it (the Platonism of the intelligible form and the agent intellect): since our concepts are unable to be modes of participation in the (really existing) essences of things, let us stop attributing any reality whatsoever to their content, and let us reduce their existence as concepts to that of the names that designate them; for only concrete individual beings (and therefore, possibly, Christ Jesus in his actual historical presence, or in his extraordinary and supernatural presence) really exist. Second, this systematized noetic implies a kind of secularizing or profaning of the intellect. By extracting for itself the process that implements every cognitive act and by placing it at the center of philosophical reflection, we are led to neglect consideration of the degrees of knowledge and the importance of their specific distinctions: strictly from the viewpoint of the cognitive system's functioning, there is in fact no apparent difference between the conceiving of a triangle, a cat or God, except in an abstracting mode. *A priori* and as a result, a perfect atheist could be a perfect theologian, nor is there anything of the sacred in theology, at least for the intellectual operations required. As Luther affirms, it is an entirely profane exercise. Third and conversely, it becomes difficult to qualify as intellectual what is rightly mystical and supernatural, to the extent that intellectual activity is characterized by the use, in knowing an object, of a conceptual mediation, whereas the highest mystical states—but all theologians are not in agreement—seem to exclude any intermediary, and even concepts. Debates on this lasted from the seventeenth century to the twentieth; we will say nothing about them, but they clearly result from the introduction of a noetic into a realm for which they have little affinity. Summarizing the three just listed consequences, we will say that everything transpires as if we were invited to proceed with a triple dichotomy: between knowing and being, science and faith, intellect and prayer.

The Mystical Way

Certainly, the schematic character of this description should not be misunderstood: it distills the logic of a certain evolution, but, between 1350 and 1700, other aspects might be stressed that partially contradict this evolution, and I will say something about this presently. Moreover, we should never forget that the reality of the spiritual life, within each mystic, eludes the theoretical working draft traced out for it by philosophers and theologians. Nonetheless, it being specifically a question of the mystical life, it will be granted that the concept of an intellect reduced to abstractive activity, devoid of the mysterial sense, and therefore stricken with theological impotence, inclines the mystic to possibly seek for signs of his encounter with the divine at the level of those psychic, or even corporeal effects that might occur in him. Thus the sapiential capacity of the intellect is relied upon less and less.

Borrowing the expression *virtus gnostica* from John Scotus Eriugena, but in a somewhat derivative sense,[1] it might be said that what is thus weakened is the 'gnostic virtue' inherent to the intellect, or again, if preferred, its contemplative power; the cognitive act has surely not been modified in its very *nature* (the intellect is what it is), but in the representation made of it, and, for a conscious being, that is enough to open up or close down certain possibilities. The *virtus gnostica* thus understood is, in reality, nothing but the capacity proper to every intellect for carrying out semantic experience. No evolution can abolish it, but we can forget to exercise it, or cease to believe that it exists. However it is this virtue that establishes the possibility for a symbolist and poetic vision of the universe; it is as if an indelible memory of Adam's paradisal intellection, under the light of which heaven and earth sing the glory of God. Clearly then a natural capacity of the human intellect for the supernatural is involved here. And this is precisely why such a capacity needs to be awakened and exercised by a truly supernatural, that is to say

---

1. Eriugena makes use of the *virtus gnostica* formula on many occasions (for example: *The Division of Nature*, III, P.L., t. CXXII, col. 633A; 'gnostic power' in the Sheldon-Williams translation, op. cit., p249) to designate the creative power of divine knowledge. Cf. Jean Trouillard, '*La virtus gnostica* selon Jean Scot Erigène', a 32-page typewritten copy.

revealed object. Lacking this, we would fall into that generalized naturalism of spiritual vision exemplified by certain esthetic ecstasies: they avoid neither pantheism, nor the confusion between the psychic and the spiritual, whatever the illusions in this respect.[1] To the contrary, the revealed Object of faith and the grace of the liturgical habitus, although originally passing as foreign to the order of common experience, are, by this very fact, able to reveal in the soul the supernatural dimension inherent to its intellective capacity and make us cognizant of our transcendent destiny. Conversely, the *virtus gnostica* thus awakened and exercised enables the mystical life to stay connected to the very life of the adoring and praying intellect, thus situating it in the continuity of a faith understood in its inexhaustible profundity.

The Mystical: The Refuge of Christian Platonism

Nevertheless, as was mentioned a moment ago, the evolution that we are retracing is neither linear nor uniform; it is even profusely complex. By becoming solidified, the Aristotelian noetic lost its living strength. Not only, by an unintended consequence, did it lead to the Nominalist reaction, but also its sclerosis and progressive marginalization (cf. Paduan Averroism) made possible a reawakening of Platonism—on occasion taking the form of a return to St Augustine. But—with the exception of Nicholas of Cusa—we must wait for the beginning of the seventeenth century, and the advent of Descartes, to see this platonizing awakening give birth to a new philosophy of nature and to a new noetic; it is in this way that Cartesian intuitionism will rediscover, in the *contents* of the idea of God (and only

---

1. The best illustration of this illusion is provided by Goethe in his 136th Proverb: 'Whoever possesses science and art, also has religion' (*Wer Wissenschaft und Kunst besitzt/Hat auch Religion*) (Cited by Etienne Gilson, *The Spirit of Medieval Philosophy* [Notre Dame: University of Notre Dame Press edition, 1991], p23). Nothing testifies better to the spiritual unawareness of an exceptionally intelligent, modern European.

The Mystical Way

there), something that transcends the mental order and that is capable of ontologically reconnecting the concept to infinite Being, because its actual imprint.[1]

As for the mystical order, it becomes the preeminent site where what remained of the Platonic noetic could assert its rights, with the risk however that its opposition to Aristotelian intellectualism, or to the scientific rationality of Nominalism, constrained it to avow its idealist and even its illuminist or supernaturalist leanings. But, however that may be, we would be seriously mistaken to see this, among the mystics themselves, at least the most important ones, as only a psychologization of interior states, and a reduction of the spiritual life to extraordinary and passively experienced phenomena. Quite the contrary—and we will read irrefutable testimonies of this—the properly spiritual capacity of the intellect, its ontological value and the central place that it occupies in the mystical life are expressly underscored by a majority of them. Undoubtedly—such is the price paid for breathing the air of the times—just as the intellectual life of the monasteries and convents tended to be isolated and separated from that of the universities, so the mystical function of the intellect is envisaged at the core of the soul's interior life, rather than at the core of its participation in the ecclesial mystery of dogma and liturgy. But, unless we are mistaken, one side has not been cut off from the other, as shown by the example, famous among others, of St John of the Cross' thoroughly dogmatic and biblico-liturgical mysticism.

True, the written testimonies of the mystics are sometimes objected to by philosophers and theologians: we should not, they think, rely on the declarations of a St John of the Cross, neither the terms that he uses nor the judgments that he formulates, to draw valid conclusions for theology. In short, we must distinguish

---

1. On this subject, let us recall the esteem that Pierre de Bérulle had for Descartes, how he encouraged the young philosopher to realize his 'great work' and even made it an 'obligation of conscience' for him (cf. Jacques Chevalier, *Histoire de la pensée*, Flammarion, t. III, pp109–110, who is quoting Baillet, *La Vie de Monsieur Descartes*, t. I, pp160–166). And do not forget that, for Descartes, although Divine Infinity, which he carefully distinguished from indefiniteness, is conceivable, it is not comprehensible.

between the language of the mystics and the language of the speculative sciences: the first describes subjectively lived experiences, experiences almost inexpressible in the categories offered by profane and religious culture; the second names objective realities considered for and in themselves. To attribute to the first the ontological value of the second would be to betray or miss its profound intention, which is not to speak of what something is in itself, but of what occurs in the contemplative soul.[1] There is some truth in this thesis: the account of a mystical experience is not a treatise in theology, not even mystical theology. But, without entering into a discussion that might lead too far afield (Does the theologian always know what he is talking about when he speaks of mystical experience, and should he not sometimes just be content to know *what is said?*), we will simply observe that many teachers, such as Eckhart or St John of the Cross, *never* speak (directly) of their experiences, since they always express themselves objectively and are in full possession of an in-depth philosophical and theological culture. This would be to falsify the most obvious significance of their writings, just as much as seeing in them nothing but daring approximations or confused enthusiasm. To conclude, then, we must give their formulations the full attention that they deserve and the metaphysical import that might well be theirs. Now, concerning the importance of the role played by the intellect in the doctrine of these mystics, especially those of the French school, to restate an expression of the Abbé Brémond, it is such that the texts in which this mysticism is set forth—texts more 'abstract', more denuded and less Christianly marked than those of Origen or St Gregory of Nyssa—seem strangely close to the texts of Oriental spirituality. Of this we will soon have the chance to get a better idea.

---

1. It is Jacques Maritain who has proposed this distinction (*The Degrees of Knowledge,* trans. G.B. Phelan [Notre Dame, Indiana: University of Notre Dame Press, 1995], p335 ff); it is likewise to be met with elsewhere, Father Congar, for example: 'Language des spirituels, langage des théologiens', in *La Mystique rhénane,* P.U.F., 1963, pp15–34). On this question consult among others the well-informed chapter of François Chenique: 'Voies et expériences mystiques', in *Mystique orientale et sagesse chrétienne* (Paris: Dervy, 1996), pp397–472.

The Mystical Way

Acquired Contemplation and Infused Contemplation

The same changes in the noetic system are, I think, at the origin of a debate which, at the start of the seventeenth century and until the middle of the twentieth, has occupied an important place in mystical theology: should we distinguish between an acquired contemplation and an infused contemplation, and can the former be characterized as mystical? This debate is of some interest to the extent that Guénon, following in this the most *classically modern* authors on the theology of the mystical, as well as the least careful—or the most ignorant—Patristic and medieval tradition, specifically opposes the initiatic and the mystical as active and passive respectively.

Almost everyone is in agreement on the definition of contemplation given by St Thomas Aquinas: 'a simple intuition of the divine truth.'[1] However, some think that this *intuitus* can either be progressively acquired through exercise, or, more extraordinarily, infused into the soul by a special grace of God perceived as such in the soul that receives it. The first contemplation seems to require, besides the grace of God, the effective use of our natural faculties, and therefore an act of the spirit, whereas in the second, solely characterized as mystical, the spirit stays passive and knows that it counts for nothing—save for its acquiescence—in what transpires. This distinction of the two contemplations is unknown to St Thomas and all of Christian tradition. It appeared for the first time in 1620, in a treatise by Thomas of Jesus, the *De contemplatione divina*.[2] Next it will become a constant theme for ascetical and mystical treatises and pass for traditional doctrine.

Some authors counter this doctrine with the following argument: if there is a contemplation acquired through the exercise (*askesis*,

---

1. *Summa Theologiae*, II–II, q. 180, a. 3.
2. Antwerp; cf. R. Garrigou-Lagrange, *Christian Perfection and Contemplation* (St Louis, MO: B. Herder, 1942), p 224. Thomas of Jesus, a Discalced Carmelite and disciple of St Teresa, aimed at reconciling Scholasticism and mysticism by presenting the latter as a miraculous science of the intellect (J. Orcibal, op. cit., p 231, n1).

from which comes 'ascesis', means 'exercise' in Greek) of our natural faculties applied to spiritual acts (prayer), ritual acts (liturgy) and doctrinal intellection (dogmatic theology), this is because a contemplative habitus is established within us. Now, the mark of a habitus is the ability to be exercised at will: 'this contemplation is called acquired insofar as we can avail ourselves of it whenever we want.'[1] But, specifically, it is hard to maintain that anyone might actually be able to produce contemplative acts at will. Besides, Innocent XII, by the Brief *Cum alias* of March 12th, 1699, had condemned the following proposition of Fénelon: 'there exists a state of contemplation so sublime and so perfect that it becomes habitual in such a way that any time the soul prays, at that moment its prayer is contemplative and not discursive.'[2] They therefore conclude that, either the state of prayer spoken of is acquired, but is not contemplation (this is affective prayer), or else is true contemplation, but then is not acquired; therefore there is only one form of contemplation that can be called infused or mystical.[3]

We should neither break the unity of contemplation, nor reduce it to one of its forms. That there are relatively exceptional and rightly *suffered* states that can be qualified as 'raptures' or 'ecstasies', and sometimes accompanied by bodily manifestations (levitations, etc.), is a fact. Still these states can never be produced, even among mystics who have attained a state of permanent union. This is what St Teresa of Avila generally teaches. On the other hand, she also teaches, it seems,[4] that we should speak of a contemplation entirely foreign to

---

1. Joseph of the Holy Spirit, *Cursus theologiae mystico-scolasticae, Isagoge*, I, IV, *Syntagma I*, De oratione, lectio 4, n° 22; Ed. Anastase de St Paul Bruges, 1924, p9 (cf. R. Dalbiez, 'Controverse de la contemplation acquise', *Études Carmelitaines*, D.D.B., 1949, p84). The treatise (unfinished) of Father Joseph of the Holy Spirit is comprised of six books; the first book dates from 1720.

2. Denzinger, *Enchiridion Symbolorum*, 30th ed., num. 1342, p388.

3. This is the conclusion of Dalbiez in the copious study cited above (cf. n2); his proof is weaker than the apparatus of his argument would lead us to believe.

4. The rather bitter debate that, around 1920, opposed Father Poulain, supporter of the two contemplations (acquired/non-mystical and non-acquired/mystical), to Mgr. Saudreau, 'has shown that, by means of various exegeses, St Teresa could be seen as an adversary or a supporter of acquired contemplation' (L. Cognet, *La Spiritualité moderne*, t. I, p94, n 52).

The Mystical Way

all activity: 'I call supernatural that which can be acquired neither by my industry, nor by my diligence, whatever the effort made, but to ready oneself for it is possible and that should be an important point.'[1]

That said, we clearly need to recognize that, in order to discern the different states of prayer, St Teresa abides by psychological and subjective criteria almost exclusively, at the risk of reducing mystical theology to a description of the soul's attitudes. Although this point of view may legitimize a distinction in the modes of contemplation, it should not, however, prevail over the *theological* point of view, the view according to which it is the Divine Object that defines the act by which It is seen: it is, then, Christic (scriptural, liturgical and dogmatic) revelation that actualizes and informs the innate contemplativeness of the intellect, which is implied whatever the contemplative mode, but obviously in varying degrees. The unity of the contemplative intellect corresponds to the unity of the Divine Object.

Finally, we thus understand why we should not separate the ascetic from the mystical. Guénon qualifies the relationship between these two terms as 'all too little justified'(!) and offers to 'dispel this confusion.'[2] What is he alluding to? About this we know nothing. But Guénon might be speaking here of the treatises on spiritual theology, for, although nearly all of them associate, as is only right, these terms and are entitled: *A Treatise of Ascetic and Mystical Theology*, this is certainly not a blameworthy confusion, but because the very nature of their subject imposes it on them, and so as to precisely situate them with respect to each other. Ascetic and mystical, in fact, according to the most classical definitions, are concerned with one and the same thing technically designated as the 'way to perfection', to distinguish it from the moral life.[3] But they are not concerned in the same way: the ascetic treats of the means employed (inner purification, prayer, recollection, spiritual practices, sacramental life,

---

1. Correspondence with Baltasar Alvarez, 54, §3; cf. Cognet, op. cit., p94.
2. *Initiation and Spiritual Realization* (Ghent, NY: Sophia Perennis, 2001), p99.
3. St Thomas specifies that 'the moral virtues are not concerned with the contemplative life in its essence', which is 'consideration of the truth'; but they are concerned with it as a 'disposition to this contemplative life' (*Summa Theologiae*, II–II, q. 180, a. 2).

cardinal and theological virtues, etc.), the mystical treats of what God himself effects in the human soul, whether He makes it known or not, in short, it treats of the supernatural fruit that, by means of the cultivation of ascesis, the Divine Sun ripens within us. For both there is, at once, continuity and discontinuity: if, on the one hand, we can only harvest what has been sown in a prepared and tilled soil, on the other hand the fruit bestowed by God is always more than we expected, since this fruit... it is He Himself. But surely God remains free in His gift and nothing is due to human effort which is at once necessary and useless.

True, there are authors who, identifying the mystical exclusively with extraordinary psychological states experienced by the contemplative, have completely separated it from the ascetic. However, such a way of seeing things is modern: it made its appearance in a few authors of the seventeenth and eighteenth centuries,[1] and, in some treatises, continued into the twentieth: in short, it is a corollary of the acquired contemplation controversy. Perhaps Guénon was inspired by these treatises which only strengthened him in his conviction that the mystical is nothing but pure psychic *passivity*, while the ascetic, being active, finds favor in his eyes and represents, in religious mode!, that which 'could better lend itself to an assimilation' with the initiatic way.[2] It must be stressed, however, that the great and earliest Christian tradition affirms the synergetic unity of what, in modern times, will be called ascetic and mystical: and it is so for St Gregory of Nyssa, St Denys the Areopagite, St Augustine, St Albert the Great, St Thomas Aquinas, St Bonaventure, Meister Eckhart, Tauler, Suso, St Teresa and St John of the Cross among others.

But surely, to restore this synergetic unity, we must re-situate the

---

1. Reginald Garrigou-Lagrange, op. cit., p12 ff.
2. *Perspectives on Initiation*, chap. 1, p8. Guénon cites as an example St Ignatius of Loyola 'whose mind was as incontestably unmystical as can be.' A curious remark: true, the *Spiritual Exercises* are essentially concerned with the activity of a soul desirous of entering into the contemplative life. But it is also directed 'to the loftiest peaks of prayer and divine love' (Pius XI, Encyclical of July 25, 1922 on the *Spiritual Exercises*). Besides, St Ignatius was himself favored with the most incontestably mystical graces: visions, locutions, the gift of tears, etc., which he, differing from St John of the Cross, made much of.

The Mystical Way

mystical in the lineage of the faith and its relationship to the Divine Object that determines it. For faith, an act of supernatural knowledge, is of itself already a degree of contemplation, already a beginning of the mystical life and an obscure participation in the intuitive vision of the Divine Truth. It is then, as St Thomas teaches, by one and the same act of the intellect that we ascend the stages of contemplation: 'the contemplative life has one act wherein it is finally completed, namely the contemplation of truth, and from this act it derives its unity. Yet it has many acts whereby it arrives at this final act.' Among these intuitive acts of the intellect, to start we must number a direct perception of the truth of first principles, next evidence from the deductions drawn from it for knowing such a truth; 'the last and crowning act is the contemplation itself of the truth.'[1] Undoubtedly, in the natural order of things, the intellect cannot do without images and symbols; 'but within them it contemplates the purity of the intelligible truth, and this not only in natural knowledge, but also in that which we obtain by revelation.'[2] Finally, let us add that, according to St Thomas, the intellectual act of theological contemplation gives rise to love in the soul and beauty pertains to its essence.[3] All contemplation is, ultimately, a contemplation of Divine Beauty.

The Way of Christ and 'Guénonian' Mysticism

'I am the Way'

Up until now we have retraced, since its origins, the history of a word and a notion, broaching on occasion the problems and debates raised and the solutions, whether provisional or lasting, brought to

---

1. *Summa Theologiae*, II–II, q. 180, a. 3.
2. Ibid., a. 5.
3. Ibid. a. 2, reply to objection 3.

Christ the Original Mystery

bear on them by the Christian faith. Having done this, we have seen the essential elements of a mystical theology being constituted before our very eyes. Henceforth we know a little more about spiritual doctrine in Christianity. What remains, so to complete our objectives and before letting the spirituals have their say, is to pass from a study of the mystical way considered in itself to a comparative study of it. To tell the truth, such a study, even limited to the principal religions, is beyond my competence. About them I will say almost nothing, merely recalling in such comparisons a major yet almost always neglected methodological principle. After which I will devote the essential part of my remarks, not even to comparing the mystical way with what Guénon calls the initiatic way (I contest the pertinence of this opposition), but to appreciating what he has to say about this way—presented under the guise of a caricatured mysticism—in the light of Christ.

The major principle that should preside over every comparison of Christian spirituality with any other spirituality is the following: in Christianity the spiritual (or mystical) way is Christ himself, for he has said: 'I am the Way.' Setting aside what is specific to it, this mystical way can indeed be considered in a formal manner so to compare it with other ways and list the similarities and differences. But, whatever might be the result of this comparison, it lacks the essential, namely what defines the attributes of the spiritual economy of Christianity. Thus we see authors, starting with the Hindu distinction between the ways of action, love, and knowledge, develop a general theory of these three ways, and then use it as a normative typology for judging the Christian way. Now to compare, for example, Shankara with St John of the Cross, as *the* way of gnosis with *the* way of love,[1] this is to presuppose an independence of spiritual forms with respect to the religions that make a fairly idealist use of them, as if the different ways were so many ideal *ne varietur* types running through, without being affected by them, the most heterogeneous sacred worlds. Such a comparison is perhaps not impossible for non-Christian religions, at least those in which there are, in fact, spiritual ways constituted as such. But when it comes to Christianity, which is defined by the equation: the way = Christ, it proves to be irrelevant since it then amounts to comparing, whether we know it

The Mystical Way

or not, a particular way of love or knowledge with Christ himself. If, for example, it is decided that Christianity does not include a way of knowledge as pure and complete as that of the Shankarian *jnana* is supposed to be, we are entitled to ask: what about Christ who is, for a Christian, *the* Way, and who is also *the* Knowledge of the Father, the *Logos* incarnate, and *the* Truth? Does all this mean nothing? Should this basic component of the Christian way be set aside as a 'negligible quantity', as an adventitious and non-essential element having no impact in the matter? What is most obvious, in all of this, is that those who proceed in this way have no awareness of how they have previously set in parentheses something that is, however, the 'substantific marrow' of the Christian way: Christ. This way is thus emptied of its most specific, most ontologically necessary Reality, after which it be-comes a conceptual phantom, an artificial abstraction comparable to some Eastern formulas: the result is known beforehand and is not very interesting. I am not reproaching this method of minimizing the importance of Christ, which can be understood, after all, on behalf of non-Christians. I am reproaching it for misunderstanding the radical changes that this undeniably revealed principle—absolute in its wording—necessarily introduces into the Christian economy of the spiritual ways: I am the Way, the Truth and the Life. It is decisive, in my opinion, that the very notion of a spiritual way, if the definition is to be borrowed from India, has nothing but an analogical significance in the Christian system. That said, we can now come to what Guénon calls 'mysticism'.

---

1. This is what Georges Vallin has done in his book *Voie de gnose et voie d'amour. Éléments de mystique comparée*, Ed. Présence, 1980. Interesting for what it says about Shankara, the work seems disappointing in what it says about St John of the Cross, who is seen from without and undoubtedly misunderstood in major facets of his doctrine. Read what Georges Morel has written in *Le sens de l'existence selon S. Jean de la Croix*, t. II: *Logique*, Aubier, 1960, pp 56–64, in connection with Vallin's article, 'Essence et forme de la théologie négative', 1958 (chap. v of *Lumière du Non-dualisme*, Presses Universitaires de Nancy, 1987). And above all, study the very text of the saint with the help of the remarkable index of his *Œuvres complètes* (Cerf, 1990): there will be no lack of surprises!

Christ the Original Mystery

Mystical Renunciation or Initiatic Demiurgy?

'Without doubt,' Guénon remarks,

> the word mysticism ... obviously refers to the ancient 'mysteries' [which are of] the initiatic order; [but usage forbids us to employ it in this sense] ... since the current meaning of 'mysticism' has been established for centuries it is not possible to use this term to designate anything else.[1]

As we have seen, this is a mistake: the term in question is as recent as those of 'esoterism' and 'occultism' (with nothing of the fortuitous about it) and, like them, dates from the end of the eighteenth century or the beginning of the nineteenth. As for telling us exactly to whom this term 'mysticism' applies, that is—with the names of St John of the Cross, Louis-Claude de Saint-Martin and Anne Catherine Emmerich excepted—a detail that Guénon thinks we can dispense with, since everyone has known 'for centuries' what this is all about.

The first feature which, according to Guénon, characterizes mysticism is passivity: mystical states are received passively and without method, whereas the initiatic way is traversed actively and methodically. Obviously, if asceticism and mysticism are totally separate, with mysticism reduced to some extraordinary states that invade a soul supposedly docile to every influence, and therefore independently of its will, then Guénon is right. But this is a caricature. After all, why should the distinction made by Guénon between 'receptivity' and 'passivity' be valid for the initiate subject to his master, 'like a corpse in the hands of one who washes the dead', and not for the mystic whose Master is Jesus Christ?[2]

Nevertheless, it will be objected, the fact still remains that the initiate actively realizes 'an effective taking possession' first of the 'primordial state', and then of the 'superior states of the being', which means that he has them at his disposal at will and not that he is pos-

---

1. *Perspectives on Initiation*, p9.
2. Ibid., chap. 35: 'Initiation and Passivity'.

The Mystical Way

sessed by them.[1] Such a spiritual perspective seems, in fact, foreign to the mystical way, or more simply to the way of Christian holiness. Can we, then, attempt to reconcile these two viewpoints by speaking, with relation to the mystical, 'of effectively taking possession of the superior states [but] in passive mode', that is insofar as the mystic benefits from the grace of Christ, who has Himself actively realized 'the initiatic process mentioned'?[2] I do not think so. And it is precisely because the 'solution' of the Abbé Stéphane expresses the pure Christian truth that it cannot allow for a reconciling of viewpoints.

The Christian truth recalled here by the Abbé Stéphane complies with the evangelical principle of identifying the Christian way, as a whole, with the Christic 'exploit': crucifixion, descent into hell, resurrection and ascension actively tracing the spiritual way in its integral course. All Christians, be they even the greatest of mystics or initiates, have no other choice than to follow Christ and to benefit from His grace by being united with Him, as much as possible, or to renounce being a Christian. And we do not think the masters of the Eckartian school have expressed themselves otherwise. Moreover, if there subsists the least doubt as to the Christic nature of the way under the Christian system, turning to St Paul should be enough to be disabused of this: consider how he was ravished 'to the third heaven', which indicates undeniably an access to the spiritual hierarchies and, therefore, to the 'superior states of the being', whatever might be the degree (2 Cor. 12:2). For the whole of Christian tradition this ascension is recognized as the model of mystical realization, and the summit to which, in this life, it is possible to attain: now, it is entirely accomplished 'in Christ', and according to a mode that can be, if one likes, qualified as passive. What Christian 'initiate' would dare to claim that his spiritual eminence is superior, in degree or in mode, to that of St Paul? It follows that, if Guénon was right, not only would the mystical way be contrary to initiatic progress, but

---

1. Ibid., chap. 39: 'Greater and Lesser Mysteries'.
2. Abbé Henri Stéphane, *Introduction à l'ésotérisme chrétien*, vol. 2 (Paris: Dervy, 1983), p 51.

Christ the Original Mystery

logically every form of Christian spirituality. Conversely, we would then need to conclude that 'Guénonism' and Christianity are purely and simply incompatible.

Finally, it seems that the manner in which the contradiction between activity and passivity, in the spiritual way, has been viewed remains quite exterior to the reality of things. First, as the Abbé Stéphane has stressed,[1] the passivity of the mystics is quite relative and their way incorporates numerous exercises. But, above all, what is lacking in such a conception is the sense of the dialectical relationships uniting passivity here to the activity and grace by which we can surpass their formal, if not artificial opposition. And so it should not be denied that, spiritually, the mystic is quite active and sometimes performs extraordinary deeds; but this activity only aims at making possible the renunciation of all action as well as the soul's powers, so to enter into death and nakedness. Ontologically, now, the mystic is likewise passive because the state to which he gains access, being unable to be *produced* by any act, is necessarily bestowed on him; however, having been established in this state by divine grace, the very being of the mystic becomes a spiritual act, an energy of love and knowledge. Or again: if, from a certain point of view, the spiritual way is traced out by the very one who traverses it, like a traveler who develops the road and the various stages of his journey to the extent that he nears his destination; from another point of view, the way, with all of its stages, is preexistent to its traversing—it has been traced out and completed once for all, and we only have to follow it to receive the blessing of its lodgings.

This is not all. We also must inquire about the very idea of an 'effective taking possession' of superior states (whether angelic or supra-angelic), and its relevance with respect to the needs of every spiritual way. That Christianity knows of a scale of spiritual degrees corresponding the degrees of knowledge, themselves dependent upon the degrees of realities to be known, should not be denied. The doctrine of the celestial, that is to say angelic, hierarchies is fundamental to Denys. Present beneath other forms with Clement of Alexandria and Evagrius of Pontus, it imbues medieval concepts,

---

1. Op. cit., pp 51–52.

The Mystical Way

especially those of the Victorines. St Thomas returns to the doctrine of Richard of Saint-Victor for whom the 'six species of contemplation ... denote the steps whereby we ascend by means of creatures to the contemplation of God.'[1] Even more clearly, St Bonaventure considers the stages of the angelic ladder as so many spiritual states encountered by the soul in its journey to God: 'our spirit is made hierarchical [by the sequence of purgative, illuminative and unitive ways] in ascending stages and conformed to the heavenly Jerusalem. It resembles, then, the nine choirs of angels and assumes, in turn, their functions.'[2] Thus the soul, in its last stage, attains to the station of the Thrones (this is 'admission', pronounced by God, to the ultimate ecstasy), next to the station of the Cherubim (this is 'inspection' or direct knowledge of the loftiest metaphysical realities of Being Itself *and* the Self-diffusive Good), and lastly to the seraphic station (this is 'induction', corresponding to entry into the Seventh Day). Having reached this seraphic station, the soul is enveloped in Darkness and gains access to the ultimate degree, in this life, of mystical union. If there is darkness, this is because in this degree the intellect has renounced all of its knowings which are somehow engulfed in the pure love that 'imposes silence' on them. At the same time, in such a 'union, the power of the soul is recollected, and it becomes more unified, and enters in its intimate self, and consequently it rises up to its summit.'[3] This is why this surpassing and this renunciation of every determinate knowledge is also the realization of a perfectly liberated and peaceful knowledge, of a truly sapiential and sabbatic knowledge.[4] Such is the Bonaventurian doctrine that Dante will take up again, sometimes literally, in the last canto of the *Paradiso*.[5]

1. *Summa Theologiae*, II–II, q. 180, a. 4.
2. *Journey of the Soul into God*, chap. 4, 4.
3. *Collations on the Six Days*, vol. 5, *The Works of Bonaventure* (Patterson, NJ: St Anthony Guild Press, 1970), p37.
4. I am following the explanation given by Gilson of St Bonaventure's spiritual doctrine in *The Philosophy of St Bonaventure* (Paterson, NJ: St Anthony Guild Press, 1965), pp408–425
5. Gilson provides the texts: *La philosophie de saint Bonaventure*, (Vrin, 1953), p367, n1. [All notes are not included in the English translation TR.]

Christ the Original Mystery

Now what is striking in this scalar course is that it is effected by a 'dispossession' of all the degrees of the created rather than by any effective possession-taking. It does not have to do with methodically conquering the degrees of the real so to possess them and be able to have them at your disposal, but with renouncing everything not the Uncreated Itself, in conformity with the word of Christ: 'Seek ye therefore first the kingdom of God, and his justice, and all these things shall be added unto you' (Matt. 6:33); which means, under the circumstances, that we must seek first the supreme and absolute One, and only then will the multiple and the relative be *given*. In other words, we cannot know and possess the relative and the multiple as such, no more than anyone can, in mathematics, calculate by themselves all the values of a function that varies by infinitesimal quantities; the 'integral' (or sum-limit of infinitesimal increases) must be calculated, and, having found that, then the various values integral to it can be calculated.[1] In the same way the deified will enter into possession of their cosmic heritage, and the innumerable degrees of creation will become their own property and as if modalities of their own immortal being, when they tend toward the One who surpasses the entire world and in whom the entire world is contained and finds its bounds. This transcendent Integral is Christ, as St Paul teaches on every page of his epistles, for He is the One in whom everything has been created, in whom all beings and all the visible and invisible degrees of reality, all the angelic hierarchies subsist, and who recapitulates and wholly surpasses the macrocosm. This is why Jesus has said: 'If I be lifted up, I will draw *all* things to myself' (John 12:32), which may be applied not only to His being lifted up on the Cross on Holy and Good Friday, but also to His being lifted up in the souls of those who adore Him. For those who lift him up, who exalt Him in the heaven of their soul above every creature, the entirety of creation is found to be gathered together and unified in His Divine Self. This is what Mary realized exemplarily, Mary who, in her glorious Assumption, surpasses all the degrees of the world and all angelic hierarchies, receiving in this way the

---

1. As Guénon has explained so well in his *Metaphysical Principles of the Infinitesimal Calculus* (Hillsdale, NY: Sophia Perennis, 2004).

The Mystical Way

royal crown that makes her Queen of heaven and earth, she who was nothing but the 'handmaid of the Lord'.[1]

Brought out here are the contrasts between the initiate according to Guénon and the Christian mystic.[2] Stretching things somewhat, this difference could be symbolized by recourse to the opposing figures of the Comte de Saint-Germain and St Francis of Assisi. How well we know that someone 'delivered while alive', or the true 'sufi', represents in Guénon's eyes the spiritual type of those who have reached the end of the way, which is not the case for the just mentioned enigmatic personage. Nevertheless, many of the considerations set forth seem to belong quite clearly to the 'Saint-Germain' or, if preferred, 'Rose-Cross' type, for which Guénon undeniably exhibits a visible fondness, and which, anyhow, exercises a strong attraction over his readers. A personage both mysterious and evanescent, but sufficiently attested to for it to be legitimate to inquire into his identity, a Rose-Cross is freed from the ordinary conditions of existence at the end of a methodically pursued and purely *technical* initiatic *labor*.

Thereafter he wanders through space and time to accomplish in human history timely as well as decisive tasks, with a view to realizing the impenetrable designs pursued by the supreme initiatic hierarchies withdrawn into the East.

---

1. On renunciation, see our summary of the doctrine of Evagrius of Pontus in *La charité profanée*, pp396–408.

2. In *Perspectives on Initiation,* p106, Guénon writes: 'Unlike mystical realizations, initiation is not something that falls from the clouds, so to speak, without it being known how or why; on the contrary, it rests on positive scientific laws and on rigorous technical rules. We cannot insist too much on this whenever the occasion presents itself, in order to avoid every possibility of misunderstanding as to its true nature.' And in a note he speaks of 'handling spiritual influences.' My reply is that what 'falls from the clouds' is the grace of Christ: *rorate caeli desuper, et nubes pluant justum*. As for initiation as a pure *technico-scientific demiurgy*, it betrays a basic promethianism that seems incompatible with spirituality: the Spirit blows where He will and does not let Himself be 'handled' by anyone. Besides, the great figures of Eastern spirituality have said nothing else: in Shankara deliverance is not in any way presented as the result of any technique (however positive and rigorous), but as a 'grace' (*anugraha,* from *anu-grah,* to choose) coming from that supremely real Being present in the depths of the soul: cf. P. Martin-Dubost, *Çankara*, Seuil, p105.

Christ the Original Mystery

St Francis has also acted in history in a lasting and powerful manner; he accomplished the mission entrusted to him by God of 'repairing the Church of the Lord'. But this he did as a man among men, renouncing everything, obedient unto death, poor among the poor, naked and covered with ashes, not as a concealed demiurge pulling the strings of a puppet theater from behind the scenes.

Undoubtedly some will make the observation that I am speaking here out of ignorance, and, in fact, I willingly acknowledge having no competence in what I call the realm of 'initiatic demiurgy'. What remains is that, from the Christian mystical point of view, such a demiurgy seems to be something quite exterior and, spiritually, devoid of the least interest except perhaps for a novelist.[1] Granted, this demiurgy is perhaps not to be found as such in Guénon; but, unquestionably, it is to be observed in more than one Guénonian and among the most qualified at that. Now, what is involved here? To even suppose that all this corresponds to some reality—which I do not deny *a priori*—clearly we are still and always dealing with data of a cosmological nature, and which even belongs to a diminished realm of this science, the realm concerned with the history of our times. Here we rediscover, under other modalities, a very ancient theme already encountered in the second part of this work and discussed at length: the theme of Jewish apocalyptic and the cosmological esoterism of the rabbis. In its relationship to the revelation of the Christic mystery, it defines one of the major tensions of Pauline teaching: how to make it understood that, as esoteric as doctrines relative to the 'elements of the world' might be, there is, in the Christic mystery, something more lofty and more interior that surpasses the degrees of creation and cosmic powers, because it integrates them within itself, and because it is precisely to an initiation into this mystery that we have been called? It is the same today. To the extent that he does not reject it as suspect, the Christian mystic

---

1. Cf. Sir Edward Bulwer Lytton's novel *Zanoni* (London, 1842). The author was Grand Master of the *Societas Rosicruciana in Anglia*. According to Guénon, the *Hermetic Brotherhood of Luxor* was the 'avowed enemy of the *Societas Rosicruciana*' (*Theosophy: History of a Pseudo-Religion*, [Hillsdale, NY: Sophia Perennis, 2004] p28). Helena Blavatsky will be inspired by many of Bulwer Lytton's novels.

The Mystical Way

will be inclined to see in this cosmological esoterism a distraction from the one thing necessary, a forgetting, or at least the risk of a forgetting of our highest vocation. Who can blame him? Certainly the cosmological sciences exist; they have, beyond the truth of their intrinsic value, an indispensable 'Christic' function to fulfill when they are integrated into the production of sacred art; and the scorn in which they are held by the majority of artists, for the sake of inspiration alone, explains in part this art's decadence. Now is the time to recall the famous medieval adage: *ars sine scientia nihil,* 'art without science is nothing', with the added clarification that the term 'art' is obviously to be taken in its primary technological sense. But what about a cosmological science that is no longer subordinate to its integration into a religion? It leads to the Babel-like exaltation of human power in revolt against God, and even the luciferian use of the forces of nature. After all, sacred art is not the major preoccupation of those who are enthused with initiatic demiurgy and the secret history of the West. Admittedly, in some of its aspects, Guénon's work can fuel this passion marvelously well, as proves the publication of some more or less recent books. To say it all clearly: such a preoccupation has nothing to do with baptismal initiation into the death and resurrection of Christ to which, in the East as in the West, the Church that He has founded invites us.

Jesus Christ Is Not An Avatara

The second feature that, with passivity, characterizes the mystical way is its exclusively psychic nature: it does not surpass the domain of the individuality, Guénon assures us.

As for the psychic nature of mystical states, Guénon's thinking has evolved somewhat. In a 1931 article entitled 'Magic and Mysticism' (which will become, in 1946, chapter 2 in *Perspectives on Initiation*), he writes: 'Certainly, we are far from denying that mysticism in itself may have a character much more elevated than magic; nonetheless, if we look more deeply(!), we soon realize that at least from a certain point of view the difference is not as great as one might imagine, for here again it is in fact only a matter of 'phenomena', visions, or the other tangible and sentimental manifestations that characterize the domain of individual possibilities alone.'[1] Having been thus warned that mysticism *is only* phenomena, we are somewhat surprised to read, in 1947, in an article 'Direct Contemplation and Reflected Contemplation':

> There are many different degrees of mysticism, [and] to really speak of contemplation in the true sense of the word [we must] set aside all that has a clearly 'phenomenal' character, [namely those states that] the theoreticians of mysticism ... themselves consider to be inferior. [And he concludes] There is no mystical contemplation properly speaking except in the case of what is called 'intellectual vision'.[2]

Is this a correction? We do not know. However that may be, what remains is the individual nature of this contemplation. He writes in the same article:

> In mysticism there is *never* any question of identification with the Principle, nor even with one of its 'non-supreme' aspects.... The very language of the mystics is very clear in this regard: it is *never* a question of union with the Christ Principle, that is with the *Logos* in itself, which, even without going so far as identification, would already be above the human domain; it is *always* 'union with Christ Jesus', an expression that clearly refers in an *exclusive* way only to the 'individualized' aspect of the *Avatara*.[3]

Perhaps this rightly astounding declaration has provoked comments from certain readers. The fact remains that in 1950, in his last text dealing with the mystical way ('Salvation and Deliverance'), Guénon finds that, among the mystics, 'union with God' is also involved. Then he raises this objection: 'How can a being have a higher end than union with God?' The reply is simple and revealing:

---

1. Page 16.
2. *Initiation and Spiritual Realization,* pp 82 and 83.
3. Ibid., p 85. My emphasis.

The Mystical Way

All depends on the sense in which one takes the word 'union'. In reality, the mystics, like all other exoterists, are concerned with nothing more or other than salvation, although what they have in view is, if one wishes, a higher modality of salvation.... In any case, since in mystical union individuality as such subsists, it can only be a wholly exterior and relative union, and it is quite evident that the mystics have never even conceived of the possibility of the Supreme Identity; they stop short at 'vision', and the entire extent of the angelic worlds still separates them from Deliverance.[1]

As we see, these 'corrections' or precisions hardly change Guénon's thesis. Undoubtedly they make his being in contradiction (on certain points) to Christian mystical texts less glaring, but this is at the price of a devaluation of their language which does not, we are told, admit of the highest possible meaning.

Now this conclusion seems to reveal, not only a great ignorance of mystical literature, but, more seriously, a misconstruing of Christian christological doctrine. It is this doctrine that is *really* at stake, and this is why we should broach this major point before having a chance to read, in the last section of this chapter, any written testimony. That, in this lengthy confrontation between Christian revelation and the doctrine of Guénon, we must finally come to the question of Christ is not at all surprising. It has been present, in fact, since the beginning, and comes to the fore now at the end of our reflections.

To start, I will have to say that it is rather improper to speak of an 'individualized' aspect of the *Avatara* in connection with Christ. Such a formulation seems to imply a confusion between human and divine nature. The divine nature is, in fact, by no means individualized in or by the human nature of Jesus, which, let us recall, has no human *I*, no human person.[2] One might speak, less improperly, of an '*individual* aspect' of the *Avatara*, to the extent that Christ being

---

1. Ibid., p49.
2. I can do no better than to refer to the explanation of trinitarian theology given in *La charité profanée*, pp245–275.

man necessarily possesses, like all men, an individual nature, that is a nature constituting an organic and indivisibly autonomous totality, what Aristotle calls a soul, a living form. The presence of a living form characterizes, moreover, not only a human being, but all living things: a tree or a cat do not have a nature less individual than Christ. However, the word 'aspect' is inappropriate to the extent that it might lead us to believe that this individuality has only an apparent reality from one 'point of view' (the heresy of Docetism), whereas Christ is truly man.

Secondly, and strictly speaking, neither is Christ an *Avatara*. To think so under this category is to make oneself liable to misunderstand His proper reality, despite an incontestable analogy that induces some authors to translate *avatara* as 'incarnation', whereas the term exclusively signifies 'descent' (of a god), and whereas, originally, India spoke not of *avatara*, but of *pradhurbhava*, 'manifestation'. The major difference is that, as paradoxical as it may seem, Christ is not a 'descent' or a 'manifestation' of the divine in the human; St Paul even teaches that, far from manifesting the 'divine condition' that was His, Christ emptied Himself and took on the 'form of a slave', which has no relationship with the divine descents spoken of in India. As for the dogmatic theology formulated by the Holy Spirit has formulated in the tradition of the Councils—the only formulation compatible with revelation—it teaches that Christ is the incarnation of the Second Person of the Blessed Trinity; and only through the relationship that this Second Person maintains with the Divine Nature should Jesus Christ be regarded as the manifestation of God. Nowhere does Scripture say that *God* was made flesh, but that the Word was made flesh. What matters here is not the *nature,* but the *hypostasis*. It is not Divine Nature that assumes human nature, it is the Hypostasis of the Son, and this metaphysical difference brings with it decisive consequences in the respective economies of each one of the religions. In particular, we understand why the Son could assume a human nature for which He becomes the person that it requires to exist, and why He could not assume the nature of non-personal beings, such as fish, wild boar, or rock, whereas that is possible for an *avatara*. With the Christic theophany, God's intention, dare I say, is not essentially to manifest in the visible

The Mystical Way

world the presence of the 'divine' and to signify, with the help of cosmic forms, His power, greatness and royalty, or the strength of His blessings. This cosmic mode of manifestation is that of the Old Law, and of the primitive and universal revelation (cf. Rom. 1:20). Evidently, the incarnation of Jesus Christ does not exclude this, as certain details in the Gospels prove. But what is essential is not there, and, from the point of view of what is essential, the Christic theophany represents something completely different. To envisage this theophany along the lines of prior divine manifestations is surely to grasp something of it (its most secondary and most exterior characteristics), but this misses its most profound and most specific dimension, which is truly signified only by the Chalcedonian formulation of the hypostatic union. Christ has come in the flesh not essentially to work miracles, which are *signs* (St John), but to accomplish the Father's will to save all men. This accomplishment, in its visible manifestation (the Passion and Crucifixion) has nothing very theophanic about it: surveyed from without, it is the trite story of a religious agitator condemned to a degrading and miserable death, in a far off province of the immense Roman Empire. So, from what does it draw its infinite redemptive value? From the single fact that it was lived and 'sustained in being', *invisibly,* by the very Person of the Son: invisibly—and not overtly—for no one was able to see the Hypostasis of the Son at work in the Suffering Servant. Only faith, and theological faith, discerns, behind the anecdotal and the factual, this hypostatic Principle. We must change, then, the way we look on what is in general called a 'manifestation of the divine'. We must learn, from the Christic mystery itself scrutinized in the light of dogmatic tradition, a new mode of theophany, a mode until then without precedent in the history of religions. And it is precisely this new mode that Guénon does not perceive. Having had at his disposal only the avataric category, he reduced the Christic theophany to that and mistook it in its radical singularity, that is in the mystery of the hypostatic union. In truth, all the facts of Christian dogmatics are inseparable from each other.

Thirdly, the mistaking of the doctrine of the hypostatic union draws Guénon into an error complementary to and the opposite of the first. A moment ago, he was shown to be confusing the two natures, by making human nature the individualized aspect of the *Avatara;* now, he seems to be dissociating divine nature from human nature by maintaining that, to be attached to the Christ-man, is to exclude the Christ-Logos—an error resting on the same forgetting of the Hypostasis. Although the natures cannot be mixed, neither should they be separated, united as they are in the unique Hypostasis of the Son. This is why the Council of Ephesus was able to declare Mary 'Mother of God', *Theotokos,* not because a human creature had given birth to God—which is absurd—but because she truly gave birth to a human being the Person or Hypostasis of whom is that of the Son, who likewise possesses the divine nature. Likewise, by uniting ourselves with Christ Jesus, insofar as by that we are designating the humanity of the incarnate Word, we also unite ourselves, at least implicitly and by virtue of the hypostatic union, to His divine nature and the Eternal Word. For, 'who has seen me has seen the Father,' whose principial Image is the Son. And, indeed, it is necessarily so since, being devoid of a human 'self', that is of an ontological principle of personal existence, this human nature would be reduced to a simple abstraction if it were not sustained in being by a Divine Subject, the second Person of the Blessed Trinity. Such is the logic of Christian dogma.

Undoubtedly it will be asserted that it is not Guénon that objectively separates the Christ-Logos from the Christ-man, but the mystics themselves who subjectively reduce the *Avatara* to what they can perceive of it. In the instance of such a subjective limitation, and however it might be for the divine reality of Christ in other respects, it can hardly be maintained that the mystic effectively realizes the superior degrees of being.

My reply to this is that I do not deny that, in certain mystical forms, we encounter an excessive insistence on Christ's humanity and its most contingent manifestations. But that is not the question. The question is to know if the fact of speaking about union with 'Christ Jesus' implies significantly those consequences indicated by Guénon. Now, such is not the doctrine of the Christians. Surely Christ received this Name when He was made man, whereas the Name 'Logos' belongs to Him by virtue of His divinity. But each of these Names, 'according to its quality', says *everything* about Christ:

The Mystical Way

'both are perfect and complete portraits of Christ...for each one for its part expresses everything that there is in Christ, insofar as it is possible for a name.'[1] Nevertheless, I know of no mystic who was attached to Christ's humanity to the exclusion of His divinity: if the former is loved, it is with a view to the latter.

As for the 'superior states', that is the angelic states, I am by no means maintaining—which would be ridiculous—that every Christian mystic, *ipso facto,* has realized them; but I do maintain that they possess them virtually in their union with Christ Jesus, in other words that this possibility of an ascension through the spiritual hierarchies, enabling access to 'isangelic' states, is found to be effectively included here. This is what St Paul affirms explicitly in his letters, as I have remarked, and what he calls the 'Mystery of Christ'; an unprecedented Mystery, but one that defines the center of the Christian faith, a Mystery not hidden and taught with obscure words in some rare esoteric writings, but a Mystery openly proclaimed in the best known texts of the New Testament: in Jesus, 'the Word of life' that 'our eyes have contemplated and our hands touched' (1 John 1:1), dwells the fullness of the Universal Man hypostatically, who contains all worlds within Himself. Did Guénon believe that? It seems that the question is posed, but I have found no explicit declaration in this respect. Without a doubt he teaches quite clearly the relationship of the Universal Man to the Logos, a Logos understood in a sense more Alexandrian than Christian, as is the case with other thinkers of his school. But, when it comes to the relationship of the Universal Man with Christ, he speaks rather bizarrely of a 'mystical Christ' and not of Christ Jesus: 'the "Universal Man"... is the mystical Christ, the "second Adam" of Saint Paul.'[2] It is impossible not to see here a deliberate intention not in harmony with the Christian faith, nor with scriptural data.

---

1. Luis de León, *Les Noms du Christ,* trans. Robert Ricard, Études Augustiniennes, 1978, p376. Luis de León (1527–1591) was one of the major authors of the Spanish golden age.
2. *Spiritual Authority and Temporal Power,* trans. H.D. Fohr (Hillsdale, NY: Sophia Perennis, 2004) p69, n.9.

Christ the Original Mystery

Keep in mind these just referred to few points of the dogmatic tradition: they constitute certainties of faith for all of the authors that I will now cite, authors who delineate, at the end of this book, its spiritual crown: they cling to these certainties with every fiber of their being, and to a true understanding of them they have devoted their lives and their deaths.

The Word of the Mystics and the Divine Essence

In this last article, I am intentionally abstaining from any reference to the Church Fathers or to the spiritual authors of the Middle Ages, the Rhinelanders especially. It would have been too easy, in order to show what a Christian mystic is, to appeal to the testimonies of Eckhart, Suso and Tauler. We will confine ourselves to modern times, from the sixteenth to the twentieth century, thus covering the period when the very term 'mystical' came into its most classical and most incontestable usage. Nor will we seek out rare disputed or disputable authors, marginal, obscure, allusive or hidden authors. We will cite only known (with one exception) and recognized authors of irreproachable orthodoxy, writers and saints whose often republished works have been recommended by the Catholic Church and have guided thousands of souls.

We will consult these works to be instructed on two points. The first rather secondary one, to occupy us but briefly, concerns the question of phenomena in the mystical way: should they be seen as necessary, or even essential? what kind of a case do the mystics make of them? The second incomparably more important point concerns the nature of union with God for modern spiritual writers: is it true that a totally exterior union between the individual nature of the mystic and humanity of Christ is involved, a union unaware of the scope of the angelic hierarchies and, *a fortiori,* the Divine Essence?

One last detail: we will now let the mystics themselves speak, since their language has been judged *indicative* of the irremediable limitation of their spiritual horizon. This means that we will not answer

The Mystical Way

doctrinally to these two questions posed.[1] But it seems that the texts that we will now listen to will convey this response much better than I could, at least if one knows how to hear them.

The Question of Phenomena

Despite many assertions and whatever the opinion of the ignorant in this respect, it needs to be recognized that there is no mystical author, nor any treatise on mystical theology that grants any essential importance to visions and other exceptional phenomena occurring in the life of a mystic. Doctrinally speaking, these phenomena do not, as such, pertain to the *supernatural* order, but to the *preternatural* order, which means that they stem from (exceptional) possibilities of human nature, even if they are the effects of an authentically supernatural grace. Some great saints seem to have never experienced such occurrences: this is the case for St Therese of the Child Jesus who does not *seem* to have known ecstasies, visions or locutions.[2] Other mystical Doctors even call for a rejection of these

---

1. In dealing with the first question we will, however, stress a rather surprising paradox. If an abundance of visions and extraordinary phenomena is an indubitable sign of mysticism, then we would have to rank Ibn Arabi among the mystics: his life and his work are, so to say, only an immense exploration of the 'imaginal world' (according to Henry Corbin's felicitous expression), that is of the 'locus' of theophanies, which was also, in a majority of cases, the 'locus' of angelophanies. It is to the point to wonder if something equivalent has ever existed in the history of religions (perhaps Swedenborg, at least for sheer quantity)? Now Guénon the Akbarian does not say *a single word* about this, or, in any case, leaves nothing to conjecture. Besides Corbin's book, *Creative Imagination in the Sufism of Ibn Arabi*, trans. Ralph Manheim (Princeton, NJ: Princeton University Press, 1969), the major work on this subject is William Chittick's *Ibn al-Arabi's Metaphysics of Imagination: The Sufi Path of Knowledge* (Albany: State University of New York Press, 1979). As for the second question relating to mystical union and the 'supreme identity', I have explained this point of view in *The Sense of the Supernatural* (Edinburgh: T & T Clark, 1998), pp 127–156; likewise cf. *La charité profanée*, pp 418–419, where I have already denounced any idea of a 'massive identification'.

2. On this issue some authors have asked if 'little' Therese is truly a mystic (Hilda Graef, for example: *The Story of Mysticism* [Garden City, NY: Doubleday, 1965],

phenomena: thus St John of the Cross, whose teaching is often misinterpreted: some see in this the proof of metaphysical inability to integrate the imaginal, whereas it rather has to do with an extreme spiritual goal that practices what Shankara called: 'the holy disdain for the non-Self.'[1] The soul can in fact receive these visions, locutions and understandings with a 'possessive attitude' and 'as if they belonged to himself,'[2] and this is why:

> since these imaginative apprehensions, visions, and other forms or species are presented through some image or particular idea, a person must neither feed upon nor encumber himself with them ... whether these visions be false and diabolical or whether they are recognized as authentic and of divine origin. Neither should a person desire to accept them or keep them, because with such an attitude he can not remain detached, divested, pure, and simple, and without any mode or method, as the union demands.[3]

---

p 272). The assurance with which some historians judge at times the spiritual geniuses about whom they speak without understanding them remains puzzling. In *Autobiographical Manuscript A* (83 v°5), Therese writes:

> I understand and I know by experience that 'the Kingdom of God is within us.' Jesus has no need of books or doctors to instruct souls; He Himself is the Doctor of doctors, He teaches without the noise of words.... Never have I heard Him speak, but at each moment I feel that He is within me' (*Manuscrits autobiographiques*, Cerf and D.D.B., 1992, p 268).

Let me mention this confidence related by Mother Agnes of Jesus, received on July 11, 1897, three months before Theresa's death: 'She spoke to me of her prayers in former times, at evening, during the silence of summer, and told me that she had understood by experience what a "flight of the spirit" is' (*Œuvres*, Cerf, 1992, p 1036). 'Flight of the spirit' is an expression of 'big' Teresa designating 'ravishment' or 'ecstasy' (*Life*, chap. 20, §1).

1. *Anatma-shri-vigharanam;* cf. Shankaracharya, *Hymnes et chants védantiques,* Ed. Orientales, 1977, p 25. For all that, we find a complete doctrine of symbolism in St John: cf. Jacques Chevalier, *Histoire de pensée,* t. II: *La Pensée chrétienne,* Flammarion, 1956, pp 839–840.

2. *The Ascent of Mount Carmel,* bk. 2, chap. 11, 7; *The Collected Works,* trans. Kieran & Rodriguez (Washington, DC: ICS Publications, 1973), p 134.

3. Ibid., bk. 2, chap. 16, 6; ICS, p 151. The saint specifies that, if God sends visions, this is so to raise up the soul toward Him, and not to stop there but 'bring a soul step by step to the innermost good' (bk. 2, chap. 17, 4; p 157).

The Mystical Way

Such is not, we know, the opinion of St Teresa of Avila, who was favored with quite numerous visions, locutions and other extraordinary graces, to which she attributed great value (without however lingering on them) because of our soul's weakness, which has need of being refreshed on the difficult road to perfection by the contemplation of Christ's human beauty. This beauty possesses a brightness, a glory such as could not be counterfeited by the devil without the soul rather quickly recognizing it. Furthermore, this imaginal vision is in no way opposed, but, on the contrary, leads to the intellectual vision of God:

> Though the former type of vision which ... reveals God without presenting any image of Him, is of a higher kind [than the imaginal vision], yet, if the memory of it is to last, despite our weakness, and if the thoughts are to be well occupied, it is a great thing that so Divine a Presence should be presented to the imagination and should remain within it. These two kinds of vision almost invariably occur simultaneously, and, as they come in this way, the eyes of the soul see the excellence and the beauty and the glory of the most holy Humanity of Our Lord. And, [through the intellectual vision] is revealed to us how He is God ... and fills all things with His love. This [imaginal] vision is to be very highly esteemed, and, in my view, there is no peril in it.... [These visions are] very easy to recognize; and, unless a soul wants to be deceived, I do not think the devil will deceive it if it walks in humility and simplicity.[1]

Besides, even coming from the devil, a beautiful image of Christ raises us towards Him; and it is the devil who is taken in. Thus

> contrary to his intention, this enemy of salvation does us good.... Where there is humility, no harm can possibly ensue, even though the vision came from the devil; and where there is

---

1. *Life,* chap. XXVIII, *The Complete Works of Saint Teresa of Jesus,* vol. 1, trans. E. Allison Peers (London and New York: Sheed & Ward, 1957) p183. I have taken the liberty of replacing 'imaginary' with 'imaginal'.

no humility, there can be no profit, even if the vision come from God.¹

The opposition between the two doctors seems so acute that it might be asked if they are speaking about the same thing, as if the contemplation envisioned by St John of the Cross amounted to the habitus of acquired contemplation, while St Teresa was only dealing with pure passively received mystical contemplation.² However this thesis may be, a thesis that seems arguable, we stress that, despite her favoring of visions, the saint by no means makes them essential to the mystical life:

When you learn or hear that God is granting souls these graces, you must never *beseech* or *desire* Him to lead you along this road'; however, these visions can be good, since they are sometimes granted for us to perceive 'the splendor of the Son of God ... like an infused light ... similar to that of the sun,' and thus the soul finds itself 'confronted with sovereign Beauty.³

Mystical Union

I have said enough to prove that no authentic mystic has ever made the essence of contemplative life consist in the manifesting of extraordinary phenomena. We can now, as promised, come to the second point: Is the mystical way limited to a union with Christ

---

1. *Book of Foundations,* chap. VII, *The Complete Works...* vol. 3, p 42. We see here how little the saint is obsessed by a fear of diabolical illusions: the intrinsic truth of the image alone matters, which exhibits a rather 'jnanic' character, and not at all 'hysterical' as some 'hardy souls' have supposed.

2. This is the thesis of Mother Marie du Saint-Sacrement: *Œuvres de saint Jean de la Croix* (Bar-le-Duc: Imprimerie Saint-Paul, 1935), t. III, Appendix V: 'La Mystique de saint Jean de la Croix et celle de sainte Thérèse'. This translation has been fortunately reprinted for the recent edition of *Œuvres complètes* in one volume (Paris: Cerf, 1990) unaccompanied by appendices.

3. *Interior Castle,* Sixth Mansion, chap. IX; *The Complete Works...* vol. 2, p 319 and 315. [Where the English translation differs from the French, the French is used TR.]

The Mystical Way

Jesus (to the exclusion of the Christ-Logos), and, even when union with God is mentioned, is this only concerned with the individual nature of a human being?

In 1537, at Cologne, a work of unknown authorship (perhaps a Fleming akin to St Peter Canisius) appeared entitled *The Evangelic Pearl*, the success of which was considerable. Let us listen, then, to how a Catholic mystic expresses himself:

> I believe that, from eternity, I was uncreated in your Divine Essence, in the memory of the Father, in the knowledge of the Son and in the love of the Holy Spirit, that You have created me in Your image and likeness, and to this You have united Yourself.[1]

Faithful to the tripartite anthropology of the Platonizers, *The Pearl*'s author places the spirit wherein God dwells at the soul's center. This spirit, the spark of the soul

> is I know not what of the naked and the unformed, and perpetually inclined toward its origin that makes of it an eternal and living mirror of the divinity continually receiving within itself the eternal generation of the Word and the image of the Blessed Trinity in which God knows Himself, and all that He is, in essence as much as in person.[2]

> [Hence, anyone] who wants to seek and find God, let Him be sought within, namely in the intimate depths of his soul where the image of God is, and dig up the field of his created essence very much in advance, and by this means he will find himself ideally uncreated in the Divine Essence and in the naked essence of the soil, and having done this he will return to his principle, by means of Jesus Christ who is our way.[3]

And it is, in fact, not by our own forces that we can

---

1. Liber II, Chap. 1, in the French translation of 1608; Cognet, *La Spiritualité moderne*, t. 1: L'Essor, Aubier, p 43. Cf. Appendix 1: Concerning '*The Evangelic Pearl*', p 482.
2. Ibid., Liber I, chap. 46; Cognet, p 43.
3. Ibid., Liber I, chap. 4; Cognet, p 46 ('ideally uncreated' means: he will find the uncreated Idea by which God conceived of him from all eternity).

arrive at this noble nothing and be made nothing and unite this nothing, that is my soul, with the nothing that is God;[1] [but it is] by the image of Jesus Christ [that] we have entered into the soul's abyss[2] [since] God has deigned to put on our mortal frame, so that, by the merits of His most holy humanity, He might purify us, reform all the powers of our soul, and so that, by the mirror of this God-Man, He might at last make of us a man-God.[3] [Having reached this ultimate degree] we are as if annihilated and divested of our creaturehood, that is of all that had been created in us in time, and we are made by grace what God is.[4]

The Evangelic Pearl stands at the summit, but it is not alone. The Benedictine teachings of Louis de Blois (1506–1566), the reformer of the Abbey of Liesses, in Hainaut, are no less lofty—and have had an immense success. This mystic was oriented toward the 'imitation of Jesus Christ': our labors and our trials are, in themselves

> base and valueless.... They will receive ... through their union with Christ, an ineffable dignity.[5] [And yet we must go beyond this]: every image and every thought of perishable things, even the thought of angels or Christ's Passion, as well as every intellectual reflection, constitute a hindrance for man in this mortal life when he desires to be raised to mystical union with God, which is above every substance and every intelligence.[6]

This 'surpassing' of Christ's humanity is wrought in

> this naked depth divested of all images [where the soul] is lost in the infinite solitude and obscurity of divinity—but to lose oneself in this way is to find oneself. Then ... it is, so to say, transformed and changed into God.[7] [And] the soul that contemplates this dark and obscure light swoons and takes leave of itself, and,

---

1. Ibid., Liber I, chap. 11; p 44.
2. Ibid., Liber II, chap. 19; p 45.
3. Ibid., Liber I, chap. 38; p 45.
4. Ibid., Liber III, chap. 4; p 47.
5. *Institution spiritualis*, chap. IX; Cognet, p 50.
6. Ibid., chap. XII, §11; p 51.
7. Ibid., §2; p 51.

The Mystical Way

passing away into God, becomes one same spirit in its most intimate depths; and, engendered with the Eternal Word of God, that the Father utters within it, it is renewed in a superlative way.

But this is not all, for, in the bosom of the Trinity, the soul is breathed into the unity of the Divine Essence:

> It possesses a certain supernatural unity of the spirit, in which it remains as if within its own abode, and it is swept away into the Divine Essence up to that supreme unity where the Father, Son and Holy Spirit are one in the triplicity of the Divine Essence Itself.[1]

These authors have profited by the teachings of the Rhineland-Flemish. Other authors are unaware of them: such is the case with St Catherine of Genoa (1447–1510) who is an 'autodidact of grace', but also one of the 'peaks of Christian mysticism.'[2] Rediscovering the themes of Dionysian apophatism, she tells us: 'I see without eyes, hear without understanding, feel without feeling, and taste without tasting. I know neither form nor measure.'[3] This is why divine love is rightly inexpressible:

> I cannot desire any created love, that is, love which can be felt, enjoyed, or understood... because pure love passes all these things and transcends them. [And this love says] I shall never rest until I am hidden and enclosed in that divine heart wherein all created forms are lost, and, so lost, remain thereafter all divine.[4]

In this love God attracts the soul to lead it to an 'annihilation of its own being.'[5] Then 'God alone remains; and man remains without soul or body, without heaven or earth; he eats, drinks, hears, and remembers, but all these things are accomplished without the workings of nature.'[6] What we have here is a state of perfect passivity, of

---

1. Ibid., §4; p52.
2. Cognet, op. cit., pp54, 58.
3. *Life*, chap. IX.
4. Ibid., chap. XIV.
5. Ibid., chap. XIV.
6. Ibid., chap. XXX. [As cited by Cognet, p63.]

ontological passivity, in which the soul understands that its 'being is God, not by participation only but by a true transformation and annihilation of [its] proper being.'[1]

Translated into French (1598), Latin (1626), and Spanish (1647), the work of St Catherine of Genoa is 'one of the sources of Christian spirituality for the classical period.'[2] Let us add that, in her mystical life, this woman experienced the most extraordinary phenomena.

We can now come to the two most prestigious teachers of Catholic mysticism for the modern period, and who were not only teachers, but also great saints.

St Teresa of Avila expressly distinguishes, as do all the authors cited, the soul, said to belong to the individual nature, from the 'center' or the 'spirit of the soul', the place where the spiritual marriage is celebrated and where the union of the personal being with God is accomplished.

> This instantaneous communication of God to the soul is so great a secret... that I do not know with what to compare it.... As far as one can understand, *the soul (I mean the spirit of the soul) is made one with God.*[3]

This union of spiritual marriage is perfect and permanent, which distinguishes it from the spiritual betrothals wherein the soul enjoys the Divine Presence only intermittently; here

> the soul remains all the time in that center with its God. [This union] is like rain falling from the heavens into a river or spring; there is nothing but water there and it is impossible to divide or separate the water belonging to the river from that which fell from the heavens. Or it is as if a tiny streamlet enters the sea, from

---

1. Ibid., chap. xiv.
2. Cognet, p 64.
3. *Interior Castle*, Seventh Mansion, chap. ii; p 335. Teresa knew of the teachings of the Rhineland-Flemish under the form of the *Institutions* placed under Tauler's name, and translated into Castillian in 1551. This is the chief reason for which the works of the saint were handed over to the Holy Office by Alonso de la Fuente in 1589; he denounced the presence of concepts derived from the famous Dominican, calling for a condemnation of both the Spanish Carmelite and the Strasbourg preacher (Orcibal, *S. Jean de la Croix et les mystiques rhéno-flamands*, p 47).

The Mystical Way

which it will find no way of separating itself, or as if in a room there were two large windows through which the light streamed in: it enters in different places but it all becomes one.[1]

The teachings of St John of the Cross will detain us longer, given the importance, with him, of theological considerations. After all, although St Teresa might speak only of her spiritual experiences, he whom she calls her 'little Seneca' (that is her little philosopher) never speaks of them (directly): he always situates himself in an objective point of view and expounds the doctrine of a spiritual method which, certainly, includes psychological aspects (How could it be otherwise seeing that it is a human being who is engaged in the mystical way?), but always in relation to the ontological and dogmatic order. It is good to remember this if errors in interpretation are to be avoided. Thus, for Guénon, St John's 'night' 'surely does not have the same significance' as it does among certain Sufis for whom it 'corresponds to a state of non-manifestation.'[2] Now the symbolism of night has deep roots in Christianity's most ancient mystical traditions; it is related to the symbolism of darkness or cloud, which is the place wherein God dwells, the 'manifestation' of unmanifestable essence; here, as Jean Baruzi penetratingly notes, the symbol is somehow only one with the symbolized, 'it clings directly to experience. It is not a figure of experience.'[3] St John of the Cross has, moreover, the clearest indications about the meaning he has given to night: 'We can offer three reasons for calling this journey toward union with God a night.... The third reason pertains to the point of

---

1. Ibid.
2. *Insights into Islamic Esoterism and Taoism*, pp76–76; this has to do with an issue of *Études Carmelitaines* in which Miguel Asin Palacios suggested seeing in Ibn Abbad of Ronda 'an Hispano-Muslim precursor of St John of the Cross.' This is the only place (unless we are mistaken) where Guénon mentions the name of a great mystic. In *Perspectives on Initiation*, p16, he mentions Anne Catherine Emmerich, who clearly corresponds to his conception of a mystic steeped in visions and phenomena. Obviously, Blessed Anne Catherine, wholly subject to the Divine Will, had no spiritual teaching to bestow. Her function was, I think, to provide a cure for the destruction, by Enlightenment rationalism, of the Christian image-world carried along in the European soul to nourish and imbue its faith.
3. *Saint Jean de la Croix et le problème de l'expérience mystique*, Alcan, 1921, p325.

Christ the Original Mystery

arrival, namely, God. God is also a dark night to man in this life.' And the symbolic significance becomes still more obvious as the text continues, where we learn that this third meaning of night (the first two are the purification of the senses—signified by the beginning of the night—and the comprehension of faith—signified by midnight) is represented by dawn the next day and corresponds to the moment when there transpires the union of the soul with the *Spouse,* also called the 'Wisdom of God', and therefore with the 'feminine' aspect of the Divine Essence, which is indeed the exact equivalent of the meaning of 'Night' among the Sufis.[1] As we see, there is 'esoteric' data among the Spanish mystics. This is perhaps why his commentary of *The Dark Night* closes, in a rather enigmatic way, with the recalling of this verse that the soul sings 'in an unknown way': 'On that thrice glad night. . .'[2]

The true intentions of St John of the Cross and the significance of his teaching should not be in doubt; in as much as he has taken care to make it explicit with all the clarity and precision of the philosopher and theologian that he was, and also with all the power of his spiritual genius.

The key to his mystical life is the same as that of other spirituals that we have encountered—the key of the Kingdom of God to the soul's interior:

> The soul's center is God. When it has reached God with all the capacity of its being and the strength of its operation and inclination, it will have attained to its final and deepest center in God, it will know, love, and enjoy God with all its might.

There are, then, several centers of the soul, or rather several degrees of depth to this center:

> Should it reach three, it will have centered itself in a third. But once it has attained the final degree, God's love will have arrived at wounding the soul in its ultimate and deepest center, which is

---

1. *The Ascent of Mount Carmel,* bk 1, chap. 2, 1; *Collected Works,* p75.
2. *The Dark Night,* bk 2, chap. 25, 4; p389.

The Mystical Way

to transform and clarify it in its whole being ... until it appears to be God.[1]

The union spoken of here is indeed a 'substantial' union, that is, in the scholastic language which is that of St John, a union that involves the reality or the very being of the soul and not only its faculties: it reaches the soul in its most profound ontological center (contrary to what Jacques Maritain asserts who sets aside any idea of an 'entitative contact'):

> In this high state of union God does not communicate Himself to the soul—nor is this possible—through the disguise of any imaginal vision, likeness or figure, but mouth to mouth: the pure and naked essence of God (the mouth of God in love) with the pure and naked essence of the soul (the mouth of the soul in the love of God).[2]

This union has received the name of transforming union, and rightly so for it surpasses the limits of the individual form and the soul's powers. God effects this union in the 'secret' of the being: 'The Master who teaches the soul dwells within it substantially where neither the devil, the natural senses, nor the intellect can reach,' and this is 'the mystical theology which theologians call secret wisdom.'[3] But, for God to be able to work in the soul's most hidden substance, it specifically needs to renounce all of its own workings and to divest itself of them as so many veils:

> A man makes room for God by wiping away all the smudges and smears of creatures, by uniting his will perfectly to God's; for to love is to labor to divest and deprive oneself for God of all that is not God. When this is done the soul will be illumined by and

---

1. *The Living Flame of Love*, stanza 1, 12–13; p 583–584.
2. *The Ascent of Mount Carmel*, bk 2, chap. 16, 9; p152. 'The soul asks [for a] ... certain contact of the soul with the divinity. This contact is something foreign to everything sensory and accidental, since it is a touch of naked substances—of the soul and the divinity' (*The Spiritual Canticle*, stanza 19, 4; p486). 'This communication [of God] is diffused substantially in the whole soul, or better, the soul is transformed in God' (Ibid., stanza 26, 5; p512).
3. *The Dark Night*, bk 2, chap. 17, 2; p368.

transformed in God. And God will so communicate His supernatural being to it that it will appear to be God Himself and will possess all that God Himself has. When God grants this supernatural favor to the soul, so great a union is caused that all the things of both God and the soul become one in participant transformation, and the soul appears to be God more than a soul. Indeed, it is God by participation. Yet truly, its being (even though transformed) is naturally as distinct from God's as it was before, just as the window, although illumined by the ray, has an existence distinct from the ray.[1]

Thus deified even in this life, the soul loves, wills and knows according to a divine mode: the soul's faculties

> inclined in God toward God, having become enkindled lamps within the splendors of the divine lamps, they render the Beloved the same light and heat they receive ... just as the window when the sun shines on it, for it then too reflects the splendors. Yet the soul reflects the divine light in a more excellent way because of *the active intervention of its will.* 'So rarely, so exquisitely', means: in a way rare or foreign to every common thought, every exaggeration, and *every mode and manner.* ... And according to the excellence of the divine attributes (fortitude, beauty, justice, etc.), which the Beloved communicates, is the excellence with which the soul's feeling gives joyfully to Him the very light and heat it receives from Him. Having been made one with God, the soul is somehow God through participation. ... God's operation and the soul's is one. Since God gives Himself with a free and gracious will, so too the soul (possessing a will the more generous

---

1. *The Ascent of Mount Carmel*, bk 2, chap. 5, 7; pp 117–118. Some will perhaps see, in the last sentence of the text, a reservation typically 'bhaktic' with respect to the so-called 'Supreme Identity' doctrine which goes further in its formulations. We can always 'go further' with words, but it is not certain that we then know what we are talking about. True identity should be exclusive of all duality, save for conceiving of it in a formal and solid way. Oneness-Infinity is not an instance in which the multiple would be totally annihilated. To the contrary, it is its Possibility: the maximum of identity is also the maximum of distinctiveness. The creature is truly *itself* only in God.

The Mystical Way

and free the more it is united with God) *gives to God, God Himself in God.* .... Clearly, the soul can give this gift, even though the gift has greater entity than the soul's own being and capacity.[1]

In this gift of God to God effected by the deified soul, that is the soul that has received the Holy Spirit as its own Possession, is accomplished its participation in the trinitarian circumincession, which is the flux of love eternally circulating among the three Persons. The soul receives the Breath, the 'divine spiration'.

> By His divine breath-like spiration, the Holy Spirit elevates the soul sublimely and informs her and makes her capable of breathing in God the same spiration of love that the Father breathes in the Son and the Son in the Father, which is the Holy Spirit Himself, Who in the Father and the Son breathes out to her in this transformation, in order to unite her to Himself. There would not be a true and total transformation if the soul were not transformed in the three Persons of the Most Holy Trinity in an open and manifest degree.[2]

St Teresa's and St John's doctrines penetrated into France at the beginning of the seventeenth century, thanks in particular to Madame Acarie (Blessed Marie of the Incarnation), nicknamed the 'new Teresa', who founded Carmel in France,[3] and also thanks to Pierre de Bérulle. Their doctrines were propagated through the translation of their works which marked the French School profoundly, as is attested by the texts of Fénelon that we have cited.[4] One of the major authors of this School is the Capuchin Benedict of Canfeld (1562–1610), originally from the English county of Essex, who spiritually looked after the Carmel of Madame Acarie and some of Bérulle's disciples. His most famous work is the *Rule of Perfection*

---

1. *The Living Flame of Love*, stanzas 3, 77, 78, and 79; pp 640–642. Cf. Appendix 2: *Is St John of the Cross a Voluntarist?*, p 483.
2. *The Spiritual Canticle*, stanza 39, 3; p 558.
3. Upon their arrival in Paris, the Spanish Carmelites who came to assist in the founding of the French Carmel were led in pilgrimage to Saint-Denis to venerate the author of *Mystical Theology*.
4. Cf. supra, p 423 and n1.

containing a brief and lucid summary of the whole spiritual life reduced to this single point of God's will (1609). Canfeld is, he too, a disciple of Denys and read Eckhart and the *Cloud of Unknowing*.[1] He distinguishes three wills in God, one exterior (the work of creation), another interior (the work of grace), and the third essential:

> This essential will is spirit and life, totally abstract, purified of itself, and devoid of all forms and images of created things, whether corporeal or spiritual, temporal or eternal... it is not something separated, nor yet something joined or united with God, but very God in its essence.[2]

It is with this essential will that it is necessary to be identified, through self-denial, that is by becoming aware of one's own nothingness:

> for... reason tells us that we can only be nothing (compared to God's independent being), since God is infinite; for, if we were something, God would not be infinite, for His being would have an end there where our being began.... If I am told that the creature is independent of God and therefore something, I reply that it is and is not.[3]

Benedict of Canfeld calls the contemplation to which we then attain the 'supereminent life'; and yet this life is only an extension of faith:

> This life is a pure, simple, naked and habitual faith, assisted by reason, and ratified and confirmed by experience... it has its residence *in apice animae* [at the peak of the soul] and contemplates God, without any means or intermediacy.[4] [And in fact] no act,

---

1. For his edition of the *Rule of Perfection* (1982), Jean Orcibal has established an index of the names mentioned by Benedict of Canfeld, and the three most often cited authors are, in order of decreasing frequency: Harphius, Tauler, and Eckhart. And these three authors' writings are so widely distributed in *all* of Europe that so fine an expert as Jean Dagens (editor of Bérulle's correspondence) could say that, between 1550 and 1610, 'the most important fact is undoubtedly the spread of Germanic mysticism' (cited by J. Beaude, *La Mystique*, Cerf, coll. 'Bref', p30).
2. *Rule of Perfection*, third part, chap. 1; Cognet, op. cit., p251.
3. Ibid., third part, chap. 8; Cognet, p253.
4. Ibid., third part, chap. 12; Cognet, p255.

The Mystical Way

meditation, thought, aspiration, or operation are worthwhile here ... nor should any means be a means between the soul and this essential will or essence of God.... In this place the most excellent speculations, as to the Trinity or anything else, should be left behind, not that they are not beautiful or noble, but for what there is of a higher capacity in the soul, by which alone the spirit's highest point is most excellently attained.[1]

The *Rule of Perfection* is a classic treatise on mystical life for the seventeenth century. There are other less illustrious, but just as significant. I have contributed to making known Mgr. Laneau's treatise, *On the Deification of the Just* (*De deificatione justorrum*, circa 1690), the publication of which, because of the anti-Quietist climate of those times, only took place at the end of the nineteenth century.[2]

Finally, there are a multitude of written testimonies (the majority are in manuscript and so numerous that any estimation is impossible) that admirably illustrate the astonishing mystical flowering experienced in the seventeenth century: unknown spiritual people, both religious and laity, both of the high nobility and of humble circumstances, and sometimes of modest learning compared to the masters just mentioned. Among these testimonies is that of the astonishing figure of Claudine Moine, someone that her discoverer Father Guennou has nicknamed the 'Mystic Seamstress': she experienced, amidst the world and in anonymity, the loftiest spiritual states.[3] Originally from Franche-Comté, born in 1618 into a rather

---

1. Ibid., third part, chap. 2; Cognet, p 253.

2. This work, translated and annotated by Jean-Claude Chenêt, has been published in Geneva at the Éditions Ad Solem (1993). It is a question of the work's first part, devoted to the theology of deification. The second part, devoted to spiritual method, will be published later. Some excerpts from this treatise are given in *The Sense of the Supernatural*.

3. Father Guennou (editor of the 'Louis Laneau' article for the *Dictionnaire de Spiritualité*) discovered in the Paris archives of the Foreign Missions (to which Mgr. Laneau belonged) an anonymous manuscript notebook on the cover of which an archivist at the end of the nineteenth century had written: *Notes spirituelles*. He was able to recover the author's name, and in 1959 (Cerf) published the results of his research under the title: *La Couturière mystique* [*The Mystic Seamstress*]. The manuscript's complete text was published by him in 1968: Claudine Moine, *Ma vie secrète* (Desclée).

well-to-do family, she received a good education. Next she lived in Paris where she assumed the position of linen seamstress and lady's companion in a wealthy Marais household. No testimony either of or about her remains, beyond a manuscript that she composed at the request of one of her confessors who Father Guennou has succeeded in identifying: Father Castillon, a recognized disciple of the famous Father Louis Lallement. This young woman had received a solid elementary education, but she was certainly not a theologian, and yet what firmness of thought and what mastery in expression! Claudine Moine spent her life as a servant in an aristocratic household: she writes in the most limpid and appropriate language; as literature, this mystical account is a masterpiece. As for her spiritual doctrine, that Jesus taught her interiorly, not the least extraordinary phenomenon is to be found in it. This young woman was intellectually nourished by the Bible and the sermons heard at Mass. Spiritually, she lived by the Eucharist and prayer, and experienced a permanent state of contemplation which, at her confessor's request, she described in this way:

> In this state the soul is always empty and always full. Always empty in that everything is obliterated from it, both the exterior works wrought by it, and the interior affections received, neither retaining nor preserving any idea or memory of them; and always full because of the loving affections unceasingly poured forth by God. Always empty, and this is, it seems to me, the permanent and immutable state of the soul from which it never leaves, in which is has a simple impression—gentle but strong—of its own nothingness and the nothingness of all created things, that empties it of itself and all creatures; always full, in which it has a simple impression—gentle, but just as strong—of God who fills it, and all its faculties, and recollects them entirely!... The imagination, however foolish and extravagant it may be, no longer wanders: it is somewhere bound up and enclosed and no longer sallies forth!... When I sometimes hear it said: 'Many things are pictured to oneself and imagined,' that surprises me and I am unable to understand it; for I have neither image nor figure, nor species or representation either corporeal or spiritual,

The Mystical Way

not even of the divinity and humanity of Our Lord. And when they do appear and want to be formed, there is something in me that rejects them and destroys them instantly, because I want only God and not His image or His figure![1]

This is how a linen seamstress, meager in learning but uncommon in trade, speaks who has received no other initiation than those of Baptism and Confirmation, but who, it is true, received Communion several times a week and only heard the Word of God in the Bible, from the pulpit or within her heart. To read her is to understand why mystical knowledge has been called the 'science of the saints'.

Did this science disappear with the advent of the century of the Enlightenment and triumphant rationalism? By no means. Undoubtedly written expressions of it are more rare or anyhow less remarkable. Two crises have played a major role in this respect: the Jansenist crisis and the 'pure love' quarrel.[2] Some historians even think, and perhaps they are right, that Fénelon's condemnation in particular had the heaviest of consequences for the spiritual life of modern Europe's convents and monasteries: today the mystical is still the object, on the part of the clergy, of an almost ineradicable suspicion.

Being unable to retrace the history of spirituality through the eighteenth and nineteenth centuries, I will only mention in closing some of spirituality's more recent figures. And first of all Saint Therese of the Child Jesus and the Holy Face, who entered Carmel

---

1. *Ma vie secrète*, p266.
2. It was Richelieu who, for political reasons, but under the complaint of 'illuminism', had Saint-Cyran imprisoned at Vincennes March 14, 1638. St Vincent de Paul testified in vain in favor of the accused, who blamed the political alliance of Richelieu with the Protestant princes of Germany... In 1711 the Abbey of Port-Royal (in disrepair for several centuries) was razed to the ground and the bodies of the religious buried in the cloister were cast into a common ditch. – On the effects of the condemnation of the doctrine of pure love, read René Taveneaux, *Le catholicisme dans la France classique*, S.E.D.E.S., t. 2, pp413–416: 'Fénelon's defeat... marks the defeat of the mystical, or at least a certain conception of the mystical.' The book of Françoise Mallet Joris, *Jeanne Guyon* (Flammarion, 1978) is quite informative, but at times tendentious.

Christ the Original Mystery

'to do nothing', who experienced neither vision, nor ecstasy, but has inaugurated a 'little way' of pure loving concentration, and whose presence radiates *throughout the entire world*. Therese, without having accomplished the least splendid achievement in the social or religious order, is in herself, if we would just reflect for a moment, one of the most prodigious spiritual phenomena of modern times. That a *purely mystical* figure could create such a stir well beyond the bounds of Christianity, during a period devoted to the most arrogant materialism, is something humanly inexplicable.

I will say nothing about the way inaugurated by her. But, in the image of her dear Father Saint John of the Cross, she advanced in nakedness of faith:

> Without support yet with support,
> Living without Light, in darkness,
> I am wholly being consumed by Love.[1]

This love is an extraordinary tree:

> There is on this earth
> A marvelous Tree.
> Its root, O mystery!
> Is in Heaven…
>
> To taste of its fruit is to enter into
>
> An ocean of peace.
> In this deep peace
> I rest forever.[2]

But this peace has nothing of a gentle sleep about it. It demands the highest vigilance and the utmost abasement, and the firmest faith in the promise brought to us by the nativity of the Word:

---

1. *A Gloss on the Divine*, PN 30; *The Poetry of Saint Thérèse of Lisieux*, trans. Donald Kinney, O.C.D. (Washington, DC: ICS Publications, 1996), p 148.

2. *Abandonment is the Sweet Fruit of Love*, PN 52; *The Poetry of Saint Thérèse of Lisieux*, pp 206–207. Cf. the *Baghavad Gita*, xv, 1; trans. A.M. Ensoul, Seuil, p 127: 'They speak of a sacred imperishable fig-tree the roots of which are above and the branches below.'

The Mystical Way

Also in the heavenly Fatherland
My elect will be glorious
By communicating my life to them
I will make of them so many *gods!*[1]

On May 15, 1897, musing on her approaching death, Therese Martin confided to Mother Agnes of Jesus:

> I have formed such a lofty idea of heaven that, at times, I wonder what God will do at my death to surprise me. My hope is so great, it is such a subject of joy to me, not by feeling but by faith, that to satisfy me fully something will be necessary which is beyond all human conception. [Then she added] As for me, with the exception of the Gospels, I no longer find anything in books [of the mystics and saints]. The Gospels are enough. [And lastly she declares] After all, it's the same to me whether I live or die. I really don't see what I'll have after death that I don't already possess in this life. I shall see God, true; but as far as being in His presence, I am totally there here on earth.[2]

St Elizabeth of the Trinity, who died at the Dijon Carmel in 1906 at the age of twenty-six, is less known than her fellow Carmelite Therese. Just as much as Therese however, but in a more classical fashion, she is situated in the most essential line of Carmelite spirituality. Her mission is less universal than that of Therese, but no less lofty.

The dominant theme of her spiritual vision is at once ontological and sacramental in nature: she grasps her own being as a 'praise of

---

1. This quatrain is at the conclusion of a 'mystery play' entitled *Angels at the Creche of Jesus*, 21, RP 2; *Œuvres complète*, Cerf-DDB, 1992, p818. Therese has the Angel of Judgment converse with the merciful God that is the Child Jesus. To conclude, she touches on the deification of the elect, the doctrine of which she had long meditated on in St John of the Cross; according to stanza 39 of *The Spiritual Canticle*: 'Accordingly, souls possess the same goods by participation that the Son possesses by nature. As a result they are truly gods by participation, equals and companions of God ... the soul will participate in God Himself by performing in Him, in company with Him, the work of the Most Blessed Trinity' (*Collected Works*, p559).

2. *St Therese of Lisieux, Her Last Conversations,* trans. John Clarke, OCD (Washington, DC: ICS Publications, 1977), pp43–44.

glory' in the bosom of the Trinity. This theme is both metaphysical and mystical, since the raison d'être of the creature is to reflect, by its very being, God's glory of which creation is the radiance, and to sacramentally return it to the Source from whence it emanated by its thanksgiving:

> O depths. Unfathomable mystery,
> My heart becomes your humble sacrament,
> You come into it to glorify the Father
> In silence and recollection.[1]

She chiefly drew her doctrine from the two Theresas and St John of the Cross, often as well from Ruysbroeck the Admirable, whom she 'verifies' through her own contemplative life:

> The Holy Trinity created us in its image, according to the eternal design that it possessed in its bosom 'before the world was created', in this 'beginning without beginning' of which Bossuet speaks following St John: *In principio erat Verbum*. In the beginning was the Word; and we could add: in the beginning was nothing, for God in His eternal solitude already carried us in His thought. 'The Father contemplates Himself' in the abyss of His fecundity, and by the very act of comprehending Himself He engendered another Person, the Son, His eternal Word. The archetype of all creatures who had not yet issued out of the void eternally dwelt in Him, and God saw them and contemplated them in their type in Himself. This eternal life which our archetypes possessed without us in God, is the cause of our creation. Our created essence asks to be rejoined with its principle.... This is 'why God wills that, *delivered* from ourselves, we should stretch out our arms towards our exemplar and possess it', 'rising' above all things 'towards our model'.[2]

---

1. *Dans une humble et pauvre étable; Œuvres complètes*, Cerf, 1991, p 1024. This is a poem of December 25, 1904.
2. *Heaven in Faith* (August 1906), Seventh Day, First prayer; *The Complete Works*, vol. 1, trans. Sister Alethia Kane, OCD (Washington, DC: ICS Publications,

The Mystical Way

A few days later she made her last retreat. On the first day she notes (August 16, 1906):

> *Nescivi.* 'I no longer knew anything.' This is what the 'bride of the Canticles' sings after having been brought into the 'inner cellar'. It seems to me that this must also be the refrain of a praise of glory [This is her divine name: *laus gloriae*] on this first day of retreat in which the Master makes her penetrate the depths of the bottomless abyss so that He may teach her to fulfill the work which will be hers for eternity and which she must already perform in time, which is eternity begun.... 'Those whom God has foreknown He has also predestined to become conformed to the image of his divine Son' (Rom. 8:29), the One crucified by love. When I am wholly identified with this divine Exemplar, when I have wholly passed into Him and He into me, then I will fulfill my eternal vocation: the one for which God has 'chosen me in Him' (Eph. 1:4) *in principio,* the one I will continue *in aeternum* when, immersed in the bosom of my Trinity, I will be the unceasing praise of His glory, *Laudem gloriae ejus.*[1]

In this holy ignorance (*Nescivi!*), the soul no longer knows of spiritual vicissitudes. It has entered into the 'fortress of holy recollection'. 'And the soul thus simplified, unified, becomes the throne of the Unchanging One, since "unity is the throne of the Holy Trinity".'[2]

Eight days after her entry into the novitiate, the young virgin replied to a questionnaire set 'in a recreational form' (August 9, 1901). One of the questions was: 'Will you give a definition of prayer?' She answered: 'The union of the one who is not with the One who is.'[3]

We conclude by calling on a testimony in which nuptial mysticism

---

1984), p103. The texts in single quotes are from Ruysbroeck. 'In the beginning was nothing' signifies, I think, that 'nothing' out of which the creature is drawn (*ex nihilo*).

1. *The Complete Works,* vol. 1, p141.
2. Ibid., p143. The text in single quotes is from Ruysbroeck who speaks of the Unity of the divine Essence. With great boldness St Elizabeth makes of the deified soul the Throne of the Trinity!
3. *Œuvres complètes* (Paris: Cerf, 1991), p903.

and essence mysticism are conjoined in the most obvious fashion, just as it is, moreover, for the majority of the just presented texts. Again we have the testimony of a young woman, Marie-Antoinette de Geuser, who died in 1918 at the age of twenty-nine. Like Catherine of Genoa, she too was an autodidact of grace, so much the more as she never directly benefited from the teachings of Carmel to which, despite her desire, her health prevented her from being admitted. In 1911, she experienced a spiritual state of transformation into the Holy Trinity. 'In this state,' she explains,

> it seemed that my 'self' was dead and that God alone remained: it was somewhat as if His Unity, His Immensity, and even, I know not how, His Changelessness were subsisting within me. It was God alone and nothing of myself remained.[1]

To a friend she specifies:

> If the Word was made flesh, this was not to humble divinity, but to elevate humanity. After being humanized, if it can be said, to appreciate the human through you in yourself, He wants to divinize you to make you capable of enjoying the divine with Him in Himself.[2]

In 1917, she confided to her uncle:

> My life ever flows along in the bosom of the Blessed Trinity. This ineffable union of the Father, Son and Holy Spirit enraptures me more and more and wholly absorbs me. Lost in Love, I have been transformed into Christ and there I live under the Father's gaze.... Despite the variety of personal relationships of this life in God, it is always the consummation in unity that is for me

---

1. My citations are drawn from the book by Marie-Paule Vadez and Elisabeth Rimaud, *Un itinéraire mystique. De Marie-Antoinette de Geuser à Consummata* (Geneva: Ad Solem, 1974). Marie-Antoinette de Geuser has written no treatise, just letters (several of which are to her uncle, Father Anatole de Grandmaison), and some personal notes that were published anonymously in 1921 under the title: *Jusqu' au sommet de l'union divine, Consummata*, by Father Plus. Guénon could have read it. Other editions followed that had numerous readers. The work cited contains the essentials.

2. Op. cit., p301.

The Mystical Way

the heart of the matter. Through everything I remain little Consummata 'in the *Unum*', the one thing necessary.[1]

She has had in fact a revelation of her divine Name: 'Consumed in the One', *Consummata in Unum*. That is her vocation and apostolate:

> Yes, more than ever I feel myself to be in my vocation now that I am no longer and that He alone lives in me for His greater Glory. Totally freed from servitude to myself, I give away the divine treasures that I draw from their inexhaustible Source.

And she is quite distinctly aware of this glorified state:

> I know that our great God draws from His little Consummata the fullest and most perfect praise; I know that, while she only dreams of working for Him, He is pleased to clothe her in sparkling purple.[2]

And here, to end this chapter devoted to the mystical, and to conclude this book devoted to the Christian mystery, is a fragment of what might be called her 'spiritual testament'; I am arranging it in the form of a poem, as seems to be required by its rhythm and its beauty:

> For me, Consummata is a little thing
> Lost in God,
> Who no longer lives but with His life
> And who lives it more and more…
> She sees everything in the Truth,
> She does everything in Love,
> She lives in Unity!
> She knows and loves,
> She contemplates and acts
> With an unction-filled spontaneity.
> Delivered from the obscurities
> That veiled from her God's will,

1. Ibid., p312.
2. Ibid., p332.

And from the resistance that hindered its accomplishment,
She lives no longer but by this adorable Will,
In complete freedom.
She is free because she lives no longer,
She is an apostle because in her lives Christ.
This is the attribute of Consummata—
To *no longer be but one with God*.[1]

Appendix I:
Concerning the 'Evangelic Pearl'

The first French version (1602) of this astonishing text into which all of Flemish Rhineland spirituality flows and whose streams water all of the seventeenth century's mystical schools, has just been republished (February 1997) by Jérôme Millon in the Atopia series, in an edition established and presented by Daniel Vidal. The introduction —entitled 'The Terrible Blow of Nothingness'—calls, I think, for reservations to the extent that it seems to have a tendency to overemphasize what is judged to be the 'disruptive' character of this text with respect to ecclesial and theological norms; but it also presents all items of information necessary for reading it. In particular, we find there the status of the most recent research stimulated by this work, whose author—certainly a Flemish Beguine—remains unknown. But Carthusian circles in the Netherlands, Germany and France assured its spread. On this subject keep in mind that some information given by Louis Cognet in his *Histoire de la spiritualité chrétienne* (upon which we have relied for support) is incorrect. Thus it seems that the authorship of the Latin translation (1545) needs to be restored to Surius, and that the authorship of the French translation cannot be attributed to Dom Richard Beaucousin as was thought.

---

1. Ibid., p338; it is she herself who has emphasized the last words.

The Mystical Way

Obviously it was impossible to take this new edition into account which, four centuries after its first publication, testifies to the importance of *The Pearl*, and which, nevertheless, only splendidly confirms the general thesis of my own book on the true nature of the mystical way.

Appendix II:
Is St John of the Cross a Voluntarist?

As is to be observed by the emphasized terms, the act of will is still exercised, even at that very lofty degree of mystical union, which once more proves that mystical passivity should be understood in its profound nature, and is not to be confused with inertia and abandonment to all suggestions believed to come from 'on high', as Guénon seems to assume. After all (cf. the text cited in footnote 2, p 471), the human will is in that case identified with the divine Will that is the Holy Spirit, in other words the preeminent divine Energy: this 'passivity' is, then, supreme activity. Must we conclude from this that St John's way is purely 'voluntarist', that it consists above all in the rejection of natural desires and therefore in an exclusively moral and ascetic activity, equivalent to a negation of the intellect and to a disqualification of anyone of the intellectively spiritual type? A few declarations of the saint, which affirm that the natural power of the understanding only extends to knowledge of the sensory world are cited in support of this interpretation (*The Ascent of Mount Carmel*, bk 2, chap. 3, 1; *The Collected Works*, p 110), and the typical attitude of a devotional, anti-intellectualist temperament, projecting its own limitations on the transcendent nature of the intelligence, a nature that it is incapable of recognizing, is seen in this. But this way of presenting matters is itself only expressing an antichristian prejudice that prevents a reading of the texts as written. In the cited passage St John says exactly this: 'The intellect, by its own power comprehends only natural knowledge, although it is endowed, *of itself as well*, with a potency with respect to supernatural knowledge for that moment when Our Lord might wish to establish it in a supernatural act.'[1] In *The Dark Night* he writes: 'When the sensory appetites, gratifications, and supports are quenched, the intellect is left limpid and free to understand the truth' (bk 1, chap. 12, 4; p 322). To clarify, these sensory appetites, gratifications and supports are concerned here with *spiritual* experiences! A while later (bk 2, chap. 13, 11; p 361), speaking of the creation of the new man, he explains: 'This renovation is: an illumination of the human intellect with supernatural light so that it becomes divine, united with the divine.' Moreover, we should be careful with vocabulary: if, with St John, the intellect or understanding often refers to the natural order, this is because he calls 'spirit' the peak of the intelligence, that 'superior portion of the soul which refers to God and communicates with Him' (*The Ascent of Mount Carmel*, bk 3, chap. 26, 4; p 258). And, lastly, let us recall that, as Father Louis Lallement has shown in *La voie de l'Esprit* (Paris: Albin Michel, 1982, pp 120–152), the illumination of the intellect in unitive contemplation (the 'spiritual betrothals') implicitly, and sometimes explicitly, puts it in possession of a total cosmological knowledge, as well as a knowledge of certain secret aspects of the divine Essence.

On the Feast of the Holy Rosary
Nancy, France, October 7, 1997

---

1. The French translation, rather than the English one is followed in the latter half of this sentence. TR

Scriptural Index

OLD TESTAMENT

Genesis
  6:1, 403
  14:14, 112
  18:2–7, 400
  26:19, 275
  28:12–17, 59
  32:32, 175

Exodus
  4:10, 175
  29:7, 195

Tobit
  12:7, 323

2 Maccabees
  11:21, 199

Psalms
  104:15, 196

Wisdom of Solomon
  8:2, 109
  14:15, 220
  14:23, 220

Ecclesiasticus
  18:6, 240

Isaiah
  49:2, 266

Ezechiel
  1:1–28, 240

Zachariah
  4:2, 412

NEW TESTAMENT

Matthew
  3:11, 147, 343
  5:1–8:1, 243
  5:30, 275
  6:5–6, 322
  6:33, 448
  7:6, 321
  8:11–2, 101
  9:36, 135
  10:26–7, 135
  10:27, 270
  11:27, 223, 258, 265
  13:11, 133
  13:44, 338
  15:26–8, 101
  18:10, 137
  19:11, 253
  19:17–21, 390
  22:14, 136
  23:34, 273
  26:26–9, 327
  26:27, 136
  28:19, 137

Mark
  3:6, 103
  4:11, 25, 133, 221, 257
  4:12, 25, 311
  4:13, 222
  4:34, 135, 272
  7:36, 135
  9:9, 284
  9:44, 175
  12:13, 103
  14:22–5, 327

Luke
  2:1, 121
  2:19, 410
  4:16, 235
  4:16–20, 238
  7:47, 356
  8:10, 133, 221
  8:17, 135
  9:48, 137
  10:1, 254
  11:52, 242, 284
  12:3, 136
  12:12, 120
  18:16, 137
  22:14–20, 327
  22:19, 149
  22:20, 105
  24:25–7257
  24:27, 236

John
  1:21, 242
  1:26, 343
  1:27, 147
  1:38, 274
  1:49, 243
  3:1 ff, 340

3:2, 82
3:14, 243
3:16–7, 342
4:14, 275
4:21–4, 135
4:22, 198
4:42, 136, 225
6:56, 331
7:15, 238
7:16, 238
12:32, 448
14:6, 52
14:8, 51
14:26, 120
15:15, 424
19:38, 82

Acts of the Apostles
  2:37–41, 136
  10:36, 101
  10:44–6, 100
  11:26, 194, 199
  14:11, 32
  15, 120
  15:7, 8, 138
  16:4, 122
  16:24, 22
  16:33, 376
  17:34, 351
  28:35, 322

Romans
  1:17, 24
  1:20, 455
  4:11, 161
  6:3–4, 343
  8:29, 479
  9:27, 123
  10:12, 101

Scriptural Index

11:33, 247
12:2, 119
12:6, 147
16:25–6, 225

1 Corinthians
1:12, 283
2:6–8, 268
2:6–10, 226
2:7, 133
2:15, 256
4:1, 226
4:6, 268
5:12, 274
8:5, 245
11:19, 231
11:23, 307
11:23–7, 327
11:25, 105
12:8, 109
12:8–9, 147
13:12, 50, 143, 144
15:9, 146

2 Corinthians
1:21, 160
1:22, 161
2:14, 247
3:16, 148, 242
5:17, 385
11:6, 244
11:13, 274
12:2, 445
12:2–3, 244
12:2, 4, 244
12:3–4, 44
12:4, 267, 268, 310

Galatians

1:13–4, 199
3:26–7, 407
3:28, 227
4:3, 9, 247

Ephesians
1:4, 479
1:9, 301
1:13, 161
1:17–23, 246
2:13–5, 227
3:3, 301
3:3–9, 224
3:9, 226
3:16, 71
4:22–4, 71
4:30, 161
5:32, 301

Philipians
3:12, 270
3:15, 270

Colossians
1:15–7, 227
1:16–8, 245
1:19–20, 227
1:25–6, 227
1:25–7, 224
1:26, 252
1:27, 301
2:9, 227
2:12, 350

1 Timothy
1:2, 322
1:5, 273
2:4, 358
3:16, 301

2 Timothy
  2:19, 161
  4:13, 360

Hebrews
  1:3, 113
  5:6, 197
  6:1, 268
  6:19, 142
  7:1–18, 197
  7:3, 198
  7:6, 198
  9:3, 142
  9:3–5, 144
  9:3, 7, 142
  9:11–2, 142
  9:15, 106, 142
  9:24, 142
  10:1, 242, 262
  10:10, 142
  10:19–20, 142
  13:20, 106

1 Peter
  2:5–9, 162
  2:9, 197, 359
  3:15, 284
  3:20–1, 342
  3:21, 343

2 Peter
  1:4, 349
  1:5, 284
  1:16, 284
  1:18–9, 285
  1:20, 285

1 John
  1:1, 457
  4:8, 258

Apocalypse
  1:5, 343
  1:6, 162
  1:20, 301
  5:10, 162
  7:14, 343
  14:6, 263
  17:7, 301
  20:6, 162

General Index

Abd al-Wahid Yahya ('John, Servant of the One'), the Muslim name of René Guénon: 73.
Abraham, 20th–14th c. : 101, 106, 112, 161, 250, 400.
Acarie (*called* Madame), foundress of the Carmelite Order in France, 1566–1618: 471.
Agnes of Jesus, Carmelite and sister of St. Thérèse of Lisieux, 1851–1961: 460, 477.
Agrippa of Nettesheim (Henry Cornelius), German doctor and philosopher, 1486–535: 419.
Albert the Great (Saint), O.P., bishop and Doctor of the Church, 1200–1280: 421, 440.
Alembert (Jean Le Rond d'), French writer and mathematician, 1717–1783: 33.
Alexander of Alexandria, bishop, ?–326: 116, 124, 125.
Amann (Emile), priest, patrologist and historian of French theology, 1880–1948: 112.
Ambrose of Milan (Saint), bishop and Father of the Church, 339–397: 128, 262, 304, 330–1, 381–4, 388, 399, 411, 412.
André-Gillois (Monique), French phiosopher and theologian, 20th c.: 248.

Angelus Silesius (Johann Scheffler, *called*), German mystical poet, 1624–1677: 420.
Anomeans: cf. Eunomius.
Apuleius (Lucius), Latin writer, c. 125–c. 180: 216.
Argentan (Louis-François d'), French priest, spiritual author, 1614–1680: 422.
Aristotle, Greek philosopher, 384–322: 3, 4, 7, 8, 13, 15, 27, 30, 41–43, 64, 67, 69, 70, 204, 207, 213, 252, 262, 430, 431, 454.
Arius, Alexandrian priest, theologian and heresiarch, c. AD 280–336: 114, 116, 118–9, 125–27.
Asclepigeneia, initiator of Proclus into theurgy, daughter of Plutarch of Athens, great grand-daughter of Nestorios the Great, 5th c.: 214.
Asin Palacios (Miguel), Spanish arabist, 1871–1944: 467.
Atallah (Wahib), Hellenist of Lebanese origin, professor of Arabic, 20th c.: 217.
Athanasius of Alexandria (Saint), Father of the Church, c. 295–375: 115–120, 124–128, 304, 323.
Audet (J. P.), French priest, historian of early Christianity, 20th c.: 154.
Augustine (Saint), Latin language African theologian,

Father of the Church: 13, 32, 64, 81, 97, 160, 166, 188, 197, 215, 237, 275, 293, 300, 304, 311, 313, 320, 331, 399, 402, 408, 409, 411, 422, 423, 430, 434, 440.

Avicenna (Ibn Sina), Iranian philosopher and doctor, 980–1037: 56

Baader (Franz von), German philosopher, 1765–1841: 420.

Badarayana, supposed author of the *Brahmasutra*, between 300 BC and AD 300: 123.

Baker (Dom Augustine), O.S.B., English mystical writer, 1575–1641: 422.

Balthasar (Hans-Urs von), Swiss priest, theologian, philosopher and mystic, 1905–1988: 134, 171, 276, 352, 362.

Bardy (Gustave), French priest, patrologist, Church historian, 1881–1955: 273, 309–10, 316.

Bareille (Georges), French priest, professor of patrology, 1854–1928: 315.

Barmont (Luc), French writer, expert on sacred symbolism, 20th c.: 248.

Barnabas, Apostle, supposed author of an epistle: 122, 254, 280.

Bartmann (Mgr. Bernard), German theologian, 20th c.: 294.

Baruzi (Jean), French historian of philosophy, 1881–1950: 467.

Basil of Caesarea (Saint), bishop and Father of the Church, 330–379: 118, 128, 276, 305–307, 325–327, 399.

Batiffol (Pierre-Henri), French prelate, historian of early Christianity, 1861–1929:

Beaucousin (Dom Richard), French Carthusian, 1551–1610: 482. 297, 303, 311–313, 325, 328, 332, 334, 380, 381.

Bede, Venerable, English monk, Latin scholar, 674–735: 412.

Bellarmine (Saint Robert), S.J., Cardinal, Italian theologian, 1542–1621: 313.

Benamozegh (Elijah), Italian rabbi, philosopher and historian of the Kabbala, 1823–1900: 16.

Benedict of Nursia (Saint), patriarch of western monks, 480–547: 337.

Benedict of Canfeld (William Fitch, *called*), English Capuchin, mystical writer, 1562–1610: 471.

Benz (Ernst), German historian and theologian, 1907– : 420.

Berengarius of Tours, Latin language rationalizing theologian, c. 1000–1088: 416.

Bergier (Nicolas-Sylvestre), French priest theologian and controversialist, 1718–1790: 382.

Bergson (Henri), French philosopher, 1859–1941: 425.

Bernard of Clairvaux (Saint), Doctor of the Church, mystical theologian, founder of the Cistercians, 1090–1153: 76, 409, 422, 425.

Bernières de Louvigny (Jean de), lay mystic, founder of the

General Index

Hermitage of Caen, 1602–1659: 422.
Berthier (Abbé Joseph), French missionary and theologian, c. 1840–c. 1910: 31, 164.
Bertin (Francis), French latinist and historian of medieval thought, 20th c: 237.
Bérulle (Pierre de), French Cardinal, founder of the Oratory, 1575–1629: 422, 431, 435, 471–2.
Blanchard (Pierre), French historian of Christian literature, 20th c.: 409.
Blavatsky (Helena), Russian theosophist, 1831–1891: 450.
Boethius, Latin poet, philosopher and statesman, c. 470–c. 525: 113, 248, 411.
Boehme (Jacob), German theosopher, 1575–1624: 420.
Boileau (Nicolas), French writer, 1636–1711: 419.
Bona (Jean), Cardinal and theologian, 1609–1674: 382.
Bonaventure (Saint), O.F.M., Doctor of the Church and theologian, 1217–1274: 76, 421, 440, 447.
Boniface VIII, pope, 1235–1303: 417.
Bonnet-Eymard (Br. Bruno), French religious, archeologist and exegete, 20th c.: 103.
Bonneterre (Didier), French priest, historian of the liturgical movement, 20th c.: 193.
Boon (Nicolas), priest of Dutch origin, expert on sacred exegesis, 1920–1981: 248.
Bornkam (G.), German historian of theology, 20th c.: 194, 202.
Borret (Marcel), S. J., French hellenist, Origen specialist, 20th c.: 241, 269.
Bossuet (Jacques Bénigne), bishop, French writer, 1627–1704: 254, 478.
Botte (Dom Bernard), O.S.B., French historian and patrologist, 20th c.: 111.
Boulanger (André), French historian of religions, 20th c.: 207, 211.
Boularand (Ephrem), S.J., French historian of Arianism, 20th c.: 114, 116, 127.
Bouyer (Louis), priest of the Oratory, French theologian, 1913– : 111, 193, 200, 221, 223, 276, 299, 304, 305, 310, 316, 354, 378–381, 400, 401, 403, 426.
Brachet (Robert), French historian of philosophy, 20th c.: 209.
Bréhier (Emile), French historian of philosophy, 1876–1952: 251.
Brelich (Angelo), Italian historian of religions, 1913– : 96.
Brémond (Henri), French priest, historian of spirituality, 1855–1933: 436.
Briçonnet (Guillaume), bishop of Meaux, 1470–1534: 424.
Bugault (Guy), French philosopher and Indianist, 1917– : 66.
Bulwer Lytton (Sir Edward), English writer, 1803–1873: 450.
Burckhardt (Titus), Swiss arabic scholar, specialist in sacred art and cosmology, 1908–1984: 30, 75.

Burkert (Walter), professor of the history of religions at Zurich, 20th c.: 202–204, 206–213, 216–219.

Butler (Dom Cuthbert), O.S.B., English patrologist, 1856–1934: 409.

Cabrol (Dom Fernand), O.S.B., French liturgist, 1855–1937: 111.

Caesarius of Arles (Saint), bishop and Latin writer, 470–542: 110, 380.

Can Grande della Scala, a Italian politician and military leader to whom Dante dedicated one of his works, 1291–1329: 44.

Cano (Melchior), O.P., Spanish theologian, 1509–1560: 313.

Capelle (Dom Bernard), O.S.B., French historian of early Christianity, 20th c.: 303.

Carmignac (Jean), French priest, exegete, 20th c.: 221, 388.

Carpos, a Christian of Troas, disciple of St Paul, 1st c.: 360.

Casaubon (Issac), Genevan scholar and Calvinist theologian, 1559–1614: 313.

Casel (Dom Odo), O.S.B., German theologian and liturgist, 1886–1948: 192–194, 197, 198, 213, 223, 391.

Cassian, cf. John Cassian.

Castillon (André), S.J., French preacher, 1599–1671: 474.

Catherine of Genoa (Saint), mystic, 1447–1510: 465–467, 480.

Cayré (Fulbert), French Assumptionist, patrologist, 1884–1971: 409.

Celsus, Latin philosopher and scholar, spoke both Greek and Latin, adversary of Christianity, second half of the 2nd c.: 215, 231, 261, 263, 265, 268–272.

Certeau (Michel de), S.J., historian of mysticism, 20th c.: 399, 418, 419, 422.

Charbonneau-Lassay (Louis), expert on the emblems of Christ, 1871–1946: 72.

Charron (Pierre), French moralist, 1541–1603: 419.

Chauvet (Louis), French priest, theologian of the sacraments, 1942– : 178.

Chenêt (Jean-Claude), Christian philosopher, 20th c.: 164, 473.

Chenique (François), French logician and orientalist, 1927–: 40, 181, 436.

Chevalier (Jacques), French philosopher and historian of philosophy, 1882–1962: 435, 460.

Chittick (William C.), American Islamologist, 20th c.: 459.

Choin, cf. Joly

Chrétien de Troyes, French writer, 1135–1183: 77, 82.

Cicero, Latin orator, philosopher, and statesman, 106–43: 13, 70, 97, 113, 204.

Clamer (Albert), French priest, exegete, 1877–1963: 194.

Clasen (H.), German historian of early Christianity, 20th c.: 312.

Clement of Alexandria, Greek theologian, 150–216: 15, 114, 122, 155, 191, 215, 223, 241, 244, 246, 248–260, 262, 276, 278–280, 286, 288, 292, 295, 200,

General Index

356, 388, 399, 407, 423, 446.
Clement of Rome (Saint), 1st c. pope: 161, 306.
Clichtove (Josse), Flemish theologian and mathematician, 1471–1543: 419.
Clovis the First, king of the Franks, 466–511: 125.
Cognet (Louis), French priest, historian of spirituality, 20th c.: 427, 428, 438, 439, 463–466, 472, 472, 482.
Congar (Yves), O.P., Cardinal and French theologian, 1904–1995: 123, 171, 231, 259, 436.
Constant (Benjamin), French writer and politician, 1767–1830: 425.
Constant ('Abbé' Louis, *called* Eliphas Levi), French occultist, 1810–1875: 16, 18.
Constantia (Flavia), pro-Arian Romanian princess, half-sister of Constantine, ?–333: 125.
Constantine, Roman emperor, 270–337: 94, 107.
Corbin (Henry), French philosopher and Orientalist, 1903–1978: 73, 459.
Cornelius a Lapide (Cornelius van der Steen), S.J., Belgian Hebrew scholar and exegete, 1567–1637: 141.
Cousin (Victor), French philosopher, 1792–1867: 425.
Crampon (Augustin), French priest, exegete and Bible translator, 1826–1894: 141.
Crouzel (Henri), S. J., French patrologist, 20th c.: 114, 146, 147, 241, 250, 260–267, 270, 271,

276, 288, 299, 398, 403.
Cumont (Franz), Belgian philologist and archeologist, 1868–1947: 206, 303.
Cyprian of Carthage (Saint), bishop, Father of the Church, c. 205–258: 287.
Cyril of Alexandria, bishop, Doctor of the Church, c. 376–444: 189, 403.
Cyril of Jerusalem (Saint), bishop, Doctor of the Church, c. 315–386: 196, 291, 304, 305, 307, 318, 323–325, 353.

Daillé (Jean), French Calvinist theologian, 1594–1670: 314.
Dalbiez (Roland), French philosopher, 20th c.: 438.
Damascius, Greek Neoplatonist philosopher, c. 470–c. 544: 5, 64.
Damasus of Rome (Saint), Pope from 259–268: 115.
Danann (Alexandre de), Italian esoterologist, 20th c.: 208.
Daniélou (Jean), S.J., French Cardinal, theologian, and patrologist, 1905–1974: 103–4, 202, 228, 233, 237, 243–4, 247–249, 254, 260, 261, 286, 287, 315, 319, 339, 353, 387, 401, 403.
Dannhauer (J.G.), German language Protestant theologian, 1603–1666: 32.
Dante (Dante Alighieri), Italian poet and writer, 1265–1321: 43, 44, 46, 48, 78, 447.
Darboy (Georges), bishop of Nancy, then archbishop of Paris, 1813–1871: 376.

Decentius, bishop of Gubio, 5th c.: 332.
De Lange (N.), English language patrologist, 20th c.: 241.
Demetrius, bishop of Alexandria, adversary of Origin, ?–231: 288.
Demiéville (Paul), French indianist, 20th c.: 29, 124.
Denys of Alexandria (Saint), bishop, theologian, c. 195–265: 380.
Dionysius (or Denys) the Areopagite (Saint), mysterious theologian of the 1st c.: 70, 77–79, 204, 215, 276, 292, 319, 350–367, 369–371, 373–376, 380, 387, 389, 390, 399, 404, 408, 411, 413, 419–424, 431, 440, 446, 472.
Descartes (René), French philosopher and mathematician, 1596–1650: 434.
Devoucoux (Jean-Sébastien), bishop of Evreux, archeologist, and symbolist, 1804–1870: 248.
Diderot (Denis), French writer, 1713–1784: 33.
Dilthey (Wilhelm), German philosopher, 1833–1911: 33.
Diogenes Laertes, Greek historian of philosophy, first half of the 3rd c.: 121.
Doresse (Jean), French egyptologist and orientalist, 20th c.: 289.
Dublanchy (Edmond), French priest, Marist theologian, 1853–1938: 122.
Duchesne (Louis), French priest, historian of the early Church, 1843–1922: 127, 237, 325.
Dumas (Alexander), French writer, 1802–1870: 16.
Duperron (Jacques Davy), French Cardinal, controversialist, 1556–1618: 313.
Dupont (Dom Jacques), O.S.B., French exegete, 20th c.: 194.
Dupont-Sommer (André), French orientalist and Hebrew scholar, ?–1983: 103.
Dupuis (Charles-François, *called* Citizen), French savant and statesman, 1753–1809: 314.
Dürer (Albert), German engraver, painter, and mathematician, 1471–1528: 248
Duval (Yves-Marie), French academic, latinist, 20th c.: 229.
Duvergier de Hauranne (Jean, Abbé of St Cyran), French theologian, 1581–1647: 475.

Eckhart (Johann, *called* Meister), German theologian and mystic, 1260–1327: 5, 13, 42, 76, 189, 406, 420, 421, 424, 427, 428, 436, 472.
Eliade (Mircea), history of religions, Romanian by birth, 1907–1986: 218.
Elizabeth of the Trinity (Saint), French mystic, 1880–1906: 477, 479.
Emmerich (Anne-Catherine), German mystic, 1774–1824: 396, 444, 467.
Epicurius, Greek philosopher, 341–270: 210.
Epiphanius (Saint), bishop of Salamis, heresiologist and

General Index

scholar, c. 315–403: 321, 323.
Esnoul (Anne-Marie), French sanscritist, 20th c.: 476.
Estienne (Henri, *called* Henri II), French philologist and humanist, 1531–1598: 202.
Etheria (or Egeria, or Eucheria, or Sylvia), Spainish (or Provencal) lady, author of a journal about travel to the East, 4th or 5th c.: 325.
Eunomius, Arian bishop of Cyzic, c. 320–392; his supporters, the eunomians, were also called 'anomians' (from *anomios* = dissimilar) because they held that the Son was non-similar to the Father: 118, 127.
Eusebius of Caesarea, Father of the Church, Syro-Palestinian Greek writer, 265–340: 113, 119, 125, 128, 237, 254, 262, 286, 288, 304, 306, 380, 399, 400.
Eusebius of Nicomedia, Arian bishop of Constantinople, c. 280–341: 113.
Evagrius of Pontus, monk and mystical theologian, 346–399: 387, 399, 400, 406, 446, 449,.
Evola (Julius), Italian esoterist philosopher, 1898–1974: 300.

Faivre (Antoine), French historian of esoterism, 20th c.: 1.
Faustus of Milevis, Latin language Manichean writer, 4th–5th c.: 215.
Fénelon (François de Salignac de la Mothe), French bishop and writer, 1651–1715: 420, 423, 438, 471, 475.
Festugière (André-Jean), O.P., French hellenist, history of late antiquity, 1898–1982: 27, 202, 203, 205, 206, 214, 221.
Ficino (Marsilio), Italian priest, platonist philosopher, 1433–1499: 421.
Filliozat (Jean), French Indianist, 20th c.: 29.
Flavius Josephus, Aramean and Greek language Jewish historian, 37–100: 103, 141, 143.
Fontaine (Jacques), French latinist, 20th c.: 229, 301.
Francis of Assisi (Saint), founder of the Friars Minor, 1181–1226: 449, 450.
Francis de Sales (Saint), bishop of Geneva, mystic, and writer, 1567–1622: 423.
Fraser (James George), English ethnologist, 1854–1941: 218.
Fronton (Marcus), Latin rhetorician, preceptor of Marcus Aurelius, defender of paganism, c. 100–c. 175: 320.
Funk (Francis Xavier), German priest, philosopher, jurist, theologian, historian, 1840–1907: 313.

Gadamer (Hans-Georg), German philosopher, 20th c.: 33.
Gandillac (Maurice de), French historian of philosophy, 20th c.: 352, 404.
Garnier (François), French priest, specialist in medieval symbolism, 20th c.: 247.
Garrigou-Lagrange (Réginald),

O.P., French theologian, 1877–1964: 437, 440.
Genot-Bismuth (Jacqueline), prof. of Hebraic language and literature, 20th c.: 238, 243.
Gernet (Louis), historian of religions, 20th c.: 207, 211.
Gerson (Jean Charlier *called*), French priest, preacher, and theologian, 1363–1429: 399.
Geuser (Marie Antoinette de), French mystic, 1889–1918: 480.
Ghellinck (Joseph de), S.J., Belgian theologian and historian of theology, 1872–1950: 111, 302.
Gilson (Etienne), French philosopher, historian of medieval philosophy, 1884–1978: 431, 434, 447.
Gioberti (Vincenzo), Italian priest, philosopher and politician, 1801–1852: 15.
Gœthe (Wolfgang), German writer, 1749–1832: 434.
Goichon (Anne-Marie), orientalist and historian of Arab philosophy, 1894–1977: 56.
Gorceix (Bernard), historian of German spirituality, 20th c.: 424.
Graef (Hilda), English language Catholic theologian, 20th c.: 459.
Grandmaison (Léonce de), S.J., French theologian, exegete, and historian, 1868–1927: 123.
Gregory I (Saint *called* the Great), Pope, Father of the Church, c. 540–604: 411.
Gregory of Nazianzus (Saint), bishop, Father of the Church, 329–390: 276, 299, 305, 325, 354, 388, 400.
Gregory of Nyssa, Greek theologian, brother of St Basil, c. 335–395: 276, 305, 325, 339, 353, 387, 400, 403, 404, 408, 411, 436, 440.
Gribomont (Jean), French patrologist, 20th c.: 301.
Grillmeier (Aloys), S.J., German historian of dogma, 1910– : 112.
Grunewald (Mathias), German painter, 1465–1528: 429.
Guennou (Jean), priest of the foreign missions, historian of spirituality, 20th c.: 473.
Guénon (René), French metaphysician, interpreter of eastern Traditions, 1886–1951: 1–3, 7–9, 13, 14, 17, 18, 23, 28, 30, 34, 35, 40–42, 52–57, 63, 64, 70, 72–74, 76–81, 83, 85, 89–96, 99–104, 106, 107, 112, 113, 115, 121, 124, 126, 133, 136–140, 142, 144, 145, 150–152, 155–160, 163, 166, 167, 175, 178–180, 185, 186, 189, 190, 192, 196, 205, 207, 220, 226, 278, 294, 297, 312, 326, 338, 342, 347, 348, 350, 354, 364, 375, 377, 378, 383, 384, 389, 392, 394–396, 401, 411, 420, 424, 426, 428, 437, 439, 440, 442–445, 448–453, 455–457, 459, 467, 480, 483.

Works:

The Crisis of the Modern World (1927): 394.
The Great Triad (1946): 41.
Initiation and Spiritual Realization (1952): 53, 439, 452.

General Index

Insights into Christian Esoterism (1954): 76, 78, 90, 94, 95, 102, 103, 107, 136, 157, 297, 364.

Insights into Islamic Esoterism and Taoism (1973): 31, 56, 467.

Introduction to the Study of the Hindu Doctrines (1921): 93, 189.

Man and His Becoming according to the Vedānta (1925): 78, 93.

Multiple States of the Being (1932): 30, 226.

Perspectives on Initiation (1946): 52, 93, 160, 175, 179, 294, 342, 347, 440, 444, 449, 451, 467.

The Spiritist Fallacy (1923): 13, 18.

Spiritual Authority and Temporal Power (1929): 395, 457.

Symbolism of the Cross (1931): 64.

Theosophy: History of a Pseudo-Religion (1921): 13, 450.

Guéranger (Dom Prosper), O.S.B., French liturgist, 1805–1875: 382.

Guyon (Jeanne Marie Bouvier de la Motte), French quietist mystic, 1648–1717: 475.

Hadewijch of Antwerp, Beguine, mystic, and poet, 13th c.: 427.

Hadot (Pierre), French historian of ancient philosophy, 1922– : 387.

Hallaj (Abu' Abdullah al-Hosain ibn Mansur al), Muslim mystic, 857–922: 79.

Hamelin (Octave), French philosopher and historian of philosophy, 1856–1907: 15.

Hamman (Adalbert-Gauthier), O.F.M., historian of early Christianity and patrologist, 1910– : 316.

Hani (Jean), French hellenist, historian of religions, and symbolism, 20th c.: 210, 212, 247.

Hanson (R.P.C.), English Hellenist, historian of early Christianity, 20th c.: 240.

Harl (Marguerite), French Hellenist and Patrologist, 20th c.: 134, 147, 148.

Harphius (Henri de Herp, *called*), O.F.M., mystical writer, ?–1477: 472.

Hegel (Georg W.F.), German philosopher, 1770–1831: 20, 35.

Heidegger (Martin), German philosopher, 1889–1976: 33.

Heracleon, Greek-language Valentinian gnostic, end of 2nd c.: 114.

Hermas, author of *The Shepherd* (in Greek), 2nd c.: 347.

Hermes Trismegistus, name given by the Greeks to the Egyptian god Thoth, revealer of the arts and sciences: 32.

Herodotus, Greek historian, c. 484– c. 420: 206.

Hilary of Poitiers (Saint), bishop, Doctor and Father of the Church, 315–367: 112, 128, 304.

Hilduin, Latin language chronicler, c. 770– c. 856: 411.

Hippolytus of Rome (Saint), Greek language exegete and theologian, c. 170–235: 111, 306, 316, 321, 379.

Homer, Greek poet, 9th c. BC: 205.

Hugo (Victor), French writer, 1802–1885: 16.
Husserl (Edmund), German philosopher, 1859–1938: 33.
Hypatius of Ephesus, bishop, denied the apostolicity of the Areopagite writings, ?–545: 376.

Iamblichus, Greek philosopher, neoplatonist, disciple of Porphyry, c. 250–330: 212.
Ibn 'Arabi (Mohyiddin), Arab theosopher and mystic, 1165–1240: 73, 459.
Ibn Sina, cf. Avicenna.
Ignatius of Antioch (Saint), bishop and Father of the Church, c. 35– c. 110: 122, 134, 135, 154, 155, 199.
Ignatius of Loyola (Saint), Basque mystic, founder of the Company of Jesus. 1491–1556: 440.
Innocent I (Saint), pope, ? –417: 332, 381.
Innocent XII, pope, 1615–1700: 438.
Irenaeus of Lyon (Saint), Church Father, c. 130– c. 208: 108, 111, 114, 235, 247, 256–259, 283, 319–320, 350, 384, 388.
Isidore of Seville (Saint), bishop, Doctor of the Church, encyclopedist and theologian, c. 560–636: 97.
Isocrates, Greek orator, 436–338: 211.

James (William), American philosopher, 1842–1910: 425.

Javelet (Robert), French priest, theologian and medievalist, 1914–1986: 399.
Jean de Saint-Samson, French Carmelite, 1571–1636: 422.
John Cassian (Saint), monk and Latin language theologian, c. 350– c. 435: 411.
John Chrysostom (Saint), bishop, Church Father, c. 344–407: 126, 305–6, 328–31, 380.
John of the Cross (Saint), Doctor of the Church, Spainish theologian, mystic and poet, 1542–1591: 396, 420–423, 427, 435, 436, 440, 442–444, 460, 462, 467, 468, 471, 476–478, 484.
John of Saint Thomas, O.P., Portugese theologian and philosopher, 1589–1644: 62, 169.
John the Scot (*called* Eriugena), Irish philosopher and theologian, 810–870: 411, 421, 433.
John XXIII, pope, 1881–1963: 129.
Jeremias (Alfred), German Protestant biblist, assyriologist, and theologian, 1864–1935: 223.
Jerome (Saint), Father of the Church, c. 347–420: 141, 241, 293, 301, 399, 411.
Joly de Choin (Albert-Louis), bishop of Toulouse, liturgist, 1702–1759: 382.
Jonah, Jewish prophet, 8th c. BC: 342.
Joseph of Arimathea, Jewish notable, 1st c.: 82, 83.
Joseph de Ste Marie, O.C.D., French theologian, 1931–1985: 193.

General Index

Joseph of the Holy Spirit, Spanish Carmelite, theologian of mysticism, 1667–1736: 438.
Juda the Saint (or the Prince), Mishnah scribe, 135–217: 240.
Julian the Apostate, Roman emperor, 331–363: 125.
Jungmann (Joseph Andrew), Austrian priest, historian of the liturgy, 1889–1973: 199, 317, 333, 378, 379.
Justin (Saint), philosopher and martyr, c. 100– c. 165: 217, 218, 319–321.
Justinian I, Eastern emperor, 482–565: 380.

Kant (Immanuel), German philosopher, 1724–1804: 47, 48, 120, 424.
Kelly (J.N.D.), Anglican patrologist, 20th c.: 117.
Kittel (G.), German language Protestant exegete, 20th c.: 141.

Labriolle (Pierre Champagne de), French latinist and historian, 1874–1940: 215, 216, 320.
Lacombe (Olivier), French indianist, 1904– : 29, 124.
Lactantius, Latin language Christian writer, c. 260– c. 325: 97, 304.
Lallement (Louis), S.J., spiritual director, 1587–1635: 474.
Lallement (Louis), French priest, theologian of the spiritual life, 1907–1986: 484.
Laneau (Louis), French prelat of the foreign missions, 1637–1696: 473.

Lanteri (Bruno), Italian priest, founder of the Oblates of the Virgin Mary, 1759–1830: 424.
Larchet (Jean-Claude), French Patrologist, 20th c.: 413.
Lassiat (Henri), French historian and Patrologist, 20th c.: 107.
Laurant (Jean-Pierre), French historian of esoterism, 20th c.: 14, 16, 237.
Le Boulluec (Alain), French Patrologist, 20th c.: 253.
Lebreton (Jules), S.J., French theologian and historian of early Christianity, 1873–1956: 147, 261, 263.
Le Brun (Pierre), priest of the Oratory, French liturgist, 1661–1729: 378.
Lefèbvre (Marcel), French archbishop, 1905–1991: 170.
Legasse (Simon), French priest, exegete, 20th c.: 141
Leibniz (G.W.), German philosopher and mathematician, 1646–1716: 418, 420.
Léon de Saint-Jean, French Carmelite, Dionysian and Theresian scholar, 1600–1671: 422.
Léon-Dufour (Xavier), French exegete, 20th c.: 194, 202.
Leo XIII, pope, 1810–1903: 323.
Lepelley (Claude), French historian, 20th c.: 334.
Lépin (Marius), Suplician, French exegete and theologian, 1870–1952: 193.
Leroux (Pierre), French writer and socialist, 1797–1871: 16.
Levi (Eliphas), cf. Constant.
Liberius, pope, ?–366: 125.

Lings (Martin), English orientalist, 20th c.: 74.
Loisy (Alfred), French exegete, 1857–1940: 104, 314, 407.
Lombard, cf. Peter.
Lonergan (Bernard), S.J., English patrologist and theologian, 20th c.: 118.
Louis of Blois (Dom Blossius), O.S.B., Flemish mystic, 1506–1566: 464.
Luis de Leon, Spainish priest, theologian and mystic, 1527–1591: 457.
Lubac (Henry de), S.J., French Cardinal, theologian and historian of theology, 1896–1991: 64, 120, 171, 242, 249, 339, 398, 399, 414–416.
Lucian of Samosata, Greek rhetorician and philosopher, c. 125– c. 192: 15.
Lucifer of Calgiliari, anti-Arian bishop, ?–371: 128.
Lucretius, Latin poet, c. 98–58: 97.
Luther (Martin), German monk, founder of Protestantism, 1483–1546: 178, 399, 432.

Mabillon (Dom Jean), O.S.B., Maurist, theologian and historian, 1632–1707: 378.
Macarius the Egyptian (Saint), Syro-Palestinian Father of the Church, c. 301–391: 403.
McDonnel (Kilian), O.S.B., American patrologist, 20th c.: 155, 315, 322.
Macrobius, Latin writer and grammarian, end of the 4th– beginning of the 5th c.: 212.
Madhva, Hindu philosopher, interpreter of the *Vedanta*, 1199–1278: 123.
Maldonnat (John), S.J. Spanish exegete and theologian, 1533–1583: 141.
Mallet-Joris (Françoise), French writer, 20th c.: 475.
Manes or Mani or Manichee, founder of the Manichean religion (Mesopotamia), 216–277: 116.
Mangenot (Joseph Eugène), French priest, exegete, theologian and scholar, 1856–1922: 33.
Marcus Aurelius, Roman emperor, 121–180: 320.
Marcion, Greek philosopher and Christian gnostic, c. 85–c. 160: 321.
Marconis de Nègre (Jacques Etienne), French esoterist, 1795–1868: 16.
Maréchal (Joseph), S.J., Belgian philosopher, 1878–1944: 426.
Margerie (Bernard de), French theologian and historian of theology, 20th c.: 118.
Marie du Saint-Sacrement, French Carmelite, translator of St John of the Cross, 1861–1939: 462.
Marinus, Greek philosopher, Neoplatonist, 5th–6th c.: 214.
Maritain (Jacques), French philosopher and theologian, 1882–1973: 63, 431, 436, 469.
Markus (R.A.), historian of early Christianity, 20th c.: 230.

General Index

Marrou (Henri-Irenée), French historian of pagan and Christian antiquity, 1904–1977: 125, 126, 262, 298, 306, 334, 335.

Martelet (Gustave), S.J., French thinker, 20th c.:295.

Martène (Dom Edmund), O.S.B., Maurist scholar, 1654–1739: 378.

Martimort (Aimé-Georges), French liturgist, 20th c.: 315, 318, 337, 379.

Martin-Dubost (Paul), French Orientalist, 20th c.: 449.

Matter (Jacques), French historian of Gnosticism, 1791–1864: 16.

Maximus the Confessor (Saint), Greek monk and theologian, c. 580–662: 352, 380, 413.

Méhat (André), French hellenist, 20th c.: 15, 155, 244, 252, 258, 262.

Meile (Pierre), French Indianist, 20th c.: 29, 124.

Melchisedek, priest on the Most High and king of Salem in the time of Abraham: 142, 143, 162, 197.

Meliton of Sardis (Saint), bishop, writer and theologian, 2nd c.: 237, 239.

Mesnard (Jean), French historian specializing in the seventeenth century, 20th c.: 418.

Meunier (Bernard), historian of the Church, 20th c.: 118.

Michelet (Jules), French historian, 1798–1874: 16.

Minucius Felix (Marcus), Christian apologist originally from Africa, 2nd–3rd c.: 320.

Moine (Claudine), the 'mystic seamstress', 1618– after 1655: 373, 374.

Moses, lawgiver of Israel, 13th c. BC: 263, 264, 284, 314, 327, 342, 403, 404, 412.

Montague (George T.), American Marist and bible scholar, 20th c.: 155, 315, 322.

Mora (Vincent), O.S.B., French exegete, 20th c.: 243.

Morel (Georges), French philosopher and theologian, 20th c.: 443.

Müller (Max), German Indianist, 1823–1900: 123.

Murray (Philippe), French writer, 20th c.: 16.

Mylonas (G. E.), American historian of religions, 20th c.: 205.

Nagarjuna, Buddhist philosopher, 2nd c.: 5.

Narsai, Doctor of the Church of Edessa (Diophysite), ?–502: 307, 238.

Nestorios ("the Great"), Eleusinian hierophant under Valens, astrologer, and psychotherapist, grandfather of Plutarch of Athens, 4th c.: 214

Newman (John Henry), English Cardinal, theologian, historian and philosopher, 1801–1890: 123.

Nicholas I, pope, 800–867: 382.

Nicholas of Cusa (Nikolaus Krebs, *called*), Cardinal, German and Latin language philosopher, mathematician,

theologian, 1401–1464: 13, 76, 421, 434.
Nicodemus, a "master in Israel", 1st c.: 82.
Nicolas (Jean Hervé), O.P., French theologian, 1910– : 295.
Nicomachus of Gerasa, Greek mathematician, end of 1st c.: 248.
Nimbarka, Hindu philosopher, interpreter of the *Vedanta*, 13th c.: 123.
Noah, patriarch at the time of the deluge: 342.
Numenius of Apameit, Greek philosopher, neoplatonist, 2nd c.: 212.

Orcibal (Jean), French historian of spirituality, 20th c.: 419, 421, 437, 466, 472.
Origen, Alexandrian philosopher, exegete and theologian, 185–254: 32, 109–111, 114, 122, 126, 134, 143–149, 155, 188, 191, 215, 223, 231–233, 237, 240–242, 244, 246, 248–250, 260–276, 278, 286–289, 291, 292, 299, 306, 311, 322, 326, 384, 387, 388, 398, 399, 402, 403, 411, 427, 436.
Ossius (or Hosius), bishop of Cordova, religious counsellor of Constantine, c. 257–357: 113, 117.
Ovid, Latin poet, 43 BC–AD 17: 97.

Pallis (Marco), English orientalist, specialist in Tibetan Buddhism, 1895–1989: 139, 140, 145.
Pantanaeus, Stoic convert, first head of the Christian school of Alexandria, 2nd c.: 260.
Pascal (Blaise), writer, mathematician, physicist and Christian thinker, 1623–1662: 418.
Paschasius Radbertus, French monk and theologian, c. 785–865: 415.
Patrizzi (Francesco), Italian writer and philosopher, 1529–1597: 419.
Paul of Samosata, (scandalous) bishop of Antioch, c. 200– after 273: 115.
Pépin (Jean), French historian of early Christianity, 1924– : 241.
Perrone (Lorenzo), Italian historian of Christianity, 20th c.: 113, 120.
Pétau (Denys), S.J., learned French theologian, patrologist, 1583–1652: 313.
Pétrement (Simone), French philosopher, historian of Gnosticism, 20th c.: 357.
Philo of Alexandria, Greek language Jewish philosopher and exegete, c. 20 BC–c. AD 50: 103, 241, 249–251, 256, 359, 387.
Philostorgius, Greek historian of the Church, moderate anomian, critic of Arius and disciple of Eunomius, c. 370– after 425: 127.
Photius (or Potios), patriarch of Constantinople, Byzantine theologian and scholar, c. 820–c. 895: 127.
Pico de la Mirandola (John), Italian humanist and philosopher, 1463–1494: 64.
Piedagnel (Auguste), French

General Index

priest of the Oratory, Patrologist, 20th c.: 328.
Pius XI, pope, 1857–1939: 440.
Peter Canisius (Saint), German theologian and mystic, 1521–1597: 463.
Peter of Alexandria (Saint), bishop, ?–311: 127.
Peter Lombard (Pietro Lombardo), Latin theologian, c. 1100–1160: 152.
Piétri, (Charles), French latinist and archaeologist, director of the French School of Rome, 20th c.: 229, 301.
Pindar, Greek poet, 518–438: 205.
Pirot (Louis), French priest, exegete, 1881–1939: 194.
Pitra (J. B.), French Cardinal, learned Benedictine, 1812–1889: 237.
Plato, Greek philosopher, 427–347: 4, 5, 7, 8, 27, 31, 42, 64, 65, 69, 209, 211, 215, 250, 252, 263, 272, 273, 387, 425, 430, 431.
Plotinus, Greek philosopher, Platonist, 205–270: 64, 114, 262.
Plutarch of Athens, Greek philosopher, distant successor of Plato at the head of the Academy (diadochus), "spiritual grandfather" of Proclus, c. 350–430: 214.
Plutarch of Chaeronea, Greek writer, philosopher and historian, c. 50–c. 125: 207, 210–212, 214, 305, 387.
Polycarp (Saint), bishop of Smyrna, c. 69–155: 111.
Ponsoye (Emmanuel), French hellenist and patrologist, 20th c.: 413.
Ponte (Renato de), Italian esoterist, 20th c.: 300.
Porphyry, Greek philosopher, disciple of Plotinus, c. 232–c. 305: 114, 262.
Pouchet (Dom Robert), O.S.B., French patrologist specializing in St Basil, 20th c.: 325.
Poulain (Augustin François), S.J., French theologian of mysticism, 1836–1919: 438.
Poulat (Emile), French historian of modern Catholicism, 20th c.: 237.
Poullart des Places (Claude François), founder of the Congregation of the Holy Spirit, 1679–1709: 424.
Prat (Ferdinand), S.J., French theologian and exegete, 1857–1938: 224, 225, 228.
Proclus, Greek philosopher, Neoplatonist, 412–485: 30, 64, 70, 212–214, 219, 363.
Pruche (Benoît), O. ., French Patrologist, 20th c.: 326.
Prudentius, Latin Christian poet originally from Spain, 348–c. 415: 216.
Ptolemy, Greek speaking Valentinian of the italic school, 2nd c.: 114.

Ramanuja, Hindu philosopher, interpreter of the *vedanta*, 1017–1137: 123.
Ravaisson (Félix), French philosopher and archaeologist, 1813–1900: 425.
Reitzenstein (Richard), German

historian of religions, 1861–1931: 208, 210, 314.

Renan (Ernest), French writer, 1823–1892: 103, 104, 217, 314, 407.

Renaudin (Dom Paul), O.S.B., French theologian, mariologist (the dogma of the Assumption), 1864–1947: 189.

Renou (Louis), French Indianist, 20th c.: 124.

Reyor (Jean, pseudonym of Marcel Clavelle), French esoterist, Guénonian, 1905–1985: 138.

Richard de Randonvilliers (J.B.), French lexicographer, 19th c.: 16.

Richard of Saint Victor, Latin language Scots or Irish theologian, 1110–1173: 447.

Richelieu (Armand Jean du Plessis, duc de), Cardinal, French statesman, 1585–1642: 475.

Ricoeur (Paul), French philosopher, 1913– : 33.

Riffard (Pierre), French esoterist, 20th c.: 14.

Robert de Boron, French writer, end of the 13th c.: 77, 81.

Roguet (A.M.), O.P., French theologian, 20th c.: 160, 170.

Roman (Denys, pseudonym of Marcel Maugy), Masonic writer, ?–1986: 424.

Roques (René), historian of Christian thought, 20th c.: 351–354, 358, 363, 364, 373, 374, 387, 404.

Rordorf (Willy), historian of early Christianity, writes in French, 20th c.: 154.

Rousseau (Adelin), monk of Orval Abbey, Patrologist, 20th c.: 283.

Rudhardt (J.), Swiss historian of Greek religion, 20th c.: 96, 211.

Rufinus of Aquilea, Latin language theologian, Church historian, translator of Origen, c. 340–410: 398.

Rufinus the Syrian, monk and collaborator with St Jerome, adversary of the Origenist Rufinus of Aquilea, 4th c.: 301.

Ruyer (Raymond), French philosopher, 1902–1987: 40.

Ruysbroeck (Jan van, *called* the Admirable), Flemish mystic, 1293–1381: 427, 478.

Sabellius, heresiarch priest, born in Lybia, 3rd c.: 115, 125.

Saint-Cyran, cf. Duvergier.

Saint-Germain (Comte de), time-traveller, 1707–1784: 449.

Saint-Martin (Louis-Claude de), French philosopher, 1745–1803: 396.

Sand (George), French novelist, 1804–1876: 16.

Sandaeus (Maximilian Van der Sandt), S.J., German scholar, mystical writer, 1578–1656: 419.

Sartre (Jean-Paul), French writer and philosopher, 1902–1974: 407.

Satolli (Francis), Italian Cardinal, Thomist theologian, 1839–1910: 189.

Saudreau (Auguste), French priest, theologian of mysti-

General Index

cism, 1859–1946: 438.
Saussure (Ferdinande), Swiss linguist, 1857–1913: 130.
Scheeben (Mattias Joseph), German priest, theologian, 1835–1888: 46.
Schelstrate (Emmanuel), Antwerp priest, prefect of the Vatican Library, 1648–1692: 314, 325.
Schlegel (Friedrich von), German romantic thinker, 1772–1829: 425.
Scleiermacher (Friedrich), German pastor, philosopher, and theologian, 1768–1834: 33.
Scholem (Gershom), German-born Hebrew scholar, historian of the Kaballah, 1897–1982: 240.
Schopenhauer (Arthur), German philosopher, 1788–1860: 48.
Schuon (Frithjof), Swiss thinker, 1907–1998: 140.
Scrima (André), Orthodox bishop, 20th c.: 392.
Seneca, Latin philosopher and dramatist, c. 4 B. C.–65 A. D.: 13, 113.
Sesboüé (Bernard), French priest, Church historian, 20th c.: 118.
Sévigné (Marie de Rabutin-Chantal, marquise de), French writer, 1626–1696: 418.
Shankara, Hindu philosopher, interpreter of the *vedānta*, 788–820: 4, 30, 123, 442, 443, 449, 460.
Simon (Meister), Rhineland(?) theologian, 12th c.: 416.

Smith (Morton), English hellenist and historian of early Christianity, 20th c.: 223.
Socini (Fausto), Italian humanist, supporter of antitrinitarianism, inspirer, with his uncle, Lelio Socini, of the Socinian sect, 1539–1604: 119.
Socrates, lawyer at Constantinople, Church historian, successor of Eusebius of Cesarea, c. 380–c. 450: 119.
Solon, Greek law-giver, c. 640–c. 558: 27.
Sozomen, lawyer at Constantinople, Church historian, c. 390–c. 443: 332.
Spicq (Bernard, in religion: Ceslas), O.P., French exegete and Hellenist scholar, 1901–1992: 194.
Stéphane (Henri, pseudonym of André Gircourt), French priest, theologian, 1907–1985: 9, 445, 446.
Stolz (Dom Anselm), O.S.B., German theologian, 1900–1942: 384, 409.
Stroumsa (Gedaliahu Guy), historian of religions, 20th c.: 161, 223, 230, 231, 240, 260, 261, 312, 313, 319.
Surin (Jean Joseph), S.J., mystical writer, 1600–1665: 419.
Surius (Laurent Sauer, *called*), Carthusian humanist and hagiographer, 1522–1578: 482.
Susini (Eugène), Germanist (French), 20th c.: 420.
Suso (Henri Seuse, *called*), O.P., Rhineland theologian and

mystic, 1295–1366: 427, 428, 440, 458.
Swedenborg (Emmanuel), Swedish visionary and scientist, 1688–1772: 459.
Sylvester I, pope, ?–355: 117.
Symeon the New Theologian (Saint), Byzantine theologian and poet, c. 949–1022: 348, 386.
Synesius of Cyrene, bishop of Ptolemais, Greek language poet and neoplatonist philosopher, c. 370–c. 415: 204.
Syrianus, Greek Neoplatonist, teacher of Proclus, c. 380–c. 438: 64.

Tardieu (Michel), French priest, Hellenist and Orientalist, historian of Gnosticism, 20th c.: 239.
Tauler (John), O.P., Rhineland theologian, preacher and mystic, 1300–1361: 421, 424, 427, 440, 458, 466, 472.
Taveneaux (René), historian of Classical age Catholicism, 20th c.: 475.
Teresa of Avila (Saint), reformer of Carmel, Doctor of the Church, 1515–1582: 420, 421, 427, 428, 437–440, 460–462, 466, 467, 471, 478.
Tertullian, African Latin language theologian, apologist and heretic, c. 155–c. 225: 155, 229, 303, 311, 320–323, 329, 330, 334, 388.
Theoctistus, bishop of Caesarea, friend of Origen, 3rd c.: 288.

Theodore of Mopsuesta, bishop, the greatest exegete of the Antiochian school, c. 350–428: 353.
Theodoret of Cyr, bishop, Church historian, c. 393– c. 460: 119, 127, 304, 400.
Theodotus, unknown gnostic, disciple of Valentinian, 2nd c.: 356.
Theresa of Lisieux (Saint), Carmelite, Doctor of the Church, 1873–1897: 311, 407, 459, 460, 475–478.
Thibaut (George), German born and English language indianist, second half of the 19th c.: 123.
Thiede (Carsten Peter), German paleographer, 20th c.: 103.
Thomas (Dom Corbinien), O.S.B., German language exegete, 1694–1767: 32.
Thomas (Edmé), French canon, archeologist, 17th c.: 248.
Thomas a Kempis, Flemish mystical writer, 1380–1471: 427.
Thomas Aquinas, Catholic theologian, 1225–1274: 3, 13, 43, 76, 141, 148, 149, 159–162, 164, 168–170, 189, 197, 275, 292, 293, 385, 391, 421, 431, 432, 437, 439–441, 447.
Thomas of Jesus, Spainish Carmelite, 1564–1627: 419, 437.
Thomas Gallus, Dionysian theologian, ?–1246: 421.
Thomassin (Louis), French priest of the Oratory, theologian, 1619–1695: 380.
Tiberius, Roman emperor, c. 42

General Index

BC–AD 37: 100.
Tourniac (Jean, pseudonym of Jean Louis Granger), French writer, 1919–1995: 136, 138.
Touttée (Dom A.), O.S.B., learned Maurist, 1677–1718: 324.
Trouillard (Jean), French priest, historian of Neoplatonism, 1907–1984: 433.
Turcan (Robert), historian of religions, 20th c.: 218.
Turchi (N.), Italian Hellenist, historian of religions, 20th c.: 204.

Vacandard (Elphège-Florent), French priest, historian of Christianity, 1849–1927: 312.
Valens (Flavius), Roman emperor, Arian, c. 328–378: 128.
Valentinus, Egyptian-born Gnostic theologian, taught at Rome from 135 to 165: 147, 357.
Vallabha, Hindu philosopher, interpreter of the *vedānta*, 1479–1531: 123.
Vallin (Georges), French philosopher and sanskritist, 1921–1983: 443.
Valmont or Vallemont (Pierre Le Lorrain, *called:* de), French priest, historian, 1649–1721: 378.
Vâlsan (Michel), Romanian writer, Arab scholar, disciple of Guénon, 1907–1974: 138–140, 143, 144, 147, 152, 392.
Van den Eyden (Damian), historian of early Christianity, 20th c.: 256, 288.
Vatican II, 1962–1965: 391.
Vian (Francis), French Hellenist, historian of religions, 20th c.: 205, 209.
Vigouroux (Fulcran), French Suplician, exegete, 1847–1915: 33.
Viguerie (Jean de), historian specializing in the eighteenth century: 382.
Vincent of Lerins (Saint), theologian born in Lorraine, ?–c. 450: 189
Vincent de Paul (Saint), founder of Daughters of Charity and the Lazarites, 1581–1660: 475.
Voltaire, French writer, 1694–1778: 103, 281, 407.
Vuillaud (Paul), French scholar, historian of the Kaballah and Christian esoterism, 1875–1950: 16.

Wolfson (Harry A.), American historian of philosophy, specialist in Philo of Alexandria, 1887–1974 : 249.
Wölker (Walther), German historian of early Christianity, 20th c.: 257.

Zum Brunn (Emilie), historian of medieval thought, 20th c.: 406.

www.ingramcontent.com/pod-product-compliance
Lightning Source LLC
Chambersburg PA
CBHW031424160426
43195CB00010BB/605